THE POWER OF DENIAL

BUDDHISMS: A PRINCETON UNIVERSITY PRESS SERIES

EDITED BY STEPHEN F. TEISER

A list of titles in this series appears at the back of the book

THE POWER OF DENIAL

BUDDHISM, PURITY, AND GENDER

BERNARD FAURE

PRINCETON UNIVERSITY PRESS

PRINCETON AND OXFORD

Copyright © 2003 by Princeton University Press
Published by Princeton University Press, 41 William Street,
Princeton, New Jersey 08540
In the United Kingdom: Princeton University Press,
3 Market Place, Woodstock, Oxfordshire OX20 1SY

Library of Congress Cataloging-in-Publication Data

Faure, Bernard.
The power of denial : Buddhism, purity,
and gender / Bernard Faure.
p.   cm.   — (Buddhisms)
Includes bibliographical references and indexes.
ISBN 0-691-09170-6 (alk. paper) — ISBN 0-691-09171-4 (pbk. : alk. paper)
1. Women—Religious aspects—Buddhism. 2. Sex—Religious aspects—Buddhism.
3. Buddhism—Doctrines. I. Title. II. Series.
BQ4570.W6   F38   2003
294.3′082—dc21   2002066257

This book has been composed in Sabon

Printed on acid-free paper. ∞

www.pupress.princeton.edu

Printed in the United States of America

10 9 8 7 6 5 4 3 2 1

To Adèle, Gaëlle, and Anaïs

CONTENTS

ACKNOWLEDGMENTS

I WISH to express my heartfelt thanks to all those who have, in one way or another, helped me to bring this book to completion. There is no way of acknowledging each and every individual who has participated in this dialogical process. A short list of the usual suspects would include: Wendi Adamek, Alice Bach, Ursula-Angelika Cedzich, Wendy Doniger, Jennifer Dumpert, Hubert Durt, Hank Glassman, Allan Grapard, Janet Gyatso, Linda Hess, Kuo Li-ying, Kawahashi Noriko, Susan Klein, Miriam Levering, Irene Lin, Ellen Neskar, Fabio Rambelli, and Mimi Yengpruksawan.

Undergraduate and graduate students, over the years, have stimulated me through their questions and discussions. The first draft of the book was written during a year well spent at the Kyoto Center for Japanese Studies in 1994–95, and I am grateful for the institutional support I received from the Director, Terry MacDougall, and from his staff. Likewise, the Department of Religious Studies at Stanford, and its successive chairs, Arnie Eisen and Carl Bielefeldt, have been most supportive. I am finally grateful to my editor at Princeton University Press, Brigitta van Rheinberg, for her kindness and patience.

INTRODUCTION

THIS BOOK is the second part of a project on the place of sexuality and gender in Buddhism. The first part, published under the title *The Red Thread*, dealt with the question of monastic discipline, especially the rule against illicit sex and its transgression. It also addressed the question of the so-called degeneration of the monastic order in Japan, in particular with the widespread practice of monks marrying or having concubines, and the equally prevalent monastic homosexuality (or rather pedophilia). Sexuality, denied in principle, became crucial, and Buddhism attempted to coopt or transform local cults (in which women played a large role), being in turn transformed by them. In the case of Japan, for instance, Buddhism tried to specialize in imperial rituals dealing with the prolificity of the imperial body and the prosperity of the imperial lineage.

Whereas *The Red Thread* focused on male monastic sexuality, this work centers on Buddhist conceptions of women and constructions of gender. Although this artificial dichotomy between sexuality and gender is somewhat unfortunate, and potentially misleading, it is used heuristically, as a tool for sorting out the staggering complexity of the issues.

The present volume deals more specifically with the status and agency of women in a typically androcentric tradition like Japanese Buddhism. My general argument is that Buddhism is paradoxically neither as sexist nor as egalitarian as is usually thought. Women played an important role in Buddhism, not only as nuns and female mystics, but also as mothers (and wives) of the monks; in addition, in such capacity, they were the representatives of local cults, actively resisting what was at times perceived as a Buddhist take-over. Among these women, we also find courtesans and prostitutes, who often were the privileged interlocutors of the monks.

Women were divided, not only due to their own separate agenda, but also as a result of male domination, and some were clearly more oppressed than others. Preaching nuns, for instance, seemed to side with the male institution in threatening other women with eternal exclusion from deliverance. Thus, we are faced with a broad spectrum of situations: from exclusion to inclusion (or the other way around, depending on one's viewpoint, with discrimination as a case of "inclusive exclusion"); from agency or passivity within the patriarchal system to "life on the borderline"; to passivity or agency in the "ténèbres extérieures," rejection or voluntary departure from the patriarchal Eden or Pure Land.

Until now, the story or history of women in Buddhism has been represented in a relatively linear fashion: as a shift from oppression to freedom, a teleological narrative of progress and liberation (from so-called Hīna-yāna to Mahāyāna, or again, from an elitist ideology to a more open and democratic one). While some scholars see Buddhism as part of a movement of emancipation, others see it as a source of oppression. Perhaps this is only a distinction between optimists and pessimists, if not between idealists and realists. In both cases, the identity of Buddhism (and of women) is seen as rather unproblematic. Things, however, are unfortunately (or fortunately) more complicated. As we begin to realize, the term "Buddhism" does not designate a monolithic entity, but covers a number of doctrines, ideologies, and practices—some of which seem to invite, tolerate, and even cultivate "otherness" on their margins; it also refers to various levels of discourse (ideological, institutional) that, although globally related at a given period, have relative autonomy and distinct dynamics. Thus, even the most reactionary ideology, while operating according to its own repressive dynamic, can be put to very different uses (some of them ironic, subversive) when it is articulated to specific cultural and institutional contexts, and manipulated by antagonistic historical agents. These tactics and strategies of inclusion, exclusion, and/or discrimination were permitted (yet constrained) by a certain number of models, whose combinations are, if not endless, at least more numerous than usually recognized by partisans on both sides of the gender divide. Among them, we can mention:

1. male power (androcentrism, misogyny, patriarchy)
2. female power (biological, religious, political)
3. equality through conjunction of sexes (yin/yang)
4. complementarity through conjunction of sexes (Tantric or Daoist ritual)
5. rhetorical equality through denial of sex/gender (Mahāyāna doctrine)

"SOARING AND SETTLING"—TOO SOON?

Many studies have been produced over the past twenty years about practically every aspect of women's lives in Western societies. Reacting against what she perceived as a certain female parochialism in gender studies, Nathalie Zemon Davis insisted that the focus should be on the relations between sexes rather than on women only. In the case of Buddhism, however, there is no need yet to worry about having too many studies focusing *only* on women. We are still at the first stage, where we may need to listen carefully in order to hear the voices of women, in the interstices, or through the "italics" (the specific slant) of men's discourse.

Studies on Buddhism and gender have begun to appear, but they are usually limited to one tradition (in general Tantric or Tibetan Buddhism), or in pushing a specific agenda. I will not give here a survey of previous scholarship, but will simply point out some of the advances and remaining problems. Most recent studies tend to adopt one of two approaches: the first discusses the Buddhist bias against women, or the more or less successful Buddhist attempts to overcome this bias, while the second consists mainly in attempts to reveal the active role of Buddhist women, to emphasize female agency and thus counter the stereotype of women as passive cultural subjects. The latter is still a Western-centered approach, since a major Buddhist criticism revolves around the notion of woman as seductress; that is, precisely her active (and damning) influence. The present work combines these two types of approach, while keeping their limitations in mind.

It is worth bearing in mind Susan Sered's remark that "the writings of most feminist anthropologists carry either an implicit or explicit message that the blurring of gender categories is what will lead to the demise of patriarchy." Sered's findings suggest a different scenario: according to her, "women's religions" stress rather than play down gender differences—even if "they tend to choose the less sexist ideology available." In these religions, Sered argues, "the women's sphere is considered as good (if not better) than the male sphere, and women fully control the female sphere."[1] Going one step further, Sered argues that it is ironic that few scholars interpret women's religiosity in terms of motherhood. She wants in particular to emphasize motherhood over sexual intercourse, which she sees as a "lurking phallocentric obsession in Western scholarship."[2]

Historically, Buddhism has monopolized the afterlife and the major rites of passage—birth, death, and rebirth—while leaving the sacraments of life (adulthood, marriage) to Confucianism or Shintō. This is why we have Confucian "precepts for women," whereas Buddhist attempts—for instance Mujū Ichien's *Mirror for Women* (*Tsuma Kagami*)—remain general descriptions of Buddhist morality and practice, common to both sexes. Thus, women could find little in the Buddhist teaching that they could apply to normal life. Outside of monastic life, Buddhism was a teaching for times of crisis (childbirth, illness, death). Its impact on women was, on the whole, negative, inasmuch as it asserted the sinfulness of female sexuality and gender. What, then, would it mean for Buddhism to truly become a "woman's religion" in the sense emphasized by Sered?

Many feminist scholars have emphasized the misogynistic (or at least androcentric) nature of Buddhism. The point is almost trivial. By presenting Buddhism as a monolithic ideology, however, there is a danger of repeating the same gesture by which Buddhist ideologues attempted to construct a seamless orthodoxy. This alleged unity is what we must undermine, in order to find—within Buddhism itself, and not only outside—the many voices that have been covered, to let them contribute to the deconstruction, both internal and external, of Buddhist orthodoxy. Buddhism cannot simply be ignored, or suppressed; this would be to fall in to the same scapegoating mechanism one criticizes. Rather, we must live with it, and provide a more in-depth critique that would attempt to nip its sexism in the bud. At the same time, we need to recognize that the egalitarian ideology of Buddhism, even if it has until now mostly been ignored in practice, can indeed be used to subvert the existing gender hierarchy—unless, taking the hard-core feminist approach, one considers that the genealogical flaw of this unequal egalitarianism makes all dialectical overcoming impossible?

Not surprisingly, feminist interpretations of Buddhism vary considerably, and are even sometimes at odds with one another. I have to defer to others in discussion of specific points, but I will simply emphasize the methodological problems in this type of work. First among these is a certain hermeneutical naïveté or wishful thinking that insists on taking texts at face-value and on reading them through one single code; second, a certain ideological problem, the danger of ventriloquism when speaking in the name of a silent other; third, a problem due to the lack of sociohistorical context.

The search for the women "hidden from history" cannot, as such, justify an egalitarian reading of the tradition. As John Winkler remarked, sentences of the type "Men and women enter this visionary world together" must be taken with a grain of salt.[3] Or again, to quote feminist authorities, Sandra Gilbert and Susan Gubar: "Since creativity is defined as male, it follows that the dominant literary images of femininity are male fantasies too."[4] Furthermore, as Toril Moi points out, "it is not an unproblematic project to try to speak *for* the other woman, since this is precisely what the ventriloquism of patriarchy has always done: men have constantly spoken *for* women, in the name of women.[5] Joan Kelly notes that "we could probably maintain of any ideology that tolerates sexual parity that: 1) it can threaten no major institution of the patriarchal society from which it emerges; and 2) men, the rulers within the ruling order, must benefit from it."[6] There are, as we will see, various examples of egalitarian discourse in Western and Asian cultures, but they usually have failed to translate into social realities. The Buddhist "rhetoric of equality," in particular, remained general and abstract, never becoming a collective, social and political equality.

It might be difficult to retrieve the social context in the Indian/Tibetan case(s), and thus to prove or disprove the egalitarian rhetoric. To make sense of the active role of woman (in the form of *śakti*) in Indian Tantrism, scholars like Agehananda Bharati have argued that in certain parts of India women were actually known to take the active role in sexual matters. This, however, does not mean that women had a higher status. Furthermore, a comparison with the Chinese and Japanese contexts, where a similar rhetoric clearly conceals male power, inclines us to think that the same, mutatis mutandis, was taking place in India and Tibet. Some have also argued that Tibet constitutes an exception, as admittedly Tibetan culture was much less misogynistic than Chinese and Japanese cultures. But in Tibetan Tantrism at least, women were not represented as active energy (śakti), but as passive wisdom (prajñā). Susan Sered has documented the existence of religious traditions in which women played a major role (for instance Okinawan religion).[7] These traditions are few and far between, however, and Tantrism does not seem to be one of them, despite what a superficial glance at its egalitarian rhetoric may suggest.

There has been a tendency to exaggerate female submission, without recognizing women's capacity to play and subvert the (male) game well and to laugh off "small men." Is it not, in last analysis, to interiorize in a subtle way the male contempt toward women, these women who are said, a little hastily, to be utterly passive? This, however, does not allow us to deny, or excuse, the relentless sexism of the Buddhist tradition.

Attempts at retrieving female agency or women's voices, when not checked by interpretive vigilance, may end up in presenting just another biased image (or hearing voices). As Joan Scott points out, it "also runs the risk of conflating valuation of women's experience and positive assessment of everything they did."[8] The question then may boil down to this: do two biased images counterbalance each other, and are they the same thing as a "neutral" account (assuming that such an account would be possible)? From a political standpoint, a feminist counterargument to patriarchy, even biased, may be seen as legitimate. From a scholarly standpoint, things are a little different, even though we now know that all accounts are gendered, and no "neutral" account is possible. But the supposed "differend" comes from the fact that we are not dealing simply with a debate opposing the male position to its female counterpart. In both camps, we also find wolves in sheep's clothing and sheep in wolves' clothing.

In their search for role models and a "usable history," feminist scholars tend to project current normative conceptions and ideologies onto past cultures, and to thus perpetrate anachronisms. In order to avoid cultural fallacies, it is therefore important to look closely at the historical and anthropological records. This close scrutiny should, however, itself be informed by feminists insights, and question its documents in terms of gender. It ought to be an ideological critique, or lead toward it. Such critique must be a genuine critique of ideology (in the text as well as in its own discourse), not merely an "ideological" critique denouncing one ideology (Buddhism) in the name of another (feminism).

Retrieving the female voice, what feminist scholars have dubbed as "her/story," is a legitimate approach, but not exclusive of others. There are more women in the Buddhist tradition, and they have been more active and influential, than is usually assumed. Yet it is precisely the need to retrieve these voices that suggests the tradition, at least from a certain point onward, has tended to cover them—and it is this cover-up that we must examine. A mere denial of the sexist nature of the scholarly tradition (leaving intact the Buddhist tradition) seems misleading, even if it has some tactical and political usefulness. In the black-and-white world of gender ideology, one-sided arguments will always be more attractive than nuanced analysis.

Much feminist work on Buddhism has been concerned with "singing the praises of exceptional women" or chronicling the indignities suffered by women. This approach, however, is increasingly criticized as being blind to cultural and historical contexts and inequalities other than those related to gender, and so as being complicit in perpetuating the image of women as passive victims. A more nuanced reading would acknowledge that, while some women were passive victims, others were not. The responsible historian needs to attend to both sides. All models, whatever their initial validity, become counterproductive when they are determined by an ideological or political agenda, and are flawed from an historian's viewpoint.

THE CULTURAL APPROACH

Feminist works on Buddhism have not yet achieved the level of sophistication evident in feminist works not only in Western social history, but also in recent works on Chinese and Japanese women's history.[9] In *Teachers of the Inner Chambers*, a study on women and culture in seventeenth-century China, Dorothy Ko makes several points about Confucianism and Chinese society that seem equally valid for Buddhism and Japanese society. She notes, in particular, that the normative discourse of Confucianism and the imposition of a patriarchal ideology do not mean that women were "silenced."[10] Furthermore, as Priscilla Ching Chung puts it, "subservience of women to men did not mean total subordination of all women to all men but the subordination of specific women to specific men within their own class, and only in terms of personal and family relationships."[11] Thus, "any historical study of women and gender should be class-, locale-, and age-specific."[12] The theory of male domination should also be nuanced: men also dominate other men, women dominate other women, and social institutions repress both to various degrees. As Norbert Elias has well shown in his study of curialization, life at court was self-imposed misery, a kind of "noblesse oblige." The fact that it was self-imposed may alienate our sympathy, but it does not alleviate the misery.

The current criticism of the "woman-as-victim" model is prefigured by the work of earlier anthropologists such as Margery Wolf. Wolf convincingly argued that women could wield power in ways that were not recognized in a patriarchal gender ideology. She also showed that women's status varied at different points of their life cycle: there was little in common between the new wife and the elderly mother; whereas the former was stripped of any power, the latter was empowered by the Confucian family structure.[13] But Ko equally rejects the alternative model of "woman-as-agent," and offers a more flexible "range of constraints and opportunities that women in 17th century China faced."[14] As Emma Teng remarks, it is clear "that recent scholarship overturns older stereotypes of the Chinese woman as uniformly oppressed and unempowered. As such, this kind of research represents a powerful challenge to Eurocentric assumptions about the backwardness or victimization of the Chinese woman. A challenge to common assumptions about the nature of Chinese culture, it is also a challenge to the feminist model of liberation from tradition."[15]

Like the seventeenth century for Chinese women, the Edo period in Japan seems to have been the best and the worst of times for Japanese women. The normative literature and legal codes suggest that women were increasingly repressed. We already need to differentiate between classes, and between high and low culture: the patriarchal spirit that was a dominant trait of warrior culture may not have affected peasant culture to a significant degree. But even in the elite culture, women may have retained much more informal power in their social and domestic lives than is indicated in these sources. The "logic of practice" that governed these lives may have allowed them in many cases to turn a basically unequal situation to their advantage. What they had lost on the outside, in the public realm, they may have gained on the inside, in the domestic realm. I will return to this point. I just wanted to emphasize here that women's culture, for all the patriarchal ideology transmitted by Confucianism, Buddhism (and soon Shintō), was not as passive as we have been led to believe. We need to take into acccount real practices and subjective perceptions before passing judgment. We also need to get a better understanding of the actual dialectics at play in the exercise of power, and how boundaries between genders were constantly renegotiated.

Patriarchy is by no means as monolithic or univocal as certain feminist critics have claimed. It has its own contradictions, its fault-lines, and women are not always simply its silent, passive victims. As Toril Moi points out, "Feminists must be able to account for the paradoxically productive aspects of patriarchal ideology (the moments in which the ideology backfires on itself, as it were) as well as for its obvious oppressive implications if they are to answer the tricky question of how it is that some women manage to counter patriarchal strategies despite the odds stacked against them."[16]

Power relations obtain inside both sexes, and we should avoid demonizing one and idealizing the other, even if the need to repair the injustices done in the name of patriarchy seems more pressing at this time. Women are not all sisters. This truth is hinted at in many tales involving young girls and their stepmothers, or their grandmothers, like Cinderella, Snow White, or Little Red Riding Hood. The story of Cinderella (and its Japanese Buddhist variant, that of Princess Chūjōhime) could be read according to several codes, the gender code being only one of them. It can be seen as the fruitless competition for male recognition in a patriarchal society, where man "divides to rule." It can also be read in terms of alliance and kinship, as a tale about a mother who sees her child's marriage (and her own future) threatened by a rival. The jealousy between the stepmother and the girl can also be interpreted according to the age code as a form of the generation conflict—as in the tales of Snow White or of Little Red Riding Hood.[17] In the case of Buddhism, too, women were divided (and the division was, if not created, at least maintained by monks), and some were more alienated than others. Some (the nuns) sided with the male institution against the "wandering women," mediums, and so forth.

GENDER REVISITED

One of the primary questions informing this book is that given that Buddhism is essentially a discourse on salvation and holiness, to what extent is this discourse hopelessly (or hopefully) gendered? How do the models for men and women differ? It is more difficult, in the case of Buddhism, to see to what extent holiness shows in itself the marks of sexual difference, and this for one reason in particular: the fact that the Buddhist *Golden Legend*, unlike its Christian analogue, is essentially masculine. We are constrained by the available sources: we may want to write an alternative history, but we have (and will have) no alternative corpus. There are very few "Lives of Eminent Nuns" in comparison with the abundant hagiography of eminent monks. We may hope to discover some Buddhist Hildegard of Bingen, but the fact of the matter is that Buddhist female saints wrote relatively little. Neither did they bleed as much as their Western *consoeurs*, although they did use their blood to write, whereas for Western saints writing became a substitute for the blood of martyrs.[18] But one can still safely assume that, in the case of Buddhist women, another notion came to superimpose itself on the idea of holiness, which one could perhaps define as a rejection of sexuality and of the body: that of the need for purity, or rather purification, and above all purification from (and of) their blood. In the contact with popular religion, Buddhist holiness (and its implied rejection of the body and sexuality) gives way to sacredness, which implies purity, or rather purification from all defilement (in particular the defilement from blood). Both elements, holiness and sacredness, and the attendant defilement from sexuality and from blood, converge in the case of women. Such is the twofold truth of Buddhism: as a discourse about holiness addressed *also* to women (this discourse is what I focus on in the first part of the book) and as a recipe for better life (or "worldly benefits," Jp. *genze riyaku*), with its arsenal of techniques (love rituals and the like).

Like most clerical discourses, Buddhism is indeed relentlessly misogynist, but as far as misogynist discourses go, it is one of the most flexible and open to multiplicity and contradiction. In early Buddhism, for instance, genders are not fixed, but fluctuating, and cases of transsexualism seem a common occurrence. Buddhist attitudes toward women are part of monastic attitudes toward society and lay people. We find two types of antifeminism in Buddhism: first, the early ascetic or monastic attitude, which posits that "a bodhisattva should wander alone like a rhinoceros." In principle, female ascetics are accepted, but in practice, it is difficult for them to follow this ideal. Lonely women tend to get raped, and the Vinaya reports how, after such a case, the Buddha is said to have prohibited women from wandering alone in the forest. The second type results from the fact that when Buddhism becomes more worldly, it tends to accept the social prejudices of the patriarchal societies in which it tries to take root.

It may not be necessary to emphasize the double entendre of the subtitle of this study, "Buddhism, Purity, and Gender"—a reference to Mary Douglas's seminal book. Joan Scott has made a convincing point for the use of the notion of gender as an analytical category. But in the process, this analytical mode tends to become overly purified, epistemologically but also morally, severed from its rowdier elements, turning at times into a rather aseptic notion almost as dogmatic as some of the traditions which it claims to deconstruct. It may have been necessary to detach gender from sex, but the oblivion or obliteration of sexuality has its own dangers, when the real need is to connect the two (or more) discourses on women/gender and on sex/sexuality. As it is commonly used, the concept of gender seems to accept uncritically the nature/culture split which stipulates that whereas nature is given, culture is fluid. But as Thomas Laqueur has shown, whereas the conception of biological sex changed drastically over time, that of gender remained stable. "Gender" is not only a proper, serious synonym for "women," it also tends to leave out sex and desire, and to give a clean, expurgated (and at times puritan) version of history. Sexual relations are seen as peripheral at best. The term "gender" itself (as opposed to biological sex) is not as neutral as the claims made on its behalf would suggest. It implies a rather abstract, clean view of what's really going on between man and woman (or any other genders).

My approach, while duly emphasizing the *primacy* of gender as an epistemological or experiential given—the fact that all beings are gendered, or, more precisely, that the self (mine and that of others) is gendered—will attempt to focus on the social construction of a specific gender (woman), but also show that gender difference is only *one* among various socially constructed differences (class, race, age among them). This difference, when it is seen as the only one, may come to obscure the others. In contrast with reified differences, I want to emphasize the "differance" of gender as a root metaphor for, and a privileged access to, the notion of difference in tradition and society. I have for instance, in my earlier work, tried to deconstruct the Chan (Zen) tradition in order to show its inherent multiplicity, and to value its *differance*. Looking at the role and status of women in this particular tradition, and in Buddhism in general, is to look at the heart of the differentiating process. This emphasis on the process of differentiation is a way to always destabilize any particular type of exclusive difference. At the same time, one must avoid dematerializing actual differences, as if everything were possible; as if, for instance, sexual difference became immaterial, as if the exception (transsexualism, androgyny, the sexual freedom of the "sky-walker"—a reference to the *ḍākinī*, not the Star Wars figure) could become the norm without in turn becoming oppressive. We need to reflect on what Susan Gubar calls the "disjunction between the nowhere of the cyborg's utopian fluidity and the everywhere of ordinary people's embodiment."[19] Or again, in Susan Bordo's words: "Denial of the unity and stability of identity is one thing. . . . The epistemological fantasy of achieving multiplicity—the dream of limitless multiple embodiments, allowing one to dance from place to place and self to self—is another."[20]

We are confronted with two diametrically opposed and equally plausible models of interpretation. In the first, the sexual difference is fundamental, irreversible, dominating everything—and so forces us to reinterpret, rewrite everything—even and above all the theoretical egalitarism of Mahāyāna. In the second model, the sexual difference is secondary, derived at the level of ritual. Let us be clear about this: the point is not to express full agreement with the abstract egalitarism of Mahāyāna, but to note that, on the ritual level, the difference is merely used as an expression of a more fundamental fault-line between human and nonhuman (for instance, human and animal, the familiar and the strange, the profane and the sacred). It becomes properly symbolic. Sexual difference is according to this view not only an empirical phenomenon, but more radically the first and fundamental stage of difference as such. It allows us "to free ourselves from the fascination of the One and to opens to the law of the 'two.'"[21] Which is appropriate to Buddhism? Is sexual difference the red thread that runs throughout Buddhist thought, or is it merely one expression of a more fundamental rift? For instance, the stories of fox-women or nāga-girls, which we will discuss, can be seen as encounters with the nonhuman, in which women serve merely as symbolic markers, as figures of the other.

With respect to the first model, which relies on the feminist insight that all human beings are "gendered" and considers the sexual divide profound and beyond mitigation, Carolyn Bynum notes that "experience is gendered. In other words, not only do gender symbols invert or reject as well as reinforce the gender values and gender structures of society, they also may be experienced differently by the different genders."[22] This "differend" dominates everything, and obliges us to re-read (and rewrite) the entire tradition, even, or above all, the theoretical gender equality found in Mahāyāna or Vajrayāna literature: in a word, the entire history of "man." Every book, like Milorad Pavic's *Khazar Dictionary*, should have two versions, a male and a female. No more generic "homo religiosus" or Buddha. The buddha-nature in all sentient beings is also a male or a female one. Furthermore, this divide is not neutral; it always implies a hierarchy, a different potential of desire and pleasure. The Greek myth of Tiresias illustrates the point nicely. The Theban Tiresias once was taking a walk when he saw two snakes mating; he separated them and instantly became a woman. Seven years later, at the same spot, he saw again two snakes mating. He (she) separated them again and became once again a man. Having become famous for these metamorphoses, he was called by Zeus and Hera who were having an argument as to who, man or woman, had more pleasure in love. Tiresias only could tell. He did so by revealing women's best-kept secret, saying that, on a pleasure scale of one to ten, woman had nine, man only one. This could be read as a plea for androgyny. But, although he was fortunate enough to experience a change of sex, even Tiresias could not become an androgyne—not even the gods can. Tiresias eventually became blind after being successively a man and a woman. This story, which shows among other things that the sexes are not equal, and that for once men can be shortchanged, doesn't sound like a story invented by them.

It has become almost trivial to emphasize that all scholarship is gendered, and that there is nothing like a value-free knowledge. As Thomas Laqueur observes, "Sexual difference thus seems to be already present in how we constitute meaning; it is already part of the logic that drives writing."[23] Even awakening, the ultimate goal of Buddhism, might be gendered. It might designate a state in which, instead of perceiving gender differences as mere indices of a social and spiritual hierarchy, one has, on the contrary, the feeling of "being male or female in relation to primordial or ultimate truth." Paraphrasing, one could say that, like the narrative according to David Lodge, awakening is too often conceived as the culminating point of mystical experience, a kind of—male—orgasm. As such, it may have little to do with the multiple female *jouissance* and its "thousand plateaux," a kind of intensely pleasurable gradualism. "Sudden awakening," according to this perspective, looks suspiciously like precocious ejaculation.

According to the second interpretation, the sexual polarity is derived, secondary. Let us make no mistake here: this does not mean that we are simply returning to the Mahāyāna ideology or rhetoric of equality (that would be a third, or rather a first, interpretation, which we do not wish to retain here). It is not a metaphysical argument, but an anthropological constatation that, in the mythical, ritual, and symbolic contexts at least, the male/female polarity is used mostly to express a more fundamental cleavage: between man/woman and animal, familiar and strange. The cleavage itself becomes symbolic. According to Maurice Bloch: "The symbolism of gender and sexuality . . . should be understood as being used in rituals in an ad hoc manner to act out a more fundamental and central logic concerning the establishment of a form of human life which has apparently escaped the biological constraint of death. . . . The conjunction between human[s] and animals can be used to exactly the same ends in rituals as the conjunction and disjunction between female and male."[24] As Bloch points out, gender and animality are alternative symbolic resources that can be used together or separately to signify or create the transcendental. What speaks there is not so much gender, but ideology, and ideology can work with either gender.[25]

Paradoxically, the same feminist scholars who claim that gender is fundamental often end up reducing gender to its sociological parameters alone. Thus, we keep hearing that gender is socially constructed. Of course it is, but this is a somewhat trivial and trivializing truth, which privileges a rather insipid sociological approach. There may be more in sexual difference than meets the sociological eye. From a philosophical or existential viewpoint that emphasizes the subject, sexual difference is not only an empirical phenomenon, but the primary difference itself, the very secret of our being, the blind spot, this *differance* that produces us, as well as our vision or our speech, and as such cannot simply become the object of our discourse. We can reach only reified phenomena, not their source. Being a man or a woman is not simply the result of some political or social scheme imposed on us, something I might decide to change at will. Even my will to change it would be gendered, would be part of this mystery which is lost in sociological approaches. Thus, the problem is, as Thomas Laqueur has it, to "see difference differently."[26]

We can thus reconcile the two apparently contradictory viewpoints: the gender difference is in the last instance determined by ideology, but the sexual difference is real and fundamental (although it appears late on the ideological scene, and as derivative of gender difference). It is a more originary sexual difference, which Buddhism (as well as Western philosophy) must try to let resurface as the very *differance* if it wants to escape its dire destiny as an orthodoxy of the age of the Final Dharma. In this sense, the Buddha was justified to say that the admission of women in the saṅgha (that is, the ideological differentiation of genres) marks the beginning of the end. Women are now submitted to the "unisex" ideological model, in which they are viewed as inferior men. Their entry into the saṅgha, their emulation of a masculine soteriological model centered on the mind, marks the forgetting of their sexual difference, of their feminine "spirituality," which denies the male/female, mind/body dichotomies. Ideally, women's spirituality is more centered on the body, more open to the corporeal, fluid, porous, organic aspects of religious experience (where awakening can be conceived, not as a vision detached from the senses, but as an orgasm implying all senses, not only an *excessus mentis*, but an *excessus corporis*, hybris and hybridization). In practice, however, spiritualization usually means masculinization (and euphemization).

The unisex model described by Thomas Laqueur in the case of the West can be seen at work in Buddhism, as well. According to this model, woman does not constitute a distinct ontological category; she is merely a lesser man. In this form of male humanism called Buddhism, as in ancient Greece, man remains the "measure of all things." In the West, as Laqueur shows, the distinction of genders has preceded that of the sexes, although the latter has now become the norm and foundation. Buddhism has not yet taken the full measure of this ontological-historical change. The distinction between genders is an abstract, ideological model (based on a certain political relation) that is inscribed on corporeal reality (as a relation between yin and yang, male and female, and so forth). It is not based on a clear awareness of the sexual distinction. In this sense, even the emphasis on gender difference, as it is currently advocated, and precisely because it is socially founded, is a kind of idealism or ideology that asserts the spiritual experience to the detriment of the sensible, corporeal experience, as of the irreducible difference, of the bodies.

The gendered approach to Buddhist history is not simply to try to retrieve or rediscover a feminine world ("her/story"), one that would stand next to the male world as another self-contained territory, but to reveal how feminized the dominant male world already is—to deconstruct it from within, and to see the fault-lines in its discourse.[27] I am attempting neither a history of Buddhist women nor of women in Buddhism, but rather a revised history of Japanese Buddhism (one that includes women as a vital element of its developmental dialectic, and not only as a fetishized object of its discourse). Thus, it is not enough to retrieve women as a separate object of study, to see that they had their own history within and outside Buddhism; the point is rather to see how the history and doctrine of Buddhism were changed because of its relationship with women, and to examine how gender "gives meaning to the organization and perception of historical knowledge."[28]

The Buddhist saṅgha was (and remains) a patriarchal institution, and as such it lends itself to the type of approach (and reproach) used by feminist theorists of patriarchy, in which male domination is seen as "the effect of men's desire to transcend their alienation from the means of reproduction of the species."[29] One could, for instance, point out the importance of the Buddhist discourse on embryology and on the "bitter trap" of reproduction.[30] Hence a tendency to see sexuality (for instance, Tantric sexuality) as an escape from that trap, a key to freedom. But here again, more often than not nonreproductive sexuality has been another trap, whereas in some cases motherhood can give women a key to power. Other feminist scholars (as well as linguists), in various "seminal" or "engrossing" works, have shown how inequality is "imbedded" in the sexual relation; indeed, in the syntax itself. As Catherine McKinnon succintly summarizes: "Man fucks woman; subject verb object."[31]

Joan Scott observes that gender, as an analytic category, is connected to sex, but neither is it directly determined by sex nor a determining factor in sexuality. According to her, however, the two basic types of inequalities, male appropriation of motherhood and sexual objectification, are based on a fixed definition of the body, a rather rigid physical determinism. This explains the feminist desire to disconnect gender from sexuality, but, as I pointed out, it also runs the risk of repressing the sexual element, rather than simply acknowledging the relative autonomy and connection between sex and gender.[32]

What relations inhere between inequalities of gender and other types? How pertinent are the other ritually invoked categories, class and race, to my work? What for instance, is the relation between women and *hinin* (outcasts), children, and other oppressed categories in pre-modern Japan, and the role of Buddhism in that regard? Buddhist works on women tend to be oblivious to class and political power, and the use of gender as analytical category—in the case of nuns, for instance—may at times even obfuscate the issue of class. On the other hand, race is not as much of an issue in a relatively homogeneous traditional society like pre-modern Japan as in our modern societies. This other approach, which has been increasingly taken by recent Japanese historians such as Taira Masayuki and Wakita Haruko, considers gender to be not purely determined by patriarchy, but traversed by other types of determinism, changing and developing in relation to socioeconomic conditions of production.

Similarly, I try to combine these two approaches: that of patriarchal theory (where gender is seen as an independent category) and the socio-historical (and loosely Marxist) approach where gender is seen as the by-product of the economic and social structure.[33] Despite my reservations regarding some aspects of the notion of gender outlined above, I am comfortable with Scott's twofold definition of gender: first, as an element in social relationships based on *perceived* differences between sexes, and implying four constituents: a) culturally available symbols; b) normative concepts; c) institutions such as kinship, economy, and politics; and d) a subjective identity. The contextualization implies not only kinship systems such as the household and family, but also the labor market, education, the polity; but for traditional society, kinship remains a predominant factor. Second, Scott's definition views gender as a primary way of signifying relations of power. There is, not only a "di-vision of the world" (Pierre Bourdieu), but a "di-vision of Buddhism" (a "dual yet non-dual" teaching). The Buddhist worldview is a dual view of nondualism. The relations of gender and politics will become obvious when we examine the case of Japanese empresses. In Japanese patriarchal society, as it finds its classical shape under Tokugawa rule, the authoritative power is symbolized as power over women; at the same time (and around the same period), the utopian counterpower (in the Fujidō and other "New Religions," for instance) is symbolized by the sexual equality and freedom of women. But in both cases, women are only symbolic markers in a male political debate.

GENDERING BUDDHISM

Gendering Buddhism means, first of all, to gender (and endanger) the Buddhist orthodoxy, the tradition and the concepts on which it thrived (like enlightenment), but also to gender scholarship. It is to show the role played by bodies in constructions of gender and the transformation of women into sexual objects;[34] it is also to illustrate how (some) women, far from being passive recipients of such gendered constructs, were able to play with them, to turn the tables, by becoming sexual and gendered subjects. In this way, Buddhism, the ascetic religion, was "domesticated," becoming a household commodity.

The Chan master Linji is well known for his praise of the "true man of no rank" (*wuwei zhenren*). We could, of course, easily argue that he is still referring to "man." Woman always has a rank, and usually a low one. But does "man" here mean *homo*, not *vir*; or could we eventually have, next to the "true man of no rank," a "true woman of no rank," expressions in which both "man" and "woman" could stand for *homo*? We will see that the so-called Five Obstacles were originally the cause of the impossibility of women obtaining five exalted ranks (including that of buddha) in the Buddhist hierarchy. In that case, "buddha" is only a rank, even if it is the highest; whereas the enlightened man should be the "man without rank." For the time being, we will have to read the canon, and the entire Buddhist tradition, *en double bande*, taking into account male and female (not necessarily in that order) receptions of the teaching, and men's and women's elaborations on it.

The object, collectively called "women," is, as noted earlier, far from monolithic. The factual (and fatal) divergences between women are compounded by masculine domination, which generates cleavages and opposition within each sex. The danger would be to reify this opposition. For instance, Pierre Bourdieu, in a recent book on the question, tends to fix the rupture between the two poles of domination without taking into account the speech of the dominated and the cultural autonomy of certain fringes of the subaltern culture.[35] Instead of some master-slave dialectic, we find in this model an insurmountable barrier between the centers of domination and the world of the dominated. According to one of Bourdieu's critics, Olivier Mangin, such a sociology of domination "becomes the slave of its own grids of analysis, an analysis resting on a simple idea that domination is a 'transcendental.'" Thus, political domination is regarded in the same mode as sexual domination.

There are, however, some deep fault-lines in feminist discourse. We often find, for instance, a radical opposition between egalitarian and differential conceptions. According to the egalitarian conception, male and female roles are social constructions. According to Bourdieu, the strength of the "male *sociodicée*" (theory of the origins of society) comes from the fact that it cumulates and condenses two operations: it legitimizes a relation of domination by inscribing it into a biological nature, which is itself a naturalized social construction.[36] According to the differentialist conception, motherhood inscribes the female population with an irreducible mark. We must denounce the fictitious universalism of "a masculine vision, cygenetic and warrior-like, of the relations between sexes."[37]

Two basic conceptions of gender can be found in feminist works. According to the first one, gender is a social construction, which must be deconstructed, or denied. This model leads to a kind of androgynous, or rather neutral, conception of subjectivity, not so different from the kind we see at work in Mahāyāna. According to the second conception, gender, even if socially constructed, is the reality from which we, as subjects, emerge, and with which we must work. The cards we have been dealt might be reshuffled, but the game still has to be played. Gender cannot be wished away, but on the contrary must be asserted. Instead of a history of gender (and its social construction), we have a gendered history. Or rather, any history of gender is always already a gendered history, even androgyny—as some feminists, as well as some philosophers since Plato, have dreamt it to be—remains a gendered androgyny. Gender, in this sense, is fundamental. The point here is to question how gendering *works*, not to deny gendering as such; in other words, to criticize the hierarchy between genders, and to reverse, or rather subvert, it. And, further, the difference must be asserted, instead of denied in the name of a unisex model, whether male or female.

Another feminist dilemma may be that, one the one hand, speaking to ordinary women about ordinary things that matter to them seems to be condoning women's exploitation (if, for instance, motherhood is seen as part of their "biological" exploitation). On the other hand, to propose a "superwoman" model seems to betray the cause of ordinary women, to assert an elitist view addressed to religious virtuosos (who tend to be educated, leisurely, Western, or Westernized women). A similar dilemma confronts Buddhism. Contrary to other great religions, it has little to say about the domestic sphere. Unlike Christianity, for instance, it did not try to legislate with respect to marriage and the rules of alliance. Buddhism limited its interventions to the entry and exit points of being (birth and death), or to specific times when relations with the ultramundane were needed for the well-being of the household. Thus, although Buddhist magical rites played a crucial role in the strategies of alliance and reproduction, they did not become the object of a specific (valorized) discourse, and thus have been neglected by scholars. It is, however, in this area that Buddhism had the most contact with "ordinary" women, at the risks of compromising its orthodoxy with "heterodox rites" (*gehō*) and of confusing its priests with marginals. When it comes to conjugal matters, Buddhism is strangely silent, almost indifferent: it lends its arsenal of love rites to men and women, in particular to women in search of a husband or desiring a male child. Buddhism also heals "feminine" (that is, venerial) diseases (related to menstruation and so forth). The soft underbelly of Buddhism has to do with the soft underbelly of women. Tantric sexuality, as it has been extolled by some feminist scholars, is also a rejection of "normal" (that is, conjugal and procreative) sex, and by the same token, of women's traditional status (and, which is not quite the same, of traditional women).

The question of gender leads to the question of transcendence (beyond polarity). If male/female constitutes a root metaphor for positions (not essences), there will always be a high/low, a tendency to valorize in sexual/

gender terms. One may dream of a purely postmodern *differance*, but even that approach needs a logocentric discourse to deconstruct. Georges Lakoff and Mark Johnson did not emphasize enough the sexual side of the "metaphors we live by." Gender (male/female) is the root metaphor we live by. It is also this metaphor that was put into play by medieval Japanese Buddhists when they argued that women had to be reborn as male in order to obtain salvation. The tendency to reduce gender to other social data is often at the detriment of the fundamental feminist insight that all history, every experience, is gendered. To contextualize it is to neuter it.

The study of Buddhist teaching through the lens of gender leads us to question what we call "Buddhism." Too often we identify it with orthodoxy, which is only the "straight" and rigid *doxa*. The most creative part of Buddhist discourse might be originating in the margins. Thus, it is important to explore less conventional elements of Buddhist discourse, as long as one remains aware of their marginality, and does not try to pass them off as orthodox, or even mainstream, Buddhism.[38] But we are here at the limit, where Buddhist discourse risks dissolving into its "others." Egalitarian elements in Buddhist discourse are like embers that could be fanned into a fire, but this does not mean that there ever *was* such a fire. Any tradition, in order to survive, has to play with fire, to flirt with otherness, at the risk of losing itself. And Buddhism did lose itself in India, to take one example. But would it have been better, or even possible, to preserve identity through misogyny and other forms of xenophobia?

Finally, I cannot avoid a personal question, namely: can a male scholar, being both judge and interested party (but who is not?), write about women? Perhaps not, but about gender, yes. As long as we recognize that there is no neutral ground: this makes the situation of a male speaking about sexuality and sex/gender difference quite uncomfortable, and, in a sense, too easy—a little like a bourgeois claiming to work for the proletarian revolution. This book, like any book, is a gendered history—more precisely, a male-gendered one. It has no pretense of being "neutral" or "objective." But again, I offer no apologies: I like differences, and I dislike the monolothic discourse of ideology, whether in patriarchal or in feminist garb.

The feminine viewpoint is probably forever (or at least in this present reincarnation) beyond my reach. Is to be a woman, however, sufficient to speak in the name of these silenced voices? The impossibility, if it is one, may extend to scholars of both sexes. To speak in the name of women is only to assume the same right as Buddhist monks, to reproduce the same effects of power. As noted earlier, there is a certain well-intentioned ventriloquism in the work of some feminist scholars who claim to make Asian women of bygone ages "speak." As far as I am concerned, it would probably be safer to limit myself to deconstructing the dominant discourse of the tradition and to poach on Buddhist (as well as feminist) preserves, rather than attempting to break new ground and open new territories. But in so doing, I may find the traces of other, past poachers, and, not so surprisingly, discover that these elusive poachers were women. What we have in common, if not gender, would be a certain pleasure in crossing the lines, enjoying the thrill of transgression. Of course, my transgression remains timid and textual, whereas theirs was quite real. If, as Hélène Cixous once stated, "feminine texts are texts that 'work on the difference,' strive in the direction of difference," then my work can be said to possess a certain feminine quality, one apparently at odds with my gender and sex. Not surprisingly, the kind of feminism I feel attracted to is a form of deconstruction that, in the words of Julia Kristeva, teaches us how to "recognize the unspoken in all discourse, however revolutionary, how to emphasize at each point whatever remains unsatisfied, repressed, new, eccentric, incomprehensible, that which disturbs the mutual understanding of the established powers."[39] Here is the transferential part that objectivist historians tend to forget: To every Buddhist, as well as to the author of these lines and the reader—the words used by Derrida in the case of Nietzsche could be applied: "Il avait affaire en lui à tant de femmes"—castrated women, castrating women, affirmative women.[40]

The first part of the book addresses the normative and symbolic discourses about women. The "common Buddhist" perspective described in this section reflects the standpoint available to a literate Japanese Buddhist, not the historically specific perspective that may satisfy a Western historian of religions. Chapter 1 examines the evolution of the female monastic order in Asia, and the constraints imposed on nuns. The next four chapters deal with what I have called the Buddhist rhetorics about women. Chapter 2 studies the Buddhist discourse on gender; it takes up the "rhetoric of subordination," based on patriarchal topoi such as the Five Obstacles and the Three Dependences that denied full autonomy to women, not unlike the Eight Strict Rules had done to nuns. Another serious constraint was allegedly "biological," and therefore this chapter also examines the blood taboos that developed around women, as well as the gendered bias of Buddhist "embryology." Chapters 3 and 4 focus on what I call the "rhetorics of salvation and equality": in particular, the soteriological discourse of Buddhism developed around themes such as the buddhahood of the *nāga*-princess and the promise made by the Buddha Amida to accept women in his Pure Land (with the "minor" condition that they should first be reborn as males). The Tantric and Chan egalitarian discourses are then exposed as ideological, and complementary to the rhetoric of subordination, rather than opposed to it. The second part (chapters 5 and

6) looks at various positive images of Buddhist women, as well as negative Buddhist images of women, to reveal that these images, in both cases, are much more ambivalent than they may look. Of particular interest is the image of the monk's mother: this is the subject of chapter 5.

The third part of the book emphasizes the role played in literature and society by "transgressive" women, examining the cases of various categories of women who, unlike the Buddhist nuns, were living on the fringes of or outside the Buddhist saṅgha. It shows how, with the implantation of Buddhism in Japanese society, a kind of Buddhist "dialectic of transgression" was able to develop in response to women's infringements. Chapter 6 analyzes the role and status of female mediums. Chapter 7 takes up in particular the logic of exclusion that characterizes the "prohibition against women entering sacred areas" (*nyonin kekkai*), focusing on the case of sacred mountains. Chapter 8 emphasizes the importance of courtesans and other "wandering women," and considers their colorful relations with Buddhist monks. Chapter 9, finally, relies on folkloric sources to explore the theme of the liminal woman in her many incarnations.

PART ONE

BUDDHISM AND WOMEN

Chapter One

THE SECOND ORDER

BUDDHIST GENDER discrimination is usually traced back to the founding story of the female saṅgha, in which Śākyamuni repeatedly denied entrance into his community to his own aunt and adoptive mother, Mahāprajāpatī Gotamī, arguing that it would bring about the decline of his teaching.[1] The historicity of this well-known episode is quite dubious, if only because of its parallelism with that of the foundation of the Jain female order, initiated by Mahāvira's aunt Canda. At any rate, this precedent has set the tone of many tales about nuns. There are of course exceptions, like those recorded in the *Therīgāthā*, but on the whole the Buddhist saṅgha has been suspicious about nuns, and women in general.

The Buddha's alleged distrust of women was inscribed institutionally in the Eight "Strict (or Heavy) Rules" (*gurudharma*), which served as conditions upon the ordination of women. According to these rules, nuns must ask the monks about the disciplinary rules twice per month; they cannot hold a retreat, nor close it, in the absence of monks; they must be ordained in front of the two assemblies of nuns and monks; they cannot admonish monks officially; they must confess twice per month in front of the two assemblies; lastly, whatever their age and seniority, they have to show respect to all monks, even to those that have just been ordained. These prerequisites to ordination, which Mahāprajāpatī is said to have "gladly" accepted like a "garland of lotus flowers she placed upon her head," share one characteristic: they require the nuns' subordination to monks in all matters.

Although the status of nuns usually has been regarded as a convenient index to the importance of women in Buddhism, the representative nature of these nuns is problematic. Before attempting to determine whether the status of nuns reflects the role played by women in (or through) Buddhism, let us consider the historical development of the female order in Asia and its sociological background, with an emphasis on medieval Japan. A caveat is in order. As a group, nuns (and monks as well) constitute an elusive subject, and what looks at first glance like a linear evolution turns out to be a problematic, discontinuous narrative, in which a single name ("nuns") covers a variety of referents, as groups with different goals and functions replace one another on the historical stage. Nevertheless, if only for heuristic purposes, I found it useful to begin with a kind of historical survey, even if to undermine it in the end, by questioning whether—and to what extent—we are actually referring to the cause of "women in Buddhism" when we take the nuns as emblems, or silent "spokesmen," for all Buddhist women.

THE EVOLUTION OF THE FEMALE SAṄGHA

In a seminal article entitled "The Case of the Vanishing Nun," Nancy Falk argued that the Eight Strict Rules, through their structural and economic effects, actually brought the decline of the female order in South Asia: by implying that only monks deserved honors and offerings, they deprived the female saṅgha of donations necessary to its development, and at the same time prevented nuns from playing an active role in the Buddhist community.[2] At the beginning of the eighth century, the Chinese monk Yijing, returning from India, contrasted the lowly status of Indian nuns with that of Chinese nuns. According to him, the former received very little support from society, and many convents could not even feed their members.[3] Epigraphic evidence found at Sanchi and elsewhere suggests, however, a quite different picture. According to Gregory Schopen, even though the emergence of the Mahāyāna in the fourth–fifth century C.E. seems to have coincided with a marked decline in the role of women in Indian Buddhism, until that time, "nuns, indeed women as a whole, appear to have been very numerous, very active, and, as a consequence, influential in the actual Buddhist communities of early India." Jonathan Walters argues from similar epigraphic evidence that nuns continued to play significant religious, political, and economic roles in Indian Buddhism right up to the medieval period.[4] He questions the "simplistic notion" that one-half of the Buddhist saṅgha could have simply "disappeared" and sees this as exemplifying the general neglect that Buddhist women have suffered in modern studies." For him, their eventual "disappearance" becomes part of a larger (and still largely unexplained) phenomenon: the demise of Buddhism in India.

Although the actual impact of the Eight Rules on the female clergy is difficult to ascertain, it remains that they created a fundamental asymmetry between nuns and monks. As Liz Wilson remarks, however, it is crucial to understand that these rules, apparently aimed against the female renouncer, contained "buried tributes to her disruptive power."[5] Inasmuch as they represent an attempt by monks to check the increasing autonomy of the nuns, they suggest that, contrary to Yijing's perception, the female order was thriving. Trying to downplay their negative character, Falk herself admits that they did not compromise the essential, a practice leading to spiritual freedom. Even so, the implication that nuns were more protected than monks against corruption because they could not receive generous donations sounds rather paradoxical. Schopen has shown, for instance, that nuns could be the object of real violence on the part of monks, who went as far as destroying the stūpas worshipped by these nuns and assimilated their devotions to heretical practices.[6] Nuns, however, were far from passive, and they could at times be quite combative.[7]

The stringent limitations imposed on women's ordination—most notably, the required presence of ten fully ordained monks and nuns—paradoxically forced female religiosity to find other ways to express itself. The sociological reality of nunhood was also much more diverse and complex than what official sources (Vinaya, hagiography, and so forth) would let us believe, and, despite the emphasis on proper ordination, the line between laity and clergy was sometimes blurred. Even as the female order began to decline in South and Southeast Asia, other women continued to play an important role, as is shown by the generous gifts made by pious laywomen.[8] Thus, the case of the "vanishing nun" might simply reflect a shift from one type of female religiosity to another rather than a total eclipse of women. This is why, while acknowledging the strong desire of contemporary Theravāda nuns to restore orthodox ordination and condemning the strong resistance of patriarchal societies against such claims for a higher status, it is important to keep this in perspective and to look beyond the recurrent debate about "official" nuns.

To understand the evolution of the female saṅgha in Japan, a few words about the evolution of the saṅgha in other Mahāyāna countries (Tibet, China, Korea) are in order. Probably because orthodox Vinaya transmission already had been interrupted in India when Buddhism entered Tibet, regular nun ordinations were never performed.[9] This situation did not prevent some women from rising in the hierarchy. A recent case in point is that of the "abbess" of Samding Monastery, who, as a "reincarnation" of the deity Dorje Phakmo, enjoyed considerable prestige and privilege and even had male disciples, until she chose to return to lay life after the destruction of Samding Monastery in 1959. On the whole, however, the Tibetan institution of "reincarnations" has remained predominantly male. Furthermore, for most Tibetan nuns, joining the order was not a matter of personal choice, but the result of parental decision motivated by a desire to preserve patrimony. In the best cases, a wealthy family would build for its ordained daughter a comfortable residence near the latter's convent, and provide her with regular income.[10] The majority of nuns were not as fortunate, and for them life could be hard, as convents were at times unable to feed them. They often had to resort to hard work in the fields or even to mendicity.[11] Thus, while participating in the convent's main religious events, they continued to work at home.

The case of the Chinese female saṅgha seems quite different. Although it remained dependent on the male saṅgha, it was a rather unique institution, managed by women and for women. Significantly, it seems from the start to have recruited from among the elite: whereas the male clergy developed progressively from the lower to the higher strata of society, most of the members of the female clergy were daughters of the aristocracy. The first Chinese convents were established in Nanjing in the mid-fourth century C. E. At the turn of the eighth century, nuns accounted for almost half the Chinese clergy (estimated at 120,000 persons).[12] Nevertheless, there is very little information on their role in the development of Chinese Buddhism and on their conditions of life. The evolution of the female saṅgha in the early period of Chinese Buddhism is known to us through the *Biqiuni zhuan* (*Lives of the Nuns*), compiled in 516 or 517 by a literate monk of the Liang named Baochang, which documents the "lives" of sixty-five eminent nuns over a period of 150 years.[13] The tension between ritual orthodoxy and individual charisma is well reflected in Baochang's Preface: "These nuns . . . whom I hereby offer as models, are women of excellent reputation, paragons of ardent morals, whose virtues are a stream of fragrance that flows without end."[14] Although Baochang's nuns are idealized, they are shown in their real context, with specific data regarding their social milieu, their education, and their ordination. Thus, despite its hagiographical nature, this work constitutes an invaluable source.

The *Biqiuni zhuan* evinces a simple typology of Chinese nuns: "When, during the second age of the Buddhist religion, the faith spread east to China, the nun Zhu Jingjian became the first [Chinese Buddhist nun], and for several hundred years nuns of great virtue appeared in China one after another. Of these nuns, Shanmiao and Jinggui achieved the epitome of the ascetic life; Fabian and Sengguo consummately excelled in meditation and contemplation. Individuals such as Sengduan and Sengji, who were steadfast in their resolution to maintain chastity, and Miaoxiang and Faquan, who were teachers of great influence, appeared very frequently."[15] Apart from the figure of the influential abbess, coming from (and supported by) a rich family, the main clerical types described by the *Biqiuni zhuan* are the visionary and the ascetic. The visions of the former were often obtained after the methodical practice of concentration. Vegetarianism, relatively marginal in monks' biographies, plays a prominent role in their biographies. The ascetic nun sometimes verged on "holy anorexia."[16]

With their rapid increase in numbers, nuns eventually became quite influential—so much so that, like their male colleagues, they became a target of anticlerical criticism. According to the *Jin shu*, as Buddhism flourished in Jiangnan under the Eastern Jin, nuns came to receive protection from the empress, a development that led to clerical corruption.[17] Likewise, under Emperor An (r. 397–418), a close connection existed between metropolitan nunneries and the court, especially the imperial harem. In 398, Xu Yong denounced male and female clerics and their role in court intrigues. One nun in particular, Miaoyin, came to exert a great influence on Emperor Xiao Wudi, and she was made abbess of Jianjing monastery in 385. From that time onward, "people of talents and virtuous conduct, clerical as well as non-clerical, depended on her to obtain advancement. She received innumerable gifts (from them), and her wealth upset the capital."[18]

Unfortunately, whereas Huijiao's *Gaoseng zhuan* (*Lives of Eminent Monks*) was emulated in almost every successive dynasty, the *Biqiuni zhuan* has had no worthy successor.[19] Thus, the evolution of the Chinese female saṅgha after the Six Dynasties has not been well studied, although epigraphical materials, still virtually untapped, provide interesting information. I will give just one example, that of two Tiantai nuns, Huichi and Huiren. These blood sisters became famous at the turn of the eighth century for their criticism of the Northern Chan master Puji (651–739).[20] When one of Puji's lay disciples petitioned to have them censored, Emperor Xuanzong ordered the tantric priest Yixing, a former disciple of Puji, to investigate the matter. After questioning the two nuns, Yixing allegedly paid obeisance to them. On the basis of his report, Emperor Xuanzong made large donations to them. The stele inscription also records that their deaths were accompanied by auspicious signs, and that, some forty years later, one of their disciples, a nun named Benjing, built a nunnery near their grave and commissioned the funerary inscription in question. The inscription contrasts the initial subordination of the nuns with the eventual recognition of their spiritual superiority and institutional autonomy. Benjing, too, was clearly a nun of some standing.[21]

This case and others drawn from similar epigraphical material suggest that the female saṅgha flourished under the Tang, as many women from elite families joined its ranks. The same remains true during the Song, and Miriam Levering has recently shown that Chan nuns at that time were usually from wealthy families.[22] After the Yuan rule, under which Buddhism prospered, the rise of "neo-Confucian" orthodoxy and the growing disjunction between Buddhism and the literati seems to have caused a diminution of status for the Buddhist clergy. In the Ming and Qing periods, with a few exceptions, Buddhist convents recruited nuns from the poorest families. As Susan Mann notes, " 'getting to a nunnery' was not an appropriate choice for a young woman of elite status."[23] Buddhism continued to play an important role for women, but it was increasingly through teachings and rituals that, in tune with the dominant Confucian ideology, reinforced traditional social roles and family lineages. Perhaps one can apply to these periods the comment of Steve Sangren concerning the modern period; namely, that Buddhism, with its rituals of "post-par-

enthood," offered a "practical" new direction "for middle-aged and elderly women."[24] Even if the lineage-oriented discourse of Confucianism
was insufficient for some strong individuals, most women subscribed to
its ideology of chastity and resignation; they no longer drew their inspiration from Buddhist tales of female ascetics and mystics, but from formulaic tales of celibate widows dedicated to their parents-in-law.[25]

After Baochang's *Biqiuni zhuan*, no attempt was made to create a
coherent model for female practitioners before the *Shan Nüren Zhuan*
(*Biographies of Laywomen*) compiled by Peng Shaosheng (1740–96) during the Qing dynasty.[26] For the first time, we are shown women who seem
at first more human, less perfect than their clerical colleagues. Their conversion to Buddhism is in many cases due to a long illness or some other
life crisis. Rather than abandoning the family to follow the hard way of
ascesis, they fulfill their traditional social functions—procreating, caring
for their family. In the midst of these social duties, however, they are able
to maintain and develop a strong faith that will save them. For Peng, this
faith puts them on a par with men, whatever their weaknesses as women
may be.

According to tradition, the first Korean nun, Lady Sa, was converted
by the monk Ado. She later became a nun and spent the rest of her life in
reclusion, in a hermitage that was later turned into a convent for the
consort of King Pŏphŭng. During the subsequent reign of King Chun-
hŏng, whose consort also became a nun, many women of the aristocracy
converted to Buddhism and supported the foundation of temples by their
donations. In the Koryŏ period, Buddhism thrived under official sponsorship, and a few eminent nuns appear in historical documents. Owing
probably to the Confucian bias of the official historians, however, they
have generally been erased from the record. Arguing from the moral decline of the clergy, King Hyŏnjong (r. 1009–31) prohibited women of all
social classes from making donations to temples, or even visiting them,
much less becoming nuns. The situation seems to have grown even worse
after the thirteenth century, with the introduction of Zhu Xi's "neo-Con-
fucianism" and the anti-Buddhist policies of the Koryŏ dynasty.

THE FEMALE ORDER IN JAPAN

The complex history of the female saṅgha in Japan can receive only cursory treatment here.[27] Early Japanese nuns faced the same problems as
their Asian sisters, but in their case the question of state support took
precedence over that of proper ordination. When the court was interested
in state ritual performed by nuns, the female order flourished; when this
interest waned, it declined.

Japanese nuns are first mentioned in the *Nihon shoki* entry for the year 584, under the reign of Emperor Bidatsu, that is, half a century after the official introduction of Buddhism.[28] We are told that the influential Soga no Umako ordered the daughter of one of his retainers to be ordained under the religious name Zenshin, together with two other girls, in order to perform religious services in the Buddha Hall where he had enshrined the icons received from the Korean state of Paekche. Japanese scholars usually emphasize that, in contrast with those of India, the first Japanese clerics were female, and consider this to be an auspicious beginning. Closer scrutiny reveals, however, that these young girls (they were twelve at the time) had little choice in the matter, and that they were hardly different from shrine priestesses. In a sense, the status of these "nuns" was even lower than that of Indian nuns: they owed obeisance to their clan, and their religious fate was determined by the political rivalries of the time. Their life was even threatened when two powerful rivals of the Soga clan accused Buddhism of causing an epidemic and argued that it should be suppressed. The hapless "nuns" were defrocked, imprisoned, and flogged. Fortunately, when the epidemics continued, Soga no Umako was able to convince the emperor that Buddhism had nothing to do with it and should be allowed to be practiced privately. The nuns were released, and Umako built a new temple for them.[29] It seems nevertheless paradoxical to exalt these "first Japanese nuns" as precursors of Japanese feminism.

Despite these early ordeals, nuns came to play an important official role during the Nara period. Although the system of regular ordinations had not been realized, the ordination procedure established by the Codes (Ritsuryō) justified the existence of "official" monks and nuns, performing state rituals side by side in provincial monasteries (*kokubunji*) and convents (*kokubunniji*). The nuns' prestige reached its apogee during the Tenpyō period (729–49), under the influence of Empress Kōmyō, who had been instrumental in the creation of these provincial nunneries. Kōmyō also founded an official convent in Nara, Hokkeji, which was to play an important role throughout the medieval period. In the series of lectures on the *Avataṃsaka Sūtra*, which she commissioned in this convent, all offices were performed by nuns.[30]

After the "Dōkyō incident" (769) in which a Buddhist priest, Dōkyō (d. 772) attempted to usurp the throne, the state became more strictly separated from Buddhist influence. Moreover, the reform promoted in 754 by the Chinese Vinaya master Jianzhen (Jp. Ganjin, 688–763), leading to the first ordinations "in conformity with the Dharma" at Tōdaiji, also had a restrictive effect on both male and female ordinations.

The state-sponsored nuns of Nara were in principle equal in status to the monks. Yet a close examination of nun ordinations during the late Nara and early Heian shows a steady decline of officially sanctioned ordinations: whereas as many as one thousand women were ordained during the years 730–50, and about 1,200 during the period 790–810, the number is only twenty-five for the period 810–30. This decline was not prevented by the upsurge in bodhisattva ordinations for women.[31]

At the beginning of the Heian period, the female saṅgha was still supported at court by such powerful *dames patronesses* as the consort of Emperor Saga, Tachibana no Kachiko (better known as Empress Danrin, 786–850) and her daughter (Seishi [Empress Junna], 809–79). According to tradition, the former invited from China the Chan master Yikong (Jp. Gikū), for whom she built Danrinji, a monastery also sheltering nuns.[32] She herself took monastic vows there at the end of her life, after the death of her son, Emperor Ninmyō [r. 830–50]. This is how she became known as Empress Danrin. Danrinji was destroyed by fire in 928, and it is not until 1321 that a nunnery by that name was established there.[33]

After Seishi retired to Junna-in, she sponsored social activities (particularly on behalf of orphans) and held large meetings on the *Lotus Sūtra*. When the monastery was reduced to ashes in 874, she turned her father's villa, Saga-no-in, into a Shingon monastery, Daikakuji. Danrinji and the restored Junna-in, together with smaller convents such as the nearby Giōji, were eventually placed under Daikakuji's jurisdiction.[34] The consort of Emperor Junna is also remembered for her failed attempt to build an ordination platform for women.[35]

These isolated attempts to establish official nunneries during the Heian period constitute a rear-guard fight. Seishi's ultimate failure did not, however, mark the end of female vocations. The decline of official nunneries facilitated the emergence of another type of convent, those for "household nuns" dedicated to the salvation of deceased relatives. Although their number rapidly increased after the end of the Heian period, their status remained significantly lower than that of their predecessors. Deprived from official support, these new convents, as well as the older ones that had managed to survive, became economically dependent on male monasteries. For instance, when Sairyū-niji, a convent founded by Empress Shōtoku in the Nara period, came under the control of the Ritsu monastery Saidaiji in 880, its nuns, who once performed state rituals, were reduced to menial tasks, such as washing the robes of Saidaiji monks.[36]

During the Kamakura period, the Ritsu school in particular encouraged the emergence of this new type of convent. The most representative was Hokkeji, a convent whose abbess, Jizen, was a daughter of Emperor Go-Toba.[37] In 1243, when the nuns of Hokkeji obtained authorization to restore it, they created an "inner sanctum" forbidden to men. Two years later, however, they demanded full ordination from Eizon (1201–90), the reformer of the Saidaiji branch. After that, their community grew quickly, from the initial sixteen members to twenty-six in 1249, sixty-four in

1259, and to one hundred eighty-three in 1280, eventually disseminating over fifteen nunneries.[38]

One of the women who received ordination from Eizon was Shinnyo, the daughter of a poor scholar-monk of Kōfukuji named Shōen.[39] When Shōen died, Shinnyo was left without any means of subsistence. In 1243, she visited Eizon at Saidaiji, and told him of a dream she had had seven years before, in which a kami had foretold Eizon's work of reviving the precepts for *both* male and female practitioners. Afterwards, Shinnyo founded Shōbōji. She also restored Chūgūji, a nunnery whose foundation was traced back to Prince Shōtoku Taishi. She attracted the court's patronage when she discovered in Tenryūji a tapestry representing the Pure Land. This tapestry had been created by Prince Shōtoku's consort, in memory of her late husband. With the support of the court, Shinnyo launched a campaign to preserve the tapestry and create copies, thereby spreading the cult of Shōtoku Taishi. In the restoration of Chūgūji, as in her ordination, a dream played a crucial role. But this time, the dreamer was the priest Sōji (d. 1312), a nephew and disciple of Eizon. Sōji also wanted to restore Chūgūji, but to turn it into a monastery. He changed his mind, however, after a dream revelation in which Shōtoku Taishi himself appeared and told him that Chūgūji, being originally a nunnery, should be restored by a nun. Sōji consequently selected a group of nuns for that purpose, Shinnyo among them.[40]

In Mujū Ichien's *Zōtanshū*, the interest shown by Shinnyo for the dances and songs of the female mediums (*miko*) of Kasuga Shrine suggests that she was not simply an orthodox nun, looking down on her shamanistic colleagues.[41] Indeed, her initial decision to be ordained, on the basis of a dream, has itself a shamanistic flavor. She is by no means an isolated case. Medieval nuns shared some affinities with the *miko* officiating at nearby shrines. Eizon was acutely aware of the shamanistic capacities of some of his nuns and respected their visions as a form of sacredness, a skillful means (*upāya*) used by the deity to save people. In his *Hokkeji shari engi*, Eizon records, for instance, how a nun named Jitsua used to have auspicious dreams in which Empress Kōmyō, the founder (*hongan*) of Hokkeji, told her about the miraculous efficacy of the Buddha's relics.

Jitsua's case reflects the ambivalent nature of Hokkeji nuns—in some respects seen as channels of sacred power, in others as women discarded by their lineage—in their relation with Buddhist relics (*śarīra*). A case in point is that of the nun Kūnyo (formerly Takakura no tsubone) and her companions. Eizon recorded their religious experiences upon contact with the relics, in particular their oracular dreams.[42] Kūnyo worked to spread the cult of relics and the influence of Hokkeji among women. If Eizon mentions her role in relic worship, it is apparently because he considered her one of the artisans in the renewal of the Ritsu school.[43] Nishiguchi

Junko, pointing out that relics of the Buddha were transmitted among nuns of the imperial clan, has argued that it was a way to link these women with their families and to compensate for the state of relative abandonment in which they had been cast.[44]

This relic transmission is related to Ritsu monks and to the cult of relics in Ritsu monasteries, which were places of reclusion for princesses and women of the court. According to Hosokawa Ryōichi, many women related to the emperor entered Hokkeji. Possession of these valued relics by these nuns, who had at one time belonged to the imperial palace, provided them with supernatural protection. It also brought some consolation to these secluded women, now estranged from the court. Hosokawa argues that for these nuns relics were keepsakes of the glorious days spent in the palace. The relics connected them to the court, constituting a fictitious "house" whose center was the emperor. They also established a genealogical—truly physical—tie between these nuns and the Buddha, a concrete proof that they were "daughters of the Buddha." Thus, the relics were at the same time an instrument of empowerment (both in the Buddhist sense of *kaji*, ritual empowerment, and in the feminist sense), and the silver lining of their reclusion, otherwise a sign of dereliction.

Although old nunneries like Hokkeji were restored, and new ones constructed, during the Kamakura and Muromachi periods, they were no longer the official institutions of the Ritsuryō state. According to Matsuo Kenji, two group of monks coexisted during the medieval period: official monks (*kansō*), who had been ordained on the official platforms of the great monasteries (Enryakuji, Miidera, Tōdaiji, and Tōji) and who performed state rituals, and others monks (referred to collectively as "recluse monks" (*tonseisō*), a mixed category including monks of the Zen and Ritsu schools, as well as various types of ascetics who stood outside the official clergy. The nunneries mentioned above were founded or restored by monks of the second group. As Taira Masayuki points out, they were built or restored as institutions for unmarried noble women or widows who had lost the protection of the patriarchal system.

The initiative for the founding of new convents often came from widow-nuns. Women who had been struck by a familial tragedy often wanted to spend the rest of their lives praying for the salvation of their deceased male relatives (fathers, husbands, or children)—as well as for their own salvation. This specific purpose explains in part why many of these new foundations proved short-lived. A case in point is Henjōji, a convent founded by the daughter of Minamoto no Sanetomo, better known as the "Hachijō nun." Dedicated to the memory of her father, it was primarily a refuge for orphaned daughters and widows.[45] After the death of its founder, the convent seems to have been rapidly handed over to monks.

Yet as convents gradually became a part of the broader community, and received continued economic support from local patrons, they became the places where the daughters of the donors' families would receive ordination. This development led to the constitution of lineages that were both familial and spiritual. Many of these convents were gradually absorbed by the Zen and Ritsu schools, remaining largely outside the framework of *kenmitsu* Buddhism. After the mid-Kamakura period, however, as the Zen and Ritsu schools were gradually accepted within the greater Buddhist establishment, their convents also gained official recognition.

In the Kegon school, the most representative case is Zenmyōji, a convent founded in Yamashina by Myōe as a shelter for the wives and daughters of nobles who had died in the so-called Jōkyū Disturbance of 1221. One of the women who joined the Zenmyōji community, Myōgyō, was the widow of the military commander Yamada Shigetada. She was in her early thirties at the time, and she remained at Zenmyōji until her sixties. She copied various scriptures in memory of her late husband, and in the memory of Myōe himself after the latter's death in 1232. She participated in particular in the copying of the famous "Nuns' Sūtra" (*ama-gyō*).[46]

Perhaps with the exception of those of the Saidaiji lineage (Hokkeji, Chūgūji), convents of the early Kamakura period were not always able to develop a "genuine" religious purpose beyond their role as sanctuaries for women. From the fourteenth century onward, however, they were established more durably under the auspices of the main schools, although their sectarian affiliations were sometimes unclear. Most convents seem to have belonged to the Rinzai sect, under the system of the "Five Convents" (*ama gozan*) patterned after the "Five Mountains (*gozan*) of medieval Zen. Most of these convents were located in Kyoto and Kamakura. In the Sōtō school, we also find a group of "five convents," most of them founded toward the end of the Kamakura period under the impulsion of Keizan Jōkin (1268–1325) and his disciples. Next come the Ritsu convents, about twenty, also dating from the Kamakura period, and belonging to the branches of Saidaiji and Tōshōdaiji in Nara, or Sennyūji in Kyoto. Like Eizon, his disciple Sōji received donations from women, many of them nuns. In 1249, Eizon conferred the precepts on a dozen nuns, who in turn founded numerous convents; we recall that Hokkeji was restored by one of them.

From the late Kamakura period onward, owing to the support of the bakufu and of the court, Rinzai nunneries came to play an official role. These nunneries enjoyed a number of privileges, and their main functions were to pray for the welfare of the shogunal or imperial family and the prosperity of the state. In the following periods, despite the emergence of nunneries in the Nichiren, Jōdo, and Ji schools, the overall predominance of the Rinzai school remained unchanged.[47] The *bikuni gosho*, or imperial convents, became extensions of the court administration. Inasmuch as they were closely connected with powerful families and with the court, these institutions were of the same nature as the Five Convents in the capital.[48]

One of these convents, Keiaiji, was founded by the nun Mugai Nyodai, a disciple of the Chan master Wuxue Zuyuan (Jp. Mugaku Sogen). Born into the Adachi family, she was educated in both Chinese and Japanese and married into a branch of the Hōjō clan. After joining the order and receiving the Dharma transmission from Wuxue, she became the first female Zen teacher in Japan. Her position as abbess of Keiaiji led her to assume control of the convent network, *ama gozan*.[49] Even though the later Zen tradition attempted to erase Mugai from its official record, in her lifetime she received all the recognition a woman could hope for; indeed, she belonged to a social, intellectual, and spiritual elite.

In the biographies of the nuns of the *bikuni gosho*, we find, apart from the usual Zen emphasis on meditation and lineage, references to a rather elitist type of practice focused, as was the court, on "flowers and poetry." One may even wonder whether their attraction to Zen was not in part motivated by the fact this teaching was perceived as the latest intellectual and artistic fashion.[50] For instance, all of the nuns who joined the lineage of the renowned Zen masters Musō Soseki and Shun'oku Myōha were of high birth: Musō-ni was an imperial consort; Karin Egon, the founder of Hōkyōji and restorer of Kenfuku-niji, was a princess; and Musetsu, founder of Honjō-in, was a scion of the Ashikaga family.[51] These women were by all standards quite privileged. The preservation of their privileges was guaranteed by the strictly regulated access to nunhood; at the same time, the monastic rules could be bent for these high-ranking nuns, whose political connections could be useful. As for those convents that did not belong to this network, they usually depended on a particular family, and abbotship was determined by familial ties.[52] At a time when the aristocracy was losing ground to the warriors, ordination was more often determined by economic reasons than by spiritual vocation. To some, nunhood may have given access to a life of leisure, but even among aristocratic women, entrance into the *bikuni gosho* was rarely the result of free choice.

In the Sengoku and Edo periods, the *bikuni gosho* became increasingly elitist. Among them were convents like Keiaiji, which received women of imperial birth. If a samurai's daughter wanted to enter there, she had to be adopted by an aristocratic family. Several daughters of Emperor Gomizunoo (r. 1611–29) joined these convents; the same is true of shogunal daughters like Rishu-ni or Rigei-ni, whose ordination, in the mid-sixteenth century, allowed the creation of close ties between the *bikuni gosho* and the Ashikaga family. The ordination of Rikō-ni in 1558 also marked the beginning of the convents' relationship with the Tokugawa family. Again, in 1540, a nun named Rihō concocted a lineage connecting Keiaiji (Mugai Nyodai's convent) to Hōkyōji. Because imperial princesses entered Hōkyōji, this convent was established as the center of the conventual network, while other convents became its sub-temples. In the Edo period, these convents were perceived as part of court institutions, fulfilling at the same time religious and secular functions.

The important role played by such convents, owing to their ties with the imperial family and the nobility, should not obscure the existence, and manifold functions, of many other kinds of convents throughout Japan. At Myōshinji, a Rinzai convent in Kii peninsula built toward the mid-fifteenth century, and the headquarters of the Kumano *bikuni*, nuns were particularly active in raising donations. Another interesting nunnery in that respect was Keikō-in, whose nuns received from the emperor the title of Ise Shōnin, and the further honor of the purple robe as reward for their efforts in restoring Ise Shrine.[53] A few other nunneries, like Zenkōji in Shinano and Seiganji in Owari, received similar imperial favors. Among the *ama gozan* in Kyoto, the only convent to have received such favors during the Muromachi period had been Mugai's convent, Keiaiji.

The *ama gozan* convents, in which daughters of good family were cloistered from their childhood, were only the most visible institutions. Unlike them, other convents were usually populated with widow-nuns. The development of these two types of institutions was largely a response to societal changes. The multiplication of convents for widow-nuns, for instance, reflects a change of perception regarding the status of single women. With the progress of patriarchal ideology, it became increasingly difficult for widows to remarry; the best solution for them was to live the rest of their lives in a nunnery. The fact that these nunneries belonged in general to the Zen and Ritsu schools may be due in part to the common perception that these schools advocated a strict discipline. It was probably not, as Matsuo Kenji has argued, a mere outcome of the concern of "recluse monks" (*tonseisō*) for women's salvation. As urban convents tended to acquire official status, the gap between them and small provincial nunneries increased. Therefore, it is important to keep in mind the differences between the various institutions to which we refer by the vague terms "convent" or "nunnery," as well as those between their inhabitants. Stringent inequalities existed between, on the one hand, daughters from the nobility and the shogunal family, who lived a leisurely life in the *ama gozan* and the *bikuni gosho*, and, on the other hand, the nuns of small provincial convents.

The Meiji Restoration, by emphasizing the right of monks (but not of nuns) to marry, caused the emergence of a new category of religious women: priest's wives (called *jizoku* in the Zen sect).[54] These women rapidly came to play a crucial role in the management of temples, which no longer received governmental support. Their status nonetheless remained ambivalent in a religious movement that still adhered to the idea (if not the practice) of ascesis and celibacy, and refused to acknowledge the existence of conjugal ties. Only quite recently, in 1995, did *jizoku* become officially recognized by the Sōtō sect.[55] Yet discriminatory practices are resilient: even today, *jizoku* do not have the right to be buried with their husbands, as do ordinary wives.[56] Through an ironic turn of events, they have become, in their claim for recognition, a thorn in the flesh of "regular" nuns, who are struggling for their own elevation of status. The rivalry between the two groups has been used by the male clergy to resist any change. The main obstacle to a recognition of the *jizoku* seems to lie in the unrealistic expectation that Buddhist priests behave as world-renouncers, an ideal that flies in the face of Japanese reality. The *jizoku* question compels us to return briefly to that of female ordination before examining the sociological context(s) of Japanese female monasticism.

THE ISSUE OF ORDINATION

Throughout its evolution, the question of origins has returned to haunt the female order. The *Biqiuni zhuan*'s hesitation concerning the criteria for regular female ordination shows that this question was perceived as vital for the female saṅgha insofar as it determined the authenticity of its lineage. Whereas in Tibet and Southeast Asian countries, orthodox transmission was rapidly interrupted, or never achieved, Chinese nuns were eventually able to reach the quorum for regular ordination, but for this they had to wait for the arrival of a contingent of South Asian nuns, some seventy years after the emergence of the Chinese female order. Strictly speaking, then, the first Chinese nuns were not regularly ordained, a fact that has led "orthodox" Buddhist scholars to call them "false nuns."[57] Such uncritical acceptance of Vinaya orthodoxy, however, has a high cost, since it condemns us to ignore a significant portion of Chinese monastic history.

Although intent on establishing the orthodoxy of the Chinese order of nuns, Baochang adopts a more liberal approach, claiming, for instance, that the nuns who had received ordination prior to 434 were perfectly legitimate. He traces the emergence of the feminine order in China back to the nun Jingjian (ca. 292–ca. 361). The latter received the Ten Precepts from a Vinaya master and was ordained in 357 by the assembly of monks. Although she did not receive the full ordination in presence of an assembly of regular nuns, this did not prevent her from becoming the abbess of a prosperous convent.[58] To clear doubts in the minds of his readers, Baochang reports that, on the day of Jingjian's partial ordination, "a remarkable fragrance filled the air." This auspicious sign is confirmed by Jingjian's final apotheosis: a heavenly woman appears on a red cloud to welcome her, and she and Jingjian ascend heaven in broad daylight—in typical immortal fashion.[59]

Baochang reluctantly acknowledges that the first full ordination came much later, with a nun named Huiguo (ca. 364–433). Indeed, despite her tonsure, Huiguo remained uncertain as to her status. Thus, when the Central Asian missionary monk Guṇavarman arrived in China in 429, she asked him whether female ordinations only taken in the presence of the monks' assembly were valid. Guṇavarman reassured her. When a group of eleven nuns arrived by ship from Sri Lanka, however, Huiguo had to defend her orthodoxy. She claimed that her model was Mahāprajāpatī, "who was deemed to have accepted the full monastic obligation by taking on herself, and therefore for all women for all time, the eight special prohibitions incumbent on women wanting to lead the monastic life."[60] Nevertheless, she eventually requested Guṇavarman to "reordain" her, together with some three hundred *consoeurs*, in the presence of the foreign nuns.[61] Baochang himself seems to have had some second thoughts about the matter, as he returns to it in the biography of the nun Baoxian: "[Guṇavarman] had not said that the first transmission to China, from the Assembly of Monks only, was invalid. He had said, rather, that the second transmission was augmenting the value of the obligation that had already been received."[62] This "logic of the supplement" reflects the predicament of the first Chinese nuns. The irregularity of their initial ordination was perceived to impinge on their morality, since only the full ordination entailed the observance of some 350 (or 500) precepts. Again, perhaps questions already raised at the time about clerical morality made it necessary for the nuns (and Baochang) to emphasize their observance of the Vinaya.

In Japan, the question of regular ordination does not seem to have played a major role at first. It became more pressing with the reform of the monastic ordinations by the Chinese Vinaya master Jianzhen (Jp. Ganjin). We recall that the first Japanese nuns, Zenshin and her two companions, were simply tonsured by an ex-priest from Koryŏ. This apparent lack of credentials was compensated for by auspicious signs, as that of the apparition of relics of the Buddha, an irrefutable proof of the authenticity of Zenshin's lineage. Nevertheless, the three nuns were sent to Paekche in 587 to receive full ordination. Although they returned within less than two years, the lapse of time needed for this, Zenshin is said to have ordained many nuns afterwards.[63]

When Ganjin arrived in Japan in 752, there were only three nuns in the group of Chinese disciples who accompanied him. Thus, the quorum of ten female preceptors required for regular female ordinations was still not reached. Ganjin's uncompromising attitude posed serious problems for Japanese nuns. Not only were former ordinations invalid, but new ordinations seemed impossible. We have no clear indication of how the issue was resolved. Although a clear causal relationship cannot be proved, the fact remains that the nuns' participation in court rituals, and therefore government support, declined sharply after Ganjin's arrival.[64]

In the Heian period, the development of bodhisattva ordinations on Mount Hiei, the headquarters of the Tendai school, seems to have offered one alternative. There was no canonical restriction to female bodhisattva ordinations, unlike in the case of traditional precepts. In 1027, a platform was erected at Hōjōji at the demand of Shōshi, the consort of Emperor Ichijō. It was unfortunately destroyed by fire in 1058, and was never rebuilt. At any rate, the *endonkai* ("sudden and perfect precepts") ordination of Tendai allowed the ordination of nuns without a quorum of ten male and ten female preceptors. This solution, however, was never accepted by the older Nara schools.[65]

In 1249, twelve nuns received from Eizon the full Ritsu ordination. In his autobiography, Eizon comments, "This marks the first time in which the seven groups of Buddhist practitioners as originally instituted by the Buddha became complete in the country of Japan."[66] In other words, Eizon is claiming that the first regular ordinations in Japan, and therefore the creation of an orthodox female order, begin with him. This rather extreme claim bears closer scrutiny. As noted earlier, the leading figure among these nuns was a charismatic young woman, Shinnyo. The strange episode concerning her ordination deserves to be mentioned.[67] When she asked to be ordained, her teacher Kakujō was first reluctant, fearing criticism. Even after having an auspicious dream, he was still embarrassed by the fact that there was no other "orthodox" nun to serve as witness. Then a heavenly being appeared to Shinnyo's brother, a monk named Kyōen, and prompted him to turn into a nun. Twenty-one days after Shinnyo's ordination, Kyōen is said to have returned to his original gender.[68] Eizon, tongue-in-cheek perhaps, marvels at this event in his autobiography.[69] This story, which emphasizes the quasi-magical nature of ordination, is a response to the tradition regarding the first Japanese ordinations, and it sounds in particular like a rebuttal of Ganjin.

SOCIOLOGICAL CONTEXT(S)

Although we lack a "history" of the female saṅgha, as that of the *Biqiuni zhuan* in China, the devotional practices of Japanese nuns are described in various documents: biographies, wills, vows, epitaphs. From the mid-

Heian period onward, women called "nuns" (*bikuni* or *ama*) took a variety of precepts, or sometimes no precepts at all.[70] Among them, some were recluses, while others lived a devout life at home as "lay nuns" (*zaizoku no zenni*). The woman known as the "Hachijō Nun" (Nishi Hachijō no zenni, 1193–1274) belonged to the first group. The daughter of a courtier, she married at a young age the shogun Minamoto no Sanetomo. After the murder of her husband, she took monastic vows and retired to a convent located on Heian-kyō's Western Eighth Avenue (Nishi Hachijō). When she died, at the advanced age of eighty-two, she left a "declaration of intent" (*okibumi*) that reveals her deep faith. In the second group, we find Mikoshibe no zenni (1171–ca. 1252), a poet whose work is representative of women's poetry at the time of the *Shin kokinshū*. In her old age, she lived in Saga on the outskirsts of the capital.[71]

We noted that many Japanese nuns, particularly after the Heian period, were widows. While they were in theory dead to the world, in practice they continued to play important sociopolitical and socioeconomic rules, at least during the Kamakura and Muromachi periods. A well-known case is that of Hōjō Masako, the "nun-shogun" (*ama-shōgun*), who continued to hold the reins of power after the death of her husband, the first shogun Minamoto no Yoritomo.[72] Unlike monks, women usually became nuns late in life, and often continued to live at home: these women, called *ama-nyūdō*, *ie no ama*, or *ama-nyobō*, cut their hair, without shaving it off completely.

Often there was a close relationship between domestic economy and ordination. In many cases, a woman could not be ordained right away after her husband's death. If she happened to be pregnant, if she had children to bring up, or in-laws to take care of, she was expected to manage the households as before. Often, ordination remained incomplete, and the "nuns" continued to run domestic affairs. Thus, the ties between nuns and their households were no longer as neatly severed as before. Widow-nuns, who had in principle "left the family," were still very much part of their husband's family. Although ordination meant breaking up conjugal ties if it took place while the husband was still alive, such was not the case after the husband's death. The widow also inherited duties toward her husband's family.

Most widows were unwilling or unable to abandon all worldly ties. The *Bunpoki*, a commentary on the rules for mourning at Ise shrine, discusses, on the basis of a concrete case dated 1095, whether a widow had to observe mourning for her mother-in-law; and whether, when she herself died, the children of the husband's second wife had to mourn her as their stepmother. The *Bunpoki* ruled that there was no such need, and this rule was reiterated in the *Eishōki*, a commentary compiled during the Muromachi period.

Usually, family duties continued for the widowed nun, who was obliged to pray for her husband's rest. Many "joint vows," reflecting a Buddhist conception of marriage, show that ties between husband and wife (as "friends in karma") were not severed by death. After the fourteenth century, however, things began to change in this respect, with the appearance of convents in which nuns could practice independent of their husband's family.

Thus, two conflicting conceptions have successively prevailed regarding whether the death of a husband interrupts the conjugal duties of his widow. From the Heian to the Kamakura period, widow-nuns were required to exhibit fidelity and chastity; even after their husband's death, they continued to assume their position in the marital lineage, while praying for his soul. After the Kamakura period, one sees an increasing number of cases in which a widow severs all ties with her husband's family and dedicates herself to religious practice after entering a convent.

Motivations

Obviously, the number of nuns in convents cannot be taken as an index of the role of religious women in medieval Japanese society; however, the scholarship in the field has been dominated by the tendency to focus on "regular" nuns. The role of nuns tends to be misunderstood in particular because of an idealized or normative perception of nunhood.

Too often, nuns are credited with a single-minded spiritual purpose that takes little account of the psychological and sociological complexities involved. Describing the modern Sōtō Zen community, Paula Arai argues, for instance, that nuns show a more authentic motivation than monks, who often get ordained to inherit their father's temple, By contrast, the nuns' ordination would reflect their search for the Dharma. Arai's description is insufficient, at least in the case of premodern Japan.[73] Recent studies have called into question this idealized image of nuns and fostered a better understanding of the socioeconomic role of convents in medieval Japan. Without denying the existence of true religious vocations, we must avoid idealizing the rank and file members of Buddhist convents, thus creating an inverted image of the anticlerical caricature.[74]

The composition of the female saṅgha varied significantly with times and places. The monastic hierachy to some extent reflected the diversity of origins and motivations of the nuns. Women became ordained for various reasons, not all of them equally noble. Some motivations were purely personal, whether selfish or altruistic: they could result from concerns about old age, sickness, death, or from a desire for rebirth in the Pure Land; or again, from the desire of interceding for a dead husband, child, or lord. In many cases, the entry into a convent took place during childhood, and these young girls were destined to become professional nuns. Finally, there were also cases where "leaving the family" was perceived as a way to divorce a husband, or as a punishment for some crime. Most of these motivations did not change between the Heian and Muromachi periods, but some new characteristics emerged. After the Kamakura period, as the hope for rebirth in the Pure Land spread, more people wanted to spend their last years or last moments in a clerical context. Indeed, apart from a minority of women who may have entered the order motivated by a spiritual quest, many took the vows for purely practical reasons.

Barbara Ruch has argued that, for Japanese women, convents were the highway to freedom.[75] One should keep in mind, however, that, in the rude context of late medieval Japan, outside the safety of the official institutions freedom was bought at the cost of many hardships—in the worst case, starvation. One could just as well argue the opposite; namely, that ordination was often for single women an "escape from freedom," a way to put themselves under some kind of authority. This situation was by no means specific to Japan. From the beginning, in Asia as in Europe, nunhood (even more than monkhood) was often motivated less by spiritual than social, economic, or psychological reasons, even if in the end it may have had spiritual rewards. A case in point is that of the nun Caṇḍa, in the *Therīgāthā* (*Songs of the Elder Nuns*):

> Formerly I fared ill, a widow, without children. Without family or relations I did not obtain food or clothing.
> Taking a bowl and stick, begging from family to family, and being burned by the cold and heat, I wandered for seven years.
> But having seen a nun, who had obtained food and drink, approaching her I said: "Send me forth into the houseless state.[76]

In medieval Japan, too, monastic life, however precarious at times, was judged preferable to more hazardous female trades. For instance, when Lady Nijō stayed with a monastic community of former prostitutes during her travels in 1302–1303, she remarked: "On the small island of Taika, there was a row of small huts belonging to women who had fled from lives in prostitution. . . . I admired them for having renounced that way of life and come here to live in seclusion."[77] Other examples of motivations are described in medieval literature. In the *kana zōshi* entitled "Seven Nuns" (*Shichinin bikuni*), for instance, each of the female protagonists lists her reasons for leaving the family: prostitution, death of a child, death of a husband at war, realization of impermanence, feminine jealousy, suicide of someone in a triangular love relationship, death of a lover. This list is by no means exhaustive, but it is sufficient to show that nunhood meant different things to different women. To some it may have been an end in itself, the ultimate refuge; to others it was primarily a means of sociopolitical empowerment. Motivations thus ranged the whole gamut from spiritual aspiration or dedication to the soul of a deceased one to escape from the duties and pressures of normal womanhood or consolidation of socioeconomic power over a household. Although nunhood was often judged with suspicion as a mild form of deviance from the regular duties of women, it was on the whole accepted, and even at times encouraged. In the absence of other social institutions, nunneries provided a precarious shelter for women in times of war. In times of peace, they also provided a better education and a certain leisure for women interested in poetry and literature.

Status

Nunhood could also provide varying degrees of upward mobility. Although many women became nuns in the hope of improving their lot in life, ordination did not automatically translate into higher status. The diversity of statuses, ranging from the professional nun (for instance the abbess of official convents) to the mendicant, was already characteristic of the Indian nuns described in the *Therīgāthā*. In Japan, too, convents fostered the rich and poor, the old and the young, mothers and daughters, widows and courtesans, as well as servants. Even after ordination, this diversity remained visible through monastic hierarchy.

Such status differences were reflected for instance in the various types of tonsure.[78] Shaving one's hair was a very powerful symbolic act that removed an individual from his or her normal social duties, and to some extent from his or her gender roles. At the time of tonsure, nuns usually adopted nongendered, or rather neutered, religious names. Perhaps this symbolic erasure of gender/sex characteristics reflected a kind of identification with the rather asexual buddhas or bodhisattvas. It was also an identification, not so much with the transcendence of awakening as with the alleged transcendence of the institution. When focusing on these "neutered" women, however, scholars run the same risk of erasing gender (or rather sex) from their own scholarship.

Even though tonsure symbolizes the radical shift from one social role to another, it was often a negative one, characterized by social debasement. In medieval Japan, this rite of passage was not always freely chosen: actively sought by some, it was feared by others. A shaved head was perceived as a degradation of the body, it indicated that the person in question had been shunned by society. Monastic tonsure could thus be a mark of punishment, and nunhood, in effect, a disposal system for burned-out women. Young women could also be forced into it after a grave offense, such as illicit pregnancy or adultery.[79] We learn, for instance, of a palace servant who was sent to Hokkeji in 1432 after becoming involved in a love affair.[80] A slightly different case is that of Lady Nijō, a former favorite of Retired Emperor Go-Fukakusa, who became a nun after being rejected from the court. Her famous work, *Unasked-for Tales* (*Towazugatari*), seems influenced by the image of the young lady-in-waiting Kōgō in the *Heike monogatari*: because she was loved by Emperor Takakura (the husband of two of Kiyomori's daughters), Kōgō was banished from the palace and forced by Kiyomori to become a nun.[81] Significantly, Lady Nijō also tells of the dishonor suffered by a young courtesan who was harshly dismissed by Emperor Go-Fukakusa, and subsequently became a nun.[82]

Even though tonsure symbolically erased sex and gender, in actual practice, nuns were still bound by traditional conceptions of femininity. Kawahashi Noriko explains, "A nun's newly acquired religious identity is never seen as socially constructed, but instead is fundamentally defined by her sexual identity grounded in biological givens."[83] Unlike nuns of patrician background, who were able to enjoy the sheltered life of official convents, ordinary nuns often lived in precarious conditions. In the worst cases, a lack of resources or protection could mean mendicity or prostitution. During times of civil strife, convents were often attacked, and their nuns raped; monks were not infrequently murdered. The *Taiheiki*, for instance, describes the end of the Taira kinsmen during the Kenmu Restoration: "From temples they fetched out Heishi kinsmen who had forsaken the transient world to become monks, and stained their holy robes with blood. Likewise in diverse places they violated the chasteness of the widows of the dead, who had cut off their hair to become nuns, resolved never to wed again."[84] Such acts were motivated not only by men's sexual desire, but also by their desire to degrade their enemies.

Indeed, even in times of relative peace, nuns remained sexual objects for monks. Sexual desire is highly versatile and has no difficulty fetishizing a body represented as essentially sexless. Although the nuns' bodies were in theory de-eroticized by mortification (through tonsure and austerity, rather than maternity, as in the case of ordinary women), in practice, it was easily re-eroticized: in the case of younger nuns, precisely because they did not have to go through childbearing. Nuns, however, were not only the passive objects of male desire. According to Karen Lang, "The nun's commitment to shaving her head indicates her control over her sexuality and her potential fertility."[85] This is perhaps true of regular nuns, living in reclusion, but there were other types of nuns, whose sexuality was not nearly so constrained. Indeed, the nuns' commitment to monastic vows was not always as total as one would expect, a fact also reflected in the mode of haircutting. Instead of the symbolic gender-erasure of total tonsure, different hairstyles could be adopted, corresponding to a gradation of commitments, and consequently to a monastic hierarchy. Even the smallest status differences could be reflected by different haircuts, ranging from complete shaving to the cutting of shoulder-length hair to bangs (*ama-sogi*). Often, a pro forma ordination accompanied by a slight shaving of the head (or by a mere cutting of locks) was performed as part of an exorcism. Full tonsure was resorted to only at times of imminent danger (childbirth, illness). It implied that one was dead to the world—this was no trifling matter, since such metaphorical death could either prevent real death, or foreshadow it. Women who were not entirely ready to abandon all worldly ties would cringe before this ultimate sacrifice, and compromise by receiving only the half-tonsure. Thus, the full tonsure, which was in some cases a mark of infamy for a woman, could also be a mark of exalted spiritual status, the proof that she had symbolically become a *monk*: that is, an allegedly genderless being. In that sense, it remained a powerful symbol of commitment.

As noted above, the decision to become a nun was often taken at a time of personal crisis. Women were perceived to be intrinsically frail beings, more vulnerable to the threat of evil forces, particularly at the critical time of menstruation and childbearing. Ordination was a way to create quasi-magical ties with the Three Jewels, in order to protect oneself against such demonic intrusions. Thus, when assailed by a severe illness or facing a difficult delivery, highborn women would often take monastic vows in the hope of a safe outcome. In the most desperate cases, ordination functioned as a kind of extreme unction, providing a viaticum for the journey to the other world. If they recovered or had a safe delivery, many of these women, blissfully forgetting their vows, returned to lay life.[86] This custom explains the vogue of the bodhisattva precepts among medieval Japanese women. Religious motivation was obviously not the determining factor, even though the solemn act of receiving the precepts may have modified the religious feelings of the individual.

Not all women were entitled to such apparent fickleness, however. Whereas in the Heian period most ordinations were those of married women, in the medieval period, many young girls were dedicated to the saṅgha by their family, with or without vocation. Their number increased particularly during the Muromachi period, perhaps due to increasing concerns about the patriarchal household (*ie*). At that time, next to official convents like the *bikuni gosho* and the *ama gozan*, or the "cloisters" (*in*) reserved to nuns in large monasteries like Ninnaji and Tennōji, there existed many small hermitages (*tatchū*) or convents with specific ties with families. Because the entry into a convent required the shogun's authorization, the request had to come from the convent itself. The age for the noviciate varied with the convents, although it was usually around eight. Even after she became a novice, the young girl maintained close relations with her family. As she moved through the stages leading to her full ordination, she came to play an important role as spiritual intercessor for her relatives. Although all nuns went through the same stages, their status was to a large extent determined by the social and economic capital of their family. The complex relationships between worldly hierarchy and religious hierarchy explain why social distinctions continued to prevail within the convent.

Freedom

Being no longer confined at home, the newly ordained nun acquired a much greater freedom of movement. She could, through her alms-begging and preaching, come into contact with a greater variety of people. This relative freedom, coupled with a progressive decline in status, is not sufficient to explain the existence in the Edo period of tonsured prostitutes who claimed to belong to the lineage of the Kumano nuns. Both nuns and prostitutes were women who had rejected the familial norm, and they tended in turn to be rejected by society, or at least to be perceived negatively.

As gender discrimination increased in medieval Japan, women were gradually evicted from public functions. By becoming a nun, however, a woman acquired a certain autonomy vis-à-vis profane rules and domestic roles, in addition to being excused from conjugal duties. Inasmuch as her role as a religious specialist was recognized, she gained a certain freedom of action. She could travel to meet the needs of religious practice, and receive some respect when she appeared in public places. Nonetheless, she continued to be subordinate to male authority in her religious community. Significantly, a nun's robe remained black—the color of a novice's robe—throughout her life, whereas the color of a monk's robe changed when he attained a higher rank. Nuns of inferior status—those who had left the family in order to escape marriage, to get a divorce, or as the result of some misconduct—were held in low esteem in secular society. Furthermore, the need they had of the financial support of lay people prevented them from severing worldly ties. In the end, they could not escape gender and class discrimination.

The same social reasons explain the privileges of the monastic "leisure class"—for instance, those of the nuns of the *ama gozan*. The recent inventory of the library of an imperial convent, Hōkyōji, reveals that it contains not only "spiritual" treatises on Buddhism and Confucianism, but also a large number of poetic anthologies, books on medicine, tea ceremony, flower arrangement, famous sites, and subjects of the kind.[87] Like the nunneries of Tang China, the official convents of late medieval and early modern Japan were often seen as aristocratic venues.[88] One could probably apply to these nuns what Susan Mann wrote of Chinese women writers of the eighteenth century: "Many lived lives of privileges that few of us can imagine, separated as they were by leisure and learning from the other 99.9 percent of women in the late empire."[89]

Dirty Laundry

Most Japanese nuns, however, were not as privileged. One major difference between Japanese monks and nuns had to do with "domestic" work. In order to support themselves, many nuns came to perform specific tasks such as washing the clothes of the monks. A number of stories mention women who, having become nuns at Amano, at the foot of Mount Kōya, continued to wash the clothes of monks who were their fathers, brothers, or husbands. According to the Vinaya, a monk could have his clothes washed only by a woman of his family. In practice, though, it seems that this rule was not strictly followed in Japan. For instance, a document entitled "Rules of Zenrinji" (*Zenrinji shiki*) forbids monks to importune villagers with their laundry, implying that it was a common habit.[90] In the *Yamato monogatari*, we are told about a monk of Mount Hiei who returns to his village in order to get his clothes washed because he has found no woman on the mountain who could do it.[91]

Washing clothes is a strongly gendered activity in most cultures. Katsuura Noriko emphasizes the ritual aspect of the washing of monastic robes, which was said to take place "once a month," like the washing of the women's clothes soiled by menstrual blood.[92] She suggests that such activity may have had magical connotations: in particular, the fact that such "purification rite"—akin to the *misogi* or *harai* of Shintō—was reserved for women may, from the perspective of a "cultural history of washing," imply a male recognition of the "power of women." In the French case studied by the anthropologist Yvonne Verdier, "washing-women" were in charge of the important rites of passage: the washing of newborns and the dead.[93] Katsuura tries to apply Verdier's interpretation to the case of Japanese nuns, but it seems that the latter's role was strictly limited to washing the monks' robes and did not extend to the rites of birth and death. In other words, their function seems to be a purely ancillary one, and, even though some of them may have played a mediating role and acquired a greater symbolic significance, on the whole one gets the impression that they were largely exploited, and were held in particularly servile and subaltern positions.

Divorce

As noted earlier, entering the monastic order was the only way for a woman to get a divorce. Monastic tonsure was not only an expression of the will to become a nun, but also a way to symbolically cut the ties between husband and wife. Such divorces were often attributed to female jealousy, which was very much a part of the medieval image of woman and often served as a pretext for divorce for women who wanted more independence.[94] For instance, we read in the *Entairyaku* that the wife of Takatsukasa Morohira cut her hair and became a nun at Hoanji; in other words, she took the initiative in the divorce.[95] She was twenty-six at the time, and she had been married for eleven years.

Sometimes, the intervention of a charismatic priest was required to overcome the obstruction of the husband and his family, as shown in the following story. At the end of the Muromachi period, the Tendai priest Shinsei attracted many disciples, both monks and nuns. He supervised sixteen temples dedicated to the "constant nenbutsu" (*fudan nenbutsu*), among which were five nunneries.[96] In 1485, after lecturing on Genshin's *Ojō yōshū* at the imperial palace, he gained Empress Karakumon'in (the mother of Emperor Tsuchimikado) and her daughter as disciples, as well as many highborn women. At the funeral of Karakumon'in, he recited the Devadatta chapter of the *Lotus Sūtra* which contains the episode of the buddhahood of the nāga-girl. When he himself died in 1495, several nuns tried to drown themselves, apparently in the hope of following him to the Pure Land. One of them, a young nun of twenty-two, Shinhan, did succeed, throwing herself into the water after facing toward the West. A purple cloud appeared above the pond, an unmistakable sign that she had been reborn in the Pure Land. The *Shinsei shōnin ōjō denki* gives some details about her. She had produced the thought of awakening in 1493 at the age of twenty. Resenting her husband's infidelity, she tried to kill his concubine. Her attempt failed, but this dramatic event determined her "leaving the family." She met Shinsei as he was on a pilgrimage to Ise Shrine with a group of 150 monks and nuns. Shinsei accepted her among his disciples, and she cut her hair. Her in-laws, however, refused to accept her decision, claiming that it was motivated by jealousy. Shinsei eventually convinced them that she was sincere. She then wrote a "Letter of Repentance" (*zange jō*) and eventually obtained a divorce.[97]

SORELY MISSED

According to the *Taiheiki*, after Toshimoto committed suicide for having plotted with Emperor Go-Daigo, his wife, having performed the forty-nine day rites, "put on the deep black robes of a nun, that early and late behind the brushwood door of a rustic retreat she might pray for the enlightenment of her dead husband."[98] We have already noted the growing number of widow-nuns in medieval Japan. Apart from the pious desire to pray for their dead husbands, their choice of conventual life was often the result of the patriarchal pressure regarding women's chastity, which made it increasingly difficult for widows to remarry. Consequently, many of them spent the rest of their lives in convents. Furthermore, owing to the lack of a regular procedure for divorce, it was hard for a married woman to withdraw from her conjugal roles—sexual relationships, education of children, management of the house—while she was still young. Thus, not surprisingly, old women and widows were the best candidates for ordination. But then, the husband's family often imposed it. Although we tend to think of widow-nuns as mature, post-menopausal women, such was not always the case. The wife of Ogawamiya, for instance, had become his concubine at the tender age of fourteen. Although she was only sixteen when he died in 1425, her father-in-law forced her to enter a convent.

Medieval literature abounds in formulaic stories of young women who become nuns after the death of their beloved ones, whether father, husband, son, or lover (rarely a mother or a sister). Thus, in the *Heike monogatari*, we are told that, after the death in exile of Bishop Shunkan, "his daughter became a nun forthwith at the age of twelve, and thereafter devoted herself wholly to prayers for her father and mother at the Hokkeji nunnery in Nara."[99] One may wonder whether these women entered nunhood because of a survivor's feeling of guilt, or—and this is perhaps not very different—in order to placate the malevolent spirits (*onryō*) of their dead.[100]

A paradigmatic widow-nun is Empress Kenreimon'in, one of the few survivors of the battle of Dan-no-Ura, which sealed the fate of the Taira clan. Thomas Cogan has shown the similarities between her destiny, as told in the *Heike monogatari,* and that of Tora Gozen in the *Soga monogatari*. Both were chaste widows who prayed for the salvation of their dead lovers or relatives. Kenreimon'in becomes a nun after the defeat of the Taira and the death of her son, and she withdraws in an isolated hermitage temple in Ōhara, at the northeastern outskirts of Kyoto. Tora becomes a nun after the death of her lover, one of the Soga brothers, and she secludes herself at Kōraiji.[101]

According to the *Heike monogatari*, after the execution of Shigehira, the Taira warrior accused of burning the Nara temples, his wife, Lady Dainagon-no-suke, sent a palanquin to fetch his remains. "She cremated both the head and the body, sent the bones to Mount Kōya, and made a grave at Hino. Then, most touchingly, she became a nun and prayed for Shigehira's welfare in the afterlife."[102] The tragic fate of Shigehira is presented as the inspiration for several other instances of the kind. One of them, the daughter of Chikanori, the minister of popular affairs, "was a peerless beauty, with a warm, affectionate nature. Sadly enough, when she learned that Shigehira had been taken to the southern capital and beheaded, she promptly cut her hair and donned coarse black robes to

pray for his enlightenment."[103] Another young woman bereaved by Shigehira's death was the young courtesan Senju no Mae. At the time of
Shigehira's arrest, she had been asked by Munemochi, a kindhearted Minamoto warrior, to spend the night with his prisoner to entertain him.
"For Senju-no-mae, the encounter seems to have led to sorrow. As soon
as she heard that Shigehira had been sent to the southern capital and
executed, she pronounced Buddhist vows, donned deep black robes, and
began a life of pious exercises on the Middle Captain's behalf at the Zenkōji Temple in Shinano. In the end, she attained her goal of rebirth in the
Pure Land."[104] The story of Senju no Mae is followed by that of Yokobue,
one of Empress Kenreimon'in's lesser attendants who had fallen in love
with the Taira warrior Tokiyori. When Tokiyori became ordained, she
tried to see him in his Saga hermitage, but he avoided her and left for
Mount Kōya. She eventually becames a nun at Hokkeji, but soon died,
perhaps of a broken heart.[105]

Although the motif of eternal chastity underlying nunhood (as a kind
of live burial) never led to the extremes of the Indian institution of widow-
burning (sati), it did find its ultimate expression in stories of suicide in
China and Japan. The *Taiheiki* describes the predicament of warrior
women after the defeat of their kinsmen: "There were wives who cast
their bodies into deep waters, unwilling to marry anew when the loss of
their husbands made their vows as vain things. And there were aged mothers, lingering on after their sons were dead, who fell over into chasms by
their own will, since they had no more means of living and could not
find a day's food."[106] The *Heike monogatari* tells of the last moments of
Kōzaishō, a court lady who had lost her husband Mochimori in the Genpei war: "Then, with her tearful gaze fixed on the distant heavens, she
uttered a supplication: 'Hail, Amitābha Tathāgata, Teaching Lord of the
Western Paradise! Lead me to the Pure Land in accordance with your
vow; assure me rebirth on the same lotus as the dear husband from whom
I parted too soon.' As she spoke the last word, she cast herself into the
sea."[107] The *Heike monogatari* adds a significant comment to her story:
"Among the many women who have lost husbands, it has long been common practice to enter the religious life, but few have gone so far as to
drown themselves. Might this be the kind of thing that is meant by the
saying, 'A loyal vassal does not obey two masters; a chaste wife does not
serve two husbands'?"[108] The *Heike monogatari* seems at times to hesitate, however: in the story of Empress Kenreimon'in, a woman rescued
after throwing herself into the sea, survival is presented as the only hope
for the salvation of the dead and the living. The same source goes one
step further in reporting the admonition of the Taira warrior Koremori
to his wife: "Don't think of becoming a nun if you hear I have been killed.

Find another husband—anyone at all—so that you can save yourself and care for the children."[109]

All of these accounts are largely fictitious, however, and we do not know for sure whether bereaved women chose death over "live burial" in a convent. Sometimes, the two were closely connected, as in the case of the nun Myōtatsu. This disciple of Myōe spent twelve years at Zenmyōji, praying for the souls of her husband and her son, both killed during the Jōkyū Disturbance. After Myōe's death, she participated with other nuns in the copying of the *Avataṃsaka Sūtra* (the so-called *Nuns' Sūtra*, Jp. *ama-gyō*). The night after copying the section under her responsibility, she threw herself into the Kiyotaki river, at the age of forty-seven.

Single women were often deemed useless to society, and subject to subtle (and not so subtle) forms of ostracism. Even a former empress like Kenreimon'in or a former imperial concubine like Lady Nijō, having no relatives to support them, had to live a relatively frugal life. The secluded woman's comment on the vanity of worldly existence sounds at times like a "sour grapes" argument. Indeed, reclusion offered a way to keep face after being rejected, and to justify the rejection as a self-imposed withdrawal. The point is clearly made in the *Heike monogatari*'s story of the lady-in-waiting Kogō, who was forced by Kiyomori to become a nun when one of his sons-in-law fell in love with her: "Although she had wanted to repeat the sacred vows, it was quite a different matter to be compelled to do so. Thus, at the age of twenty-three, she went to live at Saga, a shabby figure in deep black robes."[110]

As noted earlier, the *Towazugatari* also tells the story of the young prostitute summoned by Go-Fukakusa, only to be left waiting all night in her carriage at the gate in the rain. "Only a year later did we hear that she had indeed entered a religious order at the Saraji Temple in Kawachi province where she was observing the five hundred precepts befitting a nun. Her sorrow thus resulted in joy, for it led her to the true way."[111] Lady Nijō herself would soon meet a similar fate, although she refused to be cloistered. Relating a visit to Hokkeji, she tells about her meeting with the abbess Jakuenbō Son'e, a daughter of Lord Fuyutada: "She talked to me about the relentless cycle of life and death, causing me to consider remaining in the cloister. . . . But realizing that it was not in my nature to quietly devote myself to scholarly pursuits, and aware of the unending confusion that still dwelled in my heart, I decided to leave."[112] It is interesting to note in this respect that she was perhaps a younger half-sister of Son'e.[113] Both were orphaned early, and this would explain their discussion about impermanence. Son'e is the very type of these single women of aristocratic birth who were forced to nunhood by the patriarchal rule, whereas the resilient Nijō is the exception to that rule.

Although Lady Nijō refused to enter a convent, her account is paradoxically one of the rare ones revealing the "insider's story." According to

Abe Yasurō, the similarities between the *Towazugatari* and the "Kanjō no maki" chapter of the *Heike monogatari*, centered on the tragic fate and ultimate redemption of Empress Kenreimon'in, are not coincidental. Lady Nijō's use of the Buddhist theory of karma as narrative framework of her own life suggests that she had the model of the *Heike monogatari* in mind. She may have felt that she was fulfilling the same kind of destiny as Kenreimon'in, whose prayers on behalf of the Taira clan and of her dead child, Emperor Antoku, became the justification of her lonely existence.[114] Nijō, however, does not seem too afflicted by the loss of her own child, and she does not seek refuge in a hermitage. When she hears about Go-Fukakusa's illness and death in 1304, she feels powerless. Recalling how the priest Chikō, having fallen gravely ill, was saved by the intercession of his disciple Shōkū, she grieves: "Chikō recovered from his illness, and Shōkū also lived a long life. The debt I owed His Majesty was far greater than the debt Shōkū owed his teacher. Why then had my offer been fruitless?"[115] Her frustration contrasts with the peaceful resignation of her model Kenreimon'in, revealing the distance between autobiography and fiction.

The *Towazugatari* ends with the account of Lady Nijō's efforts copying scriptures and of her participation in the funerary rituals for Go-Fukakusa. She has to sell her last treasured possessions, keepsakes from her parents, in order to pay for the expenses. Yet she feels a sense of accomplishment when she goes to Kumano to finish copying the scriptures. She has a dream in which her father and Go-Fukakusa appear, and the latter seems cheerful. Empress Yūgi also appears, and she gives her two gowns to repay her for the loss of her parents' keepsakes. On waking up, Lady Nijō goes to a service for Nyoirin Kannon, and finds a white fan beside her. One monk, to whom she mentions the dream, tells her that the fan, being a symbol of Kannon, is an auspicious sign.[116]

Lady Nijō's confession can be read as an affirmation of a dearly bought independence. Of course, since it is autobiographical, there can be no closure or apotheosis, as in Kenreimon'in's case—Lady Nijō can only hope that her writing will bring her some form of immortality that would justify her life a posteriori. Her account of court life was, however, too critical; as a result it was never circulated, and the medieval literary tradition failed to canonize her.

NUNHOOD AND FEMINISM

The history of the female Buddhist order is that of a long struggle against the deleterious effects of the eight *gurudharma*, and, in particular, that of the attempt to establish (or reestablish) the legitimacy of regular ordination and to elevate the status of nuns within and outside the monastic context. Japanese nuns can be characterized, like their Western counterparts, by their "remarkable ability . . . to adapt their spiritual need to the whimsical contours of the patriarchy."[117] Yet the Buddhist female order was far from monolithic, divided between secluded and wandering, submissive and recalcitrant nuns; between "insiders" who interiorized male norms and marginals who smuggled women's religion into Buddhism; between elite nuns, some of whom were able to transform themselves into "great men in male perception," and nuns of lower rank who remained objects of sexual harassment on the part of monks (and perhaps of other nuns, as well).

The idealized description of the Sōtō female order given by Paula Arai makes no mention of power relations. It is true that the stricter rules for nuns—in particular the interdiction of marriage—has helped (or compelled) them to keep a more ascetic lifestyle. As Arai describes it, this lifestyle is characterized not only by meditation and ritual, but also by artistic achievements such as poetry, calligraphy, or flower arrangement. But can we take this portrait of female monastic life at face-value when we are dealing with premodern Japan? The nuns' Vinaya, admittedly the product of male writers, gives a rather grim image of the early female saṅgha. To what extent was the Japanese situation different? Certain medieval sources, like the *Mizu kagami* and the *Nomori no kagami*, do point to the existence of *amitiés particulières* among nuns. In the Edo period, many satiric verses (*senryū*) referred to the use of olisboi in convents and in the imperial *gynaeceum*.[118] Although such blatantly biased tales of monastic depravation cannot be taken uncritically they ought not be simply dismissed, either.

Scholarly discussions of monastic life usually reflect the orthodox view of nuns that holds that the only criterion of authenticity is full ordination. This may explain the lack of research concerning other types of female religious specialists, but does not explain why there are so few Japanese nuns today in comparison with Korean or Taiwanese nuns. The usual argument, according to which the latter nuns were the only ones (excepting Sri Lankan nuns) to receive regular ordination, does not seem sufficient to justify the contrast.[119]

Nunhood can have an ambiguous meaning when viewed as a form of control of female celibacy. As Susan Sered puts it: "Cross-culturally, celibacy is a two-edged sword: it can be used to promote an image of women as carnal and polluting, or it can offer liberation from the bonds of marriage, motherhood, and dependence on men."[120] Thus, a feminist could question whether the ideal Buddhist nun would be a genderless woman, a kind of superwoman who has transcended the limitations of gender and sexuality; or a woman who, by denying her womanhood, has interiorized patriarchal ideology. Is the nun's very desire to shed human limitations (including gender) a progress toward buddhahood, or a mere denial (in the Freudian sense)? The answer will depend on our implicit definition of womanhood. Hosokawa Ryōichi, for instance, thinks that convents are institutions that, while paying lip service to the cult motherhood, welcome women who have repressed their procreative nature.[121] The recent debate about *jizoku* (priests' wives) in Japan, leaving apart its social and historical roots, alerts us to the fact that misogyny in the form of a condemnation of female sexuality and fertility may not be the strict prerogative of the ascetic monks, but may also taint the nuns' attitude about priests' wives.[122]

Why should scholars who try to retrieve female voices in such an androcentric tradition as Buddhism merely focus on the women who—once in a while—had a say in the matter (or, as the French put it, *voix au chapitre*, a voice in the monastic chapter's decisions)? What if they were only the "spokespersons" of a dominantly male tradition, and so complicit in the silencing of other female voices?

The case of the Kumano nuns, who worked on behalf of women, yet at the same time contributed, albeit unwittingly, to their debasement, should remind us that things are never simple. Women can in some cases be their own worst enemies, as feminist scholars, confronted with such extreme cases as foot-binding and clitoridectomy, have been forced to admit.[123] Although fortunately we find nothing of the sort in Buddhism, it is difficult to join the chorus praising "eminent nuns," when the latter seem to weaken women's cause by relentlessly inscribing themselves into male structures, disguising their voice by speaking in alien tongues, or even seem to disparage ordinary womanhood and sexuality. We should therefore not consider that regular nuns represent the entire female tradition in Buddhism.

The cause of women is as multifaceted as are women themselves, and no single group can claim to represent it in its diversity. We have therefore to pay more attention to the other women, those who have not been granted access to official language, to the dominant symbolic system, those who have not been deemed significant. Although it is important to acknowledge the literary talents of medieval nuns, too much emphasis on literacy entails a risk of downplaying oral traditions—for instance, those of female mediums.

Within the Buddhist saṅgha, the rule of ordination has constituted the most efficient instrument of control, by maintaining "regular" nunhood as the privilege of a social elite. This elitist system was a form of institutionalized power. The fact that a few women may, under certain conditions, be accepted into it does not fundamentally change its oppressive nature. If such is the case, instead of attempting to force the gates of this bastion of male privilege, it may be more productive to develop alternatives, to simply bypass the whole structure as largely irrelevant and assert the right of women to appropriate the Buddhist teaching outside of a monastic framework. Emblematic fights and symbolic victories may serve a politicized and mediated form of Buddhist feminism, but they do little to address the larger issue of female religious experience. To believe that such experience *must*, to be valid at all, be mediated by adherence to a single, unbroken lineage stemming from a mythical event—the ordination in illo tempore of Mahāprajāpatī—actually reduces the richness and variety of such experiences to one single, and still androcentric, type. As Dale Spender puts it, since men have determined the traditional parameters, "the process itself can reinforce the 'authority' of men and the deficiency of women."[124]

Even if one grants the importance of the lineage, the emphasis of feminist struggle should be on Dharma transmission rather than on ordination; that is, unless one believes that the two moments are simply two sides of the same coin. Even so, there seems to be no point to the technical rule requiring the presence of ten monks and ten nuns for a female ordination, when only one priest (the spiritual master) is required for dharma transmission. Why not simply argue that the Vinaya has evolved with times and places, and that the early rigorist approach did not prevent male and female religious experiences from developing in manifold ways, giving rise to other, more egalitarian modes of legitimization? After all, if everyone, in Mahāyāna at least, can become a buddha, one should not forget that the Buddha himself reached awakening without ever having been regularly ordained. The same is true of Huineng, the sixth patriarch of Zen, and of many other male figures. Why should it be different for women? As long as the traditional conception of lineage is not questioned, however, it seems paradoxical to emphasize, as feminist Buddhists have done, universalist and international modes of legitimization such as international conferences. Indeed, most feminist discussions on Buddhist women belong to a kind of Westernized neo-Buddhism that has little to do to with the traditional forms of Buddhism (whether monastic or lay) from which it claims to stem, and such discussions could therefore just as well develop freely, outside of all monastic constraints. Why should Buddhist feminist identity lay itself in the Procrustean bed of a male monastic tradition? Women's education is indeed essential and long overdue in traditional Asian societies, but why should it have to pass through the loops and hurdles of the traditional male monastic circus, when so many new avenues and forms of lay practice seem to be available? It is more important to question the male (and female) monastic privileges by showing that there are many ways to be a female Buddhist, and that nunhood is only one of them. So women, and nuns among others, must indeed, as Paula Arai states, "innovate for the sake of tradition." Indeed, the type of innovation for which she credits Sōtō Zen nuns, although quite important as a first step to "awaken nuns from their deep slumber" (as one of these reformer nuns put it), is still too ensconced in conservative patterns of thought, not quite innovative enough to "shake monks from their torpid complacency."

Chapter Two

THE RHETORIC OF SUBORDINATION

Frailty, thy name is woman.
—*Hamlet*, 1.2.150

Get thee to a nunnery. Why wouldst thou be a breeder of sinners?
—*Hamlet*, 3.1.131

I N HIS *Mirror for Women* (*Tsuma kagami*), Mujū Ichien provides a good summary of the Buddhist grievances toward the "weaker sex." He lists as the "seven vices" of women their lack of compunction about arousing sexual desire in men, constant jealousy, deceitful ways, frivolous attachment to their own appearance, duplicity, shameless desire, and, last but not least, their defilement by menstrual blood and blood of childbirth.[1] Mujū's enumeration is actually borrowed from the Chinese Vinaya reformer Daoxuan, who, in his "Rules to Purify Mind and Maintain Insight," also observed: "The four hundred and four grave illnesses have their origin in last night's undigested food; the suffering in the eight places where one is unable to see the Buddha or listen to the Dharma has as its source—woman."[2] Significantly, most of these sins are attributed to the ability of women to arouse sexual desire in men. Thus, what should be perceived as a male problem becomes the cardinal sin of women.[3]

The Buddhist essayist Kamo no Chōmei (1155–1216), a contemporary of Mujū, was also convinced that women are "all by nature perverse."[4] It is worth noting that, at least in his case, this conviction seems to stem from a deeply rooted feeling of inferiority with respect to women. Chōmei's own list of female weaknesses is intended as an antidote to a kind of male anxiety illustrated by the case of a courtier who felt ridicule because of his own shyness in the presence of a servant maid. Chōmei argues: "Why, therefore, should any one feel abashed before a woman? If there be such a thing as a perfect woman [to whom the above does not apply] she must be a freak of nature."[5] Both Chōmei and Mujū, despite their upper-class backgrounds, were steeped in popular prejudice. The same is true of the author of the *Konjaku monogatari shū*, a work in which women are constantly treated as sexual objects. As Tonomura Hitomi has pointed out, in medieval Japan not only bodies, but also minds and subjectivities were gendered differently. To take but one example, emotions were described quite differently, depending on whether the subject is male or female. Jealousy, for instance, was perceived as a strictly female attribute.[6] Arguably, women had more reasons to be jealous than men, as their jealousy was exacerbated by unequal sexual relationships. This is particularly true in the case of this most patriarchal institution, the imperial gynaeceum. Many tales describe the cruel fate of a favorite consort punished due to the jealousy of her rivals, and some stories dwell on the harsher punishment these women received in the end. To give just one superlative instance, the *Konjaku monogatari shū* attributes the foundation of 84,000 stupas by King Aśoka to his remorse for ordering the execution of his 84,000 consorts, guilty of driving his favorite concubine out of the palace and murdering her child.[7]

Women in Buddhist texts are not only stereotypically jealous but also lustful, deceitful, and defiled.[8] In early Buddhist literature, the Buddha himself keeps repeating that the female body "is a vessel of impurity, full of stinking filth. It is like a rotten pit . . . like a toilet, with nine holes pouring all sorts of filth."[9] A locus classicus is the episode in which the Buddha spurns the daughters of Māra, characteristically named Craving, Discontent, and Lust. In another well-known example, he tells the following story to a Brahmin who wants to offer him his daughter:

> Māgandiya, when long ago I beheld these three daughters of Māra, possessed of bodies comparable to masses of gold, free from phlegm and the other body impurities, even then I had no desire for the pleasure of love. But as for your daughter's body, it is a corpse filled with the thirty-two constituents, an impure vessel, as it were, painted without. Were my foot smeared with filth, and were she to lie on my threshold, I would not touch her even with the sole of my foot.[10]

I have discussed elsewhere Buddhist conceptions of the female body, and Liz Wilson has also exhumed the "charming cadavers" and various hidden skeletons from the cupboards of the Indian Buddhist tradition, so there is perhaps no need to linger in this sepulchral atmosphere.[11] Like her, I do not share the optimism of those who want to see such statements as aberrant and not truly Buddhist, or as mere "skillful means." This charitable view is represented, for instance, by Nancy Schuster, who thinks that such statements should be taken simply as adjuncts to meditation on the impurity of the human body (never mind that this body is usually a female one), and are "very carefully restricted to the goal of taming the meditator's own mind." While Schuster concedes that occasionally "an irate writer steps over the line and accuses woman, the object of lust, rather than the lustful mind of the meditator," for her misogynist outbursts remain "aberrant growths within a particular literary genre. And they do not seem to be very common."[12] Although Schuster may be right in arguing that antifemale sentiments were part of a clerical criticism toward lay life in general, this explanation tends to be used as a justification.

A Theodicy of Disprivilege

A common trope of male discourse, misogyny can easily be detected in practically all of the major religions. As noted earlier, Buddhist historians have been particularly embarrassed by the story regarding the foundation of the nuns' order. Even if this Vinaya tradition is apocryphal, it remains to evaluate to what extent early Buddhism was misogynistic. The usual argument, that the incriminated story is a later interpolation, is a transparent attempt to exonerate the Buddha himself from any bias that might have characterized his successors. Even so, the suggestion that early Buddhism might have been sexist is still judged sacrilegious by many scholars intent on promoting an idealized and normative vision of Buddhism. The traditional opposition between the alleged pristine purity of early Buddhism and the decadence of later tradition is a convenient but flawed schema. Depending on the historian's particular interest (and field of specialization), the beginning of degeneration may be said to coincide with the emergence of Mahāyāna or Vajrayāna in India, the acculturation of Buddhism in China (with various turning points such as the Six Dynasties, the mid-Tang, the late Song, or the barbarian Yuan or Qing dynasties), or with the new developments of Buddhism in Japan (during the late medieval or Edo periods). Most of the arguments in favor of early Buddhist egalitarianism rest on rare documents such as the *Therīgāthā*, a text allegedly recording the "triumphant songs" of women. We have no evidence that these verses were actually composed by the women to whom they were attributed, however, and the text was compiled, edited, and annotated by a monk, Dhammapāla.

Various authors have emphasized the fundamental ambivalence of the Buddha as a religious reformer who, while opening his community to women, singularly diminished the boldness of his move by relegating them to a subaltern position. Perhaps this ambivalence reflects specific socio-historical conditions, and in particular the antagonism that existed among various clerical factions. Such is the view of Alan Sponberg, who, in an interesting attempt to elaborate a typology of Buddhist attitudes toward women, distinguishes among Indian monks four typical attitudes: a "soteriological ecumenism" that gives an equality of chances to men and women regarding the final salvation; an "institutional androcentrism" that, in practice, relegates women to a secondary rank; an "ascetic misogyny" that considers women as the incarnated evil; and lastly, under the influence of Tantric Buddhism, an attempt to rehabilitate women through "soteriological androgyny." This typology has the merit of emphasizing the diversity of Buddhist attitudes toward gender. Sponberg, however, assumes too readily that in the case of ascetic misogyny we are probably dealing with the influence of pre-Buddhist ascetic traditions.[13]

Sponberg argues that soteriological ecumenism was already present in early Buddhism, and has survived in spite of all vicissitudes. This ecumenism, which in his opinion constitutes the most fundamental view of Buddhism, corresponds to the Buddhist "rhetoric of equality" (soon to be discussed in the cases of Tantric Buddhism and Chan/Zen). Paradoxically, as Sponberg himself points out, this ecumenical perspective, characteristic of Mahāyāna Buddhism, often goes hand in hand with the most radical gender prejudices. Indeed, as Max Weber already noted, "The fact that a prophet such as the Buddha was glad to see clever women sitting at his feet and the fact that he employed them as propagandists and missionaries . . . did not necessarily carry over into an evaluation of the whole female sex. A particular woman might be regarded as sacred, yet the entire female sex would still be considered vessels of sin."[14]

Sponberg emphasizes that misogyny was not the fate of Buddhism: women played an important role in the early Buddhist community, not only as donors, but also as practitioners and teachers. Despite their institutional inferiority, they were recognized as having a spiritual status equal to that of men. The *Therīgāthā* is usually read as a poetic tribute to the spiritual achievements of some of these women, who reached awakening and became "saints" or arhats. Such is the case of Khemā, the consort of King Bimbisāra, who obtained deliverance long before her virtuous husband. Yet, even if one granted such egalitarian beginnings, it remains to explain the trend reversal, and the progressive hardening of the Buddhist community toward its female constituents.

Buddhist soteriological universalism and egalitarianism remained largely theoretical positions, sustained by a clear perception of the constraints inherent in the social context of the Buddhist order. Even so, it did create a deep tension, which sometimes shows on the surface of Buddhist discourse. Yet Sponberg's way of accounting for such discursive tensions, for instance by reducing the diversity of early Buddhist judgments on women to dissensions between rival monastic groups, verges on a form of sociological reductionism, which sees the history of ideas determined by purely external, socioeconomic factors. Although sociological factors obviously contributed to doctrinal developments, they are not sufficient to explain them. While attempting to account for the complexity of the tradition, this type of explanation tends to underestimate individual complexity and to confuse ideal-types with particular social groups, whose existence remains at any rate largely speculative.

Sponberg argues that Buddhist misogyny should not be overestimated, as it is always counterbalanced by a more healthy egalitarianism. Rather than emphasizing the ambivalence of the older texts in this regard, he rightly stresses the multiplicity, the rich multivocality of the tradition. He also wants to argue that Buddhism was always a source of (social and spiritual) liberation for women. Unfortunately, the reverse is also equally true. Indeed, at least in the case of medieval Japan, much of the Buddhist discourse on women amounts to what we could call "strategies of containment." These stategies can take at least three different forms, an obvious one, the rhetoric of subordination, and more indirect and ambivalent ones, the rhetorics of salvation and of equality.

But before we turn to these strategies, let us return briefly to the founding story. Why did the Buddha initially reject Mahāprajāpatī Gautamī, his aunt and stepmother? Buddhist scholars have tried hard to justify his apparent ingratitude, advancing all kinds of pragmatic reasons for his behavior.[15] It is the handsome Ānanda who deserves all the credit—some orthodox Buddhists would say the guilt—for convincing the Buddha to change his mind. Significantly, this change is not presented as stemming from his realization of the truth of Ānanda's point, but from his desire to avoid disturbing his disciple's peace of mind. He allegedly reflected as follows: "If I reject [the request formulated] three times by Ānanda, his mind will be disturbed and will come to confuse things that have been taught to him. It is better if my true Dharma lasts only a thousand years and if the mind of Ānanda, son of Gautamī, is not disturbed."[16] After the Buddha's death, Ānanda's fellow-monks reproached the latter for interceding on behalf of women.

The sexism of early Buddhism clearly asserts itself in this story, where Ānanda plays the role of a scapegoat. As a young man sensitive to the predicament, and charms, of women, Ānanda sharply contrasts with his puritanical elders. His image became more positive in Mahāyāna. In medieval Japan, for instance, a ceremony called "Ānanda's repentance rite" was held twice per year in many monasteries in order to commemorate Ānanda's intercession on behalf of women, and it is still held today in Sōtō convents for the benefit of all women.[17] This tradition has even been traced back to the Buddha himself, who allegedly advised his female disciples that "in the future, women who want to become nuns, as well as those who have this virtuous intention, must keep in mind their debt toward Ānanda by invoking his name, making offerings and singing his praise." The *Sūtra of Repaying One's Debt* (*Baoen jing*) points out that, in order to perform this rite (on the eighth of the second and eighth months) women must purify themselves and observe the Eight Strict Rules of respect during the six watches of the night. Ānanda will then answer their prayers and protect them.[18]

Another reason ritually invoked for the Buddha's initial reluctance to admit women in his community is his pragmatic respect for local customs (and prejudices). The principle "In India, do as Indians do" was invoked to justify the Eight Strict Rules.[19] Clearly, the notion that an enlightened being should in all matters conform to the customs of an unenlightened society raises a few questions. After all, is not the Buddha usually praised for rejecting the most fundamental ritual of Brahmin society, animal sacrifice? Could one not expect more from a religious reformist who, or so we are told, did not hesitate to question an institution as well established as the caste system? We recall the Buddha's prediction that the decline of the Dharma, triggered by the admission of women, could not be prevented even by the Eight Strict Rules. Ironically, some later texts try to downplay the discriminatory nature of these rules by underscoring that, due to their scrupulous observance by women, the duration of the True Dharma increased from five hundred to one thousand years. In other words, these texts implicitly acknowledge the importance of women in the preservation of the Dharma. Quite paradoxically, however, even these qualities of women are now negatively read as an unmistakable sign of the times, the topsy-turvy reality characteristic of the Final Dharma: "When the dharma is about to be extinguished women will be zealous, constantly doing meritorious deeds, while men will be lazy and indifferent, will not engage in religious discourses, will look on monks as manure, and will not have believing minds."[20]

Woman as Temptress

One locus classicus for the misogynist position is found in the *Vijñaptimā-tratāsiddhi-śāstra*: "Woman is an emissary from hell. It is forever impossible that she becomes a buddha. Outside, she may look like a bodhisattva, but in her heart she is like a *yakṣa* [demon]."[21] Male practitioners who set their bodies and minds on the path to liberation were advised to keep women at a distance. In one of many instances, the Buddha admonishes his disciples, "Monks, beware of women! . . . Put on fire, milk swells, boils and pours out; likewise the ascetic at the contact of a devout woman."[22] Another oft-quoted admonition appears in the *Sūtra of Forty-two Sections*: "Be careful not to look at women. If you happen to see them, do not look at them. Be careful not to talk to them. If you talk to them, be sure to guard your mind and behavior." These warnings were versified for the sake of easier memorization:

A serpent full of venom
Can still be seized with the hand;
The woman who deceives men
Must not be touched.
The man who has knowledge
Must not look at her;
Or, if he is forced to see her,
He will treat her as his mother or sister.

Looking at her objectively,
He will hold the woman
As a heap of impurities.
Not to reject the fire of lust
Is to [condemn oneself] to
Perish from its burn.[23]

The same metaphoric vein is exploited ad nauseam in passages like the following: "It is better for a monk to face a cobra than a woman; because the snake can only kill, whereas the woman plunges [one] in the ways of expiation. . . . How many times have I told you, with many comparisons, that love is as dangerous for a man as fire is for straw; as a poisonous fruit, as a venomous snake, as a brandished sword, as the sharp stake from which one cannot extricate oneself. It would furthermore defile my order, have I told you."[24] As one might expect, the early Buddhist diatribe against women, repeated and amplified by later commentators, had a deep impact on the mentality of its practitioners and wide-ranging social repercussions.

The early Buddhist ambivalence has to do with the attempt to reconcile two contradictory conceptions of sexual difference. In the first, sexual difference is the product of some kind of fall of humankind, and it is supposed to disappear as one proceeds toward spiritual realization. According to this model, women gradually become equal to men (or even, become men), as they reach higher stages. This ideal is expressed in the *Therīgāthā*, where women are said to have become arhats. In the second conception, the subordination of women to men is based on the Hindu notion of dharma, according to which the women must always be subordinated to a man (father, husband, or sons). Ascetic women were not well tolerated in Hindu society, nor women who strayed away from their ideal role (celibate women, sterile women, widows who often took refuge in the Buddhist community). Thus, the Eight Strict Rules may have been an attempt by early Buddhists to stay in line with the common practice of the time.[25] Women were judged too fragile for monastic life, in particular for wandering monasticism. In the society of the time, as today, single women were an easy target for male desire. This is not sufficient, however, to explain why the objection against women's ordination remained long after monasteries and convents had been built.[26] Thus Buddhism, for all its much-vaunted egalitarianism and its departure from the caste system, endorsed the dominant ideology at times a little more than was needed.

Narratives like that of the foundation of the female saṅgha, although denigrating with respect to women, were perhaps not simply caused by the monks' misogyny. They may also have constituted a sociopolitical choice, an attempt to present laywomen more positively and raise their status at the expense of the nuns'. Thus, next to Mahāprajāpatī, we find the figure of Viśākhā, the daughter and spouse of rich merchants, who was among the first converts, but never received ordination. As noted earlier, it seems that the early saṅgha preferred laywomen to nuns, and considered the latter as a potential source of embarrassment. [27] At the same time, early Buddhism, while admitting that female renouncers could become arhats, denied them the highest spiritual realization, insofar as they remained attached to the cycle of birth and life through motherhood. It is also worth noting that, in India at least, Buddhism avoided glorifying the function of motherhood.[28] And yet, the Buddha did not encourage women to remain celibate, as he had men.

THE FIVE OBSTACLES AND THE THREE DEPENDENCES

In Japanese Buddhism, three distinct ideological elements came to be connected into a relatively coherent discourse on women: the political/ontological theory of the Five Obstacles; the social notion of the Three Dependences; and the biological/religious concept of the blood taboo. These elements, merging with the notion of karmic burden and traditional gender stereotypes (like the so-called Seven Sins of women), justified the institutional submission of women, and their exclusion of women from sacred places (*nyonin kekkai*), or even, in the worst-case scenario, from paradise and buddhahood.[29] Most influential here is probably the theory of the Five Obstacles.[30] This expression refers to the five types of rebirth that are out of reach of women: rebirth as the god Brahma, as the god Śakra, as Māra, as a universal monarch (Wheel-Turning King, *cakravartin*), and, last but not least, as a buddha.[31] Hōnen, giving a slightly different version, writes:

> On careful reflection, we must admit that there are great hindrances in the way of woman's attaining enlightenment, so that unless she is dealt with in an especial way, she will be liable to become a victim to doubts. The reason is that her sin is grievous, and so she is not allowed to enter the lofty palace of the great Brahma, nor to look upon the clouds which hover over his ministers and people. She is always taken down to a lower seat than the soft-cushioned one of the divine Indra, and she can never behold the flowers of his Thirty-Three-Citied Heaven, nor sit upon the throne of King Māra in the sixth heaven. She cannot succeed to the throne of the four Wheel Kings, nor even have a hope of such a thing. A woman cannot hope for any fortunate position even in this perishable and defectible world of birth and death, how much less must be her hope of attaining to Buddhahood! No matter what sūtra or śāstra you look at, she is always spoken of in terms of scorn, and everywhere despised. There is no place

for her to go but to the three painful states and the eight misfortunes, and there are no shapes for her to assume but those of the six ways and the four modes of birth.[32]

Significantly, this was one of the arguments by which the Buddha tried to justify the eight *gurudharma*.[33] These rules meant, among other things, that women, because they must at all times remain under the dependence of men, cannot hope to ever attain the exalted positions listed above.[34] In the Vinaya version of the Five Obstacles, we find mention of the "Four Kings" instead of Māra, and of "non-retrogressing bodhisattva" instead of "buddha." According to Kajiyama Yūichi, the reference to the rank of buddha among the Five Obstacles seems to point to a period, around the first century B.C.E., when the conception of buddhahood had already developed. Formerly, the highest goal, arhathood, was open to both men and women, and there was therefore no point in such limitations.[35] Furthermore, the notion of the Five Obstacles was at first merely a kind of technical or juridical restriction. It is only later that it came to be read as a moral and ontological inferiority, and was associated with various female moral characteristics—deceit, greed, vanity—which were themselves both the causes and consequences of a negative karma.[36] Thus, through its linkage to karmic guilt and biological inferiority, the meaning of the Five Obstacles, or rather, the rhetorical use of this notion, drastically changed over time. This evolution was achieved in Japan toward the ninth century, a period characterized by significant changes in the perception of women. Whereas in early Buddhism the theory of the Five Obstacles was merely a limitation to women's upward spiritual mobility, in medieval Japanese Buddhism it became an outright exclusion from buddhahood, and, more concretely, from sacred places.

To make things worse, this motif came to be coupled during the Kamakura period with the patriarchal notion of the Three Dependences (Jp. *sanjū* or *sanshō*), a notion that seems to have predated Buddhism both in India and China. Indian women were expected to live in complete subservience to their parents in childhood, to their husbands after marriage, and to their sons after the death of their spouses. In the *Laws of Manu*, for instance, we find clearly expressed the idea that the woman must be under the tutelage of a man (father, husband, son) at all ages.[37] Likewise, Confucian teachings emphasized the "Three Dependences" or "Three Followings," a term found in the *Yili* (*Book of Rites*). It is Buddhism, however, that appears to be responsible for its spread in medieval Japan.[38] As noted earlier, in his *Commentary on the Sūtra of Infinite Life* (*Muryōjukyō shaku*), Hōnen notes that internally women have five obstacles, externally three dependences.[39] The same idea appears in such Buddhist texts as the *Dazhidulun*, the *Yūyenü jing*, and the *Huayan jing*.[40] Paradoxically, many women turned to Buddhism in the hope of escaping from these dependences.[41] Those women who joined the Buddhist order, however, were in many cases merely accepting another form of dependence: toward the monks whom they would eventually serve as they had their fathers (as a source of authority), theirs sons (washing their clothes and feeding them), and sometimes their husbands (as sexual partners). Furthermore, often "leaving the house" was not sufficient to escape domestic responsibilities, and the nuns, willingly or not, remained a member of their lineage or of their husband's household, as noted earlier.

Female Reception

How were these theories received in Japan? Although the discourse on the Five Obstacles constitutes a textbook case of gender discrimination, even more disturbing perhaps is the fact that many women seem to have uncritically accepted and interiorized it. The theory was influenced by autochthonous notions and received a distinctive Japanese slant, eventually taking on a life of its own. This semantic drift results in part from the Japanese interpretations of the Chinese character *zhang* (Jp. *shō*), read as *sawari*, a term meaning "obstacle," but which also has the connotations of "passion" (moral flaw), and "menses" (biological, and eventually karmic, flaw).[42] This unfortunate drift paved the way to reinterpretations in terms of moral and biological defilement; however, it was probably as much a result of changing perceptions as a contributing cause of such changes.

In due time, the expression "Five Obstacles" became a standard way of referring to the allegedly deep guilt of women. It became part of catchphrases like "clouds, fog, mist, the darkness of the Five Obstacles." A similar development occurred in China, as we can see from the "Chants of Shame and Embarrassment" (*Cankui yin*): "I am ashamed that I did not cultivate virtue in my last life: / And so received this [female] body with its five obstacles. / Still, I was fortunate enough to have aquired a human body. / Why should I object that it is a female one?"[43]

The female belief in the Five Obstacles is well reflected in female "vows" (*ganmon*) and donation letters (*kishinjō*). Actually, the oldest known vow mentioning the Five Obstacles and the Three Dependences was written in 883 by Sugawara no Michizane at the request of a lady of the Fujiwara family in memory of her dead parents.[44] But the *Kōyasan monjo*, for instance, contains many documents written by women, including vows asking for cure or rebirth as men, as well as for deliverance from the Five Obstacles and the Three Dependences. In the Heian and Kamakura periods, women possessed property, fields, and so forth, which they could bequeath to temples. Thus, economic motivations may explain in part why certain priests were ready to question the theory. Nevertheless, the dominant monastic interpretation is that, although women are very handicapped beings, they can be saved by the power of the Dharma. Although this interpretation is often put in the mouths of women in literary works such as the *Heike monogatari* or the *Soga monogatari*, it is a form of male ventriloquism.

The reception of the theory among women, however, was more complex than it appears, and there are cases where it was accepted with a grain of salt (a powerful purifying agent, as we know). Thus, within the basic interpretive framework, various interpretations emerged. In particular, we must distinguish the interpretations of literati-monks from those found in women's literature, especially poetry. Women found a powerful counterargument in the Buddhist notion of nonduality, as examplified by a verse said to have been sent by the priest Shōkū to the poetess Izumi Shikibu: "Since in Buddhism there is neither two nor three, how could there be five obstacles?"[45]

The acceptance of the notion by women was by no means passive and monolithic. Edward Kamens has shown, for instance, that the topos of the Five Obstacles was primarily used as a poetical device. He writes:

> If the Buddhist discourse increased guilt, and many women interiorized this guilt, not all women accepted the negative image which was offered to them. Many must have seen it for what it was, a male fabrication. However, rather than rejecting it, they played with it, transforming it into a literary topos. Self-depreciation is after all a common feature in Japanese culture, and can easily turn into false modesty. Thus, the female complaint about their own inadequacy may have had a quite different meaning from the male assertion of the five obstacles.

Kamens illustrates the point with the case of the Kamo priestess Senshi, a renowned poetess. In a poem entitled "Devadatta," she reflects on the enlightenment of the *nāga*-girl in the *Lotus Sūtra*: "Here is the example of one who was not obstructed by the Five Obstructions, / so I, too, can hope that no more clouds will block my way."[46]

Another well-known example is that of the verse attributed to Izumi Shikibu: "When a priest passed her house carrying a maidenflower (*ominaeshi*), she asked him where he was going, and when he said, 'I am taking this flower as an offering for the nenbutsu rite on Mount Hiei,' she wrote this and attached it to the flower: 'If this is truly its name, it faces the Five Obstructions, and yet / how enviable this flower that mounts the heights!' "[47] Here, we see how the Five Obstacles were associated with the notion that women were to be excluded from sacred space, to which we will return. A similar poem was written by Fujiwara no Mototoshi (1060–1142): "A certain woman, says the *kotobagaki*, wanted to send an *ominaeshi* as an offering for a 'nonstop' nenbutsu in the eighth month and asked Mototoshi to compose a poem for her to submit. He wrote [on behalf of the woman]: 'How can this flower, which, like me, faces the Five Obstructions, / be made into a being who can be born anew on a lotus?' "[48]

These poems, while they suggest that there may have been a custom of sending *ominaeshi* to Hiei rituals as substitutes for or representatives of real women, also show how the Five Obstacles were used as a poetic topos.[49] Let us mention another poem by Kianmon'in (d. 1357), the consort of Emperor Kōgon: "How I rely on it—the Buddha's single vow, / which nonetheless does not entirely rid me of the Five Obstructions."[50] According to Kamens, this poem "poses one doctrinal tradition of exclusion, that of women from buddhahood per se, against another doctrinal tradition of inclusion, that of women among those who can attain eternal rebirth in paradise."[51] But, as we will see shortly, the two traditions go hand in hand. The Five Obstacles could also be removed magically, with the help of the bodhisattva Kannon, as in the case of a woman ascetic from Tosa province, who, we are told, obtained magical powers owing to the power of the *Lotus Sūtra*: "Coming for the miraculous efficacy of Kannon, she secluded herself in one of the caves, / To cast off her woman's body with its five hindrances, she chanted the wondrous Sūtra of the One Vehicle, and attained a body with the ability to fly."[52]

A CASE OF BLOOD POISONING

> Rain has not been falling
> But Yamada river is dirty.
> Yamada women's
> Skirts' juice.[53]

One domain in which Buddhist misogyny seems to have found an ideal breeding ground is that of the defilement related to female bodily functions. As Michelle Rosaldo explains, "Because women are more involved than men in giving birth and mourning death, feeding, cooking, disposing of feces, and the like, . . . cultural notions of the female often gravitate around natural or biological characteristics: fertility, maternity, sex, and menstrual blood. And women, as wives, mothers, witches, midwives, nuns, or whores, are defined almost exclusively in terms of their sexual functions."[54] By drawing on male phobias, Buddhism helped to reinforce the visceral male repulsion toward female blood. Menstruating women across cultures have long been said to have a putrefying power. In Japan as in premodern Europe, people believed that menstrual blood could hinder natural maturation processes. Thus, the brewing of sake—like the maturation of wine in Western wineries—was said to be spoiled by the mere presence of a menstruating woman.[55] The same is true of the blood of childbirth. In Chinese medical conceptions, women are said to be "led by blood." Popular imagery justified the blood taboo by invoking embryological conceptions, according to which it is the blood of menses that constitutes the foetus (by accumulating instead of flowing away), becoming, properly speaking, the child's body. The blood of childbirth is therefore a mere residue of menstrual blood that was not used by the foetus. According to a probably late version of the *Sūtra of the Blood Bowl*, which inherits Chinese conceptions of the three "worms" dwelling inside the human body, the menstrual blood is none other than the elimination of the waste coming from worms that feed on the bones and blood of women. It is the presence of these worms in their body that makes women impure beings; we will return to that scripture in greater depth. From India to China, Korea, and Japan, the "politics of menstruation" thus became an essential part of the male discourse on female sexuality.[56] Analyzing the Chinese case, Emily Ahern argues that Chinese pollution beliefs are intimately connected to the kinship system.[57] Women's defilement was used to justify their marginal position in their father's and husband's lineages. Yet while Japanese patriarchal ideology shared many features with Chinese patriarchal ideology, the kinship systems were quite different in both countries. Again, in Korea, where women were also perceived as strangers in a male-centered system, the pollution of female blood, albeit the object of temporary taboos, never became inherently defiling as in Japan.[58]

Is the belief in blood impurity internal or external to the question of gender? To what extent is it related to the social position of women, in particular to their allegedly divisive, hence threatening, role, in stark contrast with that of post-menopausal women, who, in being perceived essentially as ageing mothers rather than wives, were no longer considered a threat, and so represented as a unifying force in the family? Emily Ahern considers three different interpretations for Chinese belief in the dangerous power of menstrual blood: "The first looks to the emotional significance of death and birth, the second to women's social role, and the third to the system of ideas about pollution."[59] Accepting the first and third, Ahern rejects (with qualifications) the idea that belief in the power of menstrual blood reflects the social role of young women because, while young women may manipulate family relationships to ends antithetical to the ideals of patriliny, they do not consciously and deliberately manipulate the power associated with menstrual pollution to these ends.[60] Arguing against Ahern's view, Steve Sangren emphasizes the social interpretation of women's blood. According to him: "As one might expect, there are positive as well as negative qualities associated with femininity in

China; yet female deities [are viewed] as unambiguously positive. As ideal-
izations of womanhood, then, female deities must overcome the stigma
of pollution associated with menstruation, sexual intercourse, death, and
childbirth."[61] Sangren continues "[T]hat there is a closer association between women's roles in domestic groups and female pollution than that
posited by Ahern follows from viewing these pollution beliefs as part of
a larger contrastive set of ideas about female gender in Chinese religion,
a set of ideas that encompasses positive as well as negative female qualities."[62] Sangren also claims that the negative and positive qualities are
represented by the wife (or daughter-in-law) and the mother (or sister),
respectively; but, unlike in India, only the positive (unifying) qualities
seem symbolized as female deities, whereas the negative (divisive) are
merely represented in pollution beliefs.[63] Perhaps this contrast needs to
be more nuanced, as there are Chinese female deities, like Linshui Furen,
who are clearly associated with sexuality and childbirth and are not as
unambiguouly positive as Sangren argues.[64] This is even more so in the
case of medieval Japan, to which we now turn.

In the medieval period, among the taboos listed in the "Ordinance to
Subjugate the Spirits of the Dead" (Goryōsha bukkiyō, 1403), we find
the impurity caused by blood during a woman's monthly periods. At such
times, a woman was sheltered from public view for eleven days , whereas
childbirth only required a ten-day confinement.[65] There seems, however,
to have been no particular blood taboo in ancient Japan. Although the
mythical hero Yamatotakeru, for instance, has sexual relations with a
woman during her period, he is not explicitly condemned—yet his tragic
ending seems related to this perceived impurity.

Nishiguchi Junko argues that the concept of defilement first developed
in the rituals for the kamis.[66] During the Heian period, the concern with
ritual purity and defilement among the nobility was based on Onmyōdō
(yin-yang) teachings. At the same time, this growing concern was viewed
as specifically Japanese by Fujiwara no Sanesuke, who wrote in his Shōyūki (1027): "Yorimichi says that in India people are not afraid of defilement. I answer that the fear of defilement is Japanese, and that in China,
one does not fear it."[67] Yorimichi was clearly mistaken so far as India is
concerned, but he may be right in his perception that the Japanese notion
was distinct.

The medieval period saw the development of the notion of kegare ("defilement"), which implies not only something dirty, but also encompasses
the idea of exhausted energy. According to Miyata Noboru, the "red impurity" (aka fujō, a common epithet for menses) is simply a particular
case of kegare. It was also seen as a sign of fundamental gender difference,
and in that respect it seems to reflect a fear of female otherness.[68] Menstrual blood is especially impure inasmuch as it bears the mark of exclu-

sively female powers. The biological phenomenon of menstruation led to
the view that the female body is essentially porous, and that its "out-
flowing" is practically beyond control. Menopause, by stopping the flow
of menstrual blood, seemed to make women more appropriate vessels for
the Dharma. Indeed, it is often after reaching that state that women became nuns; however, this was more in recognition of the fact that they
moved beyond the threat of being female by fulfilling their procreative
duties. This kind of fear is by no means limited to premodern Japan.
According to Mary Douglas, the emphasis on female pollution is a direct
function of male dominance. It came to be emphasized in societies where
male power was "contradicted by other principles such as that of female
independence." In societies where male dominance was guaranteed by
other social institutions, however, this ideological way of disempowering
women was superfluous.[69]

Until the Meiji period, and even later in remote areas, menstruating
women had to seclude themselves in special huts (*bekka*, lit. "separate
fire"), a practice that can be traced back to the medieval period. We read,
for instance, in the *Shasekishū*: "The taboos observed at Ise differ somewhat from those of other shrines. Childbirth [lit. *ubuya*, "parturition
hut"] is spoken of as 'bearing spirit' (*shōki*), and those involved are under
a fifty-day pollution; likewise, death is spoken of as 'death spirit,' and
also creates a fifty-day pollution. Death proceeds from life, and life is the
beginning of death. The shrine official informed me that this was handed
down as the reason for birth and death to be both taboo."[70] We recall
that the list of the seven womanly sins that Mujū gave in his *Mirror for
Women* ended with blood pollution.

Mujū, however, tries to downplay the aspect of ritual defilement:
"Thus, to speak of placing birth and death under a taboo is the same as
saying that we do not foolishly create the karma of delusive conduct
which causes the painful cycle of birth-and-death."[71] Mujū's point seems
to reflect the ancient belief that the impurity of childbirth did not have to
do with blood per se, but with the fact that at childbirth the woman ventured closer to the other world, and therefore to the impurity of death.
Thus, through a network of symbolic associations, childbirth came to be
associated with the defilement of death.[72] Outside of canonical scriptures,
the taboo against women has to do with blood pollution and death pollution (the latter being not limited to women). The *Shingiryō* and the *Jōkan
gishiki* do not mention childbirth and menstruation. The *Engishiki* gives
an interesting scale of pollution: thirty days of pollution at the time of a
person's death; seven days at the time of birth; five days for the death of
the six kinds of animals; three days for their birth; three days in the case
of meat-eating, and so forth. In this text, however, defilement is limited
to the individual; it does not yet extend to its family; and there is not yet

a notion of contagion, as in the case of the defilement of death. It is with the establishment of shrine Shintō during the medieval period that the taboo becomes stricter.

It is precisely the taboo that explains the soteriological value of menstrual blood in Tantrism, a teaching that emphasizes the power of transgression.[73] In this context, even though menstrual blood remains a sign of impurity, the very notion of defilement is dismissed as a false view that must be overcome through ritual inversion. Thus, low-caste washerwomen, familiar with the impurity of menstrual blood, are often mentioned as sexual partners of choice for male practitioners.[74] The *Canda-mahārosana-tantra* indicates that the male participant should suck the blood and other fluids from his partner's vagina. Hindu and Buddhist Tantric texts are usually written from the standpoint of the male practitioner. The Hindu Tantrika, for instance, is encouraged to identify his semen with the god Śiva and the woman's menstrual flow with Śiva's *śakti* (deified energy), and, in order to unite these two primordial powers within himself, to retain within his own body both fluids discharged during intercourse.[75] In the Indian alchemical tradition, male semen and female blood are assimilated to mercury and sulphur (the semen of Śiva and the blood of his *śakti*, respectively).[76] In medieval Daoism, in order to obtain immortality, women were told to "slay the red dragon," that is, to restore the lost menstrual blood through the practice of inner alchemy (*neidan*).[77] After "slaying the dragon," the breasts of the female practitioner become flat and her menstrual blood is purged, and she emerges with a male body—or sometimes with a child's body, that is, a degendered (yet ungendered body).[78] Thus, Daoist women had to deny their biological process, whereas men simply had to store their seminal essence. Although this is not the place to examine the debated issue of mutual influences between Tantric and Daoist alchemy, it will suffice to point out that alchemical notions gained widespread currency in Chinese culture. Thus, in Ming China, the "red lead" (i.e., female blood), originally an alchemical substance, was seen as a powerful regenerating fluid whose consumption was advised by some doctors.

Blood was not simply valued for its transgressive power, however. In some cultural contexts, female blood was even considered sacred for its apotropaic power. It was a multivalent symbol from the start, which, in local cults that could be described as more akin to women's religions, was valued as a prerequisite for procreation. Thus, whereas from the standpoint of men the menstrual flow was defiling, from that of women it was purifying. In such contexts, sexuality was inherently auspicious, as the source of the regenerative powers of women, of the earth, and, by metaphorical extension, of the cosmos. Menstruation indicated the beginning of a period of fecundity and constituted a rite of passage to womanhood.

The regularity of this biological process was a clear indication that women, like the moon (another symbol of yin), were in tune with the underlying rhythms of the cosmos. This more positive interpretation was developed in Chinese medical discourse after the Song, but it apparently had little influence on "ritual" medicine and folk beliefs.

In Japan, too, these conceptions are reflected in the magical role of the color red, the vermilion used as a symbol of life in exorcisms, for instance, against pestilence deities.[79] The red cloth used by women in white-magic rituals is explicitly associated with their menses.[80] "Red magic" was also used in rituals at the time of first menstruation, or that of the first pregnancy, during which women wore a red loin cloth or underskirt, or a red belt (haraobi).[81] It is worth pointing out here that, among Okinawan mediums, prolonged menstruation is a sign of divine election, and their name kamichi means "divine blood." Thus, not only is menstruation not considered an obstacle, but it is the very condition of female priesthood. This makes the contrast with Japan even more striking. In Shintō, the priestesses of high rank (monoimi) were selected before puberty, and not only were they supposed to remain virgins for life, but they were also believed to have no menses.[82] The apparition of menstrual blood was a sign that they had broken some taboo and thereby incurred the wrath of the god.[83] Menstrual discharge thus came to mean discharge from office, whereas in earlier periods it was only a temporary restriction: the miko could not perform when pregnant or menstruating.

Thus, from the Heian period to the Kamakura period, the combined influence of shrines and temples, on the one hand, and of Onmyōdō theories, on the other, increased blood pollution. As we will see in the case of the legend of Princess Chūjōhime, prolonged menstrual periods and other female ailments came to be seen as the result of a bad karma, implying some kind of sexual transgression; for instance, adultery.[84]

More generally, blood defilement or pregnancy prevented ordinary women from getting close to shrines. Even in such cases, however, ritual devices afforded remediation. When the miko of Tsushima menstruated at the time when they had to perform a ritual, they merely recited a particular norito in order to "correct the defilement" (kegare-naoshi).[85] Buddhism, however, was relatively lacking in such purification rituals. The main ritual available was the so-called "Ususama's Rite of Dissolution of Defilements" (Ususama kaie hō), centered on the Tantric deity Ususama (Skt. Ucchuṣma).

Buddhist priests had some reasons to be wary of blood defilement insofar as it could ruin the efficacy of their rituals, and thus cost them state sponsorship. The question received diverse treatments from the new schools that emerged in the medieval period. Blood defilement is denied by Hōnen in his Kurodani shōnin wago tōroku. When someone asks him whether women can recite the sutras and are allowed to visit the temple during menstruation, Hōnen merely answers that in Buddhism there are no such taboos, which have been spread by shrine priests and Onmyōdō masters.[86] This, however, did not lead Hōnen to reject entirely the exclusion of women from sacred places. Later on, however, we find the popular belief that menstrual defilement could be alleviated by the nenbutsu.

The question was brought to the forefront in the Nichiren school. In *Gassui gosho* (A Letter on Menstruation), addressed in 1264 to the wife of Lord Daigaku Saburō, Nichiren takes a rather ambivalent position on this matter. After having affirmed that the worst sinners—consequently, even women—would be saved from hell if they firmly believed in the redeeming power of the *Lotus Sūtra*, Nichiren replies to the woman's specific concern, whether she should continue reciting the sutra during her periods: "Having read almost all the Buddhist scriptures, I, Nichiren, have found clear references in them against drinking liquor, eating meat and five very spicy vegetables, or having sexual relations on specific days and months, but I can't think of any sutra or discourse showing dislike of menstruation."[87] Nichiren then remarks that menstruation is a purely physiological phenomenon, and that it is indispensable for procreation, yet he compares it to a long illness, which should not be seen as an external defilement. He argues, however, that although menstruation has not been perceived as defilement in India and Japan, it is so regarded in the local religious context, and therefore women should refrain from appearing before the gods during their period.[88] While concluding that "daily practice of Buddhism should not be obstructed by menstruation," Nichiren offers some caveats: for instance, even though a woman may chant the title (*daimoku*) of the *Lotus Sūtra* during her periods, she should not recite the sutra itself, nor perform daily services in front of it.[89] Furthermore, by arguing that menses "are not an impurity coming from outside," but merely the "usual infirmity of women," that is, a "principle that must have been inherited from seeds of saṃsāra," Nichiren does in fact interiorize the sin of menstruation. With him, the ritual impurity of menstruation has become the moral defilement of woman.[90]

As in the case of the Five Obstacles, the blood taboo was not accepted by all women without resistance. The legend of Izumi Shikibu's pilgrimage to Ise, for instance, seems to bear testimony to the resistance of women to contemporary notions of defilement. As the story goes, the poetess, surprised by untimely menstruation during a pilgrimage to Kumano, was about to turn back, when an oracular verse of the goddess Amaterasu revealed to her that she was not ritually impure and could therefore proceed to the shrine. Izumi wrote: "Beneath unclear skies, my body obscured by drifting clouds, / I am saddened that my monthly obstruction has begun." To which the deity responded: "How could the god who mingles with dust / suffer because of your monthly obstruction?"[91]

Similar statements are put in the mouths of Buddhist priests who, perhaps in an effort to outbid rivals, claimed the high metaphysical ground by resorting to notions such as nonduality (between purity and defilement, for instance) or innate enlightenment (*hongaku*). Thus, a woman in labor ceased to be perceived as an immediate threat to the people assembled at Atsuta Shrine since, as Mujū again reminds his readers, "if only the heart is pure, the body likewise is not defiled."[92] In this domain, as in others, the Buddhist tradition is far from monolithic. For instance, various esoteric documents (*kirigami*) of the Sōtō school criticize the very notion of female impurity and sin in the name of the Mahāyāna principle of nonduality. As one of them states, "When one receives these words, which are those of the Buddha, how can one consider as a sin the menstrual flow that follows parturition?" We will, however, have the opportunity to examine more closely this rhetoric and question its social effects. As late as the Edo period, a popular religious movement like the Fujidō insists that menstrual blood is not polluting. This movement, centered on the cult of Mount Fuji, exerted a significant influence on the subsequent "New Religions," in their attempt to reform society from a perspective presupposing the "spiritual power" of women.[93]

DRINKING FROM THE BLOOD BOWL

Nevertheless, mainstream Buddhism remained strongly sexist. The most blatant case of Buddhism's relentless enforcement of the blood taboo is the propagation of the *Sūtra of the Blood Bowl* (Chin. *Xuepen jing,* Jp. *Ketsubongyō*). This short apocryphal scripture of Chinese origin opens with the arhat Mulian (Skt. Maudgalyāyana) descending to hell in search of his mother. Upon discovering a blood pond full of drowning women, Mulien asks the hell warden why there is no man in this pond, and is told that this hell is reserved for women who have defiled the gods with their blood. Having found his mother, Mulian is unable to help her. In despair, he returns to the Buddha and asks him to save his mother. The Buddha then preaches the *Sūtra of the Blood Bowl*.[94] This scripture first explains the cause of women's ordeals: women who died in labor fall into a blood pool formed by the age-long accumulation of female menses, and are forced to drink that blood. This gruesome punishment is due to the fact that the blood that was spilled at the time of parturition contaminated the ground and provoked the wrath of the earth god. The text goes on to explain that blood pollution occurs in two ways: first, when the blood shed at childbirth touches the ground, it contaminates the earth god; then, when the garments stained by that blood are washed at the river, it pollutes the water used for tea offerings to the buddhas and other worthies. This repeated pollution is thus the cause of the infernal torments of the "blood pool."

There was a Daoist version of this scripture, entitled *Xuehu jing* (*Scripture of the Blood Lake*), as well as popular versions contained in the *baojuan* (Precious Scrolls).[95] The themes of the *Blood Bowl Sūtra* found their way into popular literature. In an oft-read tract of the *baojuan* genre, the *Zhongxi baojuan*, it is said that sinners falling into this hell are men and women who have committed murder in a past life, women who died after childbirth, women who transgress taboos, women and men who fornicate during forbidden periods, and so forth.[96] Whereas in the Buddhist text, only women fall into hell, in the Daoist *Xuehu jing*, even if women are the main target, men, too, can be victims—in particular, men who died a violent death. The text says, "without distinguishing men and women," or, "men go to the men's pond, women to the women's pond." On the whole, however, most texts reserve the Blood Pond Hell for women (in a structural opposition to Amitābha's Pure Land). The notion of a Blood Pond Hell meant strictly for women seems to appear during the Song period.[97] In earlier recensions of the scripture, the sin of childbirth was attributed for three parts to the man, seven parts to the woman. If sexual union had taken place during the four taboo periods, both man and woman were to be condemned to the Blood Pond Hell.

The motif of the Blood Pond found its most developed expression in the tale of Woman Huang, the subject of several *baojuan*. In one of them, her husband accuses her as follows:

> When you gave birth to your children you also committed a sin:
> How many bowls of bloody water, how many bowls of fluids?
> For every child, there were three basins of water;
> three children, and thus nine basins of fluids.
> You dumped the bloody waters into the gutters,
> And so you polluted the Sprite of the Eaves.
> Three mornings and you were already back in the kitchen,
> And so you polluted the God of the Hearth.
> Before ten days were up, you went into the front hall,
> And so you polluted the household gods and ancestors.
> Before a month was up, you went out of doors,
> And so you polluted the sun, the moon, and the stars.
> You washed the blood-stained clothing in the river,
> And the tainted waters polluted the Dragon King.
> You spilled these waters on to the ground,

And the spirits of Hell had nowhere to hide.
After washing the clothes, you laid them on the bank to dry,
And so you polluted the Great Yin and the Great Yang.[98]

The karmic burden of Woman Huang is particularly heavy: not only does she feel polluted by childbirth, but she also happens to be married to a butcher. In the *Huangshinü dui Jingang* (Woman Huang explicates the *Diamond Sūtra*), when she reproaches her husband for his sins of slaughtering animals, he turns the tables on her. After listing her sins, as we recall, he concludes: "In vain you rely on your reading of the *Diamond Sūtra*— / The sins of a lifetime will not be easily redeemed."[99]

Thus, women go to hell, not because of some intentional sin, but merely because of bodily functions over which they have no control. The point of the *Blood Bowl Sūtra* was not to condemn women to hell, however, but rather to offer an easy way out of the mess that they had created (with some Buddhist help) for themselves. Thus, the Buddha tells Mulian that, in order to be a filial son, he has to hold a Blood Bowl Feast for three years, with the participation of monks reciting the sutra for a full day. When he does so, the blood pond will turn into a lotus pond, while sinful women will be reborn in a better place. In conclusion, the Buddha addresses women: "As for the *Blood Bowl Sūtra*, if you, with a believing mind, copy and keep this sūtra then you will be causing, as far as possible, the mothers of the three worlds to gain rebirth in heaven, where they will receive pleasures, clothes, and food naturally; their lives will be long, and they will be rich aristocrats."[100] It is worth noticing that the focus has shifted from the relationship between a filial son and his sinful mother (whose crimes were not limited to blood defilement) to ordinary women whose only crime was to have given birth. Thus, women cannot escape the double-bind: they have to procreate and they are doomed because of this. In the Chinese context, their only hope of redemption is at the same time the cause of their sin: by producing children, especially filial sons, who, by repaying their debt to them, will be able to perform the rituals on their behalf. Actually, some interpretations give more weight to female agency and to the redeeming value of the sutra itself.

In one version of the story, her recitation of the *Diamond Sūtra* (and not the *Blood Bowl Sūtra*) was not in vain, since her zeal eventually attracted the attention of King Yama himself. Thus, after she died, she was allowed to return to the world of the living. But because she could not regain her former body, she had to be reborn in a male body—an ironic twist on the topos of male rebirth. She became an official, who later learned in a dream of his former identity, and took care of his/her former husband and children. Woman Huang became a popular heroine, whose story is told by the nun Xue, a midwife of sorts, in the *Jinpingmei*. It is also part of the "Morality Books" (*shanshu*) repertoire, under the title *Nü zhuan nan shen* (*The Woman Who Was Transformed into a Man*).

Woman Huang is also described as a filial daughter, a female Mulian, who rescues her own mother from the Blood Pond Hell. As Beata Grant points out: "When Woman Huang jumps into the Blood Pond, silk skirts and all, to embrace her mother, she is saving herself as well as her mother, and indeed, all women. Like Mulian, she is willing to drink from the blood bowl on behalf of her mother, and her good intentions are enough to bring Dizang to the rescue, as with a puff of his Dharma breath the Blood Pond is transformed into a Lotus Pond and Woman Huang's mother as well as all the other women are saved."[101] According to Grant, although the original objective of these texts was no doubt a didactic one, "in the course of popularization, a definite subtext began to emerge as the choice between pollution and purification came to be seen as a source of great conflict and anguish and not a simple moral imperative."[102] In a version of the ritual inspired by this scripture, and still performed today in Taiwan, the children of a dead woman, at the time of the funeral, redeem their mother's sin by symbolically drinking the blood that was spilled during their childbirth.[103]

The *Blood Bowl Sūtra* seems to have spread in Japan during the medieval period.[104] The fact that Japanese commentaries emphasized menstrual blood rather than parturition blood has led to the somewhat misleading translation of the scripture's title as "Menstruation Sūtra." In this reinterpretation, the pollution caused by blood now affects the entire pantheon, and it becomes the symbol of woman's cardinal sin. As one version of the text explains, "Because they were born as women, their aspirations to buddhahood are weak, and their jealousy and evil character are strong. These sins compounded become menstrual blood, which flows in two streams each month, polluting not only the earth god but all the other deities as well." Another source specifies the length of the nefarious period: "This red blood flows for seven days each month. In twelve months this amounts to eighty-four days." Because men have no part in this form of defilement—unlike in the case of the parturition—only women are condemned to pay the price of blood.

The *Blood Bowl Sūtra* played a prominent role in the Shin and Sōtō schools. Its themes were found in Jōdo devotional hymns (*wasan*) such as the *Ketsubongyō wasan*, sung by associations of women (*kō*).[105] Women, constantly exposed to the dangers of childbirth, were particularly vulnerable and had little leisure for skepticism. References to the Blood Pond Hell crop up in the hymns addressed by women's associations to deities of easy childbirth, such as Santai-sama, which emphasize female defilement and offer nenbutsu to alleviate it.

The widespread cult of the *Blood Bowl Sūtra* is attested to by legends like the following, found in the *Ketsubongyō engi* of Shōsenji in Shimosa Province. The thirteen-year-old daughter of a parishioner is possessed by the spirit of the nun Hosshō, a daughter of Hōjō Tokiyori. The spirit calls for the priest of nearby Hosshōji (a temple founded on Hosshō's behalf by her father), and tells him that she has fallen into the Blood Pond Hell; she requests that he recite the *Blood Bowl Sūtra* to save her. The priest asks advice of a statue of Jizō, the main object of worship of Hosshōji, and the bodhisattva appears to him in a dream and tells him to go to the pond of Teganuma. When the priest goes there, he discovers a copy of the sutra on a lotus leaf. After he has it copied and recited during a seven-day service, the spirit of the nun departs from the girl.[106]

Similar stories of ghosts explaining their crime and punishment to a living witness are found in Sōtō sermons. One such story tells about a young girl who lived near a bridge at the foot of Tiantong shan. Because she died prematurely, her spirit hovered near that bridge. In order to placate her, monks read the *Diamond Sūtra* and the *Blood Bowl Sūtra*, and gave her a lineage chart. Owing to this, she was able to obtain salvation.[107] The *Blood Bowl Sūtra* was even introduced into Sōtō ordination rituals, and thus into the very heart of monastic discipline. This was in response to the fact that women, because of their intrinsic defilement, cannot ascend the ordination platform without committing an offence.[108] Likewise, the Sōtō *kirigami* describe talismans that women had to carry or swallow to purify themselves from blood defilement when they attended religious ceremonies. There were two types of talismans: one to temporarily stop the menses, the other to restore them.[109] Similar practices were performed during Sōtō funeral rites, such as placing a copy of the *Blood Bowl Sūtra* into the coffins of women as a talisman to save them from hell.[110]

The Blood Pond Hell also appears in a text related to Tateyama, a place believed to be the gate to the other world: the *Ashikura chūgo onbason engi*. In this "origin story," the god, assuming the form of an old woman called Onba-son, comes to dwell at Ashikura-dera at the foot of Tateyama. This became a place where women, who were forbidden to set foot on the mountain, performed a preliminary ritual called *nunobashi daikanjō-e* (Great Unction of the Cloth Bridge), in order to obtain salvation. After this ritual, which was supposed to free them from their sins and from retribution in hell, women received a copy of the *Blood Bowl Sūtra* (or *Blood Lake Sūtra*), as well as a talisman that certified their transformation into males.[111] This symbolic transformation, however, was apparently not sufficient, since the mere possession of the talisman did not allow women to ascend the mountain and take part in the main ritual of deliverance from the Blood Lake Hell. They had to give the copies of the *Blood Bowl Sūtra* piously copied by them to the monks who would then take these scriptures to the mountain and throw them into an earthly replica of the Blood Lake. The talisman, the *Blood Pond Sūtra*, and a shroud inscribed with the *Lotus Sūtra* in Sanskrit characters (*kyō katabira*) were put in a woman's coffin.[112] Another legend connected to Tateyama is that of the mother of Jikō shōnin, the founder of this cultic center, a woman who had after death fallen into the Blood Pond Hell.[113]

As noted earlier, itinerant female preachers (Kumano bikuni), even if they simultaneously preached deliverance from these hells and rebirth in the Pure Land, were nontheless instrumental in spreading the fear of the Blood Pond Hell among women. They tried to conceal the sexist nature of the dogma by presenting their message as one of feminine emancipation. For all their talk about final deliverance, and their enrollment in the feminist cause by some scholars, these nuns contributed to the subjection of women to Buddhist male ideology.

In making women responsible for the pollution of childbirth and menstrual blood, Buddhism was not only sexist, but it also undermined one of its fundamental principles: the belief in the individual responsibility of acts, which rests on intentional action. If menstruation is defiling, it is nonetheless involuntary and should bring no retribution. By emphasizing the sin of gender, Buddhism seems to return to earlier notions of ritual pollution, which it tries to legitimize by considering this female vice of form (or of substance) as the effect of a karma that is both collective and individual.

Of course, one may argue that such representations are mere "skillful means" (*upāya*), a sort of shock-treatment meant to eradicate the disease. At the same time that it reinforces female guilt, Buddhism claims to offer absolution. By its magic power, the *Blood Bowl Sūtra* allowed women to avoid the ritual pollution of menses and childbirth and to come into the presence of the gods and the buddhas. But at what price? It was now for the duration of the entire menstrual period, and no longer simply at childbirth, that women needed the priests. Although the function of the sutra was originally a funerary one, it was eventually diverted to the benefit of worldly values, and the text, having become a talisman for pregnant women, was reinscribed in a natalist strategy. At any rate, the Japanese of the Edo period came to adopt a ritual that heightened the pollution of female blood and of death, in order to better erase it, all in return for a strict ideological control of women by Buddhism. Such is the contradiction—or ventriloquism—of a religious teaching that on the one hand affirms blood pollution while on the other praises motherhood. The case of the *Ketsubongyō* shows that Buddhist soteriology is based on male superiority, exploiting female fears, more than on compassion. This should not surprise us, since a great part of the success of Buddhism in Asia has been due in part to the priests' ability to capitalize on human fears, in particular that of death.

THE "FACTS" OF LIFE

The blatant injustice of the Blood Pond Hell was accepted by women as just another "fact of life" (or rather, of death)—a woman's life of toil and trouble. In the *Samyutta-Nikāya*, the Buddha enumerates five extra forms of suffering for women: menstruation, pregnancy, childbirth, having to wait upon a man, and being subjected to the authority of in-laws.[114] An interesting story is that of the woman who remained pregnant for seven years, and, because of the suffering she endured before giving birth, realized the truth of suffering and the value of Buddhism as a way to end suffering. Her son eventually became a monk, and was praised for having endured suffering seven years in the womb. Interestingly, we find no mention in such Buddhist traditions of Rāhula, the son of the Buddha, who is said to have remained six years in the maternal womb, perhaps because the womb of the Buddha's wife, like that of his mother, cannot be such a bad place.[115]

In Chinese popular culture, too, there were many popular songs and stories emphasizing these "facts of life," conveniently mixing biological "facts" with social oppression. In the *baojuan* (Precious Scrolls), for instance, we hear of women at odds with their shared destiny, trying to fight back or to find an escape. The *Liuxiang baojuan* relates the story of Liuxiang nü, a saintly girl born into the family of a restaurant owner, and who keeps from childhood a vegetarian diet.[116] The heroine hears a sermon about karma, salvation, and the toils of womanhood in a nearby convent. She convinces her father to open a vegetarian restaurant. Later, she agrees to marry a young man, Ma Yu, if he agrees to ten moral conditions.[117] But once she moves into the new household, she has to confront the animosity of her sisters-in-law and mother-in-law, who beat her and accuse her of adultery. She is eventually driven out of the house, and has to beg for food, staying at night in temples. Despite his love for her, Ma Yu ends up taking a new wife, and he leaves for Guangdong. The rest of the family dies of meat intoxication during the birthday feast for the mother-in-law. In the end, the family is rescued from purgatory thanks to Liuxiang's intercession, while she, her husband, and his second wife are reborn in Amitābha's Pure Land.[118]

We find here the ethical teachings of lay Buddhism. But the chief value is not conventional, as the text is devoted to courage, freedom, and the salvation of women. Liuxiang nü breaks social custom and succeeds in the end. She never really has a normal marriage. The text does not say that she did not sleep with her husband just after the marriage, but she remains celibate afterwards. What she values is meditation, not sex and children. She offers a strong resistance to marriage and to the toil and submission it requires. The text also gives us the sermon of an old "nun" on the sufferings and dangers of pregnancy and childbirth, as well as other difficulties a wife must endure: "We women are despised for troubling our mother's bodies, and for not caring for our parents. When a girl grows up she abandons her parents and is married to another man."[119] Likewise, the nun of the *Jingpingmei* draws a dark image of a woman's destiny:

> When a woman is married to a husband for her whole life she is controlled by him. All her joys and sorrows derive from him. After they are married she necessarily suffers the pains of childbirth, and cannot avoid the sin of offending the sun, moon, and stars with a flow of blood. Now I will speak with you in more detail about the sufferings women endure in childbirth.[120]

> Now the suffering of giving birth which I have discussed, the sufferings of ten months of pregnancy and of three years of nursing, and after birth, the bitter toil day and night of exchanging dry and wet [clothing], these are what is called "in loving a child, there is nothing one won't do."[121]

The nun then recites the "Precious Scroll on Pregnancy" (*Huatai bao-juan*), a detailed month-by-month account of the pains and anxiety of pregnancy.[122] The explicit conclusion is that children should repay the suffering and pains through which their parents have gone; however, this material might also have led some women to question marriage itself. This description of childbirth as suffering, already found in the *Public Teaching of Huiyuan on Lushan*, will find echoes in medieval Japanese texts such as the *Ise nindenki*.[123] This text shows a hesitation between two metaphors: in the first part the five stages of gestation are described as a smooth process of awakening; but in the second part, among the "eight sufferings," gestation and birth are described as "pure hell" (Avici hell). In the *Heike monogatari*, we read that "People say nine out of ten pregnant women fail to survive the ordeal of giving birth."[124] Even if the figure is exaggerated, it is quite telling.

Whereas popular tradition considered "the facts of life" from the standpoint of the woman, the early Buddhist tradition also emphasized the standpoint of the newborn child—or rather, of the human being undergoing rebirth. The *Visuddhimagga* (*Path of Purification*), for instance, takes gestation and birth as illustrations of the Truth of Suffering. To give just an idea, here is how it describes the first stage of gestation, the "suffering rooted in the descent into the womb":

> When this being is born in the mother's womb, it is not born inside a blue or red or white lotus, etc., but on the contrary, like a worm in rotting fish, rotting dough, cess-pools, etc., he is born in the belly in a position that is below the receptacle for undigested food (stomach), above the receptacle for digested food (rectum), between the belly-lining and the backbone, which is very cramped,

quite dark, pervaded with very fetid draughts redolent of various smells of or-
dure, and exceptionally loathsome. And on being reborn there, for ten months
he undergoes excessive suffering, being cooked like a pudding in a bag by the
heat produced in the mother's womb, and steamed like a dumpling of dough,
with no bending, stretching, and so on.[125]

One could contrast the notion of childbirth (actually a rebirth) according to Theravāda Buddhism (as expressed, for instance, in the *Visuddhimagga*) and to Tantric Buddhism. Medieval Tantric embryology completely washes away the stigma of blood, making gestation a purifying
process of enlightenment. Strangely, the defilement remains connected
with childbirth itself, where, as we have seen, the traditional blood taboo
remains.

THE RED AND THE WHITE

The overvaluation of the father's role in reproduction is reflected in the
belief that only women could be infertile. Such was not always the case,
however. A cosmological model also determined fertility and sterility. The
normal sterility attributed to old age was one thing, the abnormal sterility
in a young or mature couple was another. Chinese "correlative thinking"
claimed to distinguish between auspicious and inauspicious times for co-
itus, based on the Five Phases theory. Conception was said to take place
when the essences of man and woman reach their fullness. This relatively
equal treatment of man and woman is still characteristic of the *Ishinpō*,
a medical text which explains sterility as the result of an imbalance between the respective coldness and warmth of blood and breath.[126] If the
"essence" of man is too liquid or too cold, for instance, conception cannot
take place. In many medical texts of the Edo period, infertility has become
the dubious privilege of the woman, and it is now the result of some moral
deficiency. Although conception was clearly the crucial phase, various beliefs contributed to relativize its importance, in particular the notion that
the gender of the embryo could be changed during gestation.[127]

Buddhism introduced a new element in this well-established model: the
presence of an "intermediary being" (Skt. *antarābhava*) at the moment
of conception.[128] Buddhist embryological conceptions revolve around the
"harmony of the three things": the mother's health, the sexual act itself,
and the presence of the "intermediary being." This idea was absent in
the theories of the non-Buddhist medical tradition; however, the *Huangdi
neijing taisu*, compiled in the seventh century by Tang Shangshan, argues,
with a reference to Buddhist notions, that the spirit (*shen*) must descend
into the womb before birth. In his *Godan shō*, the Pure Land priest Shōkū

describes the father as the "generating cause of birth" [*nōshō no in*], and the mother as the "condition for being generated" [*shoshō no en*].[129] He also describes the condition of the "intermediary existence" [*chūu*] between the moment of death [*shiu*] and the moment of birth [*shōu*]. The descent of the intermediary being into the womb is also described according to the theories of the *Abhidharmakośa-śastra*.[130] Regarding this descent, we are told that the "intermediary being," wandering into the intermediary realm, sees a man and a woman engaged in sex, and is irresistibly attracted to one of the partners, while he hates the other. This is due to the fact that this intermediary being, because of his past karma, is gendered. When he is male, for instance, he wants to make love to the woman instead of the man, and when the man ejaculates, the intermediary being believes that it is he himself who did it. This error renders him coarse and heavy, causing him to descend into the womb. In this particular conception, the fetus is also, consequently, gendered from the start. A male fetus is placed on the right side of the womb, facing backward, whereas a female fetus is placed on the left side, facing forward. In the particular case when the intermediary being is a bodhisattva waiting to be reincarnated, he chooses his father and mother with due knowledge, and he enters his mother's body through her right side.[131] The fact that ordinary "intermediary beings" enter the womb through the vagina explains in part the belief that conception is impure.

This conception of conception was not entirely specific to Buddhism: we also find it in a late *Upaniṣad*, the *Garbha-upaniṣad*, according to which the father's semen (*śukra*), which produces the embryo when united with the mother's blood (*śonita*), already contains, from the very start, the four elements. Yet, in order for an embryo to form, the body's substances (*dhātu*) are not enough, nor is the union between semen and blood. A more subtle element—*manas*, karma or *ātman* for the Hindus, *vijñāna* or *antarābhava* for the Buddhists—is needed. As Lakshmi Kapani queries, "Are these two causal series, the one physical, provided by the parents, the other psychological, provided by the individual himself, entirely distinct—or do they in some ways intersect? In effect, by stating that one is born a boy or a girl according to the proportion of the two semens and that a cripple results from the parent's mental troubles, the *Upaniṣad* makes the individual's entire destiny, in particular his social and religious destiny, depend on the physical series and all the psychophysiological material it provides." She adds, "Where does the strict law of karma fit in? In order to resolve this problem it would be necessary to reconcile the two causal series into a single schema, which in turn would necessitate the hypothesis that the subtle body chooses its own womb, according to its latent desires (*vāsanā*) and motivations (*saṃskāra*) already accumulated from past lives."[132]

Let us return to the red and white, which colors have had metaphorical resonance across Asia, from ancient Iran to Japan.[133] The Chinese conception, reflected in the funerary rituals, is that the (red) flesh comes from the mother, whereas the (white) bones come from the father. More specifically, the mother's "red drop" contributes the skin, blood, flesh, fat, heart, and various soft, red viscera; whereas the father's "white drop" contributes the hair, nails, teeth, bones, veins, arteries, ligaments, semen— in other words, all that is white, hard, structural. This is very much like the Greek conception, described by Aline Rousselle, in which semen goes to build the "noble white parts." Therefore, a woman who wants a son must "whiten" or "masculinize" herself. According to Aristotle, "Man produces sperm because his is a warm nature, such that he possesses a capacity for bringing about an intense concoction of the blood, which transforms it into its purest and thickest residue: sperm or male seed. Women cannot perform this operation. They lose blood, and at their warmest they can only succeed in turning it into milk. . . Thus, the ultimate difference between the sexes lies in the fact that one is warm and dry, the other cold and wet, qualities that reveal themselves in their aptitude or inaptitude for achieving concoction."[134] Incidentally, this distinction is presented as the ultimate rationale and justification of the androcentric social order. The Egyptian theories of reproduction, too, ascribed the bones to the male principle and the flesh to the female.

Although the bones are clearly more valued than the flesh in the Chinese context—since the whole purpose of the "double-burial" is to get rid of the flesh in order to keep the bones—one can argue that this conception is relatively egalitarian in that both the man and the woman are seen to participate fully in the procreative act. According to Maurice Bloch and Jonathan Parry, death rituals, aimed at the regeneration of fertility, can serve as an index to kinship practices. They provide an attempt to solve the "problem" of affinal and matrilineal relations. For the Chinese, bones come from the father and his ascendants, while flesh is given by the mother. In this exogamous society, bones are treated as very important, and at the time of the second burial all remaining flesh is removed from them. By contrast, endogamous societies studied by Maurice Bloch, like the Merina of Madagascar, take great pains to retain the entire body. The same was true of ancient Confucian funerary rites, where the entire body (including nail clippings) was preserved in the coffin. In a society like that of the Chinese, which emphasizes the distinction between kin and affines, the custom is to rid the bones of flesh to make them the object of the ancestral cult. Thus, "the final triumph over death is also a triumph over the necessity for affines and over the world of sexual reproduction they represent."[135] Since this opposition between affines and agnates is also expressed symbolically in terms of red and white (flesh and bones, but also blood and semen, yin and yang), the outcome of the funerary ritual can be seen as a victory of the white over the red, or, as Evelyn Rawski puts it, a victory of ritual propriety (*li*) over chaos and decay: "In the process of restoring order through *li*, *yang* overrides *yin*, men affirm symbolic superiority over women, agnates over affines."[136]

Similar conceptions were already found in India outside Buddhism, particularly in Hinduism and Jainism. The *Caraka-saṃhitā*, for instance, explains that if there is a superabundance of blood at the moment of conception, the embryo will be female; of semen, the embryo will be male. Anatomical sex is produced by an imbalance of substances. In later texts, perfect balance results in production of a hermaphrodite (*dviretas*, "a being with two emissions"; that is, one who can simultaneously menstruate and ejaculate). This is, however, a rather exceptional case. Thus, as Anne Chayet points out in the case of Tibetan medicine, the role of the parents is complementary, but cannot be equal. This inequality is alternative, however. During the development of the embryo, the paternal seed produces the bones, the brain, and the spinal chord, whereas the maternal blood produces the flesh, the organs "full and empty," and the viscerae.[137]

A similar conception of paternity ("Like father, like son") is illustrated in Buddhist stories in which a child instinctively recognizes his true father.[138] The most famous such story is of course that of the recognition of the Buddha by his son Rāhula, who finds him without hesitation among five hundred magical doubles. Things were not always as easy, however, and the recognition of fatherhood could lead to serious inheritance disputes. These conceptions were still alive and well in late medieval Japan, as one can infer from the following *senryū*: "No wonder / they quarrel: the placenta / like a hunting map."[139] In the hunting parties of the shogun, the guests of each clan were distributed on the ground according to protocol, their place being indicated by their blazon on a map. According to popular belief, the blazon of a child's father appeared on the placenta at the time of childbirth. This placenta was carefully preserved by the family as proof of the authenticity of filiation. Things got worse when several blazons appeared on the placenta, like on a hunting map.[140]

We can observe a shift to a more egalitarian notion of yin and yang as two equally active seeds in the Tachikawa teachings, which speak of "watering life" with the white and red fluids. In a Tachikawa text like the *Konkōshō*, as in the *Abhidharmakośa-śāstra*, the gender of the child is said to depend on that of intermediary being. This theory, which attributes all of the agency to the *antarābhava*, implies the equality of the red and the white, and therefore of man and woman, in the procreative act. Yet, the same text, in a section entitled "Male and Female are not equal," seems to indicate that the gender of the child depends entirely on the outcome of the "battle of the sexes," at the cellular level:

The *Taitaku ron* (Treatise on the Reliance on the Womb) states: "If the male essence first opens, then the female essence strives to it and the yang encompasses the yin, and it becomes a boy. If the female essence first opens, then the yang essence strives to it, the yin encompasses the yang, and it becomes a girl. . . . Because it corresponds to the original form, if the intermediary being is male, then as a result of sexual union the female essence must open first, then the male essence proceeds, and the male form of the original state will be formed. If the intermediary being is female, as a result of lascivious pleasure the male essence opens first, the female essence then proceeds, and the female form of the original state is formed."[141]

In a strange inversion of the traditional roles of the white and red, the *Konkōshō* concludes: "The male essence is always responsible for the formation of the outside red flesh, the female essence is accumulated inside to form white bones. When the female and male essences flow out, neither of them comes ahead or behind."[142]

Other conceptions present the red and white in "competition." These conceptions also derive from Indian medical theory. According to the *Garbha-upaniṣad*, for instance, "An excess of the father's semen produces a male, an excess of the mother's semen, a girl, and an equal amount of the two semens, a eunuch [or rather, a hermaphrodite, *na-puṃsaka*]. A troubled spirit produces the blind, the lame, hunchback and dwarfs. When the sperm is crushed by the wind and splits into two, twins are born."[143] According to an interesting (and widespread) Japanese belief, the gender of the child is said to depend on who gets most pleasure from the sexual intercourse. According to the *Shasekishū*, for instance, the conscience is formed by the fusion of the "white drop" of the father and of the "red drop" of the mother; and, depending where the sexual pleasure was, the child will resemble the father or the mother. This conception is vividly expressed in the following anecdote about "embarrassing sermons":

> A nun in Mutsu province lost her son called Saemon no Jō and held a memorial service, at which the celebrant spoke of the causes of resemblance between parent and child. "The causal relationship between mother and child is splendid. When the father and mother have relations, a boy is produced through love on the part of the mother; a girl, when the father predominates. If at the time of conception the father's mood is ecstatic, the child will resemble him; if this is the mother's mood, then the child will resemble her. Since Saemon looked exactly like his mother, she must have had a good time conceiving him!" It is embarrassing to go into such detail about a person who sponsors a religious service.[144]

The complex embryological relationship between parents and child described (tongue in cheek) by the author of the *Shasekishū* differs from the simplistic beliefs that came to prevail in the Edo period, which emphasized paternal genetic transmission, and according to which, as the saying went, "a woman's belly is merely borrowed." The secondary wives of the Tokugawa shogun and of his *daimyō* were called *ōharasama* (lit. "Mrs. Womb"), and their primary function was to produce an heir. Women were seen as totally passive in the reproductive process. They were the receptacles of a sacred deposit, which they merely caused to fructify, or, to use another common (and cross-cultural) metaphor, a fertile soil fecundated by man.[145] Ironically, this notion bears superficial resemblance to the feminist argument that procreation is ancillary to women; in other words, that women are not defined by motherhood (or maternity). In the Chinese and Japanese cases, a distinction should be made between social motherhood and biological maternity. Conversely, there are feminists who criticize (male) attempts to dissociate the embryo from women's body (and thus make women ancillary to the procreation process).[146] This, in turn, resonates with the idea, often encountered in medieval Japanese literature, that mother and son form a single body.[147] In the Fujidō, however, a millenarian cult that developed during the Edo period, gestation was said to take place in the bodies of both parents. The name of the movement itself was based on a play of words on "Fuji," meaning both the mountain of that name, and "nonduality." Such nonduality implied a reversal of the symbolic attributes of yin and yang. Nonetheless, the Fujidō remains an exception that confirms the patriarchal (and quasi-Aristotelian) rule, under which women were essentially "borrowed wombs," providing "room and board."

In the patriarchal context, women were viewed not only as the foreign element in a household, but also the weak link in the lineage. Childbirth was a very risky business, and it was believed that nine out of ten women would die in labor. At times of high mortality rates and minimal life expectancy, the reproductive function of women was valued. There were many beliefs about the womb and its reproductive capacities, and magical ways to interfere with the natural process of reproduction. Thus, the womb was viewed as a potential target for occult powers, against which it needed magical protection. The body of the pregnant woman, and particularly her womb, were always at risk from evil influences. Since gestation was part of the "intermediary period" between death and rebirth, the womb was sometimes assimilated to a tomb or a stupa.[148] Not surprisingly, this grave attracted restless ghosts. Unless well protected by magical means, the weakened body of the parturient was easy prey, and Japanese medieval tales like the *Eiga monogatari* abound in stories of court ladies possessed by vengeful ghosts (*onryō*) during labor. Uterine magic was also used to control timely aperture and closure of the womb, in both good and evil ways, and thus both as a contraceptive and abortive method. Tantric Buddhists, in particular, used spells to close the womb for a long period, causing harm to the woman. One is reminded of Māya's long pregnancy, but in her case it is not seen as entirely negative (albeit strange), nor as required by the fetus's maturation.

The contrast between these views of conception is reminiscent of that between Aristotle's "monoseed" theory and Hippocrates' "two seeds" theory. Aristotle's pronouncement that women did not produce sperm meant that half of the human race were eunuchs incapable of transmitting life or reproducing except insofar as they provided the environment in which the male sperm might develop. But in the struggle against desire, in contrast with procreation, women became men's equals and were accorded a new dignity.[149]

The yin/yang theory at the basis of the Chinese "red and white" metaphor looks Aristotelian, in that the woman is viewed as being purely passive: "The yang leads, the yin follows." This definitely has a misogynistic ring, and it is indeed reminiscent of the Aristotelian theory of the two causes, efficient and instrumental, which gave the backing of science to misogynist theories.[150] As noted previously, woman, in her purely passive function, gives only "room and board." This theory brings to mind the aforementioned motif of the borrowed womb (hara wa karimono).[151]

On the contrary, the theory of the double-seed undermined any misogynist interpretation of procreation. Thus, one can contrast the "phallocentric seminism" of Aristotle with the dual seminism of Hippocrates, which implied an equality of the sexes. Similarly, the embryological discourse of Buddhism duplicates the egalitarian/unegalitarian rhetoric of its philosophical discourse. For instance, the theoretical equality advocated by the Zen master Dōgen (1200–1253) is reproduced in the embryological equality that he borrows from the "science" of his time. But this "equality" of the red and the white is undermined by the implicit hierarchy of yin and yang.

The insistence on male procreation is not specific to Buddhism; it also characterizes Western patriarchal ideology.[152] Thomas Laqueur has shown how, in the West, "a biology of cosmic hierarchy gave way to a biology of incommensurability, anchored in the body, in which the relation of men to women, like that of apples to oranges, was not given as one of equality or inequality, but rather of difference."[153] Likewise, in Japanese Buddhism, the old unisex model where a woman could, by improving her karma, become a man, seems to be denied in texts such as the Ketsubongyō, where a woman is intrinsically defiled by her karma/biology, and doomed to fall into hell (despite her good karma she can no longer become a man). Her only hope is now a miraculous intervention, some buddha ex machina, in this case the magical power of the Ketsubongyō. But the underlying conception, with regard to the sexual difference, is a radical departure from earlier models.

The Hippocratic system implies an equivalence of the sexes. The embryo results from the mixture of male and female seeds—hence the name "seminism." Until the end of the seventeenth century, Hippocrates was the ultimate authority. According to the Hippocratic tradition, gender is determined by a kind of battle between male and female seed. The gender of the child was the result of a subtle dosage of the two seeds. When the male seed dominates, a male child is born. The right is specific to the male embryo, the left to the female embryo. According to Laqueur, "Two-seed theories, like those of Hippocrates and Galen, hold that 'seeds' from both parents are necessary to vivify the matter provided by the mother. One-seed theories, of which Aristotle's was the most influential, hold that the male provides the *sperma* (the efficient and, more problematically, the formal cause) in generation while the female provides the *catamenia* (the material cause). The female ejaculate in this model had no purpose because by definition the female provides no seed."[154] Although Aristotle integrated Hippocratic theories into his philosophical system, he thought that the female ejaculate was devoid of life. The vital principle was contained only in the male ejaculate. The role of the female was reduced to providing menstrual blood, a lifeless matter, but necessary to feed the embryo. Thus, Aristotle's theory rests on the superiority of the male in the reproductive process. He was not the first one to show this androcentric bias. Greeks generally believed that the woman was merely a receptacle, but fertile soil fecundated by the man. But Aristotle was the one who gave this prejudice a scientific form, whereas until then medical science, with the two-seed theory, had undermined such prejudice. "For Aristotle . . . and for the long tradition founded on his thought, the generative substances are interconvertible elements in the economy of a single-sex body whose higher form is male."[155]

Perhaps these simplistic notions will make us smile.[156] As Laqueur observes, however, "much of the debate about the nature of the seed and of the bodies that produce it . . . [is] in fact not about bodies at all. . . .[but] about power, legitimacy, and fatherhood.[157] Or again, in Jean-Joseph Goux's words, "The legacy of a patrimony of signifiers is thus symbolized in the language of fertilization and sexual reproduction, in the belief that it is the father . . . who confers both visible and invisible form upon the offspring, while the maternal contribution, both physiologically and socially, has the neutrality of an excipient, the inert negativity of earth."[158]

The above discussion has shown that the procreative role of women—in conception proper, in gender determination, and in the gestation process—has always been a source of contention. This is due in part to the fact that Buddhist ideology, in this domain, borrowed from other discourses (medical embryology, patriarchal conceptions of lineage), and was not as consistently androcentric as in other, purely symbolic areas like the blood taboo.

The development of the notion of defilement from the tenth century onward is not purely a Buddhist fact, but was intimately related to the conceptions of the ruling class.[159] As Nishiguchi Junko notes, the taboos of blood and death are notions that Japanese Buddhists developed in order to participate in royal rituals, inheriting in the process the repulsion toward defilement that characterized the nobility and the cult of the kami. Yet Buddhists themselves came to transgress taboos (for instance, the defilement of death), and they even in some instances justified killing. As ritual specialists, Buddhist monks entertained relations with *senmin* (outcasts, specialists of impurity). They also came to perform all kinds of rituals to protect the daily life of nobles. In their funerary services for noble women, for instance, they had to look for scriptural passages implying the possibility of female buddhahood. Thus, they came to praise woman as the "mother of the buddhas," and to allow the possibility of "gender change" (even in the postmortem form of bones). Inasmuch as they remained in the canonical framework, however, they could not avoid gender discrimination, and Buddhist hells remained paved with good intentions.

The Buddhist obsession with defilement had perhaps less to do with Buddhist teaching itself than with the fact that Buddhism, in the process of becoming the official ideology, inherited (and amplified) traditional concerns about ritual defilement and purification. The development of the red and white symbolism reminds us that symbols have their own dynamics and can sometimes subvert the manipulation of the ideologues. Buddhist priests tried to extend their ideological grip from rituals performed for women who died in childbirth to childbirth in general, and beyond to the entire realm of embryology and gynecology. On the one hand, they contributed to the bias against supposed female impurity and to "naturalize" the social injustice of patriarchal society, while on the other they opened the door to a return of local cults in which women and women's issues played a central role. In the process, Buddhism was to some extent subverted by female values.

It is clear that we need to revise traditional narratives: not only is the teleological schema of the rise of patriarchy too simple, but, among women themselves, "le malheur des unes fait quelquefois le bonheur des autres." At the ideological level, female inferiority was the result of two types of discourse, which may overlap with, or contradict, each other. There was first a kind of inferiority that we may call "clanic" because the woman was perceived as a commodity for the lineage: she was not asked for her opinion, and did not even possess her body, a mere instrument of procreation. Her only hope to reclaim her body and mind was to free herself from familial and clanic constraints by entering a different lineage, the Buddhist order. The second type of female inferiority was a product of widespread misogyny. It was the *imbecillitas sexus,* in which the woman was despised because she was feared: she was seen as evil (or prone to evil), and judged impure because of her blood; she worried males because she served as an intermediary with the world of the dead. Her alleged powers are the cause of her disempowerment.

The fact remains that all of these discourses are about women, not by women. Despite a few exceptions, like the networks of literate women in Heian Japan, women were on the whole increasingly subjected to patriarchal ideology, in its Confucian and Buddhist varieties. This explains why the experience of women can only be reconstructed from iconographic and sociological documents, and is rarely told in the first-person. But here again, there are significant exceptions. After deconstructing Buddhist rhetorical strategies, we will see in the last part of the book—"Women against Buddhism"—how certain female voices were able to reassert themselves.

Chapter Three

THE RHETORIC OF SALVATION

T HE NŌ play *Genzai Shichimen* describes the encounter between the holy monk Nichiren and a female *nāga* on Mount Minobu. A woman regularly comes to listen to Nichiren's teaching and to make offerings to the Buddha. One day, as Nichiren resorts to the exemplum of the *nāga*-girl to illustrate the possibility of female buddhahood, she expresses her gratitude for the fact that she, too, will now be able to free herself from the "Three Fevers." As these Three Fevers precisely refer to the sufferings of the *nāga*, Nichiren realizes that she is no ordinary woman and asks her to reveal her true form. She leaves the stage and soon returns, wearing a *hannya* (demoness) mask, symbolizing her transformation into a female *nāga*.

> She has become a great hideous snake
> Whose eyes shine like the sun and the moon,
> Who turns around the seat of the reverend priest,
> Wrapping him in its numberless coils.
> Its attitude is all of shame and repentance;
> Lifting its head before the priest,
> It raises toward him imploring eyes.[1]

Nichiren then takes the *Lotus Sūtra*, and reads: "In one instant, true awakening can be found." Upon hearing these words, the snake/dragon instantly metamorphoses into a heavenly maiden (*tennyo*), "identical to a buddha," as celestial music is heard and lotus flowers fall on the stage. To thank Nichiren, she dances a *kagura*. After this, she promises that she will become the tutelary deity of Mount Minobu, warding off calamities and guiding sentient beings toward salvation. In a final apotheosis, she ascends in the sky. This Nō play brings together a number of motifs related to the theme of the salvation of the *nāga*-princess, which finds its classical expression in the *Lotus Sūtra*.

The Legend of the Nāga-girl

> Women have five obstacles;
> Far from them the purity of the Pure Land.
> But even as the lotus blossoms in black mud,
> So the daughter of the Dragon King has become a buddha.
> (*Ryōjin hishō*)[2]

As this *imayō* ("modern style") song from the *Ryōjin hishō* shows, the sexist topos of the Five Obstacles was often coupled with the theme of the buddhahood of the *nāga*-girl, as found in in the Devadatta chapter of the *Lotus Sūtra*. This verse suggests that the "rhetoric of inequality" and the "rhetoric of salvation" work hand in hand. In the *Lotus Sūtra*, when the bodhisattva Mañjuśrī descends to the palace of the *nāga*-king Sagara to preach the Law, the king's eight-year-old daughter produces the thought of awakening and in no time reaches the bodhisattva stage of nonreturn. Upon returning to Vulture Peak, Mañjuśrī tells the disciples of the Buddha assembled there about the event. When the arhat Śāriputra refuses to believe him, on the ground that the gender of the *nāga*-girl would prevent her from obtaining enlightenment, she appears before the assembly and tells him that she will turn into a buddha right before his eyes. She then offers a wish-fulfilling jewel to the Buddha, and suddenly turns into a *man*; in this new form, she cultivates the bodhisattva practices and goes to the "undefiled realm" in the South. There, sitting on a jewel-lotus, she reaches ultimate awakening, becoming endowed with all the marks of a buddha. Marveling at her apotheosis, all the beings of the *sahā* world rejoice and worship her.[3] Śāriputra, a representative of orthodoxy, may have had some reasons for skepticism, in light of the fact that early Buddhist scriptures like the *Mahāvagga* considered the *nāgas* unable to practice Buddhism. In most Buddhist texts, the *nāgas*, despite their magical powers, are said to be the embodiment of ignorance and passions.

The metamorphoses of female *nāgas* are not limited to this story, however. Indeed, the *nāga*-girl of the *Lotus Sūtra* belongs to a family of female snakes and dragons, beings that have haunted the Japanese imagination.[4] The motif of the *nāga*-girl has inspired many Japanese commentators from the ninth century onward.[5] Kūkai mentions it only in passing in the *Sangō shiki* (797) and the *Jūjūshinron*. Not surprisingly, it is in the Lotus-centered Tendai and Nichiren schools that such commentaries have flourished. In his *Hokke shūku* (821), Saichō comments on the story thus:

> This passage concerns those beings who can realize buddhahood only with difficulty and reveals the power of the *Lotus Sūtra* to help them. She is an animal, one of the six destinies, obviously the result of a bad karma. She is female and clearly has faculties which are not good. She is young and thus has not been practicing austerities for a long time. And yet, the wondrous power of the *Lotus Sūtra* endows her with the two adornments of wisdom and merit. Thus we know that the power of the *Lotus Sūtra* reveals it to be the jewel among the scriptures and a rarity in the world.[6]

Significantly, the *nāga*-girl's realization becomes here the *Lotus Sūtra*'s achievement. Saichō argues that her example is significant for all sentient beings. He was primarily interested in arguing that the rapid attainment of buddhahood was possible through the power of the *Lotus Sūtra* and that Tendai practices were superior to those of the Hossō school. The *nāga*-girl and others around who were converted, "through the wondrous power of the Sūtra," all realized buddhahood with their bodies just as they are (*sokushin jōbutsu*).[7] In other words, Saichō apparently had little interest in the salvation of women as such.[8]

Nichiren, on the other hand, has left a number of texts in which he affirms the salvation of women. He seems to emphasize a strongly feminist reading of the story, asserting that the buddhahood of the *nāga*-girl means the potential buddhahood of all women.[9] Nichiren, however, here and there also expresses disturbingly patriarchal conceptions of women, and his emphasis on the power of the *Lotus Sūtra* remains in line with Saichō's interpretation.

At this point, it is worth noting that the *nāga*-girl is mentioned in the *Lotus Sūtra* in connection with Devadatta, the Buddha's cousin and the arch-villain of Buddhist mythology. Devadatta's future buddhahood is justified by the fact that in a past life he was a hermit who taught the *Lotus Sūtra* to the future Śākyamuni. Nichiren, following that line of thought, establishes an explicit parallel between the enlightenment of Devadatta and that of the *nāga* princess. He makes an interesting slip, however, when he argues that "only with the preaching of the *Lotus Sūtra*, in which the *nāga*-king's daughter attained buddhahood, did it become evident that the attainment of buddhahood was a possibility for *all the mothers* of the world."[10] Significantly, although the *nāga*-girl's mother is conspicuously absent in the story, the women who are saved are mothers, and womanhood is redefined as, or definitively associated with, motherhood. We will return to the place of mothers in Buddhist soteriology. Suffice it for now to point out that, in Nichiren's mind, there was a significant parallelism between the salvation of "evil men" and that of ordinary women. For him, the salvation of Devadatta is no longer merely the karmic result of his having been once the "good friend" of Śākyamuni. It now illustrates the redeeming power of the *Lotus Sūtra*, a scripture able to save the worst criminals (and, by the same token, women). The underlying logic, according to which women are fundamentally evil and thus naturally associated with evil men, is hardly new. Although Nichiren seems to have accepted the notion of the Five Obstacles, he also argues that the *nāga*-girl reached awakening in her female body, without having to be reborn as a man.[11] Furthermore, for him, pious women who believe in the *Lotus Sūtra* are superior to profane men: the saving power of faith relativizes the "natural" gender hierarchy and allows him to bypass the theory of "rebirth as man." Nevertheless, the fact that Nichiren does not mention a change of sex does not mean that he entirely denies its necessity; rather, in the context of the *hongaku* (innate awakening) theory of Tendai, such a change is no longer seen as a sine qua non condition of buddhahood.

These commentaries alert us to the fact that things may have been a little more complex, and that the two aspects, salvation and discrimination, may be intimately connected. Here again, as in the case of the *Blood Bowl Sūtra*, soteriological inclusiveness presupposes (and reinforces) gender discrimination; it is only the other face, or the silver lining, of discrimination. The Janus-faced logic at work here could be expressed as follows: women are inferior; yet, since even those women can become buddha owing to the power of the *Lotus Sūtra*, this sutra is the foremost scripture. It has often been remarked that, in the *Lotus Sūtra,* the Buddha spends more time asserting the scripture's superiority than expounding a particular doctrine. In a strangely autoreferential fashion, much of the doctrinal content of that scripture seems to be precisely the promotion of a cult of the *Lotus Sūtra*. The paradox here is that the truth of the *Lotus Sūtra* lies in its affirmation that this scripture speaks the ultimate truth. At any rate, whereas Devadatta is said to represent evil men, the *nāga*-girl's representativity is more elusive: she might be said to symbolize such diverse categories of beings as children, animals, and women. Owing to the power of the *Lotus Sūtra*, all these beings can become buddhas. Although the traditional emphasis has clearly been on the buddhahood of women, the fact remains that the text, rather than saying clearly that the *nāga*-girl is *by nature* equal to men, seems to insist on her multifaceted inferiority, which only the *Lotus Sūtra* can redeem. This kind of rhetorical device is not one that emphasizes either pure salvation or pure discrimination: rather, it stages a dramatic process of redemption, according to a logic of proselytism.[12] Thus, the other side of the "saving power" of the *Lotus Sūtra* is the assertion of the negativity of women. As noted earlier, the arhat Śāriputra refuses to believe in the *nāga*-girl's achievement, because for him "a woman's body is soiled and defiled, not a vessel for the Law."[13] Even though he eventually has to concede, the subliminal message of the text remains that "women are filthy," even if, owing to the purifying power of the *Lotus Sūtra*, some of them can indeed become vessels of the Law.

Should the *nāga*-girl story be read only through a gender code? The folkloric richness of the theme goes much beyond the mere soteriological promise for women and its sexist background. Yamamoto Hiroko, for instance, argues that the point of the *nāga*-girl story is not that women can become buddhas, but that animals (and more generally nonhumans, *irui*) can, as well.[14] After all, despite the fact that the *nāga* princess can appear in a human form, the *nāga* is usually classified as an animal. This point is elaborated in the *Keiran shūyōshū*. After pointing out that the *nāga*-girl has a female body, the essence of which is lustful desire, Kōjū writes:

As for her species, her body is that of a poisonous snake, the essence of which is great anger. Among the six destinies, she belongs to the animals, the essence of which is stupidity. The very shape of the snake embodies the three poisons. Its frightening aspect represents anger, attachment stands for desire, and impurity for stupidity. As for her gender, the female body is stupidity. She is young, which also means stupidity. The essence of stupidity is ignorance, and ignorance is the root of all afflictions.[15]

The symbolic multivalence of the *nāga* may explain why the theme of the *nāga*-girl, reaching to the religious roots of medieval Japan, reveals a world that goes far beyond (or rather, conveniently pushes aside) the "all too human" question of the possibility of buddhahood for women. Admittedly, Yamamoto's argumentation rests mainly on scholarly literature, and it may not accurately represent the common medieval perception of the *nāga*-girl. Undeniably, for many women, as for priests like Nichiren, the *nāga*-princess, despite her animality, was a spokesperson for women. In other words, her femaleness overshadowed her animality. Nevertheless, the symbolic elaborations of Japanese Tantrism struck a deep vein in the Japanese imagination.

The *nāga*-girl takes impressive shortcuts in her spiritual quest, becoming very rapidly (and temporarily) a man before moving on to buddhahood—the supreme manhood. She never had the time to really become a woman, to fully experience the female predicament. Being physically immature, she is spared the guilt of "blood defilement." The message here, which a number of Mahāyāna tales about young virgins reaching awakening seem to reiterate, is not so much about the curse of being born a female, as about the predicament of crossing the threshold of puberty to accede to the status of biological and social womanhood.

The importance of *nāgas* and other reptilian creatures in the medieval imagination explains the symbolic multivocality of the theme, and the impossibility of reducing it to a clear-cut—whether sexist or egalitarian—interpretation. The story of the *nāga*-girl has given rise to all kinds of allegorical interpretations in medieval scholastic literature. For instance, the motif of her offering a jewel to the Buddha takes on a new meaning when we read that this jewel was actually one of the Buddha's relics (*śarīra*), preserved in the *nāga*-palace. Thus, the *Keiran shūyōshū* assimilates the jewel of the *nāga*-girl with the *cintāmaṇi* and with the Buddha's relics, and connects the theme with that of the *nāga*-palace as a hidden repository of Buddhist treasures.[16] In this interpretation, the jewel (as a Buddha relic) becomes a metaphor for the buddha nature inherent in all beings. Another oft-encountered theme is the identification of the *nāga*-girl with Benzaiten (Sarasvatī), an Indian goddess of reptilian nature, and with the sea-goddesses of Japanese mythology. Through such associations, the *nāga*-girl became a symbol of fertility and wealth, and a source of royal legitimacy—quite a departure from her image as a virgin candidate for enlightenment.[17]

But perhaps the most interesting development is the use of the *nāga*-girl theme to illustrate the Tendai theory of "innate awakening" (*hongaku*). According to this interpretation, the Three Evil Paths—passions, karma, suffering—are identical to the Three Aspects (or Virtues) of *nirvāṇa*. The *Shinnyokan*, a medieval work attributed to the Tendai priest Genshin, explains, for instance, that when the *nāga*-girl heard Mañjuśrī preach that "all dharmas are ultimate reality," she realized that, despite her *animal* body, she was fundamentally enlightened and was consequently able to reach buddhahood without discarding her femaleness.[18] Here, the *nāga*-girl's achievement is the realization of her innate awakening, which nullifies her current limitations. It is what Buddhist scholars call the standpoint of "principle" (*ri*), or ultimate truth. By contrast, the *Keiran shūyōshū* emphasizes the standpoint of "phenomena" (*ji*); that is, the Three Imperfections—being an animal, a female, and a child—that constitutes her personality.[19]

The allegorical reinterpretation of the *nāga*-girl story along the lines of the *hongaku* theory took some rather complicated twists and turns, which I will spare the reader.[20] An outline will suffice. The general idea seems to be that her journey to the undefiled realm in the South should be read according to the Tantric symbolism in which the South, correlated with the element fire, symbolizes the burning of all defilements. The point of this allegorical reading is to show that, since in Chinese cosmology the South symbolizes the yang, going Southwards means to become yang, that is, to become male. In this fashion, the reference to the "undefiled universe" in the South becomes more logical (in a strange way), the implicit assumption being that this universe is a place without women. Because in Tantric maṇḍalas the South also corresponds to the realm of the buddha Ratnasambhava (Jp. Hōshō) and to the stage of "practice" (the second of the "Four Gates" of the spiritual path), the undefiled southern universe also means the destruction of all female impurities, by entering through the gate of "practice" (*shugyōmon*).

According to one interpretation, the body of the *nāga*-girl is only a "provisional" one, of the type adopted by enlightened beings as an *upāya* to teach people. According to another interpretation, the *nāga*-girl is able to reach awakening "without changing her deluded animal mind" precisely because, in the *hongaku* context, "passions are awakening."[21] The situation is radically different in the case of the *nāgas* seen by Kenreimon'in in her dream, since they are *actual* reincarnations of former members of the Taira clan. Owing to their karma, these people have to experience painful rebirth as animals before being eventually reborn into the Pure Land.

The *Keiran shūyōshū* extends the notion that Japanese gods are the local manifestations of Indian buddhas by arguing that gods reveal themselves as snakes/dragons in order to "hide their light and mix with the dust."[22] In the case of the *nāga*-princess, however, it is the contrary that happens: whereas everyone sees her as an eight-year-old girl, the Buddha alone sees her true form, which is that of a monstruous snake.[23]

The mythological *nāga*-palace is also read allegorically as a realm of darkness, but because this realm is identified in *hongaku* hermeneutics with the primordial, undifferentiated chaos—that is, a state prior to any duality or discrimination—it is paradoxically interpreted as the realm of the enlightened mind. The metaphor recurs in several chapters of the *Keiran shūyōshū*, to emphasize the idea that the *nāgas*, precisely owing to their defiled nature, are the symbols of nirvāṇa, emphasizing the Mahāyāna identity between defilement and awakening (*bonnō soku bodai*). In that sense, the *nāga*-girl becomes an allegory of awakening (for all sentient beings, not only for women)—that is, the realization of the identity between nirvāṇa and saṃsāra, as expressed by the *Lotus Sūtra*.[24]

Perhaps more important for our purpose than male scholarly commentaries and their hermeneutical overkill are the documents that reveal to us something about the female interpretations of the *nāga*-girl story. Although they are less voluble than scholastic commentaries, they are quite numerous. It is only toward the tenth-eleventh centuries that the story spread among the people. It is tempting to read this as a form of banalization, a sign that the legend has become a mere literary topos that does not necessarily affect the conceptions and practices of women. Female reception was by no means monolithic, however. The frequent mention of the *nāga*-girl in such vows clearly shows that, for many women, its emotive power transfigured it into something vital, and that it was not merely a cliché. This power can still be felt in the *imayō* songs collected in the *Ryōjin hishō*:

> Through Mañjuśrī's work, I hear,
> the Dragon King's daughter became a buddha,
> that's what they say!
> Leaving the palace of King Sāgara,
> she had to change into a man,
> but finally she found the buddha path.[25]

> Even the daughter of King Sagara
> only eight when she first heard
> the ultimate and wonderful *Lotus Sūtra*,
> came near the buddha path.[26]

If the Dragon King's daughter became buddha,
why can't we, too, somehow?
A thick cloud, the five obstacles, yes,
but buddha nature shines through like the moon.[27]

The theme of the *nāga*-girl flourished in medieval Japanese literature. In the "Consecration Scroll" (*Kanjō no maki*) chapter of the *Heike monogatari*, the former imperial consort Kenreimon'in, having been prevented from taking her own life at Dan-no-ura, spends the rest of her days as a nun in Jakkō-in, a convent in Ōhara, on the northeastern outskirts of the capital. When the Retired Emperor Go-Shirakawa pays her a visit, she confides to him her hopes of escaping her female predicament, symbolized by the Five Obstacles and the Three Dependences, and refers to the story of the *nāga*-girl. More interestingly, she recounts a dream in which she saw that all of the members of the Taira clan had been reborn as *nāgas*:

> When I was returning to the city after the warriors captured me, we stopped at Akashi Shore in Harima Province. There I dozed off, and in a dream I saw the Former Emperor and the Taira senior nobles and courtiers, all in formal array, at a place far grander than the old imperial palace. I asked where we were, because I had seen nothing like it since the departure from the capital. Someone who seemed to be the Nun of Second Rank answered, "This is the Nāga Palace." "What a splendid place! Is there no suffering here?" I asked. "The suffering is described in the *Ryūchikukyō Sūtra*. Pray hard for us," she said. I awakened as she spoke. Since then, I have been more zealous than ever in reciting the sutras and invoking Amida's name so that they may achieve enlightenment. I think it has all been exactly like experiencing life in each of the Six Paths.[28]

When Kenreimon'in dies in 1191, auspicious signs suggest that she has achieved her goal of rebirth into the Pure Land, while her two female companions are said to have attained the *nāga*-girl's wisdom. This reference to the *nāga*-girl in their case is significant. As noted earlier, the nun Myōtatsu is believed to have drowned herself upon the death of her teacher Myōe in order to become a *nāga*, and perhaps therefore, emulating the *nāga*-girl, to obtain buddhahood. Could the desperate gesture of Kiyomori's wife—the Nun of the Second Rank, who threw herself into the sea with the young Antoku Tennō and the regalia at Dan-no-Ura—be interpreted in the same way? According to the *Heike monogatari*, her last thought was directed toward rebirth in the Pure Land, but her last words to comfort the child were, "There is a capital under the waves, too."[29]

In medieval Japan, the *nāga*-palace was perceived as the repository of all treasures, including the relics of the Buddha (corporeal as well as written—the sutras).[30] Thus, in the *Towazugatari*, Lady Nijō's lover, the imperial priest Ariake no Tsuki, vows to copy the sutras of the Five Sections with his own blood to deposit them in the *nāga*-palace. The *nāga* kingdom, symbolizing ignorance, was indeed the source of all *saṃsāra*. At the same time, since in Mahāyāna teaching the cycle of life and death (*saṃsāra*) is no different from *nirvāṇa*, the *nāga*-palace became the threshold of enlightenment.[31] This may explain its power of attraction for forlorn women, who could identify with the *nāga*-girl. But their deliverance was at the cost of their lives.

Even though the negative connotations of the figure of the *nāga*-girl were muted in the *Lotus Sūtra* story, the associations between this figure and other representatives of the snake and dragon lore were too deeply embedded in popular Japanese culture to remain submerged for long. Thus, it is difficult to read this character and its destiny merely in terms of the salvation of women. Not that it matters very much in the present context. Whichever interpretation one chooses to emphasize, the Buddhist message remains fairly sexist. There is a difference in that regard between early Buddhism and Mahāyāna, however. Whereas early Buddhist discourse, in its sexist mode, advocated an outright rejection of women, Mahāyāna sexism is more subtle, pairing as it does discrimination and salvation, and tying both to a logic of proselytism.

BECOMING MALE

> Just once, if all women heard
> a voice chanting this chapter,
> they'd climb the lotus by midnight,
> long out of their female bodies.[32]

Even though Indian Buddhist texts concede that women can attain a spiritual realization, they usually deny the possibility of a female buddha.[33] Thus, although Buddhism has been characterized by its rejection of social discrimination (in particular, of the Indian caste system) on soteriological grounds, not only did it "naturalize" gender discrimination, but it also contributed to "demoralize" women by moralizing their gender according to karmic factors. Actually, it is as if there was only one gender, femaleness, since maleness was not stigmatized as "gender."

As noted earlier, however, such Mahāyāna scriptures as the *Lotus Sūtra* allowed the possibility of buddhahood or ultimate salvation for women. Yet we must keep in mind that, in early Buddhism, arhathood is the highest stage that could be reached by men and women alike. Thus, according to the *Sūtra of the Mother of the Buddha*, Māyā obtained the fruit of arhathood without changing her female body. Although the *pāli* tradition says that, when she reaches the Trāyastriṃśa Heaven, she becomes a male god, this gender change is glossed over in the Chinese translation.[34] One easy way to finesse that impossibility was to rephrase it, saying that women could attain buddhahood on the condition of being first reborn as men. In some texts, the change of gender is merely predicted, and will take place in a higher realm (a paradise). The locus classicus, to which we will return, is Amitābha's thirty-fifth vow in the *Sukhāvatīvyūha-sūtra*: "In my land there will be no women; if you want to be reborn in my land, you will become men."[35] Although, strictly speaking, only men can become buddhas, the transformative stage can be so shortened as to be almost emptied of its content. But this caveat could constitute a real stumbling block at times.

The canonical motif of women's necessary rebirth as men was related to that of the Five Obstacles, and the story of the *nāga*-girl was one of its main vehicles.[36] We recall that, when confronted with Śāriputra's objection that, as a female, she had a filthy body subject to the Five Obstacles, the *nāga*-girl immediately turned into a male, and eventually became a perfect buddha endowed with the thirty-two marks. The Sanskrit version of the *Lotus Sūtra* describes this transsexual moment in almost voyeuristic fashion: "Then, at that moment, before the elder Śāriputra and the entire world, King Sagara's daughter's female organs vanished, and the male organs became visible. She appeared as a bodhisattva."[37] Significantly, the reference to the girl's sexual organs is missing in the Chinese translation by Kumārajīva, which "emasculates" the passage in the same gesture as it emphasizes the "manhood" of the bodhisattva. This way of simultaneously asserting sexual/gender difference and resolving it through a legerdemain constitutes a radical departure from the early Buddhist tradition. Indeed, in early Buddhism, the gender fault-line was easily crossed, but in both directions. The narrative theme known as "transformation of sex" (*paravṛttavyañjana*) was not referring to a one-way transformation, as it later became in Mahāyāna.[38] Early Buddhists, while they considered the male sex the better one, also believed that this superiority was not, so to speak, carved on flesh: it could easily disappear owing to unethical behavior; conversely, the female sex could easily disappear as the result of ethical behavior.[39] Although gender was determined by past karma at the time of conception, it could also be modified by acts committed during the present life.[40]

Various Mahāyāna scriptures emphasize the possibility of transformation from female to male, and the subsequent achievement of buddhahood by the transgendered individual. In such scriptures, however, something else seems to be at stake: they are no longer talking about simple karmic rewards, and the fault-line between genders runs much deeper: only young girls seem able to cross it.[41] The motif appears, for instance, in the *Asheshi wang nü jing* (Skt. *Aśokadattavyākaraṇa*, T. 12, 337), where the twelve-year-old daughter of King Ajātaśatru, having vowed to become a bodhisattva, sees her body transformed into that of a boy, and receives the prediction that (s)he will become a buddha. In the *Ligoushi nü jing* (T. 12, 338), the daughter of King Prasenajit, also at the tender age of twelve, vows to become a buddha; she turns into an eight-year-old boy, who receives the prediction of his future buddhahood. In the *Xumoti pusa jing* (Skt. *Sumatīdārikāpariprcchā*, T. 12, 334, 335), it is the eight-year-old Sumati who, by cutivating bodhisattva practices, sees her body turn into that of a novice and receives a similar prediction.[42] But the most influential scripture was probably the *Sūtra on the Transformation of Women into Buddhas* (Skt. *Strīvivartavyākaraṇa-sūtra*, Chin. *Zhuannüshen jing*, Jp. *Tennyoshingyō*, T. 14, 564), in which a pregnant woman named Jōnichi has come to hear the Buddha.[43] Realizing that the unborn daughter in her womb also hears and understands his sermon, the Buddha praises her and teaches her how to become a man in order to reach awakening. The girl eventually is born as a male and becomes a bodhisattva.[44] This scripture was read during women's funerals, along with other famous scriptures. Its name appears in many vows compiled by Ōe no Masafusa on behalf of elite women.[45]

The Kamo priestess Senshi composed the following poems about the *Tennyoshingyō*: "All the evil karma from previous lives will be extinguished, / and she will certainly attain Great Bodhisattvahood; / in the end, her female body will be transformed, / and she will reach the Ultimate Way"; and, "Since I have encountered this teaching given specially for me, / it is certain that my body will be transformed—what joy to hear it!"[46] Senshi was also strongly influenced in her beliefs by the *Lotus Sūtra*. In one verse on the "Bodhisattva Medicine King" chapter, she writes: "If a woman, hearing this chapter . . . , can accept and keep it, she shall put an end to her female body, and shall never again receive one."[47] She continues, "Since there is, after all, a way for me to hear this rare dharma, / I know that there is an end to all my sorrows."[48] Elsewhere, she writes about the "Bodhisattva Fine Sound" (Myōon Bosatsu): "[Whoever is] . . . in any other troublesome place, he can rescue them all. Even in the inner quarters of a king's palace, changing into a female body, he preaches this scripture."[49] She adds: "Only you, Bodhisattva Fine Sound, would change into a despicable, sorry body like this one, for the dharma's sake."[50]

In Japan, the references to canonical examples of gender change must be placed in the proper ritual context. Medieval rituals often included the recitation of a powerful mantra, the *kōmyō shingon*. This mantra, advocated by Myōe, allows a fast rebirth by destroying all obstacles. Since a woman, by using it, could become the god Brahma, this implies that she could also become a buddha.[51] The gender change could be brought about by other forms of Tantric ritual, involving, for instance, the visualization of the lotus inside one's chest and its symbolic overturning; or by a strict observance of the Vinaya (which amounts to a denial of sexuality and of one's femininity). In some cases, the ordination ritual itself—the monastic tonsure and the donning of the *kāṣāya*—is said to symbolically (or magically) transform women into men. The belief spread through various rituals aimed at women's awakening, such as the *hokke hakkō* (*Eight Lectures on the Lotus Sūtra*) or the Ānanda penance ritual. It is a recurrent motif in funerary rituals (*gyakushu* and *tsuizen*), in priests' sermons, or in the vows of aristocrats. It is also found in literature, for instance in such influential texts as the *Hosshin wakashū* (1012), which also mentions the *nāga*-girl; or in the *Ryōjin hishō*, a collection of *imayō* songs, dating from the end of the Heian period. Such transformation can also be achieved after death, through post mortem ordinations, transference of the merits (*ekō*) produced by donations and prayers, or stupa worship. In the *Shoekō shingishiki*, for instance, a passage related to stupa worship begins as follows: "Respectfully we ask the suppression of obstacles, and the realization of non-birth. May we suddenly turn the five obstacles of the female body, to obtain the way to the land without defilement."[52] But above all, the transformation in question may be achieved, metaphorically, through enlightenment. As we will see in the next chapter, however, to realize the nonduality between man and woman is to become a "true man," not a "true woman." Thus, the Qing reformer and social critic Tan Sitong (1865–98) was clearly mistaken when he wrote that "though the idea of 'transforming women into men' is found in Buddhist scriptures, it is confined to the Hīnayāna teaching. Written in such Mahāyāna Buddhist sūtras as the *Garland Sūtra* and the *Vimalakīrti Sūtra* is the assertion that the female body should remain as it is, not needing to be changed into that of a male. There is nothing to suggest men are superior to women."[53]

In the case of the male rebirth of women, as in that of the *nāga*-girl's apotheosis, various scholastic interpretations seem to depart radically from the common reading. We are told, for instance, that "becoming a man" does not require a physical change, but rather that it is a metaphorical way of saying that a woman has come to realize her buddha nature: which is neither male nor female. The *Keiran shūyōshū* gives a bizarre explanation of the gender change in terms of a literal "revolution of the heart." Here, becoming a man means that the downward-facing lotus of the heart turns upwards.[54] The same theory is found in the *Hokekyō Jikidanshō* (1546), a commentary on the *Lotus Sūtra*, where it is credited to the Tendai master Annen: "In the chest of every sentient being is an eight-petal lotus flower. In the case of a man, that lotus is opened and facing upwards, whereas in that of a woman, it is closed and facing downwards. However, when the *nāga*-girl became a buddha, the lotus in her chest opened up, facing upwards. Such is the meaning of 'turning into a man.' "[55] The metamorphosis of the *nāga*-girl is therefore interpreted in

Tendai esotericism as a turning upward of the lotus, corresponding to perfect awakening (*tōshōgaku*).[56] A striking feature of these scholastic glosses is that, although they seem to be speaking of women, they are in the end more interested in their abstract intellectual musings than in real, flesh-and-blood women and their predicament.

INTERPRETATIVE DIVERGENCES

Japanese Buddhist scholars have tried to interpret positively—and in some cases, to explain away—the strange prerequisite for salvation of rebirth as a man.[57] To be sure, the meaning of this notion, depending as it does on use and context, is not always as clear as it would at first glance appear. Numerous problems arise when we try to pin it down. For instance, is this gender change a prerequisite for women's buddhahood, or is it a mere sign (admittedly a sexist one) that buddhahood is already achieved, despite a transitory stage? In other words, should we emphasize the goal or the process? Does it confirm male superiority, or does it already tend to indicate, as we will see later in Mahāyāna literature, that gender distinction is no longer truly significant, as it is about to change, and can from a certain stage onward be changed at will? Is this sex change a mere technicality, as some would think, or the main objective?

According to Nancy Schuster's charitable interpretation, "changing the female body" was probably developed as a narrative theme by Mahāyānist writers in order to confront the traditional Buddhist view that women could not reach buddhahood.[58] One could argue just the opposite, namely, that Mahāyāna Buddhists were much more restrictive in this respect than were their predecessors. Apart from the fact that Schuster seems to buy into a problematic teleological view of Buddhism, she does not see the requirement of sex change as a sexist imposition, but interprets it as a symbol of the abandonment of ordinary existence for women entering religious life. According to her notion, such religious life offers an alternative to both maleness and femaleness, a "new birth into a new kind of creative living." She argues that, despite the maleness of these new bodies, "it seems fair to assume from the context that the transformation signifies the transcendence of ordinary worldly life and the sex distinctions that are part of it."[59] Perhaps then it would not be fair to ask why the abandonment of ordinary life for a man is not symbolized by the reverse sex change. To argue that although transcendence tends to be defined in gendered terms in any given society, it should nonetheless not be reduced to gender, is not quite the same thing as to insist in phallocentic fashion that the body of any candidate for transcendence must be equipped with a male sex organ.

Like the *nāga*-girl, the "women" who are the heroines in the scriptures mentioned above are all young girls. Schuster suggests that "the point of presenting a wise young girl as the Buddha's interlocutor is to demonstrate that this child is really a bodhisattva, has already pursued the bodhisattva career through many previous existences, has reached a high level of attainment, and nonetheless is now reborn in female form." Femaleness is therefore not incongruent with the highest levels of understanding. These girls, however, who have yet to reach puberty, have not begun to participate in a woman's traditional "way of power," or rather of powerlessness. Indeed, this adult female life, which Schuster describes as "a life committed to creating and nurturing new life," could as well be seen, in the context of patriarchal society, as a life of hardship and exploitation. By entering the bodhisattva path, the girls in question may indeed commit to "a different kind of creativity than that available to them as a result of their biology." To simply claim, however, that "their choice is symbolized by the sex change these children undergo in the sūtras," and that "their maleness is used as an image of commitment to the religious life," seems to beg the question.[60] Their magical metamorphosis from female to male is perhaps "a metaphor for the enlightened way of dealing with the utter fluidity of reality," and it may indeed be "dramatically effective and intellectually compelling in its implications."[61] That said, it could just as well be seen as a magical flight of imagination, an evasion of harsh social realities. In the case of these girls, as in that of the *nāga*-princess, commentators have attempted to downplay the biological event by claiming that they were bodhisattvas from the start. Indeed, a bodhisattva can manifest itself in any form he or she wants, but such transformations belong to a different topic, and they no longer bridge the gap between women and enlightenment. Inasmuch as these girls are not "real" persons, but simply the "provisional" manifestations of some transcendent being, the message conveyed by these texts seems hardly to be a feminist one.[62]

There is no denying that Buddhist scriptures valorize masculinity. For one thing, the body of the Buddha is always described as a male one. The fact that, even when he is represented as naked, his sex organ allegedly remains hidden is not so much a sign of androgyny as one of a superlative virility—the capacity to come into full action as suddenly as a horse or an elephant.[63] There are practically no female buddhas, and even when the buddhahood is predicted for a woman (like Queen Vaidehī or Queen Śrīmaladevī) and no sex change is explicitly mentioned, the goal remains very distant and does not necessarily translate into the concrete image of a female buddha.[64] Furthermore, when a bodhisattva assumes a female guise, it is usually a skillful means to convert people, and his feminization remains limited in its practical effects on the status of women. Clearly, the belief in the imperfection of the female body inhibited positive feminine representations.[65] Although Buddhism offered some women an escape from traditional constraints (like their procreative duty), Buddhist priests considered these constraints as natural for most women, and were unable or unwilling to distinguish between biological constraints and the arbitrary constraints imposed by society.

Salvation for women was therefore projected onto a utopian realm beyond gender. The Buddha declares in the *Lotus Sūtra* that a woman who hears this scripture and practices accordingly shall be reborn "on a jeweled throne among lotus blossoms, never again to be tormented by greed, never again to be tormented by anger or folly, never again to be tormented by pride, envy, or other defilements."[66] Edward Kamens observes that "the implication is that such a woman will cease to have the putative female characteristics that mar and limit her capacities to achieve what men may achieve: in the Pure land, these faults will be neutralized, which may mean that the woman herself will be, in a sense, neutered."[67] According to Kajiyama Yūichi, the alleged absence of women in Amitābha's Pure Land is not meant to exclude women or to suggest that they are unable to reach awakening; quite the contrary, the prerequisite gender change is to free them from the various ailments of a female body.[68] Kajiyama argues that, in this context, the male body is emphasized as a symbol of deliverance simply because it is more "wholesome" than the female body; the latter, conversely, becomes a symbol of rebirth into an inferior realm. Even if one chooses not to emphasize the sexist bias contained in this "natural" view of the female body, it remains that Kajiyama's interpretation, echoed by Simone Heidegger, sounds overly optimistic.

Part of the problem arises from the fact that, in the contrast between man and woman, the former is seen as closer to the goal of genderlessness (androgyny); for all practical (or spiritual) purposes, he is *less* gendered, and in a sense already *beyond* gender. Thus, whereas women need (and usually want) to be reborn as men, the goal (or next step) for men is to become androgynous (a state including both genders) or to pass altogether beyond gender, two ways of transcending gender limitation. Even though buddhahood (and, more generally, holiness) is seen as essentially genderless in stories of the *nāga*-girl type, there are also hagiographical accounts (for instance, the tale of Chūjōhime) in which femininity, and feminine ailments, play a significant role. Such legends seem to unfold simultaneously on two very distinct registers. At one level, the most obvious, that of hagiographical glorification, the heroine is described in terms identical to those used for male saints; but at another, deeper level, we find at play notions of purity and defilement, expressed through specifically female features such as menstrual blood.[69] Here, the highest truth may be, paradoxically, that of defilement, and the hierarchy between the two levels is the reverse of that between the two truths of the traditional schema, where defilement is said to represent the superficial, conventional truth, whereas genderlessness of the female ascetic is regarded as the ultimate truth. Simone Heidegger mentions the tendency to associate sexuality and responsibility in sexual matters with femininity, and asexuality and the overcoming of passions with masculinity. Along this line of interpretation, gender differences are not limited to the body, but apply to the mind, as well. The sex change thus comes to reflect (or produce) a change in the state of mind, a passage from mental passivity to activity, from the incompleteness of corporeality to the freedom of the spirit.[70]

Like the Five Obstacles, the theme of the "transformation into a man" (*henjō nanshi*) could at times be manipulated for specific purposes. An interesting subversion of this theme is found in the "New Religion" Ōmo-tokyō. In 1892, its female founder, Deguchi Nao (1837–1918), then aged fifty-seven, was suddenly possessed by a god, who entered her womb. The deity declared itself to be Ushitora no Konjin, the "Primordial god," who, because he had remained silent for three thousand years, had come to be feared as an evil god in popular religion. After initial resistance, Nao began to write down the words of the deity: thousands of pages of oracles, compiled under the title *The Tip of the Brush* (*Ofudesaki*). Among them, various apocalyptical, antigovernmental, and anti-imperial prophecies led to her repeated arrest. Asserting that sex and gender are not necessarily isomorphic, Nao insisted that she embodied both male and female characteristics. Punning on the old Buddhist topos, she claimed to be a "transformed male" (*henjō nanshi*), or a male in the guise of a female, whereas her male disciple Onisaburō was a "transformed female" (*henjō nyoshi*).[71] The latter stated: "I am a man with a female nature, but my hair is long and thick, my beard thin, my body soft, and my breasts large, so I even resemble a woman physically."[72] He envisioned himself as a mother goddess, and liked to disguise himself as Benten (a popular version of the goddess Benzaiten).[73] Together they would preside over the coming millenium, bringing about the realm of Ushitora no Konjin. Although rather exceptional, this case is significant in that it reveals the endless possibilities of gender symbolism.

AMIDA'S VOW AND ITS IMPLICATIONS

In the *Soga monogatari*, the courtesan Tora, having become a nun after the death of her lover, one of the Soga brothers, meets his mother and tries to convert her to the Pure Land teachings:

> Women are disparaged in both the Buddhist and Confucian canons. Amida Buddha pledged, however, that the most evil of men may achieve salvation merely by chanting his name; he also vowed that women may attain bud-

dhahood. If we do not believe in the compassion of the Buddha and fail to carry out our religious duties, we shall end up in the Three Evil Worlds.[74]

Pure Land scholars have long claimed that the emergence of their schools in the thirteenth century marked a radical progress in the Buddhist discourse on women's salvation. Their claim rests essentially on a much-quoted passage of Amida's soteriological program, relative to his Thirty-Fifth Vow.

> O Bhagavat, if, after I have obtained *bodhi*, women in immeasurable, innumerable, inconceivable, immense Buddha countries on all sides after having heard my name, should allow carelessness to arise, should not turn their thoughts toward *bodhi*, should, when they are free from birth, not despise their female nature, and if they, being born again, should assume a second female nature, then may I not obtain the highest perfect knowledge.[75]

The most standard, and uncritical, exposition of the spiritual "progress" represented by the Kamakura "new Buddhism" was offered by the Pure Land scholar Kasahara Kazuo, whose theses have for that reason recently become a target for "revisionist" scholars. Kasahara notes that because in the "ancient Buddhism" of the Nara and Heian periods women were perceived as imperfect and defiling, they were prohibited from entering the sacred mountains, a prohibition that remained in place until the Meiji Restoration. Thus, before the Kamakura period, monks living in mountain temples had little opportunity to come into contact with women and as a result felt no need to develop soteriological means for them. By contrast, the founders of Kamakura "new Buddhism," who left the mountains and mingled with the populace, were led to produce soteriological methods and to promote them among the people. This is allegedly how the salvation of women first came to be advocated by leaders of Kamakura's new Buddhism such as Hōnen, Shinran, Ippen, Dōgen, and Nichiren.[76]

Kasahara contrasts the pre-medieval religious conditions (based on pantheistic, syncretistic attitudes) and human conditions (defined as compassion, honesty, suppleness) with those that became predominant during the medieval period—a period in which new schools distinguished themselves by their emphasis on a single and easy soteriological practice. In the Pure Land schools, in particular, there was only one buddha, Amida, and a single path to rebirth in his Western paradise. This new practice involved a rejection of all earlier complicated forms of syncretism. In the world of the Final Dharma (*mappō*), traditional human qualities are less valued; the only thing that counts is faith in Amida. Whereas in early Pure Land hagiographies like the *Ōjōden*, women endowed with qualities such as compassion, purity, and chastity received auspicious signs at the time of death or before, in the new Pure Land teaching, the nenbutsu became the main condition for rebirth into the Pure Land.

According to Kasahara, the implications of such radical change for women were momentous. Whereas women had been until that time neglected by Buddhism, they could now become buddhas or be reborn in the Pure Land. Salvation was near at hand, owing in particular to Amida's Thirty-Fifth Vow. The belief that Amida saves *even* women developed into the idea that Amida saves women *first of all*. The Thirty-Fifth Vow is, in a sense, a vow to transform women into men. The apparent contradiction between this vow and the Eighteenth Vow, which implied salvation of all *equally*, is downplayed. At any rate, women acquired a soteriological priority, along with "evil men" (*akunin*). Kasahara's main thesis, shared by most Pure Land scholars, is that the emergence of Kamakura's "new Buddhism" is characterized by a "democratization" of Buddhism, extending the benefits of salvation to all equally, and more particularly to evil people and women.

Critique of the "New Buddhism"

The evaluation of Buddhist attitudes toward women in medieval Japan is fraught with difficulties, because it crisscrosses with an ongoing debate regarding the nature of Kamakura Buddhism. Japanese scholars have brought to this debate a variety of teleological schemas, in which Kamakura Buddhism marks a kind of apex. Although few of them continue to describe the new Buddhism of that period as a kind of Reformation, much of the debate has revolved around the nature of old Buddhism, redefined more positively by Kuroda Toshio as *kenmitsu* (exoteric-esoteric Buddhism). In particular, the question of women "turning into men" has served as a litmus test by which to judge the claims and ideals of medieval Buddhism. Too often, these claims have been judged on the basis of doctrinal statements of a few eminent Buddhist thinkers, without paying sufficient attention to the ritual, political, socioeconomic contexts of such statements. Recently, however, historians have begun to examine the social impact (or lack thereof) of such doctrines on the basis of existing archives, which suggest that such ideas did not always have for the medieval minds the importance attributed to them.

Kasahara's thesis raises two types of questions, historical and ideological. From the historical standpoint, to what extent was the so-called *kenmitsu* Buddhism discriminatory toward women? Were the theories of female buddhahood or female rebirth in the Pure Land preached in *kenmitsu* Buddhism or merely in the new schools of Kamakura? From the ideological standpoint, can we say that the theory of female rebirth, as such, constitutes a soteriological teaching that lays to rest traditional prejudices against women?

The debate in question implies a reevaluation of the opposition between old and new Buddhism, or rather, a criticism of teleological schemas such as "old" and "new" with respect to Buddhism. Assuming there was a radical change, perhaps it should not be judged solely on a doctrinal basis. Depending on one's focus, the turning point may not be necessarily at the beginning of the Kamakura period. For instance, if one chooses to focus on Buddhist conceptions of women and of defilement, it would be, according to Taira Masayuki, the ninth century; if one wants to emphasize, like Kasahara, "democratization" (which does not mean gender equality), it would be much later, during the Muromachi period.

Kasahara argued that Kamakura reformers preached salvation to common people. Their soteriological discourse was not, however, free of a certain condescension toward the populace. Conversely, one finds little evidence of the canonical contempt toward women in the Buddhism of the Nara and early Heian periods, a time when women still had access to sacred mountains. It is apparently during the ninth century that the relative equality between monks and nuns gave way to a more hierarchical structure, reflecting the progressive establishment of the patriarchal system. Thus, to credit the Kamakura new Buddhism with a kind of feminist agenda, as Kasahara and others have done, is at best anachronistic: not only was the salvation of women discussed long before Kamakura "reformers," but, as we will see shortly, the soteriological discourse of the latter suggests some serious problems.[77]

With the emergence of Buddhism as the dominant ideology during the Heian period, women became increasingly dependent on priests for their salvation, and they could no longer claim the status of official religious specialists. References to the Five Obstacles, to the *nāga*-girl, and to male rebirth all appear during the eighth and ninth centuries in female vows and prayers—a few signs, among others, indicating a growing gender discrimination. *Kenmitsu* priests did attempt to address such changes, however. Yet such attempts sometimes had perverse effects, inasmuch as Buddhist soteriological discourse and practice contributed to reinforce sexist notions that they were meant to redress. A case in point is that of the Ritsu school, whose action on behalf of women and social outcasts (*hinin*) led to the unwanted result of pigeonholing both groups in the same category.[78] Although Ritsu priests cannot be held entirely responsible for this ideological contamination, the fact remains that it is owing to Buddhism that the status of *hinin* and that of single women came to be closely related in the medieval period.[79]

Various authors have emphasized that, whereas established Buddhism was by and large sexist, individual priests like Kyōkai, Ryōgen, Eizon, or Myōe did their best under such constraints to help women. They are perhaps exceptions that confirm the rule, but they nonetheless worked to obviate the rule. Scholars, however, disagree as to their significance. Matsuo Kenji, for instance, in an attempt to exempt Eizon and Myōe from the characterization that they represented *kenmitsu* Buddhism, distinguishes between official monks (*kansō*) and "recluses" (*tonseisō*) who have left the official system. In the latter group he includes "heterodox" monks (like Hōnen, Shinran, and Nichiren) who came up through *kenmitsu* Buddhism and reformers within *kenmitsu* Buddhism (Eizon, Myōe). Matsuo considers this group of recluse-monks (*tonseisō*) to be representative of Kamakura new Buddhism.[80] This alignment allows him to argue that it is only among such *tonseisō* communities that one could find genuine concern for women (and *hinin*).[81]

Let us take a closer look at the teachings of the founder of the Pure Land school, Hōnen, whom Matsuo, like Kasahara, describes as a kind of feminist *avant la lettre*. In 1190, at the demand of Chōgen, a typical *kansō*, Hōnen commented on the three Pure Land scriptures at Tōdaiji. These sermons led to the compilation of the *Muryōjukyō shaku*, in which he speaks of Amida's vow for women who have the Five Obstacles and Three Dependencies. Except for that text, he hardly mentions women. Hōnen recognized the karmic obstacles that burden women, and he developed a theory of "male rebirth" for women.[82] He writes:

> This is the reason that the Buddha Amida made a separate vow particularly for women. The following is the venerable Zendō's [Shandao's] interpretation: "By virtue of the merit of Amida's great vow, women who call upon the sacred name, may, when they come to the end of life here, have their bodies changed into those of men. Amida holds out His hands to them, and the Bodhisattvas help them to seat upon a lotus stand, on which they are carried into the Pure Land. . . . Apart from the power of the Great Vow of Amida, a woman cannot have her body changed to that of a man in a thousand kalpas, nay, not even in as many kalpas as there are sands in the river Ganges. This expresses the beneficent power of Amida's merciful Vow, by which woman may escape pain and receive the gift of blessedness.[83]

Here, the Pure Land scriptures rival the *Lotus Sūtra* in their attempt to attract a female audience; that is, after enrolling all men, including the evil ones (like Devadatta in the *Lotus Sūtra*, and Ajātaśatru in the Pure Land scriptures) in their soteriological scheme. In the *Nenbutsu ōjō yōgi shō*, attributed to Hōnen, the Pure Land is said to be open to all, men and women, good and evil people alike; and in the *Jūni kojō mondō*, we read that Amida saves *even* women afflicted with the Five Obstacles.[84] As the *Kurodani shōnin gotōroku* states, "We reject neither women nor the *icchantika*."[85] We have noted earlier the ominous parallel between women and evil men, symbolized here by the *icchantika*.

A story often invoked in the Pure Land tradition is that of the encounter between Hōnen and the courtesan of Muro Station (Muro no shuku).

Matsuo sees stories of this kind as proof of the genuine concern of Hōnen for women, and therefore of the moral superiority of the Pure Land schools; however, it may be somewhat naive to take such stories at face-value. Without being too hermeneutically suspicious, one might just as well think that the Jōdo rhetoric tends to distort the real situation. Conversely, the relative absence of such rhetoric in *kenmitsu* Buddhism cannot simply be construed as a lack of concern for women. The *tonseisō*, because they lacked the institutional support enjoyed by the *kansō*, had to rely on the donations of the people, and, if only for that economic reason, they were obviously *interested* in the fate of individuals, including women.[86]

Distinctions such as that drawn by Matsuo between *tonseisō* and *kansō* remain insufficient to account for the complex strategies of medieval priests. All *tonseisō* were not preoccupied with the cause of women, nor were all *kansō* indifferent to it. Established priests like the Hieizan abbot Ryōgen, for instance, are known to have devised specific rituals for women. Matsuo accepts uncritically the tradition according to which Kamakura new Buddhism worked for the salvation of women, without examining the meaning of such "salvation" nor its actual impact on the social status of medieval women. Despite Matsuo's insights, his new paradigm is flawed by his desire to promote the specificity of a new Buddhism (admittedly one different from Kasahara's) against the preeminence of ancient Buddhism (and more precisely, Kuroda Toshio's *kenmitsu taisei* paradigm). Although he pays more attention to social and institutional realities, in the end he tends to map the institutional divisions along doctrinal fault-lines. Apologetic visions of Kamakura Buddhism are perhaps an unavoidable by-product of any dualistic approach in terms of accepting an opposition between so-called ancients and moderns. They end up enrolling the cause of women in support for a certain form of Buddhism.

Another scholar who has focused on the development of the theory of female salvation in the Ritsu school is Hosokawa Ryōichi. Hosokawa examines, for instance, the thought of the Saidaiji priest Sōji (1232–1312). Like his master and uncle Eizon, Sōji had lost his mother when still a child. By the age of nineteen, explaining that he viewed "all women as his mother," he compiled a Vinaya commentary for the nuns of Hokkeji.[87] According to his biography in the *Honchō kōsōden*, when he completed this work more than twenty grains of relics (*śarīra*) materialized. This small miracle led Eizon to praise Sōji's filial piety. The text was printed in 1302 by another of Eizon's disciples, Eishin, in memory of his own mother. All of this seems to indicate that in the Ritsu sect the salvation of women was centered on mothers.[88]

In 1256, Sōji printed the *Tennyoshingyō*, using it to preach the theory of male rebirth to the nuns of Hokkeji. Significantly, rebirth in the Pure Land and female guilt seem associated in his mind. Many donations to

Saidaiji came from women, in particular from nuns of Hokkeji who had interiorized Sōji's and Eizon's theory of " salvation for women." By donating the domains they had inherited from their families, they prayed for (male) rebirth in the Pure Land and buddhahood, as well as for the salvation of their parents, their former patrons at court, and their fellow nuns.[89] Even after years of practice, Ritsu nuns were still trying to deny their womanhood and hoped to be reborn as men.

Thus, even though they had been able to escape their destiny as "mothers," it does not mean that they obtained their independence. Having left home, they became prisoners of another system, in which motherhood was the highest value. In this sense they were hardly different from the widow-nuns. Their practice had very little to do with their self-realization, and, unlike Ritsu monks, they were not allowed to perform rituals related to the public sphere, for instance to the safety of sea-traffic. They remained confined to their cloister, like ordinary women were confined to their homes. Eizon and his disciples, while developing the female saṅgha, kept it subordinated to the male saṅgha. Even though Ritsu monks worked on behalf of women in memory of their beloved mothers, they did not see these women as independent subjects in social relationships, because such women were still burdened with the karmic fetter of the Five Obstacles. Thus, the salvation of such women presupposed their motherhood and their male rebirth. As Sōji puts it in his colophon to the edition of the *Tennyoshingyō*, at the time of death a woman cannot hope for rebirth in the Pure Land if she does not first transform into a man. This is not specific to the Ritsu teaching, as we have seen. At any rate, the Ritsu sect, through the publishing activities of priests like Sōji, played an active role in the propagation of the rhetoric of salvation throughout medieval society. Consequently, it is difficult to argue that such rhetoric was the monopoly of either Kamakura new Buddhism or *kenmitsu* Buddhism.

The current debate reveals the fallacy of attributing to Kamakura new Buddhism a soteriological inclusiveness that can already be found in *kenmitsu* Buddhism. Unfortunately, it also tends to fall back onto old models inasmuch as it attempts to give precedence to one form of Buddhism over another. Hidden scholarly agendas tend to distort the fundamental gender issues. Nevertheless, such debates mark progress to the extent that they force scholars to confront doctrinal statements with the the reality of social practices.

The Ideological Debate

Before turning to some of these social practices, let us examine the performative impact of the Buddhist rhetoric of salvation. Even if it is difficult to follow Kasahara when he argues that *kenmitsu* Buddhism used women as a symbol of those excluded from salvation, it remains that the emphasis on motherhood and on gender change, by reducing women to their procreative function and by assuming their inferiority, doubly denied them their intrinsic dignity and freedom as human beings. Even women who rejected in principle the constraint of motherhood—for instance Ritsu nuns—were unable to preserve a healthy respect for their own bodies and minds. Thus, the salvation offered to women came at a very high cost. Taira emphasizes that the theory of female rebirth or buddhahood always goes hand in hand with that of female guilt (at least from the ninth century onward). The discrimination against women is always tied to the theory of female salvation. Consequently, in Japanese society, the notion of female guilt did not lead to the impossibility of salvation; on the contrary, it turned out to be a rhetorical device paving the ground for a female soteriology. The more despicable and guilty the women were, the more dramatic was the catharsis of salvation. Discrimination allowed salvation, and salvation presupposed discrimination. And the expression "buddhahood of women" remained rather ambiguous: does it refer to women in their present biological make-up, whether sexually active or not, or did these imperfect women require slight magical surgery to become "eunuchs in the Buddhist kingdom of heaven"?

Take, for instance, the often invoked theory of the "precedence of women" (nyonin isen). As the Pure Land priest Zonkaku formulates it in his Nyonin ōjō kikigaki: "Although the Tathāgata's compassion extends to all beings, it extends first to women." This does not mean, however, that the Pure Land schools rejected female guilt. On the contrary, this theory must be interpreted against the background of the rise of patriarchal ideology in late medieval Japan and its debasement of women. Feminist scholars have pointed out that it actually constitutes a development of misogyny under the guise of soteriology. Thus, it is a development of the rhetoric of salvation of kenmitsu Buddhism rather than a genuine Pure Land product. Inasmuch as the actual status of women is concerned, however, it must be said that this rhetoric works both ways, and that any attempt to close this ambiguity, albeit justified on feminist grounds, is bound to distort the complex reality. Here, a history ad usum Delphini will not do. The feminist critique is particularly powerful, however, when it reveals the limitations of Buddhist egalitarianism. In that respect, even priests like Eizon and Myōe cannot be entirely exonerated: for instance, inasmuch as their soteriological discourse and social practice are directed primarily at mothers, they contribute, however indirectly, to keep other women in ideological servitude.

The desire to be reborn as man was solidly anchored in women themselves, and kenmitsu Buddhism has, in some respects, only used women's own beliefs to trap them in the magic web of female guilt. The discourse on female rebirth or buddhahood penetrated deeply into profane society, and when the founders of the new schools of Kamakura Buddhism appeared, these ideas were as widespread in the Buddhist saṅgha as in lay society. It is not that before the Kamakura period women were reduced to despair: *kenmitsu* Buddhism, while emphasizing female guilt on the one hand provided hope for salvation on the other. In its own way, it attempted to respond positively to increasing gender discrimination.

The general acceptance of Buddhist prejudices against women after the ninth century was not the result of a general decline in the status of women, but rather one of its causes. Nevertheless, the rise of the patriarchal system provided a basis for such prejudice in social reality. In the literature of the time, one can hear echoes of the self-loathing of women. In this respect, a comparison between two texts belonging to the same genre, although to different periods, the *Nihon ryōiki* (ninth century) and the *Konjaku monogatari shū* (mid-twelfth century), is significant. Whereas the motifs of the stupidity, malice, and guilt of women are practically absent from the former, they pervade the latter. It shows that such motifs, initially invoked to allegedly protect the virtue of monks, had by the twelfth century spread to the entire society.

Thus far the discussion has revolved primarily around ideology. It remains to consider how this ideology was received, and what its social impact was. It is not entirely clear whether the ideology actually penetrated the core beliefs, let alone the practices of common people. For instance, when we closely examine the actual reception of Pure Land beliefs, it seems that women who hoped to be reborn in the Pure Land usually did not actually envision their rebirth in a male form. The question of female reception is a complex one, but it seems that in many cases (at least in the higher social strata) the Buddhist rhetoric was perceived as a literary topos. In the popular imagination, scholastic discussions about the Pure Land may not have had as strong an influence as an androcentric reading of the sources would lead us to believe. Other questions need to be addressed, among them whether women were simply victims and whether they were at all responsible for their debasement. While women were at times accomplices in the establishment of patriarchal ideology, they also developed various forms of passive or active subversion. Assuming that Buddhism had, on the whole, a negative impact, the question that remains is how to evaluate the role of Buddhism in comparison to those of larger societal issues (such as the rise of the patriarchal system).

From the viewpoint of women, what did this ideology mean? In the *Hokke kenki* biography of the nun Ganzei, the sister of the Tendai priest Genshin, we read that "although she received a female form, it can truly be said that she is a man of faith." Eminent nuns were perceived as having overcome their gender by symbolically becoming men. Although such cases remain exceptions, even ordinary nuns can be said to have loosened the gender constraints, inasmuch as ordination was a way for them to transcend their gender. Tonsure was believed to have the same effect as cremation, providing access to the Pure Land by transforming women into men.

Rather than discussing the hermeneutic fine points of such theories, it is better to focus on their actual effects. We have first what we may call the "perlocutionary" effects: insofar as the message is ambivalent, it means more (or less) than it says. Women may be saved, even though they are unworthy. Or rather, they have first to admit that they are unworthy in order to deserve salvation. Furthermore, they cannot get salvation by themselves and so need the compassionate power of the buddhas; in other words, they need monastic intercession. We can detect here a kind of spiritual blackmail. One cannot, however, simply endorse the simplistic views that all priests are good, or all bad. Some priests (as well as some women) clearly saw a door open in the doctrinal wall of Buddhism that made it possible to genuinely care for women's destiny.

The shift from the code (*ritsuryō*) system to the manor (*shōen*) system, in which nunneries lost their official character and gradually became private institutions, coincides with the time Buddhist ideologues begin to talk about "deliverance for women." For all the talk, male supremacy was not questioned, and gender discrimination was by no means diminished. Actually, the spread of notions of impurity through all levels of society stimulated the resurgence of Buddhist prejudices such as the "Five Obstacles" or the need for a "male rebirth."

Nishiguchi Junko, while emphasizing the sexist nature of Buddhist discourse, shifts the responsibility (and the merits, as well) from Buddhism to the society at large and its patriarchal ideology. She points out that, canonical claims to the contrary, there is some evidence that women believed in the possibility of being reborn in the Pure Land in their present female body.[90] Yet references to the Five Obstacles abound in the vows (*ganmon*) accompanying funerary ceremonies and other rites for women.[91] Such vows were usually written by literati on behalf of women, and became respectable clichés. Thus, they really prove that women believed in the necessity of being reborn as men. In a number of visions, dead women appear to their relatives and tell them that they have been reborn into the Pure Land, but they usually appear in their past feminine form. Likewise, judging from the objects found in graves (combs, mirrors, and the like), the assertion of female gender beyond the grave seems to have remained strong throughout the medieval period. There seems therefore to have been some discrepancy between the genderless Pure Land envisioned by monks in their treatises, and the gendered—and, so to speak, more mundane—paradises seen in people's dreams. In parallel, one observes the development of notions of "other worlds" (paradises and hells) contiguous to the human world in sacred mountains like Kinpusen or Tateyama. Although the influence of the idea of male rebirth is undeniable in the Heian poetry written by women, it seems that, apart from nuns and a few other pious laywomen, most women did not pray for a gender change, finding it more natural to believe in rebirth as they once were. Thus, even though the Buddhist doctrine penetrated the feminine elite, it apparently did not have such a deep influence on most women.[92]

When founders of the Pure Land school declared that women could be reborn in Pure Land, what they had in mind was a postmortem salvation: in other words, the only good women are dead women. It also meant that these women's purified remains, in the form of ashes, could be buried near the buddhas in the sacred space of the mountains. Although many different types of women (nuns and laywomen, all honest and compassionate) were said to have been reborn in the Pure Land in texts such as the *Ōjōden*, the orthodox truth of the matter is that no women are found in the Pure Land.[93] Another way to say this is that, although there may be women in paradise, they no longer have a female body. Their genderlessness was symbolized by their ashes. At the end of the twelfth century, at Daijō-in, a cloister built at Mudōji on Hieizan for the repose of the soul of Kōkamon'in (alias Shōshi), the hair of the imperial consort was deposited inside the *honzon*, and the vow written on that occasion expresses the belief that she had been reborn as a man and reached the ultimate stage of the bodhisattva career.[94] Thus, the same mountain cultic centers that refused access to living women saw no problem in accepting their remains and ritually assuring their rebirth into the Pure Land.

A FEMININE TOPOS

Women, most notably courtesans, can be manifestations of bodhisattvas or other deities. To what extent did these ideal types constitute role models for ordinary women, or simply the spinning of male fantasies? The ideological nature of the *henjō nanshi* theory is attested to by the fact that these texts pay no attention to real or imaginary cases of transsexualism. As noted earlier, the possibility of an actual sex/gender change in the present life was routinely accepted on karmic grounds by early Buddhism. It is hardly mentioned in later Buddhist literature, however, and only outside of Buddhism proper—for instance, in literary works of the Edo period—do we hear of similar cases. Even when they involve monks and nuns, they seem to happen at random, without any moral or karmic significance, and receive a pathological interpretation, outside of any soteriological framework. We find such cases mentioned in the *Mimibukuro*, under the title "Becoming a Man, or a Woman" (Henshō nanshi mata nyoshi), which recalls the Buddhist theme, but clearly indicates that transsexual change can go both ways.[95]

In all of the cases discussed above, the salvation of women is based on the negation of their femininity. Although, with the *hongaku* theory, Buddhism came to revalorize human reality as an expression of the absolute, it failed to revalorize femaleness, as it could have done on the basis of its logic identifying defilements and awakening. Indeed, if all phenomena are the expression of ultimate reality, why reject blood and other such female hindrances? Tantric Buddhism had begun to revalorize sexuality along these lines, but, paradoxically, it also contributed to the development of blood taboos in medieval Japan. Furthermore, this emphasis on sexuality did not not lead to a reevaluation of women's status: on the contrary, it tended to constrain them to their sexual or procreative roles. The Tantric revalorization of the human world is double-edged, for it may provide an alibi for a social status quo, a "naturalization" of socially constructed inequalities. Not only did the allegedly equalitarian notion of *hongaku* arise in androcentric institutions, but sexist elements can be found at its very core. At the same time, like most Buddhist teachings, it also contained its antidote, a negation of the karmic justifications of social inequality.[96] It can therefore not be held responsible for notions such as the Blood Pond Hell, which constitute an hyperbolic expression of karmic thought.[97]

Around the three main axes contituted by the notions of the Five Obstacles, of female rebirth into male, and of Amida's specific vow in favor of women, a Buddhist discourse developed, which, under the guise of salvation, emphasized the ontological, moral, karmic inferiority of women. It thus reinforced the motif of their properly biological inferiority, stemming from other impure sources, that its negative valence made more difficult to recuperate into a soteriological discourse.

Perhaps Buddhism simply provided a convenient vocabulary for conceptions that were deeply rooted in a patriarchal imagination. This repressive aspect was not always clearly perceived, however, as scholars still emphasize the soteriological component—indeed, not negligible—of such discourse, without paying due attention to its premises.

This double-speak is what made Buddhist discourse so efficacious, and caused the adhesion of the principally concerned party, women, who interiorized patriarchal values while they believed to be working for their salvation. The importance of that theme is also due to the fact that on its interpretation depend all the judgments that one can pass on the evolution of medieval Buddhism, and in particular the attempts to promote a revamped version of the old opposition between old and new Buddhism.

This analysis goes beyond the question of gender proper, however. In the *Lotus Sūtra*, the implicit connection between the case of Devadatta and that of the *nāga*-girl suggests that the hope for salvation presupposes for the individual (male or female) the recognition of his/her primordial debasement and the need to resort to the mediation of Amida and his priests. The much-vaunted "democratization" of Pure Land Buddhism and other similar movements does not lead to individual autonomy, but on the contrary to voluntary servitude, to submission to the saving grace of Amida and the intercession of his earthly representatives. The interest of these religious movements in the common people (and women) and their salvation was by no means disinterested. Although such ideological underpinnings have to be scrutinized, they do not entirely detract from the value of concrete priestly actions in favor of oppressed categories. *Faute de mieux*, such actions did produce local relief, even if they unconsciously propelled an ideology that was partly responsible for the suffering itself—not unlike these doctors who, while attempting to help the victims of an epidemic, contribute to its spread.

Chapter Four

THE RHETORIC OF EQUALITY

Such majestic equality in front of the law, which allows rich and poor alike to sleep at night under the bridges.
—Anatole France

ACCORDING TO Max Weber, the "equalization of the sexes in principle . . . may coexist with the complete monopolization by men of the priestly functions, of law, and of the right to active participation in community affairs; men only are admitted to special professional training or assumed to possess the necessary qualifications."[1] The same view can be found among feminist historians like Joan Kelly, who sees the notion of sexual parity as a mere alibi for patriarchy, rather than a potential threat to it.[2] At the other end, the anthropologist Susan Sered is disappointed to find that the so-called women's religions "do not proclaim egalitarian gender ideologies. They usually buy into prevalent unegalitarian notions of gender and gender roles."[3]

We have seen that there are two related Buddhist responses to perceived female inferiority, the first one being a "rhetoric of inequality" that accepted the status quo, the second a soteriological discourse on women's salvation, a "rhetoric of salvation" that seemed to question this status quo but in practice reinforced it. The same can be said about the third approach to which we now turn, the "rhetoric of equality," an attempt to solve the problem by denying it. This denial was made in the name of Mahāyāna nonduality, by asserting the nondifferentiation between man and woman from the standpoint of ultimate truth. This approach could be qualified as "sudden" in Chan terms, and it has lent itself to various forms of antinomianism. Like most forms of antinomianism, this "sudden" approach had very little social impact, and actually left the structure of domination intact, or even sometimes reinforced it. By negating the gender difference that prevails in our world in the name of a higher reality (or rather, a higher perception of reality), it contributes to maintain gender discrimination. We need to pay special attention to it, for it is too often taken at face-value—or at least used in performative fashion—by feminist scholars bent on finding hope for women in Buddhism. This rhetoric of equality found its main expressions in Tantrism and Chan, as well as in popular religious movements on the margins of Buddhism. Although it is usually considered to be specific to Mahāyāna Buddhism, it was already found in early Buddhism. In the *Therīgāthā*, for instance, when Māra tells Somā, a female disciple of the Buddha, that "a mere woman" could not gain enlightenment, she replies: "What harm is it / to be a woman / when the mind is concentrated / and the insight is clear?" And she concludes: "If I asked myself: / 'Am I a woman / or a man in this?'/ I would be speaking Māra's language."[4]

GENDER EQUALITY IN MAHĀYĀNA

As is well known, in Mahāyāna, forms are said to be empty; consequently, so is gender difference. This viewpoint was prefigured in early Buddhist notions concerning the instability of gender, although these ideas were never developed as a rationale for transsexuality. The locus classicus for this notion is the following passage of the *Vimalakīrti-nirdeśa*, which rejects gender difference as illusory. The arhat Śāriputra, the same disciple who refused to recognize the enlightenment of the *nāga*-girl, is confronted this time by a goddess. When he asks her what prevents her from transforming herself out of her female state, she answers that her female state is nowhere to be found because it is empty. And, to make him understand concretely, she magically turns into him, and makes him turn into her.[5] Through this trading of places and gender roles, she shows that buddhahood should no longer be identified with maleness. The *Vimalakīrti-nirdeśa* passage appears to be a development of the *nāga*-girl's dialogue with Śāriputra in the *Lotus Sūtra*. Despite (or because of) its radicality, it never became as popular as the latter. Simone Heidegger argues that the gender change of the *nāga*-girl does not so much indicate male superiority as signify the "unsignificant" character of formal gender differences. She points out the suddenness of the transformations described: the girl's awakening, but also her gender change.[6] This suddenness suggests that the *nāga*-girl had already fulfilled all the conditions for awakening; in other words, her gender change was a technical formality, the external or physical manifestation of an inner, spiritual transformation. Indeed, in some versions of the story, the *nāga*-girl is enlightened before the gender change takes place, and her transformation only reflects her capacity, as a bodhisattva, to change form at will.[7]

   The encounter between an arhat and a supernatural maiden is a topos in various scriptures. Likewise, in the *Sūtra of the Nāga-King Sagara*, the *nāga*-girl replies to the objection of the arhat Mahākāśyapa that "if one cannot become buddha in a woman's body, one cannot become buddha in a man's body. . . . When one knows through awakening and possesses the Dharma, there is neither man nor woman." And she reveals to him that the Buddha predicted that she will become a buddha without any gender change at the end of three hundred kalpas.[8]

This expression of Mahāyāna egalitarianism is seen by many to constitute the apex of Buddhist literature. The *Vimalakīrti-nirdeśa* and the *Śrīmaladevī* have been singled out as representative of these scriptures "that accept women as advanced Bodhisattvas and imminent Buddhas."[9] The *Śrīmālādevī*, however, despite (or because of) its radical egalitarianism, never had the impact of the *Vimalakīrti-nirdeśa*. The influence of the latter was due more to its comical subversion of gender roles than to its groundbreaking (or ground-removing) philosophical dialectic.

Earlier we encountered several other Mahāyāna scriptures that, as Nancy Schuster has shown, contain one version or another of the same topos. Schuster remarks: "Perhaps the most striking evidence for the very different attitude toward women found in Mahāyāna Buddhist texts is the fact that a woman is no longer identified merely by her sexual function; when she performs a truth act it is grounded on the fact of her true aspiration to the attainment of Buddhahood and her unshakable commitment to the Bodhisattva career."[10]

We recall, for instance, how in the *Sumati-sūtra* the eight-year-old daughter of a householder of Rājagṛha, Sumati, questions the Buddha about bodhisattva practice. When the arhat Maudgalyāyana objects that such practice is too difficult for a young girl, Sumati performs an "act of truth," taking the earth as witness of her resolve that she will soon become a buddha.[11] At this point, Mañjuśrī intervenes and asks why she does not first transform her female body into a male one. She answers that such a body "cannot be apprehended, for dharmas are neither male nor female." To remove the arhat's doubts, however, she first turns into a young novice monk. Then, vowing that in her future buddha-land there will be nothing having to do with Māra, in particular no "women's demeanor," she performs another act of truth and turns into a thirty-year-old monk.

In the *Vimaladattā-sūtra*, the daughter of King Prasenajit, Vimaladattā, defeats a group of eight arhats and bodhisattvas in Śrāvastī. She is then taught by the Buddha and resolves to practice the bodhisattva path. When Maudgalyāyana intervenes again, arguing that she cannot do so with a female body, she performs an act of truth. When he asks why she has not changed her female body, she turns the tables, asking him why *he* has not changed his *male* body. As he remains silent, she concludes, "Neither with a female nor with a male body is true enlightenment attained . . . for there is no achieving perfect enlightenment in any way."[12]

In the *Gangottara-sūtra*, a laywoman of Śrāvastī named Gangottara engages in a dialogue with the Buddha at the Jetavana. When he asks her where she comes from, she answers that his question is irrelevant: does one ask a magically created being where he comes from? Being herself in no way different from a magically created being, she is neither coming from nor going anywhere. The Buddha approves of her, and declares that his question was on account of ignorant bystanders. The dialogue moves on to a higher level of understanding, and reveals that Gangottara, while not quite the equal of the Buddha, is definitely enlightened.

Finally, we have the heroine of the *Strīvivarta-sūtra*, an unborn girl, who questions the Buddha from within her mother's womb, and, owing to his teaching, is able to turn into a male.[13] In one recension (T. 564), she tells the puzzled Śāriputra: "You must understand that I am not actually female or male, that maleness and femaleness are not real in an ultimate sense. . . . Nonetheless, in this world male and female bodies exist empirically, and a woman has good reason to choose *not* to go on living as a woman." In all of these texts, the conventional distinction between maleness and femaleness is shown to be empty from a higher standpoint. The practitioner who has entered the bodhisattva path is no longer either female or male. Gender differences and gender discrimination are negated, or rather relativized. Such differences characterize the world of forms, and they are as ontologically deficient as this world itself. Even so, they continue to obtain in this world, and in the end male superiority, while denied in principle, is reasserted in practice—according to a now familiar logic. Indeed, as Simone Heidegger observes, the distinction between maleness and femaleness tends to overlap with that between the two levels of truth. In a self-replicating move, maleness is associated with the higher truth of emptiness or suchness, and femaleness with the conventional truth of gender differentiation. The same gender code prevails in the motif of the bodhisattva manifesting himself in a female body as a skillful means to save sentient beings.[14] Never do we find a female bodhisattva manifesting herself in a male body.[15] In short, the realization of genderlessness becomes implicitly, for a woman, a way to transform into a man—a spiritual transformation in this case, rather than a physical one.

GENDER EQUALITY IN VAJRAYĀNA

Before attempting to evaluate the effects of Mahāyāna egalitarian rhetoric in Japanese Tantrism, let us examine briefly its expression in Indo-Tibetan Buddhism. The renowned "madman of Druk," Drukpa Kunley, emphasizes for instance the superiority of women from a philosophical standpoint:

> Someone said: "Some women are superior to men, but in our age of decadence, it is not good that women have more power." To this reflection, I replied: "How could this be due to the change of kalpa? From the earliest ages, everything that belongs to the female gender had generally much power, and this in religion as

well as in the world. . . ." In religion too, [the female gender] is the best. Thus one does not say Father Prajñāpāramitā, but Mother Prajñāpāramitā. In the secret mantras as well, one always says: "The Body, Speech and Thought of all the Tathāgatas abide in the womb [or: the sexual organ] of the Vajra Queen," and never in [the sexual organ] of the father. . . . Among the deities called Protectors of Buddhism . . . , the spouses [*yum*] are the most terrible; and if the lamas who have wives exert themselves as much as they can, like bees, is it not because they have to feed a Lady?. . . The *Kālacakra* [*tantra*] also speaks of "Emptiness . . . , our Mother, the best of all states.". . . Thus, whether in the religious realm or in the world, it is the female gender that is in fact important. . . . Better, one says that excellent lamas who practice the path of sexual union must revere their "woman of gnosis" [*vidyā*, ritual partner] as an indispensible instrument.[16]

The examples invoked by Kunley are often cited as proofs of the sexual egalitarianism of Tantrism; however, they deserve closer scrutiny. The fact that wisdom (*prajñā*) or emptiness (*śūnyatā*) are referred to as "Mother" of all the buddhas, for instance, needs to be placed in a broader social and ideological context. The presuppositions that govern Kunley's metaphors are brought to light in a passage of the *Lam rim chen mo*, in which Tsongkhapa (1357–1419) comments on the symbolic gendering of wisdom (*prajñā*) and skillful means (*upāya*) as "mother" and "father": "Just as a mother can bear children of different castes or nationalities, depending on the ethnicity of the various men who father them, so too can wisdom bring forth a variety of spiritually accomplished individuals: śravakas, pratyekabuddhas, and buddhas. Because the mother, wisdom, is the same in all of these cases, the father will determine the spiritual lineage of the adept."[17] Only if the "father" is skillfull means (*upāya*) will the son, that is, the adept, be a buddha. In other cases, the son will only be a saint of the Lesser Vehicle (Hīnayāna). As José Cabezon contends, even if the maternal metaphor seems to lead to a revalorization of the status of women, we must see that this revalorization is seriously limited by the use of the said metaphor. Tsongkhapa actually says that "the altruist mind is like the father's seed, whereas the wisdom that is the realization of selflessness is like the mother. For example, if the father is Tibetan it is impossible for the child to be an Indian or a Tartar and so forth. Hence, the father determines the ethnicity of the son."[18] Cabezon continues: "If we take into account all the aspects of the symbol, we cannot overlook that at the root of the metaphor is an implicit assumption demeaning the status of women, namely that a woman's ethnic heritage is of no consequence in determining the ethnic heritage of her children, that the man's ethnic background is the sole determinant of the child's ethnicity. Just as man is 'more important' in determining the ethnicity of the child, so too is father-love in the spiritual realm."[19] In short, in such doctrinal couples as wisdom and compassion, or wisdom and skillful means, the first term, the feminine (wisdom), is common to the two Vehicles, whereas the second one, that is, the masculine (compassion or skillful means), is specific to Mahāyāna and valorized as such. Thus, if wisdom is represented as feminine, it is because of its inferiority in the determination of Mahāyāna "ethnicity," and because of the emphasis on emotional states perceived as a characteristic of Mahāyāna.[20] Therefore, far from extolling wisdom and women as a superficial reading would suggest, this imagery presupposes and reinforces the inferiority of women. Max Weber had already noted that the symbolic abrogation of gender difference usually goes along with a dichotomic system of gender segregation.[21]

The gender equality of Tantric ritual works usually to the advantage of men. The same is true in yogic or alchemical practice, where the "outer" or physical woman is ultimately depreciated in favor of an "inner" or spiritual woman, as a fundamental symbol of ideal androgyny. Having realized his female inner side, the Tantric practitioner reaches the much-wanted autonomy: "What need do I have of another woman, when I have within me an Inner Woman?"[22] Thus, androgyny is not simply an accepting of femaleness, it is at the same time a denial of real womanhood. Such male-centered androgyny is a way for men to appropriate the biological powers of women, and it goes along, in actual practice, with a strict subordination of women. As to the sexual symbolism of Tantric ritual, it is often governed by a logic that is relatively indifferent to gender. Such logic strives primarily to establish, through the conjunction or disjunction of various polarities (such as man and woman, but also man and animal) a kind of human life that transcends biological constraints, and, above all, death. In this context, the sex/gender differences brought into play by ritual might be in last resort secondary.[23]

An obvious example of the essential ambivalence of symbols is the omnipresence in Indo-Tibetan Tantric iconography of representations of divine couples in sexual embrace (yab-yum).[24] In Hindu Tantrism, the god's "female energy," his śakti, is personified as his female consort. The same seems true in the case of the mudrā, the sexual partner of Tibetan Tantric gods. As Agehananda Bharati and Alex Wayman have pointed out, however, this female mudrā, contrary to the Hindu śakti, is a symbol of prajñā (wisdom), and as such she is utterly passive and inferior in status. Bharati remarks,

> The Buddhist tantrics utilized two different types of goddesses—pure Indian śakti, who preserve their dynamic function in their new Vajrayāna locale, as well as other Indian, Buddhist and non-Buddhist models (like Tārā and Locanā) which came to function in a manner more representative of the polarizing doctrine of Vajrayāna (as Prajñāpāramitā, Nairtyā, etc.): these goddesses came to

be purely Buddhist in conception, expressing the notion of absolute quiescence, and are far removed from the offices of a *śakti*. Iconographically, they are shown in a sitting posture.[25]

The division of labor is well marked in Hindu and Buddhist Tantrism: in both cases, the redeeming function is assigned to the dynamic principle and its mythological manifestations. In other words, in Buddhism it is the deity personifying the *upāya* (male), and in Hinduism the deity personifying the *śakti* (female), that guide the adept.[26] Thus, the Tibetans invariably assign the dynamic function to the male principle, the passive or static function to the female principle.[27] Another point worth noting is that although Tantric Buddhism emphasizes sexuality, it is an essentially nonprocreative sexuality. In that sense, the female deities of Tantric Buddhism are quite distinct from the mother-goddess images usually invoked in utopian visions of a primordial matriarchy.

The iconographic representations of *yab-yum* deities are said to be the model for sexual rituals. Miranda Shaw has argued that, in the Hindu context, the Tantric practitioner is enlightened by strange, strong women. Yet he tends to remain the main character in all of these stories.[28] Even if he is not bent, like Daoist practitioners, on "stealing" the energy of his female partner, the fact remains that the idealization of women in a ritual context does not necessarily translate into their higher status in ordinary life. Actually, it presupposes social inequality if we take into account the contrast between the sacred and the profane, the discrepancy between ritual and nonritual arenas. A comparison with the tradition of "courtly love" in medieval Europe might be useful here. For all the knight's idealization of his lady, and the real power it gave to some women over some men, women in general continued to occupy a subaltern position. The medieval knight was merely flirting with taboos. Tantric discourse has more to do with the soteriological value of transgression and ritual inversion than with gender equality per se.[29] As is well known, Tantric practitioners were fascinated by transgression. Tantric texts abound in passages like the following: "One who unites with mother, sister, and daughter / will attain the extensive perfection and truth / at the pinnacle of the Mahāyāna."[30] But these are symbolic images, and the partners of Tantric practitioners were usually low-caste women with hardly any chance of upward social mobility. Furthermore, Tantric sexual intercourse was not only a *coincidentia oppositorum*, but a powerful opportunity to merge with the "dark side"—lust, deceit, filth—of woman.[31] The woman becomes a sacred altar, a temporary embodiment of the goddess, a stepping stone from the profane to the sacred.[32] Thus, the ritualized union of the Tantric practitioner with his *mudrā* is less a sexual union with a woman than an imagined union with the goddess.

The utopian quality of this tradition is evident, and the freedom it claims for its female adherents is equally problematic. The real woman is only a means to an end, a kind of "transitional object." She is denied, inasmuch as she has to hide behind a divine mask. Admittedly this kind of double-role, like that of female mediums, might constitute a form of power, a way to assert one's voice—but always in the name of another, under a false identity. It remains a form of alienation. In short, Tantric ritual offered a role to women, as long as they observed the rule of the game. Admittedly some women, under favorable circumstances, were able to play this game well and turn it to their own advantage, but they remain the exception that confirms the rule, and their success is to their own credit as individuals, not as passive followers of some egalitarian teaching.[33]

In order to understand how the Tantric tradition represented itself, we need to pay due attention to the motivations of its ritual and hagiographic literature. The women described in this literature are extraordinarily powerful demonic beings called *yoginī* or *ḍākiṇī* (Tib. *mKha' 'groma, kha-droma*, lit. "those who go into space," usually translated as "sky-walkers"). Whether they can serve as role models for Western women remains an open question. Apart from these ideal "women" and their wondrous powers, very little is said about ordinary women and *their* agency, their woman-specific problems (menstruation, abortion, childbirth, and dependence). It may be believed that all women are embodiments of Vajrayoginī, but it is unlikely that many of them actually saw themselves (except in their wildest dreams) as such.[34] How relevant to such women are the *ḍākiṇī*, whose traces, once found, are said to be "incandescent, exhilarating and provocative as they beckon to their seekers from a spacious realm of sky-like freedom?"[35]

The Tibetan *ḍākiṇī* may be a symbol of wisdom (*prajñā*). She is not ipso facto a symbol of woman, however, but simply a symbol defined as feminine, in order to underscore the complementarity that goes along with duality.[36] The same can be said of other similar female figures of Tantric Buddhism who, unlike the Hindu *śakti*, are relegated to a passive role. The desexualization or disempowerment (I dare not say "emasculation") that characterizes such symbolic redefinitions of local deities by Buddhism can be seen at work in the transformation of Srin-mo, the progenitress of ancient Tibet, into a "neutral" Tārā.[37] The "Terrible Mother," Genitrix/Progenitress of Tibet, becomes in Buddhism dPal-ldan lHa-mo (Palden Lhamo, "the glorious goddess").

Ancient Tibet was conceived like a demoness lying on her back, who needed to be subdued. Twelve Buddhist monasteries were erected at places corresponding to the significant parts of her body to pin her down. Significantly, her vagina is not listed among these places, perhaps because it would have looked too much like a rape.[38] The sexual symbolism is present, however, in the fact that one of the structures that pinned her down was a *lingaṃ,* the phallic symbol of Śiva, erected in the East, at a place said to be like the goddess' pubic hair.[39] According to one tradition, the "bodhisattva of compassion" Avalokiteśvara (Tib. sPyan-ras gzigz, Chenrezig), assuming the form of an ape, tamed her through sexual intercourse.[40] Here, copulation is first and foremost a method of domination. As a result, she was reformed and assumed a new identity, that of Tārā, the "Savioress." In the process, however, she has also been neutered.[41] Looking like a typical bodhisattva, she may have become a model of perfect femininity, smiling serenely upon her worshippers, but her threatening femaleness, the expression of her dark chthonian powers, has disappeared. Paradoxically, she seems to have turned into a male (or androgynous) figure.[42] Her transformation is one of the indices that local cults have been tamed by Buddhism.

But the story does not end there, and local cults do reassert their influence. The chthonic powers of the supine Srin-mo, tied up by Lilliputian Buddhists, were revived with the rise in the Gelugpa tradition of the goddess Palden Lhamo, a Tibetan version of the bloodthirsty goddess Kālī or Durgā.[43] She is nevertheless an exception, being the only high-ranking *dharmapāla* described as riding over a sea of blood: a metaphor that, in her case, probably refers to menstrual blood and fertility.[44] Nevertheless, in one of her representations, this "mother goddess" is depicted as an old woman with sagging breasts, sitting on the skin of her slaughtered son.[45] The fifth Dalai Lama's attempt to strip her of her destructive chthonian powers—by associating her with pre-Buddhist cosmology and turning her worship into a sky-cult—failed, and she remained a symbol of demonic sexuality.[46] As Rosemarie Volkman points out, "the subjugation of the chthonic/telluric Genitrix/Progenitress through the process of the demonization of her sexuality did nothing whatsoever to diminish her power but, paradoxically, increased it."[47] Her case seems suggestive of what happened to many other lesser deities of the ḍākinī type. In this scenario, an archaic chthonic goddess is dissociated into two distinct personae: one being literally "elevated into the sky" (like a "sky-walker"), while the other is demonized and continues to roam the earth as a demoness. Those who cling to the positive side of the picture as a model are not only oblivious to the dynamics of religious symbolism, but, in depriving the bloodthirsty demoness of her worship, they also end up worshipping a lifeless substitute—if not attracting the goddess's revenge.

CHAN/ZEN EGALITARIANISM

Let us now turn to the Buddhist discourse on gender equality as it found its expression in the Chan/Zen tradition. This discourse rests on two theoretical bases, Mahāyāna nonduality on the one hand, and the "sudden" teaching that denies traditional conceptions of karma on the other.[48] One of the justifications of gender discrimination in Buddhism had to do with the notion of karma, the belief that one's past acts determine one's social position. Thus, the social hierarchy merely reflects the karmic hierarchy. To the extent that Chan rejected the notion of karma in the name of the higher principle of sudden enlightenment, it also (theoretically) denied gender differentiation, as well as all gendered (gradual) stages—for instance, rebirth as man—on the way to enlightenment. This kind of ideal found its expression in notions such as Linji Yixuan's "true man of no-rank" (*wuwei zhenren*).

We noted earlier, however, that equality presupposes (and at times reinforces) inequality. The Chan position is reminiscent of the words of Saint Jerome: "As long as a woman is for birth and children she is as different from man as body is from soul. But when she wishes to serve Christ more than the world, then she will cease to be a woman and will be called man."[49] Many Chan/Zen texts emphasize the equality between man and woman, and above all equality as it pertains to the ultimate goal, awakening. The fact that such texts were written at times and places where the status of women was perfectly subaltern should no longer surprise us. It means that, as in the Tantric case, such equality should not be taken too literally insofar as this kind of discourse had little impact in practice. Gender difference is denied in Chan rhetoric, but perhaps to deny it was still to give it too much reality. From the standpoint of ultimate truth, this paradigmatic duality was rather considered to be fundamentally unreal and irrelevant to awakening. In spite of all this, very few women found their way into Chan chronicles. Among the exceptions is the case of the nun Zongzhi. She was one of Bodhidharma's four foremost disciples, and she is said to have obtained the "skin" of her thick-skinned master, while the three others obtained the "flesh," the "bones," and the "marrow," respectively. It is hard to avoid the feeling that the "skin" serves as a metaphor for a relatively superficial understanding, and consequently implies a relatively inferior status as disciple.[50] This led a later commentator, the Japanese Zen master Dōgen—in a chapter of his *Shōbōgenzō* entitled "Bowing and Obtaining the Marrow" (Raihai tokuzui)—to argue in typical nondualist fashion that there can be no difference in depth between skin, flesh, bones, and marrow. Following Dōgen, this story has become an obliged reference in all claims of gender equality in Zen.

The episode regarding Zongzhi's attainment is first mentioned in the *Lidai fabao ji* (ca. 774), a text that makes a strong case for gender equality. For instance, we are told that the disciple of the Chan master Wuzhu, a woman named Wei, was called a "great male" (*dazhangfu*) by him. She allegedly obtained awakening after Wuzhu explained the truth of nonduality to her. This is probably the first example of the rhetoric of equality in Chan texts. Significantly, the *Lidai fabao ji* gives her educational record. She was a daughter of the administrator Mu Rong of Qingzhou. Having heard of Wuzhu's great compassion, she came with her mother to pay obeisance to him. After Wuzhu preached the basics of Buddhism to the two women, she begged him for further instruction, arguing that she was a woman "with the three obstructions and the five impurities, and a body that is not free." In order to obtain freedom from this karmic burden, to "cut off the source of birth and death," she now paid allegiance to him. Impressed by her resolution, Wuzhu told her: "If you are capable of such [resolution], then you are a "great male" (*dazhangfu*), why [think of yourself as] 'a woman'?" Then he taught her about the essential truth of "no-thought" (*wunian*): "In no-thought, there is no 'male'; in no-thought, there is no 'female'. In no-thought, there is no obstruction; in no-thought, there is no hindrance. In no-thought, there is no-birth; in no-thought, there is no-death. At the very moment of no-thought, no-thought itself cannot be found. This is to cut off the source of birth and death." Wuzhu eventually gave her the religious name of Changjinjin ("Constant diligence") and allowed her to take the tonsure, together with her mother.

Wei's example inspired one of her relatives, a young woman who was the granddaughter of Grand Councilor Su. Her story follows the same pattern. She went to see Wuzhu, who immediately recognized her qualities. Seeing that she was "obdurate and determined on chastity," he taught her the principle of nonduality, emphasizing that no-thought transcends body and mind (and therefore gender). Upon hearing his words, she wept profusely, and told him: "Your disciple is a woman whose karmic hindrances are heavy. But now that I heard the Dharma, all defilements and obstructions have vanished." She received from him the religious name of Liaojianxing ("She who perfectly sees her nature") and she "tonsured herself," a rather unprecedented act. Like Changjinjin, she later became "a leader among nuns." The point made by Wuzhu is that, as soon as a woman produces the thought of enlightenment, she enters the bodhisattva path, and ipso facto transcends all duality, all gender limitations. This is the realm of innate enlightenment (*benjue*) or "sudden awakening" (*dunwu*), the ideal domain of no-thought, in which there is neither male nor female, neither master nor disciple. And yet, Wuzhu remains a male master answering his female disciple, a patriarch who, even in his wildest dreams, has never met (and is not prepared to meet) a matriarch. Despite his name (Wuzhu, Non-Abiding), he still abides in the world of forms, in which enlightened beings are "great men."

As Wendi Adamek has pointed out, the place given in the *Lidai fabao ji* to these two female disciples of Wuzhu is quite prominent. Adamek even suggests that they may have written the text in question.[51] Unfortunately, we have no way to verify this provocative hypothesis. Furthermore, despite the positive image of these two nuns, they still seem to be considered as second-rank citizens in the Chan community. The former is referred to as a "great male" by Wuzhu—an ambivalent expression of praise, which implies a denial of her sex, as well as a valorization of maleness (as more "genderless" than femaleness). They come to him in the belief that their female body has plagued them, and he in turn teaches them how to go beyond this duality.[52] Yet the nonduality expressed here is never translated institutionally into full equality of status. There may indeed be no male or female in the realm of no-thought, but neither Wuzhu nor his female disciples are able or willing to bring this realm down to earth and to make it a reality. In a certain sense, no-thought may be seen as an escape from reality, or an alibi, a good reason not to change this reality. The "revolutionary" teaching of Wuzhu—like all forms of antinomianism—turns out to be socially quite conservative.

Wuzhu's two female disciples in turn became teachers, but teachers of women. In the end, they were not officially listed as Wuzhu's successors because his lineage was in essence patriarchal. These women who, perhaps against their father's will, had refused to marry were still defined primarily by their relationships with male kin (father, grandfather) and their place in patriarchal society. They did not rebel against male authority. On the contrary, they were quite submissive, learning how to keep their place in a male-centered Chan community. They seem to have no recorded inscription either, and they did not leave any trace in popular imagination as thaumaturgic teachers. A close examination of Chan epigraphy reveals that a number of eminent nuns reached awakening, but they are usually recorded simply as Chan masters and the stele omits mention of their gender.

Miriam Levering notes that these stories were included in Chan preaching and teaching at a time when Chinese society and its Confucian leadership were trying to confine women to the inner quarters.[53] As noted earlier, Buddhism was the ultimate refuge for women who wanted to escape their destinies as spouses and mothers. Although it did not acknowledge femininity as a positive value, it produced a great number of conversions among women, most of them from higher social strata.

Buddhist scholars usually take the Chan/Zen rhetoric of equality at face-value, quoting authors such as Dahui Zonggao (1089–1163) and Dōgen. Speaking about his successful lay student, Lady Tang, Dahui declares: "Can you say that she is a woman, and women have no share [in enlightenment]? You must believe that this matter has nothing to do with [whether one is] male or female, old or young. Ours is an egalitarian Dharma-gate that has only one flavor."[54] And he concludes: "For mastering the truth, it does not matter whether one is male or female, noble or base. One moment of insight and one is shoulder to shoulder with the Buddha."[55] Despite—or because of—the theoretical gender equality it advocates, Chan was an essentially male discourse, structured as it was by a patriarchal tradition in whose pedagogical tradition "matriarchs" are unheard of.

Chan egalitarianism may derive as much from an institutional need for aristocratic support as from theoretical premises. The sudden increase in references to women in Dahui's sermons is indeed related to the fact that these were addressed to nuns or influential laywomen. Although Dahui named five nuns and one laywoman among his fifty-four successors, none of them appears in the official lineage of his school. Gender biases were too deeply entrenched to be shaken by mere theoretical contradictions, or by fictional subversion of Mahāyāna scriptures like the *Vimalakīrti-nirdeśa*.

In order to document the radical change in status of Chan nuns during the Song, Levering has focused on the role and perception of Chan abbesses as literati women. One of them, Miaocong (alias Wuzhao) even received a purple robe.[56] The same thing happened in Japan in the case of nuns of the *ama gozan*, and Miaocong's is one of the obvious Chinese precedents for the Rinzai abbess Mugai Nyodai, who received the robe and the portrait (*chinzō*) of/from Mugaku Sogen. Likewise, the robe of Shun'oku Myōha was transmitted within Tsūgenji, a Zen nunnery. Thus, these nuns received the symbols of transmission, and to some extent the status of authority that went along with them. As was noted earlier, however, these nuns became female replicas of the masters, and they tried to erase the marks of femininity in themselves. For all that, even in the most open-minded currents of Rinzai Zen, such as the Daitokuji branch, they had no access to orthodox succession, and their actual status remained inferior. Thus, it is hard to follow Barbara Ruch when she argues that the fact that Mugaku Sogen named Mugai Nyodai as heir to his teachings "is clear indication that he . . . believed that religious enlightenment was genderless."[57] Or rather, even if such was indeed the case, it is irrelevant, inasmuch as it failed to translate into practice.

The metaphor of the "great man" applied to women was part of the rhetoric of equality that runs through the Chan and Zen traditions. As Levering has indicated, it definitely has an androcentric ring.[58] Even if this condescending tone is not as blatant in the *Lidai fabao ji*, it is certainly not entirely absent, and the women's voices in these texts are voices of consent, not of dissent. Chan stories involving women imply male dominance, and do not let us hear the female voice. There are, as always, some exceptions. We recall the inscription for the two Tiantai nuns Huichi and Huiren, discussed in chapter 1. This inscription seems to echo a distinctive female voice, and it does so at the expense of the Chan master Puji (651–739), a man who liked to think of himself as the seventh Chinese "patriarch" of Chan. The two nuns did not think so highly of him, however, and they let it be known. The anger of Puji's partisans in front of this crime of lèse-majesté led to their investigation on imperial order by the priest Yixing, who eventually exonerated them. Perhaps it is significant that this voice, while emanating from within the Buddhist saṅgha, would resonate outside of the Chan tradition. The claim of this inscription is that a Buddhist nun, known for her strange powers and perceived as the manifestation of a bodhisattva, initiated her disciples to a truth of a higher order than that preached by one of the foremost Buddhist authorities of the time. Here we may hear the distant echo of a higher esoteric tradition, one that was always in danger of being eclipsed or erased by the political power of established Buddhism, but one that always resurfaced in the popular tradition. The significant point is that this hidden tradition of wonder-workers is represented here by two women, two blood-sisters, who end up buried at Longmen (like Shenhui and most prominent Buddhist priests of the time). We find similar stories of nuns with psychic powers in the *Biqiuni zhuan*: for instance, the story of Jingcheng, who was always accompanied by a tiger.[59] But rarely do we hear, even from these superior beings, the voice of dissent that we hear in the case of Huichi and Huiren. Yet, the problem with this kind of account is that we are still dealing with exceptional women—and nuns at that—who had, like Wuzhu's female disciples, surpassed (or denied) their sex, and who in that sense could not provide models for ordinary women. Female voices of consent or dissent remain confined to the Buddhist saṅgha. All this points to the urgent need for a careful assessment of the role played by women, lay and clerical, in Tang and Song Buddhism (and namely in "patriarchal" Chan).

Most of the records of the Chan nuns are found in the hagiographical collections known as "Records of the Transmission of the Lamp" (*chuan-denglu*). Among the hundreds of Chan masters included in this pseudohistorical literature, we only find a few brief mentions of nuns. Most of the time, there are short dialogues between a Chan master and his female disciple. But, whereas the norm is to give further dialogues in which the disciple is now the master, the enlightened nuns never reappear as full-fledged masters. As Dahui said in his instruction to his female disciple Miaoyuan: "Concerning this matter, every one is equal, regardless of being a man or woman, noble. Why? At the assembly for the preaching of the *Lotus Sūtra*, the buddha simply helps one girl to become a buddha, and at the assembly for preaching the *Nirvana Sūtra*, he only helps one butcher to become a buddha."[60] Also worth mentioning is Dahui's eulogy for Lady Tang, one of his lay disciples:

> You will know that although Lady Tang was born years ago, she fundamentally was never born; her extinction today likewise fundamentally did not extinguish

anything. Born and not born, like a reflection in a mirror; extinguished and yet not extinguished, like the moon in the water.[61]

Levering points out the two contradicting themes of karmic retribution (rebirth in the Pure Land) and the emptiness of birth and death. Far from reconciling them, however, Dahui seems to play them off against each other, interweaving the two levels of truth. But the main problem is that these words are not said of a living woman, but of a deceased patron. Lady Tang has the "beauty of the dead."

Despite the inherent bias in Chan rhetoric, the message seems to have had a liberating effect on some women. Chan literature often shows us arrogant male practitioners defeated by a sharp-tongued woman. While this may be read as an indication of women's self-confidence and spiritual achievement, it is difficult to know how much of this to attribute to the Chan teaching itself. In the chapters to follow, we will discuss examples of encounters in which a monk is challenged by a woman, and loses face as a result. Like these examples, the cases recorded in Chan literature may be seen as instances of female reaction to male patriarchy, as well as an attempt to coopt some figures of recalcitrant women. It is hard to follow Shih Heng-ching, herself a Chan nun, when she reads these stories as unambiguous expressions of "the liberal and open-minded attitude of the Ch'an School toward women."

How is gender equality expressed in classical Chan literature, for instance in the "Records of the Transmission of the Lamp"? Significantly, the only woman who is given a record of her own in the *Jingde chuandeng-lu* is Liaoran, the abbess of Moshan. When the monk Guanqi Zhixian, during his peregrinations, arrives at Moshan, the following exchange takes place:

> Liaoran sent an attendant nun to ask: "Are you merely sightseeing, or did you come for the Buddha Dharma?" Zhixian replied, "For the Buddha Dharma." Liaoran then ascended to her seat. Zhixian asked for instruction. Liaoran asked, "Where did you start your journey today?" Zhixian replied, "From the entrance to the road (lit., from the mouth of the road)." Liaoran said, "Why didn't you cover it?" Zhixian had no reply. He then for the first time performed a kneeling bow to her. He asked, "What is Moshan (lit., summit mountain)?" Liaoran said, "Its peak is not exposed." Zhixian said, "What is the occupant of Moshan like?" Liaoran replied, "(S)he has neither male nor female form (*xiang*)." Zhixian shouted, "Why doesn't she transform herself?" Liaoran replied, "She is not a spirit, nor a ghost. What would you have her become?" Zhixian at this could only submit. He became a gardener at the nunnery, where he stayed for three years.[62]

Here, Liaoran truly assumes the position of the master, and Zhixian feels compelled to acknowledge her authority. His taking up the lowly position of gardener is somewhat funny, when one recalls the Western anticlerical topos of the sexual relations of the nuns and the convent's gardener. At any rate, it implies that gender distinctions still obtained in real monastic life.[63] Another interesting point is that the abbess speaks authoritatively from her high chair (that is, in the symbolic function of a living buddha). What would have happened if she had not occupied this position? An indication is perhaps given in the following story, where the egalitarian rhetoric, although used correctly, fails to work and discrimination seems to take place.

> When an anonymous *bhikṣuṇī* wanted to give a formal Chan lecture, the monk Tangong said to her, "A nun, being a woman, should not give a Chan teaching." The nun said, "What do you have to say about the eight-year-old *nāga*-girl becoming a buddha?"—"The *nāga*-girl can do eighteen kinds of transformations. Can you just make one transformation for this old monk?"—"Even if one can transform oneself, one is nothing but a wild-fox spirit," said the nun. Tangong then kicked her out.[64]

This story suggests that what was emphasized in Liaoran's case was perhaps more her abbatial function than her gender itself. The fact remains that Liaoran was one of the rare women able to gain access to such a privileged position.

Outside of the Chan monastic tradition, Tao Shan and Peng Shaosheng offer two different views of the same topos. In his preface to the *Shan nüren zhuan*, Peng writes that "only the most virile of women (*nü zhong hao*) are able to uproot their emotional attachments in the manner of 'great fellows' (*da zhangfu*)."[65] We have here a patriarchal adaptation of the classical ideal of the *virago*, the female military hero who achieves equivalence, or indeed eminence, in the world by becoming not a great woman but, as it were, a man (*vir*).[66] Tao Shan's case shows a tension between male and female spiritual ideals. On the one hand she identifies herself with the tradition of wise females such as Mahāprajāpatī and Lingzhao. On the other hand, she is ashamed of her female limitations.[67] She has a sense of inadequacy and alienation, perhaps as a result of having to negotiate a double-identification with paternal and maternal narratives. Peng Shaosheng writes: "[Tao Shan] was like a flower in the sky, like the moon [reflected] in the water. Neither the same nor different, neither the self nor the other." Peng no doubt meant to illustrate Tao Shan's spiritual transcendence of all dualities, including gender. It is ironic that his words in fact express the double-bind in which her profoundly spiritual aspirations left her suspended.[68]

Peng was motivated to compile this work in 1775 by the religious faith of the women in his family (his wife and daughters, and Tao Shan, the wife of his nephew). He intended the work as a model for his two daughters. His fatherly love may explain why he seems less convinced by the traditional prejudice against women, and argues that faith is more essential for rebirth in paradise than birth as a man. Arguing about the irreality of appearances as explained in Mahāyāna, and therefore of the irreality of the gender distinction, he appeals to the Buddhist condemnation of women as it had been formulated by the Buddha himself.[69] For him, women are freed from their traditional vices once they are good practitioners, which seems to be begging the question, since it is precisely because of these weaknesses that women are deemed unable to become good practitioners. He believes that women are the equals of men in wisdom and in faith. He has no difficulty finding in canonical literature and in Chan texts examples of pious women such as Queen Vaidehī. Although Peng provides a more realistic description of his laywomen than other authors dealing with monks and nuns, he tends toward hagiography. A singular process of democratization seems at work. As Gabriele Goldfuss notes, the characteristics of Chan masters—oneiric capacities, premonitions of their death, thaumaturgic powers, voluntary death, mumification, relics—are now found with laywomen.[70]

The case of Tao Shan, the wife of Peng's nephew, is particularly significant in that respect. A talented poetess, she was initially reluctant to marry:

> When she turned twenty-three, [her parents] wanted to marry her. From then onward, she sang unceasingly the name of the Buddha. She composed ten poems entitled *Cankuiyin*. . . . When she came as new bride to the family of her husband, she spoke the whole day with them of the Law of Emptiness and of the evanescent nature of the passion. She wanted to "preserve her child body." This led to a conflict with her family, and in the end she walked the "way of the bride." While meditating and reading scriptures, she found herself pregnant. She gave birth to a child, and fell ill. She died "en odeur de sainteté" at the age of twenty-five.[71]

Despite his empathy with Tao Shan's tragic destiny, Peng thinks that she has chosen the right path and achieved saintliness by fulfilling her duty as daughter and wife. Although a Buddhist, he remained deeply influenced by Confucian values, and his entire work is a glorification of the social function of motherhood.

Let us now turn to Japanese Zen. The exemplum of Moshan Liaoran is quoted by Dōgen in "Raihai tokuzui" (1240) a text that, as noted earlier, is often read as a precursor of Buddhist feminism. This story (and the assertion based on it) deserves some scrutiny. In his early proselytizing years, Dōgen seems to have strongly advocated the equality of the sexes. An oft-quoted passage in this context is the following: "What demerit is there in the fact of being a woman? What merit in being a man? There are bad men and good women. If you wish to hear the Dharma and put an end to pain and turmoil, forget about such things as male and female. As long as delusions have not yet been eliminated, neither men nor women are free from them; when they are eliminated and reality is experienced, there is no longer any distinction between male and female."[72] Again, in "Bendōwa" (1231), when someone asks him whether laymen and laywomen can practice zazen, or only monks, Dōgen answers that there is no distinction between man and woman, or between high and low, in the Dharma.[73]

Dōgen apparently had only a few female disciples, and perhaps it is for them that he wrote the *Shōbōgenzō* in "feminine" script (*kana*) and delivered the sermon recorded in "Raihai tokuzui" (1240).[74] In this fascicle of the *Shōbōgenzō*, Dōgen expands on this theme, giving examples of awakened nuns, and declares: "Both men and women can realize the Way. In any case the realization of the Way should be respected, regardless of sex."[75] He adds: "For example, the *nāga*-king's daughter is said to have realized the Way. We should make a venerating offering to her as if to the buddhas. This is a traditional manner in Buddhism."[76] In the same chapter, Dōgen also criticizes the notion of *kekkai* (a restricted sacred space), which, in a typical hermeneutic move, he reinterprets and absolutizes as meaning "without limits, including all beings."[77] But the period when he emphasizes the theory of female buddhahood (*nyonin jōbutsu*) corresponds to the ten years he spends at Fukakusa on the southern outskirts of Kyoto, after his return from China, trying to spread the True Dharma among lay people. After his departure for the distant province of Echizen and his emphasis on ascetic monastic life, this theory will no longer be mentioned, or rather, it will be strongly denied.

We may suspect that Dōgen's egalitarian discourse reflects a typically masculine point of view. However that may be, as his initial proselytism gave way to a preoccupation with establishing a distinct sectarian lineage, gender equality, along with the equality between monks and laymen, disappeared from Dōgen's discourse. Toward the end of his life, he seems to have drastically changed his view on the question of the salvation of women: In "Shukke kudoku," he declares: "In some sūtras it is said that laymen can become buddhas and that women can do the same. Such statements, however, are not the true transmission of the teachings of the buddhas and patriarchs. The true transmission is that buddhahood can be realized only after having entered the monkhood."[78] For him, monastic ordination, and more precisely the donning of the *kāṣāya*, had the quasi-magical power to cancel all human flaws (gender-related or not). This contradicts the established view, initially asserted by Watsuji Tetsurō, that Dōgen had overcome the traditional Buddhist prejudice against women. The same master who was allegedly "by far the most uncompromising on asserting complete equality between the sexes" also believed that "one cannot become a buddha in a woman's body." In this, he remained in line with the androcentric discourse of the *Lotus Sūtra*.[79] Even if these excerpts are inconclusive, they are enough to show that Dōgen cannot be enrolled into the feminist cause without undue reductionism.

Apart from normative texts, it is difficult to know what Dōgen's attitude toward women may have been in practice. Even in the beginning he remained very aware of the dangers that the presence of women could bring to his community. The *Eihei kōroku* contains a sermon related to one female disciple, a nun named Ryōzen: "Although she is a woman, she has the willpower of a 'great male'. . . . She does not spare the effort to nourish the way, that is why I have shown her the meaning of [Bodhidharma's] 'coming from the West.'"[80] Thus Dōgen seems to consider her the equal of a monk (despite the rhetoric of the "great male"). But if one looks at the Rules he formulated for his community, nuns cannot live in the same hermitage as monks. It is not clear what their position at Kōshōji or Eiheiji was.

Uchino Kumiko argues that Dōgen emphasized the equality of men and women in attaining buddhahood. Yet when Dōgen advises his disciples to take a woman as a master, it is much as when he says that one must not hesitate to take a wild fox as master as long as one has faith. Thus, he seems to go beyond the conventional representations of women while simultaneously reaffirming them (a move we have already seen in many texts like the *Lotus Sūtra*).

Dōgen liked to recount the exchange between the Chan master Deshan Xuanjian (782–865) and an old woman. Here, Dōgen talks about men being taught reluctantly (the French expression *à corps défendant* captures this superbly) by women. The story calls to mind the transgression motif that we will see recurring in later Japanese literature: women— usually virgins or old women, never housewives—engaging in Dharma battle, not remaining in their prescribed place. The old woman, however, after defeating the young Deshan, reassumes her traditional position, acknowledging (with some false modesty perhaps) that she cannot be a master because of her "female obstacles."

Even allowing for more diversity in Dōgen's text—a self-deconstructing and often self-contradictory text—it may be instructive to contrast the abstract egalitarianism of Dōgen to the influence of female images in the teaching of Keizan. Keizan seems to have been more willing to put into practice the theoretical equality to which Dōgen paid lip service. We know, for instance, that he built a nunnery, the Enzūin, on the land of his newly-founded Yōkōji. This nunnery was entrusted to the woman who had given him the land, and who had in the meantime become his disciple under the religious name of Sonin. Yet, despite his interest in the spiritual guidance of female disciples, nuns were still on the margins of his male monastic community. Even if Keizan wanted to save women, was he able to overcome the prejudices of his time? Given the documentation now at our disposal, it would be premature to pass definitive judgments, but it is certain that women played a crucial role in Keizan's thinking and career. It was no doubt due in part to the presence of women at Yōkōji that Keizan put into practice the theory of equality between men and women that had already been preached (though without much effort at practicing it) by his predecessors. The importance of the mother and the intercession of the female figure of the bodhisattva Kannon for Keizan brings to mind other cases, such as those of Myōe and Shinran.[81]

Keizan, while remaining within the framework of the Mahāyāna discourse about nonduality, seems to have been more willing to take a few risks in order to bring this gender equality to pass, in particular when he founded the nunnery at Tōkoku.[82] Women were not excluded from his "mountain," as was the case in many other mountain temples, although his female disciples remained on the margins of the masculine community of Yōkōji.[83]

Some documents of the early Sōtō community at Yōkōji tell us about the relations between Keizan and the nun Sonin. As we may expect, Keizan leaves out any information about her that is not strictly connected to his monastery, and thus we can only conjecture about her life. Of his relationship with her, Keizan simply says that the two of them were "as close as the magnet and the iron."[84] But he does insist on the spiritual progress made by this able disciple, "whose pure acts every day increase in number, while her thought of awakening is steadily refining itself and ripening. Having received the Buddhist precepts and become aware of the spiritual essence, she has cut through and rejected all passions and thoughts of desire, and she is intent on the pure practice of those who have 'left the family.' "[85] Toward the end of the year 1321, Keizan notes a "dialogue" in the course of which Sonin pronounced her "first extraordinary words," the preliminary signs of her awakening. In 1322, when Keizan built a nunnery on Yōkōji land, it was Sonin who was charged with running it. This convent fulfilled several functions: it was a place of prayer (bodaiji) for the soul of Keizan's grandmother and, in accordance with the wishes of his mother Ekan, for the salvation of women and for the success of Keizan's conversion work. In 1325, just before his death, Keizan named Sonin the mother superior of Hōōji, in Kaga province. She survived him and died in her eighties. Her tombstone was recently found, along with several others, just outside the precincts of Yōkōji. Yet despite her intimate relationship with Keizan, and the fact that she received his Dharma transmission, Sonin was not included in the official lineage of his school. Only one late source, the *Nihon Tōjō rentōroku*, attests that she really had received the robe of the Dharma (thus the succession) from

Keizan. The latter's progressive thinking was all but forgotten by the To-kugawa period, although the egalitarian rhetoric of Zen fared well.

Dōgen's earlier views on women also disappeared in the process of the expansion of the Sōtō school, and the head temples refused admission to women until the Meiji era. This discriminatory policy was strengthened and institutionalized under the religious control of the Tokugawa shogun-ate in the seventeenth century.[86] Paradoxically, one may think that, if the Sōtō tradition became increasingly sexist, it is largely due to the "return to Dōgen" and his "pure Zen" that marked the reform of Zen in the Edo period. This "pure Zen" was purely monastic, and basically hierarchical.

In a short piece by the Edo Zen master Suzuki Shōsan entitled *Two Nuns (Ninin bikuni)*, a young woman, after experiencing the traditional soteriological paths of Buddhism, discovers the ultimate nondualistic truth of Zen owing to the kind of rough treatment that Zen masters call the "kindness of an old woman." Her spiritual journey begins when, at seventeen, she loses her husband, a twenty-five-year-old warrior. This is followed by the death of the young woman who had given her shelter, and with whom she had planned to go on pilgrimage. She sees her friend's corpse decay, week by week, following the traditional pattern of the Nine Faces of Death.[87] This is in itself significant, as one rare example of a woman who meditates on impermanence through the decaying body of another woman. Finally she becomes a nun in a mountain temple and meets there another nun who criticizes the decadence of Buddhism, but also tells her that there is no difference between man and woman: "Never, in any case, should you think your body real. For all that you are a woman, then, before whom need you feel ashamed or inferior? It is clearly taught that there is no fundamental difference between man and woman."[88] She finally meets another old nun who teaches her about the ten worlds and, again, about the impurity of the body. Then she teaches her the *nenbutsu*. But when even this does not work, the old nun changes tactics, and resorts to Zen maieutics. Seizing the young nun's robe, she asks "Who are you?" and presses her to speak. She then knocks her down twice, shouting: "It's nothing, nothing at all!" Upon which the young nun suddenly reaches awakening, recalling a dream she had had one night near a chapel, when a skeleton danced and sang "It's nothing, nothing at all." Lest we misinterpret this touching bildungsroman, we must recall that Suzuki Shōsan was one of the strongest advocates of the patriarchal values of "Tokugawa ideology," and his gruesome description of the decay of the female corpse draws on standard misogynistic Buddhist ac-counts of the female body.

Even though it was rarely translated into social practice, the egalitarian principle could justify various forms of female rebellion. This principle may explain in part the appeal of Zen to women. Rhetoric is not necessarily always empty. In the "dialogue" of the nō play *Sotoba Komachi*, for instance, Komachi replies in Zen terms to two Shingon monks who scold her for behaving improperly as a woman. Once again, an old woman of lower status resorts to Zen rhetoric to defeat arrogant monks. Zen thought seems to have been used at times by women to resist the dominant ideology.[89]

The egalitarianism of Zen, just like its apparent opposite (the sexist discourse of traditional Buddhism), can be read as condoning the established order, preempting any attempt at social change and rebellion. It also allows, however, for the creation of a space of inner freedom, a distancing from social roles and norms that could have a dissolving effect and threaten social order. Like most religious beliefs, it can be used by both conservatism and anarchism, undermining as well as strengthening the social and ideological order. It is therefore more ambivalent than the traditional sexist discourse. It is also more dangerous, inasmuch as it looks like a liberating doctrine, and its ideological nature usually remains unseen: for most scholars, Western and Japanese alike, Dōgen, for instance, is a truly egalitarian thinker. Such optimism is perhaps outdated. Rather than wondering if medieval Zen masters named some exceptional women as heirs to their teachings because they believed that enlightenment is genderless, we might precisely question whether enlightenment is, or ever was, genderless, and further whether the enlightened person should transcend gender (*and* sexuality).

Things and people are not always what they seem. Looking at real practices, we find that egalitarian rhetoric did not imply equality, but conversely, that inegalitarian rhetoric was not always followed to the letter. To give just one example, while the Five Obstacles became for some a mere topos, the deliverance from these obstacles tended to remain a sexist ploy. Consequently, we should be wary of any teleological schema that privileges one of these rhetorics.

Perhaps the two rhetorics differ only in appearance. Actually, in many cases, the one is merely the continuation of the other. Even when the Buddhists' assertions seem positive—for instance, when they assert the possibility of the salvation of women and argue that sexual difference does not obtain at the level of ultimate truth—they are weakened by the proselytizing context and the afterthoughts of the preachers. Often, what we find is not an interest for women as such, but a desire to broaden one's territory, to encroach on the preserves of rival sects, and to differentiate oneself from others by offering more radical theories. Although these theories are rarely followed by practical effects, they have the merit of opening the door to changes.

The alleged interest of Buddhist reformers for the people is usually confused by scholars with an interest for the cause of women. Such is not the case, inasmuch as antifeminist representations circulated among the people themselves, even if these representations were less powerful in the lower strata of society than in the ruling elites. Conversely, the implication of women in monastic life (as it can be observed in the Ritsu, Rinzai, and Sōtō schools) does not reflect a greater opening toward the people, but results from a renewal of monastic interest in discipline (*vinaya*). The interest in women, like that in outcasts (the *hinin* and other subhuman categories) is sometimes the mark of an authentic Buddhist compassion, but it can just as well be a kind of noblesse oblige, an elitist approach to the question of poverty, a condescending humanitarian attitude cofirming the status quo (the nobility of the helpers, the debasement of the helped). It creates or maintains the status (and gender) difference while diminishing some of its effects.

The discourses on inequality and on salvation are usually considered separately—one being seen as negative, the other as positive. It appears, however, that these two discourses are intimately related; the salvationist discourse presupposes the guilt and therefore is not purely emancipatory. Conversely, the discourse on female guilt is not as plainly negative as it seems since it leads to salvation. They are two dialectical moments: inequality leads to equality (salvation), but salvation itself becomes rhetorical, since it takes place in the future and justifies present injustice. When we turn to the rhetoric of equality, we may suspect that a similar dialectic is at work. In other words, the denial of gender at the ultimate level presupposes its preservation at the conventional level.

The story of the *nāga*-girl (or the rhetoric of salvation) in fact connects the two rhetorics of inequality and equality. As long as it is used in the first discursive field (inequality), it is seen as a gradual development. When it is used in the second field, it is a sudden realization: gender differences are not gradually obliterated (in practice), but purely and simply denied— in principle. Yet because Chan, unlike traditional Mahāyāna, no longer accepts the dialectical value of conventional truth (and upāya), it deprives its egalitarianism of its dialectical element: instead of having two faces (each of which contain the other), it has only one face (itself Janus-faced): its rhetoric of equality can be judged as a tool of oppression. But its conventional/sexist aspect no longer leads to salvation (because the passage between conventional and ultimate—like that from gradual to sudden— is denied in principle in the name of a strict adherence to the ultimate/ sudden teaching. This prevents Chan masters from paying attention to the real predicament of women.

More important than the blatantly sexist theory are the real practices: those of Buddhist monks, but also those of the women who are the object of the theory, and their reception of the latter. The whole question is to know whether Buddhism was liberating *despite* its sexism, or whether liberation is merely an *alibi* for its sexism. Actually, the two positions are not exclusive, and Buddhism cannot be reduced to a single position on that matter. We should therefore attempt to avoid the reductionism that characterizes most commentators.

In the Buddhist model, man comes first (and last); that is, after and before the Buddha. In Mahāyāna soteriology, one thus has the schema: buddha (nature) → man → woman → man → buddha. Maleness is the mandatoy stage in preparation for buddhahood—just like monks are the necessary mediator between women and the Buddha. Thus, woman is secondary in relation to man. Yet in another sense, it is the sexual difference that is secondary in relation to the primordial unity or nonduality: even in Tantrism, the primordial duality is always derived from a more primordial unity. And it is this sexual difference that *simultaneously* creates man and woman. Thus, *in principle* man has no logical, ontological, or chronological priority.

Hence there remains the possibility of an ethics that does not take gender into account. But Derrida, for instance, deconstructs the apparent "neutrality" of this transcendence.[90] The transcendent (beyond or prior to) any duality is already marked by masculinity. There is therefore no contradiction between the two discourses (of inequality and equality). One can acknowledge the importance of the utopian quality in Buddhism—as long as it is a "well-tempered" utopia—neither pure immanence nor pure transcendence. Awakening itself, as a realization of transcendence, is by the same token strangely masculine insofar as it remains the metaphysical abstraction of the "neither . . . nor." Yet as a vibrant affirmation of reality in its elusive emptiness it may actually be gendered. Is sexual difference therefore a quasi-ontological difference, which at the same time deconstructs any ontology, in typical Buddhist fashion?

PART TWO

IMAGINING BUDDHIST WOMEN

Chapter Five

MONKS, MOTHERS, AND MOTHERHOOD

ONE TYPE of woman that the Buddhist monk could not simply ignore or debase was his mother. The feeling of guilt or longing toward the woman he had left behind to enter the Buddhist order forced him to confront the issue of motherhood. Maternal imagery, of the type found in Christian monachism, where the abbot of a monastery often described himself as a "mother," is not totally absent in Buddhist monachism. As the monk Zhiwei put it, "My father and mother engendered my physical body, my Dharma-Master engendered my Dharma-body."[1] The relationship between a monk and his master was described rather as the tie between father and son. Thus, to "leave the house" was to leave the mother (and more generally, woman and kinship) but it was also to enter another house (this time a "male," *that is* not a gendered one), the saṅgha. The presence of women in this order was only accepted inasmuch as they had been "purified," and their gender symbolically erased. The newly ordained monk was welcomed into a new (male) descent group, with the ancestors' blessing given by the elders. Buddhist masters were symbolic fathers, and the ritual of initiation sometimes involved a vivid representation of male procreation.[2] Buddhism (or at least some Buddhists) dreamed of a male lineage in which spiritual fathers would beget sons—sometimes literally, as in the cases of the "true disciples" who were both the biological sons and Dharma heirs of a priest.

Although one would expect fathers to be exalted as begetters in a patriarchal tradition like Buddhism, they are conspicuously absent, perhaps because the biological father is displaced by the spiritual master.[3] The case of the father of the Buddha, King Śuddhodana, is only partly an exception, perhaps because the Buddha did not have a master. According to a tradition concerning Śuddhodana, "When he died, the Buddha and Nanda were at his pillow, and Ānanda and Rāhula were at his feet. And now at the time of his father's obsequies, the Buddha shouldered his father's coffin, in order to admonish sentient beings in our latter age against ingratitude for our fathers' and mothers' loving care."[4] Even so, Śuddhodana was only nominally Śākyamuni's father, since the latter's conception was "immaculate," involving an oneiric white elephant. Many other birth stories of eminent monks deny entirely the role of the father as begetter. A typical case is that of the mother of the priest Gonzō, who became pregnant after dreaming that a bright star entered the bosom of her dress.[5]

The Sōtō Zen master Keizan also tells us how his mother, Ekan, was impregnated during an auspicious dream.[6] She dreamed that the light of the sun entered her mouth (the mouth becoming the displaced sexual organ, through which immaculate conception occurs). The mother of Keizan's disciple Gasan Jōseki prayed to the bodhisattva Monju (Mañjuśrī) to obtain a "child of wisdom," and she became pregnant after dreaming that she had swallowed a "sharp sword." The mother of Gennō Shinshō, Gasan's disciple, was also granted a handsome boy in response to her prayers to Kannon.[7]

As the notion of filial piety penetrated Buddhism, both parents were included in their children's prayers. Yet, although we often hear of mothers who have fallen into hell, and of sons who want to save them, rarely do we hear of sons saving their fathers, or daughters their mothers. This suggests the extent to which faith itself came to be gendered. In a few cases, the relation between father and child is more developed, but it is also more conflicted. Thus, although Miaoshan's father was saved by his daughter, according to Steve Sangren Miaoshan "preserves her purity, but only at the expense of filial piety. As Kuan Yin, her true identity, she intercedes on behalf of not only her father, but all souls tormented in hell. . . . In the process of attaining bodhisattvahood, Kuan Yin has essentially denied her role as daughter and wife and taken on the role of mother."[8]

BAD MOTHERS

Buddhism abounds in stories of helpless mothers who have become hungry ghosts and need to be rescued from hell, usually by their son. Probably the most famous instance is that of the mother of Maudgalyāyana (Chin. Mulian, Jp. Mokuren).[9] Mulian's efforts on behalf of his mother are presented as the origins of the festival of the "Universal Salvation" of the dead, a festival that greatly helped to anchor Buddhism in Chinese society. Thus, contrary to the Confucian cult of ancestors, Buddhism seemed concerned with female forebears. This is perhaps more a manifestation of remorse than a radical change, however, to the extent that the Buddhist "cult of ancestors" remained essentially patriarchal. Mulian's mother was no paragon of virtue, and the description of her wickedness only serves to highlight the virtue of her son.[10] In most Chinese versions of the legend, she is described as "greedy," and guilty among other things of having refused to offer food to monks. In a Japanese variant found in the *otogizōshi* "Mokuren no sōshi," by contrast, Mulian's mother is portrayed as a model mother. Yet, she is reborn as a hungry ghost as a punishment for her obsessive maternal pride.[11] The "sin of motherhood," based on blind love of a parent for a child, is expressed by the topos of the "darkness of heart" (*kokoro no yami*) of the mother.[12] Another case is that of the mother of the Chinese monk Zilin (fl. 765), a woman damned because of her motherly love: when she gave birth to him, she ate chicken eggs, and smeared egg whites on the sores of his head. When Zilin implored the god of Tai shan to forgive his mother, the god told him: "If you go to Mao shan [in Zhejiang] and worship at the stūpa of King Aśoka, she may be forgiven." The next morning, Zilin, following the god's instructions, went to the Juzhang Mountain Monastery where he kowtowed and cried out sorrowfully . . . forty thousand times. He finally heard someone call out his name. Looking up into the sky, he saw his mother amidst the clouds, thanking him and saying: "By the force of your efforts I have been born in Trāyastriṃśa, and so I have come to thank you." Upon these words, she disappeared.[13]

The desire of a mother to protect her own child was fanned by a patriarchal polygamous system in which women had to compete for men's favors and in which the mother's own identity was derived from that of their child. Stories of stepmothers abusing their stepchildren to benefit their own offspring are another expression of the perpetuation of the same reality. This "darkness" (and the sense of ephemereality that provokes it) is reflected, to take one example, in the *Kagerō nikki*, the diary of the "mother of Michitsuna," whose entire life revolves around the whims of an increasingly estranged husband and the uncertain future of her child. She is trapped in her role as a mother, and all her fears grow in a kind of vacuum, loosely connected with reality. Because she live in quasi-reclusion, her son becomes everything for her. This explains why madness is a potential outcome for such women: their love for their child, turned into obsession, could lead them to a kind of living hell—let alone to damnation after death.

The motherly love for a child can sometimes become pathological, and turn into its opposite. The dark side of motherhood finds its extreme expression in the story of a Japanese monk named Sanuki-no-bō, who, during a visit to hell, ran into a hungry ghost who tried to devour him. He was rescued by the bodhisattva Jizō, who revealed to him that the ghost was his own mother, who had fallen into an evil destiny, and for whom he should henceforth hold memorial services.[14] The story is reminiscent of that of Mulian's mother, but the point here is that, transforming the mother into a kind of ogress, it reveals the deep ambivalence of the son toward his mother. The ogress-like qualities of motherhood also appear, inverted, in the story of Hārītī, the motherly ogress, who, once converted by the Buddha, became a protector of children. As Hārītī's figure suggests, there is a fine line in Buddhist legend between blind love and ghoulish desire: even oggresses feel motherly love, but conversely, even loving mothers have something of an ogress in them.

The Ambivalent Mother

Alan Cole observes that "sometimes [the mother] is presented as the only woman without sin, at other times she is the most sinful of women. Even more interesting are presentations in which she is both."[15] A case in point is the story, mentioned earlier, of the consort of King Bimbisāra, Queen Vaidehī, whose is represented on lateral panels in the Taima maṇḍala. Here, I want to briefly examine Vaidehī's ambivalent relations with her son Ajātaśatru (Jp. Ajase). The prediction that her husband, King Bimbisāra, would be killed by his own son led Vaidehī to try to abort, but the child survived. This episode, when Ajātaśatru discovered it later, led to his hatred for his mother, a sentiment referred to by Japanese psychoanalysts as the "Ajase complex," and extolled as the Japanese counterpart of the Oedipus complex. It is supposed to express the unresolved animosity felt by Japanese men toward their mothers as a result of the prevalence of the "maternal principle" in Japan.[16] Ajātaśatru, however was also jealous of his father, and had him put in jail. To save her husband from starvation in his cell, Vaidehī found a rather interesting expedient: she spread a paste of milk and honey all over her body, so that the king would be able to gain nourishment by licking her fragrant body.[17] When Ajātaśatru wanted to kill Vaidehī for disobeying his orders, his ministers reminded him that, although according to the Veda, numerous kings were parricides, none ever killed his own mother.[18] They argued that such a despicable act would necessarily mean his banishment from the *kṣatriya* caste and cause him to fall to the rank of outcast (*caṇḍala*).[19] Ajātaśatru eventually changed his mind, but nevertheless put his mother into jail.

The rest of the story explains the presence of Vaidehī on the Taima maṇḍala. The forlorn mother prayed to the Buddha for help, and he appeared to her in her cell. When she asked him where she could find refuge from such evil, he told her about Amitābha's Land of Bliss and taught her how to visualize it. Subsequently, Vaidehī obtained salvation.[20] Despite this "happy ending," Vaidehī remains a rather ambivalent figure. The motif of the mother who attempts to get rid of her son in order to protect her husband, as also that of the woman who defies death to nurture her starving husband (in a way that has strong erotic overtones), deserves further study, and not only by psychoanalysts.

Mater Dolorosa

We recall that Māya, the Buddha's biological mother, died soon after his birth. Her premature death is usually explained by the belief that the mother of the Buddha could not allow herself to be sullied by sexual intercourse. According to another tradition, her death afforded a way to avoid the terrible pain that would have been caused by the "great departure" of her son Gautama. The *Lalitavistara*, for instance, states: "The mothers of the Bodhisattvas of the past also died seven days after giving birth. And why so? Because the Bodhisattva, having grown up and in the fullness of his strength, when he leaves the family, his mother's heart would break."[21] Thus, although we are told that she became an arhat in her female body, even Māya could not escape the grief of motherhood.

Despite her early death, Māya retains the features of the *mater dolorosa*. The story of the former life of Śākyamuni as Prince Sudhana suggests what Māya's grief could have been had she not died first. As the prince is about to leave, the queen weeps and says:

> My body is like a stone, my heart is no longer within me. You are my only child. Even if I could gaze upon you forever, I would never tire of it. Since I heard that you must go so far away, my spirit has faltered, and I have lost my senses. When I was pregnant with you, I was happy as a tree when it bears blossoms. Since I gave birth to you, I have doted on you as a tree dotes on the fruit it bears. I never thought that you would leave this kingdom and go so far away, abandoning me here.[22]

Despite this heart-rending scene, the prince leaves with his wife and children. To show his unflinching generosity, however, he gives them away as slaves. Fortunately, he finally listens to his father and returns home after one year, and is reunited with his whole family.

We hear very little of Māya's sister, Mahāprajāpatī, in her maternal role, perhaps because she was reunited with her adoptive son when she became a nun and eventually obtained salvation. In one text, however, we are told that she became blind because of weeping over Gautama's departure from the palace. She recovered her vision upon the Buddha's return to Kapilavastu, when his wife Yaśodharā bathed her eyes with water that had flowed from his body at the time of the "twin miracles" of water and fire.[23]

Despite the sharp contrast between Māya and Mulian's mother, both need the intercession of their sons. The legend of the Buddha shows him concerned for the salvation of his mother—this woman whom he compares to a "jade woman"—one of the seven treasures of the *cakravartin* king. In a famous legendary episode he ascends to the Trāyastriṃśa Heaven in order to preach to her. His triumphant return to earth came to be staged in China as part of the festivities at the end of the summer retreat, implying that the act of repaying the mother is consummated in a public festival on the fifteenth of the seventh month. There is an interesting parallel between the Buddha's ascension to the Trāyastriṃśa Heaven and Mulian's descent into hell.[24] Later, at the moment of entering *parinirvāṇa*, when he is already apparently gone and stiff in his coffin, the Buddha returns temporarily to life in order to preach one last time to the woman who has given him life. In the Japanese tradition, Māya became even more important. In the *Shaka no honji*, for instance, Gautama's religious quest is said to have been motivated by his desire to save his mother and to be reunited with her. Indeed, it is now the realization of her absence that leads to his initial aspiration for enlightenment, and not, as in the mainstream hagiographical tradition, his four "encounters" (with a sick man, an old man, a corpse, and a monk) during excursions outside the palace.

Chinese Mothers

Alan Cole has described the Buddhist recuperation of Chinese family values such as filial piety and mother-son love. He shows how Buddhist authors drew on nearly all aspects of reproduction including parturition, birthing, breast-feeding, and child-care to construct various forms of "family values" that clearly sought to problematize, and even demonize, biology for Buddhist ends.[25] Buddhist texts increasingly asked sons to feel indebted to their mothers for the kindness (*en*) shown by giving birth to them and breast-feeding them.

Cole does not distinguish between "social" motherhood and "biological" maternity. Motherhood was not perceived as being as "natural" as fatherhood in China, however. The "natural" mother (*shengmu*) was eclipsed by various socially determined mothers, and she was recognized only when legitimized by marriage.[26] In this way, Chinese patriarchy tried to weaken the biological bond between mother and child and to privilege the father. The role of the mother was limited in some cases to serving as a receptacle for the child procreated by the father, giving it birth and "nurturing" it. In Cole's words, Buddhists "asserted that the womb acts as a landing strip which allows the new person, in the form of gaseous consciousness, to spin out of the intermediate realm between death and rebirth and take up residence on the human plane."[27] While Buddhism tried to capitalize on the mother-child relationship, it also subscribed to Confucian notions. Thus, an early Tang apocryphal scripture, the *Sūtra on the Importance of Parental Love*, declares

> The Buddha said, "In this world our parents are closest to us. Without parents we would not be born. We are lodged in our mother's womb for ten months, and when the time is ready, the child is born and falls on the mat. . . . When he is hungry and needs food, only the mother will suckle him. When the mother is hungry, she swallows her bitterness and gives out sweet words; she allows the baby to sleep in a dry place while she herself occupies the wet spot. Only the father will love him, only the mother will nurture him. . . . Vast and bound-

less indeed is the love of a mother for her child. How can one repay such a loving mother?"[28]

On the whole, however, Buddhism downplayed the role of the father. By emphasizing the pivotal mother-son relationship and providing ideological support—against Confucian etiquette and patriarchal conceptions of motherhood—for what Margery Wolf has described as the "uterine family," Buddhism was properly encouraging a form of "incest" (in the etymological sense according to which *incestus* is the antonym of *castus*, "educated," "who conforms to rules and rites").[29] Wolf concludes that "the structurally 'troubled' reality of the Chinese family is due to the friction between the patrilineal interests and the uterine family's."[30]

Likewise, Cole argues that "the uterine family" of mother and son found a voice with the emergence of Buddhist-style filial piety.[31] In a sense, Mulian can be seen as a spokesman for uterine family dynamics, and all he did, when saving his mother, was repay the "milk-debt."[32] Significantly, much of Chinese Buddhist discourse revolves around such notions as birth-debt and milk-debt and displays a fairly explicit mother-son eroticism.[33] The image of lactation, in particular, became a prominent motif in Buddhist images of motherhood. For instance, when Māya understands that the Buddha is coming to visit her in her heavenly abode, she spontaneously begins to lactate. The milk pours into the Buddha's mouth, albeit from a distance. When Māya sees that she is again suckling her son, she goes into raptures of delight that "shake heaven and earth."[34] The motif of motherly milk as proof of kinship is a recurrent one in tales of miraculous birth.[35] In the *Konjaku monogatari shū*, for instance, we find the story of the consort of King Pañcala, who gives birth to five hundred eggs. Later on, these eggs hatch into five hundred boys, who recognize their mother when she presses her breast and milk spurts into each of their mouths.[36]

Maternal milk not only provided nourishment for the child; as "transformed yin blood," it was also believed to transmit genetic characteristics.[37] The emphasis on breast milk, with its erotic connotations, also represents a radical expansion of traditional conceptions of filial piety. Lactation is no longer perceived as a simple physiological fact, but is now construed as a miraculous event revealing the karmic bonds between mother and son or as as intentional sacrifice on the mother's part. The *Sūtra on the Filial Son*, for instance, elaborates in significant fashion on traditional clichés about the self-sacrificing mother: "She was so completely sincere [in her caring for her child], even to the point that she turned her blood into milk."[38] The theme of the milk-debt, described in the Chinese context by Cole, was also found in Japan, as shown by the following verse attributed to the priest Gyōki: "If I do not now repay / My obligations to my mother / Who nursed me with her abundant breasts / Then when shall I? / For the years fly by as quickly / As the passing of one short night."[39] Above all, a mother's milk symbolized her love. Yet this very physical maternal imagery could sometimes lead to a kind of regressive fixation. In the *Nihon ryōiki*, for instance, we are told of an adult son who, as he was dying from a fatal disease, said: "It will prolong my life if I drink my mother's milk." The mother consented to his desire. Sucking her breast, he lamented, saying, "I am abandoning the sweet milk of my mother and dying!" and breathed his last.[40]

THE FORSAKEN MOTHER

The tension between uterine and monastic lineages, and the pains of the separation between mother and son, are poignantly expressed in a song entitled "Farewell Mom!" (*Haozhu niang*), retrieved among the manuscripts found at Dunhuang:

> Let the mother work hard to keep the empty house!
> Farewell Mom!
> The son wants to enter the mountain in order to cultivate the Way.
> Farewell Mom!
> Let the brothers work hard to watch over their mother.
> The son wants to enter the mountain to sit in dhyāna.
> Turning his head, he prosternates toward Wutai shan.
> On Wutai shan are planted pine trees and thuyas.
> He sees them truly reaching heaven.
> Arriving to the high mountain, he sees the Four Seas in the distance.
> Tears fall from his eyes by several thousands streams.
>
> The separation during this life cuts their lever inch by inch.
> They have left each other this morning, and they are separated for ever.
> He has just separated from his mother, and they will no longer be together.
> When will come the time to see each other again?
> The milk debt has not been repaid.
> He vows to become a buddha to repay his mother's kindness.
> Father and mother think of their son—their entrails are going to break.
> The son thinks of father and mother—a thousand streams of tears.
> He has renounced the love of father and mother.
> The only company he needs is his monk's robe.
>
> Farewell Mom![41]

Cole argues that the Buddhist discourse about mothers is one of indebtedness. As the above example shows, however, the motif of indebtedness is sometimes intertwined with an assertion of independence from family ties. When he "leaves the family," the new monk becomes in principle "unbound" (Jp. *muen*) and no longer obeys the "law of the house" (*oikonomia*), the "general economy" of the karmic debt. In practice, however, Chinese monks vainly fought to assert this principle, arguing that they were no longer bound by filial piety, or at least did not have to show respect to their parents. In many cases, ordination must have been experienced as a mixture of nostalgia and remorse, and this may explain why the image of the abandoned mother so haunts Buddhist literature.[42] As Cole points out: "What really shocks the historian is the way that many authors sent, narratively speaking, their mothers to [hell]." Yet the mother "is also released from hell by her loving son and therein lies the heart of the complex."[43] Accusations of a lack of filial piety have long plagued Buddhism. Already in India, the Buddha was accused of destroying families. In China, monks were accused of abandoning their parents and of interrupting ancestral rites by refusing to produce offspring. They attempted to reply to Confucian criticisms by arguing that "leaving the family" was more efficacious and more ecumenical than Confucian filial piety because it assured salvation, not only to a few generations of ancestors, but to the larger family of all sentient beings.

"Kill Your Mother"

In Chan/Zen literature in particular, the tragic fate of the mother seems above all to enhance the intransigent virtue of her son. The best known—and, to a Confucian ear, the most scandalous—example is Linji's injunction to kill one's parents. Linji himself emphasized, however, that his statement was not meant to be interpreted literally, but allegorically, and explained that the "father" in question is ignorance, and the "mother," concupiscence. Nonetheless, his words resonated at a deeper level with his disciples' experience. The symbolic murder of the mother, in particular, is often staged in Chan/Zen stories. A case in point is that of Huangbo Xiyun, who had left his old mother to become a monk. One day, during an alms-begging round, he happened to pass through his native village. His mother, having recognized him too late, ran after him and eventually drowned while crossing a stream at night. Huangbo, aware of the accident, came back to the river bank, and threw a torch into the water. At that moment, the body of his mother floated to the surface, which he interpreted as a sign that she had obtained salvation. The "throwing of the torch" subsequently became an essential element in Chan/Zen cremation rituals.

Another pitiful story is that of the mother of the Chan master Dongshan Liangjie (807–69). Abandoned by her son, she was reduced to begging. Having found his whereabouts, she called on him, but he refused to receive her. She died of grief on the threshold of his monastic cell. Liangjie collected the rice found near her and mixed it with the morning gruel of the monks as a funerary offering. Subsequently, his mother appeared to him in a dream and praised him for having shown such firmness: owing to it, she had been able to put an end to her illusory attachment and as a result she had been reborn in heaven. The story is quoted by Keizan Jōkin, who comments: "Zen masters are all equal in virtue, but Dongshan, the founder of our school, made Zen particularly prosperous. This is owing to the merits obtained by leaving one's parents and keeping one's determination."[44] Although Keizan tried to emulate Dongshan Liangjie in all things, he maintained a more ambivalent attitude toward his own mother, the nun Ekan, and he remained deeply attached to his uterine lineage. The first convent founded by him, Enzūin, was dedicated to the memory of his maternal grandmother, and its main object of worship (*honzon*) was a statue of the bodhisattva Kannon that he had inherited from his mother.[45] Thus, the relations between Keizan and his mother seem caught in the double-bind between familial ideology and monastic ideal. The gap between the monastic ideal of autonomy vis-à-vis the mother and the psychological or sentimental reality could not be so easily bridged.

Monastic conceptions eventually spread outside the monastery. Thus, the legend of the miraculous birth of the Fifth Patriarch, Hongren (601–74), as it was told to laywomen by Buddhist nuns, contained a message of resignation for mothers. In the *Jinpingmei*, for instance, a nun by the name of Wang tells women how master Zhang, a former incarnation of Hongren, abandoned his eight wives to become the disciple of the fourth patriarch Daoxin.[46] The gist of the story is as follows: After six years of ascesis, Zhang receives the Dharma transmission from his master. As he is too old to now spread his teaching, however, he decides to reincarnate himself one last time. He therefore asks "shelter" from a young girl who is washing clothes by the river. When she refuses, he throws himself without a word into the river. Upon returning home, the girl finds herself mysteriously pregnant. At this point in the story, the narrator inserts a supposedly reassuring comment: "The fifth patriarch [Hongren] has chosen to be reborn in this maternal belly for the salvation of living beings. Do not regret anything! The ancient buddha, when descending into this world, finds himself commonly reincarnated in the womb which he borrows, and only much later will he save his mother." In the meantime, the girl is expelled from home and she soon gives birth to a boy. Mother and son find refuge in the house of a Mr. Wang. After six years, the son, "no longer looking after his mother, went straight away to the dried-up tree by the side of the muddy river, collected the Three Jewels and went to hear the predication of the fourth patriarch at Huangmei Monastery. Thus, the fruit of his destiny was accomplished. Later, he achieved the salvation of his mother, who was reborn in paradise."[47] The moral of the story seems to be that a monk, as long as he has not reached awakening, has no time to waste on filial piety or on remorse. True, the mother is saved in the end, but this fact is mentioned almost incidentally, and seems irrelevant to the plot.

The same viewpoint is expressed by Dōgen, in what constitutes a remarkable piece of Buddhist casuistry. When one of his lay disciples asked him what he should do about his mother, since he was her only son and she could not be expected to survive alone, Dōgen advised him to find some way to provide for his mother's livelihood and to become a monk. He further asserted the disciple's responsibility by declaring that, if his desire was sincere, he would find a way to get out of his predicament with the invisible help of protecting deities. To illustrate his point, he brought up the story of the Sixth Patriarch, Huineng, who had abandoned his old mother in order to study with the above-mentioned Hongren:

> The Sixth Patriarch was a wood-cutter in Xinzhou prefecture. He sold firewood to support his mother. One day, at the market place, he aroused bodhi-mind while listening to a customer recite the *Diamond Sūtra*. He left his mother and went to Huangmei. It is said that he obtained ten ounces of silver and used it to supply clothing and food for his mother. I think that this was given from Heaven because of the sincerity of his aspiration. Ponder this thoroughly.[48]

Dōgen's desire to prove the superiority of monastic life leads him to contrast the figure of Huineng with that of Layman Pang, another famous Chan master. He argues that the latter could not have been enlightened since he had not severed his ties with his family: "Layman Pang gave up his treasures, but not the dusty world. He must be called an utter fool!"[49] Dōgen concedes that it would be preferable to first fulfill one's filial duty and to become a monk after burying one's mother. The mother may outlive her son, however, and in such a case not only would the opportunity to become a monk have been wasted, but both the son and the mother would feel guilty about it. On the other hand, becoming a monk now would bring great merit for both:

> If you abandon your present life and enter the Buddha Way, even if your mother were to die of starvation, wouldn't it be better for you to form a connection with the Way and for her to permit her only son to enter the Way? Although it is most difficult to cast aside filial love even over aeons and many lifetimes, if you give it up in this lifetime being born in a human body, when you encounter the Buddha's teachings you will be truly requiting your debt of gratitude. Why wouldn't this be in accordance with the Buddha's will? It is said that if one child leaves home to become a monk, seven generations of parents will attain

the Way. How can you waste an opportunity for eternal peace and joy by cling-
ing to your body in this uncertain ephemeral world? Consider this, and ponder
these points thoroughly on your own.[50]

Incidentally, Dōgen's mother died while he was still a child, and this
perhaps explains why he could be so adamant in such matters. Despite
his advice to forsake traditional filial piety, some of his disciples felt otherwise. Gikai, for instance, is said to have left the abbotship of Eiheiji to
care for his mother, and his disciple Keizan, as we will see, remained very
attached to his mother.

Despite the relative efficacy of Buddhist rituals—such as those based on
the Mulian legend or on Huangbo's story—the salvation of the monk's
mother remained on the whole a pious wish. Maternal love was indeed
often sacrificed by the monk on the altar of awakening. In a family-centered
society, this situation led naturally to intense feelings of regret and guilt.

Those stories of mothers abandoned to their tragic destinies by their
sons must have sounded particularly scandalous to Confucianists. Chan
advocates such as Guifeng Zongmi or Qisong worked hard to prove not
only that Buddhists did not relinquish filial piety, but also that theirs was
superior to Confucian filial piety because it was not limited to relatives,
but included the incomparably larger family of all sentient beings.[51] In
their ecumenism, however, they overlooked one of the primary functions
of filial piety: to preserve and differentiate family lineages. Referring to
the Chan/Zen monks' abandonment of their mothers, the Edo scholar
Tominaga Nakamoto offers the following criticism: "Śākyamuni's teaching certainly takes filial piety seriously. However there really were mad
inversions in later times such as the affair of the Ōbaku monk [Daigito,
who took no notice of his mother's starvation]. It was for such fellows
that hell was invented. In general, in the Buddha Dharma in China there
is much estrangement of parents. This arose out of [a desire to] frustrat[e]
the Confucians and in India it is not evident at all."[52]

Japanese Mothers

In Japan, despite Dōgen's statement, monastic ordination did not always
imply a radical break with the mother. Such a break did at times occur,
however, when a monk went to study in China. An eloquent example of
maternal grief is provided by the poetic diary of the mother of the Tendai
monk Jōjin, after her son's departure for China in 1072, where he was to
die nine years later. Her personal name is not known, and her identity as
"Jōjin's mother" derives from her son. She was apparently a member of
the Minamoto lineage stemming from Daigo Tennō (r. 897–930). She had
two sons, whom she pushed into the Buddhist order after the death of her

husband. At the age of eight, Jōjin became the disciple of a Tendai master named Mongyō, and succeeded him as abbot of Daiunji in Iwakura. In 1054, he was nominated *ajari* (instructor), and was thereafter often called to the palace. He was also one of the four chaplains of Byōdōin, and went back and forth between the two places. After the death of Go-Reizei Tennō in 1068, Jōjin returned and called his mother near him. Everything went well for her until the fateful day in 1070 when he told her of his desire to go on pilgrimage to Mount Wutai. Although he was already seventy at the time, this did not deter him. After Jōjin's departure, it was Jōjin's brother who took care of their mother, but he never occupied the same place in her heart, and she only refers to him as the "Vinaya Master" [*risshi*].

In her diary, Jōjin's mother tries in vain to understand the disaster that has befallen her. Ironically enough, she attributes her son's project to some bad karmic cause. Interestingly, she compares her state of dereliction to that of Śākyamuni's father, Śuddhodhana, after his son "left the family," since Śākyamuni's mother, who died just after his birth, did not have the time to get attached to him.[53] She remembers Jōjin's childhood and her constant care for him. She also recalls how he refused to let her accompany him to Kyushu, and how, when she reproached him for neglecting his filial duty, he replied that those who search for awakening must reject everything. She oscillates between despair and hope, and prays for their ultimate reunion in the Pure Land. She rejoices when she receives a letter from Jōjin, soon after his arrival in China. In 1073, she notes that her health is failing, and tries to find comfort in the thought of the Pure Land. She closes her diary on a note of hope: "If my sins like dew / That disappears in the morning sun / Came to disappear entirely / Why would not the evening moon / Take me away?" On the whole, however, her diary is the bitter record of her abandonment, experienced as absolute disaster. Despite the soothing effect of poetry, it seems essentially motivated by resentment, and intended to remain as a ghost haunting her son.[54] Jōjin, however, hardly seems to have been haunted by his mother's memory. Only two passages in his own diary refer to his mother. In the first one, he sees a mantra of Amitayus on the wall of an inn and wishes that he could "transmit to Japan the causes and conditions for women to change their body [into a male one]";[55] in the second, the sight of the eighty-five-year-old mother of an inn-keeper reminds him that his mother is the same age.[56]

There are other examples of Japanese monks who abandoned their mothers to go to China. The *Shoku Nihongi* (766) mentions that an official title was conferred upon the mother of Fushō, one of the two monks who went to invite the Chinese Vinaya master Jianzhen (Jp. Ganjin) to Japan. She was probably promoted because of her son's achievements—although her promotion is dated 766, twelve years after Fushō's return.[57] Another well-known case is that of the mother of Chōnen. Before embarking for China in 983, Chōnen performed a Buddhist service on her behalf, and offered the following written vow:

> In the heart of this son of the Buddha [Chōnen], there are things difficult to endure. Let the Tathāgata elucidate them. My old mother is at home, and she is sixty. My gratitude for what I have received from her is truly deep. If I abandon her to go to China, it goes against the way of filial piety. But if I stay with her without going to China, it goes against my long-cherished desire to go to China. Thus I first had many thoughts about this, and I finally talked about it with my mother. Not only did she manifest no anger at the thought that I may abandon her to go to China, but she advised me to do so. At times I rejoice at the thought that she advised me thus, at times I cry at the thought of my mother's heart. My mother is not an ordinary mother, but a predestined mother, who strengthens good causes, namely my trip to China. Even though many people may try to dissuade me from going, I cannot listen to them.[58]

Chōnen was forty-five at the time, his mother sixty, and his father was probably already dead. Like Jōjin, Chōnen asked his brother to take care of her, and, in the event of her death, to take charge of the funeral. Before returning to Japan in 986, he obtained a replica of the statue of Śākyamuni made on order of King Udayana when the Buddha visited his mother in the Trāyastriṃśa Heaven. After his return to Japan, he enshrined the statue at Seiryōji, on the western outskirts of Kyoto.[59] When he obtained the statue, Chōnen must have had in mind the image of the Buddha preaching to Māya. It is not known whether his own mother was still alive when he returned with the statue in 986.

Mothers as Teachers

In Buddhist discourse, the functions of giving birth and nurturing are often contrasted. In their role as educators, the mothers of monks sometimes emulate the classical paradigm of Mencius's mother. A case in point is that of Genshin's mother: when her son sent her a gift after performing lectures at the court, she rebuked him, saying that she wanted him to become a saint and not a prelate.[60] Likewise, Keizan's mother watched carefully over the spiritual and monastic career of her son, whom she believed was promised to an exceptional destiny. According to Keizan's own testimony, it was his mother's lifelong prayers and admonitions that helped him to overcome all karmic obstacles. She becomes not only a "good friend" (kalyāṇamitra), but a replica of Māya and an earthly double of the bodhisattva Kannon.

> When she was thirty-seven, my merciful mother dreamed that she was swallowing the warmth of the morning light, and when she woke up she found that she was pregnant. She then addressed the following prayer to the Worthy

[Kannon]: "Let the child I am carrying become a holy man or a spiritual guide. If he is to become a benefit to men and gods, give me an easy delivery. If not, o Kannon, use your great divine power to make the insides of my womb rot and wither away." With this prayer on her lips, for seven months she prostrated herself 1,333 times each day, reciting the *Kannon Sūtra*. At the end of this time, she had a natural, painless childbirth. . . . Later, all the events that marked my life were determined by maternal prayers to the Venerated [Kannon]. I was able to reach adulthood without any problems, leave my family and study letters, cultivate the Way and produce wisdom, and finally inherit the Dharma and become an abbot, and come to the aid of men and gods—all this due to the prayers [that my mother addressed] to Kannon.[61]

Toward the end of his life, Keizan pronounced two "adamantine vows," one of which was "to respect the final words of my merciful mother, the elder sister Ekan. She was a bodhisattva who worked for the well-being of women, and I would not dare disappoint her. I must dedicate myself to her last wishes and respect them."[62]

From the standpoint of an eminent priest like Keizan, the idealization of motherhood (or rather, of one particular mother, his own) could have several motives. He may have been simply responding to the topos of the "milk-debt." He may also have wanted to enhance his own self-image as a Zen master. Unlike the hagiographical image of the ascetic as a man who wants to sever all of the ties that keep him bound to this world—and in particular, the bond between mother and son—the image of the priest as holy man implies a glorification of his mother, who becomes the channel through which greatness (*his* greatness) entered the world.

The Sublimated Mother

In Freudian terms, the figure of the mother is ambiguous because it represents extreme safety and supreme risk, life and death, tenderness and sensuality.[63] When this ambivalence becomes objectified as an opposition between the distinct figures of the virgin and the whore, each of the mother's attributes is dissociated from its complement. The act of dreaming, however, reassociates that which had been dissociated through the effects of repression or denial. For Freud, therefore, the whore is a mere substitute for the mother and she retains all of the characteristics of the latter. This ideological double-bind of male perception—women as pure mothers and defiled whores—may explain in part the uneasy attitude of Buddhist monks toward those women who followed "the way of all flesh," falling into sin to give birth to their sons, as was required for the latter's eventual salvation. Only in a few hagiographical cases were the mothers of eminent monks perceived as remaining free from the defilement of sexual intercourse. We have already discussed in the case of Māya and other "sublime" mothers the topos of immaculate conception (which associates the motif of "purity" with that of "auspicious event"). As such monks, being temple founders, became the objects of local cults, their mothers came to be glorified as local deities, mediating between ordinary women and their saintly sons. From the standpoint of a female follower, the founder's mother was in the best position to intercede on her behalf with the former's saintly son, and thus it is not surprising that the mother became in turn the object of a female cult.[64]

Women prayed to the holy man in order to be reborn in the Pure Land, but they also prayed to his mother for more mundane benefits, such as easy childbirth and abundant lactation. These superlative mothers became the symbols of mountain temples and shrines and contributed to their prosperity. For instance, the mother of Kūkai, who, as we will see, was worshipped at Jison-in (at the foot of Kōyasan) as a deity of childbirth, received ex-votos (ema) representing female breasts. Similar images were also offered at Mikumari Shrine in Yoshino, whose most important icon was Tamayorihime, the mother of the mythical ruler Jinmu. This development was partly the result of a play on words: the name of the shrine, read originally as mikumari (water-dividing), came to be read mikomori (protecting children).

Although Kūkai had nothing to do with the growth of the cult of his mother, there were cases in which a priest would address his prayers to a sublimated image of his absent mother. The well-known story of the priest Myōe cutting off his ear in front of an image of Butsugen Butsumo (Skt. Buddhalocanā, a deity whose name, in Japanese, signifies "Buddha-Eye, Mother of the Buddhas") is perhaps the most extreme case. Myōe wrote afterwards: "I take refuge in mother, my mother. / The beloved child of Śākyamuni, Jōben, / Who has been forsaken after the Buddha's entrance into parinirvāṇa. / [Signed] With reverence, the mountain beggar of Kishū."[65] Although Myōe's case can be seen as a typical case of sublimation, we must resist the temptation to force our materials into the procrustean bed of Freudian or Jungian theory.[66] The image of the mother in Buddhism is not merely an archetype in the "uncharted deep," but also a historical representation that varied considerably depending on time and place.

THE CHANGING IMAGE OF MOTHERHOOD

Ōsumi Kazuo has noted that, whereas the mothers of Chinese monks are rarely mentioned in Buddhist hagiography, those of Japanese monks often play a significant role in the lives of their sons. In the biographies of eminent Japanese monks, where the point is often to show that the monk in question had been a child bequeathed by the buddhas (mōshigo), little is said about the father as begetter, nor about family lineage. These "biographies" usually emphasize the miraculous signs preceding the conception and birth of the future holy man. This hagiographical structure may reflect the influence of native cults, in which women played a crucial role.[67] There are, however, other reasons that may explain why mothers play such a prominent role in the lives of Buddhist monks. On the basis of our earlier discussion, we could argue that monks cared so much about their mother precisely because they had lost (or abandoned) her, and because of their ambivalent feeling toward a person to whom they were deeply indebted, but whom they saw as (physically and sometimes morally) defiled.

Many scholars have noted that mothers were highly respected in early medieval Japan. The legal codes of the Kamakura period, for instance, paid much more attention to the role of the mother than those of subsequent periods. Paradoxically, the avowed respect for motherhood developed in aristocratic circles, precisely where women were most crudely the objects of male exchange. In his *Gyokuyyō*, for instance, Kujō Kanezane argues that women are superior to men because every woman is the true mother of the buddhas of the three periods, whereas no man is their true father.[68] With the sublimation of motherhood, motherly love received a new ethical significance as a symbol of the boundless compassion of the buddhas and bodhisattvas.[69] In *Gukanshō*, Jien (1155–1225) emphasizes the suffering of the mother during delivery, and he urges his readers to express indebtedness and gratitude to mothers, since all people owe their existence to their mother. He also describes the central role of women—both as daughters and mothers—in Heian politics:

> The truth of the old saying that women provide "the finishing touches" (*nyonin jugan*) in this country was revealed by the appearance of [. . .] reigning Empresses.[70] In trying to understand the basis for this in the Buddhist teachings, I conclude that the phrase "birth of the human world" clearly points to the meaning of the fact that people are all born from the wombs of women. The pain that a mother suffers in childbirth is indescribable. . . . So the principle that a person should try to take care of and revere his mother was followed. Reigning Empresses Jingū and Kōgyoku were placed on the throne because each was the wife of the previous Emperor and also the mother of the Crown Prince.[71]

Thus, Jien justifies the existence of female rulers (from Jingū and Suiko to Shōtoku) and the subsequent Fujiwara consorts by the fact that they were "mothers of the country" (*kokumo*), not by their own capacities or charisma. In other words, even though motherhood was highly honored, and Japanese rulers of the Heian period may have considered their consorts the apples of their eyes, these women were mere instruments in the matrimonial strategies of the Fujiwara or Taira regents. How little status women gained from their part in these matrimonial strategies can be seen in the following story, reported in the *Ōkagami*. Having heard that one of the daughters of Kaneie was pregnant, the retired emperor Sanjō asked Michinaga whether this was true. Michinaga went to see the young woman and told her that he wanted to make sure that she was pregnant: "So saying he forced open her breasts and twisted them, whereupon what should happen but [the milk] squirted quickly over his face. Without saying another word, he left the scene at once. Coming to the Crown Prince he reported, "It is true!"[72] We need to qualify Jien's earlier statement: only legitimate motherhood was to be extolled. Although in this case the pregnancy was illegitimate, it does not change the fact that women were treated as commodities. These young women may not have perceived their situation in this light, as we can see from Kenreimon'in's words: "As Chancellor Kiyomori's daughter, I became the Emperor's mother and held the country in the palm of my hand."[73] This instrumental image of motherhood (and daughterhood) as a commodity in matters of kinship—daughters used as progenitresses—is at first glance rather different from that of the mothers idealized by Buddhist priests. The medieval emphasis on motherhood can be seen paradoxically as a symptom of women's loss of status.

The Buddhist attitude toward motherhood was particularly ambivalent: while valuing it to some extent, Buddhism also turned it into a cardinal sin. Although they may have been uttered by sincere monks and filial sons, passages like "the Buddha himself was born from a woman" or "all women are the true mothers of the buddhas of the three periods" should not be misconstrued as feminist statements. Even when Buddhism seems to show respect for motherhood, as it did in medieval Japan, this does not mean that the status of women was improved. On the contrary, we have seen that the sphere of action for women diminished in the patriarchal system of late medieval Japan. Indeed, their value was gradually limited to the procreative function.

The monastic discourse about motherhood proliferates around an absence, and is reinforced by feelings of nostalgia and survivor's guilt. The mother, as vanishing mediator, is memorialized (and commemorated) through rituals or priestly concerns for women in general.[74] Many women, after the deaths of their husbands, became "widow-nuns" under the spiritual guidance of their sons. We also hear of monks, who, after the deaths of their mothers, performed funerary services on their behalf every year. We have letters of vow (*ganmon*) written on this or other occasions, like donations of fields or icons, and the copying of sutras for the mother's memory.[75] The *hokke hakkō*, a series of eight lectures on the *Lotus Sūtra*, were initiated in the eighth century by the priest Gonzō (754–827) in memory of the mother of his friend Eikō. The latter, a Daianji monk, had for years sent food daily to his aged mother, who lived in the vicinity of his temple. When Eikō died unexpectedly, Gonzō, fearing that the shock would prove fatal to the old woman, kept his death secret and continued to send food to his mother. She eventually found out the truth, and died soon thereafter. Full of remorse, Gonzō devised the eight lectures in her memory.[76]

The question of finding out the postmortem destiny of their mothers was a matter of some urgency for many monks. A particularly interesting case is that of the Shingon priest Ningai. After his mother's death, she appeared to him in a dream and told him that she had been reborn as a horse. Ningai, after a frantic search, eventually found the horse, but the latter died before he could do anything for it. Ningai then drew two mandalas on the horse's skin, thus symbolically connecting the deceased (mother and horse) to the realm of the buddhas.[77] A variant of this story involves the monk Shakunō, who, having come to Kyoto in search of his mother, arrives at the Sekidera Pass. There, he finds a recalcitrant mare that its former owner had abandoned after cutting one of its ears and its tail to "cut its ties" and disengage his responsibility. Shakunō feeds the mare for thirty days, then dreams that he is riding it with a young monk, when the latter pushes him down, saying: "This is your mother." The mare then confirms that it is indeed his mother, and that she has been reborn as an animal because she once refused to give water to someone. When Shakunō wakes up, he expresses his filial piety by worshipping the mare, but the latter soon dies, and Shakunō eveually draws a mandala on its skin.[78] Another example worth mentioning in this artistic context is the funerary service performed by the Zen master Musō Soseki for his mother when he was still a novice. According to the *Sangoku denki*, on this occasion, Musō made a painting of the "Nine Phases of Death."[79] The *Musō kokushi nenpu* adds further details: Musō is aged thirteen, and the nine phases (or "faces") of death are more precisely those of his mother's body.[80]

VARIETIES OF MOTHERLY EXPERIENCE

As Tonomura Hitomi has pointed out, although the reality of parturition and motherhood may form a continuum from a woman's perspective, "the discourses concerning them, however, developed along two separate lines for different social and economic reasons, and they seem to impart meanings that are mutually contradictory."[81] Even though the discourse on motherhood seems limited to biological mothers, in the social practices of the time the notion of motherhood extended beyond biological maternity to include various types of socially defined "mothers," such as the stepmother and the wet-nurse. Perhaps the blood-relationship between mother and son was emphasized precisely because other "mothers" threatened to displace the biological mother. In patriarchal society, maternity is not identical with motherhood. Significantly, the woman who nurtured the future Buddha is not the one who gave birth to him. Although the delivery is said to have been very easy, Māyā died soon after, and thus she probably never had a chance to suckle her newborn child. As noted earlier, this role fell to Mahāprajāpatī, Gautama's stepmother (and maternal aunt). In all likelihood, the newborn prince also had one or several wet-nurses. Perhaps we should also recall in this context that, after his strenuous asceticism, a young maiden offered him milk, creating another sublimated milk-debt by nourishing his exhausted body and allowing him to reach enlightenment (itself a kind of initiatory rebirth).

The two parallel figures of the wet-nurse and the stepmother loom large in the imagination of medieval Japan. The wet-nurse is usually represented as a paragon of abnegation. Although the fact is rarely mentioned, she, like the biological mother, is tied to the child by lactation. Since milk was believed to transmit genetic traits, the milk-debt toward her must also have been a deep one. Due to the increasing patriarchal reluctance to leave boys with their mothers, wet-nurses were also the primary channels of cultural transmission. They were indeed a perfect commodity for patriarchal society, even though some of them, owing to their close ties with the child, were at times able to exert in turn a considerable influence on the clan's destinies and on court politics. Their image eventually merged with folkloric motifs, which we will discuss later.

With the exception of Mahāprajāpatī, stepmothers are usually represented as evil women in countless stories of "stepchild abuse" (*mamako ijime*), as that of Chūjōhime. Another tale, even closer to the Cinderella motif, is the *Ochikubo monogatari*, in which everything revolves around the rivalry between sisters in their quest for a husband.[82] Lady Ochikubo is the daugher of an official with the rank of *chūnagon,* and of a secondary wife of royal blood. After her mother's death, her father's main wife treats her like a servant and keeps her in an annex room (*ochikubo*, hence her name). The son of an influential family, Michiyori, hears about her and, visiting her at night, falls in love with her. The stepmother, discovering their relationship, becomes enraged and calumniates Ochikubo, telling her husband that she had sexual relations with a servant. The abused father breaks with his daughter, who is locked up by the stepmother and betrothed to an old man. Michiyori kidnaps her, however, and begins humiliating the *chūnagon* and his family. When Ochikubo gives birth to a child, she becomes Michiyori's main wife. Michiyori eventually reconciles himself with the aging father. After the latter's death, Ochikubo takes care of her stepmother and her half-sisters, and she herself becomes the mother of a royal consort.

Another (in)famous stepmother is that of Semimaru, the blind musician of Ausaka Barrier. In Zeami's Nō plays (*Semimaru* and *Ausaka mono-*

gurui), the blind beggar Semimaru is actually a prince abandoned by his father, Emperor Daigo. In Chikamatsu's play *Semimaru*, his blindness is said to have been caused by the jealousy of his wife when she discovered his love affair with a young woman named Naohime. The maternal nature of Naohime is revealed at the beginning of the play, when Emperor Daigo, during an inspection tour, sees her breast-feeding, not only her infant (who will turn out to be Semimaru's child, and therefore Daigo's grandson), but also her aged mother—a literal repayment of the milk-debt. The play, appropriately enough, ends with her second pregnancy and the apotropaic recitation of the *Ten Months of Pregnancy*, a scripture describing gestation as a ritual process under the protection of the buddhas. A related tale is that of Shuntokumaru, the young son of a rich householder, who, because of the calumnies of his stepmother, is driven away from home. Having become a blind beggar, he wanders like a madman and ends up at Tennōji. His remorseful father, believing him dead, goes to Tennōji during the spring equinox to pray for him. Now the deranged Shuntokumaru appears and begins to dance and sing, and his father, having recognized him, brings him back home.[83]

The stepmother's evil nature has been toned down in the *Ochikubo monogatari*. Likewise, in the Semimaru plays, the stepmother is replaced by Semimaru's main wife, and the "stepchild" in danger of being harmed by the latter is the yet-unborn child in Naohime's womb. The evil stepmother resurfaces in a Kabuki play entitled *Female Semimaru*, where Naohime replaces Semimaru as main protagonist. She is abandoned on Mount Ausaka by order of her stepmother, after the latter has gouged out her eyes. Here, the motif for the stepmother's cruel act is her desire to marry her own daughter to the ruler.

These poignant tales, influenced by the medieval motif of the "suffering god," have one Indian precedent in the story of Aśoka's son, Prince Kunāla, who was exiled after being accused of incest by his stepmother. In this case, the motif of her action is not jealousy, but unrequited lust turned sour. Pursued by her hatred, Kunāla has to gouge out his eyeballs to obey a royal edict bearing an apparently unmistakable proof of authenticity— Aśoka's own teeth marks. These marks, however, were surreptitiously taken by Kunāla's evil stepmother while the king was inebriated.[84] Kunāla is eventually reunited with his father and recovers his eyesight.

In all of these legends, the stepmother's plot is eventually discovered, and familial harmony restored with the reunion of father and child. The figure of the stepmother is not only what, from the point of view of the tale's structure, one could call an essential "actant" or narrative function, she is also a reflection—perhaps a distorted one—of certain social realities, or at least an expression of medieval conceptions about a certain type of woman. In the polygamous patriarchal context of early medieval

Japan, the main wife exerted power over all of the children in a family, even when the biological mother of her stepchildren was still alive. She felt threatened by younger wives and concubines, however, and this could cause her to harbor negative feelings toward these younger women and their offspring. Thus, the emergence of stories about evil stepmothers in medieval Japan can be read, not simply as the resurgence of a traditional folkloric motif, but rather as an index of the tensions generated by the patriarchal system.

In tales of abused children, two distinct motifs can be distinguished, depending on whether the stepmother's jealousy or hatred is expressed toward a male or a female child. Sometimes, she is jealous of both together, as in these stories of persecuted brother and sister.[85] In the case of a female child, if we consider the stepmother as a narrative substitute for the mother, another reading, whereby the motif is employed to euphemize the conflict between female generations (mother and daughter), is possible. The emphasis on menstrual blood, in Chūjōhime's story, seems also to point in that direction: the appearance of menses, marking puberty, is the clear indication that the time for the change of generations has come.[86] In the case of a male child, it is clear that the stepmother, if she does not herself have a son, will be overpowered when he reaches maturity and becomes the head of the house. Even in that case, however, another reading can apply that sees the stepmother as a veiled reference to the mother, and her lust for the boy as an allusion to the danger of mother-son incest.

Even if we do not choose this kind of reading, we may, instead of simply accepting these stories' description of the arbitrary power of the stepmother, emphasize her sense of powerlessness; for instance, her awareness that she is no longer attractive to her increasingly distant husband.[87] The debasement of the stepmother may represent, in veiled terms, that of the main wife, a perception of her arbitrary power from the standpoint of other spouses.[88] The story of the abused stepchild can point toward (at least) two radically different situations. The evil stepmother can either be the main wife, seen from the standpoint of secondary wives; or she can be the contending secondary wife herself, in the case of the death of the first (that is, main) wife.

In the divine world of these tales, normal relations of power no longer obtain: stepmothers are eventually punished, whereas abused children experience a final apotheosis that reveals their divine nature.[89] The emergence of such stories seems to coincide with that of the *ie*, a "house" founded on the *yometori-kon*, a type of marriage specific to the aristocratic class, in which the stepmother and the child do not live together.[90] In the microsociety of the "house," the main wife is represented as an evil woman who tends to abuse her power. This may be a case of blaming the victim, however, in which the stepmother plays the role of a scapegoat. These apparently simple fairy-tales tend to invert real relations of power, and ought not be read as transparent reflections of social reality.[91]

Mad Mothers

A recurrent theme in Nō plays is that of the mother separated from her child. The separation results in the mother's madness, which can only be cured by the reunion with her (usually male) child. Even when this reunion fails to occur because of the death of the child (for example, in *Sumidagawa*), a semblance of presence can be obtained through oracles and mediums who bring his spirit momentarily back. Thus, contrary to an aristocratic society that emphasized the sinful nature of motherly love, the world of popular arts maintained a more positive relationship between mother and child, and the dances of the miko or *shirabyōshi*, as well as those of Nō plays, constituted ways of praying for the reunion of mother and child.

The emergence of the theme of the maddening bereavement of the mother separated from her child to some extent reflects the social reality of a period when the privileged bonds between the biological mother and her child, threatened by the development of patriarchal society, were becoming increasingly tenuous. In late medieval Japan, the blessings of the mother were no longer emphasized, and women were gradually losing the traditional support from their matrilineal lineage for giving birth and raising children.[92]

The motif of the deranged mother is already found in early Buddhist literature. Its locus classicus is the story of Kisāgotamī, a woman who had lost her mind because of her child's death, and who, upon meeting the Buddha, realizes the universality of her predicament and takes refuge in the Three Jewels. In the *Therīgāthā*, too, we hear the testimony of Vāsiṭṭhī, a woman led to madness by the hubris of material love:

Afflicted by grief for my son, with mind deranged, out of my senses, naked and with dishevelled hair, I wandered here and there.

I dwelt on rubbish heaps, in a cemetery, and on highways. I wandered for three years, consigned to hunger and thirst.[93]

In Japan, however, the loss of a child was not always the result of a death; it could also have social causes such as abduction. Likewise, the madness that often ensued was a socially codified way to express bereavement. To make things even worse, the loss of a child for a mother often meant her rejection by her in-laws' house and by society, her "banishment" and condemnation to vagrancy and perhaps madness—an ordeal during which she often acquired some shamanistic characteristics.

Mad mothers appear in a large number of Nō plays.[94] In the play *Hyakuman,* for instance, Zeami depicts the devastating effects of the separation between mother and child. He writes that, just as the Buddha ascended to Trāyastriṃśa Heaven to preach to his mother, all children should long and mourn for their mothers. The main protagonist, Hyakuman, is a dancing-girl from Nara, who was separated from her son near Saidaiji. Her wandering leads her to Seiryōji, on the western outskirts of the capital, where she prays to find her son at a great *nenbutsu* ceremony. She dances like a madwoman in front of a crowd, in which her son happens to be. He recognizes her and they are finally reunited. The play seems based on the story of the priest Engaku, who founded Dai-nenbutsu celebrations at Kiyomizudera in Saga, the setting for the play. Engaku had been an abandoned child. Even after becoming an eminent priest, he still longed to find his mother, and asked the bodhisattva Jizō to grant him that boon. When his prayer was answered, he built a Jizō Hall at Kiyomizudera.[95]

In the play *Kashiwazaki,* a woman of the Kashiwazaki district learns that her husband has died and that her son Hanakawa has become a priest. In her grief, she wanders through Japan, eventually arriving at Zenkōji. She carries a bamboo branch on her shoulder, a traditional emblem of madness, and suffers the heartless laughter of local children. When she tries to enter the inner sanctum, forbidden to women, a priest stops her. She accuses him of narrow-mindedness and presses closer. Finally, she puts on the keepsake garment and hat of her dead husband, and she offers a dance to the Buddha. The priest, who is none other than Hanakawa, recognizes her and eventually mother and son are happily reunited.[96] As Erika Bainbridge remarks, "Many women could project their personal situation onto the deranged mother's characterization, find vicarious atonement in her derangement, and gain catharsis through witnessing the final reunion with the lost child."[97] Bainbridge also points out that all of the mad mothers depicted in such Nō plays lack husbands, and that the children they lose and frantically try to retrieve are all boys, not girls.[98] Thus, motherly love itself was gendered, and the mother's search for her son was also an attempt to retrieve a rank in society (together with her sanity) by finding the only male relative who could protect her.

THE LAW OF ALLIANCE

Faced with a widening of gender asymmetries from ancient to premodern Japan, historians have tried to conceptualize this complex transformation as a narrative of the growth of patriarchy. This narrative seems at first glance to make sense, even if it requires considerable nuance at times. There is undeniably a connection between the increasing subjection of women and the development of the feudal system (patriarchy being only one aspect of the latter). In ancient Japan, women occupied a central position in the local community organization. Until the medieval period at least, women were relatively less subaltern in Japan than in most other Asian cultures.

Scholars have tended to confuse feudalism, patriarchy, and the *ie* system—related but distinct phenomena. Wakita Haruko argues that "the subordination of women began with the establishment of the *ie* or family system, on which patriarchal authority was based."[99] If one emphasizes changes in marriage practices, one tends to see the shift toward patriarchy taking place in the late Heian and Kamakura periods. If one focuses instead on inheritance practices, the shift takes place later, toward the Muromachi period.

The Kamakura period was characterized by an efficient administration, and as long as this state of things endured it was quite safe to leave landed property to women, who could appeal to respected authority for protection. The situation changed in the Muromachi period, due to the breakdown of peace and order: as the central authority grew weak, military power became the only guarantee of safe possession. The Muromachi period appears as a turning point in several respects: changes in marriage forms, as well as changes in inheritance practices, and consequently in the familial structure, led to the emergence of the feudal system. Thus the period signaled the deterioration of the position of women in various ways: they were reduced to economic dependence, subordinated in the feudal hierarchy, and increasingly subservient to their in-laws.[100]

Another telling sign of rising patriarchal authority was the exclusion of women from official functions. Though basically patriarchal, Tang law, on which the Ritsuryō system was based, had been more tolerant of women in China than were the new institutions in Japan. Hitomi Tonomura has recently argued, however, that, contrary to established opinion, women continued to play an active role in public life during the medieval period.[101]

Although female subjection seems to have reached its peak with the "feudalism" of the Sengoku period (1482–1558), in one sense it became more extreme during the Edo period, as the situation was "naturalized" and given a philosophical basis. The rules of the warrior class gradually permeated the nobility, and eventually the merchant and peasant classes. Women of the merchant class retained greater individuality because of their economic role.[102] At the same time, the return to law and order that marked Tokugawa rule offered some protection to women by stabilizing their status.

Lineage and Family

The term "patriarchy" is too general to describe the specificity of Japanese social structure after the Heian period, in contrast with other "patriarchal" societies like that of Confucianist China. Although the Chinese norm was always patrilineal kinship, things took a turn for the worse in the Song period, when women were gradually excluded from inheritance.[103] As sexual segregation increased, men came to monopolize access to land property, and women became economically dependent on their parents and in-laws. They became an object of lineage negotiations and practically disappeared from public life by the Yuan period, which witnessed an interiorization of Confucian values: filial piety for men, chastity for women.[104] The development of the ideology of filial piety (in Buddhism as well) can be seen as an attempt to control men as well as women. For women, however, the devotion of the wife to her husband came above filial piety. The wife becomes responsible for her in-laws' honor, and the chastity of widows now acquired social and political significance.

Patrilinearity in Japan never implied an exclusive valorization of agnatic filiation; blood ties (*ketsuen*) on both parents' sides were valued. Whereas in China filial piety was turned into a kind of moral absolute, in Japan it always remained subordinated to loyalty toward the political authority. Until the end of the Heian period, on account of contemporary marriage and inheritance practices, women were also less thoroughly integrated into their husband's family than their counterparts in China.[105]

Even the notion of biological filiation lost its relevance when the field of adoption, later on, came to be no longer limited to relatives, often including strangers who were adopted to perpetuate a lineage. The lack of interdiction of marriage between agnates in Japan forms an even greater contrast with Chinese exogamous lineation. The difference with China, where barriers separating exogamous clans can be crossed only by women, is well illustrated in the following excerpt:

> Question: "Grafting is successful when a plum is grafted onto a plum or a peach onto a peach. But other trees will not take. This suggests that those of the same clan would graft, while those of different clans would not." Answer: "Your doubt sounds right, but it is based on ignorance of the essentials. Adoption of any person in Japan with a Japanese endowment of yin, yang, and the five elements is like grafting a plum tree onto a plum tree. But to adopt a person of a foreign country is like, for example, grafting a persimmon onto a peach. Certainly it would not take."[106]

Although the affirmation of patriarchal authority was a condition of the development of the state, the social role of women in ancient Japan was not initially simply a procreative one, in the service of male lineage.

Women of the upper social strata became part of the symbolic capital of their husband's family, but they also had an important role in public life because they could manage and transmit real properties, and could even become head of the house—unlike in Chinese-inspired rules.[107]

The ie System

Whereas the Chinese clan was an exogamous group, in Japan, until the Heian period, the essential element of political and social organization was the clan (*uji*), an endogamous group sharing the same name and the same ancestral deity, the *ujigami*. With the gradual penetration of the Chinese codes, the clan gave way to the co-residential family or household (*ie*), in which the rule of exogamy applied. The Japanese model remained more flexible, however, due to different adoption rules. The clan in the Heian period was a patrilineal institution, whose functions were primarily ceremonial and political in nature; it was related only tangentially to the family life of an individual. The household, on the other hand, was oriented strongly toward the female line.[108] It was essentially matrilineal and failed to coincide with patrilineal clan groups.[109] By the end of the thirteenth century, however, it had become increasingly patrilineal.[110]

The *ie* was a corporate, rather than a kinship, unit, in which the value was not so much on the continuity of the bloodline from father to eldest son as on the perpetuation of the family as a corporate group through its name and occupation. The Japanese priorities, in short, were the reverse of those of Confucian theory: maintenance of its social role across generations was in practice a more important criterion than agnatic descent in the organization of the Japanese *ie*.[111]

The *ie* of the medieval period was managed by one husband and one wife. The responsibilities of the wife included preparation of food and clothing, but also managing the household budget. Not only childbearer or sexual object, the wife of the medieval period had considerable power within the household. Status was accorded not merely as result of her biological ability to bear children, but because of her presence and involvement as manager of household affairs.[112] Perhaps the most typical example is that of Hōjō Masako, who was able to gain control of the shogunate after the death of her husband, Yoritomo.

Marriage

Since the pioneering work of Takamure Itsue, scholars such as William McCullough, Jeffrey Mass, and Wakita Haruko have revealed great differences in the character of Japanese marital and familial relations from period to period.[113] In the Nara and Heian periods, men and women enjoyed relative equality in marriage, along with property rights and membership in the village organization. Marriage as we know it was not yet codified, and at any rate the term covers a multiplicity of practices, described differently by Japanese and Western scholars. For Japanese scholars, the main distinction is between *mukotori* marriage, in which the husband comes to live in the residence of his wife's family, and *yometori* marriage, in which the wife is brought into the husband's household, and which becomes typical from the eleventh–twelfth centuries onward; another transitional type found in the Heian period is *tsumadoi* marriage, in which husband and wife live separately, the husband visiting the wife at her residence.

The main categories used by Western scholars include "virilocal" marriage, in which the wife lives with the husband's family; "uxorilocal" marriage, in which the husband lives with the wife's family; and "neolocal" marriage, in which the spouses live in their own house, apart from their in-laws. A fourth, less common, type is "duolocal" residence, in which spouses live separately, with the husband visiting his wife, but not living with her. The difference between the two types of terminologies is essentially one of perspective. Whereas Japanese categories emphasize relations between persons, Western categories focus on the modes of marital residence. Both have their advantages and disadvantages, but for our specific purpose they are interchangeable. For the sake of simplification, we find chronologically (and logically) two main types—uxorilocal and virilocal residence (or, in Japanese terminology, *mukotori* and *yometori*), with two main intermediary (and transitional) forms, duolocal and neolocal residence.

McCullough attempted to show that marriage residence among aristocrats in the Heian period was never virilocal, but uxorilocal, duolocal, or neolocal.[114] It finally became virilocal only toward the fifteenth century. The most widespread practice until the end of the Heian period was the uxorilocal residence of the husband, in which the husband resided with his principal wife, at least at the beginning of the marriage. Polygamy, which was frequent in aristocratic strata, also led the husband to visit periodically the houses of his secondary wives. The transition between ancient and medieval Japan is characterized by an overall drift leading, first, to the dominance of the neolocal residence in the last part of the Heian period, and, ultimately, to that of virilocal residence in the Kamakura and Muromachi periods.[115] Uxorilocal marriage seems to have disappeared almost entirely by the late twelfth century.[116]

The fact that, in the Heian period, marriage was not always a male-centered institution does not mean that there was gender equality in matters of sex.[117] Scholars have stressed the human anguish caused by duolocal marriage, which in fact allowed for polygamy.[118] The medieval period could thus be defined in terms of marriage practices by the extension of the practice of virilocal residence (or *yometori* marriage), a phenomenon that negatively influenced the status of women. Perhaps this was a necessary development in the evolution of military rule, in which the control of land was crucial. Not all women were equally affected by this system, however. Although virilocal marriage is usually seen as an element of patriarchy, it could mark an increase in status for women without wealth, and thus be actively desired by them. Despite the patriarchal position of her husband as head of the household, the official wife was guaranteed social status and rights in a secure position.[119]

To sum up, marriage in premodern Japan changed from a primarily sexual relationship between a woman and a man to a more publicly elaborate arrangement between two houses (or lineages); and from an arrangement that kept a woman's body stationary (at her house) and the man's body mobile to one that transferred the woman's body to a man's house. As Tonomura concludes: "The transformation in marriage practice signified, above all, the reorganization of sexuality and a social reevaluation of the woman's body."[120]

Procreation, Motherhood, Divorce

In a society where family was the predominant value, the status of women depended, more than anything else, on their aptitude to give birth and to raise children. Many texts emphasize the disgrace of women who had no child. For such women, life was extremely hard.

Female sterility was a major cause of divorce. In the Heian period, divorce was an informal matter that fell outside the scope of the law. The husband or wife who wished for a divorce simply ceased to have relations with the other spouse. Such informality was permitted in part by the financial independence of the spouses, and by the fact that the wife remained a member of her clan even after marriage.[121] Heian women retained their property even once married. The independently owned property of a woman provided her and her children with a measure of security against the loss of her husband and compensated to some extent for the looseness observed in Heian marriage ties.[122] In the event of a divorce, children followed their mother to her parental house, even though they continued to bear the clan name of their father.[123]

We cannot enter into the details of the evolution. Things, however, progressively deteriorated during the medieval period. By the Edo period, letters of divorce, called *mikudari-han* (three lines and a half) because of the manner in which they were set out, were sufficient for a husband to repudiate his wife. Their wording illustrates the arbitrary power of the husband. Here is one example, dating from 1805:

To Fuyu Dono,

It is my pleasure to divorce you hereby. Therefore hereafter there is no objection to your marrying anyone whomsoever.

Witness my hand, the 11th of the 7th month,

Tama Saburō[124]

As noted earlier, divorce was much more difficult for women. Their only hope was to find refuge in one of the few *enkiridera* ("temples for severing relations") that served as sanctuaries for women.[125] According to the *Ritsuryō yōryaku* (1471), for instance: "If a woman, hating her husband, seeks refuge in a convent and serves there for three years, and upon receiving her discharge, submits a petition, she will be restored to her parents' home."[126] In principle, only men could initiate divorce, and only women were thought to commit adultery.[127] Adultery on the part of the husband was not a crime, but the wife's adultery came to be severely repressed, particularly after the Muromachi period. The husband's rights in such cases were legally recognized. The *Tokugawa hyakkajō*, for instance, contains the following statement: "A wife who commits adultery shall be put to death with the man involved"; and, "It is no crime for a husband to kill an adulterous wife and her partner if there is no doubt of the adultery." We must keep in mind, however, that normative texts do not necessarily reflect the reality of practices.

Widowhood and Inheritance

The slow transformation in marriage practices paralleled the gradual diminution of the property rights of women in the aristocracy and in the warrior class. Initially, women were not inferior to men in matters involving property—a condition that might have continued if not for revolutionary changes within the polity. Late in the seventh century, the adoption of codes (*Ritsuryō*) modelled on those of Tang China led to the constitution of an elaborate bureaucracy. This change was translated in the social sphere by a new patriarchal orientation in the organization of the family and its succession system.[128] In the Heian period, however, women were still financially (if not psychologically, as the *Genji monogatari* shows) independent from their husbands. Property was not shared, and husband and wife bequeathed their property separately to their children.

In the civil-military dyarchy of the early Kamakura period, we find endless stories of inheritance disputes. According to Jeffrey Mass, women's gradual loss of autonomy in matters of inheritance toward the end of the thirteenth century was not caused by gender discrimination, but resulted from a simple imbalance between supply and demand: there was too much progeny, not enough property. Thus, the right to alienate property came to be denied to junior heirs (both male and female).

After a short remission at the beginning of the Kamakura period, in which Yoritomo's reforms gave power to warrior women (and his wife and widow, Masako, was the one who most benefited from them), the decline resumed by the late thirteenth century, in particular with the appearance of "life-tenure" inheritances. Widows were obliged not to remarry under penalty of surrendering land rights conveyed to them by their spouses. Women were unable to consummate divorce except by flight, which was a punishable offence leading to the loss of property from a spouse; and, as widows, women were unable to remarry without surrendering their late husbands' lands.[129]

Women's slide downward accelerated in the fourteenth century, as unigeniture (in which the father still had a choice as to which of his sons would be his heir) paved the way to primogeniture. Although women were not eligible for political office, and widows were ineligible to remarry, many women refused to be passive victims: they sued—and were being sued. The striking fact about the Kamakura period is the importance of widows, and their considerable power in certain cases. Women inherited estates and engaged in lawsuits over land. As noted earlier, they continued the work of their deceased husbands, and remained a member of his family. Once again, a prime case in point is that of Hōjō Masako, who, as the "nun-shogun" (*ama-shōgun*) of the Kamakura Bakufu, took the reins of government into her own hands upon the death of her husband, Yoritomo.[130] As noted earlier, many women who entered the monastic ranks during the medieval period were widows (*goke*).

With the military rule of the Kamakura period, a new warrior family unit emerged, in which the family head (*sōryō*) exercised leadership over the extended family.[131] This system, studied by Mass, was a transitional model, different from the later practice of transmitting the *ie* to the eldest son. Patterns of marriage changed together with patterns of inheritance (the chicken-and-egg problem)—as widows or daughters began to receive inheritance limited to their lifetimes, the property reverting to their sons afterwards. This evolution paved the way to the single inheritance.

According to the legal code of the Kamakura Bakufu, "though male and female are different, the debt owed to father and mother is the same."[132] Within the *sōryō* house itself, single inheritance and inheritance for one lifetime only by widows and daughters were becoming common in the mid-fourteenth century. Subsequently, women's inheritance rights came to be limited to one lifetime, and even this was not universally observed.

Even in the late Kamakura period, as the principle of partibility gradually gave way to unigeniture and primogeniture, wives and daughters were still receiving property, both as settlements in perpetuity and life tenures.[133] Signs of drastic changes, however, appeared as early as 1286, when the Bakufu decreed against female inheritances out of a desire to maintain a continous anti-Mongol guard effort. Despite survivals and counterexamples until the beginning of the fourteenth century, primogeniture came to dominate inheritances, from which junior males and all females were excluded.

Already by then, and even more decisively during the fifteenth and sixteenth centuries, the continuous warfare led heads of warrior households to prefer to bequeath the totality of their property to their (male) heir. The principle of the single heir, usually the eldest son, put the daughters in the second rank with wives and diminished their powers. As succession through male primogeniture became the rule, women lost their right to inherit or bequeath property. They were integrated into the households of their husbands and subordinated to their in-laws. All of the authority within the *ie* passed into the hands of the father.[134]

Even though they could inherit, women of the aristocracy and the warrior class were—with a few exceptions—excluded from political office, and thus prevented from accumulating property.[135] By the late fourteenth century, they had also lost their inheritance rights. Among merchants and artisans, however, women's property rights remained strong, and were normally passed from mother to daughter; that is, at least until the end of the sixteenth century, when the holding of commercial property eventually passed into the hands of men. The decisive blow against female property holding was struck with the establishment of a unified polity by Oda Nobunaga, Toyotomi Hideyoshi, and Tokugawa Ieyasu.[136]

The system of primogeniture, prevalent in the warrior class, was never completely followed in peasant or merchant families. In the rural context, women retained in practice a certain authority in business, and were never entirely subordinated, as Confucian ideology wanted, to their parents, husbands, and sons. The image presented by Kaibara Ekken (1630–1714) in his *Onna daigaku* (*Great Learning for Women*) reflects the Confucian ideology of the elite, but this image remained wishful thinking in the case of village life. Indeed, women retained a considerable power of decision in the village until well into the Meiji period.

Women and Japanese Patriarchy

The institution of the *ie* system, characterized by virilocal residence and by primogeniture, has been described as the establishment of patrilineal hegemony. This image, however, is incomplete. As noted earlier, the rights of women to inherit property during the Heian period were not so much a proof of their freedom as a way to compensate in part for female vulnerability caused by unequal sexual relationships. The Heian period was not, as has been often argued, an age of matrilineal hegemony. The role played by women in matrimonial strategies during the Heian period is well known. When the Tendai priest Jien, in his *Gukanshō*, refers to women as providing "the finishing touches" [lit. "inserting the eyes"] in Japanese politics, he has in mind imperial consorts of the Fujiwara clan. In the context of the late Heian court, however, the role of Fujiwara women at court can hardly be described as female agency—they were mere instruments for the political prominence of their clan.

As Haruko Wakita notes, all of these roles and beliefs related to women are centered in the definition and ideology of the *ie*, in which women appear both as mothers and managers. Thus, compared to the unstable position of wives in Heian marriages, the position of the official wife in medieval Japan was quite secure. Wakita argues, quite paradoxically, that the depiction of the medieval *ie* as patriarchal is one-sided, a product of male-oriented analyses that emphasize the role of patriarchy.[137] Indeed, the power of the main wife was not diminished, but increased by the patriarchal authority of her husband, at least in some respects. She became a matron, and a patroness. She ruled over the household's other women and had a more stable situation than in previous periods. Her dependence was a price to pay for domestic security and power. As Wakita has shown, the development of the *ie*, an institution concerned primarily with reproduction processes (sexuality, childbearing, child rearing), explains why women's reproductive processes were depicted in a more positive light in late medieval texts such as the *Shintōshū*.[138] Despite Wakita's assertions, however, there were spheres in which women were disadvantaged. The principal wife was, for instance, often neglected sexually, to the benefit (or the detriment, depending on the case) of younger secondary wives or concubines. Furthermore, Wakita's analysis is limited to the main wife. Here again, the danger is to consider that all women share the same interests, without paying due attention to the divisions created between them by patriarchy. The number of women married into households and becoming official wives remained limited. Most women in households were no more than servants. Moreover, many women who were not considered useful to their households were sent to monasteries, while others became prostitutes or entertainers.[139]

Many factors contributed to put increasing pressure on the patriarchal system in the medieval and Edo periods, and Buddhism was only one of them. This pressure weighed more heavily on the higher classes, due to a kind of noblesse oblige reminiscent of the European process of "civilization" studied by Norbert Elias. Despite the Bakufu's attempts to establish a rigid system of control, women's sexuality remained relatively free throughout the Edo period. Judging from the account of the Jesuit missionary Luis Fróis, one could believe that Edo women did not seem to attach great importance to chastity.[140] In this respect, village women had much more leeway than the daughters of warriors, condemned to chastity by strict Confucian norms. It is not until after the Meiji period that things begin to change, as village life deteriorates under the influence of modernization, and the puritanism of the patriarchal system becomes predominant. Even then, old values and attitudes were resilient, as we can see in John Embree's ethnographic study of the village of Suyemura.[141] It is also toward that time that feminist consciousness began to develop in the upper social strata, and women began to use their sex to vindicate their rights. For the elite, the equality of rights became more real after Taishō (1912–26).[142] Even though the Japanese patriarchal system was not nearly as monolithic as has been too often assumed, and many pockets of freedom remained through the Edo period, the general trend seems unmistakable.

The Role of Buddhism

As a social group and as an ideology, Buddhism was at the same time the oppressor and the victim. It implied a repudiation of familial values—a radical break with civil society and kinship. Although this ideal was never completely abandoned, the necessity of adaptation to patriarchal societies had, from very early on, led to some rather drastic changes. Unlike the Christian Church, which claimed to legislate the relations between husband and wife, parents and children, Buddhism remained discreet in its dealings with the Japanese family. Buddhist priests followed the general practice in prohibiting widows from remarrying, but otherwise they hardly intervened in family affairs.[143] Local communities maintained their hold on people, and Buddhism was never able, like Christianity in Europe, to constitute an ethical horizon that would transcend politics and allow the emergence both of the individual and a private familial sphere.[144]

Buddhist ambivalence toward women was partly determined by social factors such as the primacy of filial piety and patrilineal lineage, into which women were integrated as mothers and spouses. Chinese monks, although they had in principle "left the family," remained more dependent than did their Indian counterparts on social and familial structures. Eventually, despite some initial reluctance, they became the ideological keepers of Chinese society. They came to advocate on the one hand what they denied on the other: the importance of family continuity, and of the procreative role of women, upon which the fate of the lineage depends. At the same time, they offered to some women a means to escape this role—a particularly unrewarding role in a patriarchal society—through ordination as nuns. This ideological double-bind (women as mothers and women as wives, that is, as defiled by sexuality) explains the uneasy Buddhist attitude toward those women who were perceived as transgressing the bounds of their social role.

Yet, Buddhism was especially popular among aging women, whether widowed or not. It offered them a transition to the "third age" and the "third gender"—a third world in which they no longer played an active parental role. With its emphasis on severing worldly ties, Buddhism fostered resignation and provided an alternative support group, constituted of other women, to replace household or kinship ties.[145] Buddhism integrated marginal women, and only in some rare cases pushed normal women toward marginality.

We have seen that the emphasis on motherhood did not reflect an improvement of the status of women. Indeed, as has often been observed, the identification of woman with motherhood contributed to maintain women in a secondary status. It was also one of the reasons that prevented them from entering the Buddhist orders. It seems therefore paradoxical that this view would have been promoted by the Buddhists themselves. But we have noted the enduring reluctance of the male-centered Buddhist tradition to accept women within its ranks. Yet, even if motherhood is usually coopted by the dominant male ideology, it is an important element of women's religion. Therefore, it should not simply be seen from the male viewpoint. Susan Sered, for instance, emphasizes motherhood as the typical female experience and as the source of a polytheism of values that prevents any absolutist, transcendental drift: "The realities of motherhood lead women to diverse sorts of deities that 'fit' the diversity of mothering experiences. Motherhood is not a matter of absolutes, but of particular sorrows, joys, decisions, and personalities. The same factors that encourage the development of immanent deities in women's religions discourage the development of either a male omnipotent god or a female great goddess. Grounded in the here-and-now, in particular relationships, the deities of women's religions tend to be as ambiguous as life itself."[146] In this sense, one could argue that the ideology of motherhood, even if it played a part in the development of patriarchal society, forced Buddhism to hold its fundamentalist tendencies in check and to open itself to the multiplicity of local religions. Thus, women may in turn have been able to use and subvert that male ideology. Not every woman fell into the trap of patriarchal discourse, and accepted her "destiny" as a mother. Owing to the longer view provided by Buddhism, some realized that motherhood is merely one stage within a woman's life cycle, or one of the roles every person will have in one life or another. In the final words of the royal nun Mahāprajāpatī: "Formerly I was mother, son, father, brother, and grandmother. . . . This is my last life."[147] Buddhism's attitude toward mothers is marked by a fundamental ambivalence, which reflects its ambivalence toward the world of immanence (the mother being one of the symbols of immanence and debt). And this ambivalence turned out to be, in the end, a productive double-bind.

I should also reiterate that motherhood is not a simple concept, and that Buddhists, by emphasizing (and at the same time denying) the "uterine" relationship, were far from simply reflecting the complex reality of mother-child relationships. Whether one chooses to affirm motherhood (as limitation) or deny it (repression) in the name of a male vision of experience, one is confronted in both cases with a kind of repression. The ideology of motherhood can serve as well to affirm the power of women as to entrap it. Or rather, it served some women (elite women, social mothers) to obtain a certain freedom at the expense of other women (women of lesser status, biological mothers). As noted earlier, maternity (biological motherhood) was by no means a guarantee of legal (or social) motherhood. In the case of a concubine or secondary wife, her biological motherhood, even if it insured her a more secure position in the house, did not entitle her to legal status as mother. It also did not give her any hope of ever rising to the rank of main wife, who remained the real mother of the husband's recognized sons. Despite this legal hierarchy, each mother tended to favor her own children and to resent those of her rivals, a situation well reflected in the many legends about evil stepmothers.

The ideology of motherhood not only pitted some women against others within the patriarchal family, but also demarcated fertile women from others who rejected (or were rejected from) the procreative path. From this ideological standpoint, which represents the mother as the ideal woman, both the professional nun and the courtesan are deviants. They may differ in their attitude toward sexuality, but they agree in their rejection of procreativity, and in that sense they both constitute challenges to the patrilineage. From a slightly different angle, however, both the wife/mother and the nun accept patriarchal institutions, albeit different ones—the family and the monastery, respectively.

From the foregoing discussion, it is clear that the Buddhist discourse on motherhood, despite its apparently positive tone, often went hand in hand with the subordination of women and their reduction to their procreative function. Nevertheless, as Dorothy Ko illustrates in her analysis of the Chinese context, there are two ways (at least) to look at it: "Cults of domesticity and motherhood may have been promoted first by male literati, but they acquired concrete meaning only as women embraced the ideals for their own reasons. Their affirmation of the Confucian tradition, or their interpretations of it, did not simply serve the interests of the patriarch."[149]

Chapter Six

CONFLICTING IMAGES

THE VARIOUS forms of Buddhist rhetoric discussed so far represent aspects of the normative discourse of canonical Buddhism. Parallel to this, popular tradition offers a slightly different, and at first glance more positive, attitude toward women.[1] Thus, after discussing the theoretical Buddhist discourse about gender, we need to examine emblematic representations of women. Whereas normative theories attempt to constrain the interpretation of gender symbolism, these popular representations tend to acquire a dynamic of their own. Thus, they sometimes reinforce the doctrinal rhetoric, and at other times undermine it. Both movements may even be simultaneous. To give just an example, we recall how, in his rather distorting *Mirror for Women*, Mujū Ichien lists the seven "sins" of women. In the same passage, he provides us with some classical instances of female duplicity. In China, "national calamities" were caused by three women, the most well known being Yang Guifei, the courtesan who brought about the downfall of Emperor Xuanzong (r. 712–56) and jeopardized the Tang dynasty. In Japan, Emperor Go-Toba died in exile after the failure of his coup—the so-called Jōkyū Disturbance of 1221—allegedly instigated by his lover, a dancer named Kamegiku.[2] Mujū, however, also offers as counterexamples cases of female compassion and religious fervor such as the edifying story of Lady Vaidehī in the *Sūtra of the Meditation on the Buddha Amitāyus*, or the episode of the awakening of the *nāga*-girl in the *Lotus Sūtra*. Consequently, Mujū argues, if a woman becomes conscious of the sins inherent to her sex, she may reject the world and find salvation in Buddhist practice.

Earlier generations of feminist scholars attempted to highlight female figures that could serve as potential role models for modern women. One feminist strategy has been to search for remarkable women, divine or human.[3] Although female figures have a lot to tell us, the research of "great men" of female sex seems insufficient. First because as exceptions they tend to confirm the rule.[4] Not only is the model that they offer not very practicable, it contributes to the occlusion of the real problems faced by ordinary women. Such attempts to retrieve (historical or mythological) role models, although valuable, have a tendency to wax hagiographic. An alternative is to consider how official history and popular patriarchal tradition have "demonized" some women—often precisely those women who came to exert real (political or spiritual) power—while glorifying others. One can also focus on the charismatic women who are often the founders of the "new religions," but in many cases we must note the socially conservative character of their teachings.[5]

WOMEN IN THE LIFE OF THE BUDDHA

> And that's just half the story
> of the women in my life
> —Randy Newman

The First Lady of Buddhism is of course Māya, the "biological" mother of the Buddha, although the spiritualized birth of the future Buddha hardly involved any biological process: "Just as though a gem of beryl in a crystal casket were placed on her curving lap, so does his mother see the Bodhisattva like a body of pure gold illuminating her womb."[6] The same is true of the Buddha's son Rāhula, whose birth, according to the *Mahāvastu*, left him and his mother, Yaśodharā, undefiled: "Now Rāhula, passing from Tuṣita [Heaven], came down into the womb of his mother, the Kshatriyan maiden—this my pious friend is the tradition."[7] In Buddhist legend, the role of the Buddha's mother is essentially posthumous, and her death became a paradigmatic element of the birth story of all buddhas: "The mothers of all Bodhisattvas die on the last of the seven days following their delivery of the Supreme Men. Now what is the reason why mothers of an Omniscient die so soon after giving birth to the Best of Men? While he is still dwelling in Tuṣita the Bodhisattva makes this his care as he searches for a mother whose karma is good. 'I will descend," says he, 'into the womb of a woman who has only seven nights and ten months of her life remaining.' And why so? 'Because,' he says, 'it is not fitting that she who bears a Peerless One like me should afterwards indulge in love.' "[8] This is perhaps the first occurrence of a theme that we will encounter again: the denial of the sexuality of Buddhist women considered as *mothers*.

Exit Māya, enter Mahāprajāpatī, the Buddha's aunt, adoptive mother, and first "daughter" (female disciple). In her classic work on women in Buddhism, I. B. Horner hardly paid any attention to Māya, but chose instead to emphasize the role played by Mahāprajāpatī. More recently, Jonathan Walters has presented Gotamī Mahāprajāpatī as a female buddha (or more precisely, as a buddha for women), and underscored the importance of her "life," the *Gotamī-apadāna*, "in the general process of extending Buddhist soteriology to women in all walks of life."[9] According to him, Mahāprajāpatī was held up as the female counterpart of the Buddha. Walters sees as an indication of this the fact that, whereas in earlier Buddhist literature, her name is always given as Mahāprajāpatī, the

Gotamī-apadāna only uses her clan name Gotamī, the female equivalent of Gotama (or Gautama), by which the Buddha was known.[10]

When Gotamī is about to enter into final extinction (*parinirvāṇa*), she bows to the Buddha and says: "It is thought, chief of the world, / that women are all flawed. / If there should be some flaw in me, / compassion-mine, forgive it." She then explains why she has chosen to part with life: "My ears and eyes weren't satisfied / to see you or hear you speak. / But now that I've become perfect, / my mind is quenched by dharma-taste."[11] She consoles the grieving Ānanda, her biological son. The Buddha then says: "Yet still there are these fools who doubt / that women too can grasp the truth. / Gotamī, show miracles, / that they might give up their false views."[12] Gotamī then leaps into the sky and displays her special powers. Having done so, she tells the assembly about her past lives, the prediction of her future enlightenment, and her penultimate rebirth in the Trāya-striṃśa Heaven: "All the other Śākyan women / also went there then. / But of them all I was the best; / I was the Victor's nurse. / My son, once he had left the world, / became the Buddha, the instructor." Gotamī, having forever surmounted all emotional attachments, finally takes leave from the Buddha with these words:

> This is my last look
> at the lord of the world;
> your face, a fountain of ambrosia,
> won't be seen again.
> No more homage to your soft feet;
> I won't touch them again.
> O hero, chief of the world,
> today I go to nonexistence!
> Who needs your face and body,
> with things such as they are?
> Everything conditioned changes;
> it provides no comfort.[13]

Then she finally enters *parinirvāṇa*, to the assembly's grief. The scene concludes with the Buddha's eulogy of this perfect woman—or rather, perfected nun—who has put an end to all rebirths.[14]

Walters' claim that Gotamī Mahāprajāpatī is a female buddha seems exaggerated. Despite her final apotheosis, she remains a mother and a widowed royal consort.[15] In the *Gotamī apadāna*, she contrasts the Buddha's present role as her teacher with her former role as his wet-nurse and nurturer:

> I nurtured your physical body . . . , but this flawless dharma-body of mine was nurtured by you.

I suckled you with milk / which momentarily quenches thirst. / From you I drank the milk of the Dharma, / continually at peace.[16]

Here, Mahāprajāpatī's pride as "the best of the Śākyan women" and the "Victor's nurse" gives way to a more appropriate humility, in her realization that she is the one who has been actually nursed by the Buddha. According to the *Mahāvastu*, Gotamī even became blind because of the tears she shed when her adoptive son left the palace, and was cured only when he returned to Kapilavastu and when Yaśodharā bathed her eyes with water purified by him.[17] Thus, even if Gotamī is a female counterpart of Gotama, she is so in the same way as the physical world is a counterpart of the spiritual world. She plays the role of mother and intercessor, which we will find again in the case of the mothers of eminent Japanese priests. As Liz Wilson points out, "Gotamī encompasses in her life all that Gotama rejects in his. She represents the social locations of consort, wife, and parent—in short, everything that Gotama must renounce in order to become the Buddha."[18] Furthermore, her entry into nirvāṇa does not really outshine that of her adoptive son, as Walters argues. Her motivations are quite different. As she herself states, it is not because she has achieved her mission, but rather because, having placed herself in the care of the younger men of her lineage after the death of her husband Śuddhodana, she is afraid of being left behind when they die: "I can't bear to see the Buddha's final passing, nor that of the two foremost disciples, / nor that of Rāhula, Ānanda, and Nanda."[19]

Even if she was not a "buddha for women," Mahāprajāpatī remained a role model, in particular for nuns, and she seems to have been the object of a cult. In China, for instance, Tao Shan (1756–80) writes in her *Chants of Shame and Embarrassment*: "Mahāprajāpatī Gotamī made a vast and limitless vow / To save every last woman in this world of Jambudvīpa."[20] Although Mahāprajāpatī's death is sometimes associated with that of Lingzhao, daughter of the Chan layman Pang, she entered *nirvāṇa* before her father, and at any rate the meaning of the two episodes differs. Whereas Gotamī chose to die because she did not want to witness the disappearance of her foster-child and spiritual master, Lingzhao tricked her father and disobeyed (or transcended) filial piety by preempting his ultimate move.

The Buddha, when he left home to embark on his spiritual quest, did not only abandon his father and foster-mother, Mahāprajāpatī. He also broke his conjugal ties. His abandoned wife (or wives) did not disappear so easily from his life, however, or from his legend. There is no consensus as to whether Śākyamuni had one or several wives. According to one Vinaya tradition, after his main wife Yaśodharā, Śākyamuni had married two girls of the Śākya clan, Gopikā (var. Gopi or Gopī) and Mṛgaja (or Mṛgarājanyā)—and, incidentally, he also had no less than 60,000 concubines![21] As Mujū Ichien, in his *Mirror for Women*, summarizes: "Although the Buddha Śākyamuni alone is exalted in the Three Worlds and is a tathāgata since remote antiquity, he had three children by three women. These were the monks Upavāna, Rāhula, and Sunakkhatta. Yet we do not speak of the Buddha as being impure."[22] Curiously, it is only when he was about to leave the palace that he decided to impregnate Yaśodharā—in order, we are told, to prove his virility to those who might question it.[23] Yaśodharā is said to have remained pregnant for six years. She eventually gave birth to a child named Rāhula upon hearing that her estranged husband had finally reached awakening. The tradition remains silent about the two other sons of the Buddha.

According to the *Lalitavistara*, the mother of Rāhula was Gopī, and her pregnancy was induced by a mere touch of her belly by Śākyamuni. He did so, again, in order to show his masculinity, but this time without even renouncing his continence.[24] The Tantric tradition, however, explains that the Buddha had reached enlightenment even before leaving the royal palace, through sexual play with Gopī. Thus, Gopī is presented as a sexual initiator into Tantric mysteries, not unlike the "jade woman" of the later Sino-Japanese tradition.[25]

Although Yaśodharā, "The Glorious One," came to play the part of the main (or only) wife, she is practically absent from the early accounts of the Buddha's life. Her initial role is limited to pointing to the Buddha, when he returns to Kapilavastu, and telling her son Rāhula that this is his father.[26] In the later tradition, however, her role develops greatly and she becomes one of the three main figures in the holy family of Buddhism, next to King Śuddhodana and Queen Mahāprajāpatī. We now learn that the love between Yaśodharā and Śākyamuni has been following its course over many lifetimes, and that it is because she was bound to him by karma that she became his wife in his last life. Furthermore, she is now presented as a domestic ascetic, instead of as an erotic tempter. Thus, when she hears that Śākyamuni is practicing austerities in the forest, she starts doing the same in the palace. As a result, the growth of the embryo in her womb is stopped. Only when she hears that Śākyamuni has interrupted his ascesis in order to practice the "middle way" does she resume her normal life, and the embryological process, in turn, is able to reach its term. This contrived plot is supposed to explain why Rāhula was born on the same night Śākyamuni reached awakening.[27] This delayed childbirth led, however, to accusations that Yaśodharā had had an extramarital affair—being abandoned for six years was deemed insufficient for a woman to resume a normal sexual life—and she was about to be condemned to death. In order to prove her innocence, she had to perform an "act of truth." Thus, she put her son on a stone in a pond, and the stone floated. Her innocence was further confirmed when the Buddha returned to Kapilavastu and magically produced five hundred replicas of himself: Rāhula, having been told by his mother to bring a gift to his father, went directly to him.[28]

Nevertheless, the Buddhist tradition has retained an ambivalent image of Yaśodhara. Her desirable beauty could be seen as a negative element from a Buddhist standpoint, but in the broader Indian context it tended to be read positively. On the one hand, because she was initially an obstacle in Śākyamuni's quest, she is depicted as a deceitful temptress; on the other hand, people felt some sympathy for her when they heard of her ordeal, and of the fact that she remained faithful against all odds. She is described as a kind of Indian Penelope, who has to resist the advances of Devadatta, Śākyamuni's cousin and nemesis. Devadatta is eventually evicted when the Buddha temporarily returns from his spiritual odyssey. Finally, even Yaśodhara's attempts to seduce her husband offer insufficient ground to condemn her. Not only does she fail to bring him back, but also she remains lovesick. Thus, whereas all of the other members of the clan convert to the Buddha's teaching—beginning with her cherished son Rāhula, who drinks the love potion intended for his father and falls under his charm—she longs desperately for her husband as a result of an enduring passion provoked by her past karma.[29] Her tragic destiny, however, finds a spiritually correct resolution in some variants of the legend, in which she becomes a nun and eventually reaches enlightenment. In the Vinaya of the *Mūlasarvāstivādin*, in particular, the "glorification" of Yaśodhara causes her to lose some of the human appeal she had in the *Mahāvastu*: she has now become a semi-divine being, endowed with supernatural powers.[30] Along the same lines, the tendency to represent Śākyamuni and Yaśodhara as a model couple eventually prevailed. Another version of the Buddha's karmic relations with Yaśodhara was circulating in Japan, however. The *Konjaku monogatari shū*, for instance, reveals why, although the Buddha treated Yaśodhara with sincere care, she was never pleased or appreciative. According to the Buddha's own explanation, this was the result of a grudge from a past life. There once was, the Buddha tells his disciples, a violent king who was driven out of his palace, and who wandered across the land with his wife. As they were about to starve, he caught a large tortoise. He sent his wife to fetch water, and, while she was away, he ate the tortoise. It is not too hard to imagine her reaction when she found out about his deception. "I am the prince who ate the tortoise," Śākyamuni concludes. "Yaśodhara is my wife who went to bring water. Owing to our karmic relationship in our previous lives, we do not get along well when reborn as man and wife for generation after generation. A mere piece of tortoise meat could cause anger and falsehood."[31]

Female Disciples

If the early Buddhist saṅgha was somewhat reserved in its praise for nuns, such was apparently not the case when it came to famous laywomen, on whom it depended for its existence. Here again, however, things are not so simple. Two such women are Viśākhā and Āmrapālī, whom the tradition contrasts sharply. Āmrapālī (var. Ambapālī) was a courtesan of the city of Vaiśālī whose lavish gifts to the Buddha eclipsed those of all other donors.[32] A well-known episode is that in which she outshines the Licchavi in her giving to the Buddha. According to Georges Dumézil, the structure of this account reflects the Indo-European ideology of the three functions (religion, war, and fecundity). We may note here in passing Dumézil's remark that these functions, represented here by different male individuals or groups (in this case the Licchavi), are sometimes also represented synthetically by one single female figure, human or divine.[33] Yet the monastic tradition, which greatly benefited from these gifts, has not been very grateful for Āmrapālī's, insofar as it has emphasized her hubris rather than her generosity, and described the end of her life in a rather negative fashion. Āmrapālī, we are told, was a courtesan because in a past life she had once referred to a nun as a "public woman."[34] According to the Vinaya tradition, "She charged fifty pieces a night and as a result the city of Vesālī became very prosperous. She bore a son by King Bimbisāra who became the *thera* Vimalakodañña. . . . Having heard her son preach the doctrine, she strove for insight, using her own ageing body as a symbol of impermanence."[35] In the *Therīgāthā*, the verses attributed to her illustrate the aging process of a prostitute.[36]

Although Āmrapālī was wise enough to use her own life for a didactic purpose, she was not as fortunate as Viśākhā, who, it is implied, as a result her generosity produced many offspring and never grew old: "And even as the crescent moon waxes great in the sky, even so did Viśākhā become great with sons and daughters." We are given the figure of 8,420 children, grandchildren, and great-grandchildren. "She herself lived to be one hundred twenty years old . . . [yet] she always seemed to be about sixteen years old."[37] Thus Āmrapālī, the prodigal courtesan, eventually became an old hag—not unlike Ono no Komachi in Japan—whereas Viśākhā, the good wife, brings forth many offspring and remains forever young (a typical feature of the third function according to Dumézil).

The erotic overtones of many of the female figures closely related to the Buddha are striking. Māya herself, the pure mother, is described in terms that recall, not only the Indian *yakṣiṇī*, but also of the daughters of Māra—images of temptation. Like them, Yaśodhara is prisoner of her worldly passions, and in the end redeemed by her love. Her effort to tempt the Buddha brings to mind the case of Ciñcā, a young nun of surpassing beauty. Ciñcā's destiny, however, ends more tragically. Having become a disciple of the infamous "heretic monks"—a group of monks jealous of the Buddha who became the villains of early Buddhism—she began spreading the rumor that she was having an affair with the Buddha. Then she feigned pregnancy by attaching a wooden bowl (or a wooden disk) over her belly. She confronted her alleged lover, accusing him in front of his disciples of having seduced her, "even as a woman with a mass of dung in her hand might seek therewith to defile the face of the moon."[38] Śākyamuni received help from the god Śakra (or, in a variant, from the arhat Maudgalyāyana), who turned into a mouse and chewed through the cord that fastened the bowl (or disk). When the latter fell on the ground her deception was revealed. In a farfetched variant, the disk falls upon her feet and cuts off two of her toes. Then she is brutally driven out of the Jetavana, and as she passes from the Buddha's sight, the earth splits open and she falls alive into Avīci Hell.[39] There is also a *jātaka* version, in which Ciñcā is one of the consorts of the father of Prince Mahāpadma, the Buddha in one of his past lives. She invites the prince to sleep with her, and when he refuses, she wrongly accuses him. The prince is condemned and thrown from a cliff, but he is miraculously saved by the mountain deity and receives shelter in the palace of the *nāga*-king. Afterwards, he goes to the Himalayas to practice ascesis. His father, having heard that he is alive, goes to see him and learns the truth. Upon returning to his palace, he orders Ciñcā to be flung from the same cliff.[40]

Another variant of Ciñcā's story is that of the nun Sundarī.[41] In her case, however, after spreading the rumor that she is having an affair with the Buddha, she is killed by the heretic monks, who abandon her corpse near the Jetavana. They then accuse the Buddha's disciples of having eliminated her to cover up their master's fault. Fortunately, the deception is discovered when one of the murderers, drunk, boasts of his crime. Here, her guilt seems redeemed by her tragic end. In both cases, we are faced with wandering nuns, particularly vulnerable women. Both Ciñcā and Sundarī are merely instruments in the hands of "heretic masters." They do not count, they just serve, like Māra's daughters, as foils for the Buddha's innocence.

QUEENS, EMPRESSES, AND OTHER IMPRESSIVE LADIES

Queen Māya and her sister Mahāprajāpatī inaugurate a type of royal devotee that figures prominently in the Buddhist gallery of female portraits. The portrait, however, was not always so positive. In China, one female ruler stands out as such: it is Empress Wu Zhao (better known as Wu Zetian).

A Two-Edged Paradigm

We noted earlier the ambivalence of feminist efforts to retrieve female role models in high places. Perhaps the most misguided of such attempts is Diana Paul's rehabilitation of Wu Zhao.[42] In order to provide a "more balanced" image of Wu Zhao than that left by a male-centered Confucian tradition, Paul emphasizes her political astuteness and her Buddhist devotion. In so doing, however, she chooses to ignore the long list of political crimes perpetrated by this despotic ruler, and the Machiavellian features by which she outsmarted most male Chinese rulers. One may not accept at face-value the *Jiu Tang shu*'s account, according to which the imperial concubine Wu Zhao, upon giving birth in 654 to her second child, killed it in order to raise suspicion about Gaozong's principal spouse. At any rate, she replaced the latter as imperial consort in 655, and she already held the reins of power even before the death of Gaozong in 683. Even if we do not believe Confucian sources when they denounce her affair with the Buddhist priest Xie Huaiyi, the fact remains that she did not hesitate to resort to violent means to keep the power to herself, while keeping her own sons in a kind of house-arrest. For instance, she decimated the Wei family, the in-laws of her son Zhongzong, including the seventeen-year-old Princess Yongtai, whose only crime was a few critical remarks.[43]

In 688, Wu Zhao had a "Luminous Hall" (*mingtang*) built, perhaps in an attempt to assert her status as Son of Heaven.[44] It has been argued that, in order to erase her gender, she resorted to a prophecy found (or inserted) in an apocryphal sutra, the *Dayun jing*, in which a bodhisattva manifests as a woman to save sentient beings.[45] Buddhism, with its notion of "skillful means" (*upāya*) used by the bodhisattvas, may have helped her to bend the gender rule that Confucianism had used against her. Yet the status of universal monarch (*cakravartin* king), which Wu Zhao also claimed for herself, was one of the five ranks that Buddhism denied to women.

Steve Bokenkamp takes a different tack, emphasizing the Daoist elements in Wu Zhao's ideology. He first points out that Wu became the first (and the last) woman to participate in the Feng and Shan rites on Tai shan in 666, and that she repeated the same rites on Song shan ten years later. On these occasions, she presented herself as "mother of the realm," a role for which she seems to have long prepared herself.[46] Thus, Bokenkamp argues, "While a few Buddhists may have wished to view Wu Zhao as a crypto-male, the extent to which her gender is asserted throughout the texts written by and for her reveal that this was never a part of her projected image."[47] This is reflected, for instance, in Li Jiao's celebration of her Feng and Shan rituals on Song shan: "To provide beneficence to a suffering age, she debased herself to ascend the throne as a female sovereign." The "debasement" mentioned here, Bokenkamp argues, is her descent from divine status, not an assertion that Wu Zhao was somehow really a man. To quote again from Li Jiao: "She entered riding a mare, but now pilots flying dragons. / From the scattered sand of dynastic decline she has forged the stones of Nü Gua to repair Heaven."[48] According to Bokenkamp, it is clear that Wu Zhao not only accepted archetypal explanations of the nature of woman, but "took them seriously in a way that had not been contemplated before." For example, her interest in the Central Peak (Song shan) may be another indication of her deft use of the symbolism of the center (or the "inner") as the place of the woman, the secret place where life begins. This control of the symbolism of the center justified her rule of the Central Kingdom.[49]

Female Rulers in Japan

In the case of Japan, we must distinguish between female *tennō*, who reigned officially, and royal consorts, who sometimes exerted a lot of occult influence, but had to take a back seat in public life.[50] Famous consorts include Kōmyō Kōgō, the consort of Shōmu Tennō; Danrin Kōgō, the consort of Saga Tennō; and Junna Kōgō, the consort of Junna Tennō.[51] In the first centuries of Japan's centralized rule (sixth to eighth centuries), women became tennō as frequently as men. After the Nara period, however, women no longer ascended the throne, and most high administrative functions were reserved for men.[52]

Wu Zhao's image seems to have inspired that of the last Japanese female ruler, Kōken Tennō, who returned to the throne under the name of Shōtoku Tennō.[53] In particular, the scandalous relationship attributed by Confucian critics to Wu Zhao and the Buddhist priest Xie Huaiyi was replicated in the alleged love affair between Empress Shōtoku and the priest Dōkyō. In both cases, the sexual scandal was aggravated (or provoked) by the Buddhist encroachment of royal power. Thus, political rivalries were conveniently hidden behind alleged sexual misbehavior. By an ironic turn of things, Empress Shōtoku received a taste of her own medicine. The daughter of Emperor Shōmu and Kōmyō, a consort of Fujiwara birth, she was able, after the death of her father, to evict her brother by disclosing his affair with a court lady during the mourning period. According to Tanaka Takako, the contrast between Shōtoku and her mother Kōmyō reflects the difference in status between a royal consort and a female tennō, a difference hinging on the ability to produce a male heir. Whereas the royal consort who gave birth to a male child was extolled as a "mother of the country," a celibate female *tennō* was seen as a kind of freak and a potential source of troubles. Jien's *Gukanshō*, for instance, contains recurring praises of the "mother of the country" who upholds the *sekkanke*

(Fujiwara) family, as well as criticisms of Shōtoku Tennō. Jien's remark, according to which Japan is the country where women "put the final touch" (lit. "the pupil of the eye," *nyonin nyūgen no kuni*) is by no means an appreciation of female freedom. The reference to the "final touch" is only an appreciation of the role of women as mothers, tying the royal family to the Fujiwara clan.[54] The same type of criticism appears in the *Jinnō shōtōki* by Kitabatake Chikafusa. Significantly, Chikafusa, when he mentions Shōtoku, does not give her the title of *tennō*, and refers to her simply as *johei*, "imperial consort." He reproaches her, not only for having clung to power, but also for having failed to engender a male heir—two points on which she differed from her mother.[55]

Empress Shōtoku allegedly received karmic punishment for burning Buddhist Scriptures out of anger. Her wrath is said to have been triggered by a misogynistic statement attributed to the Buddha in the *Nirvāna-sūtra*.[56] Although she managed to avoid hell, she had to suffer retribution in her living body. She could still hope to be saved in the end, however, because she experienced auspicious signs in response to her pious donations to Saidaiji. The *Mizukagami* (ca. 1200) describes the event as follows:

> Saidaiji was built in 765, and bronze statues were made of the Four Heavenly Kings. Three were successfully cast, but there were seven failures in casting the fourth. Finally the Empress made this vow: "If I can discard my womanly body and become a buddha through the Buddha's virtue, may the next casting be successful as I put my hand into the molten copper. And may my hand be burned off if my prayer is not to be granted." Not the slightest injury was found on the Empress's hand, and the fourth statue was then cast successfully.[57]

Even the *Gukanshō* seems willing to blunt its criticism: "This Empress was no ordinary person. A story is told of her vow with Amoghapāśa at the Saidai Temple. The things she did were gossiped about, but they were not thought of as precedents. Her actions really should be understood as the actions of a Buddhist incarnation (*gongen*)."[58]

The reign of Empress Shōtoku is linked in the *Gukanshō* with that of another female ruler, Empress Saimei (also known as Kōgyoku)—in both cases with negative comments.[59] Whereas Shōtoku had to suffer in this world, Kōgyoku is said to have fallen into hell.[60] The mention of Kōgyoku appears in the legend of Zenkōji, a temple founded by Honda Yoshimitsu to house a miraculous Amida triad. We are told that Yoshimitsu's son, Yoshitsuke, died, but shortly after returned from the dead. During his descent into hell, he met the empress among the damned, and offered to take her place. Both were ultimately saved by his gallant gesture.[61] To show her gratitude, after they were both restored to life, Kōgyoku helped Yoshitsuke and his parents to establish Zenkōji. The image of an empress suffering in hell is disturbing, but already in the *Nihonshoki*, Kōgyoku's image was a little strange. We are told, for instance, that, during her funerals, a demon (*oni*) appeared at the top of a nearby mountain—a rather ominous event. Kōgyoku is the only female ruler said to have fallen into hell, allegedly because of her arrogance and her jealousy, but also because of the Five Obstacles, that is, because of her gender.[62] By the Muromachi period, her damnation had become the punishment for having been unable to have children.

It may be worth noting that the Five Obstacles, emblematic of female dependence, raise a problem in her case because they contradict her imperial status. A female ruler should not submit to any man—this was precisely Empress Shōtoku's crime. Furthermore, one of the Five Obstacles is that a woman cannot become a universal monarch or *cakravartin*. This seemed to preclude the possibility of a woman becoming *tennō*, the medieval equivalent of the *cakravartin*. It certainly made the position of a female tennō a critical one, and probably explains in part why, after the Nara period, such oxymoronic beings disappeared. None of this seems to explain why Kōgyoku and Shōtoku were singled out for infernal punishment. Perhaps it has to do with the fact that they both, like Wu Zhao, clung to the throne. Not surprisingly, such women, who wielded power over men and refused to abdicate, were obvious targets of jealousy and criticism, and they were therefore abused, if not physically, at least symbolically.

A Good Woman Is Hard to Find

By contrast with the cases described above, some royal consorts were singled out as saintly women. Empress Kōmyō is one such case. Whereas her daughter Shōtoku, the patroness of Saidaiji, was demonized by later tradition, Kōmyō was idealized as the saintly woman who founded Hokkeji in Nara. She was well known for her pious works, and was apparently instrumental in her husband's decision to erect the Great Buddha of Tōdaiji. Thus, her legendary aura grew rapidly. The *Genkō shakusho* explains her name as a reference to her radiant beauty. In the *Kenkyū onjunrei ki*, another work of the Kamakura period, she has become an incarnation of the bodhisattva Kannon. This text is actually an *engi* of the Nishi Kondō of Kōfukuji, the Golden Hall built by Kōmyō for her deceased mother. According to this legend, an Indian king who had wanted to worship a manifestation of Kannon had a dream that this bodhisattva had manifested itself in Japan under the form of Kōmyō. He sent a sculptor to copy the features of Kōmyō, but the latter, in turn, asked the sculptor to make a statue of Amida on behalf of her mother. The sculptor answered that Shaka (Śākyamuni) was better suited for such a purpose, and carved the statue of Kōfukuji's Western Golden Hall.

The scale of this story, unfolding from India to Japan, is a testimony to Kōmyō's glory. Likewise, in the *Kōfukuji ranshōki*, it is said that the statue of Jūichimen Kannon at Hokkeji has the features of Kōmyō. And yet the *Kenkyū onjunrei ki* mentions that Kōmyō saw in a dream a heavenly being (*deva*), who predicted that she would be reborn in the Tusita Heaven, Maitreya's paradise.[63] The episode for which she is most well known, however, is that of the bathhouse at Hokkeji.[64] Kōmyō commissioned a public bathhouse that would be open to all without distinction of rank, and she vowed that she herself would wash one thousand people. As she was about to fulfill her vow, the last person who showed up was a leper. When she proceeded, somewhat reluctantly, to bathe him, he told her that a doctor had once predicted that he could only be cured if someone would suck the pus of his boils. Now he begged Kōmyō, in her great compassion, to do so. Overcoming her disgust, she eventually complied and sucked him "from head to toe"—or so we are told. Then, just as she asked him never to mention this to anyone, his body emitted a wonderful golden glow and a sweet scent. He turned out to be none other than the buddha Akṣobhya, who praised Kōmyō for passing the test of sainthood.[65] It is not entirely clear whether we have here a way, for a woman, to overcome bodily impurity, or rather something akin to a Tantric inversion of values. Apart from the obvious virtuous motivations—charity, humility—that led her to lower herself, Kōmyō thus mediates between sacredness and defilement by a quasi-sexual transgression. In such a "rhetoric of contrast," sacredness appears where least expected, in a leper or *hinin*, and in a woman.[66]

In most readings, Kōmyō's action is an emblem of female virtue. Such is not the case, however, for Kokan Shiren, the author of the *Genkō Shakusho*, whose reaction attests that he indeed perceived her behavior as transgressive. As a Zen priest with a Confucian bent, Shiren could not condone such an antihierarchical and grossly physical kind of hubris. Thus, he writes:

> How could the vain cleansing of dirt and sucking of pus result in Akṣobhya manifesting himself? Moreover, the constants of human relationships are that the lord be [truly] a lord, the subject a subject, the husband a husband, and the wife a wife. From antiquity there have been few to be compared with our Empress Kōmyō in wifely virtue and feminine learning, in worship of the Buddha and reverence for the Dharma. However, in washing people's bodies, she deviated from these constants.[67]

Shiren's reaction is not an isolated case. An even more openly transgressive image of Kōmyō circulated at Tōdaiji, despite the fact that this monastery was indebted to Kōmyō's husband, Shōmu Tennō, and her daughter Shōtoku.[68] We are told that, after seeing a Jizō statue at Tōdaiji, she desired to have sex with Jitchū, a young monk who looked like the bodhisattva. Thus, she had a bath prepared for him in order to spy on him.[69] Then, she dreamed that she made love to him, but in the midst of passion she suddenly realized that his features were those of Jūichimen Kannon, and she repented. The contrast between this legend and that of the bath given to the leper may reflect the opposition between Tōdaiji and Kōfukuji, The fact that access to Tōdaiji was forbidden to all women, even to empresses, is mentioned in the *Kenkyū onjunrei ki* in connection with Hokkeji: "This temple [Hokkeji] was founded owing to a vow of Empress Kōmyō. Deploring that women cannot enter the Hall of the Great Buddha at Tōdaiji, she had a temple built according to her wish." There was even a tradition according to which the ground of Tōdaiji's Main Hall opened when Kōmyō attempted to enter it.[70] By the Muromachi period, this tradition had grown into a legend that Kōmyō had fallen into hell—because she was a woman, and more precisely, because she had attempted to enter the sacred inner sanctum (*kekkai*).[71]

In the later tradition Kōmyō came to be associated with Empress Danrin (Danrin Kōgō, née Tachibana Kachiko).[72] The consort of Saga Tennō came to be known by the name Danrin Kōgō after founding Danrinji on the western outskirts of Kyoto, allegedly for the purpose of inviting the Chan master Yikong. This foundation story plays an important legitimizing role for the early Zen tradition. Musō Soseki's *Muchū mondō*, for instance, claims that Yikong was presented to Saga Tennō and his consort by the eminent Shingon master Kūkai.[73] According to the *Genkō Shakusho*, Danrin Kōgō had earlier questioned Kūkai as follows: "Is there not a Dharma which surpasses this [namely, the Shingon teaching] again?" Kūkai replied: "In the Tang, there is the buddha-mind school. . . . I, Kūkai, have also heard a little of its teaching, it is only that I have not yet had leisure to investigate it thoroughly."[74] The historicity of that story was apparently questioned very early on: "It was on this account that Danrin Kōgō sent Egaku to inquire at the Lingqi [*yuan*]. . . . The tradition handed down about it in the world is not an idle one." Thus comments Shiren, who claims to have a fragment of a tablet bearing proof of this. Danrin Kōgō is remembered, not only for her failed attempt to introduce Chan (Zen) to Japan, but also as the author and subject of a memento mori called the "Nine Aspects of Death." In its section about Ume-no-miya, a shrine founded by Danrin Kōgō, the *Honchō jinja kō* states: "The royal consort was very beautiful. At the moment of death, she said, 'Do not make funerals, abandon me in the moor, [so that] people immersed in thoughts of sex, seeing my decomposing body, will come to realize [the truth of impermanence].' Thus, following her instructions, her corpse was abandoned on the western outskirts. Later on, her fist (*kobushi*) was found and buried. This is why this place was called *ikken* ('One-Fist'), or *kobushi no miya* ('Shrine of the Fist')."[75]

The same story appears in a number of later sources.[76] For instance, in his poetical anthology entitled *Dōkashin no saku*, Musen Koji, a disciple of the Zen master Hakuin, imitates the famous anthology *Hyakunin isshū* by giving one poem from each of his selected authors: Zen masters such as Eisai, Dōgen, Ikkyū, and Hakuin, men of letters such as Sen no Rikyū and Bashō, and political figures including Hōjō Tokiyori. Among these fifty some figures, only three women are mentioned: Danrin Kōgō, the Zen nun Mugai Nyodai (1223–98), and a woman referred to as the "wife of Ninagawa Shinyuemon."[77] Here, too, Danrin Kōgō is praised essentially as the founder of Danrinji, and for her pious postmortem exhibitionism. In all of these texts, the royal consort is presented positively and she is the one who decides to let her body decompose in order to teach other people. But perhaps this is only an inversion of the signs of the Ono no Komachi story, which will be discussed in chapter 8. The story might have been euphemized by the later Zen tradition, based on some earlier (and misogynistic) tradition. The fact remains that the story, under the pretext of showing impermanence, chooses to show in gruesome detail what happens to the body of a beautiful and powerful woman after death.[78]

Kenreimon'in

The tragic story of Empress Kenreimon'in, appearing in the *Heike monogatari*, was well known in medieval Japan. We recall that she was the daughter of Taira no Kiyomori, the wife of the Retired Emperor Takakura, and the mother of the ill-fated child-emperor, Antoku Tennō. Unlike the latter, who drowned with his grandmother and other members of the Taira clan during the battle of Dan-no-ura, she was rescued in extremis by Minamoto warriors and taken back to the capital. Later on, she took the tonsure and withdrew to a hermitage at Ōhara, on the northeastern outskirts of Kyoto, where Retired Emperor Go-Shirakawa once paid her a visit. On that occasion, she told him of her tribulations on the "six paths" of existence. As the daughter of Kiyomori and the mother of the young emperor, her life at court had seemed at first like heavenly bliss: "My only desire was to live on and on—to petition the gods, if need be, for the immortals' art of ensuring long life and eternal youth, or to search out the Hōrai elixir of immortality. I thought the bliss of heaven could be no more sublime than the pleasures I enjoyed day and night." Then, however, she had to experience the sufferings of the world of men, the separation from beloved ones and the hardships of fugitive life: "The mountains and fields were broad, but there was no place for us to take shelter and rest." As things get worse, she compares her predicament to that of the hungry ghosts: "Our days were spent on the waves, our nights in the boats. Because we possessed no tribute goods, no one prepared food for me. If something did chance to be at hand, I could not eat it for lack of water. It is true that we were afloat on the mighty sea, but the salt water was undrinkable. I felt that I was experiencing the world of hungry spirits." Soon, however, the Heike seemed to regain some energy, and the fighting resumed: "There was never a time when the battle cries ceased, early or late. I felt certain that the fighting between Asura [the anti-gods] and Taishaku [Indra, the king of heaven] must be just the same." But the worst was yet to come, with the battle of Dan-no-ura: "Darkness shrouded my eyes as I saw my son sink beneath the waves: my brain seemed paralyzed. I try to forget, but forgetting is impossible; I try to control my grief, but that too is impossible. Those who were left behind uttered a great and terrible cry: it seemed that even the shrieks of the sinners under the flames in the hot hells could sound no worse."[79]

Soon after her encounter with Go-Shirakawa, Kenreimon'in died in the odor of sanctity. The *Heike monogatari* describes her final apotheosis and the salvation of her two female attendants:

> With the passing of time, the Imperial Lady fell ill. She recited Buddha-invocations, clasping the five-colored cord attached to the hand of the central image. . . . On her left and right, Dainagon-no-suke and Awa-no-naishi wailed and shrieked at the top of their lungs, overcome with sorrow as the end approached. After her chanting voice had gradually weakened, a purple cloud trailed in the west, a marvelous fragrance permeated the chamber, and the sound of music was heard in the heavens. . . . The parting brought agonies of inconsolable grief to the two attendants who had never left her side since her days as Empress. They had nowhere to turn for help, the grass of old ties having long withered; nonetheless, they contrived most touchingly to perform the periodic memorial services. People said both of them attained the *nāga*-girl's wisdom, emulated King Bimbisāra's wife, and achieved their goal of rebirth in the Pure Land.[80]

Thus, not only did Kenreimon'in obtain rebirth in the Pure Land, so did her two attendants. The contrast between their present state of grief and their ultimate salvation offered a strong message of hope for women in these troubled times, but at the same time it reinforced the image of women as grieving beings. In her prayers, Kenreimon'in's chief concern seems to be for her son, the ill-fated Antoku Tennō, and for the unhappy souls of the Taira (Heike) clan. As Helen McCullough notes, "Without challenging the sincerity of her love and grief, a modern reader might guess that she is actuated in part by a survivor's feeling of guilt. And a medieval audience, ever fearful of unquiet spirits, would have conjectured that one of her chief aims was to placate the jealous dead."[81] Some scholars have argued that the entire *Heike monogatari* was conceived and presented as an offering to the departed Taira—a record for posterity of their names and deeds, disseminated far and wide by people in contact with the other world, the blind singers known as *biwa hōshi*. This record praises their achievements, views their shortcomings with a generally tolerant eye, and offers repeated assurances that their widows, their retainers, and others are praying for them. In this way, the first twelve chapters narrate their history in gratifying detail, and the "consecration chapter" recapitulates the facts; reasserts the truths of transitoriness and karmic retribution; adds a strong assurance that prayer is the way to salvation; states that petitions on their behalf are being offered day and night by none other than the former First Lady Kenreimon'in, society's surrogate par excellence, and virtually promises them rebirth in the Pure Land.

Thus, as Kenreimon'in's image spread through the *Heike monogatari*, she became an intercessor and a sacrificer for the Taira clan, as well as a role model for aristocratic women like Lady Nijō. We have noted, for instance, the identical structures of the encounters between Kenreimon'in and Go-Shirakawa as described in the *Heike monogatari*, and Lady Nijō and Go-Fukakusa Tennō in the *Towazugatari*.[82] Yet, even though Kenreimon'in was redeemed by her grief, her image seems to have remained tainted in popular imagination by her kinship with her father Taira no Kiyomori. Kiyomori himself is a complex figure. The *Heike monogatari* introduces him as an ambitious warrior, favored by the goddess Benzaiten, but also as an evil man who commits all kinds of sacrileges and who, as he dies full of hatred for his opponent Yoritomo, seems bound for hell. The ultimate doom of the Taira is suggested at the beginning of the text in relation to Kiyomori's "heterodox" worship of the Tantric deity Dakiniten.[83] Yet the same text also remembers him as a holy man who commissioned lectures on the *Lotus Sūtra*, and as a reincarnation of the Buddhist priest Jie. [84] Kiyomori's sacrilegious actions are reflected in those of his children. The *Genpei jōsuiki*, for instance, mentions the incest between Kenreimon'in and her elder brother Munemori. In this variant recension of the *Heike monogatari*, the story is told by a leperous monk, when Munemori, having been captured during the battle of Dan-no-ura, is paraded with other Heike prisoners through the streets of the capital.[85] The monk goes so far as to say that the young Emperor Antoku was actually the son of Kenreimon'in and Munemori. The incest is also mentioned by Kenreimon'in herself, when she tells Go-Shirakawa about the six realms; it is one of her experiences in the animal realm.[86] Thus, the lewd and taboo-breaking actions of Kiyomori's children provide the finishing touch to the story of Kiyomori's indignities.

In an article on the wives of King Aśoka, John Strong argues that the multiplicity of royal consorts serves as a literary device to represent the ambivalence of (and toward) the king: "For the most part, in legend, individual wives of kings tended not to be ambiguous. They were all good or all bad, and accordingly were praised or blamed. They could be this way because they were plural and could offset one another. In this sense, royal polygamy in Buddhism made possible a network of legends and stories that allowed for the expression of multiple, and variant, attitudes toward kingship."[87] The king, according to Strong, is denied such ambivalence, as he is to remain singular and cannot be the object of direct criticism. One could argue that Aśoka is typical of the ambivalent king, with both a good and a bad side.[88] Can the same be said of Prince Siddharta—the future Buddha—and his wives? We have noted the ambivalence of Yaśodhara's figure. Likewise, the Japanese cases we have encountered suggest that, through the case of an individualized queen or empress, the ambivalence toward kingship does not need to be held back, and it can (or must) be projected onto a single person. The ambivalence of the Buddhists toward these women, expressed as the latter's ambivalent character, reflects an ambivalence toward medieval kingship, and toward women who ventured into the public sphere. Before examining these "public" women, let us take a look at the most "private" women, some of whom paradoxically were drawn into the public realm of popular imagination.

EMINENT NUNS

Like Mahāprajāpatī, Kenreimon'in accumulated in the course of her life the roles of queen and nun. In hagiographical literature, however, these roles are usually distinct, and nuns are not as clearly individualized. Often, eminent nuns are hardly more than the female doubles of the arhats, or the personification of various "perfections" (pāramitā). Some of them, however, are endowed with a strong personality. A case in point is that of the nun Utpalavarṇā (Jp. Rengeshiki, "Lotus-Colored"), who was known even in Japan for her spiritual powers, and who retained from her former life as a courtesan a certain taste for transgressive behavior.[89] As the story goes, once when she encouraged women to become nuns, some of them protested that, because of their youth, they would likely be unable to observe the rules. She replied: "If you are going to break your vows, then break them—but be nuns!" She went on to explain how, in a former life she was a "very bold woman" (a courtesan), who once, in jest, put on the monastic robe and pretended to be a nun. Paradoxically, through this apparently sacrilegious act, she earned sufficient merit to be reborn as a human in the age of the buddha Kāśyapa, and to become one of his disciples. Although her past offences resulted in her temporary fall into hell, she was eventually reborn again in the age of the buddha

Śākyamuni, under whose guidance she became an arhat. Consequently, she now urged women to become nuns, because the karmic link with Buddhism is stronger than any sin they have committed or could commit after ordination.

The dialectic of transgression and salvation is also at work in the case of two famous Japanese nuns who obtained the reputation of living bodhisattvas, Chūjōhime and Sari. Whereas Sari is described as literally "sexless," Chūjōhime's holiness is (unusually) related to her female nature.[90] Both characters have some transgressive elements, in that they both have to force their way into a male community, and they do so through their oratory talents.[91] Chūjōhime's case is interesting, and somewhat paradoxical, in several other respects. She is famous for having been granted a vision of the Pure Land by a strange nun, a female manifestation of the buddha Amida who—alone or with some help, depending on variants—waved the famous tapestry of Taimadera to give Chūjōhime a glimpse of the splendors waiting for her.[92] Chūjōhime died at the age of twenty-nine and is said to have been reborn in the Pure Land.[93] Her final apotheosis may not, however, be as significant as her earlier ordeals. Having lost her mother at an early age, she had to suffer the jealousy of her stepmother.[94] When she was invited to court, the latter accused her of having had a sexual affair (in one variant, with a monk) at the age of thirteen. Here, the point is not so much the breach of morality, as the threat to her lineage and to the law of alliance.[95] Enraged by the scandal, Chūjōhime's father ordered one of his retainers to kill her, but the man took pity on her, and, together with his wife, raised Chūjōhime in the deep recesses of a mountain. Eventually, Chūjōhime met her father again, and the latter, having realized his mistake, asked her to return home. She refused to resume her former life, however, and instead chose to become a nun. It is at this point that the Taimadera episode, mentioned above, begins.

By becoming a nun, this Japanese Cinderella forsook (or was denied) her destiny as royal concubine.[96] Chūjōhime, in a sense, had no other choice but to become a nun, inasmuch as her damaged reputation prevented her from making the princely marriage to which she was originally destined. To make things even worse, the "annoying illness" (*urusai yamai*)—in the form of prolonged menstruation or a veneral disease—that afflicted her was reinterpreted as a kind of karmic punishment. In spite (or because) of this, prostitutes and ordinary women alike looked up to Chūjōhime as an example of a suffering woman who had overcome all hardships, and as a compassionate deity who could understand their sufferings and cure their bodily ills. The fact that Chūjōhime was perceived as either sinful or a victim (or both) is precisely what gave her the capacity to cure other women. Even today, a common herbal medicine for the alleviation of a whole range of "female complaints"—from irregular and painful menstrual periods, headaches, joint pains, and hysteria, to fever, chills, dizziness, and poor circulation of the blood—is marketed under the name *Chūjō-tō* (Chūjō's medicine).[97] Thus, although as a virgin and a nun she was in theory an asexual being, because of the "female ailment" that afflicted her, she became an emblem of sexual difference.[98] Furthermore, by renouncing the world, this typical "father's daughter" ended up saving her deceased mother rather than her father. Finally, one important aspect of Chūjōhime's legend is her transgression of male boundaries. When Taimadera monks want to deny her access to the temple, she challenges them, arguing that "for the buddhas, there is no distinction between male and female." Although superficially her legend seems to be one of denial of gender, a deeper reading shows that Chūjōhime's gender, her physical ordeals—symbolized by her being under the influence of blood—are more truly what is being emphasized.[99]

The motif of transgression is also found in the case of Sari, a young woman also known as "the lump-nun of Higo province." This nickname derives from the legend that she was born as a lump of flesh. As a result, she was at first abandoned by her parents, but later she turned into a beautiful young girl—with one significant caveat: she had no vagina—or so we are told. As if this were not enough, she appears to have been unconstrained. Her rebellious nature appears in that, when rebuked by some priests for attending a Buddhist service, she fought back and eventually outwitted them. Her uncanny nature was furthermore revealed in the fact that, when two monks slandered her, they were punished right away: "A long arm, disembodied to human view, came straight down out of the sky and clawed their faces open."[100] Common people began to worship her as a female bodhisattva. Her legend belongs to the mythological topos of the supernatural birth story.[101] Her name, too, may be significant in this respect, since it evokes the relics of the Buddha (*śarīra*). Thus, Sari is a living, fleshly relic. The problem is that, as already noted, she is no longer a woman, but, metaphorically at least, a "great man." But in a way, she was never considered truly to be feminine: not only was she physically deficient, but also she had too much spirit or charisma for a woman. In a sense, her physical lack and spiritual excess were two sides of the same coin.

Another interesting case is that of a young temple servant named Chiyono. Her legend is mentioned in the *Hekizan nichiroku*, the diary of a Zen priest of Tōfukuji, Taikyoku Zōshū, in relation with a pond called Chiyonu no ike.[102] Near this pond lived an enlightened nun, who had a young servant named Chiyo. "One day, as Chiyo was fetching water, the bottom of the ladle leaked. Suddenly a voice said: 'Scoop after scoop, one exhausts the water of a thousand rivers; perfectly clear before one's eyes, the moon of the self [appears].' She was deeply impressed by this. Eventually, her name spread everywhere. Because of this the pond was called Chiyonu no ike."[103] The gist of the story is the enlightenment of the young girl as she is scooping water at the pond. In some versions, her bucket leaks, in others its bottom falls out. In most versions, she then hears a voice, reciting the following verse: "No matter how skilled you may be, when the bottom of the bucket leaks, water will not remain in the bucket, nor the moon dwell in it." Here, as often in Zen, the moon serves as a metaphor for enlightenment.

Around the fifteenth century, pictures were added to the story of Chiyono. By the seventeenth century, Chiyono was identified with Mugai Nyodai, the powerful abbess of the Zen convent Keiaiji. The *Nyodai hōgo*, for instance, begins with the story of the temple, where a group of nuns have gathered to practice Zen. "They had a young servant of twenty-four or five years named Chiyono. She was the daughter of an important man, but people at the time did not know it." The passage ends with: "Later, Chiyono met Bukkō [Mugaku Sogen], obtained his authorization, and inherited his Dharma; she was called Mujaku Nyodai *chōrō*. When someone came from elsewhere and asked her [about this], she simply said, 'When the Sun-faced Buddha [appears] and the bottom of the bucket is leaking . . . ,' that is, she composed a poem that said, like above: 'No matter how skilled you may be. . . .' "[104] We may recall that in the *waka* collection entitled *Dōkashin no saku* Empress Danrin Kōgō and Mugai are listed among its authors. Mugai has been recently singled out as the only Zen nun inscribed in the "patriarchal" lineage, a two-edged distinction when one considers that modern Zen masters have come to believe that her name is that of a man. Here, the markers of gender have been duly erased: her name is gender-neutral, and her portrait (*chinzō*), unlike many others, focuses on her supposed masculinity.

Sisters in Flames

Famous Japanese nuns often turn out to be sisters of eminent monks: this is for instance, the case of Genshin's two sisters, Ganzei and Ganshō. Of the latter, we are told that, "although she had a body with the five obstacles, she clearly understood the two truths." In the general perception, these unusual achievements were perceived as masculine. Being the sister of a monk, or displaying verbal skills like Chūjōhime and Sari, however, was not always sufficient to gain acceptance in the saṅgha. Sometimes, a much more drastic method was called for. A disturbing hagiographical topos is found in several stories in which a handsome young woman disfigures herself in order to gain acceptance into the saṅgha. One such case is that of Eshun, the sister of the Zen master Ryōan Emyō. She was already in her thirties when she asked her brother to ordain her. He initially refused, arguing that "monastic life is for the manly (*daijōbu*). Men and women cannot change their lot. If I readily ordained women, then many monks would be corrupted [by sexual temptation]." To show her determination, Eshun then defaced herself with red-hot fire tongs, and finally gained acceptance.[105]

The same motif is found in the story of the sister of Master Hosshin: "Formerly, at Shioyama in Kai, the sister of master Hosshin, wanted to become a Zen nun. As she was too beautiful, she burnt her face with fire-mongers."[106] Another case is that of Ryōnen Gensō (1646–1711), a Zen nun recognized for her skills in *waka* and Chinese-style poetry, who also painted portraits of eminent Ōbaku priests. She writes:

> When I was young I served Yoshinokimi, the grand-daughter of Tōfukumon'in, a disciple of the imperial Hōkyōji. Recently she passed away; although I know that this is the law of nature, the transience of the world struck me deeply and I became a nun. I cut my hair and dyed my robes black, and went on a pilgrimage to Edo. There I had an audience with the monk Hakuō of the Ōbaku Zen sect. I recounted to him such things as my deep devotion to Buddhism since childhood, but Hakuō replied that although he could see my sincere intentions, I could not escape my womanly appearance. Therefore I heated up an iron and held it against my face, and then wrote as my brush led me:

> Formerly to amuse myself at court I would burn orchid incense;
> Now to enter the Zen life I burn my own face.
> the four seasons pass naturally like this;
> But I don't know who this is amidst the change.

> In this living world / The body I give up and burn / Would be wretched / If I thought of myself as / Anything but firewood.[107]

The same motif is found in a variant of Chiyono's legend in the *Nyokunshō*: (*Commentary on the Admonitions to Women*). In this account, she is said to have been the wife of the Regent (*kanpaku*). It is not clear why she chose to become a nun while her husband was still alive. He was even apparently quite fond of her, since he sneaked into the convent in the hope of seeing her. At that moment, the nuns were preparing a bath, and Chiyono, when she realized his presence, took one of the fire sticks and burnt her face that she might never again elicit male desire.[108] The face of Nyodai's statue is said to show a terrible scar.

Even though these are legends, it is disturbing that most nuns who have left a name to posterity were handsome women who defaced themselves. In one case at least, such self-denial was perceived as insufficient, and had to be pushed one step further, to the point of self-immolation. We are told that Eshun, when she approached death, prepared a large bonfire and sat down in the middle of the flames. At Saijōji in Odagawara, there is a "stone of the fire samādhi" (*kajōseki*), supposedly the stone on which Eshun immolated herself. Although this episode is usually presented as a kind of apotheosis, there may be a darker sociological reality hidden behind this female suicide. Eshun's life is a testimony to male prejudices and the sexual harassment encountered by nuns. Even after she defaced herself and became a Zen nun, Eshun had to resist sexual advances from monks and confront their scorn. We are told, for instance, that a monk from Engakuji once raised his robe to expose himself in front of her, saying, "This old monk's thing is three feet long." Eshun, however, just calmly lifted her robe, spread her legs toward the monk, and said: "This nun's thing is deeper than that." She then walked away. We have here two aspects of the same topos: namely, how nuns try to deflect monks' desires by harming themselves or by seizing the bull by its horns (pardon the metaphor).[109]

Eshun's defiant nature, expressed in her burning her face and showing her pudenda, echoes that of a female disciple of the Chan master Dahui, a nun named Wuzhuo Miaozong (Jp. Mujaku Myōsō). According to the *Wujia zhengzong zan* (1254), Dahui once sent to her a disciple who was prejudiced against female teachers. She shocked the monk into realization in a rather nonorthodox manner:

Before Wuzhuo had become a nun, Dahui lodged her in her abbot's quarters. The Head Monk Wan'an always made disapproving noises. Dahui said to him: "Even though she is a woman, she has strengths." Wan'an still did not approve. Dahui then insisted that he should interview her. Wan'an reluctantly sent a message that he would go.

[When Wan'an came], Wuzhuo said, "Will you make it a Dharma interview or a worldly interview?"

The Head Monk replied: "A Dharma interview."

Wuzhuo said: "Then let your attendants depart." [Then she called to him,] "Please come in."

When he came past the curtain he saw Wuzhuo lying face upwards on the bed without anything on at all. He pointed at her and said, "What kind of place is this?"

Wuzhuo replied: "All the Buddhas of the three worlds and the six patriarchs and all the great monks everywhere—they all come out from within this."

Wan'an said: "And would you let me enter, or not?"

Wuzhuo replied: "It allows horses to cross, it does not allow asses to cross."

Wan'an said nothing, and Wuzhuo declared: "The interview with the Senior Monk is ended." She then turned over and faced the inside.

Wan'an became embarrassed and left.

Dahui said, "It is certainly not the case that the old beast does not have any insight." Wan'an was ashamed.[110]

Because of her name, Wuzhuo (Jp. Mujaku) may have been confused with Mugai Nyodai (also called Mujaku).[111] This may explain the resonance between the above passage and the biography of the Zen master Shūhō Myōchō, a contemporary of Mugai. In 1298, when Myōchō was a young monk of seventeen, he was one day lying half asleep on the bank of the Kamo River, near Gojō Bridge, when a woman suddenly stood above him, revealing her genitals, and said, "Look at the gate from which all buddhas were born!" The young monk, shocked, passed out, and when he came back to his senses no woman was around to be seen. He went away, wondering whether he had dreamed the whole thing. Here, the transgression is both justified and made worse by the fact that it is an old woman, not a pretty young one, who flashes at an apparently innocent monk.[112]

FEMMES FATALES

It seems that the only women valorized in Buddhist discourse are those who, in a way, are not truly feminine: either because their religious practice has made them manly, or because, for various reasons (permanent virginity, transgressive sexuality), they reside outside the spheres of normative womanhood and are freed from biological and patriarchal constraints, and consequently, able to symbolize aspects of Buddhist spirituality. I will return to the courtesan motif. For the moment, I want to examine some contrasting aspects of women seen as sexual initiators in the context of medieval kingship.

The courtesan, when she becomes the favorite of a ruler, can wield a lot of power, and sometimes, if she is lucky enough to become pregnant, she will become a royal or imperial consort. Her influence can be dangerous, however, as the legend of Yang Guifei attests. Emperor Xuanzong's concubine Yang Guifei almost brought him down with her, yet, she was redeemed in popular memory because of her tragic end, and was even deified in Japan as an avatar of the Bodhisattva Kannon. According to one tradition, Xuanzong even came to Japan looking for her, and eventually found her at Kumano, a place assimilated to the Daoist "Island of the Immortals," Penglai.[113]

In Japan, several courtesans were raised to the dubious status of femme fatale. One example is that of Fujiwara no Kusuko, a married woman who became the favorite of Heijō Tennō when she followed her daughter to the palace. The Retired Emperor Kanmu sent her back home to avoid scandal, but when he died in 806, she was called back to the palace. Emperor Heijō ruled only five years. In 810, he had a quarrel with his brother, the future Saga Tennō. Because of Kusuko's alleged influence, the political turmoil that ensued was called the "Kusuko Disturbance" (Kusuko no Ran).

Another case of female influence on a ruler is that of Lady Sanmi (Ano no Renshi, 1301–59), the favorite of Emperor Go-Daigo. She was the daughter of the Middle Marshal Ano no Kinkado, and she served as lady-in-waiting to the Inner Princess. Because of her, Go-Daigo was accused of "bestowing reward where merit was lacking," and as a result he alienated the warriors who had supported him during the Kenmu Restoration. Go-Daigo's infatuation for Lady Sanmi is described as follows in the *Taiheiki*:

> Not by the three legitimate spouses could the heart of the Son of Heaven be won, nor by the nine princesses, nor the twenty-seven concubines, nor the eighty-one imperial handmaidens, nor even by the beauties of the rear palace or the dancing girls of the Music Office. For not alone by her pearlike fairness did the lady captivate him [Go-Daigo], but by her words that were adroit and cajoling, and by knowing his will beforehand, and proposing novel things. . . . Alas! How shameful it is, that because of a beautiful woman we suffer the bitter disturbances of our times![114]

Despite the heavy blame laid on her by the *Taiheiki*, however, Lady Sanmi was not without merit in the eyes of its author. The latter points out that she was the only lady-in-waiting to follow him into exile in 1331, and she kept him from despairing.[115] Unfortunately, after his return to power, Go-Daigo again squandered his rewards, granting, for instance, the lands of the Daibutsu governor of Mutsu to "the lady who was an empress's peer."[116] Nevertheless, the *Taiheiki* calls her "mother of the country," owing to the fact that, at the death of Go-Daigo in 1339, one of her sons became emperor as Go-Murakami.[117] She controlled the Southern Court, together with Kitabatake Chikafusa, and alone after the latter's death in 1354.

OF WOMEN AND JEWELS

It may be argued that we find in Japanese Buddhism at least one positive image of women as initiators: that of the "jade woman." This image developed in the context of the Buddhist cult of relics and of the discourse on Japanese kingship, and appears in Chinese literature, as well as in several medieval sources.[118] Its locus classicus, however, is the famous dream in which the bodhisattva Kannon appeared to the young Shinran and told him:

> If you, the practitioner, due to past karma, must violate women,
> I will become a jade woman to be violated by you.

During your entire life, I will adorn you
And at the time of death I will guide you to the Pure Land.[119]

This dream, according to a letter by Shinran's wife, Eshin-ni, was written down in 1201, when Shinran, having left Hieizan, secluded himself for a hundred days at Rokkakudō to pray to the bodhisattva Kannon, and on the ninety-fifth day had a vision of Kannon as Prince Shōtoku. It describes the salvation of a monk by a female deity. I have discussed elsewhere the impact of this dream on the development of Buddhist sexuality in medieval Japan, and my focus here is on the image of the "jade woman." In the *Kakuzenshō*, a text compiled around 1198 by Kakuzen—therefore, before Shinran's verse—we find a very similar passage, entitled "The *honzon* changes into a jade woman":

> When false views arise in the mind, and sensual desire becomes violent and one must fall into the world, Nyoirin becomes the jade woman of our king. Becoming the intimate woman of this man, they together produce love. During an entire life, she [adorns] him with happiness and wealth, and makes him do an infinite number of good things. She [helps] him reach the . . . Western Pure Land.[120]

This passage shows that Shinran's dream must be read against the background of the Nyoirin Kannon cult that had developed in Shingon before the Kamakura period. Even if Shinran's verse is not directly inspired by the *Kakuzenshō*, it is clear that, at the time, the so-called jade woman was perceived as an avatar of Kannon. In both cases, the purpose of Kannon's apparition is to transmute sexual desire into a cause of rebirth in the Pure Land.

Another relevant source is the record of a dream by the Tendai prelate Jien. According to his *Jichin oshō musōki*, in 1203 Jien dreamt of a jade woman in relation to the royal regalia and to the imperial consecration ritual (*sokui kanjō*). Jien interprets his dream allegorically, seeing this jade woman as the *shindama* (divine jewel), or *cintāmaṇi* (wish-fulfilling jewel). Thus, in this way the sexual union between the jade woman and the *cakravartin* king seen by Jien in his dream expresses the procreative principle sustaining imperial power.[121] Yet another jade woman appears toward the same time in the dreams of Myōe. Obviously, jade women had taken hold of the imagination of Buddhist monks of the early Kamakura period.

Both in the *Kakuzenshō* and in the *Jichin oshō musōki*, the jade woman designates the wife of the emperor. According to Tanaka Takako, these jade women are related to imperial power, and more precisely to the *cintāmaṇi* as symbol of the imperium. Endō Hajime, on the other hand, interprets Shinran's verse as a promise of salvation for Shinran, and an attempt to recognize both monastic marriage and the giving up of vegetarianism, marks of a thought based on a transgression of Vinaya.[122] Thus, the power of women seems to have served to legitimize and protect imperial power, as well as the sexual lives of the members of Shinran's school. This presupposes the various theories, discussed earlier, about the possibility of women attaining buddhahood by changing into men. But what is different here is that monks obtain salvation by having sex with a woman who is an avatar of a bodhisattva.

What are we to do with the fact that, for Jien, the "jade woman" is a *shindama*? As is well known, the *cintāmaṇi* played an important role in the Buddhism of the time, and was closely associated with the relics (*śarīra*) of the Buddha.[123] Beginning with Kūkai, the esoteric tradition developed the idea that the *śarīra* were identical to the *cintāmaṇi*, and both symbols came to be associated with the imperial regalia. Tanaka argues that Shinran, who was familiar with Tendai esotericism, must have known about these associations between the jade woman, the *cintāmaṇi*, and the *śarīra*. The *śarīra*, first brought to Japan by Ganjin and Kūkai, were famous as symbols for protecting imperial power, and many women related to the imperial house participated in their transmission.[124]

The relic was conceived of as a "seed" of life. The fertility element is expressed in symbolic associations with rice. Through its fertilizing role, the relic is connected to a whole network of symbols aimed at the prosperity and continuity of the state and the imperial family, and, as the cult spread in popular strata, of the prosperity and prolificity of the people. Although, according to a tradition, the relic is essentially male, and therefore warrant of a male (patriarchal) lineage, one should not be surprised to discover that it has played an essential role also in the female imagination.

The verse mentioned by Shinran is in fact a vow of Kannon to save all beings, and she asks Shinran to spread this verse to all beings, not only to monks and nuns. The idea of salvation by a "jade woman" has thus spread from monks to the people, in parallel to the vogue of rituals related to gender/sex, which had appeared in the monastic community of the Insei period. What distinguishes Shinran from *kenmitsu* monks is that he believed himself to be charged with the mission of spreading this idea among the people. As mentioned earlier, the sexual imagery appears also in a record practically contemporary with Shinran's dream, the *Jichin oshō musōki*, which Jien offered to Go-Toba Tennō:

> On the twenty-second of the sixth month of Kennin 3 [1203], at dawn, I had a dream, that said: Among the imperial treasures are the Divine Seal and the Precious Sword. The Divine Seal is a jade woman, it is the queen's body. When the king penetrates the body of this jade woman whose nature is fundamentally pure, and sexual union occurs, both are free of sin. This is why the Divine Seal

is a jewel of pure jade. I understood this in my dream and, upon awakening, I thought as follows: This dream must correspond to the Seal of the Sword and the Sheath of King Acala (Fudō *tōshōin*). The Sword [of Acala] is the Precious Sword, it is the king's body; the Sheath is the Jewel Seal, it is the queen's body. Through the union of the Sword and the Sheath, the Seal is accomplished. Thus King Acala must be considered as the king's main object of worship (*honzon*).

I also made the following reflection: The Divine Seal is Butsugen Butsumo (Buddhalocanā), that is, the jade woman. The Holy King [turning] the Wheel is Ichiji Kinrin [Bucchō]. Thus, [this dream] seems to mean the union of Ichiji Kinrin Bucchō with Butsugen Butsumo.[125]

The jade woman is here used as a metaphor for a precious object, the "divine jewel," and it also means the body of the imperial consort—a very sexual symbolism. The sexual union has the meaning of a divine act from which the legitimate royal power of the sun-goddess Amaterasu stems. Jien considers the jade woman and the *tathāgata* Butsugen Butsumo as one single person, but Butsugen Butsumo, in Japanese Tantrism, is identical to the buddha Kinrin Bucchō, who symbolizes the force of the *cakravartin* king. On the one hand, he can be said to represent the ruler himself. On the other hand, inasmuch as Butsugen Butsumo gives birth to all buddhas, she has a female nature. This association of Butsugen Butsumo, the jade woman, and the royal consort, gives us the image of a woman protecting royal power through her sexuality. She is not only the sexual initiator of Tantric or Daoist ritual, but also the progenitrix, the woman who gives birth to royal offspring.

Although the jade woman in Jien's dream is at first glance different from that of Shinran's dream, they both share a protective and initiating nature, based on their sexuality. The former protects the royal lineage, the latter works for the salvation of individual monks. Their different roles seem to reflect the natures of the people to whom they appear: in one case, an official monk (*kansō*), in the other, a recluse (*tonseisō*).

Another contemporary example of a woman playing the role of mediator for the three regalia can be found in Myōe. In a dream he had toward the end of 1221, Myōe sees a noble woman, who holds a mirror and a great sword and wants to have intimate relations with him. According to Tanaka, these symbolic attributes represent the royal regalia, and the woman is a jade woman, playing the role of the missing symbol, the jewel. Although Myōe, unlike Jien, is not interested in examining the relations between the regalia and royal power, nonetheless his thinking is permeated by royal ideology. And yet, although Myōe is traditionally aligned with *kenmitsu* Buddhism, we recall that, as Matsuo Kenji pointed out, he shares with Shinran the status of *tonseisō*. Thus, it is not surprising that the jade woman who appears to him is more concerned with individual salvation.

We have examined the relations between the jade woman and royal power. What role does the sexual power of the jade woman play in this ideology? Let us look at the common points between the jade woman and the buddha Butsugen Butsumo. The ideal Buddhist king (*cakravartin*) is said to possess seven jewels (golden wheel, white elephant, horse, jewel, jade woman, minister, and soldiers), the fifth being the jade woman.[126] She is represented in the maṇḍala sitting on a lotus, like a buddha or a goddess. Butsugen Butsumo, on the other hand, is a personification of the buddha's eyes. This deity has a pronounced female characteristic, and is called the mother of all buddhas. It plays an important role in Myōe's dream, in which he sees himself as her child and calls her "Mother" (*haha gozen*). We find in the case of Myōe a mixture of longing for maternal and sexual love, which perhaps reflects the ambivalent nature of this buddha. At any rate, both the jade woman and Butsugen act as spiritual teachers as well as maternal protectors of the emperor or the monk.[127]

The *Genkō shakusho*, a history of Buddhism presented by Kokan Shiren to Go-Daigo Tennō, contains a section on women, whose longest entry is consecrated to a fictional character named Nyoi. This young woman is first described in terms reminiscent of Daoist immortals. She eventually enters the royal gynaeceum and becomes the favorite consort of Junna Tennō. She is a fervent believer in Nyoirin Kannon, and it becomes clear to the ruler, through a revelatory dream, that she is actually a manifestation of this bodhisattva. Eventually, she leaves the palace with two female companions and, guided by the dragon-goddess Benzaiten, climbs Mount Nyoi. There she finds the jewels deposited by another mythical figure, Empress Jingū.[128] Later on, she invites the Shingon priest Kūkai and asks him to perform the Nyoirin ritual, as well as to carve a statue of Nyoirin Kannon in her image. The symbolic connections between Nyoirin, the *cintāmaṇi*, Benzaiten, Empress Jingū, Kūkai, dragons, and rain rituals suggest that this tale is a kind of founding legend for imperial rule. The role of Nyoi as a "jade woman" is further suggested by Shiren's "commentary," in which he discusses the meaning of Nyoi's "purple cloud chest" and its relationship with the *nāga*-palace, connecting it with the legend of the fisherman Urashima, which will be discussed shortly.

Whether she is seen as protector of the royal lineage (as in the case of Jien) or as an individual protector (as in the case of Shinran), the jade woman motif seems to be a positive one. The emergence of these two different images may reflect the sociopolitical changes of the Insei period, but these changes failed to translate into changes in the status of real women.[129] The image of the jade woman remains in the same realm of ideality as that of the mother, examined previously. This jade woman, who performs the roles of mother and lover, seems to reflect, through the detour of the dream, the unconscious medieval image of women. As noted earlier, when monks like Jien praise women, it is always mothers they have in mind. As we have seen, the maternal image developed simultaneously with the increasing marginalization of women in society, in festivals, and at court. Likewise, the jade woman exists only in the gaze of men. Thus, she is an "oppressed body," locked up in the royal and Buddhist value systems, and from this viewpoint her paradoxical "power" resembles that of another initiator, the young novice, or *chigo*, often represented as a divine child. The fact that women can be put in the same sexual category as children, and that both are at the same time a source of power and powerlessness, shows that their sexual power is culturally determined and has nothing to do with biological femininity. Furthermore, the image of the jade woman was partly coopted by imperial ideology with the development, in the late medieval period, of the legend of Empress Jingū.

The "jade woman" played an important ideological role at court, but the reality of court women was rather different. Tonomura Hitomi has recently studied the case of Hino Meishi (d. 1358), the wife of Saionji Kinmune (1310–35), and the author of a memoir entitled *Tamemukigaki* (*Facing the Bamboo*). She points out that, unlike ladies-in-waiting such as Lady Nijō, who, in *Towazugatari*, records her sometimes forced sexual relationships with emperors and aristocrats, Meishi does not mention any instance of sexual servitude.[130] Of course, she may simply have been more discreet, or merely cautious. Recording the enthronement of Prince Kazuhito in 1331, Meishi is concerned above all with the imperial regalia. Because the deposed emperor, Go-Daigo, had managed to take the sacred sword and the jewel in his flight, a substitute sword had to be used. When Go-Daigo's capture finally brought the regalia back to the palace, it is Meishi and two other attendants who received them. Describing in detail the condition of the box that contained the regalia, she recounts how deeply moved she was by the idea that they had come down to her time since the days of the gods, and how she took turns with another attendant to guard them day and night. Meishi's memoir, Tonomura concludes, demonstrates that women bore much responsibility in running the royal administration.[131]

A Walk on the Wild Side

A warrior equivalent of the "jade woman" is Tomoe Gozen, a young woman who was the attendant of Kiso no Yoshinaka. The *Heike monogatari* describes her as "especially beautiful, with white skin, long hair, and charming features." But this seductive young woman was also "a remarkably strong archer, and as a swordswoman she was a warrior worth a thousand, ready to confront a demon or god, mounted or on foot."[132] An illustration of this is given when Yoshinaka, who has rebelled against Kamakura, is defeated by the troops of Yoshitsune. At the moment of committing suicide, he forces Tomoe, who has remained by his side, to flee, and she does so reluctantly and not without one last demonstration of her indomitable spirit:

> As she sat here, thirty riders came into view, led by Honda no Hachirō Moroshige, a man renowned in Musashi province for his great strength. Tomoe galloped into their midst, rode up alongside Moroshige, seized him in a powerful grip, pulled him down against the pommel of her saddle, held him motionless, twisted off his head, and threw it away. Afterward, she discarded armor and helmet and fled toward the eastern provinces.[133]

Tomoe's case is somewhat ambiguous, as she is both faithful to her lord and lover, yet threatening to other men. Another interesting case is that of the "Gion Consort" (Gion Nyogō), a woman said to be Kiyomori's mother. According to the *Ima kagami*, she was a woman of unknown origin and was made a consort of Retired Emperor Shirakawa for unusual reasons. Although she was never formally given the title of *nyogō* (consort), she was addressed as such by the people.[134] The secret of her success is said to be linked to her worship of Dakiniten, and to her relation with the priest Ningai.[135] As the story goes, when Ningai worshipped Dakiniten for a thousand days at Inari Peak, Gion no Shōnin Hōshi sent his daughter to Ningai every day with food offerings. Because of the merits thus obtained, the girl was later taken as a consort by Shirakawa, and thus came to be called the Gion Consort. Owing to her influence, Ningai was allegedly able to leap straight up the ladder to the highest clerical position.[136]

Gion Nyogō also initiated the female transmission of a specific kind of jewel, the *śarīra* of the Buddha or the *cintāmaṇi* transmitted in the Ono school of Shingon.[137] This school participated actively in the elaboration of the Insei rule of Shirakawa by lending to him its "regalia," the *cintāmaṇi* (or *śarīra*) allegedly brought to Japan by Kūkai himself. Several other sources mention that she was entrusted with important jewels by Shirakawa. After Shirakawa, these regalia were apparently transmitted by Gion Nyogō to her putative son Kiyomori—and, in some versions, to Retired Emperor Toba.[138] Gion Nyogō (and her sister) thus played an important role in the *Busshari sōjō shidai*, the chronicle of transmission of the Buddhas' relics. Tanaka points out that the figures of Gion Nyogō and her sister recall those of the two daughters of the sea-king in the *Kojiki*, who transmitted the tide-controlling jewels to Hohoderi no Mikoto.[139] Here again, the topos of the *nāga*-palace is in the background, and Gion Nyogō may have been perceived (or construed) as a kind of priestess, another "jade woman." In this mythical setting of the *Busshari sōjō shidai*, if Kiyomori is identified with the god Hohoderi, the legitimate ruler, Shirakawa, becomes the dragon-king (or, in Buddhist terms, the *nāga*-king) himself, and Gion Nyogō a *nāga*-girl.

As we will see, however, these *nāga*-girls, as are all mediators straddling two worlds, were also Janus-faced. Gion Nyogō's ambivalence, already alluded to with the mention of her association with the "heterodox" *ḍākinī* rituals, is revealed in one strange aspect of her character: she is described as an extraordinary lover of meat. We are told that, even during the period in which Retired Emperor Shirakawa was rigorously following the Buddhist precepts against the taking of life, she sent people out hunting every day so as to feed herself fresh meat.[140]

We already have received some hints about the "dark side" of the jade woman. This side appears clearly in the legend of the foxy Tamamo no Mae:

> During the reign of Emperor Toba, a beautiful woman appeared mysteriously at his palace. . . . She was an unparalleled beauty who gave off a wondrous fragrance and emitted a light from her body. The people called her Lady Tamamo no Mae. The emperor felt some fear of her, but he was overcome by her beauty and took her as a consort. Then he fell to a serious illness, for which no medicament seemed effective. He thus ordered the fortune-teller Abe no Yasunari to make a divination, from which it was learned that the cause was Tamamo no Mae. Abe said that if she were killed, the illness would be cured.[141]

Yasunari further explains that she is actually an 800-year-old two-tailed fox from the Nasuno Plain in Shimotsuke Province, and in her past existences she had become an enemy of Buddhism. She would always appear at the court of Buddhist kingdoms, seduce the king, and, taking his life, endeavor to have herself installed as the king of the land. Tamamo no Mae was forced to reveal her true nature when asked by Yasunari to perform a special *onmyōdō* ceremony. Once discovered, she disappeared, and, resuming her original shape, fled to the Nasuno Plain. The court commanded that eastern warriors track the fox and kill it. Having done so, they "deposited the rare treasures that appeared from various parts of the fox's body in appropriate temples and houses, and they sent the white needle to Yoritomo, who was then sent into exile to the province of Izu."[142]

We have noted above the association of Kenreimon'in with the *nāga*-palace in the Kakuichi recension of the *Heike monogatari*, and the influence in Japanese medieval imagination of these women who served as mediators between the human world and the *nāga*-palace. In another recension of this work, the *nāga*-palace reappears as the ultimate dwelling place of the royal sword. In this context, fisherwomen or female divers (*ama*—a term homonymous with "nun") play an important role as liminal beings who are able (or not) to retrieve regalia. According to one tradition, after the loss of the divine sword at Dan-no-ura, the retired emperor asks two fisherwomen to dive to the *nāga*-palace in order to retrieve it. They report their encounter with the *nāga*-king and his refusal to return the sword. In another legend, a fisherwoman brings back from the *nāga*-palace pearls that become the regalia of Kōfukuji (and of the Fujiwara).[143]

As suggested earlier, the story of Nyoi also brings to light the relations between jade women and the Urashima legend. Noteworthy in this respect is the following female version of the Urashima/*nāga*-palace story: A diver (*ama*) went to the dragon-palace (or to the sanctuary of the god "Isoko," that is, Izawa no Miya of Isobe) located beyond a stone gate some seventy meters deep. There, she was offered banquets during three days (variants: three months, or one year) and returned with a box that would bring her wealth and happiness if she took it to Isobe Shrine without opening it. But the curiosity of the villagers eventually caused her to transgress the interdiction. Out of the box came a large mosquito net, which could no longer be put back inside. The box and the mosquito net were deposited in the shrine. As to the woman, she became blind (or deranged, or poor, depending on the variant), and the same fate was met by one of her descendants in each generation.[144]

The image of the fisherwoman is often paired with that of the courtesan (*yūjo*), another female figure related to water (as will be seen). In Hōnen's biography, for instance, one of them appears side by side with a courtesan as a sinner (because she kills living beings), but she is able to reach rebirth in the Pure Land. In the Nō play "Ama," we find the theme of the love between a priest and a fisherwoman. In some pearl stories, courtesans and *ama* occupy the same structural position, and both perform rites related to the sea. They are intermediaries for sacred jewels and lineages that have come from the sea to the earth.[145] Thus, one legend tells how Tōgan, a royal emissary who had obtained a pearl, was showing it while on his way to see a courtesan when the pearl was stolen by a dragon. The courtesan then dived to the dragon-palace and retrieved the pearl, but she eventually died. Three temples were built in her memory, as well as to placate the dragon.[146]

The twofold truth of Buddhist hagiography is produced by the contrast between the hagiographical discourse, which describes a saintly life unaffected by sexual difference, and a darker symbolism that can be read between the lines.[147] In the case of Queen Vaidehī, for instance, we seem to have a perfect case of wifely devotion and the spiritual quest for deliverance. And yet, through the details, another story comes to the surface.

Like the painting of "Roman Charity" by Greuze (1725–1805), in which a daughter breast-feeds her ailing father, there is a kind of voyeurism in Vaidehī's giving her naked body, covered with nutrients, to her starving husband to lick. The spectacle becomes not so much that of the pious charity consciously intended by the author, but something more ambivalent, source of voyeurism. The image becomes susceptible to a double-reading. In other words, if Vaidehī had been old and ugly, her "spirituality" may not have inspired the kind of devotion it did. Even as it seems to deny her sexuality, the legend affirms it. Likewise, the pious intentions of Empress Danrin, turning her body into a memento mori, are subverted by the obscenity of the spectacle itself, and the perverted voyeurism it occasions.

In the case of Chūjōhime, whereas the manifest content of her story is that of a purification and ascension to holiness through the denial of femininity, the latent content emphasizes the pollution of blood and sexuality. The same is true in the case of Sari, and to a lesser extent, that of Māya. Mahāprajāpatī remains asexual through and through, as could be expected from the first nun, but she remains bound to her master, the Buddha, by the ties of maternal love. In the case of Empress Shōtoku, the sexuality is suggested by the physical defilement of her encounter with the leper. Even in the most unlikely places, for instance the poem of Chiyono's enlightenment, one may discern a subtext: the metaphor of the bucket that loses its bottom is reminiscent of a ritual performed in the medieval period for easy childbirth, for instance.

In other words, behind the explicit model of holiness defined by hagiographical discourse, we can discern clues to a persistent impurity, the remains of a quite different system of values, in which female blood and sexuality played an important role. It is because these figures drew on this symbolic system that they could become so pregnant, meaningful. In other words, their sanctity was the result, not so much of their spirituality, but rather from their purification from the blood and sexuality that threatened them constantly. At the same time, blood and sexuality remain constituent elements of their lives, they become, in a sense, their blason or emblem. Conversely, when this sexuality, becoming too aggressive, moves to the forefront, women, despite their spiritual quest or claim to sanctity, are demonized. The same is true when they wield too much political power, another form of female assertion. Such is the case with Empresses Wu Zhao and Shōtoku. In both cases, sexuality and political power are intimately related, and subsequently interpreted as usurpations of legitimate male power.

The above gallery of portraits reveals that even positive images, like that of Queen Māya, when looked at more closely, lose their simplicity and uncontrolled elements resurface—a kind of return of the repressed: blood, sex, desire. This complication does not allow a teleological narrative of progress: too often, pure figures hailed by feminist scholars as models become abstract, lifeless, devoid of the kind of subtlety that could pass as inner life. Female characters that emerge in the Buddhist medieval tradition prove rather ambivalent, straddling the sacred and the profane, playing the role of symbolic shifters, mediators, often through transgression. This theme will appear more clearly in the third part of the book, devoted to women who stand on the margins (or outside) of the Buddhist tradition.

PART THREE

WOMEN AGAINST BUDDHISM

Chapter Seven

CROSSING THE LINE

ONE OF THE major components in the Buddhist rhetoric of inequality was the belief that women should be excluded from sacred places (*nyonin kekkai*). Indeed, the evolution of this belief constitutes a good index of the changing perceptions of women during the medieval period. The locus classicus for the description of this *locus purissimus* called *kekkai* (restricted area) can be found in Hōnen's commentary on the *Guan wuliangshou jing,* and it deserves to be quoted at length:

> In Japan too, woman is refused admission to holy places and buildings. Around the sacred places on Mount Hiei, founded by Dengyō Daishi, he himself set boundaries by valleys and mountain peaks, within which women were forbidden to enter. From this we see that over the top of the Mountain of the One Vehicle, the clouds of the five obstacles cannot be overspread, and in the depth of the valley of the ineffable sweetness, the stream of the three obediences cannot flow. Mount Kōya is also a mountain peak set apart by Kōbō Daishi, where flourishes the Superior Vehicle of the Shingon. There the moonlight of the three secrets shines over everything, and yet not over the incapacity of woman. The water of the five wisdoms stored in the five vessels flows everywhere over the mountain, but it does not wash away woman's uncleanness. The gold and bronze image of Vairocana, one hundred and sixty feet high, erected by Emperor Shōmu, may be worshipped by women at a distance, but they are not allowed to go inside the door. The stone image of Maitreya erected by Emperor Tenchi, may be worshipped by women, but not from the platform where ordinary worshippers stand. And so there are many places of this kind, such as Mount Kinpu and the Daigo Temple near Kyōto, over whose precincts a woman may not cast her shadow. Alas! Though [you have] two feet, there are mountains of the Law which [you may] not ascend, and courtyards of the Buddha which [you may] not look at, and holy images which [you may] not worship! There are hindrances in your way to keep you from approaching even mountains made of clay pebbles, thorny shrubs and trees, and even coarse earthy, wooden images of the Buddha. How then, can you ever possibly draw near to the Buddha of the ten thousand transcendent virtues in the Pure Land of countless treasures? No wonder if woman doubts the possibility of her attaining to birth in the Pure Land.[1]

As one can see from Hōnen's account, often quoted in later Jōdo sermons because of its literary quality, women were excluded, not only from mountains such as Hieizan and Kinpusen, but also from the inner sanctums of famous temples such as Tōdaiji in Nara and Daigoji on the south-eastern outskirts of Kyoto.[2] Furthermore, the exclusion is traced back to the "founders" of Heian Buddhism, Saichō (Dengyō Daishi) and Kūkai (Kōbō Daishi), and beyond them to the Nara temples. The notion spread in the medieval period through popular literary works such as the *Soga monogatari*. The heroine of this tale, a young woman named Tora Gozen, becomes a nun after the death of her lover Jūrō, one of the Soga brothers. Later, after having visited his grave, she meets a courtesan who was close to the brothers, Shōshō of Tegoshi, and the two women become nuns at Zenkōji, before joining Hōnen's community. Later on, they encounter the mother and sister of the Soga, and Shōshō tells them what she has learnt from Hōnen.[3]

> Women bear the special burdens of the Five Obstacles and the Three Duties, and thus cannot aspire to immediate Buddhahood. They should visit the miraculous Buddhas and the sacred precincts in order to listen to the Buddha's teachings and establish a tie with him; yet there are many hallowed grounds that cannot be visited and many Buddhist statues that cannot be worshipped. At the request of Emperor Kammu, M. Hiei was established in order to transmit the teachings of the Buddha. The peak of the Great Vehicle for attaining enlightenment rises high in the sky; and the moon of absolute reality shines brightly, but it does not illuminate the darkness of the Five Obstacles. During the reign of Emperor Saga, Kōbō Daishi was given land on Mt. Kōya. The peak of the eight-petalled lotus and the eight valleys are cool; and the water is pure, but it does not wash away the grime of the Three Duties. Women never venture above the clouds on Mt. Kimpu or to the bottom of the mist at the Daigo temple; nor do they approach Mt. Fuji, Mt. Shirayama, or Shōsha temple.[4]

By emphasizing the biological and ritual impurity of women, this prohibition, initially known as *nyonin kinzei kekkai* (area forbidden to women), and later simply as *nyonin kekkai*, also reveals the ambiguous attitude of Buddhist monks vis-à-vis a popular culture in which women played a significant role. This prohibition is traditionally interpreted (or justified) as an attempt by ecclesiastical authorities to preserve the spiritual purity of male practitioners, and in particular of mountain ascetics (*yamabushi*). This prohibition endured for centuries, until its cancellation in 1873 during the Meiji Restoration. It still remains unofficially in place at Kinpusen, however, where the spring and autumn rituals of "entering the mountain" are reserved exclusively to "healthy males."

The presence of women posed a problem for a community of male ascetics. Perhaps, as Ushiyama Yoshiyuki observes, their exclusion, referred to initially as *nyonin kinzei*, was essentially motivated by a desire to enforce monastic Vinaya through a strict separation between monks and nuns (or women in general). It seems difficult, however, to follow Ushiyama when he argues that this exclusion had no sexist intent and was unrelated to the belief in female impurity.[5] Admittedly, in early texts such as the *Sanke gakushōshiki*, the exclusion of women is simply part of a larger prohibition, which also includes thieves and alcohol. Besides, the interdiction cut both ways, and nunneries were also in principle forbidden to men.[6] The alleged laxity of the Buddhist clergy made it necessary to enforce a strict separation between monks and nuns, a point reiterated by many edicts (apparently without much success) throughout the medieval period. If monasteries and convents were initially following the same rule, however, it remains to explain why only the exclusion of women came to prevail, whereas the parallel "exclusion of men" is conspicuously absent. According to Ushiyama, it is because of the changes in the *Ritsuryō* system toward the beginning of Heian, which brought about the end of the state-sponsored female ordinations and the disappearance of official convents. As a result, monastic documents retained only the rule about the "exclusion of women."

A point of terminology is in order. Ushiyama's point that the emergence of the expression *nyonin kekkai* is a medieval phenomenon and should not be read back into the Heian period is well taken. It may be better, then, to refer to such exclusion in the early Heian period as *nyonin kinzei*, in order to emphasize its disciplinary components, already found in the *Yōrō Soniryō* (Nara period), or even in the Chinese Vinaya of the Tang. Ushiyama falls into a similar type of anachronism, however, when he attemps to extend this Vinaya-centered view to the medieval phenomenon. Whereas the notion of *nyonin kinzei* remains strictly disciplinary, that of *nyonin kekkai*, referring to a full-fledged discourse about the purity of sacred space (*kekkai*), has broader implications, and is symbolically much more complex. Thus, by restricting his investigation to the disciplinary aspect of *nyonin kinzei*, Ushiyama forbids himself to consider other factors that obviously played a role in the emergence of this taboo. He also downplays gender discrimination by legitimizing the monastic need for a strict gender distinction. Judging from the violence of such rejection, and the apparent irrelevance of the arguments invoked—in particular the notion of female sin and blood pollution—something else seems at stake here. Buddhist orthopraxy hardly justifies such a rhetoric of exclusion, particularly in light of the deplorable reputation of the major mountain monasteries at the time. It is well known that cultic centers such as Mount Hiei, Mount Kōya, and Mount Negoro served for centuries as refuges for men who had problems with the law. The presence of women on these mountains, while it would not have improved this unfortunate state of things, was obviously not its cause.

THE UTOPIAN TOPOS

It seems that women were first barred from Mt. Hiei in the early Heian period, and that this exclusion rapidly extended to a number of imperially sponsored temples. The justification for it changed drastically with time. Although at first the claim was that monks can best perform state rituals when separated from women, soon the notion of female pollution came to the forefront. Finally, legends developed about women physically defiling the sacred mountain with their menstrual blood or other bodily fluid. The fact that these developments seem related to Japanese notions of purity and defilement raises the question of the extent to which they can be seen as specifically Japanese. Similar attitudes can be found in other forms of Buddhism.[7] In Tibet, for instance, women pilgrims were until recently prevented from climbing beyond a certain point on Tsari ("Pure Crystal") Mountain. According to Toni Huber, this prohibition operated on a somewhat different logic from that of sexual distraction, which justified seasonally banning the presence of women around the mountain's meditation communities.[8] The case of Tsari Mountain is particularly interesting for comparative purposes. A significant detail noted by Huber reveals the ritual value of this prohibition (and its transgression) and may shed interesting light on the Japanese case as well: upon reaching the limit (the Drölma Pass), women were permitted to walk exactly seven steps farther down the other side toward Pure Crystal Mountain before returning back the way they came. Huber compares this to the seven steps of the Buddha, and comments: "Since all women, even yoginīs, are banned because of their bodies, all will have to wait until their next birth to see if those seven steps across the Drölma La worked to give them a male body and qualify them for the whole pilgrimage."[9]

Huber goes on to add that, although women were prevented from accomplishing clockwise circumambulation of the upper part of the mountain, they had an alternative route for completing part of it, that is, by following a counterclockwise circuit.[10] In that particular instance, the claim that women's exclusion is justified to prevent male ascetics from sexual distraction is only one among several reasons invoked. One story tells how the wife of an official defied the tutelary goddess by crossing the threshold and was severely punished. As in Japanese Buddhist legends, "feminine character is presented as disrespectful, irreverent and arrogant, impetuous, and envious."[11] Huber also notes that the monks, who tend to disregard or disparage such stories, emphasize that women are prohibited because they are by nature impure and defiling, whereas the mountain is the pure abode of the deities, a maṇḍala.[12] The linkage between purity, gender, and altitude is strongly reminiscent of the Japanese case, in which it seems only to have been applied on a larger scale. In both the Tibetan and Japanese cases, the exclusion was at times actively resisted and contested by women. As at Tsari Mountain, the control of access to ritual space on Japanese mountains is that of a utopian space where gender differences are at the same time emphasized and abolished—in the sense that there are no women—in order to turn this space into the earthly equivalent of the Pure Land.

What, then, is a *kekkai*? Originally, it was a sacred space free from all defilement, and it is around the ninth century that women became the emblem of all defilement. In esoteric Buddhism, the term designates the ritual area where demons—and by extension women—cannot enter.[13] It implies clearly more than an attempt to preserve the purity of the monks. The inner sanctum, the area around the *honzon*, also constitutes a *kekkai*. Even in temples open to women (like Ishiyamadera in Ōmi), the inside of the Buddha Hall was strictly forbidden to all profanes. At Yakushiji in Nara, even monks were excluded from the inner sanctum, to which only novices (*dōji*) had access.

There were two main types of *kekkai*, one defining the sacred space of the mountain and the other the inner sanctum of the monastery. Thus, the central altar of the main hall is called Shumidan (Mount Sumeru Altar).[14] The establishment of a mountain *kekkai* was the most efficient way for a temple to assert its property rights. In 970, for instance, Ryōgen delimited the *kekkai* on Mount Hiei by forbidding monks to let horses and cows wander on the mountain, and by prohibiting all fishing, hunting, and cutting wood. Thus, the term at first designated merely a "restricted zone" prohibited to anything unclean. There were also gradations in terms of purity and defilement, defining concentric rings of *kekkai*. At the upper *kekkai* of Hikosan, for instance, it was strictly prohibited "to produce excrement of any sort, or to spit and blow one's nose."[15] On Hieizan, there were six levels of *kekkai* of increasing purity, from the bottom (Sakamoto) to the top (Enryakuji). On Kōyasan, Kūkai defined an area extending over seven *li* in all directions, which he placed under the protection of Buddhist deities, while inviting evil spirits to leave.[16] Later this exclusion came to be applied more particularly to women.

The mythological motif of the *nyonin kekkai*, according to which the mountain deity becomes angry when a woman transgresses the boundary, was a radical departure from earlier practices, in which women were admitted in temples for ceremonies held during the day. Prior to the ninth century, it is only on account of ritual impurity—menstruation and pregnancy—and during specific periods that women were refused access to shrines or temples. The early Japanese notion of pollution (*kegare*) differed significantly from that of the *nyonin kekkai* in that the resulting taboo could be lifted through purification (*harai*), whereas that of the *nyonin kekkai* could not. Buddhist notions such as the Five Obstacles, by merging with local notions of ritual impurity, allowed the emergence of the quasi-ontological form of female defilement undergirding the notion of *nyonin kekkai*.

There were also some isolated reactions to this extension of "gender cleansing." In an oft-quoted predication, Dōgen declares: "There is in Japan something laughable. It is the so-called *kekkai*, for instance around the places of practice of the Great Vehicle, where nuns and women are not allowed to enter. . . . Such *kekkai* claim to be better and purer than the Buddhist assembly at the time of Śākyamuni. We should not want them for our [school], because they are the realm of Māra."[17] Dōgen even argues that the destruction of all *kekkai* would be a form of gratitude toward the Buddha.[18] Later, however, he seems to deny the possibility of lay practitioners becoming buddhas, and he excludes women from ritual activities at Eiheiji.[19] Thus, Dōgen's statements must be taken with a grain of sectarian salt, as we recall how the inclusive attitude of his early proselytizing period was replaced by an inflexible exclusivism.

STOPPED IN THEIR TRACKS

Although female religious specialists such as the "Kumano nuns" and their non-Buddhist counterparts traveled relatively freely through Japan, their legendary ancestors were prevented from entering the mountains. Many local traditions tell the legend of a woman named Toran (or a variant of that name), usually described as a "nun" (*bikuni*) or an "old woman" (*uba*), who was changed into a rock or a tree when she tried to climb up a sacred mountain in spite of the warning she received from the mountain god himself.[20] The rock, seen as the petrified body of this woman, serves afterwards as a reminder of the line that cannot be crossed (and yet invites crossing). Once again, the female body has become a mere sign in Buddhist semiotics.

Hakusan

One of these legends, related to Hakusan, a mountain near Dōgen's monastery Eiheiji, speaks of an "old woman" (*uba*) named Tōru, who used witchcraft to deceive people. She made a living by running a wine shop at one of the gates of the mountain. Thinking that she could make more profit by selling wine at the top of the mountain, she began climbing it, accompanied by a young girl. A voice from the clouds forbade her to defile the divine peak with her impure body, but she paid no attention to it. The sky then became suddenly dark and the voice was heard again.

Tōru merely laughed and, in defiance, crouched to urinate, deliberately polluting the sacred ground. When the path collapsed, she used her magic skills to cross the ravine over a cloud. She continued climbing, even as her companion was suddenly changed into a stone. Then, an earthquake made her drop her wine provision, which crashed below. Now alarmed, Tōru decided to turn back. It was too late, however: a mist, covering the slope, caused her to lose her way, and soon a poisoned wind transformed her into stone.

Variants of this legend were told in all cultic centers of Shugendō, the tradition of mountain ascetics. At Tateyama, a neighboring mountain whose monastery was a rival to that of Hakusan, it is a "nun" from Obama (in Wakasa province), named Toran (or Tōrō), who climbs the mountain with a young woman and a girl.[21] When they cross the limit of the sacred space, her two companions are changed into cedar trees; horns grow on Toran's forehead, and she is finally turned into a stone.[22] A little above the two trees is a place called *shikaribari* where Toran crouched to urinate on the ground. Nevertheless, Toran seems to have been integrated in the sacred landscape of Tateyama as a positive marker of sacredness. In the *Tateyama mandara*, the stone and the cedars that represent her and her two companions are listed together with more orthodox Buddhist topoi such as the cave where Kōbō Daishi performed a goma ritual, the waterfall where Hōnen recited the nenbutsu, and the bridge where Dōgen meditated.[23]

Kinpusen

Similar legends are found all over Japan, reflecting various degrees of Buddhist assimilation of local sites.[24] At Kinpusen, we can follow the stages through which Toran's story was recuperated for Buddhist purposes. According to the *Genkō shakusho*,

> The nun Toran was a woman of the province of Yamato. She practiced Buddhist asceticism in detail, and at the same time she studied the Taoist arts of immortality. She dwelled at the foot of Mount Yoshino. As tradition has it, the earth of Kinpusen is pure gold, and it is protected by the bodhisattva Kongō Zaō, who will not permit women to cross its boundaries. Toran said, "Woman though I am, I observe the commandments of purity and have experienced supernatural effects. How could I be classed with ordinary women?" and so she climbed up Kinpusen. Suddenly there was thunder and lightning and it grew dark; in her confusion she no longer recognized the path. She threw away the staff she had been holding, and it took root of itself, growing at length into a great tree. Toran also summoned up a dragon with spells and tried to ride it up the mountain. She got only as far as the source of the stream and was unable to proceed. Toran

became furious and stamped on the rocky peaks until everywhere everything was crushed or split. The lake which nurtured her dragon is under a rock. Her two footprints are still there. People say that she attained the Way of Long Life, and nothing is known of how she ended.[25]

Toran's argument that she "observes the rules of purity" and should therefore "not be classed with ordinary women" will be repeated by many women transgressing the *nyonin kekkai*. Here, the "nun" Toran is described as a kind of Daoist immortal, and the legend does not say that she turned into stone. The *Honchō shinsenden* gives a more thoroughly Buddhist version, according to which she obtained longevity by practicing diligently the Dharma at Yoshino. Her attempt to climb Mount Kinpusen was prevented by the intervention of Zaō Gongen (or Konsei Myōjin in some variants), the Buddhist deity protecting the mountain, but also because, we are told, Kinpusen "is a place of precepts, hence women have no access to it."[26]

In *Gikeiki*, the warrior Yoshitsune, in his flight to Kumano, has to leave his lover Shizuka behind, because she is not allowed to climb Kinpusen. As he explains, rather lamely, to her: "This mountain, the Peak of Enlightenment made sacred by En no Gyōja, is forbidden to the impure, so it is quite possible that I have made the gods angry by letting you share the fate which has led me here." Yoshitsune's real motif is his realization that his companion Benkei and the other members of his fugitive group resent Shizuka's presence.[27]

One of the oldest texts related to Kinpusen, the *Kumano sansho gongen Kinpusen Kongō Zaō suijaku engi*, mentions the legend of the "nun" Dōran, a woman said to be the elder sister of the priest Gigen. Here, it is not Zaō Gongen, but Konsei Daimyōjin (a phallic deity!), who intervenes. When Dōran is stopped by him, she tries to climb from the side, but the mountain crumbles down and she eventually dies.[28] Another text of the same collection contains several "origin stories" (*engi*), among which is that of a girl of the Kōga clan named Meishi (probably a name of *miko*). This *engi*, which was to be transmitted to the women of the Kōga clan, was allegedly stolen by Toran, who found in it the strength to climb Kinpusen. Yet, because she confused the sequence of correct transmission, her boldness was punished with death by the god. The Toran in question was not without pedigree, however, since her brother Gigen was the third generation successor of En no Gyōja, the legendary founder of Shugendō. In light of the *Honchō shinsenden*'s statement about her magical powers and her longevity, it is significant that she is also connected to a *miko* lineage straddling the Kinpusen and Kumano regions.[29] Admittedly, the tale emphasizes that Toran did not inherit the orthodox lineage, and paid with her life for her transgression of the sacred space. Although she is shown here in a rather negative light, her name evokes the image of the female priestesses officiating at such places.[30] The *miko* of Kinpusen and Kumano, after all, had the important function of offering prayers to the local *kami*.

A young woman named Tora also appears in the *Hieizan ryakki* as a disciple of Saichō, the founder of Hieizan.[31] While obviously building on the legend of Toran, this variant constitutes a clerical reinterpretation in terms of monastic purity. The gist of the story is as follows: One day, Saichō notices that this female disciple has become infatuated with him, and withdraws to a secret place to escape temptation. She soon finds him, however, and the same scenario repeats itself several times. At the end of his wits, Saichō begs for divine help. In response to his prayers, the earth shakes, and Tora, frightened, is driven away. Resentful, she obtains an audience with the emperor and calumniates Saichō. Her attempt eventually backfires, however. When an emissary is sent to check on Saichō's purity, the priest is eventually cleared of all suspicion. After being summoned to court, he is even authorized to found a monastery on Hieizan, a mountain henceforward strictly forbidden to women.[32]

The plot of all of the above legends is basically the same. Their main protagonist is a woman of considerable spiritual power, whose name derives from the root Tor- (Tōrō, Tōru, Toran, Tora). She is sometimes called a nun or a *miko*, more often an *uba*, a term that leads one to picture her as an old woman. She is also described at times as a young woman, however, another connotation of the word *uba* (in its meaning of "wet-nurse). She usually has one or two female companions. Through the association of her image with that of the Happyaku bikuni (on whom more later), she is sometimes described as being both old—and young-looking, that is, as having reached immortality. In some cases, however, her former youth contrasts with her present decrepitude. In all of the variants, she rides an animal (usually a dragon, sometimes an ox), or at least has an animal as "magical ally" (in one case, a dog); she herself may even assume the shape of an animal—for instance, that of a tortoise. A first sign of her losing ground is when one of her magical "objects" or companions turns into vegetation or mineral: in one case, her staff takes root and becomes a large tree; in most variants, it is the young girl or woman accompanying her.

Earlier versions of the legend make no allusion to the blood pollution that will later become one leitmotif of the *nyonin kekkai* discourse. Here, the physical pollution is caused by a voluntary act of desecration, usually her urinating on the sacred ground.[33] The mountain god now really gets angry. But so does she, and in her anger, she usually leaves marks on the landscape (on a rock, precisely), before becoming herself a stone marker. In the more Buddhified versions of the legend, we find that the "nun" can be a seductive young woman who, instead of threatening the mountain god by violating his territory (that is, his body), threatens the virtue of a Buddhist ascetic who has to get help from his divine protector. The god has now become a Buddhist deity like Zaō Gongen on Kinpusen, or Sannō Myōjin on Hieizan. In most cases, the transgressing woman is a powerful shamaness who does not hesitate to challenge the mountain god. The story, as the Buddhists disseminated it, seems to represent an inversion of the initial situation: in ancient Japan, shamanesses served and represented the (often female) mountain deity, whereas Buddhist monks were the ones who dislodged the latter by taking possession of its domain to found their monasteries.

KŪKAI'S MOTHER

The *nyonin kekkai* is vividly described in the legend of Kūkai's mother, as it appears for instance in the "Kōya no maki" "Mount Kōya's Scroll." This "scroll," as it is known to us, constitutes a section of the Buddhist tale (*sekkyōbushi*) *Karukaya* (1631), but it may originally have existed independently as an *engi* of Kōyasan.[34] The plot of *Karukaya* unfolds as follows: after leaving his wife and child and consulting the saintly priest Hōnen at Kurodani, Shigeuji secludes himself on Kōyasan. His wife, Midaidokoro, having learnt his whereabouts, decides to climb the mountain, but an innkeeper to whom she has told her intention stops her by telling the origins of the *nyonin kekkai*. The "Kōya no maki" proper begins at this point. It opens with the life of Kūkai: his birth and youth, his travel to China, his vision of the bodhisattva Mañjuśrī, his return to Japan, and his divinely inspired discovery of the site of Kōyasan. It ends with the story of his mother, a Chinese woman of royal birth. She was, we are told, sent into exile and she eventually landed in Japan, where she married a villager and gave birth to one male child. Later, she had to leave the village because of the child's constant crying and subsequently wandered across Japan. After abandoning the child, she became a nun. In her old days, she eventually heard that her child had himself become a monk under the name of Kūkai and lived on Kōyasan. She therefore resolved to ascend Kōyasan. In the end, she was prevented from doing so, although she did succeed in meeting her son. Having told her story to Midaidokoro, the innkeeper concludes: if even Kūkai's mother could not climb Kōyasan, how could an ordinary woman pretend to do so? Finally convinced, Midaidokoro renounces her project to meet her husband.

The encounter between Kūkai and his mother is strongly reminiscent of Toran's legend. It shows in a paradigmatic fashion the relationship established in Japanese Buddhism between menstruation, ritual impurity, and the exclusion of women. Let us return to the moment when Kūkai's mother is about to set foot on Kōyasan. Kūkai is warned of his mother's transgressive intention by an earthquake. He goes down to meet her, and warns her that she cannot proceed further. Like Toran, Kūkai's mother at first argues that she is not concerned by the blood taboo: "I am eighty-three and I have not had periods for the past forty-two years. As I am no different from a worthy monk, there is nothing wrong in my setting foot on the mountain." Kūkai feigns to yield to her argument, but tells her that she must first step on his monastic robe, which he spreads on the ground. When she does so, a few drops of menstrual blood fall on the robe, which catches fire and flies away, taking the mother with it. Kūkai performs funeral rites on her behalf, and as a consequence she escapes from the realm of passions and becomes the bodhisattva Maitreya. In one variant, although the robe takes fire, the mother is not taken away, but she has to renounce her plan. Kūkai installs her in a hermitage later known as the "Mausoleum for Kōbō Daishi's Mother" (*Daishi bokō byō)*, or simply the "Mother's Hall" (Hahakōdō), at the foot of Kōyasan. This chapel later became a temple named Jison-in (in Kudoyama-chō). When she dies, one year later, her body does not decay; instead, owing to the efficacy of Kūkai's rites, it turns into a mummy (*sokushin butsu*, a "buddha in this very body").[35] It is then placed in a crypt to wait for Maitreya's descent, and in due time it comes to be worshipped as a manifestation of Maitreya. As its name indicates, Jison-in was centered on the cult of Maitreya (Jison, or Miroku), and it contains a statue of this bodhisattva (and future Buddha) attributed to Kūkai.[36] Thus, whereas Kōyasan was believed to be the inner sanctum or palace (*naiin*) of the Tuṣita heaven, the abode of Maitreya, Jison-in was the outer palace (*gein*), a kind of Pure Land where women could become buddhas. It became subsequently one of several places known as "Women's Kōya."[37]

All the variants of the legend mention the "twisted rock" (*neji iwa*) that Kūkai's mother "twisted" in her resentment for being prevented from climbing Kōyasan. Another related rock is the *oshiage-iwa iwa* ("lifted-up rock"). Both rocks are obviously related to the *kekkai-ishi* or *uba-ishi*, and they have become landmarks on the mountain path of Kōyasan.[38] In the case of the *oshiage-iwa*, one tradition has it that as soon as Kūkai's mother set foot on the mountain, she began to menstruate and fire rained from heaven. At the same time, Kūkai "lifted up" the rock before her to bar her advance; or, in a more charitable interpretation, to hide and protect her from the rain and lightning. Depending on the versions, the handprint on the rock is said to be that of her hand or of Kūkai's hand.[39]

The physical trace of anger left on the landscape by Kūkai's mother calls to mind the legend of Toran, but also, more surprisingly, that of Chūjōhime, the visionary nun of Taimadera. Pilgrims to that temple can see her chapel, as well as her footprint on a rock. That footprint, we are told, was imprinted in anger when Chūjōhime, wanting to visit Taimadera, was denied access to the temple by monks. She thereupon built herself a hermitage nearby, and was eventually rewarded by a vision of Amida's Pure Land. This event was subsequently appropriated by Taimadera monks and became the source of the temple's prosperity.[40] Despite her subsequent canonization, Chūjōhime represents the woman who "does not know her place" and attempts to cross the forbidden threshold.[41] Both Chūjōhime and Kūkai's mother seem to be emblems of transgression and of menstrual blood.[42]

The figure of Kūkai's mother is a mixture of the image of the forlorn mother in search of her son and that of the old shamaness (seen as a kind of hag casting angry spells). The episode involving Kūkai's monastic robe is not only a test of ritual purity, or a reassertion of fertility returning to a post-menopausal woman, but also becomes a kind of magic duel, in which the shamaness is eventually defeated by the Buddhist priest. The same woman who fails in her rite of passage (from the profane to the pure realm), however, becomes a specialist of passages from the invisible to the visible world—in other words, childbirth. Thus, the obnoxious woman becomes an obstetric deity who can heal the very ailment from which she suffered, and becomes a specialist of blood flux. The same element is found in Chūjōhime's legend, who, as we may recall, became a deity invoked for "female ailments."

The story of Kūkai's mother adds several significant elements to the theme of the woman transgressing the *kekkai*. Perhaps the most important feature is that she has become a mother, a redeeming quality in the Japanese Buddhist context. Another significant motif is that of the menstrual blood defiling the sacred ground. Despite all of these changes, the shamanistic nature of the woman is still emphasized. A telling element in this respect is the name of Kūkai's mother.[43] Early documents merely indicate her clan name. As the legend of Kūkai (Kōbō Daishi) grew, however, the need was felt to give her a personal name, and she was at first called Tamayori Gozen or Akoya. In *Karukaya*, for instance, her name is "Akō Gozen."[44] As noted earlier, she was allegedly the daughter of a Tang emperor. She is also said to have been "the worst female in the three countries." Her moral turpitude is reflected in her physical ugliness. As a result, she was abandoned at sea. Her boat eventually drifted to Japan, and she was given shelter by a fisherman from Sanuki, who married her.[45] After the man's death, she gave birth to a son called Kingyōmaru (the future Kūkai), but because of his constant crying she was eventually expelled from the village. She abandoned him—by burying him alive under a pine tree!—but he was fortunately discovered, unscathed, by an old priest. The theme of the drifting woman is typical of the origin story of a deity. Often, such a woman, after experiencing all kinds of hardships, sees her true nature revealed and is worshipped as a deity. This pattern sheds some interesting light on Kūkai's mother, a figure who subsumes both the deity and her priestess. Likewise, the name "Daishi" (abbreviation for Kōbō Daishi) is sometimes interpreted as "Taishi" (prince) a term referring to a divine child. In other words, the pair formed by Kūkai and his mother reflects the emergence of the *oyakogami* (parent-child gods) pattern.

The *Bikuni engi*, a collection of tales about the origins of the Kumano *bikuni*, includes a legend about the Miroku (that is, Kūkai's mother) of Myōhōzan in Nachi.[46] In this version, Kūkai's mother, after being prevented from climbing Kōyasan, eventually becomes a "regular" nun. The beginning of the *engi* explains the origins of the nuns (*bikuni*) in the three countries, and reveals that in Japan the female order began when Empress Kōmyō was ordained under the name Toran. She thereafter travelled throughout Japan with her servants, who became the Ise *bikuni* and the Kumano *bikuni*.

Legends revolving around the *nyonin kekkai* continued to be used in Buddhist sermons even after the medieval period. But they speak of a nun named Toran, or Akō Gozen, who lived "at the foot of the mountain" under the protection of a holy monk. Such was the case at Jison-in and Amano. By integrating this woman into their tradition as a buddha or a *kami*, these peripheral cultic centers constituted an indispensable part of the sacred space of Kōyasan. Interestingly, Jison-in was also a sanctuary for women pursued for theft.[47] In his *Zōtanshū*, Mujū Ichien says that Amano is a place where those women who had the closest ties with Kōyasan's ascetics lived as nuns. In a tale of the *Senjūshō*, the poet-monk Saigyō (1118–90) describes how he happened to meet with his wife, who had become a nun, during a visit to Hasedera. She told him that after his departure, she felt very unhappy and, having left their daughter with a maternal aunt, she eventually entered Amano convent. Perhaps because of this account, the graves of Saigyō's wife and daughter are said to be in Amano. In 1208, Hōjō Masako established there a hall (Miedō), dedicated to Kūkai (Kōbō Daishi), as a place of worship for women hoping to be reborn in the Pure Land. Amano was supported in part by the plots of land commanded by female landholders.

In the *Heike monogatari,* the lady-in-waiting Yokobue becomes a nun at Hokkeji in Nara after the man she loves, Takiguchi Nyūdō, becomes a recluse on Kōyasan. The *Genpei jōsuiki* tells us, however, that, after being ordained, she went to Amano, where she washed the clothes of Takiguchi Nyūdō.[48] In *Karukaya*, when Midaidokoro sees that her husband Shigeuji is determined to renounce the world, she pleads: "If you withdrew in a mountain temple, where you would recite the nenbutsu, I would go to the foot of Mt. Kōya, build a hermitage there, and change my appearance into that of a nun. And once a month, I would wash your dirty clothes."[49]

There are many similar stories connected with Amano. The relations between the women living at the foot of the mountain and the recluses on
its top replicate those between the goddess Niu (a double of the *miko*) and
Kōbō Daishi (the substitute of the mountain-god), immersed in perpetual
samādhi in the inner sanctum (Oku-no-in). At the same time, these
women were the heirs of Toran, the shamaness who had been prevented
from climbing to the top of the mountain.

Jison-in and Amano were the main communities at the foot of Mount
Kōya where women could get the "fringe benefits" of their devotion to
Kūkai and his mother.[50] Yet there were initially other *nyonindō* (Women's
Halls), seven in all—one at each entrance of Kōyasan (Kōya *nanaguchi*).[51]
The path that connected them (known as *nyonin michi*) ran for about ten
miles around the mountain ridge, establishing the perimeter of the *nyonin
kekkai*. Women could thus circumambulate the mountain (*nyonin michi
meguri*), and even get quite close to the Oku-no-in *from behind*, worshipping from a distance the great stupas and buildings that crowded the sacred area. The *nyonindō* eventually became useless when the ban on
women was lifted during the Meiji Restoration.[52]

The same scenario was repeated at other cultic centers. On the eastern
slope of Hieizan (Higashi Sakamoto, in Ōtsu), for instance, there is a
chapel called Hanatsumamidō (Hall where one picks flowers—also
known as Hanatsumamisha), built on the spot where Saichō is said to
have met his mother. Every year, on the eighth of the fourth month—
birthday of the Buddha, and also the day of the beginning of the summer
retreat—women were authorized to climb there to offer flowers to the
Buddha; hence the name, Hanatsumami. The place seems to have also
functioned as a *nyonindō*, that is, a place where women could seclude
themselves temporarily.[53] Again, at the foot of Tateyama, there is a small
building called Uba-dō, dedicated to the mother of Jikō Shōnin. Interestingly, she has become identified with a rather frightful female deity—although she is represented here with a smiling face—the old infernal hag
known as Datsueba, the "old woman who removes the clothes of the
dead." As Anna Seidel observes, the *miko/uba* of the Uba-dō, significantly
named Toran, "is none other than the mountain goddess relegated from
the top of the mountain to the frontier of the human world. She has lost
her transcendence (as she was replaced by the Buddha or his avatar, the
eminent priest), but in the process she has become closer to the humans
as intercessor." The Uba-dō was the focus of important ritual activities
for women, at the completion of which they received a talisman certifying
that they had been "transformed into men."[54] Although these rituals were
said to guarantee rebirth already in this life, they did not give women free
access to Tateyama.[55] Ironically, the lifting of Tateyama's *nyonin kekkai*
in 1869 was a pyrrhic victory for women: the Uba-dō was destroyed in

the process, the cult of Datsueba forbidden, and the place turned into a cultic center of "pure" Shintō. Yet the old associations were resilient, and the place has recently experienced a revival of sorts.

We have seen that most of these places dedicated to an eminent priest's mother (identified with the mountain-god) became important for women's religion as temples for easy childbirth and abundant lactation. The apotheosis of the saint's mother leads to her identification with the local deity. These women, who became the symbols of the mountain temples and contributed to their prosperity were piously described as "nuns" despite their clearly shamanistic nature and foundation in pre-Buddhist local cults.

According to the *engi* of Kongōbūji (the Shingon headquarters on Kō-yasan), Kūkai, looking for the proper site to build his temple, spent the night at Amano-miya, the shrine of the goddess Niu (or Nifutsu-hime), and received from her an oracle in which she bequeathed her domain to him.[56] Significantly, it is here the goddess, not the priest, who defines the boundaries of the *kekkai*. The exclusion of women from the sacred site would thus have been originally established by a female deity. We are even told that the goddess rejoiced at Kūkai's coming and called herself his "disciple." Although the story is quite different from that of the unruly Toran, in both cases we are dealing with a symbolic usurpation of the mountain by the Buddhists.

THE *KEKKAI* STONE

In all of these legends, a stone—said to be the petrified body of a woman—serves as a marker of sacredness. One may wonder whether it is the transgression of preexisting sacred space that causes petrification, as the legend has it, or, conversely, the petrification itself that creates sacred space. How different are these stone-markers from other lithic signs? Unlike the yin-yang stones of the crossroad deities (*dōsojin*), these "female" stones were usually not viewed as phallic symbols.[57] Instead of demarcating and protecting the human realm, they delimit the realm of the god (and of the monks); rather than symbolizing life and fertility, they are associated with death and the other world. Admittedly, there are some borderline cases, like those stone statues of the bodhisattva Jizō, which originally marked the border between this world and the other. Despite their functional differences, these two types of stone-markers were in all likelihood intimately related to local cults.[58]

The expression "stone woman" (*umazume*), usually designating sterile women, was also used to refer to a certain type of lithic marker, the so-called *uba-ishi*, meaning, in this case, stones that are endowed with the power to bring fertility. One apparent exception is the "Killing Stone," immortalized by the Nō play *Sesshō seki*. In this case, the connotations seem quite negative. Yet one tradition claims that it was brought to Shinnyodō in Kyoto and carved into a Jizō statue. This statue is today part of the *mizuko* cult for aborted or stillborn children, but is also the object of prayers for fecundity and for the health of young children.

Another type of stone known as *tora-ga-ishi* ("stone of Tora") is related to the legend of Tora (Tora Gozen, or Oiso no Tora) in the *Soga monogatari*. Although she is not known to have ever transgressed the *kekkai*, she became a nun and traveled through Japan.[59] One variant of Tora's legend mentions a nun named Tora Shinzen who, owing to her chastity (rather than her transgressive behavior), turned into stone. Yet the relation between this stone, known as *torako ishi*, and Oiso seems at first glance farfetched. After all, Tora is a beautiful young girl, whereas the legends of the *uba-ishi* usually refer to mature or old women; she is a Buddhist devotee who is eventually reborn in the Pure Land, whereas the *uba-ishi* are the "crystallization" of women bound by their passions. These stones are always the signs of the limit, however, and Yanagita Kunio may be right in thinking that they were initially put there for a specific ritual function, and that the motif of transgression was a later development.[60]

Yanagita has pointed to the similarities between the names of the transgressive "nun" of Hakusan, Toran, and the many "stones of Tora" (*tora-ga-ishi*) found throughout Japan. He argued that Toran (and its variants) is a collective name for the shamanesses (*miko*) who lived at the site of the *kekkai* stone.[61] According to him, these stones were originally related to the practice of women (*uba*, *bikuni*) who worshipped the mountain, and their meaning was negatively reinterpreted once such practice declined. In the present case, the shift from the wayward "nun" Toran to the pious Tora seems to reflect a further domestication of the shamaness. In most legends, one of the powers of such shamanesses is their ability to bring rain. This still seems to be the case with Toran, who is able to summon a dragon (a rain-deity). Tora, however, appears to have lost this power, although the tears she shed after the death of her lover were metaphorically called "Tora's rain" (Tora-ga-ame).[62] The fact that the "stone of Tora" in Oiso was believed to cause the rain to fall is a distant echo of her past shamanistic powers.[63]

The stories of the Oiso no Tora type usually tell of beautiful young girls—like Shizuka, Yoshitsune's lover—searching desperately for the men they love.[64] We also find traditions regarding older women (*oba*) turning into stone. A case in point is that of Oba Gozen Ōyamahime, the aunt of the Fujisan goddess Konohana Sakuyahime. Sent away by the latter, she climbs the mountain, sits on a stone (called *mei-ishi*, or *oi-ishi*) to contemplate the autumn moon, and finally enters the capital of the moon. Sometimes the transgressive woman, instead of turning into stone, is said to have been crushed by a rock. At Teragatake of Ibukimura in Kōshū, where En no Gyōja and Gyōki had practiced, the story is told of a nun who was struck by lightning, and, in pain, put her hand on the cliff, where the trace of her fingers can still be seen. The stone is called Tegake-ishi ("stone of the hand mark"). The fingerprint is usually the signature of eminent monks, and this brings to mind the traditions about the hand– and footprints of Kūkai on Kōyasan, as well as the *nejiri-ishi*, the stone "twisted" by his angry mother.

Conflicting Interpretations

The sacred space of the *kekkai* remains an arena of contention, claimed by different interpretations. The feminist denunciation of the *nyonin kek-kai* as proof of Buddhist misogyny is irrefutable. The importance of the gender code does not, however, rule out other, perhaps less obvious, inter-pretations. The relations between Buddhism and women are not simply determined by gender, but also by various cultural, social, and political conditions, and in particular by the relations between Buddhism and local cults. The mythological approach taken by Yanagita, for instance, empha-sizes the resurgence of mythological patterns associating the deity and the monk (as mother and son) according to the motif known as "mother-child deity." Yanagita argues that the *nyonin kekkai* allowed the continuation, under a Buddhist guise, of the ancient Japanese cults of the mountain-god performed by female attendants.

The sociopolitical reading as well can lead to different interpretations. Thus, whereas some historians downplay the gender code and argue that sociopolitical reality is much more complex than a strict feminist reading would allow, others emphasize the irresistible progression of patriarchal values and their negative impact on the status of women. From a political standpoint, the *nyonin kekkai* was merely one aspect of the temples' at-tempt to protect their own independence, or, on the contrary, to establish their legitimacy as government-sponsored institutions. It expressed in par-ticular the need for the Buddhist establishment to identify itself with per-manence and transcendence by removing itself from any association with the domestic sphere.

The *nyonin kekkai* was not only a sociohistorical reality; it also consti-tuted a literary topos and a recurrent motif in the medieval imagination. As such, in literary plots it tends to function as a dramatic device. Yet another, symbolic approach sees the *nyonin kekkai* as a ritual device of purification, providing what Durkheimian scholars claim to be the neces-sary separation between the sacred and the profane. This approach, however, does little to address the ideological legerdemain that associates purity and sacredness with maleness, and impurity and profanation with femaleness. All of these various readings have their value and need to be examined briefly. After doing so, I want to emphasize one particular aspect, that of female transgression—at least in its mythological dimensions—because it strikes at the very heart of Buddhist misogyny.

The most charitable reading is probably that of Yanagita, who argued that the *nyonin kekkai* provided a convenient way for women to get merits without having to climb all of the way to the top of the mountain.[65] According to him, ordinary women, who are not natural climbers, may not have found the limitation imposed by *nyonin kekkai* too painful, and may even have rejoiced at the possibility of worshipping without having to climb the full distance. Indeed, the establishment of a *kekkai* limit halfway to the top of the mountain may have been a means by which to attract women who were poor climbers. Yanagita's viewpoint—that the *kekkai* could be a way for women to renegotiate the exclusion by turning it into a willed and practical limitation—sounds like a kind of "sour grapes" argument. If the *nyonin kekkai* was merely a pretext to allow "weak-legged" women to rest, why emphasize the threat for those who trespass—or rather, who feel enough stamina to walk the extra mile? Yet, while Yanagita's argument sounds a little patronizing, it is not entirely without merit. Indeed, if the point was merely to exclude women, why draw the limit of the *kekkai* halfway to the top? In a sense, the exclusion of women was also their inclusion on the margin, as they were allowed all of the way up to, and welcome at, the *nyonindō*.[66]

We should distinguish between the strict logic of exclusion and its actual practice, mitigated by several factors and fraught with infringements upon the rule. As Nishiguchi Junko has shown, not only could women practice at the *nyonindō*, on the fringes of the *kekkai*, they could also live further downhill, in liminal hamlets called *bessho* or *sato no bō*. The great Buddhist centers did not completely turn them away. Admittedly, these women did not enjoy an exalted status: they usually made a living by washing and mending clothes or preparing meals for the monks. Whereas religious functions were performed in monasteries on the top of the mountain, economic functions and other mundane activities often took place at its foot. Ironically, the *bessho* were also places where the most zealous monks fled from the corruption and decadence of the mountain monastery. According to Nishiguchi, the exclusion of women was enforced more strictly in official temples that played a crucial role in the political sphere. In other words, this exclusion had perhaps more to do with politics and with the ritual purity required of state-sponsored Buddhism than with gender issues proper. Outside of the political sphere, Buddhists were more willing to take into account the spiritual needs of women.[67] Some priests held for women relic services (*shari-e*) that replicated those performed in mountain temples.[68] A well-known case is that of the Tendai abbot Ryō-gen (d. 985), who in 977 held a relic service at Yoshida-dera, near the capital, for the sake of his mother.[69] Likewise, in 1009 Fujiwara Michi-naga held a relic service on Hieizan, and in 1018 the relics were trans-ferred to various temples accessible to women. Again, in 1024, the abbot Ingen also transferred relics to Hōkō-in and Gidarinji, to offer them to the veneration of the women of the capital.[70]

Among temples accessible to women were some major cultic centers, many of them dedicated to the bodhisattva Kannon. The *Ryōjin hishō* contains a mnemonic verse listing most of them: "Temples that bear the marks of Kannon: / Kiyomizu, Ishiyama, sacred Mount Hase, / Kogawa, and Mount Hikone in Ōmi; / closer, they can be seen at Rokkakudō."[71] The possibility of women spending one or several nights in reclusion at such places raised the problem of promiscuity, however.[72] Another point worth mentioning is that the exclusion was not the same for all women, and depended in part on their stage in the life cycle. Once beyond meno-pause, women were less subject to gender discrimination, and, past the age of sixty, they were sometimes admitted on sacred mountains.[73] Death, with parturition and menstruation the major source of defilement, could also become—through proper rituals—the source of ultimate purifica-tion. Sometimes, women's ashes were deposited in the inner sanctum of a temple, the very same place to which these women were refused access while alive. Burial on Kōyasan, for instance, was deemed equivalent to a rebirth in the Pure Land, and the inner cloister (Oku-no-in) was believed to be the gate to Maitreya's paradise. Wandering priests known as Kōya *hijiri* collected the "bones" and ashes of both men and women, as well as their hair, and these remains, deemed genderless, were eventually depos-ited on Kōyasan. In some cases, these ashes could even be placed inside the main object of worship (*honzon*).

The custom of depositing bones on Kōyasan became popular in the second half of the twelfth century, and spread afterwards to other cultic centers such as Hieizan. The reason for such an evolution is not simply the priests' compassion, but also the relationships between aristocratic lineages and temples. Members of the nobility wanted to put all of the bones of their families into *bodaiji* to assure continued prosperity. The funerals of women were performed at the father's home. Thus, the prin-cesses of the Fujiwara clan, after having been cremated at Toribeno, were inhumated at Kohata. Many *bodaiji* were established on these ossuaries, at Toribe, Kohata, Hino, Funaokayama, Kitashirakawa, and Sagano. Be-cause women were warrants of the lineage's prosperity, even if a temple had refused to admit them while they were alive, it could not reject their bones. Thus, aristocratic women would sometimes commission a mountain temple and deposit therein a statue containing their own hair.[74] At Daigoji, the bones of the imperial consort (*chūgū*) Kenshi and of her daughter were deposited under the buddha-altar of Enkō-in.

Thus, better than any rebirth in Pure Land, death transformed women into males; or rather, rebirth in the Pure Land (symbolized by the *kekkai*) was ritually enacted by the transfer of bodily remains, such as ashes and hair. The author of the *Shasekishū* mentions a case in which the body of an apparently dead girl was accepted on Kōyasan—although not all of the way to the inner sanctum:

> A daughter of Michinaga (966–1027), who was being carefully reared in the hope that someday she might be empress, died suddenly in her second year after a brief illness. The Great Omuro of Kōya (Shōshin, 1005–85) was asked to help, and the child was taken up to Kōya in a brocade bag. Since it was a girl, although only a baby, the spell was performed outside the monastery gate, the child was restored to life and in time became empress. I know her name but I hesitate to mention it.[75]

In the end, women entered this place only when sexual difference had been erased and all impurities burnt away by cremations—perhaps a Buddhist way of saying that the only good woman is a dead woman.

THE SYMBOLIC READING OF TRANSGRESSION

In the case of the *nyonin kekkai*, as in that of the Five Obstacles, discussed earlier, discrimination and salvation often went hand in hand. According to this model, which seems to express the fundamental soteriological structure of *kenmitsu* Buddhism, the exclusion of women became the prerequisite for their salvation, their ultimate inclusion.

Another structural argument, and just as paradoxical, may run as follows. The mountain and the temple are symbolically equivalent. Therefore, the most extreme purity was required both in the temple's inner sanctuary and on the sacred peak. This contrasts with the profane impurity that rules at the bottom of the mountain or outside the urban temple's gate. As Abe Yasurō points out, however, when this impurity comes into contact with the Buddha realm, it is purified, transformed into something sacred. The meaning of the religious activity of the monks toward the common people is in the *power* that renders this transformation possible. In this model, monks and monastic centers become transformative agents able to purify any defilement, and therefore they do not really need to be protected from impurity. Something else may be at stake here: as I will suggest later, perhaps the transformative power does not originate with the monks, but with the women on the margins of the *kekkai*.

Let us for now acknowledge that the point of many *kekkai* stories is not simply that women were excluded from the mountains, but also—and perhaps above all—that they did not accept this prohibition and daringly transgressed it. This transgressive aspect has been downplayed by most Japanese scholars.[76] Tradition has recorded an incident that occurred during the visit of Retired Emperor Go-Uda to Kōyasan in 1313. According to the *Go-Uda'in Kōya gokyō*, Go-Uda had made a vow to go to Kōyasan after an auspicious dream, and he climbed on foot from Jison-in, prostrating himself at every stupa. On the way, a storm suddenly broke. It was attributed to the fact that some women of the neighboring village, hoping to steal a glance at the imperial devotions, had disguised themselves as men and crossed the *kekkai*. After they were driven away with staff blows, the fair weather returned. The emperor was thus given the proof of the sacred character of the mountain.[77] Having described the incident, the same source refers to the precedent of the nun Toran: "Formerly, the nun Toran wanted to go to the sacred peak. Before she had crossed Narikawa, she was already ashamed of her clumsy shape with the Five Obstructions." Another significant case, mentioned in the diary of Minamoto no Tsuneyori, is that of a "madwoman" who climbed Hieizan in 1020. Although she was driven away by the monks, one priest complained to Minamoto Tsuneyori that the lack of reaction from the mountain deity, Sannō Gongen, was a sign of the god's decline.[78]

The signs were not always clear, and the transgression itself could appear ambivalent. According to his biography, the Tendai priest Son'i had in 926 a dream in which an elegant noblewoman arrived at the Great Lecture Hall on Hieizan in a magnificent cart. Son'i told her: "Since the Great Master [Saichō] [defined its] *kekkai*, this mountain has been forbidden to women. Why have you come here?" The lady replied, "Although I am a woman, this interdiction does not apply to me. Having received help from the *ajari*, the abbot (*zasu*) Son'i, I came from Inari to express my gratitude."[79] As it so happened, Son'i had recently performed a ritual of "tranfer of merits" (*ekō*) at Inari Shrine.[80] He realized that the lady of his dream was the Inari deity, who had come to worship the relics of the Buddha and to serve the Hieizan god, Sannō Gongen. Following this dream, Son'i built a Shrine of the Saintly Woman (Shōnyo-sha) on Hieizan, symbolically allowing women on the mountain.[81] The fact remains that women had to be either mad or divine to climb the sacred mountain.

Of course, the *nyonin kekkai* of Kōyasan cannot be studied in a vacuum; it has close relationships with other facts that contributed to characterizing the place as a sacred site. Why take such troubles to climb a mountain? In the case of a sacred mountain like Kōyasan, the answer is easy. Such climbing was believed to insure salvation, owing to the numinous presence of Kūkai, immersed in *samādhi* at the Oku-no-in until the com-

ing of the future buddha Maitreya. We recall that Kōyasan came to be
identified with Maitreya's Tuṣita Heaven, and that Kūkai's mummified
body, as well as his mother's, were seen as "flesh-icons" of Maitreya. The
belief spread that, by the mere act of climbing Kōyasan, all sins were
erased and one could be reborn in Tuṣita Heaven or become a "buddha
in this very body."[82]

The legend of Kūkai waiting for Maitreya contributed to transform
Kōyasan into a Pure Land where the remains of men and of women were
deposited in the hope of rebirth.[83] The sacred site transformed the bones
or ordinary people into relics, thereby purifying the dead from their karmic burden. Thus, whereas becoming a hermit on the mountain was for
a man a way to transmute his sins, for a woman karmic purification had
to await the purification by fire of her profane remains. What relation is
there between this function and the *nyonin kekkai*? Women's defilement
does not entirely explain why blood pollution played such a crucial role
in Buddhist legends. It should rather have been a reason to accept women
in order to purify them. Women's exclusion seems to reflect a more fundamental structure of sacredness, which cannot be accounted for entirely by
the conventional argument.[84]

Women Out of Place

Women tried to transgress the *kekkai*. Like moths attracted to the flame,
they crossed the line, braving the anger of the deity. In the medieval period, the topos of female transgression leaves the mythological realm and
materializes on the literary and artistic stages. The typical transgressive
woman is no longer Toran, however, but the poetess Ono no Komachi.
The Nō play *Sotoba Komachi*, for instance, opens with Komachi arriving,
during one of her travels, near Kōyasan. Exhausted, she sits on a fallen
grave marker (*sotoba*), when two priests, considering this a sacrilegious
action, rebuke her. An exchange of wits ensues, in which the two priests
are defeated. Komachi then composes the following verse: "If the *sotoba*
was inside paradise, / it would be indeed wicked to sit on it, / but if it is
outside (*soto wa*), / can it be such a terrible thing?" In this play, Komachi
appears as an enlightened being, who can nonplus her opponents with
the highest truth of Zen and a pun (*sotoba/soto wa*). She is no longer the
beautiful courtesan of the past, however: she has become an old woman,
and her enlightenment does not prevent her from being possessed by the
sorrowful spirit of a former lover.[85]

This play seems to have been the source for the image of the old Komachi, to which we will return. Kūkai appears in another play with the
same title. In the latter, however, Komachi is a ghost, pursued by the
vengeful spirit of her lover. She has come to Kōyasan, lamenting about

her karma. When Kūkai emerges from the inner cloister (Oku-no-in), he finds her sitting on a *sotoba* and rebukes her. The exchange between them is the same as in the above Nō play, but Kūkai, losing patience, beats Komachi. Having discovered her identity, however, he eventually frees her from her karmic burden by preaching the Buddhist truth to her. At the end of the play, Komachi recites the *engi* of Kōyasan in praise. Interestingly, the play combines her image with that of the tutelary goddess Niu, mentioned in the *engi*. Komachi's profanation, and her initial defiance of Kūkai, also call to mind Toran's transgression, as well as that of Kūkai's mother. Her wit does not prevent her from being beaten and driven away by Kūkai, admittedly a more enviable fate than Toran's petrification.[86]

Another related legend, which was very early on transformed into a Nō play, is the tale of Karukaya, mentioned earlier. We recall how Midaidokoro, searching for her husband, arrived at the foot of Kōyasan, and was dissuaded from climbing the mountain by an innkeeper. In the Nō play, however, she is more daring and actually attempts to climb it. Likewise, in another play by Zeami, entitled *Kōya no monokurui* ("The Madwoman of Kōya"), the daughter of Tadatsu no Saemon, accompanied by her nurse, arrives at Fudōzaka, at the foot of Kōyasan. The two women, wearing masculine hats, resolutely trespass the *nyonin kekkai* and arrive at the Fudō Hall, where a saintly priest is performing rituals. When the latter (who is actually the girl's father) rebukes them for transgressing the *kekkai*, the girl replies, "That's precisely because we know it that we put on men's clothes." When the girl outwits the priest and wants to proceed in spite of his warning, he beats her with his staff. The climax marked by the beating recalls the scene in which Komachi is beaten by Kūkai. The priest soon realizes, however, that the girl who protests under the blows is his own daughter, and father and child fall into each other's arms. The joy of reunion, following the catharsis caused by the violence, calls to mind the ritualized beatings of Chan "encounter dialogues." Like *Sotoba Komachi*, the play ends with praise of Kōyasan's sacredness. It also unfolds the complex symbolism of transvestism. In Nō plays, transvestism is usually perceived as a sign of madness, but here it is precisely their feigned madness that allows the two women to transgress the *kekkai*.[87] We noted earlier how, in order to approach Retired Emperor Go-Uda during his pilgrimage to Kōyasan, several village women passed themselves off as men to bypass the *kekkai*.[88]

Another literary example of transgression through transvestism is the Nō play *Dōjōji*, whose *shite*, a dancer girl (*shirabyōshi*), enters the inner sanctum of Dōjōji during the inauguration of the temple bell. Her transgression causes the bell to fall on her, imprisoning her. She is, as it were, trapped at the very core of the *kekkai*. The Dōjōji priest then traces back the origins of the exclusion of women from Dōjōji to the story of a young monk who had received hospitality in a villager's house. In order to escape the advances of the villager's daughter, the monk sought refuge at Dōjōji. The young woman pursued him, and, as she reached the Hidaka river, her rage caused her to turn into a monstruous snake. She eventually discovered the monk, hidden under the bell of Dōjōji, and the scorching heat emanating from her reptilian body reduced him to ashes. At this point in his story, the Dōjōji priest reveals to his listeners that it is the endlessly burning passion of this woman that is now impeding the inauguration ceremony for the bell. When the monks, after performing rituals of exorcism (*kitō*), lift the bell again, a demon-woman attacks them. But she is finally defeated, and, consumed in her own fire, rushes toward the Hidaka river.[89] The implication of the play is that the *shirabyōshi* is none other than the resentful spirit (*onryō*) of the villager's daughter. Because, when she danced in front of the bell, she wore a male headdress (*eboshi*), she was no longer perceived as a female, and this enabled her to enter the consecrated area. The priest seems to have recognized that, as a *shirabyō-shi*, she was no ordinary woman. The particular type of dancing girls known as *shirabyōshi* were famous for their transvestism. At the precise moment when the *shirabyōshi* entered under the bell, however, she knocked down her headdress with her fan, and so became a woman again. Thus, she transgressed the *kekkai*, and her sacrilegious action provoked the fall of the bell.

The image of women transgressing the *kekkai* reappears in *kōwakamai* recitatives revolving around the legend of Tokiwa Gozen, the mother of the ill-fated warrior Yoshitsune.[90] All of these recitatives present a section entitled "Tokiwa mondō," in which Tokiwa, pressed by her enemies, replies by quoting the *Lotus Sūtra*.[91] In *Tokiwa mabiki* (*Tokiwa's submission*), for instance, the heroine yields to the advances of the Taira warrior Kiyomori in order to save her son. She then goes to Kuramadera, where the latter has taken refuge. Going straight to the Main Hall, she ascends the high seat and begins to perform a ritual. The priest Tōkōbō, seeing this, scolds her. Without losing countenance, Tokiwa replies somewhat ironically: "It is because I am a dumb woman that, in my illusion, I have crossed the *kekkai*. So please teach me, holy man!" He then delivers a sermon to convince her to leave her seat. Tokiwa feigns to agree, but she turns the tables on him: "If there are in these sūtras passages which praise the woman instead of depreciating her, I won't have to climb down. If I win, I take the seat of the master, and if I lose, it is because of female delusion." Tōkōbō then cites various canonical passages of the type "All the passions of men in the three thousand worlds are not equal to the karmic obstacles of a single woman," and also lists famous Chinese and Japanese cases of *nyonin kekkai*.[92] His circular argument is fueled by self-righteous indignation and threats. Angered by his bigotry and narrow-mindedness, Tokiwa retorts: "Since you know nothing, why don't you shut up? For a noble man to calumniate a lowly woman is an act which brings a karma of transmigration." She eloquently demolishes his sexist sophistry, and counterattacks with the classical Mahāyāna argument for sexual equality: "In illusion, there is man and woman; in awakening, there is neither man nor woman." She also brings up the nonduality of the two Shingon *maṇḍalas* as an illustration of gender equality. These are only preliminaries, however. Tokiwa now resorts to ad hominem attacks. Then, taking a different tack, she asks him about the origins of the temple. Tōkōbō tells her that Kuramadera was founded at the time of Emperor Kōtoku when a Nara priest named Kanjun built a mausoleum for women (*nyonin no mihakadō*), whose main deity was the god Bishamon. This provides Tokiwa with one last argument: "How could this temple, centered on a female mausoleum, and whose *honzon* Bishamon is usually paired with a goddess [Kichijōten], be forbidden to women? If you, Tōkō[bō], reject women, you must also reject the mausoleum and Kichijōten's image. Then, I will build another temple for them." The text ends there. In her diatribe against male prejudice, Tokiwa deconstructs the sacredness of Kuramadera, revealing that the presence of women was inscribed in the very "foundation vow" of the temple, as well as in its ritual practices.[93]

Abe Yasurō argues that the narrative structure of this dialogue reflects the fundamental structure of performance arts (*geinō*) and the ambivalent sexuality and gender of their actors. The figure of Tokiwa crossing the line was skillfully transformed into the image of the Nō heroine enacting a play about the fundamental vow and the benevolence of the god. Tokiwa is presented as a feminist *avant la lettre*, but the narrative also suggests that, because of her transgression, Kurama became eventually the prey of war. It is why, having taken refuge on the mountain, Tokiwa there accomplishes her tragic destiny. In the *monogatari* tradition, however, Tokiwa is not only a rhetorical expert. She also guides, beyond death, her son Yoshitsune, appearing to him in a dream to predict his future. Her figure was thus eventually absorbed into the narrative of Yoshitsune's tragic destiny. Like that of Toran, it expressed the ambivalent nature of these unruly women who attract divine retribution because of their trespassing all bounds, but whose very presence and transgression empowers the mountain as a sacred site.[94]

THE *KEKKAI* AND THE LOGIC OF MUEN

Some of the *kekkai* stones were inscribed with the formula "forbidden to *kun* and wine"—in which the double-entendre (*kun/gun*, spice/military) expressed the temple's claim of independence from both aphrodisiacs and warriors. The lengths to which large temple complexes like Hieizan and

Kōyasan went to preserve their independence by arming themselves constitutes a fascinating chapter in the history of "warrior-monks" (sōhei),
but it also shows the ultimate failure of the prohibition. We find at work
here a principle that Amino Yoshihiko defines through the terms muen
(unrelatedness) and yūen (relatedness).[95] As official institutions, belonging
to what Kuroda Toshio called the "exoteric-esoteric system" (kenmitsu
taisei), such large monastic complexes entertained intimate relations with
the court and the military government, and they were traversed by the
same mundane forces that ruled civil society. At the same time, they always perceived themselves as utopian, ultramundane spaces, and attempted to claim an exemption from civil laws.

These claims raise the question of the articulation of the nyonin kekkai
with the notion of muen. As the troubled history of warrior-monks attests, sacred mountains like Hieizan, Kōyasan, and Negorosan offered a
refuge to many people running away from the law, and in this respect
they presented some characteristics associated with muen centers. According to Amino, however, women played an important role in muen
places. Clearly, the dialectics between "public" and "private," or between
freedom and hierarchy, worked right at the heart of the Buddhist institution. Although the utopian spirit of muen was gradually "domesticated,"
the Buddhist attitude cannot be reduced to an "ideological manipulation." The ambiguity of funyū ("nonaccess")—a notion that was originally applied to the intrusion of military authorities, and later came to
be extended (or limited) to women—is a good example of this dialectical
tension.

Was the kekkai actually threatened by female transgression, or did it
depend on it? To what extent did the above stories of female transgression
constitute unsettling incursions, a kind of poaching on the preserve of
male transcendence? Did they reflect real acts of resistance on the part of
women who felt themselves increasingly marginalized, or, on the contrary,
did they express a topos that reinforced a structural polarity and contributed to the sacredness of the place? Admittedly, the two types of interpretations are not mutually exclusive, inasmuch as real events, even if they
momentarily disrupt the status quo, eventually tend to be reabsorbed into
the old patterns. I have argued elsewhere that transgression was an essential feature of Mahāyāna Buddhism.[96] In the case of the nyonin kekkai,
however, transgression was no longer the privilege of male tricksters. In
the stories mentioned above, Buddhist priests are clearly on the defensive.
They seem unable to contain shamanistic intrusions. They may succeed
in evicting the shamaness from her domain, even as they preserve her
altar, the kekkai stone, as a mark of their symbolic victory. But it is precisely around this altar that ancient cults resurfaced in Buddhist guise.

Buddhist normalization attempted to define a transcendent realm, the sacred space of the mountain. In practice, it succeeded merely in demarcating a new territory, in which the principle of the *kekkai* came to overlap with that of *muen*. The initial deterritorialization was followed by reterritorialization, the antistructural heretotopia was restructured, and the structure was in turn subverted from within, as well as threatened from outside. The process by which a space supposedly transcending all norms becomes a kind of fortified camp, a normalized realm—a no-woman's land—is not entirely clear to me. It seems that, despite its ideal of transcendence, Buddhist monks—men who had in principle "left the family"—felt constrained to invest the saṃsāric realm symbolized by family and kinship, and as a result Buddhism came to be penetrated by kin relations (for instance, the institution of princely abbots, *monzeki*). As we have seen, Buddhist ideological and physical space was also traversed by female incursions. The borders of the *kekkai* came to define an eminently structural principle, a kind of heterotopy; that is, a field that owed its existence to its surroundings, or better, to its being surrounded. As Samuel Weber points out, "Any closed system presupposes that there is a framework that encloses it. This framework inevitably opens up the closed system. That is to say, the fictions of completeness and self-possession that any system spins for itself must be founded on exclusions and repressions, on willfully ignoring the 'outside' that frames the 'inside.'"[97]

Although legends about *kekkai* stones reveal recurring sexist strategies on the part of monks, this does not mean that Buddhism was monolithic in that regard. Taboos exist in order to be transgressed: either frontally, as in the case of women's transgression of the *kekkai*, or obliquely, for instance, through slight reinterpretations that radically modify their nature. Thus, the site of the *kekkai* stone became, or perhaps was simply restored to its original function as, a place of worship for female mediums, and women in general. Monks were symbolically encircled, contained. Although female transgression was condemned, it was implicitly understood as a structural prerequisite of the site's sacredness.

The meaning and function of the *nyonin kekkai* changed radically in the course of the motif's development from early Buddhist legends to medieval literature, which quoted these legends to advocate female resistance. Whereas Buddhist legends emphasized the agency of female mediums to better deny their rights, in medieval literature the *nyonin kekkai* topos came to play an essentially dramaturgical function, and served to enhance the plot of the narrative. From the institutional standpoint, it also expressed the dialectical relationship between Buddhism and local cults, a relationship that resonated with (but also subverted) the Mahāyāna "logic of transgression."

We have here a structure in which women, excluded from the mountain-top, lived on its slopes or at its foot. Although they still played an eco-nomic role and continued to take care of the monks, only after death could they hope to be saved, when their bones would be taken to or near the inner sanctum. This structure rests on their accomplishing the function of the sacred site that the ascetics preach about and embody. In these legends, they sustain the sacredness of the site while being at the same time de-prived of it—a rather peculiar form of alienation. That this is so is sug-gested by the fact that these women appear usually as nuns flanking the local goddess. They are in this way connected to the lineage of the priest-esses (*miko*) who serve the tutelary deity, and are perceived as the descen-dants of the goddess who initially bequeathed her domain to the monks. If one assumes that such women were somehow related to the sacredness of the place, their exclusion takes on a new dimension. It is not a mere rejection; on the contrary, it is precisely through their estrangement that the sacred site is constituted. Seen from this particular angle, the *nyonin kekkai* looks like a space invested by women. We must imagine women circling or circumambulating the mountain, going from one *nyonindō* to the others, while ascetic monks are locked up inside their ivory tower. While the latter were allegedly trying to protect themselves from disorder and transgression, we know from medieval chronicles that they lived in constant strife. In the end, women provided the meaning, structure, and order of the *kekkai* even as they seemed to threaten it.

The exclusion of women became a paradoxical "inclusion on margins," a kind of "inclusive exclusion." Contrary to what the "manifest content" of Toran's story suggests, the question of defilement is perhaps not the main point, since the mountain is in principle able to purify anyone who sets foot on it. The hidden purport, or "latent content," of such transgres-sion stories may be rather that women, through their very transgression, *empowered* the sacred site. In that way, they were still the representatives of the goddess. The transgression paradigm finds its most achieved expres-sion with headstrong women like Ono no Komachi and Tokiwa, who, by defeating the monks, reveal the sacredness of the place.

The exclusion of women from sacred places may be precisely what sets them into motion. Rejected to the periphery of the mountain, they do not remain passive, but begin to circumambulate it. The symbolism of circumambulation (*pradakṣiṇa*) implies a mastery over the four direc-tions, and, by extension, over the center. In a sense, women, by symboli-cally encircling the monks, confined monks to their ivory tower. The *kek-kai* boundary, having turned into a circumambulation path, became, like the Great Wall, both a barrier and a circular highway; unlike the Great Wall, however, it was used mainly by intruders who, walking that liminal high ground, were no longer really outsiders. In topological terms, one could say that the *kekkai* both caused and interrupted one process (the vertical movement of ascension and transgression) to facilitate another (the lateral, circular movement of circumambulation): in other words, it replaced one type of sacredness with another. Either way, the authority of the monks was constantly subverted, inasmuch as women not only transgressed the *kekkai* frontally, but they also "turned" it, approaching the inner sanctum through the back door. Thus, while male power was displayed on the front stage, it was denied on the back stage—a situation reminiscent of Japanese domestic life. It may be worth recalling in this context that the cultic practices of the "back door" (*ushirodo*) in medieval Buddhist temples became as important (or perhaps more) than the official cult performed at the front of the Buddha Hall.[98] The fact remains that it is through the relation of women with the Buddhist gender code that their subversive potentialities came to light. Left to itself, women's religion tends to be conservative. Although gender discrimination has no excuse, it can be said to have, in this case, given a new dimension to female religiosity.

When we emphasize the topological character of female transgression, we come to realize that the exclusion of women from sacred places is reminiscent of what Giorgio Agamben has analyzed as the structure of the "ban," from the Old French *ban*, the threshold that defines (and perhaps produces) at the same time the inside and outside of society.[99] The ban refers both to the inside (the "banal"—etymologically, that which belongs to the ruler, or to a collectivity) and the outside (the "banished"). It is the "threshold from which inside and outside enter into these complex relationships that make possible the validity of order."[100] Buddhist women, for instance the mothers of monks, were, strictly speaking, a-*ban*-doned, *ban*-ished, marginalized. But at the same time, they were, as the French has it, "en rupture de ban" (an expression translated as "illegal return from banishment" or "in defiance of the accepted code of conduct"); they rejected the constraints of womanhood, they refused to be banished or banalized. As such, they became the mediators between inside and outside, or between the profane and the sacred, understood in Durkheimian (spatial) terms.

The threshold, being in-between, is what separates (and actually creates) both the inside and outside. Over against the "realm"—defined etymologically by a "rule"—we have the realm of *muen*. The latter is not exactly a "realm"—since it is "un-ruly," "un-related," or out-lawed— and as such attracts and/or produces outlaws or marginals (for instance the outcasts or "nonhumans," *hinin*, of medieval Japan). It is an "anti-structural" space serving as mediation between (or even a matrix of) two "mediated" or structured realms, both ruled by the principle of *yūen* (relatedness): the sacred space of the *kekkai* above and the profane world below. The range of *muen*, however, tended to extend to the *kekkai* itself, while in the political sphere it came to be increasingly restricted by the military government.

Women, beginning with female mediums, became the keepers of the threshold, the symbols of "inclusive exclusion." The structure of the *kekkai* is therefore elliptic, determined by these two centers: the inner sanctum (Oku-no-in) and the threshold, themselves symbolized by the priest and the shamaness, or by the charismatic founder and his transgressive mother. The latter is properly "a-*ban*-doned"—by no means forgotten, but relegated to the margin, the ban, held in reserve—prisoner of a threshold, a paradoxical site that is not, strictly speaking, a place. Such women are properly "dis-placed" (and "dis-located"), being in two places at the same time, belonging to both the inside and the outside (or neither, like on a Moebius strip). What was at first a "de-localization," a rejection outside of sacred space, came to express a more fundamental "un-localization," a kind of utopian sacredness. Women who live (willingly or not) on the threshold truly establish their home in homelessness: despite the appearances, they are neither spouses nor mothers. Yet they are also the symbol of the home, of the place, and, to a certain extent, of Buddhism. The allegedly "un-localized," universal teaching gets "domesticated" as it becomes grounded in local culture. Marginalized women, however, always "en rupture de ban," refuse "the constraints of status," and so they avoid banishment or banalization. In this way, they become perfect mediators, and Buddhism, through them, is in turn dis-located, in two places (sacred and profane, local and universal) at the same time.

This topographic reading helps to explain the "elliptic" structure of the sacred place: for instance, the inner sanctuary (Oku-no-in) and the outer sanctuary (*ge-in*) of Kōyasan (as an earthly version of the Tuṣita Heaven), or the Inner and Outer Shrines of Ise. As the long controversy between the two Ise shrines suggests, this structural polarity expresses a relationship that was at times strongly agonistic. Thus, this "deep" structure, which tends to resurface in spite of historical vicissitudes, is by no means ahistorical, and it must be submitted to an ideological critique.

This structure also resembles that of current scholarship, and, more specifically, that of the present chapter, oscillating between two interpretive modes. In the first mode, women are seen as transgressing and trying to get to the top (of the mountain or of the hierarchy). In the second, they symbolically encircle men and create their own circuit of power. Depending on the interpreter, the *nyonin kekkai* can be seen as a sign of oppression and failure, or as a successful irruption and subversion of male territory. To those who emphasize women's power, it is easy to object that the crucial role of women in the sacralization process did not translate into actual equality of status. It was in the end coopted by the monks, diverted to their own profit. Although the transgressive ("mad") logic of transvestite women seems to subvert the dichotomic logic of men, the latter finally obtained. Each of these interpretations is in some respects lacking, and at this point it is worth recalling that all interpretations are ultimately performative. Thus, in the present case, the interpretation of women's transgression can have both subversive effects (by showing female agency even in the midst of an oppressive ideology), or conservative effects (by revealing the structural necessity of female transgression, it undermines the liberating impact of the latter, and may contribute to the status quo). Despite its survival in a few places, the *nyonin kekkai* is no longer really an issue. It remains, however, a useful metaphor for the enduring problem of the (relative) exclusion of women in Buddhism, and for the multifaceted notion of women's power (or powerlessness).

Chapter Eight

WOMEN ON THE MOVE

THE "NUNS OF KUMANO"

DURING A JOURNEY from Nagasaki to Edo in 1692, the Dutch doctor Engelbert Kaempfer came across a group of "singing nuns" who, despite their shaven heads, behaved like prostitutes:

To this shav'd begging tribe belongs a certain remarkable religious order of young Girls, call'd Bikuni, which is as much as to say, Nuns. They live under the protection of the Nunneries at Kamakura and Miaco [Miyako; that is, Kyoto], to whom they pay a certain sum a year, of what they get by begging, as an acknowledgement of their authority. Some pay besides a sort of tribute, or contribution, to the Khumano Temples at Isje [sic]. Their chief abode is in the neighbourhood of Khumano, from whence they are call'd Khumano no Bikuni, or the Nuns of Khumano, for distinction's sake from other religious Nuns. They are, in my opinion, by much the handsomest girls we saw in Japan. . . . The Jammabos [*yamabushi*], or begging Mountain-Priests, . . . frequently incorporate their own daughters into this religious order, and take their wives from among these Bikuni's [sic]. Some of them have been bred up in bawdy-houses, and having serv'd their time there, buy the privilege of entering into this religious order, therein to spend the remainder of their youth and beauty. . . . Their voice, gestures, and apparent behaviour, are neither too bold and daring, nor too much dejected and affected, but free, comely, and seemingly modest. However not to extol their modesty beyond what it deserves, it must be observ'd, that they make nothing of laying their bosoms quite bare to the view of charitable travellers, all the while they keep them company, under pretence of its being customary in the country, and that for ought I know, they may be, tho' never so religiously shav'd, full as impudent and lascivious, as any whore in a publick bawdy-house.[1]

Scholars of Japanese Buddhism often describe the Edo period as a time of decline and degeneration for the religion. It is during this period that the term for Buddhist "nuns" (*bikuni*) came to designate a particular type of prostitute. Indeed, many of these "nuns" affiliated with Kumano fell into prostitution toward that time. They nevertheless continued to perform religious functions such as *etoki*, predication through picture scrolls of the Buddhist Hells, and traveled through Japan, fund-raising (*kanjin*) for the reconstruction of temples and shrines.[2] It is owing to them, for instance, that Ise Shrine, which had lost the economic support of the court during the Muromachi period, was restored. Functionally, these women— sometimes called *uta bikuni* (singing nuns)—offered many resemblances to other categories of women, such as mediums (*miko*) and courtesans (*yūjo*), who traveled through the provinces, making a living with their arts. Although their purpose and ideology were usually more in line with orthodox Buddhism, they were perceived as just another type of "wandering women."

Some of these *bikuni* were, however, female mediums who had little, if anything, to do with conventional Buddhism. At the ideological level, what distinguished the *bikuni* of Kumano and Ise from their Shintō homologues? Were they truly nuns, or merely female mediums in Buddhist guise? Despite the similarities, or perhaps the genealogical filiation between *miko* and *bikuni*, what made the latter typically Buddhist was their preoccupation with the other world, the world after death, and in particular their ties with the cult of the bodhisattva Jizō. Kumano had been the land of the dead even before the advent of Buddhism. According to Hagiwara Tatsuo, however, the disjunction between the two groups of female religious specialists was achieved when the Kumano *bikuni* advocated the Jizō cult toward the beginning of the Edo period, and emphasized in their sermons the "spiritual contemplation of the ten realms" (*kanjin jikkai*).[3] Unlike them, female mediums usually dealt with solving the problems of this world, and their function normally did not extend to the other world.

One could nevertheless argue that the Kumano *bikuni*, like the *miko* who survived in official Shintō, were examples of the domestication of the "ancient sybil," or rather of her absorption by Buddhism during the Edo period. At the same time, while the so-called Ise *bikuni* became quite successful and even enjoyed imperial patronage, other types of *bikuni* sunk gradually to the bottom of society, and were rejected at the periphery of Buddhism, there joining the irregular female mediums and prostitutes. One interesting consequence of this domestication of the *bikuni* is their relation with fertility cults and motherhood, a rather paradoxical development for women who, as symbols of purity, had originally nothing to do with fertility and motherhood. This is, for Hagiwara, another sign of the historical transition from the *miko* to the nun.[4] According to him, a goddess like the deity of easy childbirth (*koyasugami*), represented as an ordinary woman with swollen breasts who gives birth and feeds children, could not have appeared among the *miko*; furthermore, their function of protecting children suggests an influence from the Jizō cult.

As we will see, the role of these nuns can be interpreted from two opposite standpoints: mediating between Buddhism and local culture, they can be seen to serve or betray the former or the latter depending on the cases. They were not the only women of this kind. In the Edo period, women known as "wandering *miko*," many of them loosely affiliated to large shrines, traveled through Japan, alone or in groups, until their activities were suppressed in 1873. The main characteristic of these women was that they were in motion, which contrasts with the relative immobility of monastic reclusion or of domestic life. The social evolution that transformed certain nuns into loose women, however, is by no means characteristic of Buddhism alone, since the priestesses (*miko*) of Shintō shrines suffered the same fate. Originally, these *asobime* (courtesans; lit. "playgirls") were perhaps sacred prostitutes. The relation, however, between the *asobime* and the *asobibe* (religious specialists tracing their origins to the goddess Ame-no-Uzume) is by no means certain. Admittedly, sexuality and the sacred were intimately connected in archaic Japanese religion. Yet with regard to the *bikuni*, this ideological aspect apparently played a minor part, and their degeneration was due mainly to their extremely precarious material conditions within Tokugawa society.

Whatever their origins and their evolution, these nuns played an important role in the diffusion of popular Buddhist culture. Like their Chinese counterparts, described without kindness in novels such as the *Jinpingmei*, they had access to the women's quarters and served occasionally as specialists in sexual matters and providers of magic talismans and recipes. Nevertheless, they never entirely lost their religious character: even when they transmitted the puritanical message of Buddhism, they continued to be perceived as the emissaries of the Kumano deity. Through their dual role as nuns and prostitutes, they contributed to the blurring of the borders that the orthodox Buddhist clergy tried to draw between religion and sexuality.

In his cultural comparison of Europe and Japan, the Jesuit missionary Luis Fróis (d. 1597) mentions that Japanese women often travel alone and do not seem to put a high price on their chastity. If they are "raped," their reputation is not tainted by that and they can still find a husband. Chastity, as the supreme value for daughters of a patriarchal system, does not seem to have been solidly established yet. It is against this background that we must consider wandering women—nuns, *yūjo* and *miko*: they were not perceived as radically different from other women, at least until the Muromachi period. Sources such as illustrated scrolls (*emakimono*) frequently show women on the road, in pilgrim's clothes. In most cases, women were going to temples and shrines to spend a period of several days in reclusion (*komori*). Iconographic and literary evidence suggests that there was some sexual promiscuity in these places. Amino argues that these cultic sites were also places of sexual license. The recurrence of imperial edicts ruling that men and women should not mingle during vigils (*tsūya*) seems to indicate that precisely the opposite was customary.[5]

Traveling alone, for a woman, must have been dangerous in those troubled times. How did single women avoid danger, on the road as in the pilgrimage centers? Amino thinks that, in the liminal time and space of pilgrimage, the usual sexual taboos were no longer observed, neither by men nor women. It seems to have been customary to consider that a woman alone was permitted prey despite laws against rape. In most cases, there seems to have been a general perception that having sex under these circumstances was natural.[6] Amino's claim has raised a number of objections. Hosakawa Ryōichi, for one, emphasizes that these women always traveled in groups of two or three, and that single women were perceived as deranged (and disturbing); this is also indicated in Kaempfer's account of the *Bikuni* he had met on the road: "For distinction's sake, from other begging Nuns, they are call'd Komano Bikuni, because they go always two and two, and have their stations assign'd them only upon the roads hereabouts."[7] The situation was probably not drastically different in the medieval period.

The helplessness of women traveling alone is well illustrated by Lady Nijō's narrow escape from being taken hostage as a servant. In Bingo, she stayed at the house of a lady whom she had met at Itsukushima Shrine. The master of the house, taking a fancy to her, refused to let her leave and came to treat her as a servant. She was fortunately rescued by a visiting lay priest, who realized who she was: "Before long I reached the capital, where I pondered the strange experience I had had. What awful fate might have befallen me had not the lay priest arrived? That man at Wachi was certainly not my master, but who would have defended me? What could I have done? I realized how dangerous pilgrimages can be."[8] Lady Nijō also describes her encounter with former prostitutes, who had become nuns and lived in reclusion on an island. Likewise, the *Kagerō nikki* describes the encounter between a woman of high birth and low-caste wandering women. Thus, it seems that the higher and the lower strata of female society met (and could only meet) during such pilgrimages: rich women go on pilgrimage to escape from the bustle of the court, poor women are vagrant, while middle-class women stay at home.

The emergence of the Kumano *bikuni* was brought about by the very special nature of Kumano as a cultic center free of the usual taboos against death and women. From the Insei period onward, imperial consorts and other women of the aristocracy made pilgrimages to this place, known as "Women's Kōya."[9] Thus, because women were welcome at Kumano, this cultic center played an important role until the Edo period. The earlier female religious who lived at Kumano, the *miko*, were superseded by the *bikuni*.

The relation between the female mediums of folk-religion, the *miko* of Shintō, and a certain category of *bikuni* is suggested by the famous legend of the Happyaku bikuni (Eight-hundred [-year-old] *bikuni*; or, according to a graphic variant, the "white nun," "hundred" and "white" being homophonous in Japanese). From the Muromachi period to the Edo period, the periodic apparition of this quasi-immortal woman who wandered through the mountains struck people's imagination. This old "nun," whose face remained as white as that of a sixteen-year-old virgin, was said to have obtained eternal youth after eating the flesh of a mermaid (or merman) from the sea-god's palace.[10] Despite the Buddhist connotations of her name, she seems to be a typical shamanistic figure, and her image must have influenced that of the Kumano *bikuni*.

What's in a Name

The line separating the figures of the nun, the *miko*, and the courtesan was a blurred one, for instance in the case of the *aruki-miko* (walking miko) who traveled through the provinces and combined their religious function with entertainment or even prostitution.[11] In the late medieval and Edo periods, courtesans were often designated by the term *bikuni* (nun), or, upon occasion *maruta* (round[-headed] ones), an allusion to their tonsure.[12] The *uta bikuni*, for instance, were itinerant prostitutes who specialized in song and dance. Medieval female entertainers were known by a variety of other names such as *yūjo*, *asobime*, *ukareme*, *kugutsu*, and *shirabyōshi*. Among these, the oldest terms referring to courtesans are *ukareme* (wandering women) and *asobime*. The first term, already found in the *Man'yōshū*, implies the notion of drifting, and was sometimes written in Chinese characters as *yūgyō jofu*—probably the origin of the more common *yūjo*.[13]

Although it may be exaggerated to speak of "sacred prostitution," it seems that religious services in ancient Japan implied a sexual element. The term *hitoya-zuma* (one-night wife) was also used for the girl or woman chosen to be the bride of the divine guests (*marebito*) for one night. Shrines like Kitano and Yasaka in Kyoto, or Tennōji in Osaka, were usually close to the red-light quarters. To give just another example, in the Genroku era (1688–1704), the priestesses of the god Ōhara Myōjin in the provinces of Echigo and Tanba began traveling through Japan to raise donations. They eventually fell into prostitution, and were called *obara-miko* or *kama-harai* (stove-exorcists).[14] The sexual appeal of the *miko* is evident in the following song of the *Ryōjin hishō*: "This shrine-maiden / she is an eyeful! / Her robe with slit sides above / and loosened behind / she's raving. / Look! / The gods have got hold of her!"[15] Another song is even more explicit: "Before the shrine the bamboo grass / is lush, though the horses chomp it. Her real love never comes, but / she is young, her bed is never empty."[16]

The term *yūjo* (women entertainers), however, did not originally mean "prostitute" in the modern Western sense. As Barbara Ruch has pointed out, the gender bias that informs the label "prostitute" distorts our perception of these women, not only of those who did engage in selling sex, but also of various types of unmarried, independent medieval female artists (some of whom were quite chaste and ascetic).[17] The hesitation in the translation (courtesan or prostitute) has to do with the fact that the meanings of the Japanese terms, as well as the social realities behind them, are quite different from their Western counterparts.

These *yūjo* formed independent groups, under the direction of a matron (*chōja*). They were said to depend on the court because they served in court ceremonies. Thus, because they served "sacred beings" (the *kami* and the emperor himself), they participated to a certain extent in sacredness. These specialists of "deep play" (*asobi*) took on all of the meanings of the word *asobi* itself, with its broad semantic field, ranging from the religious to the sexual and artistic domains. This semantic spectrum was discussed by Johan Huizinga in *Homo Ludens*, and indeed we find in Japanese mythology intuitions close to those of Huizinga on the ritual importance of play, or of Georges Bataille on the relations between eroticism and death.[18] The term *asobi*, used concurrently with *ukare* (also read *yū*) in the medieval period, implied an artistic talent related to music, song, and dance. But it would also be misleading to read the *yū* of *yūjo* as mere entertainment. The term *asobi* seems to have first meant a ritual to console the soul of the departed (and those of his relatives). Thus, *asobime* claimed to descend from the *asobibe*, court-ritual specialists. The fact that medieval courtesans tried to claim legitimacy from their ancient relationships with the imperial family or with important temples or shrines, cannot, however, be taken at face-value.

In the medieval period, the *yūjo* or *asobi* (or *asobime*), despite her sexual characteristic, was often represented as a kind of poetic Muse, and her songs (the *imayō*) were praised for their oracular nature.[19] The point is emphasized by Retired Emperor Go-Shirakawa himself, who so reveled in such songs that he compiled an anthology of them, the *Ryōjin hishō kudenshū*. The sacralization of the *imayō* (and of the *asobi* who specialized in them) was part of a broader trend, which led to the belief that Japanese poetry was the principal vehicle of expression of the gods. Thus, despite the Buddhist warning against "wild words and specious phrases" (*kyōgen kigyō*), medieval Japanese came to believe that the main poetic form of the time, the *waka*, were none other than *dhāraṇī*—the true utterances of the buddhas.[20]

Although courtesans could become the mouthpieces of the gods or buddhas, they were usually perceived as sinners who could gain redemption through Buddhism. In the *Yūjo no ki* (*Record on Courtesans*), a short tract on *asobi* compiled around 1087, Ōe no Masafusa (1041–1111) writes:

> *Asobi* row their small boats toward the passengers boats and invite the travelers to their beds. . . . This must simply be the best pleasure under heaven. . . . Aboard their boats, they indulge in love and seek man's favor by adorning their costumes and using poles to steer their boats. They sink deep in sin with no thought except to please people with their songs, nor do they know how to reach the yonder shore of enlightenment. But once a spark of faith is awakened in their hearts, even these women have attained salvation. How much more, then, would this not be true for people like us?[21]

Ōe no Masafusa's text may be read superficially as an incitement to yield to the exotic charm of these women, but there is also a warning against the threat they are to home and family. The temptations with which they lure the traveler recall those of Circe bewitching Ulysses' men: "Those who stop, invariably forget their homes. . . . High and low are seduced by [the women's] charms. They lose themselves in pleasures; some take the women as wives and consorts. Not even wise men and princes can avoid this fate."[22] As Thomas Keirstead notes, however, "Women, movement, and their corrollary, trade, mark these pleasure zones as alien and enticing; they also define them as hazardous, especially to the likes of Masafusa."[23] According to Keirstead, "The opposition that [Masafusa's] texts invoke between a central (centered) male observer and wandering (marginal) females provides the blueprint for a series of other divides central to the medieval imaginary (as well as much of the scholarship on it): oppositions that pit motion against fixity, those without established homes against the propertied, and commerce (shown to be a particularly discordant form of acquisition) against natural wealth (real estate)."[24]

Orikuchi Shinobu is the first Japanese scholar to have emphasized the sacred character of the *yūjo*'s sexuality, whereas his contemporary Yanagita Kunio avoids any explicit reference to sex, and yet judges the *yūjo* negatively.[25] More recently, scholars like Saeki Junko have emphasized both the sexual and aesthetic appeal of the *yūjo*. The visionary power of these female artists must have been quite compelling to incite a sovereign, Go-Shirakawa, to become the disciple of a former courtesan. The latter, named Otomae, was in her seventies at the time, and she was known as the "Gojō Avenue Nun."[26] After Go-Shirakawa performed funeral services with *imayō* for her, she appeared to his consort in a dream, wearing a nun's robe. Go-Shirakawa was convinced that *imayō* singing possessed a kind of magical potency: "The *imayō* that are popular these days are not intended simply for entertainment. When they are sung with sincerity at shrines and temples, they bring about divine revelations and fulfill our wishes. They obtain for people their desire for official positions, prolong human life, and immediately cure illnesses."[27] Although Go-Shirakawa was impressed by such experiences and his infatuation with *imayō* was genuine, we must also take into account the erotic element. The fact that he sought the company of the *asobi* of Eguchi and Kanzaki shows as much the "domestication" of the marginals as the "marginalization" of the imperial rule.

Michele Marra emphasizes the notion, made explicit by Go-Shirakawa in his *Ryōjin hishō kudenshū*, that the courtesan's love songs (and sometimes even sexual practices) constituted a kind of skillful means for the sake of ordinary people.[28] We are told, for instance, about Tonekuro, a courtesan of Kanzaki who reached the Pure Land after singing a song. Here, the courtesan's song is transformed into a medium for enlightenment. The case of Go-Shirakawa is particular, however, in that he was perhaps closer to the *miko* than to the Buddhist establishment. Thus, what we have here is perhaps not "the Buddhist version of the *miko* practice"; or, at least, this Buddhist version may be subverted by popular practices.[29]

Kugutsu

One particular category of female entertainers was called *kugutsu* (puppeteers) because they combined their sexual trade with a particular form of entertainment, the puppet-show.[30] They are also described by Ōe no Masafusa in a short text entitled *Kugutsu no ki* (or *Kairaishi no ki*):

> The *kugutsu* are those who have no fixed abodes, no proper homes. They pitch their tents under the sky, following water and grass, rather like the customs of the northern barbarians [of China]. . . . As for the women, they make up their eyebrows to appear sad and grievous. They wiggle their hips when they walk, flash devilish teeth when they smile, and use vermilion powder on their cheeks. They act and sing of licentious pleasures, and lure you with their sorcery and magic. Their fathers, mothers and husbands know this and do not admonish them, yet help them in their meetings with travelers. The travelers do not hate to spend a night in beautiful union with them. If they find the women's charms agreeable, they give them lots of money, clothes sewn of brocade fabric, gold ornamental hair-pins and lacquered boxes. There is no one who would not consider this different. They do not cultivate a single section of land, nor gather a single branch of mulberry. Consequently, they have no connections with the government, and are one and all landless people. Moreover, they don't know who the sovereign is. The emperor does not know of them either and they enjoy an entire life of not being taxed. At night they worship a lot of deities [*hyaku-*

shin] with drumming and dancing and a great deal of boisterousness.[31] They pray to a large headed male god for good luck. . . . They kick the dust when they sing, and all the noise they make permeates the rafters. The listeners soak the very tassels of their garment and are unable to calm themselves. . . . The *kugutsu* are one of the things under heaven. How could one not be moved by them?[32]

The *kugutsu* are here represented as emblems of freedom, exoticism, and otherness. The text reveals a kind of fascination with these gypsy-like nomads. Keirstead notes, however, that such avowed fascination may have been in large part a literary device. Masafusa's suggestion that these puppeteers are not really Japanese, aims, it seems, at distancing them even further from the author and his society.[33] Soon, their perceived otherness becomes a source of discrimination. In the thirteenth-century *Chiribu-kuro*, for instance, they are no longer a source of fascination, but are characterized as low-born prostitutes. Furthermore, their freedom must have been slightly exaggerated. They were probably not as free of worldly ties (*muen*) as Ōe no Masafusa (or Amino Yoshihiko) would have us believe. In 1249, for instance, there was a lawsuit against Minamoto no Yoritomo by the *kugutsu* concerning taxes required of them for a ceremony, which they did not intend to pay.

Another sexual element is suggested by the fact that *kugutsu* or *asobi* worshipped a deity named Hyakudayū, apparently a phallic god related to the *dōsojin* (crossroad deities), and represented by a phallus of wood, paper, or stone.[34] The *Yūjoki* notes that *asobi* kept hundreds and even thousands of these objects.[35] *Asobi* also went on pilgrimages to shrines famous for their Hyakudayū rituals, most notably those of Hirota (in Nishinomiya, Hyōgo Prefecture) and Sumiyoshi (in Osaka).[36] They worshipped other sexual deities like Konsei Myōjin, Kangiten, Aizen Myōō, and Benzaiten. Among them were the *oshiragami*, represented as crude male and female dolls.[37] The ritual manipulation of such dolls suggests that the medieval *kugutsu* still had a mediumistic character.

The Shirabyōshi

Another popular type of female entertainer in medieval literature is that of the *shirabyōshi*, women who danced to their own poetry compositions to dressed in male attire, who occupied a position structurally similar to that of the temple novices (*chigo*).[38] The *shirabyōshi* appeared during the Insei period and became popular during the Kamakura period. Their origin is described as follows in the *Heike monogatari*:

Now, the first *shirabyōshi* dances in our country were performed during the reign of Emperor Toba by two women called Shima-no-senzai and Waka-no-mai. In the beginning, the dancers dressed in men's *suikan* overshirts and high

caps and wore daggers with silver-decorated hilts and scabbards: their perfor-
mances were thus called "male dancing." In more recent times, they have worn
only the overshirts, dispensing with the cap and the dagger. The name *shirabyōshi* [white rhythm] comes from the color of the overshirts.[39]

The *Heike monogatari*'s explanation serves as a background for the
pathetic story of the *shirabyōshi* Giō: "In those days there lived in the
capital two famous and accomplished *shirabyōshi* performers, sisters
called Giō and Ginyo. They were the daughters of another *shirabyōshi*,
named Toji. Kiyomori took an extravagant fancy to the older one, Giō;
and the younger, Ginyo, found herself a popular favorite as a result."[40]
Enters the young Hotoke, uninvited (an impertinence that, as we will
see, seems to characterize the behavior of courtesans). Giō, who had the
bad idea of pleading on her behalf with the angry Kiyomori, soon finds
herself relegated to semi-oblivion. Convoked one last time to the palace,
she sings a nostalgic song, involving a wordplay on her rival's name (Hotoke means "Buddha"): "In days of old, the Buddha / was but a mortal; /
in the end, we ourselves / will be buddhas, too. / How grievous that
distinctions / must separate those / who are alike in sharing / the buddha-
nature."[41] Then Giō and her sister withdraw into a hermitage in Saga, on
the western outskirts of the capital, and, trying to forget their brief glory,
dedicate themselves to the worship of the buddha Amida.[42] Moved by
their example, Hotoke eventually joins them, and in due time they all die
in the odor of sanctity. The author concludes: "I have heard that all those
nuns achieved their goal of rebirth in the Pure Land, each in her turn.
And so it was that the four names, 'the spirits of Giō, Ginyo, Hotoke,
and Toji,' were inscribed together on the memorial register at Emperor
Go-Shirakawa's Chōgōdō Temple."[43] Lady Nijō, in her *Towazugatari*,
also describes two *shirabyōshi* sisters, Harugiku and Wakagiku, who entertained Emperor Go-Fukakusa in 1277 during two nights of a party.
Although she shows some sympathy for them, she reveals her perception
of the women's social position by referring to them as *keisei*, or "prostitutes."[44]
Another account of the origins of the *shirabyōshi* is found in the *Tsurezureguza* by Urabe Kenkō (1283–1351). In this work, the institution is
said to go back to an episode in which Fujiwara Michinori chose a talented
dancer and had her taught by Iso no zenji. Then, Iso no zenji's daughter,
Shizuka, inherited her art, and became famous as the lover of Yoshitsune.[45]
We have seen how Yoshitsune, pursued by the warriors of his brother
Yoritomo, decided to leave Shizuka behind when he ascended Kinpusen.
Soon deserted by her escort, Shizuka stumbled all night long over mountain paths. She eventually arrived at Zaō-dō, a major Shugendō cultic
center, on the day of the Kinpusen festival. There she joined a group of

shirabyōshi and *sarugaku* dancers. She was recognized by one monk, who recalled how she once danced at Shinsen'en for a rain ritual at the request of Retired Emperor Go-Toba: "In the capital, there was one year a drought that lasted a hundred days. Though the ex-Emperor offered prayers and a hundred *shirabyōshi* were commissioned to perform, not a drop of rain fell until Shizuka danced. Then there was a great downpour which lasted for three days and earned her a special imperial commendation."[46]

According to the *Azuma kagami*, Shizuka was summoned to Kamakura in 1186 to be questioned on the whereabouts of Yoshitsune. She left on the third month with her mother, Iso no zenji. After her interrogation, in the fourth month, she was, although pregnant, forced to perform a dance at Tsurugaoka Hachimangu Shrine. Three months later, she gave birth to Yoshitsune's child, who was killed on Yoritomo's order. Afterwards, she returned to Kyoto with her mother on the ninth month, and she is no longer mentioned in the *Azuma kagami*. The *Gikeiki* (Muromachi period) claims, however, that after returning to Kyoto she received the tonsure at the age of nineteen and lived in a hermitage near Tenryūji; soon afterwards, owing to her recitation of the nenbutsu, she obtained rebirth in the Pure Land. The circumstances of her final moments recall those of Giō. The point is that, with the penetration of patriarchal values in the Muromachi period, Shizuka becomes a "chaste woman" who must live in reclusion after the death of Yoshitsune.

The legends develop, however, by emphasizing not only Shizuka's love for Yoshitsune and her tragic destiny, but also, like in the case of Oiso no Tora, her wanderings. In this, she is emblematic of these wandering women first described by Yanagita Kunio, and it is possible that her story, like those of Tora, Izumi Shikibu, and Ono no Komachi, was spread throughout Japan by wandering women (*miko*, *bikuni*). The legend of Shizuka's travels through Japan is found, for instance, in the tradition of Kōryōji, a Jōdo temple in Kogashi (Ibaraki Prefecture).[47] After leaving Kamakura, instead of returning to Kyoto, Shizuka traveled with her servant Kotoji in search of Yoshitsune, all of the way up to Shimohemi in Shimōsa. Only after hearing that Yoshitsune had died at Takadachi in Hiraizumi did she decide to return to Kyoto, but she died of exhaustion on the way. Her servant, Kotoji, buried her at Kōryūji (later renamed Kōryōji), and planted a branch of *sugi* on her grave. She left to the temple the robe (*amaryō*) that Emperor Go-Toba had given to Shizuka after her dance at Shinsen'en.[48]

Hosokawa has emphasized that, like the *shirabyōshi*, Shizuka never travels alone, but always with a female companion. The *shirabyōshi* and other itinerant female specialists such as the *miko* and the *bikuni* traveled in tandem for obvious reasons of safety. It is also, however, because their legend, in order to be told, needs a narrator, someone who was an eyewitness to their tragic destiny. The two women are sometimes related by blood (mother and daughter like Iso no zenji and Shizuka;[49] sisters like Giō and Ginyo, or Harugiku and Wakagiku), sometimes not (like Giō and Hotoke, Shizuka and Kotoji, or Tomoe and Yamabue, the two female companions of the warrior Kiso Yoshinaka).[50]

In most sources, young women become *shirabyōshi* after experiencing various miseries (the death of their father, for instance). Because their youth prevents them from becoming nuns, this is usually the only alternative. All the same, their lives at court reveal to them the transient nature of existence, and prepares them for conversion. At the same time, the role played in medieval literature by the *yūjo* and the *shirabyōshi* and other courtesans recalls that played by the female mediums. The association is triggered by the term *shirabyōshi* itself, used both for the dances of the *miko* and those of the female entertainers metonymically called *shirabyōshi*.

DOWN BY THE RIVER

Row, row, row your boat
Gently down the stream.
Merrily, merrily, merrily
Life is but a dream.

"Down by the river," a muddy river at times, lived the courtesan. By contrast, the *miko*, according to Yanagita, performed her rites near a pure spring. While the partners of the courtesan are usually men, those of the *miko* are usually gods, but the line sometimes is blurred. At any rate, both types of women were marginals, and their evolution must therefore be placed in the context of the rise of the marginalized during the medieval period.[51] The riverside, like the various places where the *yūjo* plied their trade—road-stations (*shukuba*) and harbors—is by nature a liminal space. This is even truer of the river itself—many prostitutes worked on small boats. Furthermore, many of these places where people passed (roads, bridges, fords, stations) were perceived as "sacred places" with particular traditions where ordinary law did not avail. Not surprisingly, many courtesans settled in such places, or near shrines and markets. The most famous were the stations of Eguchi and Kanzaki on the Yodogawa River. For all of their marginality, the social status of courtesans was by no means a low one, at least until the Kamakura period. Indeed, they often gave birth to the children of the nobles, and even of the emperor, and their *waka* were sometimes included in imperial anthologies.

There were many categories of women on the road. The fact that they were to some extent perceived as "sacred individuals"—distinct from ordinary women—probably made their travels easier.[52] All *yūjo* were not of the wandering type, however, and in either case they were organized in corporations.[53] But after the Muromachi and Sengoku periods, the prestige of the emperor and of the buddhas and *kamis* declined drastically, which also brought a decline of the social status of the specialists in religious and artistic matters (the *geinōmin*), like the *yūjo* and the *miko* who depended on such prestige. Discriminatory attitudes toward formerly sacred individuals began to develop.[54] Although women continued to travel well into the Edo period, their status had lowered since the Muromachi period, and their connections with the sacred sphere disappeared; or rather, became latent, to partly resurface at the end of the Edo period in "new religions" like Tenrikyō.[55]

The aestheticization of the courtesan went hand-in-glove with the "great enclosure" of the *yūjo* that took place in a few decades at the end of the sixteenth century and the beginning of the seventeenth century.[56] The *yūjo* acquired a new role in literature. In the *ukiyo zōshi*, for instance, the closed quarter turns into a paradise on earth, whose goddesses and bodhisattvas are the courtesans. A heroine of the Nō and Kyōgen repertories like Hanako is representative of the *yūjo* as goddess of beauty, reflecting a certain aesthetic philosophy. In Kyōgen plays, Hanako works as a courtesan in the station of Nogami, and she falls in love with Yoshida Shōshō. When Shōshō has to leave, they exchange their fans as tokens of unending love. Because Hanako spends her time looking melancholically at her lover's fan, people come to call her "Hannyo," after the name of a Chinese heroine abandoned by the emperor. The patron of the brothel eventually sends her away, and destroys the fan. Nonetheless she is in the end reunited with her lover.[57]

According to Saeki, the initially religious character of the *yūjo* was increasingly aestheticized during the medieval period, and this aesthetic character in turn paled in the Edo period. With the decline of the *yūjo*, the notion of *asobi*—no longer expressing the *kami-asobi* (god play) performed in a world in which humans and gods were related—became a synonym for mere entertainment. The houses of pleasure lost their "cultural" flavor, and female aesthetic activities (*kabu*) moved to a male (yet feminized) theatrical sphere (*Kabuki*).[58] As a result, the image of the *yūjo* in literature also changed. The red-light district became the "floating world" (*ukiyo*) represented in woodblock prints, a place of escape from reality.

The Monk and the Bayadère

The relation between the courtesan and the ascetic has long been used as an expression of nonduality, and more precisely of the union of the sensual and the spiritual.[59] The Buddhist attitude toward the courtesan was from the outset ambivalent: despite her charms, she was feared as a dangerous temptress. Although the Buddha himself was able to reject the temptation of the lascivious daughters of Māra, in his former incarnation as the hermit Unicorn (known in Japan as Ikkaku Sennin), he had been rather shamefully seduced by a courtesan. Courtesans, however, were also women who, because they lived in a "floating world," were aware of the ephemerality of things. Knowing the "true nature" of men, they were no longer impressed by social distinctions such as lay and priest, commoner and nobility (with a few—venal rather than venerial—exceptions).[60]

The following verse is said to have been composed by a courtesan (who sounds strangely like the poetess Izumi Shikibu) when the holy man of Mount Shosha, Shōkū (910–1007), refused her offerings.

> In Settsu province
> anything at all
> becomes Dharma,
> even flirting, even love play—
> yes, so I hear.[61]

The story of Shōkū's encounter with Izumi Shikibu appears in sources like the *Sangoku denki*.[62] According to this text, Izumi, at the request of Empress Jōtōmon'in, had gone secretly to Mount Shosha with a group of eight court women. When they arrived at Shōkū's temple, however, the latter pretended to be absent. As the disappointed women were about to leave, Izumi composed a verse and pasted it on a pillar. Shōkū, seeing it, was deeply moved, and he called the women back.[63]

Shōkū is also famous for his meeting with a courtesan of Eguchi, who appeared to him as a "bodhisattva of song and dance" (*kabu no bosatsu*). The story of his visit to a courtesan at the ford of Muro is one of the best known of Japanese Buddhism, and, according to Yanagita, it was probably spread by professional entertainers.[64] In Shōkū's biography, the bodhisattva Mañjuśrī (Jp. Monju) appears to Shōkū and tells him that "the *chōja* of Eguchi, a woman of Silla, is a live body Fugen."[65] Shōkū goes to Eguchi and asks the courtesan to entertain him. When she sings an *imayō*, he closes his eyes and sees her revealed in her true glorious nature as the bodhisattva Fugen (Skt. Samantabhadra), singing a Buddhist song. Whereas the courtesan sings the *imayō* song "Shūhō murozumi" (In the *muro* of Shūhō), the name of the place, Muro, becomes in the bodhisattva's song a reference to *muro* (without ouflows, a technical term designating the undefiled state of the bodhisattva). When Shōkū leaves, the courtesan tells him not to say anything to anyone, then suddenly dies.[66] This "dramatic" ending, leaving the air filled with fragrance and Shōkū choked with tears, disappears from the Nō play *Eguchi*. In this play, the courtesan's boat fades into the mist, and takes the form of Fugen's white elephant—a rather awkward image, intended to suggest that the courtesan has been reborn in the Pure Land. The Buddhist topos of the courtesan as avatar of a bodhisattva may explain why many medieval courtesans—for instance, the *shirabyōshi* Hotoke—had a Buddhist name.[67] The intense sensual pleasure caused by the courtesan was believed (by some) to lead to a true mystical experience.

Muro was not only a red-light district, but also has been a sacred place since antiquity.[68] In one legend, its deity, the "Muro no myōjin," reveals itself in the form of Queen Vaidehī, the protagonist of the *Pure Land Sūtra*. This implies that she has been reborn in the Pure Land, and, further, that Muro itself is the Pure Land. Here again, we find a wordplay on Muro (the place) and *muro* (the perfect state, without outflow). Thus, the dances and *asobi* of the courtesans of Muro (the *murogimi*) are all a form of divine play.[69]

Another well-known encounter at Muro station involves Hōnen and a courtesan.[70] The standard hagiographical version explains that, when Hōnen arrived by boat at the Muro station in Harima province, a small boat drew near carrying a woman of ill fame. She asked him what past sins could have brought such karmic retribution on her, and whether there was a way to be saved. Hōnen told her that her past sins must have been indeed very great, but that she could be redeemed by Amida's power. Later on, he heard that the woman, after secluding herself in a mountain village, had died in the odor of sanctity.[71]

In an earlier version of Hōnen's encounter with the courtesan, however, things do not proceed quite as smoothly. When she tries to get an interview with the holy man, she is at first dismissed by his disciples. She only succeeds after sending him a reproachful verse alluding to the fact that the Buddha himself was not as discriminatory toward her sex since he had a wife and a son. When Hōnen, swayed by her arguments, finally agrees to meet her, she tells him about the origin of the courtesans (*yūjo*) and their relations with eminent monks. She mentions in particular a precedent to their encounter, that of an abbot of Tennōji, who, while crossing a river on a boat, received the following verse from a courtesan: "From the path with outflows to the path without outflows . . . / Śākyamuni himself / and Rāhula, we are told, had a mother."[72]

The story of the courtesan of Muro Station seems to have been added to Hōnen's biography in the fourteenth century, or in the period when courtesans came to be despised. These tales about the conversion of a courtesan by a holy monk are ambivalent. They cannot be simply read as a proof of the "feminism" of the early Pure Land school and other similar movements, as they also tend to include a strong criticism on the part of the courtesan of the initial aloofness of the priest.

Saigyō

Perhaps the most famous literary exchange between a monk and a courtesan is the one that allegedly took place at Eguchi between the poet-monk Saigyō and a woman named Tae. Saigyō's own account is recorded as follows in the *Senjushō*:

> I [Saigyō] once passed through Eguchi, sometime after the twentieth of the ninth month. The houses were pressed together on the north and south banks of the river. The inhabitants' fickle hearts were fixed on the comings and goings of travellers' boats. Gazing at the town, I was thinking how sadly ephemeral were its residents' lives, when an unseasonably wintry wind darkened the sky.
>
> I approached a simple cottage to ask shelter until it cleared. The woman who owned the hut showed no sign of granting my request, so I spoke the verse that came to mind,
>
> "Indeed it may be hard
> to reject
> the entire world,
> but you begrudge
> a temporary lodging."
>
> The prostitute replied sadly,
>
> "Seeing that you were one
> who had left his home,
> I only thought
> your mind should not dwell
> on temporary lodgings,"
>
> and promptly let me in.[73]
>
> Although I had intended to shelter there only briefly, for the duration of the shower, her poem was so interesting that I stayed all night.

The whole episode remains very chaste, and Saigyō does not even seem tempted to break his vows. The monk and the courtesan speak all through the night, and he listens patiently as she complains about life and weeps. When they part in the morning, he promises to come again. Unable to fulfill his promise, he sends her poems. In her reply, she tells him that she has become a nun.[74] In another tale, which seems to be a variant, Saigyō, passing through Eguchi, discusses the sad condition of prostitutes with another monk:

> The houses pressed together on the north and south banks of the river. The entertainers yearned for the short-lived passions of travellers. How ephemeral their deeds are! What will become of them in the next world after they have wasted their lives in this one?

It must have been karma from previous lives which determined that they become prostitutes. To preserve their fragile bodies for a short span they commit acts which the Buddha strictly prohibited. We all must bear the weight of our own sins, but how terrible to lead others to damnation. Yet among prostitutes there are many who achieve rebirth in Paradise. And many fisher folk, takers of life, die in a holy manner. How can that be?

At one point, Saigyō and his fellow-monk are surprised by rain and take refuge under someone's gate:

Looking into the house I saw the householder, a nun. She was rushing back and forth with a single board, frantic about the rain leaking in.

I jested casually,

"Struggling to roof
the humble cottage,"

The nun must somehow have heard me, in spite of her excited bustling about, for she tossed the board and added,

all the while thinking,
"Shine in moonlight,
collect in pools to reflect it, rain!"

Unable to ignore such refinement, we spent the night in her hut composing linked verse.

When they part, Saigyō reflects: "I have traveled through more than sixty provinces, and come to know many people, but never have I met anyone as sensitive as she. So fond had we become of her that, had she been a man, we would somehow have persuaded her to come with us and be a companion to commiserate with in our hunger. My companion kept remarking as we traveled on together, 'How I miss that nun from Eguchi.'"[75] Interestingly, the nun—a woman living next to prostitutes, and acting in a sense as their representative—seems to reveal the truth to Saigyō: the leaking roof is like the mind, defiled by the outside world. It is because of this, however, because of the rain that has collected in pools inside the house (or desire within) that the moon of enlightenment might be reflected inside it. This is why prostitutes may be more permeable to the truth than self-enclosed ascetics.

In this context, it is worth noting that Saigyō is often presented in folk-tales as a monk who gets defeated by a person of lesser status, usually a woman or a child. This is the case in the so-called Saigyō-*modoshi* tales, in which the wandering Saigyō is nonplussed by a person to whom he asks his way and turns back. Thus, the "Saigyō-*modoshi*" of Miyajima (Aki Prefecture) is said to be the place where Saigyō once asked a woman for direction; when she looked as if she were going to pass him by without answering, he composed the following verse: "Even if I had asked to a cicada shell, it would have told me the way." The woman merely laughed and pointed out an imperfection in his verse.

This theme of the encounter between the courtesan and the monk finds many variants in *setsuwa* literature and in Nō plays.[76] Many of these tales reveal an attempt to normalize the courtesan and to use her for Buddhist propaganda. Eventually, the female entertainer became a sublime "bodhisattva of Dance and Song" (*kabu bosatsu*).[77] Her songs evoked the Buddhist utopia, the Pure Land of lapis lazuli, the divine *asobi*, the "deep play" of the redeemed followers. The voices of the *yūjo* of Eguchi were said to "make the body shiver," as though they effected a kind of catharsis.[78] According to Saeki, this type of *asobi*, far from being mere entertainment, is only the poetic crystallization of the tradition of *kami-asobi* performed by the ancient sybils. Even if the motif of the courtesan as bodhisattva emerged against the background of shamanistic beliefs in the incantatory power of the *imayō*, however, it may have marked a radical departure from the *imayō* genre inasmuch as it was recuperated by an aesthetic theory or a Buddhist soteriology. The pathetic dance of the abandoned courtesan, having become an aesthetic or literary topos in Nō plays (featuring classic figures such as Giō or Shizuka), is now said to express the essence of Nō.

THE DISCOURTEOUS COURTESAN

We have seen how the Muro courtesan invoked the human relationships that bound the Buddha to his wife Yaśodhara and his son Rāhula. During his peregrinations, the young hero Yoshitsune falls in love with the young daughter of his host, Jōruri-hime, and tries to overcome her virtuous resistance. One of the most significant passages in his somewhat disingenuous plea runs as follows:

> The Buddha himself answered the call of love. This Śākyamuni, who goes from the path with outflows to the path without outflows, united with Yaśodhara, the daughter of the great minister Yaso, and engendered a son, Rāhula. Among the kami too, there are the "binding kami" (*musubu no kami*). [This is true] even of the kami who have sworn to protect the hundred generations of kings, in the two great sanctuaries of Ise. Again, in Atsuta-miya, the *myōjin* of Suwa, Izu Hakone, and even in the sanctuary on Mount Nikkō, there are male and female [divine] bodies. Furthermore, among the Three Jewels of all the buddhas, from the most distant past down to the present time, there have been vows of union. Such feeling of union between man and woman, how could one

turn one's back on it? Passions are awakening, *saṃsāra* is nirvāṇa. When one preaches that the one Buddha is all the present beings, this [means that] even the rotten wood in the valley becomes a buddha. When one hears that "all dharmas are the one Suchness," [it means that] even the storm on the peaks is the voice of the Dharma. When one considers that "all dharma are ultimate reality" [*shohō jissō*], it means that the Buddha and all beings are one.[79]

The chaste resolve of the young girl is shattered by these canonic arguments, and she eventually yields to Yoshitsune's desire. Interestingly, this eloquent case of Buddhist casuistry calls to mind the discourse by which Tokiwa, Yoshitsune's mother, defeated the Kurama priest who refused to admit her into his temple.[80] As we have seen in the case of the Muro courtesan, this kind of rhetoric had a long history.

The interdiction for courtesans getting close to the boat of an eminent monk seems to be of the same nature as the *nyonin kekkai*. The courtesan who strikes back and convinces the monk by using her art and the story of the life of the Buddha resembles those women in Nō plays and *monogatari* who transgress the *kekkai* and shut the monks up. Their talents of seduction—their *asobi* itself—changes the meaning of the transgression, and, by breaking the rule of the *kekkai*, they produce an inversion of values. What one sees here is, in a way, the inversion of sacred and profane through the transgressive activity of these women. This kind of transgression, however, remains a literary topos closely connected to the performing arts.[81]

Abe Yasurō discusses in this context the term *suisan*, meaning "to invite oneself," to visit someone [a superior] without invitation or to speak without being invited; not to remain at one's place, not to respect the etiquette."[82] A typical example of *suisan* is the intrusion of the young *shirabyōshi* Hotoke in Kiyomori's house. The term *suisan* often expresses the characteristic style of such courtesans. It describes the behavior expected from them, at least on the literary or theatrical stage, because in real life they must stay in their place. The term became an emblem of their particular status, and it may be related with the term *basara* that characterized originals in the "topsy-turvy" world (*gekokujō*) of the Muromachi period.[83] Through a kind of codification, the medieval spirit of *suisan* was able to survive even in the stiff realm of court ceremony. It came to characterize a type of eccentric behavior tolerated in front of the emperor. It extended to performing arts, with which it had natural affinities, and insufflated a new breath into them. It also provided new models of behavior for people exposed to such arts. It justified a radical transgression of the rules, reminiscent of the transgression of the *kekkai*.[84] Medieval artists (*geinōsha*), beginning with the courtesans (*yūjo*) and the dancers (*shirabyōshi*), embodied the irreverential spirit of *suisan*. This is perhaps due to the fact that, in their relationships with Buddhist priests, rather than begging for salvation, they were often the ones who revealed sacredness. In this they were backed by a mythological tradition that emphasized the convergence of the sacred and the profane.

PARADIGMS

In Japanese culture, two women, Izumi Shikibu and Ono no Komachi, have risen to the status of emblematic figures. Yanagita Kunio has pointed out that Izumi Shikibu, for instance, is credited with at least seven birthplaces, and even more burial sites.[85] One of them is in Jōshin-in, a small Shingon temple in downtown Kyoto.[86] Likewise, Yanagita has noted that there are today in Kyoto two temples dedicated to Ono no Komachi, in both of which her grave can be found. One of them, Zuishin-in in Yamashina, also preserves a statue of "Sotoba Komachi," represented as an old woman sitting in so-called Indian fashion, with one knee up, a position that calls to mind representations of the old hag Datsueba.[87] Yanagita thought that the legends of these two women were spread by wandering female artists such as the *uta bikuni*. His viewpoint has been accepted by some scholars, but strongly criticized by others. Katagiri Yōichi, for instance, holds such views as responsible for the decline of literary scholarship, inasmuch as they prevent scholars from reflecting upon the extant literature and textual tradition about Komachi.[88] On the whole, however, it seems that the opposite tendency has prevailed, even in recent scholarship, and that the two women have been studied mainly as literary prodigies. Thus, the argument could be turned against Katagiri himself. At any rate, I follow here Yanagita, and focus on the legendary or mythical dimensions of these two figures.

Apart from her poetic talents, Izumi Shikibu is famous for her active sexuality, and, like Ono no Komachi, she is said to have suffered from a venereal disease.[89] She was married for a while to Tachibana no Michisada (ca. 996–1004), but had an affair with Prince Tametaka (977–1002). Furthermore, she had an affair with the latter's younger brother Atsumichi (d. 1007, at 27, when she was about 29) even before the expiration of a year's mourning for Tametaka. As Paul Cranston puts it: "Not the least shocking aspect of the infatuation of the two brothers must have been the fact that the lady was the daughter of a mere provincial governor, and the gentlemen sons of an Emperor. She remarried with Fujiwara no Yorimasa (958–1036), a provincial governor. Her two husbands and her two princely lovers were by no means the only men in her life.[90]

The most striking episode in Izumi's legend is probably her incestuous relationship with the priest Dōmyō. In the *otogizōshi* "Izumi Shikubu," for instance, Dōmyō is the child born from Izumi's union with a courtier, and abandoned by her on Gojō bridge with a dagger at his side. The child was brought up by a townsman and became a renowned preacher on Hieizan. Having been summoned to court, he fell in love with Izumi, who returned his love. After yielding to him, she discovered his true identity, owing to the dagger.[91] Here is the story, as it appears in the *Uji shūi monogatari*:

> Long ago there was a priest called the Holy Teacher Dōmyō, the son of the tutor of the Crown Prince and a man much given to amorous pursuits. He had an affair with Izumi Shikibu. Now his reading of the sutra was most beautiful, and once when he had gone to spend the night with Izumi Shikibu he woke up and devoutly began to recite it. By the time he had read all eight books, it was nearly daybreak, and he was on the point of dropping off to sleep again when he sensed someone nearby and called out to ask who it was. "I am an old man who lives at the corner of Fifth Avenue and Nishinotoin Lane," came the reply. "What do you want?" asked Dōmyō. "I have been listening tonight to your reading of the sutra and I shall never, never forget it," said the old man. "But I often read the *Lotus Sūtra*," said Dōmyō. "Why have you chosen tonight to tell me this?" "When you have purified yourself before reading the sutra," replied the Deity from Fifth Avenue, "Brahma and Indra and other divine beings come to listen to you and the likes of me cannot get near enough to hear. But tonight you read it without having cleansed yourself first, and so Brahma and Indra were not there to listen. This gave me a chance to come and hear it myself, an experience I shall never forget."

The union of the courtesan and the monk came to be reinterpreted symbolically as the conjunction of two sexual deities of the *dōsojin* type. Indeed, the motif of incest may have played a significant role in this reinterpretation. As Ishida Eiichirō has shown, the motif of incest between mother and son has the character of a "sacred marriage" in Asian mythologies, and such hierogamies are often at the origin of a people.[92] In the present case, too, the moralizing conclusion seems to be a later addition.

The turning point and literary climax in Izumi Shikibu's life was her encounter with the Buddhist priest Shōkū (910–1007). According to one version, Izumi Shikibu, after losing her fourteen-year-old daughter, Koshikibu, in 1018, at the age of thirty-five, realized the impermanence of life and went to consult Shōkū on Shoshazan. According to another version, her desire to take refuge in Buddhism was motivated by her desire to atone for her incestuous relationship with Dōmyō. At any rate, it is allegedly when Shōkū refused to see her that she composed her most famous verse: "From darkness / into the path of darkness / must I enter: shine upon me from afar, / o moon above the mountain crest."[93] She was subsequently converted by Shōkū to the Pure Land teaching.

The legend of Izumi Shikibu was to develop yet further, however. A first addition was the story of her miraculous birth, illustrating the well-known motif of the human child born from an animal. Its prototype may be the story of the deer's child: deep in a mountain, a child was born, but the mother died. The child was found and raised by a doe. The animal later took her to a couple of old people, who adopted her and called her Shika-hime (Doe Princess). Later on, she worked in the house of a wealthy layman (chōja). In some variants, the animal is a she-boar, which comes to Fukusenji, to drink water.[94] One day, the monks hear the cries of a baby behind the Buddha Hall and discover that the boar has given birth to a child. Thinking that this boar may be the animal reincarnation of some former monk, they adopt the child. Meanwhile, an old monk appears in the dream of a childless couple of a neighboring village and tells them that the child they wanted has arrived at the temple. They go to the temple, tell their dream to the monks, and obtain the little girl, whom they call Izumi Shikibu. At thirteen, the girl goes to the capital and serves as lady-in-waiting at the palace.[95]

Another variant tells of an an old childless couple who went to pray at a temple dedicated to the buddha Yakushi. While they were sleeping in the temple, they heard the cries of a newborn. When they came out, they found a deer feeding a baby girl. Overjoyed, they picked up the baby and returned home. When she grew up, the child became very beautiful, but her feet were forked. She was gifted for study and poetry, and when she turned six her name reached the capital, whereby she was summoned. She soon became Izumi Shikibu. To hide her feet, she always wore a special kind of sock called tabi.[96]

The buddha Yakushi reappears in another episode of Izumi Shikibu's legend. According to the Sangoku meisho zue, for instance, the poetess, having fallen ill, went to consult the bodhisattva Kannon at Kiyomizu. The latter told her that she ought to pray at the three cultic centers dedicated to Yakushi (Komeyama, Hōraiji, and Hokkegokuji). Izumi Shikibu first performed a hundred-day reclusion at Hōraiji, but to no avail. Then she went to Hokkegokuji in Hyūga province, where she vowed to kill herself if there was no divine response, and she composed the following verse: "Hail to Yakushi, / dispeller of all ills! / I raise my prayer; / but more than my own pain do I regret / discredit to the Buddha's name."[97] As she was about to throw herself from a cliff, she had a vision, in which a strange man came and took her hand, reciting the following verse: "This passing shower / is but a momentary thing; / I bid you, take / your rain hat off / and leave it there behind."[98] She was soon cured, and she returned to this place the following year, at which time she suddenly died.[99] The theme of the courtesan who suffers from a strange illness and leaves the capital for a journey to the provinces was apparently widespread. It is found, for instance, in Hōnen's biography, as well as in the origin stories of many villages.

The thrust of these tales seems to be that Izumi Shikibu was so strong-minded that she could force gods and buddhas, let alone eminent priests like Shōkū, to respond to her verses. Conversely, she could also silence the elements. According to one local tradition, she was once able to appease with a verse the tumult of the whirlpool of Narumon in Awa. Another tradition related to Hachimangū in Yokoyama (Ōshū province) claims that Izumi Shikibu had actually stolen the verse from a shrine priest (*negi*). The story goes as follows: the ominous roar of the Awa whirlpool had caused some uneasiness at court and rituals were performed to appease it. The priest of Yokoyama received in a dream an oracular verse, whose recitation was supposed to put an end to the roar. Holding the written verse in his hand, the priest went quickly to the site. At that time, Izumi Shikibu, who had received an imperial order to appease the roar, arrived at the place. While spending the night at the inn, she lured the priest into reciting the verse. Early in the morning, she went to the whirlpool and composed a slightly modified verse, which she recited with success. The merit of the priest was eventually recognized, however, and his shrine flourished.

Izumi Shikibu and Ono no Komachi were often confused. In the Edo period, the verse of Komachi "Praying for Rain" was well known, but it was at times attributed to Izumi Shikibu.[100] This verse, like Izumi Shikibu's verse to appease the whirlpool of Narumon, was written in response to an imperial edict that ordered the composition of poems to put an end to a drought. It reads:

> Through one thousand hurricanes
> gods who see our condition
> strew tumult
> open the gates
> of the Heavenly River.[101]

The episode of the poetic exchange with Yakushi is also often attributed to Ono no Komachi. There is, for instance, in the village of Ono (Iyo province) a temple called Ono Yakushi. Ono no Komachi, following the injunction of the Sumiyoshi god, is said to have came to this place to perform a hundred-day reclusion, and to have been cured after receiving the following oracular verse: "It seemed that rain was falling, but the weather returned to fair, and the *kasa* was put aside."[102] Three years later, as she passed again through that place, she had a new Yakushi statue carved, inside whose head she inserted the verse.[103]

In his discussion of the legends of Izumi Shikibu and Ono no Komachi, Yanagita aimed at presenting a positive image of women. Thus, he examined these legends to find a description of female capacities and emotions, and he carefully avoided discussing sexual aspects that would have shed an unpleasant light on these women. In particular, he avoided determining to what kind of disease the pun on *kasa* (rain hat) referred in this case. As is well known, *kasa* is a generic name in Japanese literature for various skin diseases, including leprosy (Hansen's disease). After the epidemic of syphilis (*baidoku*) of 1512–13, however, it came to designate mainly syphilis.[104] Thus, even though Komachi's disease may have been leprosy, it was more likely syphilis. Scholars have often considered that Izumi Shikibu's disease at Hokkegakuji in Nikkō was leprosy, and that Izumi Shikibu (and Ono no Komachi) was in this way assimilated to medieval *hinin*. Komachi was perceived as a courtesan, a woman who liked sex (*irogonomi*). She was seen as a remorseless polygamous woman in a patriarchal society increasingly emphasizing chastity. Thus, syphilis was deemed a normal retribution for her, from a patriarchal viewpoint. Despite the apparent contradiction, this viewpoint was also expressed in the belief that Komachi was not sexually mature—a belief reflected, for instance, by the legend according to which she had no vagina.[105] These two extremes represent the two poles of male prejudice against women from the Kamakura period to the Edo period.[106] A woman who refused to marry and procreate could only invoke in her defense an ominous birth-date (for instance in the year of the horse) or some physical flaw, in particular a sexual abnormality (lack of periods, or the malformation of her sexual organs). Significantly, sterile women are often called "Ono no Komachi."[107] In any event, it is difficult to interpret Komachi's legend, as Yanagita does, as something "beautiful."[108]

Ono no Komachi

Literary scholars have emphasized the importance of Ono no Komachi in Japanese literature.[109] Her place in the Japanese cultural landscape does not, however, seem sufficiently justified by her literary achievements. She is known above all as a femme fatale who caused the death of one of her lovers, General Fukakusa. In this sense, she is the exact opposite of the Buddhist courtesans described earlier, who enlighten their lovers through sex.[110]

Little is known of Komachi, apart from the poems attributed to her and the tradition that she lived in the ninth century, under the reigns of three rulers (Ninmyō Tennō, Montoku Tennō, and Seiwa Tennō). According to the *Gunsho ruijū*, she was the granddaughter of Ono no Takamura, and the daughter of Yoshizane, an administrator in Dewa. She was admired, but also envied, for her insolent beauty and talent. Was she later rejected from the court, finishing her life in misery? Although there is no indication of that in the documentation, it is plausible, and it does fit nicely the Buddhist topos of vanitas. This historical vacuum was soon filled by literary sources.

Toward the end of the tenth century, a small work, known subsequently as *Tamazukuri Komachi sōsui sho* (*Splendor and Decline of the Komachi Who Cultivated Pearls*) was compiled by an unknown Buddhist monk from the standpoint of the Pure Land teaching. Like so many other works, it is sometimes attributed to Kūkai. It is divided into two parts: in the first part, a monk meets a decrepit mendicant woman, who confesses to him that she once was a beautiful young girl who lived in luxury and was destined to become an imperial consort. Her destiny took a brutal turn, however, when she lost her family and was reduced to misery. The monk responds to her confession with a few moralizing comments and tells her to take refuge in the Buddha. In the second part, a priest meets another old woman, reduced to a pitiful physical state. She wants to take refuge in Buddhism, and tells the priest that, having lost her family very early on, she married a hunter (or fisherman) and gave birth to a son. She was very happy at first, until her physical appearance began to deteriorate. When the child suddenly died, her husband chased her away and she became a mendicant. The priest tries to console her, promising her rebirth in Amida's Pure Land. Both stories are thus tales of the disillusion and suffering brought forth by old age. Gradually, their protagonists seem to have been identified with Komachi, which explains the misleading title.

In his *Mumyōshō*, Kamo no Chōmei (1155–1216) was still wondering whether the Komachi whose poems were recorded in the *Kokinshū* and the fictitious Komachi born from the *Tamatsukuri Komachi sōsui sho* were the same person. Many legends were already circulating about her, like the story of the ordeal that she imposed on her lover, Fukakusa Shōshō; or the discovery of her skeleton by Narihira. These legends were further amplified and spread in the fourteenth century with Nō plays that came to form a "Komachi cycle."[111] The myth took its classical form with the *Komachi zōshi* in the fifteenth century, becoming a popular theme of the *bunraku* and *jōruri* repertoires.[112]

It is the image of the old hag that is emphasized in Nō plays such as *Sotoba Komachi*. This play provides an illustration of the medieval topos of madness through possession. As noted earlier, fits of female madness are usually expressed in Nō through transvestism. Thus, when she is possessed by the resentful spirit of her lover Fukakusa, Komachi discards her rags to put on a man's hat and robe. Her transvestism calls to mind the behavior of the *shirabyōshi*, who wear male clothes to subvert sexual difference.[113]

In the *Komachi zōshi*, the old Komachi meets again her former lover Ariwara Narihira, but, whereas he has become perfectly enlightened, she remains immersed in delusion: "It is said that in terms of poetry Komachi was of the ancient lineage of Princess Sotoori and that she was the incarnation of Kannon, the bodhisattva of compassion and mercy. . . . [And yet] her mind was not clear and so she did not know the deep pathos of things (*mono no aware*), did not worship the buddhas or pay homage to the gods, and instead spent the months and days in vanity."[114] Narihira reveals to her that the depths of women's sin hide the truth from them.[115] Having spoken, he disappears, and Komachi wonders whether it was really him or a manifestation of Kannon. Afterwards she wanders across the land, and eventually meets a lonely death in a moor. Eventually Narihira, guided by her spirit, finds her remains. The tale ends on a hopeful note: "People listening to this story, and still more those reading it, will receive merit equivalent to having carved statues of the thirty-three forms of Kannon, the bodhisattva of compassion and mercy. Komachi was the incarnation of the Eleven-headed Kannon."[116] The wandering of Komachi has now become the result of her awakening, and the mark of her sacredness. It connects her forlorn figure to that of itinerant priests and/or poets like Saigyō and Narihira. This state of mind was already expressed in a verse she wrote before her alleged enlightenment:

Sad and lonely
I am a floating grass
whose root has been cut.
If a current would invite me,
I would follow it anywhere.[117]

Komachi's image is to some extent redeemed by her love affair with the famous poet Narihira. Yet, Japanese Buddhists seem to have never forgiven Komachi for her arrogance, her refusal to follow the norms. Thus, they either represent her suffering in hell, or visualize her corpse decomposing. The Buddhist topos of the nine stages of the decomposition of the corpse (*kyūzō*) came to be associated with Komachi in medieval painted scrolls (*emaki*). The choice of Komachi to illustrate the ravages of death may of course be explained as a didactic device to increase the effects of a memento mori, by showing her beauty humiliated by the ravages of death. Whereas in these paintings she dies in her prime, in the Nō plays the same effect is achieved by representing her as an old woman who suffers from the vivid remembrance of her youthful beauty.[118] Even in *Sotoba Komachi*, she has to suffer from her past cruelty toward her suitor. Yet, the image offered in this play is much more complex. I cannot do justice to its literary subtlety here, and wish merely to point out the tension between these different aspects of Komachi, or perhaps the consecutive phases in the development of her figure.[119]

The story of Komachi is developed in the *Mumyōzōshi*, a text whose female author is said to have been the "daughter of Shunzei."[120] Hosokawa Ryōichi argues that this text, while apparently following the legend of Komachi's skull, alters its meaning by transforming it into a tale of gratitude toward Komachi and by praising Komachi's steadfastness. Such treatment shows a small form of resistance to the patriarchal ideology of the time.[121] More often, Komachi's story was used as an argument for sexual submission. It seems to say: look at what happens to cool-hearted women.[122] Here, for instance, is what the *Heike monogatari* says about her: "In the not very distant past, Ono no Komachi's surpassing beauty and remarkable cultivation tormented every man who saw or heard her. But in the end, she found herself with no shelter from the wind and no means to keep out of the rain, suffering in retribution for the accumulated miseries of her suitors. (Perhaps it was because she had acquired a reputation for excessive cruelty that she failed to find a husband.)"[123] In the image of Komachi, as it develops from the Kamakura to the Muromachi periods, these elements are abandoned, and she becomes a single woman, without protection, excluded from the patriarchal system. Only during the Muromachi period, in the Nō play *Kayoi Komachi*, does she obtain salvation, together with her lover Fukakusa.

At the same time, Komachi haunts the male imagination, and not simply as a memento mori, as in the famous *Kusōshi emaki*.[124] Despite the title of this work, dating from the mid-Kamakura period, all of the verses have been lost. The original verses were probably the same as those attributed in another tradition to the Chinese poet Su Dongpo. But in Su Dongpo's verses, one does not find precise reference to gender, whereas here (in the pictures) one has a female corpse, that of a woman who was handsome—Komachi or Empress Danrin. The *Kusō zu* preserved at Saifukuji (a temple located at the "Crossroad of the Six Paths at Rokuhara," near the entrance of the charnel ground of Toribeno) transmitted this as the "Nine Faces of Death of Empress Danrin" (*Danrin kōgō kusō shi*). But in most cases, the protagonist is Ono no Komachi, and these images were widely used for the so-called *etoki*.[125] The theme was based on the Tendai notion of the "contemplation of the impure" (*fujōkan*). Significantly, this type of contemplation was reserved for men trying to overcome carnal desire, and there was no equivalent for women. Thus, ascesis remains a typically male prerogative. On the other hand, according to the description of a ceremony that took place in 1579 at Shinnyodō, the *kusō-e* also served as an object of repentance for women.[126] Thus, *etoki* were used differently depending on gender, for the "contemplation of the impure" (*fujōkan*) by men, for repentance (*zange*) by women.[127]

In a recent study of the motif, Gail Chin has argued that the paintings are a pictorial representation of the Tendai tenet of *hongaku* (innate awakening), according to which defilements (in this case female defilements) *are* awakening (*bonnō soku bodai*). This interpretation, however, does little to explain what the common reception of these paintings may have been. Chin falls into an overly charitable reading of Buddhist doctrine when she claims: "The Tendai view of the female sex as seen through these paintings of the decaying corpse neither completely heroicizes nor denigrates women. Rather, through *hongaku* thought, it regarded the qualities of good and evil in women not as absolute, but as relative. The female body was seen as synonymous with Buddhist truth, as interpreted by the promulgators of *hongaku* thought." Chin muddles the ideological context of the pictures by emphasizing their postmodern indeterminacy, in the name of a higher, genderless truth: "The image of the decomposing female cadaver . . . is a materialization of complex thoughts that are paradoxical, but there is no duality in them. In the same way, the symbol of the female corpse defies any brief explanation: it is polysemous. The gender of Buddhist truth in these paintings is female, yet truth also transcends gender as it is universal and resists definitions." Chin may be right to claim that "the Buddhist symbol of the female cadaver can be construed in many ways, misogynist or otherwise, in different cultural, religious, epochal, and personal milieux."[128] She does not tell us, however, what such readings could be, and how one could undermine the misogynistic reading. Her conclusion is, to me, puzzling: "Therefore, how appropriate it should be that a woman, whose life is filled with artistic creation that inspires anxious passion, should be used as a symbol of Buddhist truth. . . . In the end, who else but a woman can prove for all humanity that even the most utterly vulnerable will without doubt achieve Buddhahood."[129] Through such hermeneutical complacency, Chin completely exonerates the Buddhist representations of Komachi of all their misogynistic intent, and fails to address the conflict of interpretations by imagining some metphysical resolution of the issue in the name of *hongaku*.

If it seems difficult to read the pictorial representations of Komachi as expressions of a Buddhist truth transcending gender, as Chin does, there is no denying that, on the periphery of Buddhist discourse—for instance, in literature and performance arts—a more positive image of Komachi emerged, an image implying a resistance to the prevailing patriarchal readings of her figure.

According to Zeami, the "flower" of Nō is not limited to beautiful young women, but also extends to old women. This is an interesting recuperation of the theme of *Sotoba Komachi*. Several plays thus revolve around an old woman remembering her youth as a courtesan. But her final dance is sublime, and sublimates impermanence itself.[130] This is true of Komachi, as well: even reduced to mendicity, she expresses the "flower" of Nō, an ultimate beauty beyond the ugliness of this world. In the Nō *Seiganji*," Izumi Shikibu is represented as a bodhisattva of Song and Dance (*kabu no bosatsu*), like Narihira. Izumi and Dōmyō further become gods of yin and yang, joining the power of sex and that of poetry. Likewise, in the Nō *Kamo no Komachi*, Narihira and Komachi become an androgynous god, or (in the *Komachi zōshi*) an avatar of Kannon. By transforming Izumi Shikibu and Komachi into courtesans, the literary tradition ultimately aimed at glorifying them, not debasing them. The negative Buddhist reading of these courtesans could not entirely tarnish this positive image and its sexual power. Yanagita sees in them the image of the *yūjo*, but he sees only the art, not the sex. Yet, they assume symbolic value only with their male partner, whereupon they attest the virtues of sexuality and poetry.[131]

The medieval figure of Ono no Komachi remains ambivalent. This tension is reflected in her fate: her cruel rejection of Fukakusa ends in a tragic death whose memory will haunt her in Nō plays like *Sotoba Komachi*. Her craving for sensual pleasure, however, lent itself to a more light-hearted, ribald approach. This element, combined with a certain moralizing debasement inspired by Buddhism, explains perhaps why she is often derided in Edo satirical verses (*senryū*) like the following: "Ah! my dad Yoshizane / Gave me a good clitoris / Too bad for me."[132] In the next one, she shows regret for the cruel ordeal she allegedly imposed on her suitor: "If only I had known! / My vagina locked / for ninety-nine nights."[133]

The image of wandering that haunts the final part of of Komachi's life brings to mind the uncertain destinies of the wandering *miko* and *yūjo*. In this sense, Komachi's life, begun in the sedentary, secluded, and highly structured world of the court, and ending in the wilderness, is paradigmatic of this dialectic between sedentary life and nomadism. Women like Komachi have truly "left the family" (*shukke*), whereas the majority of Buddhist monks and nuns, despite their ordination, reentered a kind of sedentary domestic life, or at least a stable social system. They initially left the family in an attempt to leave the world behind, to reject it, whereas the ephemeral nature of the female medium was a paradoxical affirmation of the world, of truth *as* wandering, of a wandering truth opposed (and superior to) the sedentary (and sedated) truth of social life. Through their uprooting, these women were in a certain fashion rediscovering the fundamental truth of Buddhism, "nonabiding." Ironically, by driving the *miko* away from the shrines or the mountains where they used to officiate, and into a life of wandering and liminality, Buddhism confirmed them in a truth that they might have otherwise eventually forgotten—and that institutionalized Buddhism itself had long since lost.

There is no denying that wandering, in a society where "unbounded" (*muen*) places were rapidly shrinking away, became increasingly difficult and tended to degenerate into a licentious vagrancy. Having lost their religious bearings, they became loose women who were eventually enclosed, parked in sexual ghettos. The literary assumption of courtesans is merely the idealized reflection of past splendors, and of a lost truth: a truth that perhaps was never perfectly actualized, even if it seemed within their reach in the wanderings of the early medieval period.

The figures of Izumi Shikibu and Ono no Komachi may have initially reflected the independence of women at a time (the late Heian period) when patriarchal society and family were not yet established, and women retained a strong sense of agency. Komachi's image—for instance, the motifs found in the *Kusōshi emaki* and the story of Komachi's skull, as well as the motifs of old age and decrepitude found in *Sotoba Komachi* and similar plays—came to reflect the increasingly vocal standpoint of patriarchal society.

Lady Nijō between Komachi and Saigyō

Exiled from the court where she had spent happy years as a favorite of Emperor Go-Fukakusa, Lady Nijō compares herself to Ono no Komachi. Like her, she has lost her father and has no one who can help her. Visiting Kamakura in 1289, she complains about her wretched fate: "Did not the poetess Ono no Komachi, who was in the line of Princess Sotoori, end her life with a bamboo basket over her arm and a straw coat on her back? Yet could she have been as miserable as I was?"[134] Thus, the image of the fallen Komachi is reinterpreted as an affirmation of inner autonomy by Lady Nijō.

Far from the imperial Eden, owing to Buddhism Lady Nijō finds a new reason to live, becoming a female Saigyō and writing a text that will make her immortal: the *Towazugatari*—an "unasked-for tale"—which was kept secretly in the imperial palace until the modern time.[135] She thus is able to move on, beyond the world of the court and her disgrace, and her text, a long confession, has a redeeming, quasi-cathartic effect.[136] At the same time, it remains quite self-centered, and reveals a strong sense of pride. Although she is no longer a lady-in-waiting, she does not want to become a secluded nun. The only place for her is the open road. Seeing in her present destiny the effects of her past karma, she can only wander aimlessly, unbound.

Although Lady Nijō attributes her fall from grace to the jealousy of the emperor's consort and she downplays Go-Fukakusa's role, the reality may have been somewhat different. In her courtly function, she was often used as a sexual object.[137] For instance, because Go-Fukakusa and Kameyama are rivals, Nijō is passed between them as Go-Fukakusa tries to appease his brother's political advances. Despite his apparent understanding of her affair with the imperial priest Ariaki, however, Go-Fukusa did not forgive her and this affair is probably what led to her expulsion.

The second part of *Towazugatari* is thus an account of Lady Nijō's wanderings, described as a form of repentance for her past life as a courtesan. Having relinquished her role as female entertainer, she does not condemn the pleasures of the arts of entertainment, however. During her visit to Itsukushima Shrine, she remarks that the shrine maidens (*naishi*), when they dance, look like the Chinese courtesan Yuan Guifei or like bodhisattvas.[138] Significantly, she describes the god in a way reminiscent of a verse exchanged during the encounter between Shōkū and the Eguchi courtesan.[139] Through her writing, Lady Nijō mediates between her readers and the shrine maidens in their soteriological role.[140] She feels the bond between these women's tales and her own.[141] When she leaves the capital and starts traveling in 1289, she first goes on pilgrimage to Tsurugaoka Hachiman:

> From there I glimpsed Tsurugaoka Hachiman Shrine in the distance and reflected upon the bond from a former life that had caused me to be born into the Minamoto clan, which the god Hachiman had promised to protect above all others. What retribution has overtaken me, I wondered. Then I recalled praying for Father's future reincarnation and receiving the answer: "In exchange for your own good fortune in this life." I do not mean to imply that I begrudge him this, for I would not complain even if I had to hold out my sleeves and beg. Did not the poetess Ono no Komachi, who was in the line of Princess Sotoori, end her life with a bamboo basket over her arm and a straw coat on her back? Yet could she have been as miserable as I was?[142]

In 1290, she is back in the capital, but soon feels restless, and decides to leave again for Nara: "Life in Kyoto was scarcely more pleasant for me, so late in the tenth month I went to nearby Nara, still fatigued from my long travels. Not being of Fujiwara birth, I had never been here before and knew no one."[143] In 1292 or 1293, she receives letters from Emperor Go-Fukakusa, and meets him again at Fushimi Palace. She tells him that she never had any other lover since she left him: "I swear to you that though I traveled eastward as far as the Sumida River in Musashino, I did not so much as make a single night's pledge to any man. . . . I have heard that sometimes, against her better judgment, a nun will get involved with an ascetic or mendicant she happens to meet, but I have never fallen into such a relationship. I spend my idle nights in solitude."[144] In 1306, after Go-Fukakusa's death, she goes to Iwashimizu Hachiman and dedicates a service to his memory. The *Towazugatari* ends with the following passage:

After Go-Fukakusa's death I had felt as though there were no one with whom I could share my feelings. Then last year on the 8th day of the 3rd month I held a service in memory of Hitomaro, and on the exact same day of this year I met Empress Yūgi. Amazingly, the jewellike image I had seen in my dream became real. Now I am anxious about the outcome of my long-cherished desire, and I worry lest the faith I have kept these many years prove fruitless. When I attempted to live in lonely seclusion I felt dissatisfied and set out on pilgrimages modeled after those of Saigyō, whom I have always admired and wanted to emulate. That all my dreams might not prove empty, I have been writing this useless account—though I doubt it will long survive me.[145]

Here, the wandering woman is redeemed by emulating a male role-model, the poet-monk Saigyō, and by entrusting her work to posterity. Paradoxically, the spirit of independence that manifested itself in her long wanderings must in the end express itself in terms of a male ideal. She has forsaken Komachi for Saigyō.

According to Michele Marra, the transformation by Buddhist mythographers of the courtesan into a bodhisattva reflects the domestication of beliefs on female defilement and the conquest over the "pollution" of the female body. This transformation was a return to the norm, in which the danger of defiled margins was silenced and erased in the name of a process of spiritual realization.[146] Because of the paradoxical nature of the mechanisms of power, however, the presence of prostitutes within the precincts of temples—as characters in theatrical representations, as protagonists of sermons and tales, and as the actual consumers of the Buddhist discourse—continued to remain an indispensable element of the Buddhist assertion of power. Thus, "[the] basic structure of fear and discrimination had to be maintained for the alleged fighters against defilement to claim supremacy over potential challengers in the arena of ideological production."[147] The transformation of the courtesan's song into a medium for enlightenment in the *Ryōjin hishō* is interpreted by Marra as the Buddhist version of a more ancient religious practice, in which female priests were believed to lend their voices to a deity to convey sacred messages to the common people. "Modern songs" (*imayō*) took the place of oracles in this new Buddhist rendition of supernatural communication.[148] Thus, "the role played in Siberia by female spirits activating the shaman's ecstatic journey was assigned in Japan to female carriers of defilement—the courtesans—who, thanks to the outcast's special relation with threatening, supernatural forces, were well positioned to shield monks from the violent aspect of the god and to train them in the complicated rules that empower them to communicate with the deity."[149]

According to this view, the motif of the shamaness/courtesan/bodhisattva became a common one in one strain of anecdotal literature of the Japanese Middle Ages that asked the courtesan to play the role of spokeswoman for the Buddha. The Buddhist institution attempted to rationalize a disruptive cult of fertility that it condemned as a sinful practice but upheld as an accomplishment leading to spiritual enlightenment.[150] The subsumption of the famous poetess Izumi Shikibu under the rubric of Buddhist enlightenment created a historical precedent for the assimilation of "defiled" courtesans into the structure of Buddhist thought. The symbolic paradigm built around Izumi Shikibu provided a taxonomic device through which courtesans were cleansed of their impurities, accepted into the mercy of Amida, and reinterpreted as bodhisattvas.[151] Marra, however, overlooks the fact that the emergence of the topos of the courtesan as bodhisattva is roughly contemporary to the courtesan's loss of status, and was soon followed by the "great enclosure" of the early Edo period, during which they came to be parked in red-light districts.

The complementary (and at times conflicting) discourses on impurity and purification, or on equality and inequality, attest to the complexity of the Buddhist ideology in the medieval and early modern periods. Whereas Marra has chosen to emphasize the process of the Buddhist sacralization of the courtesan/shamaness into a bodhisattva, I have focused on the opposite process, which reduced both the female medium and the courtesan to the rank of common prostitutes. The discourse of orthodox Buddhism strikes me rather as an attempt to reduce the power of women, yet betrays a fascination for transgressive or marginal elements that apparently threaten this ideology, even if they eventually may reinforce it. Marra argues that the defiling elements, inherited from non-Buddhist beliefs, were silenced and erased in the name of a process of spiritual realization (whereby courtesans were transformed into bodhisattvas).[152] Although Buddhists attempted to domesticate the powers of the shamaness, they attempted at the same time to associate such powers with defilement. Thus, even though Marra's reading of the rhetoric of buddhahood in terms of Buddhist assertion of power is basically correct, the strategies may have been more complex than he believes.

Even if the *imayō* songs of courtesans superseded traditional oracles in this new Buddhist rendition of supernatural communication, it is not entirely clear to what extent this is a "Buddhist rendition" of local practices as opposed to a "local rendition" of Buddhist communication with Amida.[153] For instance, when an eminent priest like Genshin consults a female medium, he is not simply using her, but also being used by her. The message of the medium may sound quite Buddhist with its reference to Amida's lands, but the point remains that the monk is utterly dependent on her to interpret his destiny. She has become a necessary mediator between the priest and the Buddha. Clearly this is not what the adherents of Buddhist orthodoxy had in mind, and something seems amiss here. Marra acknowledges the presence of "a problem as to the subordination of the Buddhist clergy to shamans," but contends that "a solution was found by lending the shaman's supernatural characteristics to the monk."[154] Yet in stories like that of the encounter between Shōkū Shōnin and the courtesan, it is by no means clear who (or what) speaks: the bodhisattva or the medium, orthodox Buddhism or popular religion? Such stories, located at the convergence of many traditions, are open to multiple interpretations. It is worth recalling here that in early Buddhism the courtesan held a high yet ambivalent position. The courtesan's apotheosis as a bodhisattva during her encounter with a holy monk is in part an inversion of the old theme of the layman Vimalakīrti visiting brothels in order to convert courtesans. But it also calls to mind the episode in the *Vimalakīrti-nirdeśa*, where the goddess ridicules Śāriputra, or similar episodes in which a courtesan's enlightenment brings to light the androcentric prejudice of the monk.

Yet even if such stories reflect a Buddhist attempt to domesticate female power, this attempt often backfired. At any rate, the threat of defilement represented by Eguchi courtesans in the Nō play is that of sex and desire, and it has little to do with liminality, shamanic power, or blood taboos. We may be justified in merging two rather different motives, as Buddhist mythmakers (or, in this case, Kan'ami) often do the same. Just like the courtesan is not simply (or always) a mouthpiece for the god, however, authors like Kan'ami are not simply Buddhist spokesmen: they have their own textual strategies, their own ideological interests. The stories in question reflect, in some cases, a wishful thinking on the part of the Buddhists, and in others, the ambiguity or ambivalence of the results obtained, which often look like a Pyrrhic victory. The story of *Sotoba Komachi*, for instance, may reflect the viewpoint of the author, which should not be confused with that of Buddhism.[155] Ono no Komachi is the type of courtesan who provides Buddhists with a "ritualization of impurity."[156] The pollution is expressed in a very concrete form here, as she is cured from what appears to be syphilis (*kasa*) by the buddha Yakushi.[157] Her story also illustrates the Buddhist topos of the courtesan as decaying beauty, as in *Sotoba Komachi*, and even more vividly (or morbidly) in the "Nine Faces of Death" illustrations.

Nō plays were not a passive reflection of Buddhist orthodoxy, and they ought not be read as transparent expressions of the Buddhist teaching. Their authors were, at least initially, marginals, who were trying to represent other forms of marginality. Thus, Marra lends too much power to the Buddhist institution, forgetting the subtle dialectic of displacement, poaching, performed by Nō playwrights and actors, among others. However much they tried, Buddhists were never able to achieve ideological closure. The "Buddhist mythmaking of defilement" was relatively successful, however, whereas its corrollary, the Buddhist rhetoric of purification, was less so: the transformation of a few courtesans into bodhisattvas did not compensate for the negative impact of Buddhist misogyny, and at times it actually reinforced it.

The power of courtesans reached beyond the realm of sensory entertainment into the political realm and could at times threaten the established order. The question raised by wandering women is above all that of negotiated boundaries. Medieval Japanese society was governed by the inner/outer trope: women must be "inside," while men are "outside." What happens when women are wandering "outside"?[158] And how much freedom is there in this wandering? After all, even marginal places still belong to the space of the dominant ideology. And yet such women are always already elsewhere, they do not let themselves be pinned down so easily. Elusive, they forever speak from another space: "poaching" on the preserves of official culture, they constitute a figure of heterotopy, or heterology. Yet since their transgression, as it reaches us, remains essentially textual, literary, we cannot know to what extent it overlapped with actual forms of social transgression.

The answer to such questions will remain a matter of speculation: scholars like Amino Yoshihiko or Saeki Junko emphasize the social context and describe the history of courtesans as a shift from the sacred to the profane, from high to low status; others, like Marra, focus on representations, taking at face-value the increasing idealization of the courtesans and the role played by Buddhism in this evolution.[159] Such an evolution, however, resulted from the complex interaction of various forces: the rise of the patriarchal ideologies, Buddhist and Confucian, but also the subversive influences of local cults, of performing arts and literary representations. Ironically, the scholarly tendency to idealize courtesans reproduces the very same movement by which they searched to give themselves noble origins, whereas the opposite tendency to debase them reproduces the dominant Buddhist and patriarchal strategies. Despite the religious idealization of the courtesans, they remain quite profane. They may assume a religious character at times, but for whom? When this evolution takes place in a Buddhist context, to what extent is their idealization (as bodhisattva, for instance) a domestication (or even a repression)?

What is at stake in this process of classification? Clearly, these "unsettled" women (courtesans, but also itinerant "nuns" and *miko*) were also unsettling; they seemed to upset the proper social norms. Taxonomic strategies tend to transfer some of them to the Buddhist side of the divide (the nuns, but also, under some conditions, the courtesans), and at the same time to create a distinction between proper and improper wandering. Nuns (and to a certain extent courtesans) were sanctified by the Buddhist institution, whereas female mediums were considered with suspicion. In this way, Buddhist ideology created a solution of continuity in what was, from the sociological standpoint, a continuum. Nevertheless, affinities were still perceived between women on both sides of this artificial divide: for instance, between the nuns and the *miko*. We recall, for instance, how Lady Nijō and the abbess Shinnyo felt close to the *miko* of Kasuga and appreciated their songs and dances.[160]

Until now feminist scholars have tended to focus on "institutionalized" women: women within the family or within religious orders, laywomen (as wives and mothers) on the one hand, nuns on the other. They have tended to neglect those women who, as Bashō described himself, were "like bats—neither birds nor mice," and who remained on the threshold of social institutions. There have been, however, a few interesting attempts to study those women who were neither nuns nor wives and mothers: the wandering women (courtesans). The mother, the nun, and the courtesan can be opposed only as ideal-types. In concrete reality, things were more complex: there was, for instance, a continuity between laywomen and nuns, as we have seen in the case of the widow-nuns. Likewise, courtesans, as symbols of expenditure and pleasure, were not initially perceived as the "accursed share," they were not yet, as femmes fatales, the structural opposites of legitimate wives (symbols of reproduction and domestic economy). Dancer-girls and courtesans, being still perceived as "artists," often became the concubines of aristocrats, and as such went on to become mothers. Thus, the *sadaijin* Tokudaiji Sanemoto was the son of a dancer-girl named Yashame (lit. "yakṣa-girl"). Likewise, the *gon-chūnagon* Tōin Kintada was born from a *shirabyōshi* named Muryō (Limitless).[161] Perhaps these examples could be read as a "domestication" of the courtesan. The same was true for shrine maidens, who were often high-flying entertainers. We recall, for instance, that Kiyomori had a daughter with a shrine maiden from Itsukushima Shrine. The polarization between "mother" and "courtesan"—and the degeneration of the latter into a "prostitute"—was a later product of patriarchal ideology. Like the shrine maiden, the *shirabyōshi* and other entertainers were not, at first, loose women. They usually belonged to a family or a guild. With the social breakdown of the medieval period, however, they were increasingly subjected to social prejudice and rejected on the periphery, at the "ban," of society. Their case was not exceptional. The same was true of ordinary women, wives and mothers who had lost their husbands and sons, and who, lacking familial support, had been unable (or unwilling) to find refuge in a convent. During troubled periods, these women gradually fell to the rank of outcasts (*hinin*)—as exemplified by the case of Ono no Komachi. Yet their exclusion had a silver lining, in that it provided them with a perspective on patriarchal ideology that "settled" women, whether wives and mothers or secluded nuns and official priestesses, could never hope to attain. Captives of the threshold, they became, as it were, condemned to freedom: tragic figures who encapsulate male fears and female nostalgia. They also became mouthpieces for other women, inasmuch as they had found their own voice in solitude. As Toril Moi notes, "The obverse of the male idealization of women is the male fear of feminity. The monster woman is the woman who refuses to be selfless, who acts on her own initiative, who *has* a story to tell—in short, a woman who rejects the submissive role patriarchy has reserved for her."[162] They have become like the women Luce Irigaray calls "mystériques" (a neologism collapsing the notions of "mystic," "mysterious," and "hysterical" into a single portmanteau word).

Chapter Nine

THE POWER OF WOMEN

IN A SEMINAL work entitled *The Power of the Younger Sister* (*Imōto no chikara*), Yanagita Kunio discusses the religious situation in contemporary Japan:

Although world religions [like Buddhism and Christianity] have been brought in on a large scale, when it comes to the insecurity of our life and our doubts and anxiety regarding the future, there is something lacking in them. They have proved to be insufficient as methods of happiness in this world. Thus, the task of filling these lacks has been since remote antiquity the preserve of the women of the lineage. When the festival of Yamatohime degenerated into a mere ceremony, one began to invoke Empress Kōmyō and Chūjōhime. Thus, when one cultic form becomes insufficient, another method must be devised. This is why the fact that the younger sister consoles the loneliness of her brother is perhaps nothing else than a new manifestation of the great enduring power of the [Japanese] people.[1]

We have seen how the motif of the shamaness challenging the mountain-god was reinterpreted by Japanese Buddhists, and in particular by Shugendō adepts, as an etiological myth explaining the prohibition against women in the *kekkai* or sacred space of the mountain. From the late Heian period onward, Buddhist monks drove female mediums out of the mountains that, according to Yanagita, originally had been their domain. During the medieval period, women were also prevented from participating in festivals and from occupying major official religious functions at the main shrines.

Much has been written about Japanese female mediums since Yanagita, Orikuchi Shinobu, and Nakayama Tarō. The dominant motif has been the structural polarity that characterizes the *miko* institution: on the one hand, we have the priestess (*kagura-miko*) of the official cults, later collectively designated as Shintō; on the other, the marginal female mediums (*kuchiyose-miko*) of local cults, those wandering *miko* who survived as mendicants on the margins of the official system. In *The Catalpa Bow*, for instance, Carmen Blacker describes the female shaman as a "powerful sacral woman."[2] This two-tiered structure is particularly striking at major shrines like Fushimi Inari, where the official, "pure" rituals performed by shrine *miko* are complemented (and at times subverted) by the exorcistic rituals performed by female mediums (*fusegi*) on the hills at the back of the shrine.³ The question remains whether such polarization may be traced all the way back to the early medieval period. At any rate, the category of women called *miko* have long practiced all kinds of activities: not only oracles, divination, prayers, but also various "performing arts" (*geinō*). Although they were increasingly subject to all kinds of regulation, they did not entirely lose their power, and, at least until the end of the Kamakura period, they played at times a significant political role.⁴

Since Claude Lévi-Strauss, it has become commonplace to consider women as objects of exchange in patriarchal societies. Even in such societies, however, women were not passive agents, and they often performed very important functions.⁵ Yvonne Verdier has shown that, until recently, French women, and more precisely certain occupational categories of women (the washerwoman, the seamstress, the cook), were in charge of the major rites of passage (birth, initiation to sexuality, wedding, death); and she argued that patriarchal society imposed its strict rules over female activities precisely in order to contain the mystical powers of women: "As counterpart of their power, women are divided, separated, rival."⁶ Her analysis is reminiscent of that of Japanese folklorists such as Yanagita Kunio and Miyata Noboru.⁷ Yanagita attempted to retrieve the hidden power of women, a power fragmented in many figures of Japanese religion and folklore, across a spectrum ranging from Shintō and Buddhist mythology to performing arts. This fragmentation is reflected in Yanagita's own style—and it seems to have affected my discussion as well. If women create differences, fault-lines in the seamless discourse of male patriarchy, if they are—by nature or culture—heterological, then it would be paradoxical and counterproductive to try to repress the necessary fragmentation of any discourse about them. The common theme in Verdier's and Yanagita's books is that women are not naturally weak, but that they have been made so by patriarchy, by societies dominated by men who feel threatened by women and the powers they attribute to them: not only the spiritual power of women who serve as intermediaries between men and the sacred (the *hime* figure described by Yanagita), but also the physical, biological power of women's bodies (hair, blood).⁸ Thus, the power of women is only the other side of their defilement. We have seen earlier that in Buddhism the salvation of women presupposed, and increased, their guilt, expressed in the notion of the Five Obstacles. Thus, the narrative can always be read according to a double-grid of interpretation, as a story of emancipation or one of repression.⁹ Accordingly, we should keep in mind that all of the figures that we are going to encounter, and have already, in this imaginary journey—the priestess, the nun, the courtesan—are Janus-faced.

Yanagita starts from the ideal-typical couple formed in Japanese myths and legends by siblings, and argues that, in archaic Japan, the younger sister was "sacrificed" (in the etymological sense of "making sacred," but sometimes in the usual sense, as well) to the welfare of her brother and his lineage. Some young women were consecrated to the god and, through their mediation with the divine, insured the material prosperity of society. These religious duties of the women entailed certain privileges and the recognition of a power specific to women. Yanagita also argues that this power was essentially seen in their procreative capacity, a biological function that not only brought them closer to natural mysteries but also rendered them essential to the continuation of the male lineage and the reproduction of society. As mediators between gods and men, women played a major role in domestic rituals, and some of them, the *fusegi* or *miko*, were also in charge of rituals for the collectivity. The most typical case, according to Yanagita, is that of the virgin priestesses of the Kamo and Ise Shrines, respectively called *saigū* and *saiin*, daughters of the ruling family who were performing rituals for the ruler and the state. Many legends also allude, not only to the spiritual power, but also to the physical strength of women. A case in point is that of Tomoe Gozen, in the *Heike monogatari*. Elaborating on Yanagita's ideas, Miyata Noboru discusses examples of "strong women," and argues that, behind the apparent passivity of women, men suspected a dormant and potentially dangerous energy. An interesting case is the legend of the daughter of the famous Gangōji priest Dōjō, who was perceived as an avatar of the thunder-god and as a culture hero, and who transmitted his strength to his daughter.[10]

Along the same line of thought is the belief in the mystical power of female hair, in particular of pubic hair, derived from male fascination with the female pudenda.[11] Various origin stories (*engi*) include female hair among the treasures of the temples, as a source of prosperity and power. A play of words suggested that in the hair (*kami*) dwells a power, the power of the *kami* or gods.[12] In an exchange of letters between Yanagita and Minakata Kumagusu regarding the culture of nonagrarian people— a residual category including mountain-dwellers and female mediums— we find a strange discussion about the "pubic hair of the seven calamities" (*shichinan no sosoke*), allegedly preserved as the treasures of certain shrines.[13] The expression "seven calamities" (*shichinan*) is usually traced back to a passage in the *Prajñāpāramitā-sūtra of the Benevolent Kings*: "The seven calamities are destroyed, the seven happinesses are produced" (Jp. *shichinan soku metsu, shichifuku soku shō*). Yanagita, however, wants to interpret *shichinan* (often written in kana as *shichina* or *shitsuna*) as a vernacular expression related to *miko* and their ritual activities. Minakata calls Yanagita's attention to the fact that, in the legend of Izumi Shikibu, a shamaness consulted by the poetess at Kibune Shrine performed a secret rite involving a display of the female pudenda. The rites of Kibune shrine were said to be particularly powerful against love rivals.

Half-seriously (we hope), he wonders whether the length of these pubic hairs was owing to a physical cause or to the prayers (*kitō*) of the *miko*. Later on, during a survey in Mie Prefecture, Yanagita heard about the belief that outcast women (*eta*) have longer pubic hair than other women; recalling Minakata's stories, he wrote again to the latter, to suggest that ancient *miko* descended from such outcast women.[14] In his response, Minakata quoted several sources related to temples in Nara and its vicinity. For instance, Gangōji was said to keep as treasure the pubic hair of a woman, which looked "like creepers," whereas Kōfukuji claimed to possess the hair of Empress Kōmyō herself, and Tenkawa Shrine, the cultic center of the goddess Benzaiten near Yoshino, that of Shizuka Gozen, the unfortunate lover of the warrior Yoshitsune. Although the "treasures" of temples and shrines often include long female hair, it is usually not called *sosoke*. Inspired by Minakata, Nakayama Tarō went to look for *sosoke* all over Japan, and finally found one case at Togakushiyama. Yanagita eventually concluded that, for a woman, to show her pubic hair probably had ritual or magical efficacy, as in the well-known mythic episode in which the goddess Ame no Uzume lures the sun-goddess Amaterasu out of the Rock-Cave of Heaven. He related this to the fact that sailors often take on their boat the hair of a young woman (the captain's daughter or wife), which they put in a box as the *funadama* ("ship's spirit").[15]

THE MYTH OF TAMAYORIHIME

Yanagita traced the *miko* institution back to the myth of Tamayorihime, the virgin vestal of Kamo Shrine. In what looks like a Japanese version of Durkheim's "elementary forms of religious experience," he also found what he believed to be the vestiges of original Shintō in the present-day shamanesses of Okinawa and the Ryūkyū Islands. He saw in these islanders a kind of Japanese "aboriginals," representatives of a pristine form of religious organization, miraculously preserved, through which the more complex religious system of Shintō could be understood. Needless to say, this kind of teleological interpretation, deriving Japanese religion from Okinawan religion, has found many critics among specialists of both Japanese and Okinawan cultures. For one thing, Okinawa seems to be a significant exception to the rule of patriarchy, inasmuch as the religious power of women seems to have remained a reality there until today. Yet, even in this case, the status of women clearly changed with time, and Okinawan priestesses cannot be seen as a miraculously preserved image of the origins of Japanese culture and religion.[16]

Another basic assumption of Yanagita, namely, his belief that female Shintō priesthood found its origin in the myth of Tamayorihime, also needs to be revised.[17] The importance of the younger sister in this and related myths is what led Yanagita to entitle his main work on women *Imōto no chikara*. According to the origin myth of Kamo Shrine, Tamayorihiko and Tamayorihime were siblings, or more precisely, elder brother and younger sister, respectively. One day, as Tamayorihime was playing by the river, she was wounded by a red-lacquer arrow (*ninuri no ya*) flowing downstream, and subsequently became pregnant.[18] Her father suspected some divine agency behind this, and, after the child's birth, he invited all of the gods to a banquet. He then told the child to offer a cup of wine to the one among the guests whom he would recognize as his father. Holding the cup, the child flew through the roof and disappeared. He came to be worshipped at the upper Kamo shrine (Kamigamo) as the god of thunder under the name Wakeikazuchi (Young Thunder-god), whereas Tamayorihime was in turn worshipped at the lower Kamo shrine (Shimogamo) as the "August mother" (Mi-oya).[19] The child's uncle, Tamayorihiko, became the ancestor of the Agatanushi, the priestly clan of Kamo. Although the Miare festival is traced back to Tamayorihime's vow to see her son again, the term originally designates the birth of the god.[20]

The foundation myth of Miwa is strikingly close to that of Kamo. A beautiful girl comes to the attention of the god Ōmononushi. He turns into a red-lacquer arrow (*ninuri no ya*), floating downstream in the house's ditch, and pierces the girl's vagina (*hoto*). She takes the arrow and places it in her bed, whereupon it is transformed into a beautiful youth who makes love to her. He leaves in the morning, but she looks for him and he eventually reveals himself to her in the form of a little snake.[21]

An interesting variant, found in the *Hitachi Fudoki*, is the story of Nukahime. She is visited at night by an unknown man who disappears at daybreak. Having become pregnant, she gives birth to a small snake, which is placed in a vessel on the house altar. The snake grows so fast, however, that it constantly needs a larger vessel. At last Nukahime tells the snake-child that, because it was fathered by a god, she cannot raise him in her house and that he must go to his father. The child demands another boy as companion. As there is no one else in the house but Nukahime and her brother Nukahiko, his wish is refused. He then becomes furious, and strikes Nukahiko with a deadly lightning. As he is about to rise to heaven, Nukahime throws a rock at him, and wounds him in such a way that he can no longer escape. He must remain on Mount Kurefushi, where his descendants are still worshipped today.[22] These stories are of the type known in folklore typology as "marriage with a snake" (*hebi-mukoiri*).[23]

Tamayorihime is for Yanagita the ancestor of the modern shrine priestesses, whose names often bear a resemblance with hers (Tamayo-hime, Tamafuri-hime). We have seen that Kūkai's mother is sometimes called Tamayori-hime or Tamayori-gozen.[24] Even Shinran's wife is sometimes called Tamahi-hime, not to mention the courtesan Tamamo no Mae, who was actually a fox-spirit. The use of the word *tama* (spirit) in women's names (for instance, Otama) seems to point to an ancient cult of the female goddess (*himegami*). Emphasizing the recurrence of this word, Yanagita interprets the name Tamayorihime as "spirit-descending girl," and argues that it refers, not to a particular person, but to a function, that of the female mediums into whom the spirit of the *kami* descends. In this way, Tamayorihime becomes the prototype of the virgin priestesses of the Ise and Kamo Shrines.

According to Yanagita, all of these legends about a sister who guides her brother (who is also her husband) have something to say about the "fundamental nature" of women in Japanese culture. They seem in particular to suggest that, when the brother obeys the divine oracle transmitted by his sister, he lives happily; whereas when he refuses to listen to her, he is punished by the god.[25] Yanagita argues that these myths reflect a certain sociopolitical reality in which women exert political power: a situation still prevalent in Okinawa, but in the case of Japan preserved only in the medieval Kamo and Ise Shrines. For Yanagita, the later evolution of the status of the *miko* represents a "decline of the faith."[26]

Yanagita's study of the Tamayorihime figure is a sustained argument for the genus Tamayorihime (as opposed to the mythical individual). He writes for instance: "In my opinion, the name Tamayorihime itself had the meaning of 'standing entirely in the favour of the god.' It is not at all strange that noble women intimately serving the god and attending his festival finally came to bear this name. Or rather, it might be more appropriate to regard the name as originally having been used as a common appellation for female ritualists of high rank."[27] Concerning the connection between Tamayorihime, *tama*-jewels, and stones (also *tama*), Yanagita writes:

> Brilliant *tama* (i. e., jewels) bearing children were in my opinion a way of symbolizing the existence of spirits as a part of gods (*bunrei*). In trying to explain this [phenomenon] from another viewpoint, we should insist that 1. control of such holy stones was restricted to miko whose occupation was giving oracles; 2. their female ancestors, viz. the ancient miko, were so holy and wondrous that they could have intimate relations with gods and give birth to children of gods. . . . This was the origin of the Tamayori belief (and of the birth of the *wakamiya*).[28]

Yanagita Revisited

Yanagita argued in particular that the importance of women in Japan's ancient religion derived from their life-giving power: "Because women have the power to give birth, the important task of producing is entrusted to them. The union of elder brother and younger sister had in the past an important meaning: by having the sister dedicate her life to the god as his consort, one aimed at ensuring continuity to the brothers' house. Tamay-orihime is a noun that designates those high rank miko, and the *saigū* (Ise priestess) was the highest of them." Thus, instead of focusing, as Simone Verdier does, on the role of specific women in rites of passage (birth, death, initiation to adulthood, wedding), Yanagita emphasized that all women, due to their reproductive function, possess a mystical power to transmit the kami's power and thereby insure agricultural fertility. Although during the medieval period the priestly functions of women were gradually taken over by men, the early tradition, Yanagita argues, was preserved in popular cults.[29] He fails, however, to explain how the same procreative function (or at least the defilement that accompanied it) came to justify the exclusion of women. At any rate, women's "power" is hardly the natural result of their biological condition, the fact that they give birth; it is a social construct implying male dominance. Although Yanagita's focus on women was significant for his time, his conclusions have often been reinscribed in discourses that can be judged as being quite reactionary or patriarchal. Yanagita himself, bent on memorializing a vanishing past, never frontally addressed questions of power, ideology, and oppression.

Yanagita's theses have exerted a great influence, but they have also found numerous critics. One of them, Yoshie Akiko, thinks that religious authority was never exerted by women alone, but always by a couple.[30] She finds no supremacy of the "sister" at the origin, but a conjunction or equality of the sexes. Thus, the functional distinction drawn between *hime* and *hiko* (sister and brother, wife and husband) can be found within the religious sphere itself, and does not overlap with that between the religious and political spheres.[31] Even at this early stage, however, it appears that the *miko* function was repressed by men.

In rituals involving women, one must distinguish between the symbolism of childbearing and that of sexual union. It is easy to overlook that distinction, since the two types of symbolism often coexist. Unlike childbearing, however, sexual intercourse does not imply female preeminence. Yanagita downplayed sexual symbolism, despite its obvious centrality in many agrarian rituals. Yoshie, however, thinks that this (typically agrarian) symbolism is the one that prevailed in ancient Japanese rituals, and that it remained important in later popular religion.

Furthermore, the "proofs" of the power of women given by Yanagita cannot be taken at face-value. A legend such as that of the pregnant Empress Jingū conquering Korea does not necessarily reflect a period when women wielded more power. Not only can such a legend easily function as an alibi for male dominance, but also it is obviously the product of a much later period, and thus does not shed any light on the situation at the time described. It is only with the medieval growth of the *shinkoku* ("divine land") ideology that the image of Empress Jingū developed, and that she eventually came to be worshipped as a deity of easy childbirth.[32] Thus, her legend cannot be read as a proof that women monopolized religious power before the Ritsuryō period. True, some women were already perceived as threatening because of their unruly sexuality and resistance to patriarchal values. The problem arises because of the ambivalence of the expression "women's power" (*onna no chikara*) used by Yanagita and his epigons. It is easy to confuse the male fear of a vague female power (in the sense of *virtus*, a term paradoxically deriving from *vir*, "man"), a potential female threat (and therefore the urge to suppress it), with an apparent "power of women," which is merely the mask of her de facto alienation (as in the case of the Ise priestess). Nothing authorizes us to extrapolate, as Yanagita did, from this latent (and always already repressed) "power" a real politico-religious power of women.

Even granting Yanagita's thesis, it does not follow that all ancient *miko* were priestesses of the *saigū* or *saiin* type. We should recall here Yoshie's argument that fertility rites required the presence of a male-female couple. In his desire to emphasize the importance of Tamayorihime, Yanagita conveniently downplayed the role played by her brother Tamayorihiko, and the functional similitude suggested by the common element, *tamayori*, in both names. Furthermore, he transformed one particular legend, related to the origins of the Kamo shrine and of a powerful priestly family, into a general paradigm of the relations between men and women in ancient Japan. The crucial function of Tamayorihime in his eyes derives from the fact that, after her union with the Kamo god, she became the mother of the divine child, the thunder-god. In this particular case, however, the functional equivalence between sister and brother is weakened, inasmuch as Tamayorihiko, who becomes the head of the lineage, is not the father of the divine child, but his uncle. The tradition that sees Tamayorihime as the "mother of the god" (*mi-oya*) is more likely to be a later development than the vestige of the primitive tradition, as Yanagita argues. This point becomes obvious when we consider, with Yoshie, the priestly functions at Kamo Shrine. These functions, expressed by the male *hafuri* and the female *imi-hafuriko*, later eclipsed by that of the Kamo Priestess (*saiin*), lie at the very origin of the Kamo myth. In other words, they are the prototypes of Tamayorihiko and Tamayorihime, and not the other way around, as Yanagita contended.[33] The emergence of the *saiin* institution in the tenth century resulted from a political recuperation of the Kamo rituals under the rule of Fujiwara no Michinaga. This change seems to imply that the ritual was no longer perceived as a true "hierogamy," that is, a sacred sexual union between two relatively equal partners. The male figure (*hiko*) has now become the ancestor of the ruling family, whereas the female (*hime*) has become the "mother" of the god.

On the basis of genealogical documents of Shimogamo Shrine, Yoshie argues that the early Kamo priestesses, the *imi-hafuriko*, had to observe the taboos (*imi* or *monoimi*) only during the festivals. Their tenure in office was usually considerably longer than that of their male counterparts, with whom they sometimes married and had children. Thus, they were by no means the vestal virgins described by Yanagita. In this sense, they differed from the imperial priestesses of the Kamo and Ise Shrines, who were supposed to remain virgins and whose main ritual function was to perform during enthronement ceremonies. Even if priests and priestesses continued to officiate together, at least from the seventh century onward, their respective social statuses began to diverge—to the detriment of the latter, who, unlike their male counterparts, never became influential political figures.

Let us examine briefly the "hierogamic" ritual that was at the center of the Kamo liturgy. This ritual, held every year on the fourth month, was called *are-matsuri*, or *mi-are*, and the officiating priest and priestess were in this case respectively called *are-otoko* and *are-otome*. This ritual enactment of the deity's descent (or birth) began when the Kamo god, after descending into a sacred rock (*iwakura*), possessed the male priest. A wedding ceremony then took place between that priest and the priestess, who thus symbolically became the god's consort. The divine child born (again, symbolically) from their union—the Kamo god himself—eventually returned to the sacred rock and from there reascended to heaven. In other words, just as the priest becomes the god only when he is possessed, the priestess becomes the god's consort only during the annual festival. Thus, the figure of Tamayorihime, symbolized by the priestess, came to be worshipped separately as "mother of the god" (*mi-oya*). This "mystical" form of Tamayorihime as mother no longer reflects the meaning of the primitive ritual. The new ritual, having been appropriated by the ruling ideology, no longer reflects the entire community.[34]

The function of the *are-otome* changed toward the beginning of the ninth century, after Emperor Saga first appointed Princess Yūchiko as great priestess at Kamo Shrine.[35] The new institution presented the following characteristics: 1) for the first time, a priestess held a special mystical authority; 2) she was replaced every time the male figure to whom she was symbolically associated—that is, the emperor—disappeared from the front stage; 3) finally, she had to remain a virgin. Thus, she had very little in common with the former priestesses, who insured fertility through their union with the god or his priest. It is therefore misleading to see her as the origin of the living tradition of the *miko*, as does Yanagita.[36] Her symbolic elevation was a Pyrrhic victory: as a vestal, she owed her prestige only to the loss of her sexuality. Her priesthood was a golden slavery. She was oftentimes a "recalcitrant virgin." The Kamo rituals, as they were integrated into the official religion, came to depart significantly from this hierogamic model, however, perhaps because it was too reminiscent of the sexual rituals of agrarian cults. The same was true at Ise. In a sense, the recurrent scandals involving the high priestesses can be seen as a return of the repressed sexual element.

Thus, Yanagita seems to have confused the *saiin* with her precursors, the *imi-hafuriko* of Kamo Shrine. This led him to assert that all *miko* were originally virgins, and to interpret the cases of married *miko* as later exceptions, reflecting a decline. The actual evolution seems to have been exactly the opposite. It is the myth of Tamayorihime that, far from being original, reflects a later tradition that implies a new valorization of motherhood. Once again, the myth of the "pristine beginnings" turns out to be a late ideological invention. But even before the ninth century—and at least since the introduction of the Ritsuryō system—the coexistence of male and female priesthood must not hide the radical asymmetry and sexual discrimination that prevailed in and through the rituals.[37] The divergent interpretations given by Yanagita and Yoshie need not be exclusive. There is indeed a male paranoiac discourse about the "power" of women, a power believed to derive as much from women's sexual capacity as from their procreative capacity.

Although the Kamo and Ise priestesses were usually passive instruments in political and religious strategies, some of them were able to show a certain degree of female agency. A case in point is the Kamo priestess Senshi, as described in the *Ōkagami*:

The Tenth Princess (Senshi) whom [Anshi, daughter of Kujō Morosuke, wife of Murakami] left at the time she died in childbirth is the present High Priestess of the Kamo Shrines. Although there have been many Princesses who were High Priestesses, this [Princess] in particular has remained without any change [in her status]. . . . Although the Emperors have died from time to time, this high Priestess of the Kamo Shrines has continued unchanged. This too must be due to the fact that she is favoured by the deities of the Kamo Shrines, whom she serves. Although the High Priestesses of old of the Ise Grand Shrines and the Kamo Shrines abstained from mentioning the Buddhas and sutras, this Princess paid homage even to the Buddhist Law and each morning did not fail to raise offerings to the Buddha. . . . That the numerous people who gathered on the great Ichijō no Ōji on the days of the Kamo Festival would [under her bidding] one and all vow to become Buddhas is, when all is said and done, amazing. At the same time, she was not at all unconcerned with the more sumptuous activities of this world. . . . All in all she was quite elegant and flawless in her way of doing things.[38]

According to the author of the *Ōkagami*, it must have been because the deities of the Kamo Shrines had accepted Senshi so completely that she continued to prosper through five generations of rulers. Not everyone judged Senshi's achievements so positively, however: "When everyone in society was saying, 'It was a most extraordinary performance,' the former Provisional Governor-General of Dazaifu [Takaie] alone remarked, 'An old and deeply flattering fox! Oh, what cunning!'"[39]

The Erotic Virgin

The medieval theory of the hierogamy between the god and the Ise priestess seems to reflect a resurgence of the priestess (and the emergence of the so-called Ise Shintō). The paradigmatic role attributed to Tamayorihime by Yanagita derives from his focus on the Kamo Shrine and its priestess.[40] Yet despite the apparent parallelism between the Kamo priestess (*saiin*) and the Ise priestess (*saigū*), the origin and evolution of these two functions differ considerably.[41] Both priestesses were chosen among the non-married princesses (*naishinnō*), and remained in place at least until the end of the current reign. Whereas the *saiin* continued to live in the capital, however, the *saigū* went far away, to the end of the Ise Peninsula, often never to return. In the *Genji monogatari*, when the daughter of the Rokujō Miyasundokoro is appointed as *saigū*, mother and daughter both leave for Ise. But this dual departure is an exception: usually, daughters went alone—they literally "left the family." The myth of reference for the Ise *saigū* is that of Yamatohime, the young priestess who first brought the spirit of Amaterasu (the sacred mirror) to Ise.[42] The road that she allegedly followed became the road that every *saigū* had to follow.

The distinction between the *saiin* and the *imi-hafuriko* of Kamo calls to mind that between the *saigū*, who lived as a recluse and performed only during enthronement ceremonies, and the *kora*, the female attendants of Ise Shrine who performed the ordinary rites. In the case of the *saigū*, a princess was married to the Ise deity, according to a logic of marital alliance in which the *kami* is perceived like a powerful lord who must be won over through blood ties (or their symbolic equivalent). Thus, the *saigū* became both a hostage and an intercessor. An interesting problem arises here, however: how does one create such an alliance when the deity whom the princess is supposed to marry is generally perceived as female? In the *Kojiki* and the *Nihonshoki*, Amaterasu is indeed the sun-*goddess*. In this case, one may interpret the *saigū* as her earthly "double," rather than a sexual partner. Even in that case, the *saigū* plays a mediating role between the divine and human realms, channeling the religious power symbolized by Amaterasu.

Yet there was another interpretation, in which Amaterasu was seen as a male deity. The monk Tsūkai (1236–1305), for instance, notes in the record of his pilgrimage to Ise a strange story regarding the *saigū* and her relationship with the Ise deity: "The *saigū* is a person compared to the royal consort of the kami. Because the kami comes to see her every night, some say that every morning, snake's scales [fallen from the god's body] can be found under her bed. I don't know whether it is true or not."[43] The theory according to which the *kami* of Ise was a snake was widespread in the Middle Ages. The above tradition reflects the folkloric motif of the "marriage with the god," whose paradigmatic example is the origin story of Miwa Shrine. The belief that the *saigū* was the spouse of the god is combined here with that of her sexual relationships with a divine partner of reptilian nature. The notion, however, that the *kami* of the Inner Shrine could take a wife seemed strange to some, and the problem of Amaterasu's gender was often raised in the medieval period. In the *Shintōshū*, for instance, it is said that the "daughter" among Izanagi's children (said to have been two males, one female) is not Amaterasu, but the "leech-child" Hiruko. Amaterasu would therefore be male. Likewise, in his *Bizeibetsu*, the Tendai priest Jien wonders whether the Buddha Dainichi, the central deity of the two esoteric maṇḍalas, is male or female, and he invokes the example of Amaterasu: "The great kami of Ise is a goddess. According to the *Nihonshoki*, woman provides the foundation. But the nobles offer every year male clothes to Ise. When I asked Chikatsune Chūnagon about this, he told me that in the *Nihonshoki*, [Amaterasu] also has a male body."[44]

According to Orikuchi, because the Shintō tradition always imagines a sacred woman in front of a male deity, the woman tends to be deified, whereas eventually the male deity, eclipsed by her, becomes a kind of *deus otiosus*. Consequently, the worship of a female deity always implies that of a male deity, and the identity of the former results from her association with the latter.[45]

The legend of Yamatohime developed during the Insei period to serve imperial purposes, in connection with the ideological motif of the "three regalia." The symbolism of the regalia came to define her very nature: according to one tradition, Yamatohime herself is the "divine seal" (*jingi*), the most mysterious of the three regalia. As her symbolic value now derived from her alleged "essence" rather than from her hierogamic function, her sexual relations with the *kami* lost some of their importance. In the end, as a symbol of the regalia, she became totally objectified, instrumentalized, and alienated. By becoming the soul or jewel (*tama*) of medieval kingship, she lost her own soul. Likewise, the Ise *saigū* became a half-consenting victim, she was "sacri-ficed" (in the etymological sense—made sacred and secret, relegated to solitary confinement) for the sake of the

imperial lineage; however, she was not always purely passive. Some priestesses at least tried to reassert their own personality and agency, through
the only outlets traditionally open to them, namely, sex and poetry. The
same is true of the *saiin* of Kamo, in particular of Senshi, the poetess
mentioned earlier. Perhaps in a spirit of revenge, they allowed their sanctity to be profaned, thereby endangering the imperial and priestly lineages. Tanaka Takako has analyzed the scandals caused by the *saigū*, and
their lasting repercussions at the level of representations—in particular,
the love affair of Princess Katsuko with the poet and libertine Ariwara
Narihira.[46] As a result of her affair, the priestess gave birth to a child, who
was eventually adopted by a vassal. The "adultery" continued to be
widely talked about, and was still the object of literary commentaries long
after the event. This is due in part to the mention of this event in the *Ise
monogatari* and the great popularity of this work (which has otherwise
no relation with Ise).[47]

Other adultery stories involving a *saigū* struck the medieval imagination. One of them is the story of Saishi, a postulant *saigū*, who was found
to have had a love affair with a warrior while she was supposedly purifying herself at Nonomiya Shrine on the Western outskirts of the capital,
before leaving for Ise.[48] The story resurfaces in a pornographic illustrated
scroll (*emaki*) whose text was attributed to Retired Emperor Go-Shirakawa. Despite some anachronism, the mention of this ruler, well known
for his active sexuality (he was reputed for "using the two swords," that
is, for being bisexual) is significant. The title of the scroll, *Kanjō emaki*,
calls to mind the *kanjō* (consecration) symbolism found in other documents, such as Jien's *Bizeibetsu*, in which sexuality (in this case, the sexual
union between the ruler and his consort or "jade woman") is presented
as a factor of truth and legitimacy. The allegedly virgin *saigū* herself meta-
morphosed into a "jade woman," a sexual initiator of sorts.

According to Tanaka, the return to the theme of sexual intercourse (that
is, the emphasis on the couple formed by Amaterasu and the *saigū*) took
place toward the beginning of Insei period, and reflected the return of the
emperor to the political center stage. The uneasiness lingering from the
perception of Amaterasu as a male deity may explain the shift of focus
from the couple formed by Amaterasu and the *saigū* to that of Narihira
and the *saigū*. The initial sexual function of the *miko*, which had been
displaced in favor of the *saigū* in her relation with Amaterasu, was increasingly devalorized as Amaterasu became a "neutered" symbol of
kingship. Paradoxically, the female Amaterasu became rather genderless,
and her partner, the *saigū*, was accordingly neutralized; however, the latter's transgressivity resurfaced through sexuality—albeit an illicit one, no
longer reserved to the god, an adulterous relationship susceptible to punishment. Her transgression (or its divine punishment) found a biological

expression in the return of her menses. Thus, the moral failure of the high priestess was identified with physical pollution of the most severe kind—one reminiscent of the blood taboos encountered earlier in the case of the transgressive shamaness. The following passage of the *Waka chikenshū* clearly refers to the punishment of an adulterous *saigū*: "As long as she is not abandoned by the kami, the *saigū* of Ise has white menses and she lives in reclusion in a place called Take no Tsubone. However, when she is rejected by the god, her menses become red, like those of ordinary women, and defilement is produced."[49]

Yet, even the adulterous sexuality of the *saigū* as it emerged in her affair with Narihira, a particularly disruptive attempt to refuse her divine destiny, was reintegrated ideologically as a symbolic expression of the union of yin and yang. The scandalous union of Narihira with the *saigū* was watered down through heavy doses of a sexual/cosmological Tantric symbolism. Both the *saigū* and her lover, Narihira, were eventually transformed into sexual deities. Better (or worse), Narihira went on to become a bodhisattva, whose lovemaking was reinterpreted as a particularly efficient skillful means to save women. We find this symbolism in various esoteric documents like the *Ise monogatari zuinō*, a commentary on the *Ise monogatari*, in which the two Chinese characters of the name Ise are interpreted as symbols of yin and yang: "*I* is pronounced by opening the mouth, it is the the character *kai* [open], meaning the vagina. *Se* is pronounced by closing the mouth, it is the character *gō* [unite]; . . . it is therefore the penis."[50] In other commentaries, however, the sacrilege was still recognized. We find, for instance, in the *Ise monogatari* a poem in which a lady-in-waiting of the *saigū* says that she would not mind going over the sacred hedge to meet someone like Narihira. The *Waka chikenshū* offers the following explanation: "When [the *saigū*] reveals [her affair to others], the shrine attendants put her on a palanquin, which then exits backwards, without passing through the main gate (*torii*), making her pass over the hedge."[51] The transgressive sexuality of the *saigū* (and more generally of the *miko*) was also projected onto other real or literary figures, in particular that of the courtesan. The case of the Ise priestess calls to mind the relations between Izumi Shikibu and Narihira.[52] But before turning our attention to the courtesan, let us see what happened to the other, nonofficial *miko*, the female mediums of popular religion.

Other Types of Miko

Medieval courtesans (*asobime*) traced their lineage to the *asobibe* (court morticians) of ancient Japan. With the Taihō reform (702) and the rise of Buddhism, both their ritual functions at court and their social status rapidly declined.[53] The *asobibe* participated in the funerals of crown princes (shinnō): "It is a clan who mediates between the dark (realm) and the (realm of) light; [the asobibe] appease the impure and polluted. Until the end of their life they remain idle, hence the name asobibe."[54] As many scholars have pointed out, the famous dance of the goddess Ame no Uzume in the Kojiki is an asobi, a ritual performance in which sex and death are intimately related.[55] Ame no Uzume is said to be the ancestor of the Sarume clan. These female ritualists specialized in the performance of the chinkonsai, a ritual aimed at "appeasing the soul of the emperor" (mitama shizume).[56] These women also played the role of "distracting" (asobu), consoling and pacifying the souls of the dead. They were eventually replaced by male ritualists, however.

Another group of female ritual specialists, the katsurame, originating from the village of Katsura near Kyoto, were said to descend from a lady-in-waiting of Empress Jingū. This empress was herself viewed as a prestigious shamaness, and after her death she became the object of a cult at Gokōmiya Shrine in Fushimi. Generations of katsurame served as miko in this shrine, as well as at Iwashimizu Hachiman (a shrine dedicated to Ōjin Tennō, the son of Jingū Kōgō and the human incarnation of the god Hachiman). These ritual specialists, organized in female lineages, originally had a relatively high social status.[57]

The Mongol attempts to invade Japan in the thirteenth century caused a wave of national feeling, and in particular a strong resentment against the Korean kingdom of Koma for its participation in the Mongol attacks. The cults of Hachiman and of Jingū Kōgō developed in the wake of this momentous event, which triggered the emergence of a nationalist mystique. As is well known, Jingū Kōgō is the ancient female ruler who, although pregnant with the future Ōjin Tennō (believed to be a manifestation of the god Hachiman), conquered the Korean Peninsula. In order to lead her army, she put a belt around her belly, and she gave birth upon returning victorious to Japan. The cult of Jingū Kōgō as a goddess of fertility spread throughout Japan, in association with popular cults, which raised the status of their deities by assimilating them to imperial ancestral gods.[58] With the popularization of the cult of Jingū Kōgō, the katsurame lost their official function and were reduced to selling charms and belts for easy childbirth.

The Censured Medium

During the Heian period, as the integration of the gods into the state system progressed, the network of great sanctuaries was reorganized, and the Engishiki compiled (927). The goryō, vengeful spirits who had for a while disturbed the peace of the kingdom, were also eventually integrated therein, and they were accorded divine status. Their oracles, which had once "disturbed the peasantry," inasmuch as they had the potential of expressing the people's discontent, were now coopted by the dominant ideology.

With the systematization of the pantheon, as it found its expression in the *Engishiki*, the status of the *miko* began to decline and many of them became shrine attendants. Others resisted this functionalization, and the gods continued to take possession of their mediums, without caring too much whether the latter stood inside or outside of the system. In this way, divine oracles penetrated all layers of society, in the capital as well in the provinces. While in principle answerable to the shrines, female mediums, empowered by the god's voice speaking through them, predicted individual destinies, cured illnesses, and sometimes threw curses. They had direct access to the gods—or rather the gods had direct access to them—and through them to the people. Thus, their role was as important as that of male religious specialists. Being the vox dei, they could become the vox populi, and so influence the destinies of people and of the country. For instance, mediums appear in many stories of recluses at major cultic centers such as Yoshino, Kumano, Kasuga, or Itsukushima. The *otome* (priestesses) of Kasuga Wakamiya, like the *miko* of Itsukushima Shrine, performed *shirabyōshi* songs and dances. This is why Mujū mentions them in his *Zōtanshū*. They were clearly not virgins. The *miko* of Itsukushima were called *naishi*, like the ladies-in-waiting of the court, and they performed some of the latter's functions. In the *Heike monogatari*, for example, we are told that a courtier, in order to please Kiyomori (who was a devotee of Itsukushima), took with him some of these *naishi* to the capital. Kiyomori himself, for the purpose of reconciliation with Retired Emperor Go-Shirakawa, offered him his eighteen-year-old daughter, a child born from his union with one of these *naishi*.[59]

As representatives of local cults, women often possessed the powers of mediums, which understandably worried the representatives of official culture. I. M. Lewis has argued that, in various male-dominant cultures, some forms of possession are avenues for women to improve their status and mechanisms for expressing grievances and antagonism vis-à-vis men. In such contexts, possession can be defined as an "oblique aggressive strategy" on the part of women, and Doris Bargen has recently analyzed such strategies as they appear in the *Genji monogatari*. In some cases, however, female mediums (or more generally possessed women) were still manipulated by men, who served as their "managers." Furthermore, as Susan Sered argues, the "deprivation theory" does not seem sufficient to explain the phenomenon of female possession.[60]

An edict against oracles, dated 812, attempted to check the activity of such female mediums. It did not entirely outlaw them, however, and predictions concerning the protection of the state and the emperor, crops and epidemics, were authorized. Like the Buddhist establishment, the state tried to suppress mediums when they threatened its authority. When this proved impossible, however, it attempted to coopt them. A case in point is that of popular oracles related to (or emanating from) the *goryō*. Nevertheless, such oracles remained influential, and even rulers and Buddhist priests, for all of their powers of ritual and doctrinal superiority, had to pay attention. For instance, when a Kumano *miko* was questioned by Emperor Toba, she became possessed and began levitating, thereby showing the emperor that neither his power nor that of Buddhism could match that of the god.

Some of these popular *miko* exerted through their god a fairly strong influence at court. An interesting case is that of the Kamo Wakamiya, as reported in the *Ōkagami*: "At this time there was a sagacious woman who said that it was the young Deity at Kamo who was speaking through her, and told things only in a reclining position, so that everyone called her The Medium on Her Back."[61] She was so convincing that the statesman Kaneie came to rely rather closely on her: "Afterwards he came to put on his fine clothes and headgear, have her rest her head on his lap, and ask her concerning everything. . . . As he thus came to treat her with some intimacy, she became something like a lady-in-waiting in her status since she was not entirely a lowly person."[62]

These mediums sometimes posed a political threat, inasmuch as they were not simply concerned with prayers against illness, but also delivered oracles with clear political overtones. Already in the Heian period, the relentless activities of some mediums led to a confrontation with the Buddhist clergy and with the authorities. In one such case, occurring in 795, a woman of the capital began to make predictions that were deemed disturbing to the people, and she was quickly exiled to Sado. The following year, a lay nun from Echizen came to the capital and made predictions; she was eventually sent back to her province.[63] The officialization of priestesses at the Kamo and Ise Shrines was in a sense a way to quell unauthorized prophecies. In one case reported by Jien in his *Gukanshō*, the return of the Ise priestess to the political scene resulted from an extraordinary divine oracle she received during the visit of a high official. Ise priestesses were not usually possessed by the great *kami* of Ise (Amaterasu). Significantly, in this case the *kami* chose to resort to possession in order to condemn the "false oracles" that were being circulated by a popular female medium and her husband.[64] The alleged powers of female mediums, who became mouthpieces for the *goryō*, created a kind of paranoia in certain Buddhist circles:

You must never again use these fraudulent witches. Why? Because the powers of the World of Darkness come when they are named. Wise men can tell the false from the true, and in old days witches could point to the true cause and put an end to the "possession." But modern witches point to something that does not exist and create a wild havoc. If the true cause is divined, the illness stops. But if, quoted at random, the name of some spirit is invoked as "possessor," this spirit considers itself at liberty to enter upon what is its own, and the illness becomes much worse. It is therefore easy enough to tell true workers from charlatans. But if these women-diviners continually feed and flatter a certain spirit, reciting spells and beating their drums, the spirit will be ready enough to back them up and turn what they say into truth by going wherever they have said that such a spirit is at work. . . . This is the way that everyone is misled and cheated. It was for this reason that Kōbō Daishi in his "Calling to Witness" (Kishō) said: "These baleful old crones are destroying the Flower Garden of our Mystery. No one should go near them."[65]

The *goryō* cult experienced a revival of sorts during the Insei period, with the troubles that accompanied the political ascension of retired emperors. Several important oracles, allegedly emanating from the *goryō* of Retired Emperor Shirakawa, were transmitted by female mediums in 1142, during the reign of Emperor Toba. Sometimes, the oracles were transmitted by women in the lineage of a deceased ruler. Thus, in 1015, a woman was possessed by the spirit of Emperor Go-Reizei, the father of Emperor Sanjō. Summoned, the *goryō* explained that he was responsible for his son's eye trouble. Despite Sanjō Tennō's subsequent abdication, his health continued to deteriorate.[66] Another famous series of "wild" oracles delivered by women of the imperial lineage was that spoken by the resentful spirit of Emperor Go-Toba in 1248–49, more than twenty years after the Jōkyū Disturbance that had caused his death.[67] Thus, although marginalized, women (at least some of them) were far from powerless (or voiceless, even if that voice was actually that of the god); and Buddhist priests, in particular, had to pay attention. In this kind of ventriloquism, the "double-talk" implies (and serves the purposes of) two interlocutors.

THE *MIKO* AND THE MONK

Although the songs, dances, and oracles of the *miko* were at times disturbing to male monastic ears, they could not easily be suppressed. This is illustrated by a story about the *miko* of Kasuga, told by Lady Nijō in the *Towazugatari*:

> There was a high priest named Shinki who was a disciple of the high priest Rinkai, resident monk of the Kita Cloister in Kōfukuji. Shinki felt that the sound of drums and bells hindered his meditation. Consequently he made a vow: "If I ever become a head official of one of the six sects, the sound of drums and the clanging of bells will be prohibited." When, shortly thereafter, his ambi-

tion was realized and he was put in charge of Kōfukuji, he immediately carried out his wish, and for a long while no music accompanied the worship at Kasuga. Lonely silence filled the crimson gates around the shrine, while the dancers grieved with ever-deepening sorrow. Yet they steadfastly trusted in the will of the gods. Shinki declared, "No desire remains to me in this life. My only wish now is to devote myself wholly to the way." Accordingly he entered religious seclusion, confidently offering to the gods the joy his religious understanding had brought him. The god of Kasuga Shrine appeared to him in a dream and declared: "At the same time I forsook the Pure Realm and came to this defiled world of life and death determined to help ignorant mankind to achieve enlightenment, you ordered the cessation of music and dance, making it more difficult than ever for men to achieve salvation. I resent your interference in my work. I will not accept your offering." As a result of this dream, music was never again prohibited, no matter how troubled the times.[68]

Lady Nijō tells this story to express her appreciation of an all-night dance performance that she witnessed at the Wakamiya Shrine, and to illustrate her belief that "the Buddha, who joins us in this corrupt world out of his deep compassion, uses songs and stories to guide us to paradise."[69] In a variant found in the *Kasuga Gongen Genki*, the protagonist of the story is Shinki's teacher himself, Rin'e (or Rinkai, 950–1025), an ascetic so powerful that the great waterfall of Nachi is said to have reversed its flow when he recited the *Heart Sūtra* there.[70] Mujū Ichien, during a retreat at Hōryūji, heard the same story from the Chūgūji abbess Shinnyo and included it in his *Zōtanshū*.

Nuns like Shinnyo and Nijō enjoyed the *shirabyōshi*—dances and songs of the *miko* of Kasuga Shrine. Perhaps they had not forgotten their upbringing as ladies-in-waiting. Lady Nijō loved music and made sure to have music played for the gods when she dedicated to the buddhas the scriptures she had copied. Although she was a rather nonorthodox nun of the wandering type, she shared her musical taste with a recluse nun like Shinnyo. Shinnyo's father was Shōen (1174–ca. 1237), a Kōfukuji monk who had been chanting sutras at Kasuga Shrine. He is one of the monks who were summoned by the Kasuga deity when the latter wanted to be given the title of bodhisattva.[71] Perhaps because of his attachments to worldly pleasures, Shōen's posthumous reputation was mixed. Despite his fame as a scholar, he is said to have fallen into the demonic realm. His spirit even possessed a woman, but it was to praise the merits of the Kasuga god.[72]

The sense of rivalry between monks and female mediums that could be detected in Shinki's story above becomes even clearer in other texts. In a Kyōgen play entitled "Dai Hannya," for instance, as a priest begins to recite the *Prajñāpāramitā-sūtra*, a *miko* starts to dance and play music.

The priest asks her to stop because she disturbs his recitation, but she replies that her prayers are more important than his for the happiness of beings in this world. He is eventually overwhelmed by the music and starts dancing. Although the recitation of the *Prajñāpāramitā-sūtra* served to obtain worldly benefits (*genze riyaku*), as well, the point here is that sutra recitation is for salvation in the other world, whereas the dance of the *miko* is a prayer for benefits in this world.

At first glance, the *miko* (and their gods) appear as rivals of the monks (and their buddhas). As Buddhism assimilated local gods into its pantheon, however, the *miko* themselves became mouthpieces for the buddhas. This convergence between the monks and the *miko*, or between Buddhism and local religion, is particularly evident in the performing arts (*geinō*). Thus, in the *Ryōjin hishō*, a collection of *imayō* songs, we find a tradition according to which it was through the oracle of a *miko* of Kinpusen—the same mountain where the "shamaness" Toran had been turned into stone—that the Tendai priest Genshin (942–1017), author of the *Essentials of Rebirth* (*Ōjō yōshū*), acquired the certitude of his own rebirth in the Pure Land.[73] The song-divination (*uta-uranai*) that the *miko* performed then on his behalf brought, we are told, tears to his eyes. Again, here is how the *Yōtenki* (*Record of Heavenly Radiance*), a Tendai text about Sannō shintō, describes the Buddhist function of the female medium:

> Priestesses are called *mi-ko*, a term written in this shrine with graphs meaning August Child, because they serve the function of calling upon the compassion of Shaka (Śākyamuni) and Yakushi (Bhaiṣajyaguru), who appeared originally as Yin and Yang parents. Here is how this developed: in the past, a certain Jichi-in lived on the mountain. His knowledge had no boundaries. One day he gave the following instructions to a woman living in Kitsuji: "Go home and become a servant to Sannō. At the time of making offerings, you will begin an invocation with the catalpa bow which will enable you to guess the thoughts of someone without looking directly at that person. When you sound the string of the bow, Amida will come from the Pure Land, enter your mouth and tell you the thoughts and requests of those people." And so we know that the shrine priestesses (*miko*) are august children (*mi-ko*) possessed by Amida.[74]

Many stories tell of the encounter between a monk and a *miko* (and, through her, with a god). Sometimes, they have a strongly Buddhist slant, and the monk appears as an equal interlocutor to the god, whereas the female medium is reduced to a passive role. For instance, in the alleged dialogue between the Zen priest Kakushin and the god Hachiman, the god's oracle seems to have been piously manipulated to fit Zen purposes. The story can be summarized as follows. In 1278, at Nogami in Kii Province, Enmyō, the daughter of a lay adept named Shinchi, and Nyoi, the wife of his elder son, both seventeen years old, fell gravely ill simultaneously. The god Hachiman appeared in a dream to Shinchi and asked him to fetch Kakushin at Saihōji in Yura. When Kakushin, obeying Shinchi's request, arrived at Nogami, he entered into a dialogue with the *kami*, through the intermediary of Enmyō. He questioned the god about various points of Zen and *mikkyō* doctrine, and was told in particular that sitting meditation (*zazen*) was the best practice because it was the only one in harmony with the god's will. A few days later, Kakushin returned to Saihōji. The god must have had second thoughts, however, because some time afterwards, Nyoi became in turn possessed by him. At this time, the god went in person(s) to Saihōji to continue his discussion of Zen and *mikkyō* with Kakushin.

The words and actions of the *miko* were thus perceived by the monks as those of the gods themselves, and many stories speak of monks searching their way through a divine oracle. In the *Genkō shakusho*, we are told how the Shingon priest Kakuban received an oracle from the *miko* from Fushimi Inari Shrine, telling him to return to Yoshino rather than going on pilgrimage as he had intended. The same thing happened to Myōe, when he consulted the Kasuga deity before embarking on a long and perilous pilgrimage to China and India. The deity spoke through the mouth of one of Myōe's relatives, a lady of the Tachibana clan, who was pregnant at the time, a state that the god did not seem to consider as polluting. As the story goes, the medium mounted the main beam of the shrine and spoke as follows: "I am the Daimyōjin of Kasuga. Good monk, I am very sorry that you should be planning to go to China and so have come to dissuade you from doing so. You are wiser than anyone else, you see. Do please visit me sometimes. I live in the Southern Capital." Though pregnant, "she went up and came down with the greatest of ease, like a moth fluttering its wings."[75] Myōe, duly impressed, renounced his carefully prepared journey. The deity seems to have felt that he needed some further convincing, however, because the medium, soon afterwards, rose again to the ceiling, and spoke in a soft, sweet voice:

> "It is rude of me to sit so high up," she said, "but as persons like me are used to being elevated, I have raised up the one through whom I am addressing you. I am here because our last meeting seems to have left you in some doubt. . . . There is not one of the Gods, good monk," she then continued, "who does not protect you. Sumiyoshi no Daimyōjin and I attend you particularly. And I, especially, am always with you in the center of your body, so that even if you were across the sea we would not be parted, and I would not personally mind. But when I remember all the people who can be inspired by you to faith, as long as you are in Japan, my happiness at the thought turns to grief that you should mean to undertake so long a pilgrimage. . . ." Then she descended from the ceiling as silently as a swan's feather falling. The fragrance as she spoke had

grown still more pronounced. Though not musk or any such scent, it was very rich, and quite unlike any fragrance of the human world. Transported with delight, those present licked her hands and feet, which were as sweet as sweetvine. One woman's mouth had been hurting for days, but when she licked her the pain was gone. Despite everyone pressing in to lick her, the lady kept her loving expression and seemed not to mind. She never moved.[76]

In such stories, it is the the monk who appears to be rather passive. He yields to the deity's (or the *miko*'s) will, and fails to assert male Buddhist prerogatives over local cults (and women). His distant goal may be the realm of enlightenment in which gods and women have no place, but his concrete actions are utterly determined by divine oracles delivered by female mediums. Another case in point is that of the Kōfukuji priest Ichiwa (890–970), who had hoped to be chosen by the emperor to lecture on the *Vimalakīrti-nirdeśa*. When the imperial messenger selected another priest, Ichiwa, full of resentment, left Kōfukuji. As he was staying at Atsuta Shrine, a *miko* suddenly fell into trance, and through her the Kasuga deity spoke to Ichiwa, saying: "*I* have not abandoned you, why have *you* abandoned yourself? Don't you know that long ago, when the Emperor recorded the names of the lecturers on the *Vimalakīrti-nirdeśa* on his jade tablet, Enshū's name stood first, but Ichiwa's name was next!" Ichiwa then repented and returned to Nara.[77] Abe Yasurō points out that these tales praise the *miko*'s function as mouthpiece for the god, providing the priest with auspicious signs regarding his awakening or salvation. Such signs may come in the form of an oracle, through a *shirabyōshi* dance or an *imayō* song. Thus, in the religious world of medieval Japan, the sacred was often reached through the artistic techniques of performers called *miko*.[78]

Because female mediums (and child mediums) provided access to the invisible world, they came to play an important role in the relations between Buddhist monks and Japanese gods. Thus, their role in Buddhist discourse does not simply express the doctrinal position of Buddhism toward women, but also reflects changes in the complex relationships between Buddhism and local cults; however, the status of the gods in Buddhism cannot be used directly as an index to that of women. For instance, although the status of women declined with the medieval development of patriarchy, that of the native gods rose sharply owing to their alleged role in repelling the Mongol invasions. By then, however, local cults were practically integrated into the official pantheon. In this context, the ascendancy of Ise and Kamo priestesses is the inverted image of the social decline of ordinary shrine priestesses. But the power of the great priestesses was itself short-lived. The Ise priestess was ideologically neutralized, and the *saigū* institution, rendered obsolete by Go-Daigo's desire to assume all of the politicoreligious power, was eventually suppressed. The *saiin* institution did survive, but the Kamo priestess was relegated to a purely decorative function.

Within Buddhism itself, nuns in particular constituted the main point of contact between ordinary women, female mediums, the gods of local religion, and women in general. But there were also priests who, through their genuine interest in local cults, found in the gods a point of entry into the world of women and of the *miko*, as well as into the sphere of "worldly benefits" (*genze riyaku*). We must beware of simplistic schemas that oppose "Buddhism" and "Shintō" as "other-worldly" and "this-worldly religions."[79] Only in theory did monks deal exclusively with the "other world," leaving "this world" to the *miko* and other female religious specialists. In practice, Japanese Buddhism also became quite "this-worldly." On the *miko* side, we have noted the distinction between, on the one hand, high-class priestesses (of the *saiin* or *saigū* type) who are connected with royal authority (and in this sense close to Buddhist state ideology), and, on the other hand, the female mediums of local religion, who were at times coopted by the dominant ideology, but more often resisted and subverted it. Thus, although I do not wish to say that the difference between Buddhism and what one for lack of a better term may call "local" or "popular" religion (rather than "Shintō," a term better reserved to the official ideology of the late Tokugawa, Meiji and post-Meiji periods) is merely one of degree rather than of nature, one could argue that the two are merely ideal-types on a continuum of doctrines and practices; or even that, despite the political fiat of the Meiji Restoration, they were indissociable in practice from each other and from the warp and woof of Japanese religiosity. Although Buddhism has often been described as outworldly, it has tended to become, for all practical purposes, very "this-worldly." In that respect, it shares a number of characteristics with what Susan Sered calls "women's religions." We recall, for instance, that the interest in the physiological reproduction process (conception, gestation, and childbirth), usually seen as a specific feature of women's religions, received a lot of attention in Buddhism, as well. This is not to say, as Sered argues, that "the impact of gender on religion is quite limited, inasmuch as women's religions are not so different from men's religions."[80] A major difference, as she herself points out, remains that women's religions "are characterized by a this-worldly orientation that does not emphasize the difference between sacred and profane spheres," whereas Japanese Buddhism (and in particular esoteric Buddhism) was precisely constructed on that difference.[81] But again, with the institution of the *saigū* and the *saiin*, we find, in the cult of the gods also, religious virtuosi for whom virginity (or at least nonprocreative sex) was deemed more important than the fertility reserved to ordinary women. Therefore, if these cults still belong to a "women's religion," it is in a slightly different sense.

WOMEN ON THE EDGE

The Buddhist theme of the mother and her son, briefly discussed above in the monastic context, reappears in the "mother-child deities" (*oyako-gami*), a widespread motif in Asian mythology.[82] We have encountered it, for instance, in legends regarding the "women's hall" (*nyonindō*), in which the main deity, a female figure related to fertility cults, often merges with that of the mother of the temple's founder. The paradigmatic example is that of the goddess of Mount Kōya, identified with Kūkai's mother.[83] This legend is also reminiscent of the "origin story" of Kamo Shrine and similar myths. In particular, the claim that Kūkai's mother was an exiled Chinese princess abandoned on a boat with her child recalls the folkloric motif of the divine mother and child stranded on a beach. In Japan, the importance of the couple formed by the mother/ancestor-deity (*hime-gami*) and her child (the *miko-gami* or "august child-god," also known as *wakamiya*, or "young prince") has often been noted. A paradigmatic pair is the one formed by Tamayorihime and the thunder-god Takemika-zuchi in the Kamo Shrine legend.[84] The *miko-gami* is also often an autoch-thonous god who has been displaced, pushed aside—in a small peripheral shrine—by a more important deity. In the case of Mount Kōya, Kūkai can thus be perceived as a *wakamiya*, connected with the *ōji* ("princes") or *miko-gami* of local traditions. He is also the main object of worship, whereas his mother—the original tutelary deity—plays a subaltern role.

The mythological theme of the *oyako-gami* came to be related with the folkloric motif of the *uba* (a term better left untranslated for now) accompanied by a child. Yanagita Kunio has pointed out the popularity in the Kantō region of the cult of the "*uba* deity" (*uba-gami*) and of the "deity of easy childbirth" (*koyasugami*), both related to the figure of the childbirth deity (*ubu-gami*). The *uba* in question looks like a nun (al-though she is not tonsured) holding a child in her arms. We seem to have here another figure marking the transition from the *miko* to the nun. In Buddhism, this type became the "laywoman" (Skt. *upāsikā*, Jp. *ubai*) or the "female ascetic " (*me-hijiri*), which we saw represented in Shugendō legends by the "nun" Toran and her sisters. Once detached from the harsh milieu of mountain worship and transplanted to the domestic sphere, this cult took the form of a fertility cult centered on the bodhisattvas Kannon and Jizō, particularly the latter, with his reputation to suffer vicariously (*migawari*) on behalf of people. The activities of the Kumano *bikuni* were closely connected to this bodhisattva.

Divine filiation was perceived as an efficient way to "familiarize" the uncanny, the incongruous, the extraordinary, but also to universalize the local. Unruly deities such as the thunder-god were in this way put under the tutelage of Buddhism. Many human and divine relationships were subsumed in the parent-child relationships. Taking my cues from Yanagita, but without falling, as he sometimes does, under the spell of such symbolic associations, I want to turn to one such relationship.

We recall that *kekkai* stones like that of Kōyasan were often called *uba-ishi* (stones of the *uba*). We must therefore examine the relation between female mediums and these stones. Kūkai (Kōbō Daishi) appears in a number of legends in relation with an *uba*, his own mother being only one of them. What does this pairing of the so-called Daishi with the *uba* mean? In eastern Japan, one often encounters halls called Daishi-dō, in which an *uba-gami* (*uba*-deity), looking like a nun, is enshrined as an acolyte of the Daishi. It is clear that the cult of Daishi, as it spread among the people, came to actively focus the beliefs of women. According to Yanagita, the women paired with Kōbō Daishi are strongly reminiscent of the *miko*; that is, women who were often worshipping the gods by the side of a spring or pond. Japanese folklore abounds in ponds called *uba-ga-ike* (Pond of the *uba*) or *bikuni-ga-ike* (Pond of the *bikuni*). As we recall from the case of the "nun" Toran, itinerant *bikuni* were believed to possess shamanistic powers. The *uba* in these legends are almost always associated with children. Like the *koyasu-gami* (deity of easy childbirth), the *uba-gami* is usually represented holding a child in her arms. This image is also connected with the motif of the woman who gives birth to the god's child and raises him, as in the Kamo myth mentioned earlier. Kōbō Daishi himself has an uncanny affinity with ponds. Many ponds called *koyasu-no-ike* are related to his legend, and he is often credited with digging them. Pregnant women who drank from such ponds were believed to have an easy delivery. There is, for instance, the legend of the mother who stands all night long on the roadside, under a pine tree near a pond, rocking a child who cries constantly. When Daishi happens to pass by, as he lights up a pine needle, the child suddenly stops crying. This legend gave rise to the belief that women who drink from that spring will have abundant lactation and their children will no longer cry.[85] Yanagita argued that such beliefs in the *oyako-gami* and its connection with Kōbō Daishi derives from the link between Daishi and the *uba*. Yanagita's point is that, when the god appears as Daishi (divine child) in folkloric tales, his priestess becomes an *uba* who, whether young or old, is usually represented with children. Kageyama Haruki, pointing out the role of water in the myth of Tamayorihime, argues for a derivation from *mi-kumari* (water dividing) to *mi-ko-mori* (divine childrearing).[86]

The symbolic proliferation around this theme seems in part determined by the polysemy of the word *uba*—meaning "old woman," but also "wet-nurse," and, by extension, "young woman."[87] Yanagita and Orikuchi were the first to point out the importance in ancient Japan of the wet-nurse who, mediating between the human and divine realms, protects the child from evil spirits.[88] In the *Nihonshoki*, for instance, when Princess Toyotamahime returns to the sea-god's palace, leaving her child behind in the human world, her husband Hikohohodemi has to find a wet-nurse—an episode often interpreted as the origin story of imperial wet-nurses.[89] In the *Kojiki*, this role is played by Toyotamahime's younger sister, Tamayorihime.[90] We recall that, in the Kamo legend, Tamayorihime is the mother of the thunder-child Wakeikazuchi no Mikoto. Even after the latter's violent ascension to heaven, she is periodically reunited with him at the time of the Miare Festival.[91]

Ponds, Barriers, and Coughing

In all of these tales, the pond constitutes a structural intermediary between the spring and the river. Another structural constant is the presence of a woman and a male child, or sometimes of two women, an older and a younger one. A recurrent toponym for ponds throughout Japan is *uba-ga-ike* (pond of the *uba*). This name usually refers to the legend of a woman who drowned in that pond. The spot is sometimes marked by a stone, *uba-ga-ishi* (stone of the *uba*). In many cases, the woman is said to have thrown herself into the pond after the child in her care fell into the water and drowned.

Many legends also tell us of a mother (or wet-nurse) and a child, fleeing a home destroyed by war and drifting from village to village. In most cases, they are eventually killed and their ghosts may appear near their grave as will-o'-the-wisps (sometimes called "fire-of-the-*uba*," *uba-ga-hi*).[92] The following example appears in the *Taiheiki*. At the time of Kamakura's destruction by the supporters of Emperor Go-Daigo, a vassal of Takatoki named Moritaka came to take his master's son, Kameju, away from his mother and to entrust him to monks in Shinano. "Heedless of men's eyes, the weeping nurse Osai ran after him barefooted for five or six hundred yards, falling down to the ground again and again, until resolutely he caused the horse to run, that she might not find him out. And when her eyes beheld him no longer, the nurse Osai cast her body into a deep well and perished."[93] Sometimes, these ghosts need to be placated by proper worship.[94] Many such stories are related to the tragic fall of the Taira clan at the end of the twelfth century. A recurring motif is the deification of an old woman who has saved the only heir of a clan. Her relation with the child is sometimes a biological (or even incestuous) one. Thus, in the story of the origin of Hachijōshima, everyone was killed by a natural calamity, except a pregnant woman named Tanaba, who later married her own child and thus become the ancestor of the islanders.

The motif of the drowned child presents some curious developments. Thus, in the legend of the Uba-ga-ike in Suruga, a child playing near a pond, not far from his wet-nurse, was suddenly subject to a violent cough. In order to get some relief, he tried to drink water from the pond, but fell into it and drowned. In despair, his wet-nurse threw herself into the pond. Subsequently, she came to be worshipped as a deity able to cure the coughing of children. In the Edo period, people often prayed to an old woman, the "old woman of coughing" (*seki no obasama*), to cure infantile coughing.[95] Yanagita suggests that this appellation, and the cult behind it, derived from a misunderstanding of (or a deliberate confusion with) the name of the "old woman of the barrier" (*seki no uba*), a crossroad deity (*dōsojin*) originally worshipped in the form of a stone. Although the dual *dōsojin*, usually represented in the form of an old male-female couple, sometimes cure coughing and protect children, the image of the *uba-gami* seems to have developed beyond that of the crossroad deities.[96] This theme is also related to the many legends about the "water of nenbutsu" or the "pond of nenbutsu." In all of these cases, the pond is said to respond energetically—by filling suddenly or bubbling—when one recites the nenbutsu or some other prayer. In some cases, when, instead of a prayer, an insult—for instance, *oba kainai* (worthless *uba*)—is proferred, the sudden effervescence of the water is perceived as a sign of anger or jealousy.[97] Minakata Kumagusu describes this curious phenomenon as follows

> [Turning to Japan] there stands close to the hot spring at Arima what people call "The Second Wife's Spring," which, when upbraided with abusive words, suddenly becomes effervescent as if in a violent passion; whence the name [because its fury resembles that of the first wife occasioned by her jealousy of the second wife]. Further, the province Suruga has the so-called Old Woman's Pond. Legend speaks of a woman particularly peevish and jealous ending her life in it, 8 August 1593. Should one loudly exclaim to it, "You are an ugly hag," the water would suddenly rise with bubbles—the louder the cry, the stronger the agitation, which is popularly ascribed to the self-drowned woman's jealousy.[98]

In the first case described by Minakata, the victim is a young woman who died because of the jealousy of an older woman. This theme is well known in Chinese legend, where it has also given birth to the cult of the deity of the privy, a man's concubine who had drowned after being pushed into the latrines by the jealous main wife. In most legends, however, the two protagonists are a woman and a child. The pond is metonymically identified with the old woman (or wet-nurse) who has let the child drown in a pond or a well and, in her despair, follows him into death.

The Stone-Pillow

A related theme, which seems to express deeply seated male fears, appears in the legend of the stone-pillow (*ishi-makura*), a significant stone-marker that became one of the treasures of Asukadera in Edo. According to this legend, a young girl and an old woman lived together in an isolated house near the Sumida River. The girl prostituted herself, and during the night she killed her lovers in the most ghastly manner: by crushing their heads with the stone that served as a pillow. In some variants, the grisly task is performed by the old woman. In the Buddhist version of the legend, the serial killing goes on until the girl, having fallen in love with a young man (who is actually a manifestation of the bodhisattva Kannon), sacrifices herself by taking his place in the bed.[99] An even more sanitized Buddhist version runs as follows

> In this desert plain there were many bandits. Kannon ordered the dragon-king Shakara [Sāgara] to take the form of an old woman, and the third Nāga girl to take that of a beautiful princess, and through sex to seduce evil people, and with the two stones *bankyō* and *ban'yū* to kill them by crushing their heads. Beginning with the chief of the bandits, Okimaro, they killed in this way many bandits. Then the old woman flew into the pond and manifested herself as Kurikara Fudō, while the princess became Benzaiten, and both "manifested their traces" in that pond and cured the illnesses of the people: in particular to eliminate the coughing of babies, if they are made to drink sweet wine from this temple, their coughing ends right away. . . . The stone pillow *bankyō* and the mirror of the princess are still [preserved as] miraculous treasures.[100]

The young girl lived on a liminal site—the bank of a river—and her isolated house brings to mind the *uba-dō* (or *uba-yashiki*), a place on the outskirts of a village where religious women could stay.[101] The *ishi-makura* also served as *kekkai* stone, marking the limit between two worlds.[102] According to Yanagita, it was also used during funerals. But above all, the stone-pillow seems to be related to the *uba* stones or the *bikuni* stones—sacred stones upon which female mediums sat or placed their heads to listen to messages from the invisible world.[103] The stone is not only used here to mark the limit between the world of the living and that of the dead, like the rock used by the god Izanagi to block the gate to the underworld and escape the wrath of his estranged wife and sister Izanami, but also is a means of communication between the two worlds. At any rate, behind the strongly misogynistic overtones of the legend of the stone-pillow, we find the once powerful mediums of local cults, who return to haunt the male imaginary.

Datsueba

We have seen that the *uba-gami* was often worshipped in the form of the stone image of an old woman. This *uba-gami* was also called *Shōzuka no uba* (var. *Sanzugawa no uba*), a term that points to the Buddhist myth of Datsueba (or *Sōzu no baba*)—the old woman from hell who takes off the clothes (or the skin) of the dead on the bank of the Three-Ford River (*Sanzu no kawa*, the Buddhist Styx). She is usually represented as an old hag, a terrible figure with a wrathful face and sagging breasts, seated, with one knee up—a posture strikingly similar to one representation of the aged Ono no Komachi at Zuishin-in.[104] In Japan, she often has a companion, Kenne-ō (the Old Man Who Hangs Clothes).

Datsueba is the deity worshipped by women at the *uba-dō*, a building reserved for women, and traditionally marking the limits of the *nyonin kekkai*. Thus, during the autumn equinox (*higan*), a rite of passage for women known as the "great unction (Skt. *abhiṣeka*) of the bridge [covered] with pieces of cloth" (*nunobashi daikanjō-e*) was performed at the Uba-dō at Tateyama. Three bands of white cloth were spread on the path leading from the Yama Hall (Enma-dō) to the Uba-dō, crossing a stream on a bridge. This cloth, offered by the believers, was later used to fabricate clothes for the dead, so that they could appear in front of Datsueba wearing consecrated clothes, thus avoiding having their skin taken off by the terrible old hag. The stream is symbolically associated with the Sanzu no kawa, while entering the Uba-dō is interpreted as "entering the Pure Land" (*jōdo-iri*). In the darkness of the Uba-dō, women recited the nenbutsu for half a day, before an officiant threw the gates wide open, bringing the revelation of the luminous Pure Land of Tateyama, symbolized by the so-called Peak of the Pure Land (*Jōdo-ga-take*).[105]

The belief in Datsueba developed particularly in the Edo period, in relation with that of the King of Hell, Yama. In the process of acculturation, it seems that the Buddhist image of the old hag of Sanzu no kawa merged with that of the Japanese *uba*. For instance, at Asakusa-dera, there is a stone statue of the *uba* that became an object of worship for people who suffer from toothache.[106] Likewise, in the town of Takazaki (Gunma Prefecture), a stone statue of Sōzuga no Baba is worshipped by people afflicted by severe coughing. Beside her statue, instead of the Old Man, is a "Daishi stone" connected to the cult of Kōbō Daishi in his "divine child" (*taishi*) function.[107] In other cases, Datsueba has become a protector of children, and women pray to her for boons such as abundant lactation and children's health. In this function, she appears to be an avatar of the *uba-gami*. In some variants of her legend, the clothes (or the skin) that she tears off from the dead as they are about to enter hell are metaphorically assimilated to the placenta that she gave them at birth.

WOMEN, DRAGONS, AND SNAKES

Near the monastery built in the Korean kingdom of Silla by the priest Ŭisang upon his return from China, there was a large rock, said to protect it. According to tradition, it was the body of the dragon-girl Shanmiao (Jp. Zenmyō), who was once a young Chinese girl in love with Ŭisang. When she heard that the young priest had embarked on a ship to return home, however, she threw herself from a cliff into the sea and turned into a dragon. In this new form, she escorted the ship to Korea. Later on, when Ŭisang's monastery was taken over by "evil monks," Shanmiao turned into a large boulder that flew in the air above the temple, threatening to crush it. The monks fled and Ŭisang was able to return, while the rock landed nearby. The story of this Buddhist Mélusine was spread in Kamakura Japan by the Kegon priest Myōe, who saw himself as a reincarnation of Ŭisang. At first glance, the transformation of the young woman into a dragon, and later into stone, seems to be motivated by grief and love, and not, as in the case of the Japanese "nuns" transgressing the *kekkai*, the result of some divine punishment; however, there may be more in this story than meets the eye. In order to retrieve its meaning and function, we need to examine one significant aspect of the relationship between Buddhism and local cults, as expressed in the legends about women, snakes, and dragons.

The encounter between Buddhism and local belief often takes the form of a meeting (sometimes a confrontation) between a monk and the genius loci, in one of his manifestations as a woman, an old man, or a wild animal (snake, fox). Asian mythologies are replete with snakes and dragons, which usually represent chthonian powers; that is, tutelary deities converted (willingly or not) to Buddhism. Often the local god bows to the inevitable (that is, to the monk) and offers him protection. The paradigmatic story is found in the legend of the Buddha, where the *nāga* Mucilinda offers his coiled body as a seat for meditation to the newly enlightened master and protects him with his hood from a raging storm.[108] Stories involving monastic violence (albeit for the right cause) are also found all over Asia, however. The choice between conversion or violent submission is expressed in the legend of Shōbō (Rigen Daishi, 832–909), one of the founders of Shugendō, and his encounter on Mount Ōmine with two large snakes reputed for devouring travelers. We are told that the ascetic was able to convert the male snake, but the female persisted in her evil ways and he had to kill her.[109]

Snakes and dragons (or *nāgas*) are closely linked in Buddhist imagination, although their symbolic dynamics differ. In both cases, the Buddhist tactic has been to transform these chthonian powers into protectors, and eventually into abstract emanations of Buddhist principles. *Nāgas*, in particular, came to play a crucial role in medieval Japanese Buddhism. We recall the story of the *nāga*-girl in the *Lotus Sūtra* and its influence on Japanese culture. Despite their spiritual power, however, *nāgas* remain in Buddhist eyes miserable creatures, which have to suffer from their karma until they happen to meet the priest who will deliver them.

In ancient Japan, the snake was an ambivalent creature, with a potentiality for both good and evil. The distinction is usually made along gender lines: male snakes are often divine beings, whereas female snakes tend to be evil and to "persist in their evil ways." As noted earlier, a divine snake appears in "serpent-bridegroom" tales, a subcategory of the "god's bride" legends. In the legend of Miwa Shrine, for instance, the god who visits the young girl Iku-Tamayorihime at night eventually reveals his true form to her: that of a beautiful small snake. In the *Hitachi Fudoki*, the young Nukahime is visited by an unknown man, and eventually gives birth to a snake-child. She wants to send the latter off to heaven, but he gets angry and kills his uncle. Then she prevents him from ascending to heaven, and he remains in the mountains, where he receives a cult as "vengeful spirit" (*goryō*).[110]

Japanese mythology also contains many cases of "divine marriages" between a man and a female snake (or some other reptilian creature). Like the French legend of Mélusine, which was used to explain the origins of the Lusignan family, these myths, centered on the offspring of the deity, were originally family genealogies.[111] A case in point is the legend of Hohodemi no Mikoto and Toyotamahime, the daughter of the sea-king— ancestors of the imperial family. Their marital life came to an abrupt end when Hohodemi, by a fateful curiosity, violated a taboo: he surprised his wife in the act of giving birth, while she had returned to her original reptilian shape.[112]

In his discussion of the "Bell and Serpent Poem," Minakata tells the story of the origins of the bell of Miidera, "a mixture of the motif of the thankful serpent with a legend of the Mélusine type." The gist of the story is as follows: a young man, after saving a snake, is visited by a young woman, whom he eventually marries. When she is about to give birth, she tells him to build a parturition hut to hide her from sight. At the moment of delivery, however, he peeps and discovers a huge serpent. Ashamed, she leaves him, after telling him that the child holds a jewel in his hand, and that, if this child should cry, she would return. The man takes the jewel and loses it, and the child cries. The woman returns and tells him that the jewel was her own eyeball. She is willing to give him the other, even though she would become blind, but she asks that a bell be hung at Miidera to let her know the time.[113] This story is related to the belief that the wish-fulfilling jewel (*cintāmaṇi*) worn by the *nāgas* on their heads could restore eyesight.

This legend remains an exception. Under Buddhist influence, the ancient snake of myth and folklore tends to be demonized. In Buddhist tales, snakes often show a weird attraction to women's genitals. They seem to offer a metaphor for sexual relationships, or even more precisely for phallic penetration, despite a minor contradiction caused by the tendency to describe the evil snake as female.[114] A similar symbolism was already at work in Indian Buddhism, judging from the Vinaya injunction for nuns to close their vaginas with their feet while sitting in meditation, to prevent snakes from entering.[115] In an interesting reversal, the *Konjaku monogatari shū* tells the story of a monk who, having fallen asleep, dreams that he has sex with a woman and wakes up to discover that he is being sucked by a snake.[116] In the *Kokon chōmonjū*, it is the wife of a monk who, jealous because he is having sex with a woman, turns into a snake and bites his penis.[117] In these uncanny stories, the snake seems to serve as a metaphor for the evil tendencies of the human protagonists: sexual desire in the case of the man, jealousy and resentment in that of the woman.

The Revenge of the Snake-Woman

The motif of the evil female snake finds its expression in the story of the woman turning into a snake out of jealousy or anger. Already in early Buddhism, women and snakes were often associated. In several of his sermons, the Buddha asserts that women are worse than snakes. The most famous development of the theme in medieval Japan is probably the Dōjōji legend already mentioned. In this legend, we hear of a young woman who, like Shanmiao (thereafter Zenmyō), turns into a huge snake or dragon when she feels betrayed by the monk she loves. This time, however, it is not to protect him, but to take revenge on him. She pursues him all the way to Dōjōji and, as she coils around the bell under which he has hidden himself, the intense heat generated by her anger burns him to death. The gruesome ending of this story must have served as a strong warning to many a young monk tempted by feminine charms. The story, however, does not end with the death of the monk. The latter appears some time later to the Dōjōji priest in a dream, and tells him that, having been violated by the snake-woman, he has been himself reborn as a snake and needs the priest to recite the *Lotus Sūtra* on his behalf. After the priest has duly performed this task, the monk appears again to him in a dream, together with the woman, and tells him that, owing to the power of the *Lotus Sūtra*, they have both been reborn in heaven.

In the early versions of the tale, dating from the end of the Heian period, the woman remains anonymous, and she is referred to as the "evil woman in Kii province" or "the woman from Hidaka." In later versions, she eventually acquired a name, Kiyohime.[118] In the text accompanying the *engi emaki*, we learn that she turned into a snake after entering the Hidaka river (and not in her room, as in the *Nihon ryōiki* version).[119] In the *Hidakagawa sōshie*, while depicted in the text as a snake, she is represented pictorially as a dragon, whose appearance is strongly reminiscent of that of Zenmyō in the *Kegon engi emaki*. Despite the different purport of the two legends—the "evil woman" turning into a malevolent snake, the good woman into a protective dragon—their structure remains fundamentally the same. In both cases, the metamorphosis of the women is caused by the unbearable loss of the men they love. This similarity was apparently disturbing to Myōe, who chose to read Zenmyō's transformation, along the lines of the *nāga*-girl story in the *Lotus Sūtra*, as an apotheosis of sorts, an example of female buddhahood (*nyonin jōbutsu*). He presents Zenmyō as a model to the nuns who take refuge near him after the Jōkyū Disturbance (1221), in a convent called Zenmyōji. The resemblance between Zenmyō and the *nāga*-girl is superficial, however, since the latter assumes a human form before becoming a buddha, whereas the young girl Zenmyō becomes a dragon.

Furthermore, Zenmyō's conversion is caused by her love for Ǔisang—a fact that Myōe tries to explain away.[120] The sexual undertones in Zenmyō's story return to haunt him in his dreams, however. In a dream that he had in 1220, noted in his *Record of Dreams* (*Yume no ki*), Myōe sees a Chinese doll, who grows in his hands into a beautiful young woman—Zenmyō. She is grieving, and Myōe wants to console her, but another monk accuses her of consorting with snakes. Myōe argues that it is quite natural, since she has a reptilian nature. From this allusion to the close relationship between snakes and sexual desire, one could infer that, even in Myōe's mind, Zenmyō was not very radically different from the "woman of Kii."[121] Zenmyō, the young woman who "consorts with snakes," is after all closer to the women demonized by Buddhism for their sexual craving than to the virgin elected by the god (whose true nature is reptilian) to be his consort.

According to the *Keiran shūyōshū*, the snake symbolizes the fundamental stupidity of human beings, and it dwells within the human body.[122] In this sense, its presence is not entirely determined by gender. With the increasing emphasis on female impurity and guilt, however, it became emblematic of the evil nature of women. In late medieval literature, women nurture in their bosom a snake that awakes when they become jealous. Thus, one could argue that Zenmyō and other snake-women did not turn into radically different beings, but merely awakened (to) the snake that was dormant in them. We may have here a strange twist on the Tantric notion of *kuṇḍalini*, the dormant female energy coiled at the bottom of the human spine and aroused by yoga. At any rate, Myōe was well aware of the difficulty. In his commentary on the *Kegon engi emaki*, he tries to present Zenmyō as a protecting deity, and argues that her metamorphosis, unlike that of the "Woman of Kii," was undefiled by passion. At the beginning of the commentary, he inserts a dialogue with a disciple on the topic, which contrasts Zenmyō's reptilian nature with that of the woman of Kii.[123]

> QUESTION: There are other examples of women who transform into dragons, even if it is said here that she loved the master's virtue, is it not a sin caused by attachment?
> ANSWER: Although this may be true in the case of this woman of Kii, Zenmyō's case is different. Because the woman of Kii became a snake due to the strength of her passions, her sin is deep. But Zenmyō becomes temporarily a dragon to realize her vow of protecting Ŭisang, and owing to the protection of the buddhas and bodhisattvas, she respects the master and has faith in the Dharma. She is therefore free of sin. Kannon herself transforms into thirty-three bodies. The person who has produced the great vow can become anything.

In this dialogue, Zenmyō's transformation is defined as "provisional" (*gon*), whereas that of the woman of Kii is "real" (*jitsu*). The latter, "pushed by an evil karma, . . . *really* became a great snake, and the sin caused by her attachment is deep." Conversely, Zenmyō's metamorphosis is only a skillful means used by the buddhas to convert people; she is not *really* a dragon, and her seeming attachment to the monk is therefore not a sin. Myōe must have remembered his dream of the Chinese doll when he wrote this passage.[124] Yet, for all his interest in Zenmyō and in the salvation of women, her main virtue in his eyes was her devotion to (or her sublimated love for) Ŭisang. This, Myōe argues, must have been a karmic retribution for a past life, in which she had already encountered a true master (maybe a former incarnation of Ŭisang himself). Zenmyō's past merits explain why, although reborn as a woman, she could still benefit from Ŭisang's teaching. In this way, Myōe's commentary tries to reduce Zenmyō's womanly love to a disciple's untarnished respect for her master. By vowing to faithfully serve Ŭisang, Zenmyō was eventually able to free herself from attachment, and she relinquished her human body for an animal form (or even a mineral one). Thus, her animal metamorphosis is quite opposite to that of the woman of Kii. In Myōe's mind, Zenmyō should serve as a model for women who, having become nuns out of love and grief for a deceased husband, should now transmute their "false thoughts" (*jashin*) into pure devotion for a worthy priest (Myōe himself). His lengthy discussion of the topic may be a response to the doubts of the women in his Zenmyōji community as to whether Zenmyō's extraordinary case could apply to ordinary women like themselves. To assuage these doubts, Myōe argued that, although he had no proof that Zenmyō was "provisional" rather than "real," when the master has virtue and the disciple faith, all kinds of prodigies can be realized through the power of an "act of truth." Perhaps Myōe, who hoped to be reborn in Tuṣita Heaven, implicitly asked them to sacrifice themselves in order to follow him. The nun Myōtatsu, who threw herself into the Kiyotaki rapids after Myōe's death, seems to have taken him at his word. Her suicide may not have been merely motivated by bereavement, but also by her emulation of Zenmyō.[125]

Significantly, the illustrations of the *Kegon engi emaki* seem to contradict the text. Zenmyō's stubborn love for Ŭisang, as expressed in the iconographic tradition, resists Myōe's bowdlerizing interpretation. The illustrated scroll vividly describes her grief when Ŭisang's ship is leaving the Chinese harbor. The scene in which, in tears, she stamps her feet on the ground is particularly intense, and it evokes the anger of the betrayed woman rather than the resignation of the respectful disciple.[126] In the Dōjōji legend, the monk, although he kept his vow of chastity, was in a sense guilty for having broken his promise—thereby calling upon himself the wrath of the snake-woman. Ŭisang may have been more sincere, but he also seems to have benefited from a better karma. Yet the woman of Kii, having satisfied her reptilian lust, is eventually saved by the prayers of the Dōjōji priest, whereas Zenmyō seems to remain bound by her love, and nothing is said of her salvation.

The polarization of the snake-woman motif, represented by the bifurcation between the figures of Zenmyō and of the woman of Kii, suggests that Myōe attempted to use this motif for his own purpose. A similar attempt was made in Tendai circles by reinscribing the Dōjōji legend into the context of the Kumano pilgrimage. Pilgrims returning from Kumano had to pass through Kirime, a place feared because of its demon, Kirime-Ōji, who, unless properly placated, would attack travelers. Because Kirime Shrine is not far from the Hidaka River, Abe Yasurō argues that the snake-woman was a female manifestation of this demon, who could, when placated properly, become a protector of the pilgrims.[127] The Dōjōji legend thus becomes a warning as to what may happen to pilgrims if they do not perform the appropriate rituals of pacification.

Another Buddhist reading derives from the fact that, at the end of the *Dōjōji emaki*, we are told that the snake-woman and the monk were actually avatars of the bodhisattva Kannon, the main object of worship of

Dōjōji, and of the deity of Kumano. Indeed, in the illustrations, near the heads of the snake-woman and of the monk, two captions identify them as Kannon (as *honji*, "essence") and Kumano Gongen (as *suijaku*, "manifestation" or "trace"). The Buddhist reinterpretation becomes even more obvious in an illustrated scroll entitled *Kengaku zōshi* or *Hidakagawa zōshi*. The male protagonist of this *emaki* is a Miidera monk named Kengaku. When he prays to the *kami* of Izumoji, the latter reveals to him that he once had karmic relations with a woman, who has been reborn as the daughter of the madam of a brothel in the reputed Hashimoto station (*shuku*), and that he should now break his karmic bounds. Obeying a strange logic, Kengaku goes secretly to the *shuku* and kills the young girl, in order to expunge his karma and be able to "practice in peace." Later on, during a pilgrimage to Kiyomizu Temple, Kengaku encounters a beautiful woman, with whom he has sex. When he asks about a scar that she has on her chest, she tells him how she survived a murder attempt by an unknown man, and he realizes that she is the woman whom he thought to have killed.[128] At this point, Kengaku runs away, but the woman, enraged, pursues him. Having reached Hidaka River, she turns into a great snake, whose pictorial appearance is even more threatening than in the Dōjōji story because its head remains that of a demon-woman. The name of the temple where the monk takes refuge is not mentioned here, and the *emaki* seems unrelated to Dōjōji itself. Thus, according to Abe, the legend of Dōjōji seems to have taken up an old mythological theme related to sexuality, which it reinscribed in a salvation story connected to the *Lotus Sūtra*. What the *Kengaku zōshi* shows is that the relation between the two protagonists (attraction/repulsion, flight/union) is the result of a long karma, expressing not only a *honji suijaku* notion, but also the doctrine of the gods and buddhas symbolized by the love between man and woman.

The motif can be inverted in other ways. The *Jizō-dō zōshi*, a *monogatari* of the Muromachi period, tells the story of a monk who falls in love with a reptilian woman. The gist of the story is as follows: at the Jizō-dō in Echigo Province lived a monk who had vowed to copy the *Nyohō kyō* over a thousand-day period. One day, a beautiful woman came to listen to his predication, and she promised that she would give herself to him after he had finished copying the sutra. When he accomplished his task, she took him to the dragon-palace, and they lived happily together. The monk was apparently unaware of his whereabouts. But one day, he observed the woman during her sleep, and noticed a serpentine tail coming out of her dress. He suddenly realized where he was, and looked for a way to escape. Upon awaking, the woman realized what had happened, and she uttered harsh words: "I was looking for your teaching while thinking that you were a saint copying the *Nyohō kyō*, but you fell in love with me and all your practice is in vain." When he returned to the

human world, the monk turned into a snake. Having repented, he re-
gained his human form, but remained in a kind of coma.[129] This legend
resembles that of Dōjōji, in the sense that the monk who has betrayed the
woman's trust ends up falling into a reptilian destiny. Another widespread
legend, however, has a better ending: a dragon-girl falls in love with a
man of the Śākya clan who has been driven away from his country by a
usurper king. Assuming the form of a beautiful young woman, she takes
him to her father's palace. When he eventually wishes to return to the
human world, the dragon-king offers him a sword, with which he will be
able to kill the usurper. Having returned to his country, with his wife, the
man kills the king and ascends the throne. He is disturbed by the way his
wife reveals her true nature during sleep or sexual intercourse, however:
at these times, nine snake heads with flickering tongues appear from her
head. One day, during her sleep, he cuts off all of these heads. She awakes
and tells him that, although his action will bring no harm to him, it will
cause all his descendants to suffer from headaches.[130]

The ambivalent nature of the dragon-woman who, while seeking deliverance from the monk, can get very angry and dangerous when provoked,
is well expressed in one legend about the Benzaiten of Enoshima.[131] We are
told that when the priest Dōchi lectured on the *Lotus Sūtra* at Enoshima, a
nāga-woman, assuming human form, came every day to offer him food
and listen to his sermons.[132] Intrigued, he disguised himself with a wisteria
cloth and followed her the entire way to a cave. Realizing this, she became
angry and, assuming her snake form, declared that wisterias would no
longer grow at Enoshima.

Although priestesses and other female religious specialists experienced a
slow erosion of their authority from the Heian to the Edo periods, their
confused image seems to reflect their active resistance, as well as the fear
that continued to haunt male imaginations. Those women who lived on
the borderlines of society thus occupied a rather central place in patriarchal and Buddhist discourses, and continued to play a symbolic role that
strikingly contrasted with their diminished social status.

We have examined various figures, from the mythical Tamayorihime
and the pseudo-virgins of Shintō shrines, through the descendents of Ame
no Uzume and other female mediums whose oracles threatened established powers: the women—old and young—who haunt liminal places;
nuns and *uba* of all kinds (or, as the French has it, "de tous poils"); the
terrible Datsueba who officiates at births and deaths; to the various snake-
women who sometimes protect, but more often threaten, monastic purity.
All of these female types suggest how difficult it was for the patriarchal
image of the "femme au foyer" to impose itself. Through the mediation
of myth and legend, but also of art and literature, and of the more or less

marginal groups that peddled these stories, other images of women have continued to live in the popular imagination. In this sense, even if Yanagita's analyses often invite criticism—as in the case of his conception of shrine vestals—they nevertheless have the merit of calling our attention to a series of female practices that, despite all attempts at recuperation, have continued over centuries to resist patriarchal ideology. At the level of representation, the notion of female power has proved resilient. Even as it demonized women, Buddhist discourse paid a clandestine homage to female powers. Conversely, even when they exalted female virtues, Buddhists were forced to acknowledge the persistence in women of opaque areas that impeded all of their attempts at reducing these unruly women into "handmaidens of male desire."

AFTERTHOUGHTS

S TARTING FROM the most visible female group, that of the regular nuns, we ended up with wayward "nuns" and other unruly females. The brief history of the female order, and cursory survey of the various motivations of the female ordination, has revealed that it was a polymorphous group, neither as pure in its intentions nor as "regular" as has been claimed. From that standpoint, the "Kumano nuns" constitute an interesting case, a transition between regular nuns and the wandering female mediums of popular culture. As we have seen, however, their sermons conveyed an essentially male, and sometimes exceedingly sexist, discourse.

The strong reactions provoked in the past as now by the nuns' claims for a proper ordination that would restore the female saṅgha's legitimacy show that the stakes are important, and that such claims take aim at the heart of male power and privilege. At the same time, one may wonder whether the efforts of the nuns are not misguided. There is little hope for anything more than minor concessions in this domain, and even the restoration of the female saṅgha's legitimacy, in countries where proper ordinations have been for so long interrupted, is not likely to improve drastically the status of these nuns, let alone that of other women. Indeed, it will more likely lead to a reproduction of the dominating model, and in this sense constitutes a Pyrrhic victory that concedes the essential in order to obtain minor improvements. Ordination has often been considered a step toward upward social mobility, a way for a few individuals to ascend the ecclesiastic hierarchy, by distinguishing the select few from the majority of the commoners. Without denying the value of such local struggles, it seems more urgent to question the monastic model itself, and to revalorize other, nonmonastic forms of female religious experience. A first step toward such revalorization was to question the doctrinal and symbolic constraints that tended to deny the very possibility of such experiences, or at least their relevance to Buddhist orthodoxy.

By focusing as I have on a certain category of women (the marginals, wandering women, women who rejected male privileges) at the detriment of another (the regular nuns), there is the danger (which I have not entirely avoided, due to personal choice as much as to the relative paucity of documentation) of sidestepping the mass of "ordinary" women, whose experience constitutes the essential of female Buddhism. As Susan Sered notes, however, this silent majority is largely conservative, and it is more likely that the necessary changes will come from the active minorities: for instance, from the nuns or other female religious specialists. Although we should be wary of generalizations, it seems that female mediums are closer to the concerns of the silent majority than are the contemplative nuns.

Buddhist discourse has taken various repressive forms, based on a largely rhetorical view of impurity and gender inequality. Among the primary ones, we have discussed the notion of the Five Obstacles, the requirement for women to be reborn as men before reaching salvation, and the belief in the radical impurity of female blood. The largely sexist character of such ideological positions tends to override the contrary tendency, expressed through the rhetoric of gender equality. Paradoxically, the two types of discourse seem to reinforce each other; indeed, they are complementary. Even the much-vaunted rhetoric of equality leaves intact the basic opposition between a theoretical gender equality and the factual inequality. The seemingly neutral nature of such twofold truth hides its performative nature: namely, the fact that the theoretical claim of equality between men and women, as expressed, for instance, in Tantric Buddhism and in Chan/Zen, creates or sustains social inequalities. True, we also noted that in both types of rhetorical discourse—whether emphasizing equality or inequality—we encounter elements aimed at concretely improving the situation of women. These elements remain isolated, however, and amount to exceptions that confirm the rule. Although Buddhism may have contributed to the relative improvement of the feminine condition, there is no denying that it also maintained a situation of relative inequality that it could have more radically questioned. It is only outside of Buddhism, or on its margins—in popular religion and in certain liminal milieux—that we find attempts to protest against or subvert patriarchal dominance.

At the level of collective representations, the images of women—be they paragons of virtue or femmes fatales—were constantly reappropriated and reinscribed into different contexts, and thus cannot yield an univocal meaning. This is true also for current feminist attempts at reappropriation. Any feminist model, however seducing it may seem, can be submitted to radically opposite interpretations, as we saw in the cases of Queens Māyā and Mahāprajāpatī, but also in that of female rulers and famous nuns.

Another ambivalent case is the figure of the mother. Is motherhood the proof of the irrecusable ontological priority and superiority of women— all of the buddhas were born from a mother—or the instrument of their repression? The two approaches, while seemingly exclusive, coexisted in the reality of practice. The idealized image of the mother also fueled the monks' guilt and nostalgia, as well as their endeavors on behalf of women. This may be merely the silver lining of a darker social reality, namely, the increasing debasement of women. Indeed, the emphasis on motherhood also went hand in hand with the gradual loss of the social power of

women (for instance, at the level of inheritance). This irreversible movement was by no means uniform, however. In village society, for instance,
women retained a number of prerogatives until the end of the Edo period.
It is difficult to evaluate with precision the part played by Buddhism in
the general evolution of local power relationships, which is nevertheless
usually described as the expansion of patriarchy. Buddhism was in many
respects set back from the society of the time; it was gradually losing the
initiative in ideological matters. After the beginning of the Edo period, it
was no longer the dominant ideology.

The Buddhist logic of exclusion that prohibited women from entering
the mountains has retained our attention because it seems to backfire
against its promoters. As *mise au ban*, exclusion can produce perverted
effects, by displacing, as it were, sacrality from the front stage to the back
stage, from the center to the periphery. We thus see women inserting themselves into a logic of "reversal" (*ura*) that found another symbolic expression in the rituals performed at the "back door" (*ushirodo*) of Buddhist
temples. The back of the stage becomes the place where the main action
takes place, or at least the stage of an action that complements and revalo-
rizes the main action. Admittedly, these are symbolic victories, which
failed to translate into social reality. Still, they provide a powerful model
and suggest a way to come free of the old deadlocks. What is at stake
behind this reinterpretation of the contribution of women to (or subversion of) Buddhist orthodoxy is the possibility of new relationships that
would take into account the gender difference rather than denying it. It
points to the fallacy of a purely descriptive history when all accounts of
human agency are already prescriptive or performative. In that sense, my
analysis of the "ban" is clearly prescriptive. Like the current revalorization of the margins of medieval culture by Japanese historians, it aims at
restoring some dignity and agency to marginalized women. But this is not
true only of the "wandering women" who were gradually "ban-ished"
from public space. Domestic, "ban-alized" women were also "marginals
of the inside," "women of the secluded innermost" (*oku-san*, the devalorized "honorific" term for such women).

At the least, our meandering through the forests and mountains and
around the swamps of Buddhist discourse and practice has revealed that
the Buddhist doctrine itself is fundamentally ambivalent in its treatment
of gender, and it is rendered even more complex by the various strategies,
levels of use, and modalities of its reception. Even in the case of the most
often invoked role models, feminine symbols are fundamentally polyva-
lent. The acute realization that there is no neutral ground in this domain,
and the desire to resist monological discourse (whether Buddhist or feminist), have prompted me to methodically oscillate between two apparently
irreconcilable methodological approaches. My first move was to radi-
calize sexual difference by emphasizing the marginal and transgressive

aspects of the female condition and designating as essentially "feminine" the subversion of the patriarchal tradition; this gendered approach revealed the flaws of a certain Buddhist-feminist discourse about asexuality and androgyny, and brought to light the fact that there is—and perhaps can be—no agreement, even among feminists, in such vital matters. My second move was to relativize the importance of gender by considering it as one among various social and ideological paradigms. I believe that the tension between these two approaches has a heuristic value.

In the course of its long history, Buddhist universalism was forced to yield to the process of cultural integration, and, in so doing, to open itself to female values. Its doctrine, which in spite of its denials of gender and appeals to transcendence, had been initially, and, as it were, unconsciously gendered, became now more consciously so. We see the shift in emphasis, for instance, in medieval cultic practice, where the worship of an asexual Buddha gave way to that of a variety of gendered deities (*besson*, lit. "particular worthies"); or in the move away from the distant ultimate goal of enlightenment or nirvāna toward more proximate, and more obviously gendered, "worldly benefits" emphasizing lineage and family, agricultural fertility, and female fecundity.

Despite its theoretical nondualism, Buddhism has also tended to read dualistic (and therefore gendered) distinctions, such as other-worldly (transcendent) and this-worldly (immanent), as well as mind and body, in terms of sexual difference. Although, in contrast to the mind, the body was considered to be gendered, this distinction itself can be put in terms of gender: the gendered body now belongs to the female side of things (yin), whereas the "nongendered" mind belongs to the male side (yang). Yet what prevents us from imagining that the mind is as sexed (gendered) as the body? Therefore, why should we hold on to a kind of asexual (or rather, unisex) model of the mind? Perhaps our mindless emphasis on the mind to the detriment of the body is itself characteristic of a masculine vision of things.

According to Arnold van Gennep, rites of passage allow us to move from a nongendered to a gendered state.[1] If that is the case, what could be said of this ultimate rite of passage called "awakening"? Is it simply a return to some primordial asexual state, a kind of regressive denial, as claimed by canonical texts (usually written by male clerics)? Or might it not be on the contrary a passage to a state characterized by the realization (and not simply the "sublimation") of sexuality and gender? One of the merits of so-called Tantrism is precisely to have represented buddhahood under two aspects, male and female (*yab-yum*), interpreted as resulting from the union of "skillful means" (*upāya*) and "wisdom" (*prajñā*). This arrangement still makes the female the lesser half, however, and implies that buddhahood, as ultimate synthesis, transcends its two gendered components. The word "buddha" should come to designate a state in which, instead of perceiving gender differences as mere indices of a social and spiritual hierarchy, one possesses, on the contrary, the feeling of "being male or female in relation to primordial or ultimate truth."[2] In this sense, next to the buddhas defined as "great males," we need to make room for buddhas as "great females." Or, to use the Chan expression, "sun buddhas, moon buddhas." Whether or not we can still have a female transcendence, in a culture (both Western and Buddhist) where transcendence has always been marked as masculine, is another matter. But do we need to retain the quasi-monotheistic concept of transcendence, under Buddhist garb, or could we use a more polytheistic notion like "immanent transcendence"? There has been a tendency to valorize spiritual progress shown by detachment from the "immediate" and the "concrete." But Carol Christ, in her critique of Mircea Eliade's conception of religion as providing relief from the "chaotic and dangerous flux of things," rightly asks, "Who says that the transcendent is 'better' than the 'immanent'?"[3] Susan Sered concurs: "Once we fall into the trap of judging transcendent religiosity to be 'better' than immanent religiosity, it is but a short step to believe . . . that women's religions are this-worldly because women are less intelligent or less capable of abstract thinking than men. (And indeed this is an easy trap because the so-called 'great world religions' are both male-dominated and other worldly.)"[4]

The problem of equality in Buddhism is not the same as in democracy, for instance, where one has an ideal of human justice. Buddhism stands or falls on its transcendental nature, the possibility of going beyond (or fully realizing) human nature, beyond good and evil and conventional values. A Buddhism reduced to its conventional truth would no longer be Buddhism, but conversely, would a Buddhism reduced (or amplified?) to its ultimate truth still be the Buddhism of the Middle Way?

Despite (or because of) its egalitarian rhetoric, Buddhist teaching is largely patriarchal. Any form of Buddhism that resembles monotheism or preaches intransigeant transcendence (Amidism, but also "Sudden" Zen) tends to be patriarchal, inasmuch as that ultimate figure tends to be male (and will be so as long as Buddhism tries to identify with dominant social ideology). To the extent that Buddhism becomes polytheistic, however, room is made for more egalitarian practices, sponsored by increasingly powerful deities. Buddhism has thus been able to offer countermodels for subcultures, and contributed at times to the subversion of dominant ideologies.

Perhaps, then, the notion of awakening must also be modified, moving away from the grandiose, radical "revulsion" (*paravṛtti*) of consciousness, the sudden overturning of heaven and earth or the abstract negation of all duality, toward a more humble, down-to-earth, gradual realization of the beauty and mystery of life, a world in which some differences remain to be enjoyed, while discrimination is forever abolished. Transcendence has become "transcendental immanence," a realization of the "emptiness-as-form" of Mahāyāna Buddhism, but with a critical awareness of the potentially negative effects of any ideology when it is used to justify an existing social order instead of questioning its flaws.

To argue that the egalitarian principles of Buddhism have, on the whole, failed to translate into social equality does not mean that it may suffice to isolate the principles from the symbols embodying (but also allegedly misrepresenting) them, to distinguish Buddhist "spirituality" from down-to-earth Buddhism. We need rather to submit these principles to a thorough ideological critique, to recognize their ambivalent origin, in order to exploit tactically their liberating potential. To simply claim, as Buddhists have done for so long (and some scholars still do), that "the Dharma is neither male nor female" is to miss the point. Even though no assertion of any kind can be made regarding ultimate truth, it remains that, insofar as the Buddhist Dharma reaches us through human discourse and social practice, it falls within the domain of conventional truth. When conventional truth claims for itself the privilege of transcendence and in-fallibility, it becomes just another ideology whose negative effects must be denounced.

We have examined some of these effects in the context of medieval Japan. We have seen, for instance, that female figures were often used as metaphors to express male ideals, or to debase female experience. It seems paradoxical that women were, in the end, disempowered, despite the availability of a symbolism that could have been used to their advantage. Since women were prevented from seeing childbearing as "empowering," female imagery was used mainly by men. Even today, at the level of symbol childbearing remains ambivalent. Whereas some feminists reject motherhood as a potentially essentializing characteristic and a pretext for male domination, others exalt it as a form of female empowerment and a central characteristic of women's religions. As we have seen, Buddhism has tended to reject motherhood as a form of attachment, but it also extolled it as the source of buddhahood and a symbol of compassion.

We should not underestimate the powerful message of liberation of Mahāyāna Buddhism, a message that often offsets androcentric or misogynistic tendencies. This message is that all beings can become (or already *are*) buddhas: not simply all beings, in the abstract sense, but more concretely, *you* and *I*. Although the Mahāyāna notion of a universal buddha-nature (*tathagātagarbha*) is not always egalitarian in practice, neither can it be said to be solely responsible for all social discrimination, as the recent "critical Buddhist" polemic against the notion of innate awakening (*hongaku*) has claimed—or, if it is indeed so, at least not any more than the strict notion of karma advocated by early Buddhist "orthodoxy" and "critical Buddhists." In spite of all ideological uses, it retains a "liberating" potential, which may be reactivated in the proper cultural or sociopolitical environment. Some texts may be more "gendered" than others, but no text is determinant in and of itself, apart from its changing contexts and uses. The egalitarian message seems to break all social and cosmological constraints of family, race, and temporal or spatial conditions. Yet we need to keep in mind the social limits of egalitarian ideologies and the danger of interpreting them out of context. When John Locke asserted that "all men are free," he felt the need to specify that by men he meant "British gentlemen" (indeed, his liberalism was never meant to extend to Indian men and women). Likewise, the French Revolutionaries, in their "Déclaration des droits de l'Homme et du Citoyen," reserved human rights to "citizens" (a distinction that excluded women).[5]

What about the much-vaunted "social revolution" of early Buddhism? At the time of the Buddha, only men were allowed to become renouncers, and even when renunciation became institutionalized in the Hindu theory of the four *varṇa*, it remained a purely male ideal. The Buddha's call for spiritual freedom could hardly be restricted to men, however. Despite his alleged reluctance to admit women into his order, the notion of enlightenment was indeed subversive, and it could not remain for long the privilege of the "sons of good family" (as the Buddha calls his disciples); it could be restricted neither to "sons" only (to the exclusion of "daughters"), nor to "good families." Indeed, families were to be left behind. Eventually, however, one observes a "domestication of enlightenment," inasmuch as the ultimate goal of Buddhism tends to become a familial affair, not unlike ancestor worship. New Buddhist models, such as the householder Vimalakīrti or Layman Pang, reach enlightenment at home. In medieval Japan, enlightenment becomes a postmortem achievement, the outcome of a funerary ritual performed by (or on behalf of) relatives. In the same way, one can discern a "domestication" of Japanese gods, who are represented in increasingly anthropomorphic fashion, in particular as members of extended families. In this way, familial values reentered the arena of cultic worship.[6]

It is fair to say that, at least in its dominant monastic expression, Buddhism has been a fundamentally androcentric teaching, but one which, when confronted with internal and external realities, had to water down its wine. The female standpoint is conspicuously absent from normative Buddhist discourse, and women seem to have largely interiorized dominant, debasing notions, such as the topos of the Five Obstacles. But even when they seemed condemned to "poach" on masculine preserves, women were full-fledged historical actors, and we should not be too quick in concluding that they were passive victims. Some resisted with more or less success, as the legends of the "nun" Toran or of Ono no Komachi suggest, while others seem to have been "active" victims, willful agents of their own victimization (or that of their "sisters"). Although this side of the picture is understandably less often discussed, some women had their share of responsibility in, if I may use the expression, "sleeping with the enemy." The discourse of nuns, for instance, often sounds like a kind of male ventriloquism. Just like clitoridectomy is, in Susan Sered's terms, a "culturally condoned procedure for mutilating women's bodies," one could perhaps, stretching things a bit, say that some forms of female monasticism were "symbolic clitoridectomies," forms of initiation that reinforced the control of young women by older women (and men). One has to be very optimistic to interpret this denial of normal female bodily (and psychological) experience as "a somewhat feminist response to a patriarchal cultural environment."[7]

Just like men, women can be both aggressors and victims, even if social conditions put them more rarely in the first role. We are confronted here with two irreconcilable viewpoints, that of the lawyer and that of the prosecutor. The former tends to blame the system and to present the defendant as a victim; the latter looks for individual responsibility, in both the aggressor and victim. In the Hegelian master-slave dialectic, for instance, the slave is largely responsible for his situation, which is the result of what Erich Fromm labelled "escape from freedom."

I have argued in the first part of this book that there was in Buddhism both more and less equality than meets the eye; more equality because the misogynistic discourse found its limits in specific contexts—where women were able to turn the tables; and less because the egalitarian rhetoric remained rhetorical, covering up various kinds of sexism. This may be the Buddhist version of the old dilemma: the optimist viewing the bottle as half-full, the pessimist as half-empty. Depending on our focus, we might find enough data to see Buddhism as fundamentally sexist or egalitarian. Scholarship, too, becomes performative in its attempts to legitimize, reform, or undermine a given form of Buddhism. For some, Buddhism is irremediably on the side of oppression, while others credit it with "opening the eyes" of women (in the sense of the "eye-opening" of a Buddhist statue).

To argue for the possibility of reaching buddhahood or awakening from within the locus of gender—if there is such a place—is quite different from hastily jumping beyond or past gender, to soar to high metaphysical space, in the hope of getting a blissful bird's-eye view of the gendered (low) life on earth. The denial of perspectives is still a perspective that ignores itself, amounts to little more than a pleasant, and rather shallow, dream of lightness. We are reminded here of the old existentialist critique of essentialism in Sartre's famous motto, "existence precedes essence."

Existentialism may be outdated, but this insight, at least, deserves to be preserved. The advocacy of Buddhist androgyny by feminist scholars like Diana Paul or Rita Gross looks like a return to Plato's famous (and somewhat uncanny) notion of the androgyne; indeed, it amounts to Platonic idealism in Buddhist garb.[8] To recognize existential and cultural determinations is by no means to condone patriarchal conceptions of gender. Between the two main ways of going beyond gender (or rather, of ignoring it), asexuality and androgyny, Buddhist asceticism has usually chosen the first. In early Buddhism (and in Hinduism), androgyny did not mean overcoming, but rather exacerbating, the sufferings caused by gender: the passions specific to the sexes, with respect to each other, were rather additive than subtractive. The asexual model is well expressed by a female disciple of the Buddha, the nun Soma: "If I asked myself / Am I a man or a woman in this? / Then I would be speaking / Māra's language." Ironically, feminists who advocate androgyny would also be speaking Māra's language, at least according to those other feminists, who, following the Mahāyāna party line according to which "the Dharma is neither male nor female," claim to be speaking truly the Buddha's language.

The different Buddhist views on gender, subsumed as rhetorics of equality and of inequality, may seem at first glance contradictory. Indeed they are at a certain level, but at another level they are interdependent, insofar as they participate in an overall process that "leads to the representation of the unchanging transcendental group"—the Buddhist saṅgha.[9] As Maurice Bloch points out in a different context, differing representations of gender are not rival concepts, but differing kinds of knowledge. Bloch explains that, if authority is to be legitimized, it must be represented as part of a transcendental order beyond human action and life. Such an image must be created by negating "biology," which is seen as both evident and low. If such is the case, we must avoid privileging one representation as *the* Buddhist view on gender, or on women. On the one hand, the rhetoric of equality seeks to establish the transcendence of Buddhist truth and of the patriarchal tradition. In so doing, it leaves the gendered realm intact. It is essentially ideological in that it serves to legitimize authority: clerical power and state power. On the other hand, if women symbolically represent the biological world of *saṃsāra*, then the Mahāyāna identity between *saṃsāra* and nirvāṇa implies their revalorization as being identical with truth. In this light, courtesans are no longer daughters of Māra, but bodhisattvas of Song and Dance. Furthermore, as in Nietzsche's writings, such truth, qua woman, is no longer an essence.[10]

Yet, the male-centered logic of Buddhist doctrine is at times subverted by that of common representations (for instance, the old "mechanic of fluids" still at work in premodern Buddhist embryology). Gendered symbols have their own dynamics, and they can on occasion fool the ideologues who claim to manipulate them. Buddhists tried to capture female sexuality in their discursive net, which gradually extended its grip from rituals of death and birth to the entire realm of embryology and menstruation. By doing so, and despite its male-chauvinist ascetics, Buddhism opened itself to the influence of the same female values it meant to control. In almost all of the cases examined above, it added oil to the fire of beliefs about female impurity, exacerbating the problem in order to offer its self-serving resolution. It attempted to impose itself at the cultural border by imposing moral borders of its own. Japanese Buddhists, vying with Confucian reformers to "naturalize" the hierarchy and social injustice of the Tokugawa order, elaborated on the antifeminist ideology they had inherited from their Indian and Chinese precursors, but in so doing they were obliged to leave room to local cults and beliefs in which women and womanhood played a prominent role. Women have often had the last word in the realm of popular religion, this last word being inspired to them by the god, of which they are the mouthpiece—even if this word is sometimes "translated" (and betrayed) by the male specialist.

If women's religions, according to Sered, are characterized by a this-worldly orientation that does not emphasize the difference between sacred and profane spheres, Mahāyāna Buddhism, as it became more "this-worldly," came to assume some characteristics of a "women's religion."[11] Yet the same Mahāyāna logic that led to the interiorization of compassion also led to the interiorization of female defilement. Whereas in a ritualist context appropriate or inappropriate behavior is defined externally by action, and always temporarily, in Mahāyāna it becomes part of human nature, and this nature tends to polarize along gender lines: good and evil, pure and impure, male and female.

Buddhist priests were attracted to the margins in their attempts to seal the gaps and regulate passages or exchanges between Buddhist orthodoxy and various popular heterodoxies. During this process, however, Buddhism itself became in part marginal: some of its border-guards defected to the enemy, and the frontline between orthodoxy and heterodoxy was constantly moving. The tension between the centralizing discourse and the de facto multivocality of the tradition, expressed in a constant (dis)-play of the same and the other, becomes the twofold truth of Buddhism. This is somewhat ironic, in light of the fact that Buddhist discourse is explicitly based on the "Two Truths" theory, which was initially a way for Buddhism to integrate otherness, rather than to open itself to alterity.

In terms of gender, the twofold truth would be to realize that, while Buddhist discourse is undeniably misogynistic, the situation of women within it has been modified by elements external to gender. We have noted the opening of Buddhism to local cults, in which women played an important role. Once again, the causality is far from simple: although there were egalitarian tendencies within Buddhism, they were contradicted by various external factors (the rise of patriarchy, the role of popular conceptions regarding defilement, and so forth). To give just an example, civil war in late medieval Japan did probably more to lower the status of women than any sexist teaching. The rule of primogeniture, for instance, derived above all from the necessity to protect the household (*ie*) during the political chaos of that period.

How can we reconcile the gender approach (for which gender is primary) with the sociohistorical approach (for which gender is only one of the determining factors)? These two viewpoints seem irreconcilable in theory, but may be complementary in practice. This is because the gender-only approach, like an hermeneutical bracketing, can have real effects only when reconciled with actual social life and articulated with other sociohistorical factors. There is no need to make a fundamental choice; on the contrary, one must be able to shift the focus from one approach to the other, to use the "play" between subjectivism and objectivism, in order to avoid being trapped in either of them.

On the home front, the Buddhist clergy needs to address the status of its nuns. Or rather, inasmuch as the female order is an integral part of the Buddhist saṅgha, it is the Buddhist nuns themselves who need to question their own status—not only vis-à-vis male clerics, but also vis-à-vis other categories of women—and adopt a self-critical view of their own history. In particular, they must resist incitements to peddle views that disparage their own sex, but rather negotiate the difficult relationships between detached spirituality and embodied womanhood, between a (male-inspired) ascetic ideal and the needs of women in society. They have to find their proper place among other women, and to do so they must be willing to explore the potential conflicts of interest between their own group and others (like that of the *jizoku*, wives of Japanese priests).

For scholars, it is high time to focus their work equally on nuns and other, less visible female groups, and/or to realize that they are actually taking sides, and why. The analysis of Buddhist rhetorical modes has revealed the complexity of conflicting strategies within a basically androcentric framework, and the possibility of activating or reactivating certain subversive elements within this arena of contention called "sexual difference." Here, the main danger facing the scholars seems to be a certain hermeneutical naïveté, namely, the desire to "soar and settle" too soon by taking the egalitarian rhetoric at face-value. The close scrutiny of Buddhist discourse is revealing, particularly when it shows a return of repressed elements—for instance, representations of bodily fluids—that may work for and against the improvement of the status of women.

One could contrast the sexless (or rather, neutered) egalitarianism of mainstream Mahāyāna Buddhism, with the sexual conjunction (concrete sexual egalitarianism) of local cults and of "heterodox" Buddhist schools influenced by yin-yang thought, like the Tachikawa-ryū.[12] The emphasis on a yin-yang model implying the equal participation of both sexes runs against what we could call the Buddhist "gender tetralemma"—the four dialectical positions regarding sex/gender: 1) male power (phallicism); 2) female power (*onna no chikara*); 3) androgyny (male *and* female gender, which often amounts to denial of either sex); 4) neither male nor female (neutered egalitarian rhetoric). In the past, institutionalized religions like Buddhism, Daoism, Confucianism, or Shintō have attempted either to negate or to recuperate *both* the beliefs in "female power" *and* the yin-yang sexual conjunction.

In medieval texts and popular cults influenced by the Tachikawa school, the conjunction of the two primordial principles was expressed allegorically by the primordial incest of the two sibling deities Izanami and Izanagi. This sexual union took place after their staged encounter around the heavenly pillar, itself a rather obvious phallic symbol. Thus, it is symptomatic that the myth of sexual difference itself would revolve around a phallus. The sexual conjunction is described as the union of two complementary elements, like the two parts of a *symbolon*—a symbol of symbolic difference, as it were. As Pascal Quignard remarks, however, sexual difference cannot be reduced to symbolic difference.[13] It may well be irreducible, primitive, and not merely "socially constructed," as gender scholars would have it. Like the yin-yang ideology, which considers sexual difference to be derived, and therefore symbolically tame, such social constructivism seems to result from a "misunderstanding that confuses sexual difference and human language."[14]

By focusing on Buddhist conceptions concerning women, I may have ended up reiterating the Buddhist gesture of exclusion of women as subjects. I would argue that I did so in order to emphasize that Buddhist orthodoxy was bound to fail, and that it remains haunted by its significant others. I have attempted to reveal the existence of these others, and therefore to reintegrate them, at least at the level of discourse, and mark their empty place at the very core of the tradition, or on its margins. When Śākyamuni returns home, like Odysseus, his faithful wife Yaśodhara is still waiting for him, and she has borne him a child. The Buddha, reunited with woman and child, is now ready to become an old sage. He could, like Vimalakīrti, become an enlightened and enlightening householder. But, or so the monastic tradition tells us, this would have been to fall into the trap of Māra. Instead, he chooses to leave home again, taking with him the only person that matters to him: his child, a future monk and arhat. That this monastic solution was not accepted by all (in particular by women) is shown in variants of the story, which describe Yaśodhara's pregnancy and delivery as parallel to Śākyamuni's asceticism and enlightenment. The image of Yaśodhara and of other Buddhist women, while still part of Buddhist discourse, was already a departure from strict orthodoxy insofar as it was more apt than the teaching to be reappropriated by other social categories. The hagiographic tradition, however, still does not offer the viewpoint of women: a vision that is already divided to the extent it interiorizes, or not, the male viewpoint. Its deconstruction soon reaches its limits, and in order to "imagine" female strategies (for lack of "hearing (female) voices"), we had to move away from purely Buddhist texts, toward folkloric or literary documents whose motivations and audiences were diverse and not always clear.

Women on the Threshold

Transgression of gender, or the subversion of sexual difference, is not some return to a primordial androgynous nature, a kind of static perfection that may well derive solely from male phantasm. Transgression may seem more "natural" to women, not because of some innate female quality, but because of their social position as marginals in a male-dominated symbolic order. Inasmuch as "femininity" is defined as "that which is marginalized by the patriarchal symbolic order," such transgression is also open to those males who turn out to be symbolically feminine.[15] Conversely, symbolic masculinity becomes an option for those women who integrate and internalize the male symbolic order.

The image that imposed itself in the second part of this study is that of the margins, the threshold, the "ban." Women were "put on the ban" (*mises au ban*) when they were either ban-ished or ban-alized. If the whole effort of patriarchal Buddhism was to establish neat boundaries, women both marked and blurred these boundaries. Despite attempts to put them "under house-arrest," they remained infinitely mobile, versatile. The women who best symbolize such qualities are those who, willingly or not, installed themselves in such liminality. Like the shamaness figures with whom they were identified, and who were in turn feminized, such women were used as mediators by society to express the conjunction of opposites.

But they were much more than that. Sexual difference tends to overflow its boundaries; it cannot be reduced to the regulated play of yin and yang. These women transgressed, invaded male turf, trespassed male boundaries—even when, like the nuns, they tried to adopt male values, all the more so when, like the wandering women, *miko* and courtesans, they actively contested them or simply ignored them. Nuns also transgressed the bounds of their femininity by renouncing sexuality. Finally, even when they "kept to their place," as most of them did, women were not thought innocent of transgression. Thus, "women's religion," with its cult of motherhood, of blood, and so forth, was always suspect and lent itself (in the male imaginary, at least) to all kinds of drift. Yet the further one gets away from Buddhist orthodoxy (whose long-winded discourse about women revealed the latter's conspicuous silence), the better female voices are heard, for instance, in folklore or literature; at the same time, and paradoxically, it becomes more obvious that women were caught in determinisms that were not simply those of gender.

The Buddhist ascetic ideal is one of "adult" power, which rejects people outside of its mental or spiritual *kekkai*: not only women, but also children and old people. Childhood, womanhood, and old age were seen primarily as negative, weakening, powerless states against which the ascetic (a real man) must shield himself. Of course, there has been, and continues to be, a liminal recognition, which will haunt Buddhism in perpetuity, one suspects, that children and the old, and perhaps more essentially women, are paradoxically sources of power. In the Buddhist golden legend, prince Siddharta (the future Buddha) is living a very sheltered life into which illness, old age, and death are not allowed. He has to go outside of his father's palace to encounter them; but the woman is inside, in Siddharta's inner quarters. He has, therefore, to leave forever the palace (and the child he once was), but also the world (where old age reigns), to eventually find in the wilderness a place where he will become free of these constraints. The adult man is thus defined in opposition to the woman (paradigmatically), and to the child and the old man (syntagmatically): the child (not yet defined sexually), the woman, and the old man/woman (no longer defined sexually) are thus his three alter egos, his "shadows," from which he tries to run away. The woman is either seen as the fundamental other (the one closest to the adult male's inner chamber, hence the most threatening: or, from another angle, empowering), or merely as one of the "others" that must be eliminated. Like children and old people, women are dependent. Their story and history must therefore be inscribed in the broader field of the excluded other, and not seen through the lens of gender alone.[16] If we want to stick to the gender lens, we have, like Hélène Cixous, heuristically to use the word "woman" as shorthand for all those who are denied access to discourse and power.[17] The feminine is not only powerlessness, it is also, in Hegel's words, "the eternal irony of the community." It is not simply what opposes the masculine, but what seduces or subverts it, that which lies outside or deconstructs the *essentially masculine* opposition between male and female.

Paradoxically, even though it always manifests itself in gendered fashion, power seems more fundamental as an explanatory model than does gender. The binary "male/female" is used as a linguistic paradigm to express a more fundamental opposition between active and passive, or, even more crudely, between penetrating and penetrated. Thus, it opposes active males to passive females and passive males, including children and other socially or culturally inferior people, like the *hinin* of premodern Japan. In ancient Rome, as in premodern Japan, women and children were used interchangeably as sexual objects. To better understand the patriarchal debasement of women, we may need to study more closely the status of children in medieval Japan. As I have discussed elsewhere, on the one hand children were neglected, while, on the other, they were idealized: for instance, as *chigo* (young nobles).[18]

The same is true for women: their idealization went hand in hand with contempt. While being a self-proclaimed other-worldly religion, Buddhism received from the social world its basic concepts about sex and gender (even when it departs from them): its conception of women, in particular, cannot be understood without reference to larger societal developments, like political ideology, the history of the family, of children, of the aged, and so forth. Because women constitute the most consistently repressed category, the feminist reading remains extremely powerful. But an overemphasis on gender and women might contribute to the further exclusion of children and the old. Until now, Buddhism has not been able to think through sexual difference; the best it could do was offer variants of a unisex model. The Buddhist teaching has been badgered, however, shaped by sexual difference from within as well as from without, and perhaps it has not yet said its last word, or exhausted all of the implications of Vimalakīrti's "thundering silence."

NOTES

INTRODUCTION

1. Sered 1994: 210.
2. Ibid., 279–80.
3. Winkler 1990: 201.
4. Gilbert and Gubar, quoted in Moi 1985: 57.
5. Ibid., 67–68.
6. Kelly 1984: 28.
7. Sered's work on Okinawa has been recently criticized by a Japanese feminist (and the wife of a Zen priest), Kawahashi Noriko. See Kawahashi 2001b.
8. Scott 1988: 20.
9. For a useful survey of Chinese scholarship, see Jinhua Emma Teng, "The Construction of the 'Traditional Chinese Woman' in the Western Academy: A Critical Review," *Signs* 22, 1 (1996): 115–51. For Japanese scholarship, see Wakita, Bouchy, and Ueno 1999.
10. Ko challenges the oversimplified view scholars have taken on these matters. Even within the constraints of patriarchal ideology, women retained possibilities for fulfillment and a meaningful existence. The classic expression of woman's subordination, the so-called Three Dependences or Submissions (Chin. *sancong*, Jp. *sanjū*)—Ko's "Thrice Following," with the implication that "following" is not necessarily "submitting"—is a case in point. See Ko 1994: 6–10, 219–23, 249–53.
11. See Chung 1981. Likewise, Charlotte Furth tells us that the portrayal of Confucianism as hierarchic and misogynist by China scholars, by contrast to a supposedly more egalitarian and gynocentric Daoism, is not warranted by Chinese medical texts. The social paternalism of Confucians was much more protective of women as childbearers and mothers than Daoist sexual arts, which, in a polygamous society, tended to exploit women as sexual handmaidens; Furth 1994: 146. Regarding Daoism, Brigitte Berthier contrasts imaginary and real women, in a way reminiscent of Tantric Buddhism; Berthier 1988: 295.
12. Ko 1994: 7.
13. Teng 1996: 125.
14. Ko 1994: 4.
15. Teng 1996: 133.
16. Moi 1985: 64.
17. The feminist anthropologist Yvonne Verdier has shown that the traditional (gendered) reading of Little Red Riding Hood's tale may not be as pertinent as it seems. In the earlier oral variants, not expurgated by Charles Perrault, the wolf plays a rather minor role. The little girl more or less consciously desires to cook the blood of her grandmother (read mother) and eat it. Here again, the conflict of generations, revolving around a powerful female symbol (blood), is significant. See Verdier 1995: 169–97.
18. Albert 1997; Verdier 1995.
19. Gubar 1998: 899.
20. Bordo, in Caroline Ramazanoglu, ed., *Up Against Foucault*, 228–29.

21. See *Les grands entretiens du monde*, 1994 2: 29.

22. See Bynum, Harrell, and Richman 1986: 13.

23. Laqueur 1990: 17.

24. Bloch 1992 :78.

25. Bloch also writes: "The symbolism of gender and sexuality . . . should be understood as being used in rituals in an ad hoc manner to act out a more fundamental and central logic concerning the establishment of a form of human life which has apparently escaped the biological constraint of death. . . . The conjunction and disjunction between humans and animals can be used to exactly the same ends in rituals as the conjunction and disjunction between female and male." (ibid.)

26. See Laqueur 1990: 88.

27. See Natalie Davis 1971: 76, 90, quoted in Scot 1988: 29.

28. Scott 1988: 31.

29. Scott 1988: 33; see also Jay 1992; Verdier 1995: 169–97.

30. O'Brian 1981: 8.

31. McKinnon 1982.

32. Scott has been criticized by a number of feminist scholars. Judith Bennett criticizes her for emphasizing gender as "meaning," not materiality, and abstracting the inequality of the sexes. She argues that theorizing patriarchy is more important than theorizing gender. See Bennett 1989: 258. According to another critic, Uta Schmidt, gender can be misused to dissolve specific experiences of women and neutralize questions like male domination. See Schmidt 1993. For Kathleen Biddick (1993), the focus on gender renders invisible other borders and hierarchies. For Judith Butler, gender is performative and never static; it is volatile and disruptive, and there is always the danger of objectifying it. Micheline Dumont criticizes the "social constructivist" trend. For her, even if there is a need of "unhinging gender from sexual identity," there is the danger of going too far and transforming medieval subjects into desexualized bundles of socially determined behaviors (a very Buddhist—and male?—metaphor). See Dumont 1989: 114. (I am indebted for these references to Hank Glassman.)

33. In the case of traditional societies, kinship structures seem more important than economic structures in the strict sense, but because they are based on notions of exchange (for instance the "exchange of women" analyzed by Claude Lévi-Strauss), they are also based on economics, in the broader sense of "symbolic economy." On this question, see Goux 1990.

34. See for example Tonomura 1994a and 1997; Bargen 1997.

35. See Bourdieu 1998.

36. Ibid., 29.

37. Ibid., 117.

38. An example of this tendency can be found in Shaw 1994.

39. Kristeva 1990: 156.

40. Derrida 1981: 82.

CHAPTER 1

1. See I. B. Horner, trans., *Cullavagga* 10: 355. The legend of Mahāprajāpati will be examined in chapter 6. Other Vinaya sources regarding this episode include the *Sarvāstivāda Vinaya*, T. 1435, 15; the *Mūlasarvāstivada Vinaya*, T.

1415, 29–30; the *Mahāsaṅghika Vinaya*, T. 1425, 30; the *Mahīśāsaka Vinaya*, T. 1421, 29; and the *Dharmaguptaka Vinaya*, T. 1428, 48. Among sutras, see for instance: T. 60, T. 1478, T. 1565.

2. Falk 1989: 159–60.

3. Takakusu 1966: 81.

4. Walters 1994: 368–71.

5. Wilson 1996: 146, quoting Auerbach 1982: 8.

6. See Schopen 1995.

7. A good example of the nuns' combativeness can be found in a Vinaya tale illustrating their acrimonious relationships with Jain neighbors. Of course, the purpose of this story is to justify yet another rule for nuns; namely, that nuns should never use quarrelsome language with anybody, but it could be heard as a vivid echo of the "voice" of these women. See Roth 1970: 106–7; and Nolot 1991: 88–91.

8. Willis 1985: 77.

9. In spite of this, I will continue to use the terms "nuns" to designate women living a religious life in a convent or under its supervision.

10. Chayet 1993: 286.

11. Ibid., 286–87.

12. See Zürcher 1991: 46.

13. Baochang is known as the author of various works such as the *Jing lü yixiang* (T. 53, 2121) and the *Mingseng zhuan*. But because he was not credited with the authorship of the *Biqiuni zhuan* until the beginning of the Tang, it has been suggested that the work may be a later compilation.

14. See Tsai 1994: 15.

15. Ibid., 16.

16. A case in point is the nun Guangjing, who, having decided to fast, entered dhyāna to concentrate on Tuṣita Heaven. She died four months later. See T. 50, 2062: 939b. Baochang gives six examples of female autocremation. Another type, not included in the *Biqiuni zhuan*, perhaps because it emerged only later, is that of the "lay nun," also found in Japan. There seem to have been in Song China "nuns" with long hair, judging from the following passage of Daocheng's *Shishi yaoluan* (preface dated 1020) on śikṣamāṇa nuns: "The śikṣamāṇa, who are called here [in China] 'women studying the Dharma' [*xuefa nü*], have a long hair which resembles that of today's nuns." See T. 54, 2127: 262a.

17. See *Jin Shu* 64. In *Ershiwu shi*, Taipei: Xinwenfeng.

18. Zürcher 1959: 153. Quote from T. 50, 2063: 936c. See also Zürcher 1991: 83; Tsai 1994: 33–34.

19. The *Gujin tushu jicheng* (dated 1725) contains ninety-five biographies of nuns (from the Jin to the Ming), two-thirds of which are copied from the *Biqiuni zhuan*.

20. For more details, see Faure 1998b. Their stele inscription by Liang Su was preserved in the *Sokwŏn salim*, an epigraphic collection compiled by the Korean priest Ŭich'ŏn (1055–1101). See Saitō 1973: 823–49.

21. For more details, see Faure 1998b.

22. See Levering 1998.

23. See Mann 1997a: 10.

24. See Sangren 1983: 12. Along the same line, Patricia Ebrey argues that, already during the Song, post-menopausal women would often turn to Buddhism in order to assuage their jealousy toward younger rivals and to find new sources of personal fulfillment beyond the family. See Ebrey 1993: 170–71, 127–28.

25. See Mann 1997a: 2.

26. See ZZ 1, 2, 23, 1: 106a–26b; and new ed., vol. 150. On this work, see Goldfuss 1994.

27. For instance, see the recent work of scholars such as Katsuura Noriko (Katsuura 1989, 1992), Hosokawa Ryōichi (Hosokawa 1988a, 1988b, 1989b), Ushiyama Yoshiyuki (Ushiyama 1982, 1984, 1989), and Matsuo Kenji (Matsuo 1989, 1996).

28. According to the *Nihon shoki*, the legitimacy of Zenshin's ordination was proved when a relic was discovered in a vegetarian meal offered to the nuns by Umako. The incredulous Umako tried in vain to destroy the relic, and finally converted: "From this arose the beginning of Buddhism." See Aston 1972: 101–2, 134–35, and 111.

29. Aston 1972: 103–4.

30. *Sanbō ekotoba*, trans. Kamens 1988: 291.

31. As is well known, the vogue of bodhisattva ordinations was the result of Saichō's effort to overthrow the monopoly on regular ordinations retained by the Nara temples. This movement was not, as Paula Arai argues, initiated by women, and it is exaggerated to describe it as an indication that "Heian nuns took their destiny in their own hands." See Arai 1999a. 1999b; as well as Taira 1990 and Groner 1990b.

32. Regarding this point, the *Genkō shakusho* by the Zen historiographer Kokan Shiren claims, rather unconvincingly, that Kūkai was instrumental in the process.

33. On Empress Danrin's image as a pious Buddhist, see infra, chapter 5.

34. Junna-in (also known as Saiin, the Western Palace or Chapel) was still a nunnery in the tenth century, and, according to the *Sanbō ekotoba*, it was the place of semi-annual confession services for nuns, dedicated to the arhat Ānanda. With Hokkeji and a few Heian nunneries, it remained active in the Kamakura period.

35. Later on, when Jōtōmon'in (Akiko) was ordained, Fujiwara no Michinaga planned to build an ordination platform for nuns at Muryō-in. But this plan failed due to the obstruction of Hieizan. Subsequently, there was no more talk of ordination platforms for nuns in Tendai.

36. See *Nihon sandai jitsuroku*, quoted in Nishiguchi 1987: 23.

37. On Shinnyo and Jizen, see Wakita 1995: 135.

38. Wakita 1995: 138.

39. This Hossō scholar, who had been married and had several daughters, was a disciple of Jōkei (a.k.a. Gedatsu shōnin). Shōen is mentioned in the *Shasekishū* as a dissolute monk, who after his death fell into the path of demons. His spirit took possession of a woman in order to give through her mouth a description of the Buddhist hell under Kasuga, where people who believe in the kami can receive the help of the bodhisattva Jizō. See *Shasekishū* 1.6, ed. Watanabe 1966: 71–72.

40. See *Shōtoku Taishi denki*, quoted in Hosokawa 1987:114. In her *Towazu-gatari*, Lady Nijō tells how, after visiting Hokkeji, she wanted to learn more about Prince Shōtoku and his consort, and went on to Chūgūji, where she met with the abbess Shinnyo, whom she had seen once at court. See *Towazugatari*, trans. Brazell 1973: 205. After Shinnyo's death, Chūgūji was twice destroyed by fire, in 1309 and 1311. Soon after, in 1337, it passed under the jurisdiction of Kōfukuji. See Hosokawa 1989b: 142.

41. See *Zōtanshū* 10.4, ed. Yamada and Miki 1973: 307.

42. See *Yamato koji daikan*, vol. 5, Tokyo: Iwanami shoten 1978; or *Saidaiji Eizon denki shūsei*, Kyoto: Hōzōkan 1977.

43. See Tanaka 1989 and 1993: 184–89.

44. The *Tōji go-shari sōjō jidai* records that the dancer-girl Kamegiku received relics from the hands of Emperor Go-Toba himself. See Hosokawa 1988a, 1988b.

45. See Amino 1978: 207.

46. See Okuda 1999. Myōgō also copied the entire *Shaka nyorai gohyaku daigan* (The Five Hundred Vows of the Tathāgata Śākyamuni) over a period of fifty days, an ascetic feat during which she mixed her blood with ink, offering a prayer, incense, and flowers for each character copied; she finally copied the entire 600-fascicle *Mahāprajñāpāramitā-sūtra* at the age of sixty-four.

47. Ushiyama 1989: 238.

48. The *ama gozan* system, organized in 1380 after the model of the Five Mountains of the Zen school, included Keiaiji, Tsūgenji, Danrinji, Keirinji, and Gonenji. We recall, however, that Danrinji, founded by Empress Tachibana, had fallen to ruin in the eleventh century, and there is no trace of its being restored. The four other nunneries coexisted only during a short period, and most were in ruins by the end of the Muromachi Bakufu. At the end of the Middle Ages, Tsūgenji and Keiaiji remained only in name. The male "five mountains" that served as models for the *ama gozan* were Nanzenji, Tenryūji, Shōkokuji, Tōfukuji, and Manjuji. In Kamakura, a similar system developed around Taiheiji, Kokuonji, Gohōji, Tōkeiji, and Zenmyōji. The official character of these nunneries is reflected in the fact that the abbess of Keiaiji was selected by the shogun among the nuns of the branch-temples.

49. See Ruch 1990: 502–11.

50. In the Edo period, sixteen convents were officially called *bikuni gosho* because their abbesses from the start had been princesses or noblewomen; more exactly, convents directed by princesses were called *gokyūshitsu*, those directed by noblewomen, *gozenshitsu*.

51. Harada 1997: 154.

52. Ushiyama 1989: 249.

53. In the sixteenth century, the court and the shogunate were no longer able to rebuild Ise Shrine every twenty years, as had been the tradition, and as a result the shrine had fallen into a state of disrepair, that is, until the wandering nuns started raising funds to restore it. On fund-raising activities, see Goodwin 1994.

54. As is well known, Jōdo Shinshū priests have always been an exception in this respect. Their wives were called *bōmori*.

55. This question has been discussed by Kawahashi Noriko, herself a *jizoku*— and an anthropologist. See Kawahashi 1995.

56. Ibid., 174.

57. For instance, see Chikusa 1989.

58. Tsai 1994: 18–19.

59. Ibid., 19.

60. Ibid., 54.

61. Ibid., 54.

62. Ibid., 62–63.

63. Aston 1972: 118.

64. See *Tōshōden*, in Takakusu 1928–29.

65. See Groner 1990b.

66. *Kongō busshi Eizon kanshin gakushōki*, in *Saidaiji Eizon denki shūsei* 22; quoted in Hosokawa 1987.

67. See *Shōdai senzaiki, DNBZ* 64: 247–48, 286.

68. See Hosokawa 1987: 107. In the "Nuns" section of the *Shōdai senzai denki*, we are told that when Kakujō was performing the *poṣatha* in the Kangen era, a heavenly being appeared to the priest Kyōen and told him to become a nun in order to ordain other nuns, then disappeared. Kyōen became a woman right away, went back to his native village, and ordained his younger sister—none other than Shinnyo. The biography adds that with the ordination of Shinnyo the Buddhist orders were finally complete in Japan.

69. See *Gakushōki*, s.v. "Kenchō 3" (1251), in *Saidaiji Eizon denki shūsei*, 23–24; quoted in Hosokawa 1987: 107–8.

70. As noted earlier, the Japanese terms translated by "nun" cover a wide range of situations. For instance, *ama* could refer to very different groups (from regular nuns to prostitutes). Likewise, the term *zenni* ("zen nun") became a funerary title attached by Muromachi priests to the *kaimyō* (posthumous name) of women, and referred to women of low status and meager connection to the temple.

71. This nun left a collection of poems, the *Mikoshibe no zenni shōsoku*. She is also said to be the author of the *Mumyō zōshi*.

72. The following account is indebted to Katsuura 1992: 241–71; and Katsuura 1995.

73. Ushiyama, however, reacting against the recent tendency to focus on socioeconomic motivations, continued to emphasize the vocational aspect of medieval nunhood.

74. On this anticlerical imagery, see Faure 1998a.

75. See Ruch 1990.

76. *Therīgāthā*, verses 122–26; quoted in Kloppenborg 1995: 166.

77. Brazell 1973: 228.

78. The symbolic value of hair—and of tonsure—has been the subject of several recent studies. See Katsuura 1989, Lang 1995, Hiltebeitel and Miller 1998.

79. See Katsuura 1989; Kasamatsu and Katsumata 1983: 36.

80. See also *Ōkagami*, trans. Yamagiwa 1977: 164. When the wife of Fujiwara no Michimasa runs away to the palace of the Empress Dowager [Kazuko], the narrator comments. "Ah, if this old man's wife were to do something like this, I would shave off her white hair and scratch off her nose. [But] those who are known to be in high stations are so jealous of a good name that they are unable

to do anything [in these situations]." On tonsure as punishment, see also Amino et al. 1983: 35–37.

81. Abe Yasurō 1999: 75.

82. Ibid., 79–80.

83. Kawahashi 2000b: 49.

84. See *Taiheiki*, trans. McCullough 1979: 312.

85. Lang 1995: 4.

86. Many examples appear in the *Eiga monogatari* and similar sources. See McCullough and McCullough 1980.

87. See Komine 1995. There were actually few Buddhist books, apart from the recorded sayings of Zen masters, biographies of monks, or "origin stories" (*engi*) of temples. Nuns seem to have preferred poetic anthologies, novels, and, somewhat surprisingly, military tales.

88. In general, Chinese nuns do not seem to have observed too strictly the rule of poverty: they did not have to beg because convents were supported by the rent of their land properties. They had their own kitchens and refectories, with meals prepared by novices and slaves. Often, when land was given to a nun by her family, she became the permanent abbess. Some of them, who could keep individual donations, became very rich and influential. Thus, eminent nuns enjoyed relatively greater freedom and more social contacts than did lay women. This seems to have been even more true with respect to Daoist nuns. See Despeux 1986: 84.

89. Mann 1997a: 4.

90. See Katsuura 1995: 190–93.

91. See *Yamato monogatari* 27, quoted in Katsuura 1995: 192–93.

92. Katsuura 1995: 190–93.

93. See Verdier 1979.

94. See the case of the husband who takes his wife from the temple, violates her, and receives instant karmic retribution. *Nihon ryōiki* 2, 11; trans. Nakamura 1973: 175–76.

95. See *Entairyaku*, s.v. "12/8, 1348"; quoted in Katsuura 1992: 250.

96. See Katsuura 1992: 241–47.

97. See *Shinsei shōnin ōjō denki*, quoted in Katsuura 1992: 241–43.

98. See McCullough 1959: 54. Usually, the ordination took place during or soon after the forty-nine-day period following the husband's death.

99. See *Heike monogatari*, trans. McCullough 1988: 114.

100. See ibid., 471.

101. See Cogan 1987: xxxi–xxxii.

102. Ibid., 400.

103. McCullough 1988: 331.

104. Ibid., 341.

105. Ibid., 331–43.

106. See *Taiheiki*, trans. McCullough 1979: 338.

107. Ibid., 322.

108. Ibid., 323.

109. *Heike monogatari*, trans. McCullough 1988: 244.

110. Ibid., 206; see also the case of the *shirabyōshi* Giō, infra, ch. 6.

111. *Towazugatari*, trans. Brazell 1973: 86–87.

112. Ibid., 204.

113. Both were apparently born of the same mother, the lady-in-waiting Chikako. See Hosokawa 1987:140–41.

114. See Abe Yasurō 1999: 84–87; Wakita 1995: 130.

115. See *Towazugatari*, trans. Brazell 1973: 246–47.

116. Ibid., 256–57.

117. Lisa Bitel, quoted in *IMJS Report* 4, 1 (1993): 3.

118. See *Yanagidaru* 12, 19: "In the nuns' convent, / he knows they [i.e., olisboi] can be found /—the colporteur." And the variant in *Yanagidaru* 78, 29: "In the convent, / he secretly sells them—the colporteur."

119. Indeed, the female order in Sri Lanka eventually disappeared, and it was only recently revived.

120. See Sered 1994: 273.

121. See Hosokawa 1987. The denial of normal sexuality is lampooned in a parodic version of Kaibara Ekken's morality classic, *Onna daigaku*. In this pastiche, nunhood is presented as a result of frigidity induced by wrong education: "The Way of Love is the most important thing. It is because a father and a mother enjoy themselves in this Way that they have descendants. If a girl's parents are too strict with her in matters sexual, it can be unexpectedly detrimental. She will shun sex, lose her pluck, and be a disappointment to her husband . . . Then she will be driven out and become a nun [*hokkai bobo*, lit. "Dharmadhātu cunt"]. Surely this would be regrettable indeed! And all of this because, forgetting the lusty passions of their own youth, parents raise their daughters too strictly." See Fukuda Kazuhiko, *Edo no seiaigaku*, Tokyo: Kawade Bunko 1988: 13; quoted in Minamoto 1993: 105.

122. See Kawahashi 1995.

123. Dorothy Ko points out for instance the Western bias regarding foot-binding, and emphasizes the autoeroticism involved in what strikes us as mere mutilation. Yet, however autoerotic it may be, masochism is not exactly liberation, but only a more perverse form of alienation—and any form of alienation has its pay-offs, autoerotic or otherwise. See Ko 1994.

124. Dale Spender, *Man's Studies Modified: the Impact of Feminism on the Academic Disciplines*, Oxford: Pergamon Press, 1981: 2.

CHAPTER 2

1. Daoxuan, *Jingxin jie guan fa*, T. 45, 1893: 824a; Morrell 1980: 68.

2. Morrell 1985: 151.

3. Tonomura 1994a: 152.

4. *Tsurezuregusa*, trans. Keene 1967: 83–85.

5. Ibid.

6. Tonomura 1994a: 138–40.

7. *Konjaku monogatari shū* 4:3, ed. Yamada Yoshio et al., vol. 1: 271–73; Dykstra, 83–86; see also *Yichu liutie* (Jp. *Giso rokujō*). A variant tells how Aśoka killed his five hundred consorts for having damaged his vegetal namesake and symbol, the *aśoka* tree. See Strong, forthcoming.

8. A list of such stereotypes can be found in Dayal 1935: 223–24. See also Lachaud 1998.

9. See *Zhuan nüshen jing, T.* 14, 564: 919.

10. Burlingame 1921: 34.

11. See Faure 1998a; Wilson 1996.

12. Schuster 1984: 41.

13. See Sponberg 1992; see also Kloppenborg 1995: 152.

14. Weber 1963: 239.

15. Mohan Wijayaratna's book on Buddhist monasticism is typical of the pious arguments used to explain away this scandal. See Wijayaratna 1991: 160.

16. See Nolot 1991: 9.

17. Kamens 1988: 272–73. On Ānanda and nuns, see also *Jakushōdō kokkyō-shū,* op. cit., 360b.

18. The discovery of a "stupa of Ānanda" erected in 1265 on or near the site of Zenmyōji, the convent founded by Myōe in Takao, on the western outskirts of the capital, is further evidence of the existence of a cult dedicated to Ānanda during the Kamakura period. Because Zenmyōji was destroyed in 1830 by an earthquake and was never restored, the exact location of this convent remains unknown.

19. Wijayaratna 1991: 159.

20. Quoted in Overmyer 1991: 105.

21. *T.* 31, 1588; quoted in Kasahara 1983: 199.

22. *Sūtrakritanga,* quoted in Wieger 1910: 87–88.

23. Lamotte 1944–80, 2: 886.

24. Ibid., 337.

25. See Falk 1989: 157–60.

26. Chayet 1993: 149–50.

27. See Falk 1989: 158.

28. Chayet 1993: 149.

29. Regarding the assertion that there are no women in the Pure Land, see the *Lotus Sūtra,* trans. Hurvitz 1976: 407; and the *Sukhāvatīvyūhopadeśa* by Vasubandhu, *T.* 26, 1524: 232. The same idea is found regarding the buddha-land of the Buddha of Medicine: see *Bhaiṣajyaguru-sūtra, T.* 14, 451, trans. Birnbaum 1979: 155, 175, 181, 185, 188, 195.

30. The Five Obstacles are also mentioned in *Majjhima-nikāya,* trans. Horner 1975–77, 3: 109. Other sources include the *Aṅguttara-nikāya* 1.15: 12–16; the *Madhyamāgama, T.* 26: 607b; the *Ekottarāgama, T.* 2, 125: 757c; the *Mahīśāsa-kavinaya, T.* 22, 1421: 186a; the *Chaoriming sanmei jing, T.* 15, 638: 541–42; the *Lotus Sūtra, T.* 9, 262: 35c (trans. Hurvitz 1976: 201), and the *Dazhidulun* 2, 9, 56. On this question, see also: Nagata 1985, Iwamoto 1980: 82; Horner 1975: 291; Kajiyama 1982: 56–57; and Heidegger 1995: 10–14.

31. The locus classicus is the *Lotus Sūtra, T.* 9, 262: 35b–c. Note that the gods Brahma, Māra, and so forth, are described here as divine ranks or functions, rather than individual deities. See also: Kasahara 1975; Oguri 1987; and Groner 1989: 53–74. The knowledge that women cannot become an arhat or a *cakravartin,* or Indra, Māra, and so on, is also said to be one of the Ten "Forces" (*bala*) of the Buddha. See Nagata 1989: 21.

32. See Coates and Ishizuka 1949: 351. Here, Hōnen seems even to deny women the possibility of reaching the four highest realms of Buddhist practice, from the Once-Returners to the Arhats.

33. See Nagata 1989: 25.

34. The original Sanskrit text of the *Lotus Sūtra* regarding the Five Obstacles reads simply: "Women, until now, have never obtained the Five ranks" (pañca sthānāni stryadyāpi na prapnoti). See Taira 1990: 89.

35. See Kajiyama 1982.

36. See, for instance, the *Chōnichimyō sanmaikyō*, T. 15, 638; quoted in Iwamoto 1980: 53. Nagata Mizu, however, attributes the negative reinterpretation of earlier notions (as expressed in Abhidharma literature) to the Hinduization of Buddhism and the misogyny of the saṅgha. See Nagata 1989: 30.

37. On the Three Duties or Three Obediences, see *The Laws of Manu*, V, 148, in *Sacred Book of the East* xxv, 195; Doniger and Smith 1991: 115; see also Nakamura 1973: 70.

38. Although the expression "Three Obediences" is already found in the *Liezi*, its first appearance in Japanese literature seems to be in the *Genpei jōsuiki*.

39. See Hōnen's *Commentary on the Guan wu-liang-shou jing*, in *Hōnen. Ippen, NSTK* ed., 53.

40. See *Yüyenü jing*, T. 2, 142: 864; *Huayan jing*, T. 10, 293: 790; and *Dazhidulun 99*, T. 25, 1509: 748b. According to the latter text, however, the woman, when young, has to obey both parents, and not only her father. See also Nagata 1989: 14.

41. Thus, the *Biqiuni zhuan*, written by a male author, reports that when her father complained that leaving home is not filial, An Lingshou said: "My mind is concentrated on the work of religion, and my thought dwells exclusively on spiritual matters. . . . Why must I submit thrice [to father, husband, and son] before I am considered a woman of propriety?" See Tsai 1994: 20.

42. In the *Daikanwa jiten*, for instance, *shō* is translated by *hedateru*, *hedate* ("to separate," hence "a wall"), and this remains close to the original meaning in the *Lotus Sūtra* passage. But according to the *Nihon kokugo daijiten*, the term *sawari* means not only to present an obstacle, but also the passions and offences (*tsumi*) that hinder awakening, actions bringing a bad retribution (*zaishō*), troubles caused by war, epidemics, natural calamities, and, finally, menses (the "monthly hindrance," *tsuki no sawari*). Although the first meaning remains close to the Chinese, the others considerably deviate from it, and have a meaning akin to fault, crime, or sin (*tsumi*).

43. Quoted in Grant 1994: 16.

44. See *Kanka monsō* 12, quoted in Yoshida Kazuhiko 1989: 62.

45. Quoted in Yanagita 1990b: 450 and 455–56. See also Tokuda 1997: 81. This verse is a variant, however, of Izumi's own poem: "Since I have heard that there is neither two nor three [in the Dharma], / I know the five obstacles will not obstruct me." See Taira Yasuyori's *Hōbutsushū*, ed. Yoshida and Koizumi 1969: 427; trans. Kamens 1993: 432.

46. See Kamens 1990: 112.

47. *Shin senzai wakashū* 894; *SKT* 1, 618; quoted in Kamens 1990: 80.

48. *Mototoshi shū* 115, *SKT* 3, 470; Kamens 1990: 81.

49. Kamens 1990: 81.

50. *Shin senzai wakashū* 895; *SKT* 1, 618; Kamens, 1990: 81.

51. Kamens 1990: 81.

52. Foard 1977: 119.

53. See Embree 1944: 18.

54. Rosaldo 1974: 31.

55. On the French case, see Fabre-Vassas 1997.

56. On Indian conceptions, see Bhattacharya 1975; on Korean conceptions, see Kendall 1984.

57. See Ahern 1975: 206–14.

58. Kendall 1984: 175.

59. Ahern 1975: 212.

60. Sangren 1983: 11.

61. Ibid.

62. Ibid., 15.

63. Ibid., 24.

64. On this deity, see Berthier 1988.

65. The most defiling act was abortion because of the presence of blood and death. The penalty for the woman acting in the first three months of her pregnancy was seven days, and thirty days for those who underwent abortion later. See Marra 1993a: 49.

66. See Nishiguchi 1987.

67. *Shōyūki*, s.v. "Manju 4.8.25," 1027; quoted in Hérail 1995: 226.

68. Women are seen to be powerful through their bodies, the source of pleasure and of life. Yet because of their alleged powers, women must be separated, divided, and pitted against one another. See Verdier 1979: 323–44.

69. Douglas 1966: 140–42.

70. Morrell 1985: 74–75.

71. Ibid.

72. Despite their impurity, pregnant women sometimes serve as mediators with the invisible world: thus, the Kasuga deity takes possession of a pregnant lady of the Tachibana clan to reveal its oracle to the priest Myōe. See Tyler 1990: 269–84.

73. In Western culture, too, the alleged negative properties of menstrual blood make it all the more attractive to magicians. There was a genuine fear of menstrual blood in antiquity (as can be seen from spells). Pliny points out that all plants are contaminated by proximity to a menstruating woman. See Pliny, *Natural History*, 19.176.

74. See White 1996.

75. See Lang 1986; White 1996, 1999: 271.

76. See White 1996.

77. Daoist "inner alchemy" (*neidan*) was also open to certain women. A Qing text entitled *The Queen Mother of the West's Ten Precepts on the True Path of Women's Practice* describes how to "slay the red dragon": the woman must first restore the blood lost in menstruation. In order to do so, she must "cultivate the menses" by entering a state of awareness in which she becomes able to circulate her *qi* (life force) through the body, to transform her bodily fluids into blood, and ultimately to transform her blood into *qi*. See Mann 1997a: 72; Furth 1999.

78. Wile 1992: 204.

79. This symbolism was used to justify the red color of Daruma's robe, which itself symbolized the placenta. See Faure 1995. The legendary founder of Chan/Zen, Bodhidharma (Jp. Daruma) was definitely a "red monk"; even his beard is said to have been red in some sources. For a detailed discussion of this "bloody" figure, see Faure (forthcoming).

80. Miyata 1993b: 260.

81. Ibid., 256.

82. Ibid., 156.

83. This calls to mind the case of the virgin goddess Kumārī, in Nepal, on which see Allen 1996.

84. See Tanaka 1996: 50–60.

85. Hasegawa 1980: 24. See also Yanagita 1990b: 449.

86. *Hōnen's Kurodani shōnin wago tōroku*, question 145; quoted in Iinuma 1990: 40.

87. See Hori 1995: 38.

88. Yoshie Akiko has shown that Shintō menstruation prohibitions were largely a product of Nichiren's time. See Yoshie 1989; see also Cornyetz 1995: 55.

89. Cornyetz 1995: 40–42.

90. See Iinuma 1990.

91. See *Fūga wakashū* 2099 and 2100.

92. See Morrell 1985.

93. Miyata 1989: 35–36.

94. See translation in Nakano 1993: 80–82. Concerning this text, see also Soymié 1965.

95. According to the *Poxie xiangbian,* for instance, the *Blood Bowl Sūtra* was used in a Chinese "new religion" (labelled "heretic teaching"), the Hongyang jiao. On this question, see Sawada 1975b.

96. Another *baojuan* says that women "stain Heaven and earth when [they] give birth to children. . . . When you are a man's wife you cannot avoid the blood-stained water . . . and the sin of offending the Sun, Moon, and Stars (i.e., the "Three Luminaries," *sanguang*)." See Topley 1975: 75.

97. See Makita 1976: 79–80; Soymié 1965: 112.

98. See *Huangshinü dui Jingang* ("Woman Huang explicates the *Diamond Sūtra*"), quoted in Grant 1989: 267.

99. Ibid., 267–70. See also Carlitz 1986, chapter 3 ("Religion in the *Chin p'ing mei*"); Sawada 1975b; and Chen 1974.

100. Cole 1998: 201.

101. Grant 1989: 263. Insofar as we have here a relationship between mother and daughter, a more apt parallel could be that of Chūjōhime.

102. Ibid., 289.

103. See Seaman 1981.

104. See Sawada 1975b.

105. Other examples include the "Hymn of the Blood Pond Hell" (*Chi no ike jigoku wasan*), and the "Hymn of the Barren Woman" (*Umazume jigoku wasan*). See Minamoto 1993: 96; and Nakano 1993: 78.

106. Hagiwara 1988: 20.

107. See Bodiford 1993: 207.

108. See the *Shōwa Teiho Sōtōshū gyōki kihan* (ed. 1967), quoted in Nakano 1998. Although political correctness has led to suppression of this passage in the 1988 edition (*Shōwa shūtei Sōtōshū gyōji kihan*), the *Ketsubongyō* was until recently transmitted during nun ordination at Sōjiji, and it is still sometimes put into coffins in provincial funerals. See also the *Zenmon jūshiki gyōji gaku zensho* (Explanation of the Ordination Ceremony), Tokyo: Kōmeisha, 1952.

109. See, for instance, the "Ryū no daiji" (Talisman to Stop Defilement) in Sugimoto 1938: 17; see also Ishikawa 1984: 165.

110. See Tamamuro 1963: 175–77; and Takemi 1983.

111. On the *nagare kanjō*, see also *Jakushōdō kokkyōshū*, 281b; and Seidel 1992–93. The term *kanjō* (Skt. *abhiṣeka*, "unction," used for Tantric ordination) in the name of this ritual is found in other rituals concerned with the deliverance from the Blood Pool. Another type was practiced in Tochigi Prefecture to save women who had died in labor: a banner with the nenbutsu written on it was erected by the side of a stream, for passers-by to wet it with a bamboo ladle. When the writing on the banner has been washed down, the women are said to be freed from the Blood Pond.

112. See Seidel 1992–93; Soymié 1965: 145.

113. This legend gives a detailed description of the Blood Pond Hell. There are actually three kinds of Blood Pond Hells: that of the doubting mind (*gishin chi no ike*), for women who do not believe in the Buddha because of their jealous minds; that of false views (*jaken chi no ike*), for ignorant, arrogant women who do not give alms, who get angry at men, and who boast and calumniate others; and that of one's own fever (*ji netsu chi no ike*), into which fall women who have committed a crime. Although all women are bound to fall into one of these three hells, the second hell is more particularly reserved to women who commit the horrible sin of resisting men. See Nakano 1998.

114. See the *Samyutta-nikāya*, trans. Feer 1884–98, vol. 4: 239; quoted in Kloppenborg 1995: 163.

115. Burlingame 1921: 307–8.

116. See Overmyer 1985: 245.

117. This name calls to mind the story of the "wife of Mr. Ma" (*Malang fu*), another incarnation of Guanyin, on which see *Fozu tongji, T.* 49, 2035: 380c, and Stein 1986: 54–61.

118. See Overmyer 1985: 246–49.

119. *Jingpingmei* 1.1b, quoted in Overmyer 1985: 251.

120. *Jingpingmei* 1. 2a, quoted in ibid.

121. Overmyer 1985: 252.

122. Ibid., 284–85. See Carlitz 1986, chapter 3; Sawada 1975b; Chen 1974.

123. On the text attributed to Huiyuan, see Cole 1998: 194–95. On the *Ise nindenki*, see Faure 2000.

124. McCullough 1988: 321.

125. See *Visuddhimagga* xvi, 37–38, trans. Ñanamoli 1975: 569–70.

126. Niimura 1994: 272–73.

127. By the Tang with the Daoist Sun Simiao, and later with the *Furen liang-fang*, we already find suggestions as to how one might change the gender of the fetus. In the Buddhist context, this sex change was achieved by specific Tantric rituals centered on the Wisdom-King Ucchuṣma (Jp. Ususama Myōō).

128. Niimura 1994: 256.

129. See Mori Eijun, ed., *Seizan Shōnin tanpen shōmono shū*, Bun'eidō shoten 1980; quoted in Niimura 1994: 278.

130. See also Bareau 1979, and Filliozat 1991b.

131. Niimura 1994: 280. On the impurity of the womb, see, for instance, in the *Konjaku monogatari shū* the story of the future mother of Shōtoku Taishi, who dreams that a monk (actually a manifestation of Guze Kannon) wants to come into her. She objects that her womb is too unclean. The monk then enters through her mouth, and she wakes up pregnant. See *Konjaku monogatari shū* 11. 1, ed. Yamada et al. 1959–63, vol. 3: 52.

132. See Kapani 1989b: 187. See also: Héritier-Augé 1989; Keswani 1962; and Aristotle, *Generation of Animals*, trans. A. L. Peck. London and Cambridge, MA: Loeb Classical Library, 1963.

133. On the red and the white in ancient Iran, see the Pahlavi text discussed in Lincoln 1991: 218–27.

134. Rousselle 1988: 31–32; see also Augé-Héritier 1989: 168.

135. See Bloch and Parry 1982: 20–21.

136. Rawski 1988: 26–27.

137. Chayet 1993: 180–81.

138. See Waltner 1990: 29–37.

139. *Yanagidaru* 43, 8, quoted in Cholley 1996: 96.

140. Cholley 1996: 96–97.

141. See *Konkōshō*, in *Kinsei bukkyō shūsetsu*, op. cit., 247.

142. *Konkōshō*, ibid., 247.

143. *Garbha-upaniṣad*, trans. Kapani 1989a: 178; see also Kapani 1989b.

144. Morrell 1985: 184.

145. The same conception, mutatis mutandis, was found in the American South, where the fetus of a slave woman belonged to the master. Just like in modern feminism, for reasons having to do with what Foucault would call "bio-power," and what Dorothy Roberts calls "the dark side of birth control," the fetus was perceived as in conflict with the mother. See Roberts 1997.

146. See, for instance, Raymond 1998.

147. See Wakita 1985b: 186–93. From a Buddhist standpoint, in theory mother and child are one. In a Sōtō *kirigami*, for instance, we find the following exchange between master and disciple. The master asks: "When someone dies in labour, and child and mother are not distinct, is it necessary to separate them for the funeral?" The disciple replies: "Since they are fundamentally one body, what's the need to separate them?" There follows a discussion about emptiness, in which the master argues that, although all things are ultimately empty, one still distinguishes between the mother's body and the embryo within it. In such case, he asks, "Are the mother and the child one, or two?" The disciple replies in typical Zen fashion: "Coming originally from no-rank, they return to no-rank. Even if

there were myriad bodily divisions, there is only one person." The master finally approves. See Sugimoto 1938: 123.

148. In some Christian spells, the womb is compared to a tomb (and birth implicitly to resurrection): "Come out of your tomb, Christ is calling you." See Aubert 1989: 439. Buddhists do not seem to have conceived of the womb as a living animal, as has Western tradition since Plato, down to Rabelais and Montaigne (and beyond). In the West, magic aimed at "restricting the freedom of movement of the womb which, as an animal, demon, or deity, was thought to have a natural inclination to move about inside the female body." See idem, 425.

149. See Rousselle 1988: 4

150. Note, however, that in Tantric conceptions the traditional color symbolism (red yang, white yin) is inverted: because the male seed (yang) is assimilated to the semen, it is white, while the female seed (yin), assimilated to blood, is red.

151. This motif seems to appear with the *Gogin wakashū* by Ishida Mitoku (ca. 1661–72).

152. See Goux 1990: 213, 221.

153. Laqueur 1990: 207.

154. Ibid., n. 36, 255.

155. Ibid., 42.

156. After all, the spermatozoid was only discovered in 1677 by Louis de Ham, a discovery which (for a time) restored male prestige. But it is only two centuries later, in 1875, that the true nature of fecundation was established by Van Beneden, and that the old myths of "sacred embryology" were put to rest. On this question, see Darmon 1981. It is about the same time that, in Japan, the notion of the "two seeds" was practically abandoned for that of the "borrowed womb."

157. Laqueur 1990: 57.

158. Goux 1990: 225.

159. Yoshie 1995: 298.

CHAPTER 3

1. See Renondeau 1960: 44–56.

2. See *Ryōjin hishō* 116, trans. Kim 1994: 81.

3. *T.* 9:35c, trans. Hurvitz 1976: 201.

4. For more on this question, see infra.

5. The famous *Lotus Sūtra* commentary attributed to Shōtoku Taishi is based on a recension in 27 chapters, in which the Devadatta chapter is missing. The story appeared with the 28-chapter recension, which seems to date from the time of Zhiyi (a contemporary of Shōtoku) and arrived in Japan during the Nara period. Even so, the new commentaries on the *Lotus Sūtra* do not seem to pay special attention to this chapter. See Yoshida 1989: 59–60.

6. *Dengyō Daishi zenshū* 3: 261; quoted in Groner 1989: 61.

7. *Dengyō Daishi zenshū* 3: 265.

8. Groner 1989: 68.

9. See *Kaimokushō*, pt. 2; trans. Yampolsky 1990: 121.

10. Ibid., 121–22. A similar point is made by the Edo scholar Tominaga Nakamoto; see Tominaga 1990: 119–20.

11. See Nabata, ed. *Shinranshū Nichirenshū*, 460.

12. Yoshida 1989: 49–57.

13. Watson 1993: 188.

14. Yamamoto 1993: 243–44.

15. See *Keiran shūyōshū*, T. 76, 2410: 599a; and Yamamoto 1993: 244.

16. *Keiran shūyōshū*, T. 75, 2410: 544b.

17. On the relationship between the *nāga* and relics, see Tanaka 1993; Faure 1998c.

18. Yamamoto 1993: 244–45.

19. Ibid., 249.

20. See, for instance, *Keiran shūyōshū*, T. 76, 2410: 622b-624a.

21. Yamamoto 1993: 252.

22. *Keiran shūyōshū*, T. 76, 2410: 517c.

23. Ibid., 623c.

24. T. 76, 2410: 517c.

25. *Ryōjin hishō*, no. 292, trans. Kim 1994: 81–82.

26. *Ryōjin hishō*, no. 113, ibid., 82.

27. *Ryōjin hishō*, no. 208, ibid., 82.

28. McCullough 1988: 436.

29. Ibid., 378.

30. On this question, see Faure 1998c.

31. It may seem strange that in the *Heike monogatari* the *nāga* realm (normally perceived as belonging to the animal destiny) would be listed after the other planes of rebirth, and in particular after the infernal realms. It is at the same time the deepest hell and the gateway beyond hell, toward the Pure Land. As the source of all delusion, it can be identified with the ultimate principle of the world of *saṃsāra*. In Kenreimon'in's description, some aspects of the Taira flight may also be interpreted as a reference to the animal path. For instance, before killing himself, the Middle Captain declares: "We are like fish in a net; there is no escape, no matter where we go. What chance do I have of living out my life?" Thus, the animal realm became *dis*-located, presented first as the world of land and water animals preyed upon by hunters, and then as the semi-divine (yet paradoxically afflicted) realm of the *nāga*. In this light, the whole Taira epic, seen from the standpoint of the "consecration chapter," becomes an initiatory death and rebirth, and the dream of the *nāga*-palace, far from being an anticlimax, becomes the turning point of the narrative.

32. *Ryōjin hishō*, no. 117, trans. Kim 1994: 82.

33. According to the *Bahudhātuka-sutta*: "It is impossible, it cannot come to pass that a woman who is a perfected one could be a complete and perfect buddha." See *Bahudhātuka-sutta* 3:65, quoted in Shaw 1994: 27. Again, in the *Bodhisattvabhūmi*, we hear that "completely perfected buddhas are not women. And why? Precisely because a bodhisattva has completely abandoned the state of womanhood. Ascending to the most excellent throne of enlightenment, he is never again born as a woman. All women are by nature full of defilement and of weak intelligence. And not by one who is by nature full of defilement and of weak intelligence is completely perfected Buddhahood obtained." Quoted in ibid.

34. See Durt 1996. On the *pāli* tradition, see G. P. Malalasekera, *Dictionary of Pāli Proper Names*, London: John Murray, 1938, 2: 608–10. The question of Māya's blood pollution was piously avoided in East Asian Buddhism. We recall that Gautama's birth was a bloodless affair, but even so, Māya must have experienced the usual womanly predicament. The scriptures remain conspicuously silent on this point.

35. *Sukhāvatīvyūha-sūtra*, *T.* 12, 360: 368c.

36. See Taira 1989, 1990, 1992; and Heidegger 1995: 14–16.

37. See Rambelli (forthcoming).

38. Paul 1979: 170.

39. Bapat 1957: 210.

40. The *Sāratthadīpanī*, a subcommentary on the *Samantapāsādikā* (Chin. *Shanjianlü piposha*, *T.* 24, 1462), explains, for instance, that a man could turn into a woman after committing acts such as adultery. On the contrary, a woman could be transformed into a man when her negative karma was exhausted, providing that she led a pure life, and that she entertained "a strong aspiration to become a man." See Bapat 1957: 211.

41. We still occasionally hear echoes of the earlier theory, for instance in the Vinaya. Even in Japan, we find cases of men and women, in particular monks and nuns, crossing the gender line. See, for instance, the *Jakushōdō kokkyōshū*, 256b, 300–301; and Faure 1998a: 77–78.

42. The notion that becoming a man is necessary for salvation was also found in Daoism. Female Daoist adepts were supposed to "slay the red dragon" (that is, stop their menses) before being able to jump the gender divide.

43. See Schuster 1981.

44. *T.* 14, 564: 918; a variant recension is *T.* 563, entitled *Fuzhong nüting jing* (*Sūtra on a Woman Hearing [the Dharma] in the Womb*). See also Paul 1979: 175–76. Other references include the *Chaoriming sanmei jing* (*T.* 15, 638) and the *Wusuoyou pusa jing* (*T.* 14, 485). Incidentally, this legend may have reinforced the Japanese belief that gender could be changed in utero through specific Buddhist rituals.

45. See *Gōtō tokunagon ganmon shū*, by Ōe no Masafusa, quoted in Nishiguchi 1987: 106.

46. See poem no. 16, in Kamens 1990: 91.

47. See poem no. 47, in ibid. On the the Eight Vows of the Medicine Buddha in the *Lotus Sūtra*, see *T.* 9: 54c; and Hurvitz 1976: 300. See also Iwamoto 1980; Yoshida 1989: 45–91.

48. See Kamens 1990: 123.

49. No. 48; see *T.* 9: 56a; Hurvitz 1976: 308. According to the "Bodhisattva Wonder Sound" chapter of the *Lotus Sūtra*, "even in the inner courts of a king, transforming itself into a woman he preaches this Sūtra. . . . This bodhisattva Wonder Sound is one who is able to save and protect all the living in the *sahā-world*."

50. See Kamens 1990: 124.

51. We recall that the rank of the god Brahma was one of the Five Obstacles, that is, one of the five ranks denied to women. See *Kōmyō shingon giki*, quoted in Yamamoto 1993: 258. See also the Yakushi ritual described in the *Yakushi*

hongankyō, based on the eighth of Yakushi's Twelve Vows. Another important ritual centered on Ususama—the Wisdom King (*myōō*) who purifies all defilements—was performed to change the gender of a child within the womb, more precisely to transform the impure (female) fetus into a pure (male) one. See *Asaba shō*, chapter "Ususama," op. cit., 260. This sex change, however, was motivated by patrilineal strategies, rather than by soteriological ambitions.

52. *T.* 81, 2578: 668c–669a.

53. Chan Sin-wai 1985: 109–10.

54. See Yamamoto 1993: 262.

55. *Hokekyō jikidanshō*, quoted in Yamamoto 1993: 261; See also *Keiran shūyōshū*, T. 76, 2410: 609c.

56. See Yamamoto 1993: 264.

57. See, for instance, Kajiyama 1982.

58. Schuster 1984: 54.

59. Ibid., 55.

60. Ibid., 60.

61. Ibid., 56.

62. On Tiantai interpretations, see Paul 1979: 282–84; on the *Nāga-sūtra*, see also ibid., 232–41.

63. The latter metaphor was perhaps not a happy or realistic one, as pachydermic sex is by no means an easy affair, as Michel Strickmann has argued (tongue in cheek). See Strickmann 1996.

64. Queen Śrīmālādevī is hailed as female buddha by Diana Paul, who writes that "feminine images of Buddhahood are a contradiction in terms if asexuality denotes the male state. . . . The portrait of Śrīmālā is an exception to the traditional association of the feminine with sexuality and the masculine with asexuality." See Paul 1979: 287; and idem, 1980a: 100, 225.

65. See, for instance, the "Ten Ailments" of woman in the *Yuyenü jing*, T. 2, 142: 863c; quoted in Kajiyama 1982: 62.

66. *T.* 9:54c, trans. Hurvitz 1976: 300.

67. Kamens 1990: 125.

68. See Kajiyama 1982: 68–69; Kajiyama bases his argument on the *Akṣobhyatathāgatavyūha* (Chin. *Achufoguo jing*, T. 11, 313), a text anterior to the *Sukhavativyūha*, in which it is said that in the buddhaland of Akṣobhya women do not experience the pains of pregnancy and delivery. Although the dream of a female existence free from suffering seems older than that of a sex change, the fact remains that it was abandoned to the benefit of the latter. See also Heidegger 1995: 19–20.

69. For a similar structure in Christianity, see Albert 1997: 239–41.

70. See Heidegger 1995: 20; and Paul 1979: 170–79.

71. See Hardacre 1990: 52.

72. Hardacre 1990: 57.

73. Hardacre 1990: 221.

74. *Soga monogatari*, trans. Cogan 1987: 291–92.

75. See *Guan wuliangshou jing* T. 12, 365:268; and Max-Müller 1894: 19.

76. See Kasahara, 1975.

77. See ibid. and idem, 1983; see also Oguri 1987.

78. The same is true for priests like Hōnen, Ippen, or Nichiren, the latter calling himself "son of a *caṇḍāla.*"

79. On this point, see Amino 1989.

80. See Matsuo 1989.

81. Myōe's community, for instance, differed radically from *kansō* communities, and its founder can therefore no longer be simply labelled as a "reformer" of ancient Buddhism. Admittedly, Myōe worked to reform the Kegon school, and he joined *kenmitsu* priests in denouncing Hōnen's Pure Land teaching. In 1206, he received official recognition from Go-Toba Tennō. Myōe had been officially ordained at Tōdaiji in 1188, but he became a recluse-monk in 1195. His disciples, both monks and nuns, were also recluses, wearing the distinctive black robe. According to Matsuo, Myōe's biography shows that he, and therefore recluse-monks, worked actively for the salvation of women. See Matsuo 1989: 104.

82. See *Hōnen. Ippen,* ed. NSTK, 164.

83. Coates and Ishizuka 1949, vol. 2: 353.

84. See *Hōnen shōnin zenshū,* 336–44; and ibid., 344–53. See also *Ippyaku yonjūgo kojō mondō* [ibid., 380–401]. The same discourse was developed in later Pure Land tradition. For Shinran, see *Jōdo wasan* in NKBT, *Shinran shū. Nichiren shū,* 56, 78. See also *Nyonin ōjōshū* (Muromachi period), in Ryūkoku Library, edited by Kasahara, 296–300, and discussed in ibid., 244–51. On Rennyo and women's rebirth, see ibid., 254–82.

85. See Nagata 1989: 12.

86. Matsuo 1989: 111, 125.

87. See the *Shibunritsu chū bikunikai hon* (*Commentary on the Fourfold Vinaya, Precepts for Nuns*), Kanazawa bunko, *Shiryō zensho,* vol. 5, Kairitsu-hen 1, ed. Kanagawaken Kanazawa bunko 1981; quoted in Hosokawa 1989b: 142.

88. The *Fanwang jing* (*T.* 24, 1484) emphasizes filial piety. See Ishida 1971: 57.

89. Hosokawa 1989b: 153–56.

90. Nishiguchi 1991: 23.

91. In 1950, various objects were discovered in three parts of the body (head, torso, thigh) of a "nude" statue of Jizō, together with a number of dedication texts (*ganmon*) and a list of over 260 people related to the project. The only dated *ganmon* (1228) in the statue was that of a nun named Yuishin, who asks to be reborn in the body of a man in the next life. Her plea is drawn from the *Jizō hongankyō,* which states that women may petition Jizō to gain rebirth as men.

92. Nishiguchi 1991: 25.

93. An exception is the paradise of the Buddha Amitayus (Jp. Ashuku)—although there is no sexual desire there, and childbirth is painless for the blessed women who inhabit this paradise.

94. Nishiguchi 1991: 20.

95. See Minakata 1971–73, bekkan 1: 608–14, quoting the *Wakan sansai zue.* We are here in a world that, more than that of Buddhist soteriology, recalls that of Herculine Barbin, the transsexual whose tragic life-story was studied by Michel Foucault (see Foucault 1980b). Significantly, Minakata makes no connection with our Buddhist theme, and focuses on the teratological elements (sudden growth of male or female genitals and so forth). On this question, see also Faure 1998a,

chapters 2 and 5. As to bisexuality, it was seen in Buddhism as even worse than femaleness.

96. For a review of the criticisms addressed to *hongaku* thought by "Critical Buddhism" (*hihan bukkyō*), and a nuanced discussion of the issues involved, see Stone 1999.

97. For a hyperbolic criticism of the *hongaku* thought in this respect, see Nakano 1998.

CHAPTER 4

1. Weber 1963: 104.

2. Kelly 1984: 28. See also Sered 1994: 5.

3. Sered 1994: 209.

4. *Samyutta-nikāya* I: 129, trans. Murcott 1991: 158–59. See also Lang 1986: 77; and Grant 1995: 158–59.

5. Thurman 1976: 61–62.

6. See Heidegger 1995.

7. A similar viewpoint, downplaying the sex change or omitting it altogether, is expressed in various commentaries on the *Lotus Sūtra*, such as the *Fahua yishu* (*T.* 34, 1721: 592b) or the *Fahua wenju ji* (*T.* 34, 1719: 314b).

8. See *Sāgaranāgarāja pariprcchā*, *T.* 15, 598: 149–50; see also Paul 1979: 233–41. The same structure is found in the story of Vimaladatta: see *Vimala-dattapariprcchā*, *T.* 12, 338 and 339, and the recension of the same text contained in *Mahāratnakūta*, *T*.11, 310 (33). See also Iwamoto 1980: 71.

9. See Paul 1979. Paul's teleological vision of Mahāyāna depicts women's spiritual progress according to a classification into four types, illustrating the gradual improvement in the attitudes toward women. These are: 1. Scriptures that hold a negative attitude toward women (the vast majority); 2. Scriptures (like the *Larger Sukhāvatīvyūha-sūtra*) that deny women's presence in the Pure Land(s); 3. Scriptures accepting women as low-stage bodhisattvas; and 4. Scriptures accepting women as advanced bodhisattvas and imminent buddhas.

10. Schuster 1984: 52.

11. The act of truth has been defined by Burlingame as "a formal declaration of fact, accompanied by a command or resolution or prayer that the purpose of the agent shall be accomplished." See Burlingame 1917; W. N. Brown 1940.

12. *T.* 12, 338: 95c.

13. Schuster 1984: 39.

14. See the *Strītivartavyākarana-sūtra*, *T.* 14, 566, the *Aśokadattavyākarana*, *T.* 12, 337, apropos Princess Aśokadattā, and the recension of the *Mahāratna-kūta*, *T.* 310 (32); quoted in Iwamoto 1980: 60.

15. One exception to this rule is a Japanese story in which the bodhisattva Kannon (Avalokiteśvara, usually perceived as female in East Asia) manifests itself as a young boy (*chigo*) to reward an old monk. But even in this case, we are dealing with "male love" (*nanshoku*), a term that has no female equivalent. On this question, see Faure 1998a.

16. See Stein 1972: 120–22.

17. Cabezón 1992b: 186.

18. *Lam rim chen mo*, quoted in ibid., 191.

19. Ibid., 188.

20. Ibid., 190.

21. See Weber 1963: 104.

22. Quoted in van Gulik 1971: 425.

23. See Bloch 1992: 78.

24. Shaw 1994: 28–31.

25. Bharati 1965: 203.

26. Ibid., 210.

27. Ibid., 210–213.

28. Ibid., 56–57.

29. The hypothesis of Tantric inversion has been recently criticized, however; see Marglin 1982: 61.

30. See *Guhyasamāja-tantra*, quoted in ibid., 58.

31. Gyatso 1987: 248.

32. On the woman as altar, see the *Bṛhadāraṇyaka Upaniṣad*: "Her lap is a sacrificial altar, her hair the sacrificial grass; her skin, the soma press. The two lips of the vulva are the fire": quoted in Shaw 1994: 163.

33. Miranda Shaw has attempted to make a case for a feminist reading of the Indo-Tibetan Tantric tradition. She idealizes Tantrism, however, when she takes Tantric egalitarian discourse at face-value—a fixation on principle that makes one prone to overlook the actual exploitation of women. The Tantric recognition of femaleness as ontologically primary and maleness as derivative and dependent does not translate into "a deference to women in social and ritual context." Strangely, the female voices retrieved by Shaw sound very much like those of men. As to the rituals in which, Shaw argues, women were central figures, she fails to adduce any evidence of their actual performance. See Shaw 1994: 132, 174, and passim. Meanwhile the Tibetologist Anne Chayet is of the opinion that "known Tantric rituals seem to have been written for men." See Chayet 1993: 314.

34. Shaw 1994: 38–41.

35. Ibid.

36. Chayet 1993: 305.

37. See Volkmann 1995; see also Gyatso 1987.

38. These twelve points form three concentric squares whose perimeters were formed by the shoulders and hips, elbows and knees, and wrists and ankles, respectively, to which was added Lhasa's main temple, the Jokhang, a symbolic nail stuck at the heart of the demoness.

39. Gyatso 1987: 44–45.

40. Volkman 1995: 195.

41. Ibid., 196.

42. Ibid.

43. Ibid., 200.

44. Ibid., 203

45. This may point to a fertility ritual involving human sacrifice. As a figure of death, Palden Lhamo also recalls the Hindu godess Iyeṣthā, or the "old hag" of the Japanese tradition, Datsueba. On the former, see Volkmann 1995; on the latter, see Seidel 1992–93.

46. Volkman 1995: 210.

47. Ibid., 211.

48. Of course, the Chan discussion of karma is more complex than we will be able to ascertain here. For a detailed analysis, see Heine 1999.

49. Quoted in Jay 1992: 117.

50. See Ōkubo Dōshu, *Dōgen zenji zenshū*, Chikuma shobō, 1969–70, vol. 1: 252.

51. See Adamek 1996.

52. T. 51, 2075: 192a–b. See also Yanagida Seizan, *Shoki no zenshi II: Rekidai hōbōki*, Chikuma shobō, 1976: 254–57.

53. Levering 1998: 109–10.

54. *Dahui pushuo*, ZZ 1, 31, 5: 455a.

55. Ibid., 433b, in Levering 1982: 20.

56. The encounter of Miaozong (Mujaku) with Wan'an Daoyan (1094–1164) is described in the *Wujia zhenzong zan*, in ZZ 2b, 8: 475a; quoted in Levering 1997: 152–53.

57. See Ruch 1990.

58. Levering 1992: 20; quoting *Dahui pushuo*, in ZZ 1, 31, 5: 455a.

59. On Jingcheng, see *Biqiuni zhuan*; trans. Tsai 1994; see also Zürcher 1991: 67–74.

60. *Dahui Pujue chanshih yulu*, T.47, 1998a: 909b.

61. Levering 1992, 1997.

62. *Jingde chuandeng lu*, T. 51, 2076: 289a; trans. Levering 1982: 28.

63. Liaoran's story was often cited in the Dharma instructions given by Chan masters. For example, Hongzhi mentioned it several times in the *Hongzhi chanshi guanglu*. See T. 48, 2001: 16b, 32b, 42b, 44c, and 47b. Dahui and Yuanwu also recounted her story as examplary when they were giving instruction (ibid., 32b. 44c, and 94b). The *Yuanwu Foguo chanshi yulu* retells the story; see T. 48, 1997: 779b.

64. *Jingde chuandeng lu*, T. 51, 2076: 294c.

65. Grant 1994: 78.

66. Ibid., 79.

67. Ibid., 80.

68. Ibid., 34–35. See also the call to reform of Tan Sitong (1865–98), in Chan 1985: 109–10.

69. Goldfuss 1994: 23.

70. Ibid., 28.

71. Ibid., 29–30.

72. *Shōbōgenzō*, "Raihai tokuzui," T. 82, 2582: 36c; see also Terada and Mizuno 1970, vol. 1: 326, and Levering 1982: 31.

73. Terada and Mizuno 1970: 25.

74. In the Kamakura period, however, *kana* was not an exclusively "feminine" script, as is sometimes claimed.

75. See Terada and Mizuno 1970, vol. 1: 322; trans. in Yokoi 1976: 234.

76. Yokoi 1976: 355; Terada and Mizuno 1970, vol. 1: 323. This passage is not found, however, in the seventy-five fascicle *Shōbōgenzō*, but only in the twenty-eight fascicle *himitsu* ("secret") *Shōbōgenzō*.

77. Terada and Mizuno 1970, vol. 1: 327–29; see also Heidegger 1995: 82–83.

78. See Yokoi 1976: 78; Terada and Mizuno 1970, vol. 2: 323.

79. See Weinstein 1973.

80. *Eihei kōroku,* in *DZZ* 2: 155.

81. Several scholars have described Myōe's idealization of the mother figure in his worship of the female deity Butsugen Butsumo, the "mother of all Buddhas." See, for instance, Tanabe 1992: 55–57. As to Shinran's well-known dream of Kannon at Rokkakudō, see infra, chapter 5. The motif of Kannon leading men to salvation through carnal love was already widespread in China. See Stein 1986.

82. See, for instance, *Denkōroku,* T. 82, 2585: 392b, 403a. On Keizan and women, see Ishikawa 1993; Aotatsu 1974; and Sōtōshū nisōshi hensankai, ed. 1955.

83. See Nishiguchi 1987: 22–42.

84. *Tōkokuki,* in Kohō 1976: 395.

85. Ibid., 401.

86. Uchino 1983: 178.

87. For an analysis of this topos, see Lachaud 1998.

88. *Ninin bikuni,* trans. in Tyler 1977: 23.

89. See Harada 1997: 173.

90. Derrida 1992: 109.

CHAPTER 5

1. See *Xu Gaoseng zhuan, T.* 50, 2060: 541c.

2. See, for instance, Kvaerne 1975; for the Indian Tantric context, see White 1996.

3. In the *Lotus Sūtra,* the Buddha himself is presented symbolically as a father, that of the prodigal son, which is every one of us. In Buddhist legend, Śākyamuni's real fatherhood is also displaced onto the spiritual plan, making him the spiritual teacher of his son Rāhula. The relation between him and Rāhula is emphasized in early Buddhism at the detriment of the relation between son and mother; however, After Śākyamuni's return to Kapilavastu and the subsequent reunion of father and son, we hear little of Rāhula.

4. See also Tominaga 1990: 181.

5. Perhaps this story is influenced by the notion that the "intermediary being" (*antarābhava*) whose descent is necessary for conception to take place would enter the woman's body through her genitalia, not through the mouth—a case reserved to the reincarnation of the purest bodhisattvas.

6. See Faure 1996: 35.

7. See *Nihon Tōjō shosoden,* in *DNBZ* 110: 13b, 17b. An interesting variant is found in the case of Myōe's mother, who went to a temple with her two daughters to pray for another child. She dreamed that someone gave her oranges. The younger sister had the same dream, but the elder sister stole her oranges, and it is she who eventually became pregnant. See *Genkō shakusho* 5:16, trans. Ury 1971: 262.

8. Sangren 1983: 11. In the *Dizang pusa benyuan jing* (*Sūtra of the Original Vow of the Bodhisattva Kṣitigarbha, T.* 13, 777–90), the bodhisattva Dizang (Jp. Jizō) is represented as a woman, more precisely a daughter, in two previous lives. One of the stories is about a woman named Guangmu (Jp. Kōmoku, "Bright Eyes"), who, like Mulian, saves her greedy mother from hell. Among the many "relics" discovered inside a "nude" statue of Jizō (dated to 1228) in 1950, were a number of dedication texts (*ganmon*), in particular one signed by an eighty-three-year-old nun named Myōhō. Her motivation was to save her parents, especially her mother, by imitating the bodhisattva Kōmoku. See Sugiyama 1965; and Glassman (forthcoming).

9. On stories of mothers fallen into hell, see Wakita 1985b: 178–86.

10. Incidentally, the image of Mulian's mother better conformed to misogynist clichés than that of Māya, endowed with all feminine virtues. For the Chinese and Indian mythological backgrounds of monks saving their mothers, see Cole 1998.

11. See Glassman (forthcoming).

12. The expression comes from a verse in the *Gosenshū*. Misc. I, 1103. See Wakita 1985b: 183–85; Shirane 1987: 184–86; and Glassman 2001: 14–16.

13. See *Song gaoseng zhuan, T.* 50, 2061: 721b–722a.

14. Wakita 1985a: 178; see Ury 1979: 163–65.

15. Cole 1998: 57–58.

16. On the Ajase complex, see Kosawa 1954; Okonogi 1982; Vincent 1997; on Ajātaśatru's legend, see Durt 1997.

17. See *Guan wuliangshou jing, T.* 12, 365.

18. Tominaga Nakamoto uses this figure to infer that Westerners (by which he means Indians and Parths as well as Dutchmen) privileged the woman over the man. See Tominaga 1990; and Durt 1997.

19. See *Mosheng benyuan jing, T.* 14, 507: 775a; and *Caihuaweiwang shangfo shoujue wu miaohua jing, T.* 14, 510: 778a.

20. On Vaidehī, see *Wuliangshou jing, T.* 12, 260: 268; *Guan wuliangshou jing, T.* 12, 365: 341; see also Yamada 1984.

21. See Foucher 1927: 67.

22. *Sanbō ekotoba,* trans. Kamens 1988: 150. See also Durt 1996.

23. See Bareau 1982: 41; and Tatelman 1998.

24. Cole 1998: 69.

25. Ibid., 1.

26. Lauwaert 1991: 126. The Qing code, for instance, recognizes at least eight types of motherhood, among which the main one is not the *shengmu*, the birth mother who is not the principal spouse. The legitimate mother is the *dimu*, the main spouse of the father and the legal mother of the children born from all his spouses.

27. Cole 1998: 55. See also *Abhidharmakośa-śāstra,* trans. La Vallée Poussin 1923–31; English trans. Pruden 1988–89, vol. 2: 395–400.

28. See K. Ch'en 1973: 38–39; see also Lauwaert 1991: 143.

29. See Legendre 1985: 38.

30. See Wolf 1972: viii and 37.

31. Cole 1998: 36.

32. See Sangren 1996: 159–63.

33. For example, as Cole observes, in the *Mahāvastu* the Bodhisattva picks his mother as though he were picking a bride, and then enters her womb under the most romantic circumstances. See trans. Jones 1949–56, vol. 1: 158–63, quoted in Cole 1998: 38. Another significant case is that of the *antarābhava* ("intermediary being"), whose sexual attraction for one of his future parents will determine its gender at rebirth. See *Abhidharmakośa* 3, 12, in La Vallée Poussin 1923–32; English trans. Pruden 1988–89, vol. 2: 383–93. On this question, see also Wayman 1984.

34. See Cole 1998: 67.

35. The prowess of the lactating mother also appears in Japanese legends like the following, telling the bizarre origins of the youngest child of the pestilence god Gozu Tennō ("Oxhead King"). As the god, his wife, and his seven children are traveling from India to Japan, a monstruous snake blocks their way. When questioned by Gozu Tennō, it claims to be his eighth child, a daughter born from the discarded placentas of the other children. When Gozu Tennō's wife, understandably incredulous, presses her breasts, milk suddenly gushes forth and falls into the mouths of the seven children and the snake alike. Now convinced, she asks the snake to reveal his true nature (*honji*), and the latter then appears in the form of Eleven-Faced Kannon, standing on the waves. See Yamamoto 1998a: 519.

36. See *Konjaku monogatari shū* 5. 6, ed. Yamada et al. 1959–63: 356–57; trans. Dykstra 1986: 189. The same source also mentions the legend of Lady Rokumo ("Doe-Mother"), a young girl born from a doe. The girl is raised by a hermit. She is so pure that, when she walks in the forest, lotus flowers blossom under her feet. She eventually marries the king and gives birth to a lotus blossom. The king, disappointed, orders the lotus to be thrown into a pond, but the man charged with the task notices that on each of the five hundred leaves of the lotus flower, a tiny handsome boy is sitting. Thus, the five hundred princes are saved, and they later all become monks. See *Konjaku monogatari shū* 5. 5, ed. Yamada et al. 1959–63: 352–56; trans. Dykstra 1986: 183–87.

37. In the *Bencao gangmu*, Li Shizhen (1518–93) describes milk as "transformed yin blood" and goes on to say that "before pregnancy it appears as menses below; during pregnancy it provides nourishment of the fetus, and after birth it ascends as milk. The subtleties of these creative transformations are nature's marvels." See Lauwaert 1991: 44; and Cole 1998.

38. See Cole 1998: 71. See also *Majjhima-nikāya* 1.265, trans. See Woodward 1973: 29: "Then at the end of nine or ten months she brings it (the baby) forth, with great anxiety, a heavy burden. When it is born, she feeds it on her own blood: for 'blood,' brethren, is called mother's milk in the discipline of the Aryans."

39. *Sanbō ekotoba*, trans. Kamens 1988: 312.

40. *Nihon ryōiki* 2. 2, ed. Endō and Kasuga 1967: 177; trans. Nakamura 1973: 160.

41. See Demiéville 1973: 275–76, quoting the *Ci niang zan* (manuscript Pelliot 2713), ed. Ren Erbai, *Dunhuang qu jiaolu* [Shanghai 1955: 98–101]. A similar song, "Pleasure of entering (or 'dwelling on') the mountain," is found in the ms. Pelliot 2713. See ibid., 284–86.

42. Ibid.

43. Cole 1998: 57.

44. See *Tōkoku ki*, in *Jōsai daishi zenshū*, ed. Kōhō Chisan 1976: 733.

45. The bodhisattva Kannon, who had become a compassionate female figure in China, appears as the sublimated double of the mother. Significantly, Keizan placed inside this statue his own umbilical cord and birth-hair, which had been preserved by his mother.

46. See Lévy 1985, 1: 830–35.

47. Ibid.

48. See *Shōbōgenzō zuimonki*, 4.10 ed. Nishio et al. 1965: 393. In his *Shōbōgenzō*, Dōgen contrasts Huineng's merit with that of two famous Tang emperors: "Although the emperors Daizong and Suzong constantly associated with monks, they were too attached to their rank to forsake it. Layman Lu [Huineng], having forsaken his mother, became a patriarch. Such is the merit of becoming a monk." See *Shōbōgenzō* "Shukke kudoku," *T.* 82, 2582: 283a; trans. Yokoi 1976: 79. In a recension of the *Platform Sūtra*, where Huineng's story first appears, he has become a second Buddha, immaculately conceived by his mother. He does not even owe her any milk-debt, since he did not actually drink her milk, but was instead fed ambrosia by the gods. See Yampolsky 1967: 60–63.

49. *Shōbōgenzō*, *T.* 82, 2582: 283a.

50. See *Shōbōgenzō zuimonki*, 4.10 ed. Nishio et al. 1965: 393.

51. On this question, see Ch'en 1968: 15–50.

52. See Tominaga 1990: 181–82. Tominaga adds in a footnote that "the affair of the Ōbaku monk Daigito is mentioned in the *Shōjusan*." It is unclear to me at this point, however, who this monk was.

53. See Frank 1989: 480–81; and Sugano 1985.

54. See Frank 1989: 257–66.

55. Ibid., 262.

56. See Hirabayashi 1978; and Miyazaki 1979.

57. See Takagi 1988: 224.

58. See *Honchō monsui* 13, quoted in Takagi 1988: 243. The person who wrote the vow on behalf of Chōnen was a well-known scholar, Yoshishige no Yasutane, who became a monk under the name of Jakushin the same year Chōnen returned to Japan. After Jakushin's death in 1002, one of his disciples, Jakushō, went to China, where he died thirty-two years later. Jakushō's ordination was prompted by the death of the woman he loved. According to his biography, he could not bring himself to bury her body, and decided to become a monk while contemplating her decaying body, following the topos of the "nine aspects of death." Jakushō left behind a mother and a son, the latter himself a Hieizan monk. According to the *Zoku Honchō ōjōden*, before leaving Japan he performed a *Hokke hakkō* ritual for his mother. In the vow written on that occasion, he refers to the vow written by Yasutane on behalf of Chōnen's mother. See *Senjūshō* 9.2, ed. Nishio 1970: 278–79.

59. Seiryōji, more popularly known as Shaka-dō because of this statue, was initially named after Qingliangsi, Mañjuśrī's cultic center on Mount Wutai. The statue is still preserved there, and its fame has even increased since the discovery, inside it, of many objects (including cloth viscerae). On this question, see Henderson and Hurvitz 1956.

60. See *Konjaku monogatari shū* 15. 39, in Yamada et al. 1959–63, vol. 3: 356–59. Genshin was a disciple of Ryōgen (912–85), a Tendai abbot who was also concerned with the salvation of women. See Gotō 1984.

61. See *Tōkoku ki*, in *Jōsai daishi zenshū*, ed. Kohō 1976: 405–6.

62. Ibid., 432–33.

63. See Koffman 1985.

64. See Ōsumi 1983a; and Katsuura 1984. On mothers of eminent monks, see also Ōsumi 1983a and 1983b.

65. See Kawai 1992: 73. According to a private communication from Okuda Isao, however, Myōe was actually facing a statue of the bodhisattva Monju (Mañjuśrī), not of Butsugen Butsumo.

66. Kawai Hayao, for instance, has interpreted Myōe's legend in Jungian terms as a typical case of sublimation. See Kawai 1992.

67. See Ōsumi 1983a.

68. *Gyokuyō*, entry for Yōwa 1/11/28 (1181), quoted in Tonomura 1997: 162.

69. There are several stories in which a mother asks the gods to forgive her son. In the *Nihon ryōiki*, for instance, after mentioning one such case, the author adds in a note: "How great the mother's compassion was! She was so compassionate that she loved an evil son and practiced good on his behalf." See ed. Endō and Kasuga 1967: 180–83; trans. Nakamura 1973: 75–76.

70. The translation of *jugan* (inserting the eyes) by "finishing touches," however, does not entirely do justice to the importance of women in these matrimonial strategies.

71. *Gukanshō*, See ed. Okami and Akamatsu 1967: 149; trans. Brown and Ishida 1979: 37.

72. *Ōkagami*, trans. Yamagiwa 1966: 149–50.

73. *Heike monogatari*, trans. H. McCullough 1988: 434.

74. The Tendai abbot Ryōgen, for instance, is well known for his action on behalf of women. He established relic assemblies (*shari-e*), which women were permitted to attend.

75. See *Heian ibun*, section Daibatsu, 652, 1322, 1560, 1573, 1796, 2021, 2320–21, 2340–41; quoted in Nishiguchi 1987: 218.

76. See *Genkō shakusho* 2: 21, trans. Ury 1971: 241–45. See also *Sanbō ekotoba*, trans. Kamens 1988: 234–39; on the Hokke hakkō ritual, see Tanabe 1984.

77. In a variant, Ningai's mother appears as a cow. This variant is found in the tradition of Zuishin-in, a temple related to the poetess Ono no Komachi. Located on Ushikawa-yama (Mount Cow-Skin) on the outskirts of Kyoto, it was formerly known as Mandaraji ("Temple of the maṇḍala").

78. See Katsuura 1997: 37–44. The theme of the lost mother was widespread in medieval Japan in times of political turmoil and economic hardship. A number of stories tell of people going to Kiyomizudera to pray to the bodhisattva Kannon to find their lost mothers. Such is the case of Keizan's mother, who, according to Keizan himself, found her own mother again, after several years of separation, upon completing a retreat at Kiyomizu.

79. See *Sangoku denki*, ed. Ikegami 1976, vol. 1: 212–13.

80. In the *Miyako meisho zue* (1780), we finally learn that he painted this to repay his debt toward her (at the age of ten, after reciting the *Lotus Sūtra* for ten days).

81. Tonomura 1997: 161–62.

82. The literary emergence of the Cinderella motif in East Asia can be traced back to a Chinese tale recorded in the *Youyang zazu xiji* (ninth century). See Mauclaire 1984: 10.

83. Yanagita 1990a. Another Nō play entitled "The madwoman of Tennōji" has for its heroine a beautiful madwoman, the daughter of a *chōja* of Kageyama. She had fallen in love with Shuntokumaru before he became blind and was abandoned at Tennōji by his stepmother. After he becomes blind, he comes to visit her, and their reunion brings the play to a happy ending. Another version, found for instance in the *Wakan sansai zue*, differs on several points. Here, the stepmother of Shuntokumaru wants to make her own son the heir. She casts a spell on Shuntokumaru, making him leprous and blind, and orders that he be abandoned at Tennōji. The daughter of the *chōja* of Kageyama comes to see him at the temple, and, owing to Kannon's power, his sight is eventually restored. Later on, the stepmother and her son are reduced to begging.

84. On Kunāla, see *Konjaku monogatari shū* 4. 4, ed. Yamada et al. 1959–63, vol. trans. Dykstra 1986: 86–89; Matisoff 1973: 68–71 and 168–72; Keene 1962; and Strong (forthcoming). For the various recensions (*sekkyō*, Nō, Kabuki, *jōruri*) of the Semimaru tale, see Matisoff, ibid., 163–273. Another story of an abused stepchild is that of bishop Jōmu, a contemporary of Uda Tennō. When the child was two years old, his father Yamakage went to Chinzei as senior assistant governor-general. The boy's stepmother, who detested him, tried to kill him by dropping him into the sea under the pretext of embracing him, but a turtle surfaced, caught him on its back, and saved his life. See *Heike monogatari*, trans. McCullough 1988: 218.

85. See, for instance, the tale of *Sanshō dayū*, in Iwasaki Takeo, *Sanshō dayū kō: Chūsei no sekkyō-gatari*, Tokyo: Heibonsha, 1994.

86. See Mauclaire 1984: 12; and Verdier 1995: 169–97.

87. See the case described in the *Shinsarugaku ki*, in Yamagishi et al., 1977: 135–36.

88. See Wakita 1994: 93.

89. The motif of the "suffering deity" as a child persecuted by a stepmother is developed in the story of the deities of Hakone and Izu. To escape from her evil stepmother, a young princess leaves India, together with her half-sister. The two girls take refuge in Japan, where they are eventually deified. Another deity, Enmyō Myōjin, is said to have been originally a young girl who was drowned by her stepmother during her father's absence. See *Shintōshū*, ed. Kishi Shōzō, 1967: 42–46; and Wakita 1994: 89–93.

90. This is the case, for instance, with the *Ochikubo monogatari*. See Mauclaire 1984.

91. Wakita 1994: 93.

92. On this question, see Bainbridge 1992: 91; and Wakita 1984, 1993, 1994.

93. *Therīgāthā*, verses 133 and 134; quoted in Kloppenborg 1995: 162.

94. See, for instance, the plays *Hyakuman*, *Kashiwazaki*, *Sakuragawa*, *Asuka-gawa*, and *Sumidagawa*, in *Yōkyokushū*, ed. Yokomichi and Omote 1960.

95. Wakita 1985b: 196–97.

96. Bainbridge 1992: 96–97.

97. Ibid., 94.

98. Ibid., 93.

99. Wakita, 1984: 77–79.

100. Ackroyd 1959: 43–48.

101. Tonomura 1997: 144.

102. The effects of the social changes of the Muromachi period on women are not so different from those of the Renaissance in the West, acccording to Joan Kelly: "In sum, a new division between personal and public life made itself felt as the state came to organize Renaissance society, and with that division the modern relation of the sexes made its appearance. . . . Noblewomen, too, were increasingly removed from public concerns . . ., their loss of public power made itself felt in new constraints placed upon their personal as well as their social lives." See Kelly 1984: 47.

103. The complete table of kinship relations—the totality of the agnates—includes nine generations, from the great-great-grandfather to the children of the great-grandsons of ego. See Cartier 1986: 243.

104. Ibid., 272–75.

105. Beillevaire 1986: 295.

106. Atobe Terumi, *Nihon yōshi setsu* ("On Japanese Adoption," 1722) quoted in McMullen 1975: 178–79; Lauwaert 1991: 180–81.

107. Beillevaire 1986: 298–99.

108. McCullough 1967: 141.

109. McCullough 1967: 145–46.

110. Ibid., 146–47.

111. McMullen 1975: 134–35.

112. Wakita 1993: 88–90.

113. See McCullough 1967; Mass 1989; Wakita 1993.

114. See McCullough 1967: 105.

115. Ibid., 106.

116. Ibid., 118.

117. Tonomura 1997: 136.

118. Ibid., 84.

119. Wakita 1993: 87.

120. Tonomura 1997: 146.

121. McCullough 1967: 139.

122. Ibid., 124.

123. Ibid., 142–43.

124. In Hozumi Shigetō, *Rikon seidō no kenkyū*, p. 6; quoted in Ackroyd 1959: 65.

125. See Takagi 1992.

126. Hozumi, op. cit., 35; quoted in Ackroyd 1959: 65. In practice, however, things may have been more complex.

127. *Tokugawa hyakkajō*, art. 50; See also art. 50 and 51 in J. H. Gubbins, "The Hundred Articles and the Tokugawa Government," *Transactions and Proceedings of the Japan Society* 17 (1918–20), quoted in Ackroyd 1959: 58.

128. Mass 1989: 9.

129. Ibid., 75–78.

130. Wakita 1984: 89.

131. On this question, see Mass 1989.

132. Wakita 1984: 90.

133. Mass 1989: 100.

134. Beillevaire 1986: 307.

135. Ibid., 80.

136. Wakita 1984: 92–94.

137. Wakita 1993: 102.

138. Wakita 1984: 99–100.

139. Wakita 1993: 85.

140. Quoted in Amino 1989: 107.

141. See Smith and Wisewell 1982.

142. See Miyata 1983: 43–49.

143. Mass 1989: 117.

144. Beillevaire 1986: 287.

145. Sangren 1983: 18.

146. Sered 1994: 178.

147. *Therīgāthā*, w. 159–60; quoted in Kloppenborg 1995: 165.

148. The situation was similar in China; see Bray 1997: 353.

149. See Ko 1994: 19.

CHAPTER 6

1. See Falk and Gross 1980.

2. See Morrell 1985: 67–69.

3. This trend is characteristic of the book edited by Nancy Auer Falk and Rita Gross. See Falk and Gross 1980.

4. The point is acknowledged by Gross herself. See Gross 1993: 117–18.

5. The charisma of such women often derives from the passive sexual role they assume (as mediums) in their relations with the divine or the demonic. They are generally possessed by a male deity who treats them with as little respect as the traditional Japanese husband treated his wife. Moreover, as their teaching spreads, their individual charisma is often channeled, controlled by male acolytes, who, in typical Weberian fashion, emphasize the "charisma of office."

6. *Mahāvastu*, trans. J.J. Jones, vol. 2, 1952: 15.

7. Ibid., vol. 1, 1949: 121.

8. Ibid., vol. 2, 1952: 3.

9. The *Apadāna* is included in the *Khuddakanikāya* of the Suttapitaka, and is constituted of hagiographies of eminent nuns.

10. Walters 1994: 373. See also idem, 1996: 117.

11. Idem 1994: 123.

12. Ibid., 126.

13. Ibid., 132.

14. Ibid., 137.

15. The point has been made by Liz Wilson; see Wilson 1996: 30–31, 142–43.

16. M. E. Lilley, ed., *Apadāna*, 2 vols, London: PTS, 1925–27, 2: 532.

17. Bareau 1982.

18. Ibid., 143.

19. Lilley, *Apadāna*, 2: 530; quoted in Wilson 1996: 30–31, 142–43.

20. Quoted in Grant 1994: 16.

21. See *Fuli taisi yinyuan jing*, *T.* 3, 173: 13b. See also Peri 1918; Bareau 1982: 48.

22. Translation based on Morrell 1980.

23. Some traditions also report that, apart from Rāhula, the Buddha had two other sons from his secondary wives. See, for instance, the *Shishi liutie* (also known as *Yichu liutie*), Hangzhou: Zhejiang guji chubanshe, 1990: 311; *Konjaku monogatari shū* 3.13, trans. Dykstra 1995: 24; *Shutsujō kōgo*, trans. Tominaga 1990: 135. On this question, see also Peri 1918.

24. On the above, see Peri 1918: 1–3.

25. See Shaw 1994.

26. She is completely unknown in the earlier Vinaya-piṭaka (of the Theravādin, the Mahīśāsaka, and the Dharmaguptaka), but her figure grows gradually in the later Vinaya-piṭaka (of the Mahasaṅghika and the Mūlasarvāstivādin) and in the *Mahāvastu* (part of the Vinaya of the Lokottaravādin). See Bareau, 1982: 32–37.

27. See *Mahāvastu*; quoted in Bareau 1982: 41–42.

28. See the Mūlasarvāstivāda Vinaya, quoted in Bareau 1982: 44–45.

29. The Buddha, in a past life, is said to have been an ascetic named Unicorn (Jp. Ikkaku sennin), and Yaśodhara was the courtesan who seduced him. See Faure 1998a.

30. Bareau 1982: 48.

31. *Konjaku monogatari shū* 3:13, ed. Yamada et al., 1959–63, vol. 1: 220–22; trans. Dykstra 1986: 24.

32. See Willis 1985; Dumézil 1983: 17–35.

33. See Dumézil 1983: 17–35.

34. Kloppenborg 1995: 166. Note the inversion with the case of the nun Utpalavarṇā, mentioned below.

35. See Vinaya 1: 268, quoted in Kloppenborg 1995: 166.

36. *Therīgāthā*, w. 252–70.

37. *Dhirgāgama* 4.8, in Burlingame 1969, vol. 2: 76. See also Falk 1990: 134.

38. Burlingame 1969, vol. 3: 22.

39. *Dhammapada* 176, in ibid. 19–22. See also the Japanese version in Morrell 1980.

40. Ibid., 22–23.

41. Ibid., 189–91.

42. See Paul 1980b; see also Naomi 1989; and Yang 1960–61.

43. On this tragic figure, see Faure 1997a: 130–32.

44. See Forte 1976.

45. *T.* 12: 1098a.

46. Bokenkamp 1998: 385–87.

47. Ibid., 388.

48. See *Quan Tang wen* 248: 1b–2a; quoted in Bokenkamp 1998: 389.

49. Bokenkamp 1998: 390.

50. The title "Emperor"—and a fortiori "Empress"—is an anachronism in the case of ancient Japan. I will therefore use the term *tennō* whenever possible, though I retain the adjective "imperial" for lack of a better term.

51. On Kōmyō Tennō, see Tanaka 1992: 32. On Danrin Kōgō, *see Genkō shakusho* 6.1, trans. Ury 1971: 269–71.

52. Six women served as *tennō* during the Nara period: Suiko (r. 592–628), Kyōgoku (who reigned from 642 to 645, and again from 655 to 661 under the name of Saimei), Jitō (r. 690–97), Genmei (r. 707–15), Genshō (r. 715–24), and Kōken (who reigned from 749 to 758 and again from 764 to 770 under the name of Shōtoku). Although two female *tennō*, Meishō (r. 1630–43) and Go-Sakura-machi (r. 1763–70), are listed for the Edo period, their reigns were purely nominal. On female empresses, see Tsurumi 1983: 71–75.

53. See Faure 1998a and Tanaka 1992.

54. Tanaka 1992: 38.

55. Ibid., 39.

56. See *Keiran shūyōshū*, T. 76, 2410: 780c; see also Tanaka 1992: 49.

57. *NBTK* 12.79; quoted in Brown and Ishida 1979: 35.

58. *Gukanshō*, trans. Brown and Ishida 1979: 35.

59. Ibid., 37.

60. See *Zenkōji engi*. There are also cases of emperors who fell into hell, the most well known being probably that of Daigo Tennō. According to the *Imaka-gami* (1170 or 1180) and the *Hobutsushū*, the famous female novelist Murasaki Shikibu is also said to have been damned for telling lies in her *Genji monogatari*. For this reason, nuns copied sutras to save her as well as her female readers from infernal torments. Gradually, however, Murasaki came to be identified as an ava-tar of the bodhisattva Kannon of Ishiyamadera, the temple where she was said to have written her novel. As to the *Genji monogatari*, it was identified with the *Lotus Sūtra*, and presented as an *upāya* to realize the impermanence of the world.

61. See Tanaka 1992: 44.

62. Ibid., 44.

63. Ibid., 36.

64. On this question, see Abe Yasurō's compelling analysis in Abe 1998: 17–64.

65. The sexual element, latent in this story, comes to the foreground in a related story in which the famous courtesan Izumi Shikibu, emulating the bodhisattva Kannon, had vowed to make love to one thousand men to bring them to enlighten-ment. She almost failed when the last man turned out to be a sickly old mute. See also Kimbrough 1999: 204–10.

66. We may also mention in this context the Christian topos of the holiness manifested by overcoming repulsion for the abject object: for instance, the legend of Saint Francis sucking the pus of a diseased man. On this legend, see Albert 1997: 271.

67. *Genkō shakusho* 18, op. cit., 159c; trans. Ury 1971: 314–15.

68. See sect. Jitchū in *Genkō shakusho*. 9, op. cit., 112c. Kokan continues with the episode of the bath offered by Empress Wu Zhao to the two eminent Chan priests, Shenxiu and Huian. On this, see Faure 1997a: 104.

69. Jitchū is the founder of the *keka* (repentance) ritual at Tōdaiji. See Abe 1999: 168–70.

70. See *Shichidaiji junrei shiki*, quoted in Tanaka 1992: 42.

71. See *Daibutsu no engi*; quoted in Tanaka 1992: 42.

72. See for instance, *Jakushōdō kokkyōshū*, 74.

73. See *Muchū mondō*, ed. Satō Taishun, Tokyo: Iwanami shoten, 1974 (1934): 198. On the relations between Danrinji and Musō's Tenryūji, see Hayashiya 1978.

74. *Genkō shakusho* 6.1, trans. Ury 1971: 271.

75. *Honchō jinja kō*, pp. 1638–45.

76. The *Honchō nyo gan* (1661) gives a more detailed description: animals fight to devour her corpse, beginning with the hair, then arms and legs, the foul smell fills the four directions, and the whole thing is extremely impure. Passersby cover their nose, those who come nearby vomit. After forty-nine days, only the fist of one hand remains in the grass, and it is eventually buried. Later on, the consort is deified and a shrine is built, called Ume-no-miya.

77. Strangely, such famous poetesses as Izumi Shikibu or Ono no Komachi are passed over silently (despite the symbolic association mentioned earlier between Komachi and Danrin Kōgō). Ninagawa, who died in 1448, had reached awakening under Ikkyū. His wife's verse was composed after a discussion she had with him regarding Zen. Mugai Nyodai's *waka* is said to have been composed in response to a kōan by the Chinese Zen master Mugaku Sogen. My information on this text is indebted to a paper presented by Nishiyama Mika at the "Culture of Convents" conference (Columbia University, 1998). On the *Shichijūichiban shokunin uta-awase*, see also Harada Masatoshi 1997: 140–42.

78. A description of the "nine faces of death" is found in the *Danrin Kōgō kūsō zue*, Coll. of Saifukuji, Kyoto. See Kano Susumu, *Rokudō no tsuji-atari no shiseki to densetsu o tazunete*, Muromachi shobō, 1988. See also: *Saga Tennō no misaki Danrin Kōgō nijūnanasai meishū kusō no zu*, Coll. Kano bunko, Tōhoku Daigaku (1797); and *Kūsō shi emaki* (1527), Coll. Dainenbutsuji, Osaka. There is also a relation between the *Kusōshi* (Verses on the "nine faces of death"), Danrin Kōgō, and a work by the Edo Zen master Suzuki Shōsan entitled *Ninin bikuni* (Two Nuns), a tale in which we find the following verse: "A flower did she seem / She who now so soon / Alas, lies a corpse / In the open field." See Tyler 1977: 19; and Sanford 1988: 77. See also *Kusōshi emaki*, in Akiyama 1977. Regarding Ono no Komachi and the *Kusō-e*, see Hosokawa 1989a: 247–54.

79. McCullough 1988: 436.

80. Ibid., 438.

81. Ibid., 471.

82. See Abe 1999.

83. McCullough 1988: 230.

84. Ibid., 213.

85. *Genpei jōsuiki*, 1097; quoted in Minobe 1982: 230.

86. Ibid., 1205.

87. Strong, forthcoming, 24.

88. Ibid.

89. The *Sanbō ekotoba*, for instance, quotes the *Sūtra of Utpalavarṇā*, in which this nun is said to have become an arhat. See Kamens 1988: 291–92; this sutra is quoted in the *Dazhidulun* (*T.* 25: 161a-c); see Lamotte 1944–80, 2: 844–48. See also Dōgen, *Shōbōgenzō*, "Shukke kudoku," *T.* 52, 2582: 278c–279a; trans. Yokoi 1976: 70–71; see also *Jakushōdō kokkyōshū*, 248. Dōgen, however, merely quotes this story to emphasize the "quasi-magical" power of the *kaṣāya*; on this question, see Faure 1995.

90. Kyoko Nakamura interprets Sari's physical lack of gender as the persistence of the Indian tradition, though feminized, in Japan and as a stage in the process of transition from male to female. For her, "This story serves as a bridge between an early Mahāyāna trend and a later Tantric trend in which woman plays a central role as a cosmic symbol." See Nakamura 1973.

91. In the thirteenth century, Chūjōhime came to be identified with the bodhisattva Seishi (Mahāsthāmaprāpta).

92. See, for instance, the *Towazugatari*, trans. Brazell 1973: 205. Lady Nijō claims to have found inspiration in this legend, in which the two divine nuns tell Chūjōhime: "We have come because you sincerely believed in the Western Paradise. If you trust in this maṇdala, you will not suffer."

93. Like Miaoshan and Lingzhao, next to whom she appears in the *Jakushōdō kokkyōshū*, op. cit., 252b.

94. Significantly, in Muromachi variants of her legend, Chūjōhime's sufferings are not caused by her stepmother's jealousy for her Snow-White beauty, but by the latter's desire to promote the future of her own children.

95. Tanaka points to the resemblance with the legend of the goddess Awajima Myōjin, who came to suffer from an "infortunate" (read "venereal") illness and was subsequently abandoned at sea.

96. On Chūjōhime, see Tanaka 1996; and *Jakushōdō kokkyōshū*, 252.

97. See ten Grotenhuis 1992: 198; and Tanaka 1996: 19–22.

98. Tanaka 1996: 50–60.

99. In her case, however, the theme of blood may be related to Chinese medical conceptions regarding her secluded life as a nun. In a Song text, quoting Chu Cheng, we find the following passage about nuns: "Dwelling in the inner quarters, their desires germinate but lead nowhere until yin and yang contend; now Hot, now Cold, they have the symptoms of intermittent fever which, prolonged, lead to fatigue disorders. Blocked menses, filthy white leukorrhea, phlegm buildup, headaches, heartburn, facial moles and warts, pains in joints—these are the illnesses of widows . . . . the illnesses of those with ample blood." See Furth 1999: 89.

100. See *Nihon ryōiki*; 3: 19, trans. Nakamura 1973: 246–48; and *Genkō shakusho*, trans. Ury 1971: 316.

101. The motif of superior children born from eggs appear in many Buddhist tales. In one of them, taking place in India during the lifetime of the Buddha, Sumanā, the daughter of a rich householder of Śrāvastī, Sudatta, gives birth to ten eggs. From these eggs, ten male children are born, who eventually become arhats. In another tale, the wife of a householder of Kapilavastu becomes pregnant

and delivers a lump of flesh. Seven days later, the lump opens, giving birth to one hundred children, all of whom eventually take the Buddhist vows and become arhats. See the *Nihon ryōiki*, trans. Nakamura 1973: 246–48; or the *Sanbō eko-toba*, trans. Kamens 1988: 203–4. See also the *Konjaku monogatari shū*, trans. Dykstra 1986: 183–87.

102. See Tokuda 1994, and idem, forthcoming.

103. The *Chiyono monogatari* is presently known through six recensions, dated from the end of the fourteenth to the eighteenth centuries, one of which, the *Chiyono zōshi*, is preserved in the Spencer Collection of the New York Public Library.

104. See the copy in Komazawa Library dated from the end of the nineteenth century.

105. See *Rentōroku* 4, in *SZ* 16, Shiden, 1: 301–2; see also Bodiford 1993: 466–67.

106. See *Shincho monjū*, quoted in *Nihon itsuwa Daijiten*, Osaka-Tōhō shuppan, 1967, vol. 3: 2658.

107. See Fister 1988: 30.

108. See *Nyokunshō*, Tenri Library. The copy dates from the seventeenth century but the text seems to have been compiled between the end of the fifteenth century and the beginning of the sixteenth century. An abbreviated version was published under the title "Me no to no sōshi" in the *Gunsho ruijū*. The passage in question is a little ambiguous, and could be read as if the husband, by accident, burnt his face with one of the logs for the fire. But from the context it seems obvious that it is the wife who did so voluntarily, in order to escape her husband's desire.

109. Another case is that of a nun who, having been harassed by a monk, suddenly strips in the midst of the monastic assembly, daring him to come forward.

110. *Wujia zhengzong zan*, in *ZZ* 2b, 8: 455a–b, trans. Levering 1997: 152–53. Wuzhuo's repartee echoes a dialogue between Zhaozhou and a monk: "What is Zhaozhou's stone bridge?"—"It transports asses across, it transports horses across." Wuzhuo's kōan was well known in Japan, and was used, for instance, by Shōtaku, a nun teacher of the famous convent Tōkeiji. See *Shōnan kattōroku* (1545), trans. Trevor Legget, *The Warrior Koans*, 106–7 (I am indebted to Miriam Levering for these references).

111. On this question, see Yanbe Hiroki, "Mugai Nyodai to Mujaku," *Kanazawa bunko kenkyū* 301, 1998.

112. See Yanagida 1981: 125.

113. See *Kumanosan ryakki*, quoted in Yamamoto 1993: 87, n. 33.

114. *Taiheiki*, trans. McCullough 1979: 9.

115. Ibid., 126.

116. Ibid., 345.

117. Wakita 1995: 28–29. Lady Sanmi bore many children to Go-Daigo Tennō, and one of her daughters become the priestess (*saigū*) of Ise.

118. According to the *Daikanwa jiten*, "jade woman" means: 1) a honorific term for someone else's wife; 2) a beautiful woman; 3) an immortal woman, or a celestial woman; 4) a concubine given by the emperor. In Japan, the term appears

above all in Onmyōdō texts and in esoteric literature during the Kamakura period. See, for instance, the *Keiran shūyōshū, T.* 76, 2410: 736c.

119. *Shinron muki,* 201–2.

120. *Kakuzenshō, TZ* 4: 480b.

121. See Akamatsu 1957; Yamamoto 1987; and idem, 1993: 296–302; Tanaka 1992: 95–97.

122. See Endō 1989.

123. See *Kakuzenshō, DNBZ* 51: 130–31 (or *TZ* 5: 615c).

124. See Tanaka 1993: 148–75; Hosokawa 1988b; and Ruppert 1999: 192–229.

125. See Akamatsu 1957: 96.

126. See *Dhīrgāgama-sūtrā, T.* 1, 1: 21c and passim; *Fayuan zhulin, T.* 53, 2122: 617b; and *Kakuzenshō, TZ* 4: 193–94.

127. Tanaka 1989: 101.

128. The *Jinnō Shōtoki* gives the following account of the way in which Jingū obtained these jewels during her Korean expedition: "While at sea, Empress Jingū obtained a sacred stone (*nyoi no tama*) and by this means was able to delay the birth of her son, the future Ōjin Tennō, until her return to Kyushu. His future having been foreordained by the gods even before his birth, Ōjin became known as the emperor of the womb." See Varley 1980: 102. See also *Heike monogatari,* trans. McCullough 1988: 372.

129. See Tanaka 1989: 121.

130. Tonomura 1997: 143.

131. Ibid., 144.

132. *Heike monogatari,* trans. McCullough 1988: 291.

133. Ibid., 292. Her grave can be seen today in the precincts of Tokuonji, the temple dedicated to Yoshinaka in Nagano.

134. See *Ima kagami,* chapter 4, quoted in Tanaka 1993: 205.

135. Here again, we can detect an allusion to the dark side of Kiyomori, and to his main object of worship, the goddess Benzaiten (who also came to be identified with Dakiniten, the fox-deity).

136. *Keiran shūyōshū, T.* 76, 2410 : 633b.

137. See the *Busshari sōjō shidai,* quoted in Tanaka 1993: 149; see also Faure 1998c.

138. *Busshari sōjō shidai,* quoted in Tanaka 1993: 157.

139. Tanaka 1993: 159.

140. *Kojidan* 1. 81; quoted in Tanaka 1993: 212.

141. The story is connected to the legend of King Hansoku in the *Renwang jing;* for a summary, see Minobe 1982: 226–27.

142. See the otogizōshi *Tamamo no Mae,* in Nishizawa and Ishiguro 1977; and Tanaka 1993: 227. For the Zen version of Tamamo no Mae's legend, see also Faure 1996: 71.

143. See the *engi* of Kōfukuji and Kasuga, quoted in Abe 1998: 165.

144. This version of the legend was told at Shima (Kii penisula). See Bouchy 1996–97: 284.

145. See Bouchy 1996–97.

146. See *Shidōji engi*, quoted in Abe 1998: 165.

147. This schema is reminiscent of the Christian Golden Legend, on which see Albert 1997: 239–40, 257–59.

CHAPTER 7

1. See *Hōnen shōnin zenshū*, 1955: 77; trans. Coates and Ishizuka 1949, vol. 2: 351–52.

2. In another sermon, given at the time of the eye-opening (actually reopening) ceremony of the great Buddha at Tōdaiji, Hōnen gives a slightly different list of the main prohibited places: "In our kingdom, although it is a small country, there are many places where women cannot go. At Yoshino, the limit is the Fudōin; on Hieizan, Sakamoto; on Kōyasan, Fudōzaka; at Tennōji, the octagonal stūpa (Happōtō); At Zenkōji, women may enter the Hall, but not the inner sanctum." See Nishiguchi 1987: 120. Later on, male and female pilgrims seem to have been admitted for reclusion (*komori*) in the main hall of Zenkōji, and they could also circumambulate the gallery under the main altar.

3. A similar story line is found in the Nō play *Kōchō* (*Butterfly*) and in its *monogatari* version, the *Kōchō monogatari*, in which the sites of *kekkai* are again listed (with Tateyama, Togakushiyama, Shaka-no-take). In all cases, this passage is inserted in a sermon asserting the salvation of women.

4. See *Soga monogatari*, 1966: 420–23; trans. Cogan 1987: 284. My translation departs slightly from Cogan's.

5. As noted earlier, during the Heian period, the interdiction for menstruating women to participate in shrine rituals was only temporary, and implied no moral stain. See, for instance, the rules regarding pregnant or menstruating women in the *Engishiki* (927); see also Ushiyama 1994: 75.

6. Amino 1978: 23.

7. In China, according to the *Yichu liutie* (dated 954), women were not allowed to climb mountains like Jinfeng shan. In Korea, as well, mountains were the object of severe taboos. See Kendall 1984: 129–30.

8. See Huber 1999: 123–26. Ipolito Desideri, a remarkable witness on Tibet (where he lived from 1716 to 1721), during a visit to the Dakpo region in 1720, notes that "the other place the Thibettans [*sic*] venerate exceedingly is called *çe-ri* (Tseri or Tsari). . . . Troops of pilgrims, men and women, go thither to walk in procession round the foot of the mountain. . . . It is considered a sacrilege for any woman, even for nuns, to go to the upper mountains; and there is a point beyond which they are forbidden to pass. This they never attempt as they believe that any woman who dares to pass this point will be put to a fearful death by the Kha-ndro-mà [that is, sky-goers], the tutelary goddesses of the place." Among the many mountain deities of Tibet, many were goddesses, like Jomo Gangkar, the Everest. See F. de Filippi, ed., *An Account of Tibet*, reprint Taipei: Chengwen, 1971: 143, quoted in Huber 1999: 122, and Chayet 1993: 71–72.

9. Huber 1999: 126.

10. Ibid., 121.

11. Ibid., 123.

12. One monk gave Huber a particularly interesting explanation: "The reason why women can't go up there is that at Tsari there are lots of small, self-produced manifestations of the Buddha's genitals made of stone." See Huber 1999: 124. A Tibetan explanation relating this exclusion to menstruation and pollution is found in N. Chophel, *Folk Culture of Tibet*, Dharamsala: Library of Tibetan Works and Archives, 1983: 12. Regarding the perception of the mountain as a maṇḍala, it is worth mentioning the distinction made between two ideal-types: the mountain totally taken over by Buddhism—and as a result, utterly "mandalized"—and the mountain that continues to be an object of worship for the "nameless religion" and resists "mandalization." Women were probably not as entirely excluded, if at all, from the latter. See Huber 1999: 22–26, and Buffetrille 1998.

13. According to one definition, the *kekkai* (Skt. *sīmā-bandha*, or *bandhaya-sīman*) can be of three types: the first type (*sheseng jie*), limited to rituals like ordination and confession, defines the space where monks cannot stay without their three robes; the second type (*sheyi jie*), the space where they can be without robes; and the third (*sheshi jie*), the space where they can live and cook food. See *Bukkyō daijii*, vol. 2: 1038b.

14. The ordination platform (*kaidan*) is also defined as a *sīmā-maṇḍala*. The *kekkai* thus defines both ordination platform and meditation hall (*dōjō*), both being places cordoned off from the profane.

15. Hikosan's four *kekkai*, or levels of increasing purity, were marked by *torii* of metal, stone, and wood, respectively. Women could climb no higher than the second *kekkai* (and even this was forbidden during and immediately after their periods). Interestingly, the cultic center came to be ruled in the sixteenth century by an abbess, who moved her dwelling just outside the second *kekkai*. See Grapard, forthcoming.

16. See *Bukkyō daijii*, vol. 2: 1040b. The *kekkai* of Kōyasan is defined as follows in the *sekkyō* tale *Karukaya* (1631): "[Mount Kōya] is a restricted precinct, extended seven *ri*, a mountain where all alike strive toward salvation through their own efforts. For this reason, male trees grow on the peak and female trees grow in the distant valleys. Because male birds fly about the peak, female birds fly about the distant valleys. Since stags eat the grasses on the peak, does eat the grasses in the valley. Be they trees, grasses, birds or beasts, males may enter the mountain, but no female may enter. So all women are absolutely forbidden." Quoted in Matisoff (forthcoming).

17. "Raihai tokuzui," T. 82, 2582: 38a–b. See also ed. Terada 1974, vol. 1: 327.

18. T. 82, 2582: 38a; ed. Terada 1974: 329–30.

19. See "Shukke kudoku," T. 82, 2582: 278–85. See also Heidegger 1995: 81–82; and Ishikawa 1992a.

20. See Yanagita 1990b: 445–49; and 1990c. See also Miyata 1993a: 162. The name Toran (var. Dōran) first appears in the *Kumano sansho gongen Kinpusen Kongō Zaō suijaku engi*, in Gorai 1984, vol. 2: 214–15.

21. The *uba-ishi* ("stone of the old woman") of Tateyama is also mentioned in the *Wakan sansai zue* 68, ed. Wakan sansai zue kankō iinkai, Tokyo: Tōkyō bijutsu, 1970, vol. 2: 840. There, a group of "old nuns" (*rōni ichigyō*) try to climb

Tateyama, and they turn into trees and stones. Furthermore, it is said that when people tried to build a Hall for Women (*nyonindō*) at Tateyama, the wooden materials also turned into stone. The mountain of Tateyama remained off limits to women until 1869.

22. Toran's horns, a variant specific to this legend, came to be worshipped as one of the treasures of Tateyama.

23. See Seidel 1992–93: 127. In the village at the foot of Tateyama, the main sanctuary was the "Hall of the Uba" (Uba-dō), which houses three statues of the *uba*, or *onba*, as she was locally called, surrounded by sixty-six smaller statues, one for each province. A five-minute walk away, across a river, is Enma-dō, the Yama Hall. On the Tateyama maṇḍala, a group of blindfolded women can be seen, proceeding from one temple to the other, on a path covered with white cloth. It is the ritual called "The Great Ordination Assembly of the Cloth-covered Bridge" (*nunohashi daikanjōe*), celebrated each autumn on the equinox day (*higan*). See Seidel 1992–93: 128.

24. Let us review a few stories. In Sado, the god of Kinpokusan is an avatar of Shogun Jizō, and the *kekkai* is the site of a Shingon temple, the Shinkōji. We are told that a woman, calling herself a servant of the god, pretended to climb the mountain. A storm arose, and she lost her way. Afterwards, people found a large rock (*ōiwa*) that was not there before, and whose top looked like the hair of a woman. They called it *miko-iwa*. At Gassan in Dewa, there is also a *miko-ishi* (sometimes written as *mi-ko ishi*, "august-child stone") because the man who "opened" this mountain, Prince Hachiko, had performed a ritual on that spot. But another version speaks of a *miko* who transgressed the *kekkai* and was turned into stone. At Akagami-yama at Hago (in Tōhoku), we also find an "Itaku tree" (*Itaku-sugi*) and a "dog stone" (*inu-ko ishi*). As tradition has it, a *miko*, accompanied by a dog, started to climb the mountain, and as a result of her transgression she was turned into a tree, while the poor dog was turned into stone. The name Itaku is perhaps derived from *itako*, a generic term for blind female mediums in northern Japan. At Mount Horowa in the same Hago, we also find a *moriko-ishi* ("Child-keeping stone", or rather, "stone of the *moriko*," another name for the *miko*) based on a similar legend. Likewise, at Chūzenji, on Mount Nikkō, we find an "ox-stone" (*ushi-ishi*) next to a *moriko-ishi* (or *miko-ishi*). Its origin is traced back to the legend of a shamaness who, asserting her ritual purity, attempted to climb the mountain. Despite the fact that she rode on the back of an ox to avoid polluting the ground, the ox suddenly turned into stone, and, when she insulted the animal, the same thing happened to her. See Yanagita 1990c: 200.

Upon occasion, the reason for a woman's turning into stone is not transgression but grief or persecution. In the *Soga monogatari*, out of grief, after the death of her lover Jūrō, Tora becomes a stone (*Tora-ga-ishi*). The same thing happens to the dancer-girl Shizuka when she is separated from her lover Yoshitsune. Variants in which the heroine or her attendant turn into stone as the result of persecution reveal the influence of the *mamako ijime* (abuse of stepchildren) theme. This theme is found, for instance, in the *sekkyō* ballad *Sanshō dayū*, in which Anjuhime and her brother Zushio are persecuted by the infamous Superintendant Sanshō (see Iwasaki 1994). At Iwagiyama, the place where Anjuhime died and was eventually deified as the mountain goddess, the *uba-ishi* is that of her *uba* (wet-nurse), who turned into stone. At Kiso Ontake, the two abused children are Rishō Gozen and her brother Akotamaru; Rishō Gozen dies after climbing halfway to the top, but eventually she is deified as Oyu Gongen (Deity of Hot Water). Nevertheless, the place of her death marks the limit of the *kekkai*. See *Kiso Ontake engi*, quoted in Sakurai and Miyata 1975: 512–13.

25. *Genkō shakusho*, trans. Ury 1971: 312–13.

26. See *Kobon setsuwa-shū, Honchō shinsenden*, ed. Kawaguchi Hisao 1967: 347.

27. *Gikeiki*, trans. McCullough 1966: 167.

28. See Gorai 1984, vol. 2: 214–15.

29. Abe 1989b:168.

30. The mother of En no Gyōja, still worshipped at the Haha kōdō (Chapel of Lady Mother) constructed on the site of the *kekkai*, near the mountain entrance of Tōgawa, is called Torame.

31. This Kamakura text, ulterior to the Einin era (1193–99), has been preserved in the Hieizan Bunko Collection; see Abe 1989b: 173. See also *Konjaku monogatari shū* 11. 26, ed. Yamada 1959–63: 108–9.

32. Abe 1989b: 174.

33. This rather unseemingly act, which Yanagita labelled the "piss of rebuke" (*shikaribari*), is a significant motif in all of these myths or legends and it seems to constitute an apotropaic gesture. See Yanagita 1990c: 196, quoting the *Wakan sansai zue*. On the apotropaic use of excrement, see Bourke 1891; and Greenblatt 1990: 59–79.

34. Another characteristic of the *Kōya no maki* is that it is one of the rare documents that emphasize Kūkai's mother and her relationships with her son. As such, it forms a striking contrast with *Karukaya*, which emphasizes the father-son relationships between Shigeuji and Ishidōmaru. See Muroki 1977: 43–55, esp. 52–55; and Matisoff (forthcoming).

35. See Matisoff (forthcoming).

36. Jison-in was one of the administrative quarters of Kōyasan. It was built not long after Kōyasan in 816, but gradually lost its function during the Muromachi period. On the altar of Jison-in is a portrait of Kūkai, which he is said to have painted himself at sixty-one, not long before his death, from his reflection in the water; and an image of Maitreya, which his mother, at the time of dying at eighty-three, is said to have painted herself as a self-portrait.

37. See Hinonishi 1979.

38. In *Karukaya*, these stones are also called *kakushi-ishi* (hidden stone) and *kesakake-ishi* (stone where the *kesa* was hung). See Matisoff 1973: 279.

39. See ibid., 139. This motif is reminiscent of Izanagi's blocking the way to Izanami upon his return from the Land of the Dead.

40. On this story, see Tanaka 1996: 9–62; also *Jakushōdō kokkyō zokushū*, 252–53. As noted earlier, the image of Chūjōhime developed in the Muromachi period, particularly in Pure Land sermons. The various traditions regarding her were unified in the *Taimadera engi emaki*.

41. On this point, see Abe 1998: 15.

42. Similar stories are told about the mothers of such famous ascetics as En no Gyōja and Taichō. See *Genkō shakusho*, trans. Ury 1971: 514.

43. In one document, Kūkai's mother is also called Tamayorihime, famous as the name of the goddess of the Kamo shrine, the ancestor of a lineage of *miko*. Yanagita has also argued that, like Tora and its derivatives, it is a generic term referring to the priestly function, priestess, rather than to specific individuals. The name *akō*, likewise, designated in medieval Japan the shamanesses (*fusegi* or *miko*), and also often evil women or traitors. See Abe 1989b: 170. Let us also mention the name Akomachi, which is that of a goddess of love identified with the *dōsōjin* and with Dakiniten, who appeared to Kūkai and was subsequently enshrined as one of the protecting deities of Tōji.

44. In the *sekkyōbushi*, Kūkai's mother is Akō Gozen, while in the *engi* she is simply called "the nun." She is also sometimes called Jison Gozen, due to the belief that she was a manifestation of Maitreya (Jison).

45. We have here a variant of the legend of the daughter of the sea-god, washed ashore on an *utsubune*. Kūkai's mother can thus be seen as a sea-god's daughter and a *hyōchakushin*, a deity who reaches the shore after drifting at sea.

46. Myōhōzan was one of the three cultic centers of Kumano, and it was also the place where the Zen priest Shinchi Kakushin (d. 1298) had buried the ashes of his mother. This temple, allegedly founded by Kūkai himself and transferred from Kōyasan, was later restored by the wife and the daughter of Hōjō Tokiyori. As women of all classes asked to be buried there, it came to be called "Nyonin Kōya" (Kōya for women). See Hagiwara 1983: 15–20.

47. See Katsuura 1995: 171–72.

48. See *Genpei jōsuiki* 40, ed. Ikebe Yoshitaka, *Kokubun sōsho*, third ed., vol. 8. Tokyo: Hakubunkan, 1918.

49. See *Karukaya*, in *Sekkyōbushi*, Heibonsha Tōyōbunko, 1973; and *Sekkyō-shū*, ed. Muroki 1977: 15. See also Pigeot 1972: 77.

50. A third place was Kamuro (about three miles east of Jison-in, on the southern bank of the Ki river).

51. According to Hinonishi Shinjō, in the Meiji period the route via Jison-in was the main, "front" access to Kōya, whereas Kamuro was the "back" route; see Hinonishi 1989: 243.

52. Only one of them remains, at Fudō-guchi. This *nyonindō* is said to have been founded during the Enkyō era (1744–48) by a woman from Edo named Yokoyama Take. The number of female establishments around Kōyasan is also related to the fact that the limit of the *kekkai* has varied over time. The boundary now marked by the *nyonindō* (Women's Hall) and the *Daimon* ("Great Gate"), at the top of the path from Jison-in, presumably represents a shrinking of the original *kekkai*, which in the past was marked by the temple itself, or even farther down, by the Amano shrine, where Kōya *hijiri* kept their wives and children. Later on, it apparently came to be marked by the *oshiage-iwa* (lifted-up rock). On this question, see Gorai 1989: 139. Amano (present-day Katsuragi-chō) is located about three miles southwest of Jison-in. Where there was formerly a *bessho* (annex) of Kōya there is today a shrine, Amano jinja, dedicated to the tutelary goddess Niu (Nifutsuhime).

53. Likewise, at the foot of Kinpusen, a Haha kōdō was dedicated to the mother of En no Gyōja. On Mount Negoro, at Dainichiji at the foot of the mountain, there was a cult centered on the nun Myōkai, the mother of Kakuban. At the An'yōdō (or An'yōji) of Ogoto Chino, at the foot of Hieizan, is found the grave of Ryōgen's mother.

54. Two kinds of rituals were performed: funerary rituals for the dead (*segaki, ketsubongyō kuyō*) and "premortem" rituals (*gyakushu*) like the "great unction" (*nunohashi daikanjōe*).

55. See Seidel 1992–93: 130.

56. See *Kōbō Daishi den zenshū* 1: 53–55; see also Tanabe 1999: 356–59.

57. A significant exception is that of the representation of Konsei Myōjin at Kinpusen, which seems to have been perceived both as a *kekkai* stone and a *dōsojin*. For a discussion of the *dōsojin*, see Czaja 1974; and Faure (forthcoming).

58. Nowadays, stones or pillars, called *kaidan-ishi*, can still often be seen in front of the temple gate. For instance, on the slope of Hieizan near Higashi-Sakamoto, one can see pillars bearing the inscription: "*Kekkai* [forbidden] to women, oxen and horses," a rather significant taxonomy. On these stones, one usually finds a formula of the type: "Forbidden to bring spicy food, alcohol and meat within the precinct (*fukyō kunshū niku nyū sanmon*). The character *kun* (Chin. *hun*) means both "aliments of animal origin" and "hot aliments" (garlic, onion, and so forth, forbidden by Buddhism; also, figuratively, "licentious talk"), or "*Sanmon*, access forbidden to all morally corrupt [elements] such as women, fish, meat, and the five hot aliments." Other similar formulas include: "Area where one does not kill living beings" and "Forbidden to the entertainment arts." The term *kun*, referring to the five intoxicating foods (garlic and the like), is both phonetically and graphically close to *gun*, "military," and this double-entendre was probably not fortuitous during times when temples were trying to assert their independence from warriors. See Kōjin konwakai ed. 1975: 282–84.

59. Yanagita mentions another similar case, that of a stone named Oitonbo, located at the foot of Kinpusen, near Ryūsenji, at the entrance of Ōmine. The pilgrims to Ōmine, when they try to hold it, find it at times light, at times heavy. It seems alive, reacting to the way it is treated. See Yanagita 1990c: 197.

60. Ibid., 194.

61. Ibid., 190, 204. There was near the grave of the Soga brothers on Mount Hakone a stone named Tora-ishi (or Tora-ga-ishi), as well as Tora Gozen's stone stupa, both of which were said to have miraculous powers; for instance, the stone healed people who prayed while washing it, and, when moved, it returned to the same place during the night. In other cases, the Tora-ga-ishi, becoming the "stone of Tora Gozen," can cause the rain to fall. Let us also mention the "stone stupa of Torame," inscribed with Sanskrit letters, at Hōfukuji, a Sōtō Zen temple on Reikisan (Mount Sacred Tortoise) in Shimodani. Finally, there is a Tora-ga-ishi at Daijiji, a Rinzai Zen temple (in Ōsumi province) allegedly founded by Oiso no Tora.

62. Incidentally, the poetic metaphor "tears of Tora" gave its title to a famous rain scene painted by Hiroshige (mistranslated in an exhibition catalogue as "Tiger's Rain").

63. See Yanagita 1990c: 197.

64. Ibid., 193.

65. A similar view is expressed in Miyata 1975: 518; and Harada 1958.

66. Yanagita 1990c: 201–2.

67. Nishiguchi 1987: 116.

68. Several relic services were thus performed at the foot of Mount Hiei. See *Sanbō ekotoba*, trans. Kamens 1988: 303–4.

69. See *Konjaku monogatari shū* 12, 9, ed. Yamada 1959–63, vol. 3: 141–42.

70. See ibid.; and *Heike monogatari*, 22; quoted in Nishiguchi 1987: 94–96.

71. See *Ryōjin hishō* 313; trans. Kim 1994: 98.

72. On this question, see Faure 1998a; Amino 1989 and 1994.

73. See *Nanbokuchō ibun Kyūshū hen*, no. 3345; quoted in Iinuma 1990: 69.

74. Nishiguchi 1987: 83.

75. This case reveals both the compromise made by the temple and its limits—the ritual is performed outside of the temple's gate, not in the inner sanctum. See Morrell 1985: 252.

76. One significant exception is the work of Abe Yasurō (see, for instance, Abe 1989b, 1998).

77. See Abe 1989b: 191.

78. See *Kojidan* 4; and *Sakeiki* by Minamoto Tsuneyori (s.v. "Kannin 419" [1020]; quoted in Abe 1989b: 176). Women called nuns (*ni* or *ama*) in such stories were probably novices, who had received only the bodhisattva precepts, but not a formal ordination.

79. A variant reads: "Although I am a woman, I am not an ordinary person, but a saintly woman (*shōnyo*)."

80. See *Yōtenki*, in *Zoku gunsho ruijū* 48: 589.

81. Other sources mention the existence of Shōnyo-zuka (tumulus of the saintly woman).

82. Nishiguchi, quoted in Abe 1989b: 185–86.

83. On the theme of Kūkai and Maitreya, see the *Heike monogatari*, trans. McCullough 1988: 347.

84. Ibid., 187.

85. See Abe 1989b: 190.

86. Ibid., 190–91.

87. See Hosokawa 1993: 32; Abe 1989b: 174.

88. Abe 1989b: 192–93.

89. Hosokawa 1993: 176.

90. See, for instance, "Fushimi Tokiwa," "Nabiki Tokiwa," "Tokiwa mondō," "Fue no maki," and "Sanchū Tokiwa."

91. This topos recalls the story of the nun Sari, who silences the monks who want her to leave the temple where she has come to listen to a sermon.

92. These mountains/temples are: Tiantai shan, Moji shan, Yiwang shan, and Qingliang (Wutai shan) in China, and Enryakuji, Kōyasan, Hasedera, Okadera, Taimadera, and Tōnomine in Japan. This list appears nowhere else. The mention of Hasedera is surprising, since this was a Kannon temple open in principle to women.

93. In another of these "Tokiwa dialogues," dating from the Edo period, the exchange is even more developed and Tokiwa's victory more complete. Tōkōbō lists all kinds of proofs of the inferiority of women, drawn from Chinese, Japanese, Buddhist, and even Christian mythology: the myth of the demiurge Pan Gu (Jp. Banko), the creation story of the *Kojiki*, the life of the Buddha, and the myth of Adam and Eve (Adan and Eba). Tokiwa, however, turns all of these myths around to prove the superiority of women. Subdued, Tōkōbō becomes her disciple, together with three hundred monks, and the *nyonin kekkai* is abolished. See the recension in the Iwase Bunko Collection, copied in 1861. See Abe 1989b: 207.

94. Abe 1989b: 208.

95. See Amino 1978.

96. On this question, see Faure 1998a.

97. Samuel Weber, *Institution and Interpretation*, Minneapolis: University of Minnesota Press, 1987: 63.

98. On this question, see, for instance, Marra 1993b.

99. The meanings of "ban" from the Old French *ban*, are as follows: jurisdiction or proclamation of the suzerain, summons, proclamation, excommunication, exile; hence "banal," meaning originally belonging to the suzerain; and "à bandon" (from which comes "abandon") also means "at liberty." The "ban" is thus a "form of the relation," any relation; and "A ban donner" (usually translated "to abandon") originally meant both "mettre au pouvoir de" and "laisser en liberté."

100. Agamben 1998: 27.

CHAPTER 8

1. See Kaempfer 1906, vol. 2: 37–38, 340–41.

2. On the question of fund-raising, see Goodwin 1994.

3. On this question, see Hagiwara 1983.

4. Ibid., 285–86.

5. Amino 1993: 86–95.

6. Amino 1994.

7. Kaempfer 1906, vol. 2: 37–38.

8. *Towazugatari*, trans. Brazell 1973: 237.

9. Retired Emperor Shirakawa was accompanied during his third pilgrimage to Kumano by his niece (and adopted daughter) Fujiwara no Shōshi (the future Taikenmon'in, 1101–45), whom he wanted to marry to Emperor Toba, and by Shōshi's adoptive mother, Gion Nyogō. Taikenmon'in went on the same pilgrimage nine other times, twice alone. After her death in 1145, Empress Bifukumon'in (Fujiwara no Tokuko) went four times. Other imperial consorts followed suit, as well as women of the ruling classes, for instance, Hōjō Masako, the widow of Minamoto no Yoritomo, who went to Kumano in 1208.

10. In some variants, the nun's longevity is said to result from her eating the "nine-holed" shellfish offered by the sea-god. She is also said to have traveled through Japan holding a branch of white camellia, to have planted very long ago an old tree (a camellia), to have built a temple (*dō*) and a stupa, and to have preached without words. On the development of the legend, see Hori 1995, vol.

2: 689–97; and Nakayama 1930: 519–30. On mermaids, see also *Jakushōdō kok-kyōshū*, op. cit., 276.

11. See Kim 1994: 7. See also Saeki 1987: 19–20.

12. Another term borrowed from Buddhism is *Daruma*, by reference to the tumbling Daruma-dolls of popular culture. On the rather surprising posthumous destiny of Bodhidharma, the legendary founder of Chan/Zen, see Faure (forthcoming).

13. See Miyatake 1996: 33. They were also called *nagare no kimi* (Ladies of the Current), because some of them worked on small boats, but one gloss emphasizes that the expression actually refers to their "floating heart." Courtesans were also called *keisei* (lit. "loss of the castle"), in reference to the femmes fatales of Chinese history; or *jōrō*, a term originally designating daughters of the nobility. The highest courtesans were called *dayū* (or *tayū*), which in Chinese and Japanese means a high rank official, or even *oshō* (Reverend), a term normally designating Buddhist priests. In the Edo period, the red-light districts came to be called *kikenjō* (citadel from where happiness is visible), the name of the palace at the top of Mount Sumeru. By implication, the girls who lived there were all bodhisattvas. On this terminology, see Miyatake 1996.

14. Ibid., 54, 63.

15. See *Ryōjin hishō*, no. 560; trans. Kim 1994: 6.

16. See ibid., 123.

17. Ruch 1990: 530–31.

18. See Huizinga 1951; and Bataille 1986.

19. See *Yūjoki*, in Yamagishi et al. 1977: 154–56; Kim 1994: 44; and Kwŏn 1986b. See also Keirstead 1995.

20. See Pigeot 1998; Plutschow 1978; and Morrell 1985: 62–63, 71–72.

21. See *Yūjoki*, in Yamagishi et al. 1977: 154.

22. Ibid.

23. Keirstead 1995: 84.

24. Ibid., 85.

25. See "Miko to yūjo to," in Orikuchi 1975; and Yanagita 1990d.

26. Ruch 1990: 107.

27. Kwŏn 1986b: 296.

28. Marra 1993a: 52.

29. Ibid., 54.

30. On this question, see Law 1997: 19.

31. Or perhaps *Hyakushin* means "white god," another term referring to *Hya-kudayū*, or to a variant of the *oshiragami*, a deity worshipped in the form of dolls by female mediums. See Gorai 1990: 118–27.

32. *Kugutsu no ki*, 115–17. The *Kugutsu no ki* (or *Kairaishi no ki*) is translated in Law 1997: 97.

33. Keirstead 1995: 83.

34. Ōe no Masafusa writes, "In particular [these women pray to] Hyakudayū. This is one name for the *dōsojin*." On this deity, see Law 1993: 110; and Kim 1994: 9–10.

35. See *Yūjoki*, in Yamagishi et al. 1977: 155; quoted in Kim 1994: 8.

36. See *Yūjoki*, ibid. See also *Ryōjin hishō*, no. 380: "What the women of plea-sure like are, / miscellaneous arts, / hand drums, / small boats, / big umbrellas, / hair ornaments, and / Hyakudayū, to whom they pray for the love of men." Quoted in Law 1993: 113.

37. On the *oshiragami*, see Yanagita 1990e.

38. Affinities between *chigo* and *shirabyōshi* have been pointed out in Hoso-kawa 1993: 61–63.

39. *Heike monogatari*, trans. McCullough 1988: 30.

40. Ibid.

41. Ibid., 34. The allegorical nature of the girl's name, obvious in the case of Hotoke ("buddha"), is also apparent in that of Giō, whose first character refers to the gods (*gi*). Perhaps, as Abe Yasurō suggests, one could thus read the story allegorically as referring to the gods (*gi*) who are abandoned by Kiyomori to the profit of the buddhas (*hotoke*), but are saved by the buddhas (when Hotoke joins Giō). See Abe 1998: 175.

42. The hermitage, called Giōji, became a convent dependent on Daikakuji. It is located near Danrinji, another place connected with a famous woman, Empress Danrin. It contains the graves of Giō and Ginyo, and of their mother Toji; as well as a a stupa of Kiyomori. This hermitage is still popular today among romantic young girls.

43. *Heike monogatari*, trans. McCullough 1988: 36–37.

44. See Tonomura 1997: 159; and Brazell 1973: 114–15.

45. See *Tsurezureguza* 225.

46. *Gikeiki*, trans. McCullough 1966: 172.

47. It was taken up in the Edo period in *Koashi*, by Koide Jūgo, and in *Tone-gawa zushi,* by Akamatsu Sōtan. See Hosokawa 1993: 212.

48. Kōryōji still claims to possess a fragment of that robe, which turns out to be a textile of the Ming period.

49. In the *Gikeiki*, Shizuka and Iso no zenji are accompanied by two servants, who will be replaced by Kotoji in the Katsushika legend. See also the Nō plays *Yoshino Shizuka* and *Ninin Shizuka.*

50. See also, in the *Heike monogatari,* the couples formed by Shima-no-senzai and Waka-no-mae, Giichi and Gini, Gifuku and Gitoku.

51. One aspect of this context is the *basara* (flamboyant) style in the Muro-machi period; on this phenomenon, see Satō Kazuhiko 1995 and Amino 1993.

52. See Amino 1989, 1990, 1994.

53. See Amino 1989: 115.

54. See ibid., 120–24.

55. Amino 1994: 232–44.

56. The first red-light district (*kuruwa*) was created by Hideyoshi in Kyoto's Nijō district in 1589. Keisenchō became Shimabara, and in 1617 the Tokugawa shogunate sanctioned the famous Yoshiwara quarter in Edo, which housed be-tween 1,500 and 2,000 courtesans, classified in a strict hierarchy according to their status. Customers who did not want to comply with the strict rules of Yo-shiwara could go to the "night falcons" (older prostitutes, fifty to sixty years old, operating at crossroads, in particular at Yoshida-chō, east of Edo, near the Sumida), "nuns on a boat" (*funa-bikuni,* working on a small boat on the Sumida

river), and similar individual prostitutes. The traditional courtesans were now joined by prostitutes, who were mainly farm girls sold by impoverished fathers and brothers. As Joyce Ackroyd states, "The improved organization of the profession increased the demand for recruits at a time when ever-deteriorating agricultural conditions created a bottomless reservoir of surplus females." See Ackroyd 1959: 64.

57. See Saeki 1987: 102. On the "madness of love," see Hosokawa 1993: 33–38.

58. Saeki 1987: 206–8.

59. See O'Flaherty (Doniger) 1973: 43–53.

60. See Robert Darnton, "Sex for Thought," *New York Review of Books*, 22 Dec. 1994: 65–74.

61. See *Gosenshū* 1197, quoted in Kim 1994 :12.

62. See *Sangoku denki*, ed. Ikegami Jun'ichi 1976, vol. 2, chap. 6. The *engi* of Seiganji, compiled much later, toward the end of the Ashikaga regime, seems to have drawn from that source, but its content and style are more elaborate.

63. Shōkū also answered with a poem, which strangely resembles that of the god at Fushiogami in Kumano: "Since in Buddhism there is neither two nor three, how could there be five obstacles?" See Yanagita 1990b: 455.

64. See ibid., 517.

65. The story is also found in the *Senjūshō*, the *Jikkinshō*, the *Sangoku denki*, and the *Hokekyō jikidanshō*.

66. See *Kojidan* 3; Abe 1998: 150.

67. In his play *Sonezaki shinjū*, Chikamatsu writes: "At the beginning was the Bodhisattva Kannon, I mean my heroine, the courtesan Oharu." See Keene 1961.

68. See *Takakura-in gokōki*; quoted in Abe 1998: 162.

69. Ibid., 163.

70. See *Hōnen shōnin gyōjō gazu* 34, quoted in Gorai 1990: 113–14. The courtesan is presented as defiled. The courtesan who, during the Heian period, was perceived as a bodhisattva, became an impure woman in the Kamakura period, at least in appearance, for in reality, according to the Mahāyāna logic of nonduality, impurity is the very source of awakening.

71. See Coates and Ishizuka 1949: 612. In later commentaries, the place name Muro is often interpreted to mean "nondefilement" (*muro*), as in Shōkū's story.

72. See Abe 1998: 212.

73. See also the poems in the *Shinkokinshū* 978 and 979, translated slightly differently: "Here in the world / it's hard to renounce / everything; / how can you deny me / a night's borrowed lodging?" To which the courtesan answers, with a grain of salt: "From what I hear / you've left this world; / I wouldn't want / your heart to be dragged back / by a night's borrowed lodging!" See Kim 1994: 12.

74. *Senjūshō*, tale 118, in Moore 1982: 208–13. The story soon became so famous that, in the Edo period, there was in Eguchi a Kimi-dō in which wooden statues of the courtesan and of Saigyō were enshrined. Then, in the Nō play *Eguchi*, influenced by the legend of Shōkū, this courtesan became an avatar of the bodhisattva Fugen.

75. See *Senjūshō*, tale 44, in Moore 1982: 184–86. In the same collection, we hear the strange story about how Saigyō, while staying on Mount Kōya, con-

structed and animated with a spell a zombie-like creature, made out of collected bones. See tale 48, ibid., 190–94.

76. Yanagita 1990b: 510–15.

77. This story appears in various medieval sources like the *Kojidan* and the *Jikkinshō*, and in the Nō play *Eguchi*.

78. Saeki 1987: 50–52.

79. See the *Jōruri jūnidan sōshi*, a work attributed to Ono no Otsū, the semi-legendary founder of jōruri; quoted in Abe 1989b: 209–10.

80. Ibid., 210.

81. Ibid., 214.

82. The term also came to designate a ritual act of carnivalization, a kind of banquet performed during imperial rites like enthronement (*daijōsai*) or the Go-setsu festival in the eleventh month. See ibid., 219–21.

83. Ibid., 223.

84. Here is how the *Wakan sansai zue*, an Edo-period text that draws on an ancient vein, describes the origins of the *nyonin kekkai* in its section on Tateyama in Etchū province: "It is said in one tradition: Formerly, a nun from Obama in Wakasa, named Tōro, accompanied by a young woman and a girl, dared to enter [*suisan*] the mountain forbidden to women [*nyonin kekkai san*]." See *Wakan sansai zue*, ed. 1970, vol. 2: 841a.

85. On Izumi's biography, see Cranston 1969: 3–24.

86. This was at first the site of a hermitage, the Komi-dō, built by Michinaga for Izumi when she entered religious life. Originally a part of Tōboku-in, a temple founded by Michinaga's daughter Jōtōmon'in (Fujiwara no Akiko), it was named Jōshin-in after Izumi's death, and later rebuilt at Ichijō-Ōgawa. It was moved a second time to its present location during the Tenshō era (1573–92). See Cranston 1969: 22. Jōshin-in was initially a subtemple of Seiganji, a famous Jōdo-shū temple, on which see Yanagita 1990b: 437–38; and Foard 1980: 452.

87. Zuishin-in is said to have been founded in 991 by Ningai, an eighth-generation disciple of Kūkai. It was destroyed during the Jōkyū and Ōnin wars, and partly rebuilt in 1599. This place, anciently called Ono, was the domain of the Ono clan. Not far from the tomb of Emperor Daigo is a temple called Onodera, which was the *ujidera* of the Ono clan. Later in her life, Komachi retired to this place, where her suitor Fukakusa is said to have waited for (almost) one hundred nights

88. Katagiri 1975: 62. On the mysterious illness of Komachi (or of Izumi Shikibu, in some variants), see Hosokawa 1989a: 263–70.

89. See, for instance, the Nō play *Hokkejiku* (1687) in Tanaka Makoto, ed., *Mikan yōkyokushū*, 1966: 67–70; quoted in Kimbrough 1999: 12. We also recall that, paradoxically, Izumi Shikibu redeemed herself by making love to one thousand men.

90. Cranston 1969: 13, 17–18. See also Kimbrough 1999.

91. After Dōmyō's death, one of his friends saw him in a dream, on a boat on a lotus lake, chanting the *Lotus Sūtra*. Dōmyō told his friend that, although he had committed during his life many sins that prevented his rebirth in the Pure Land, he was eventually saved by the power of the *Lotus Sūtra* and could

expect to be reborn soon in Tuṣita Heaven. See *Genkō shakusho* 19: 9, trans. Ury 1971: 335.

92. See Ishida 1964 and 1984.

93. See *Kōchū kokkai taikei* 3, 1927: 64; quoted in Cranston 1969: 6.

94. Fukusenji was originally a Shingon temple, but it later became Rinzai. Even today, women cannot stay there. There is behind the temple, however, a sanctuary of the *ubugami*, and many pregnant women come to pray there for an easy child-birth.

95. Yanagita 1990a: 357–58. The same story, but shorter, is told in the *Jisha sōran* (edited in the Taishō era), where it is said that Izumi was the child of a white deer.

96. Yanagita connects this story to that of Jōruri Gozen (in Mikawa): There once was a householder (*chōja*) who wanted a child and came to pray at Yakushiji. Yakushi eventually appeared to him in a dream in the form of a great white deer, and told him that his prayer had been granted. Soon, a female child was born, and she was called Jōruri-hime. Her face was very beautiful, but she had forked feet. Her father, to hide them, covered them with cloth, thus creating a new kind of sock, the so-called *tabi*. See Yanagita 1990a: 360. This birth story calls to mind the legend of the ascetic Rishū Sennin who was practicing in the mountain behind Hōraiji (in Mikawa Prefecture). One day, as he had come out of his cave to uri-nate, a doe happened to eat the leaves touched by his urine and became pregnant, eventually giving birth to a cute baby girl. The ascetic sent the girl to Nara, to be brought up in the house of a noble. It is said that this girl grew up to become Empress Kōmyō. Because she had been carried by a doe, however, she was born with forked feet. The same motif is found in a number of Buddhist legends. See Yanagita 1990a: 361; and Strong 1992: 219–21.

97. In Japanese: namu yakushi shobyō shitsujō no gan tatete mi yori hotoke no na koso oshiminakere. See Cranston 1969: 3–24.

98. In Japanese: murasame wa / tada hitotoki no / mono zo kashi / ono ga mi no *kasa* / soko ni nugioke. The wordplay on *mi no kasa* (rain hat) explains the "passing shower" (*murasame*). See *Sangoku meisho zue* 55, quoted in Yanagita 1990a: 369. In variants of the story, the main protagonist is Ono no Komachi. See Yanagita 1990b: 458–59.

99. Yanagita Kunio discusses several variants of this story. See Yanagita 1990b: 456–58.

100. See, for instance, the *Seisuishō*: "Following an imperial order, Izumi Shik-ibu asks for rain." Quoted in Yanagita 1990a: 373.

101. In Japanese: chihayaburu / kami mo mimasaba / tachisawagi / ama no to gawa no / higuchi aketamae. See the *Koōgimi shū*.

102. In Japanese: haru ame no furu to mieji ga hare nikeri sono mi no kasa o sokoni nugioku; with again a wordplay on *kasa* (rain hat, but also syphilis). Quoted in Yanagita 1990a: 371.

103. A variant is is also found in the legend of Hiruma Yakushi in Bitchū prov-ince, one of the three great sanctuaries of Yakushi in Japan. See *Biyōki* 9, and *Bitchū junrei ryakuki*, quoted in ibid. Ono no Komachi catches a disease called *kasa* and prays to the Buddha Yakushi to be cured, but, obtaining no answer, she composes a resentful verse (above). At that point, the voice of Yakushi responds,

from the Buddha Hall ("The summer rain lasts only a moment . . ."), upon which her disease is cured. Yanagita gives similar examples, with variants of the two poems; see ibid., 371–72.

104. On this point, see Hosokawa 1989a: 263–70.

105. Ibid., 269.

106. On the "Komachi without vagina," see Higuchi 1988: 138. The same image of Komachi can be found in the *senryū* of the mid-Edo period, or in enigmas (*nazo-toki*) of the end of the Edo period.

107. Compare the sexual caricatures of Komachi, Empress Shōtoku, and the nun Sari, among numerous others.

108. On relations between Komachi legends and plays, see Kitagawa 1978: 239–49.

109. Much ink has been spilt over Komachi, and I cannot do justice to this complex figure here. For a summary of the theses, see Hosokawa 1989a: 218–28; and Strong 1994. Komachi has been studied principally from the literary standpoint, and, after Yanagita, from the folkloric standpoint (a fact deplored by some literary critics), but usually without much reference to Buddhism.

110. On the image of Komachi as femme fatale, see Strong 1994.

111. This cycle includes the following plays: "Kayoi Komachi," "Sōshi arai Komachi," "Ōmu Komachi," "Sotoba Komachi," and "Sekidera Komachi." See Godel and Kano 1997.

112. An interesting variant, inverting the "hundred-nights" motif, is found in a legend quoted in Minakata 1973: 10: 282.

113. Hosokawa 1989a: 26–28.

114. See Teele, Teele, and Teele 1993: 43–56.

115. Ibid., 48.

116. Ibid., 53–54.

117. See the *Kokinshū* 18, 938. This poem is a reply to a letter from an officer named Funya no Yasuhide, who had invited Komachi to visit him in his new location in Mikawa.

118. See *Sotoba Komachi*, *Ōmu Komachi*, and *Sekidera Komachi*, in Godel and Kano 1997. In the latter play, although she is over one hundred years old, Komachi has conserved her passion for poetry.

119. In his discussion about Nō, Suzuki Shōsan takes up the play *Sotoba Komachi*. He is puzzled by the suggestion that the old Komachi may not have been fully enlightened, and considers it a misinterpretation. To correct it, he rewrites the play, entitling it *Omokage Komachi* (Komachi in Dignity). In order to remove any ambiguity about Komachi's awakening, he eliminates the story of her possession by Fukakusa Shōshō. See Tyler 1977: 137.

120. The author of the *Mumyōzōshi* was actually Shunzei's granddaughter, born to his daughter Hachijō-in Sanjō and Fujiwara Moriyori.

121. See Hosokawa 1989a: 198; and Tanaka 1999: 108, 121.

122. See *Heike monogatari*, in McCullough 1988: 324.

123. Ibid.

124. *Kusōshi emaki*, Coll. Jakkōin, Hieizan; it is included with other *emaki* of the Six Ways in *Nihon emaki 7, Gaki zōshi, Jigoku zōshi, Yamai zōshi, Kusōshi* (Ed. Komatsu Shigemi, Tokyo: Chūōkōronsha, 1977).

125. On Komachi and the "Nine Faces of Death," see Lachaud 1995, 1997, and 1998; Chin 1998; Sanford 1988. On the "charming cadaver" topos in Indian Buddhism, scc Wilson 1995a and 1996.

126. See Hosokawa 1989a: 253.

127. Hosokawa 1989a: 253–54.

128. Chin 1998: 311.

129. Ibid.

130. Saeki 1987: 110.

131. Saeki 1987: 81.

132. In Japanese: totsu sama wa / Yoshizane naredo / oshii koto. There is a double-entendre on Yoshizane, the name of her father, which can be read as "good clitoris." See Godel and Kano 1997: 19.

133. In Japanese: to wa shirazu / akazu mon'e /kujūku ya. This is an allusion to the ordeal inflicted by Komachi on her suitor Fukakusa.

134. Brazell 1973: 187.

135. See Abe 1999: 47.

136. Wakita 1995: 67.

137. Abe 1999: 81.

138. Brazell 1973: 229.

139. Abe 1999: 58.

140. Ibid., 81.

141. Ibid.

142. Brazell 1973: 186.

143. Ibid., 202.

144. Ibid., 222–24.

145. Ibid. 264.

146. Marra 1993a: 51.

147. Ibid.

148. Ibid., 54.

149. Ibid., 55.

150. Ibid., 62.

151. Ibid., 63.

152. Ibid., 51.

153. Ibid., 54.

154. Ibid., 55.

155. On this point, see Foard 1980.

156. Marra 1993a: 101.

157. Ibid., 102.

158. This trope, however, which informs self-representations, does not define social reality. As Tonomura Hitomi has shown, there were also women in the public sphere. See Tonomura 1997.

159. See Pigeot 1998.

160. On Shinnyo, see also Nagai 1966–67, vol. 2: 255–65.

161. See Hosokawa 1992: 229.
162. Moi 1985: 58.

CHAPTER 9

1. See Yanagita 1990c: 26.
2. Carmen Blacker describes two kinds of sacred women active in modern Japan: the *nuru* and the *yuta*. "The *nuru* is a priestess who exercises spiritual power over a village or group of villages. Her office is hereditary and she does not resort to trance. Whereas the *yuta* has generally been called to sacred life through an illness, and she is a specialist in trance and possession." See Blacker 1975: 113–14. This distinction seems to overlap with that established by Nakayama Tarō between the *kannagi* and the *kuchiyose*. Blind mediums (called *itako* or *ichiko*) still act as mouthpieces for *kami* and ghosts in northern Japan. See also Nakayama [1930] 1974: 3–25.
3. For an analysis of the dual structure of Inari worship at Fushimi, see Smyers 1999.
4. Miyata 1983: 225.
5. See, for instance, Weiner 1976.
6. See Verdier 1979: 343–44.
7. Yanagita's thesis, expressed in *Imōto no chikara* (1990c) and *Josei to minkan denjō* (1990b), has constituted an unavoidable reference. See also Yanagita 1990a and 1990d; Miyata 1983, 1993b; and Hasegawa Kiyoko, *Onna no minzokushi* (1980). More recently, Katsuura Noriko, following Verdier's analysis, has focused on the role of nuns as "washerwomen," designating and analyzing them as "liminal women." See Katsuura 1995: 197–99; and Miyata 1993b: 226–38.
8. See Nakayama [1930] 1974: 561; and Miyata 1993b. On the so-called patriarchal theory, see Scott 1988.
9. Michel Foucault has suggested that the same could be said about contemporary sexual emancipation. See Foucault 1980a.
10. See *Nihon ryōiki*, trans. Nakamura 1973: 105–8, 163–64, and 197–99; Yanagita 1990c: 92–97.
11. Miyata 1983: 223–26.
12. See the discussion on "the magical power of the pubic hair," in Miyata 1983: 77–83. On the religious function of hair, see also Eilberg-Schwartz and Doniger 1995; Hiltebeitel and Miller 1998.
13. *Soso* is a slang word referring to the vagina (*inmon*, the "yin gate"), which is sometimes, according to Minakata, called the "seven calamities" (letter to Yanagita Kunio, 22 April 1944). The two scholars were not the first to notice this strange relic. The *San'yō zōki*, for instance, already mentioned "the hair of the seven calamities" kept in Izu and elsewhere, and specified that it is pubic hair. The author of the *Kasshi yawa*, on the other hand, expresses some skepticism regarding the extraordinary length of the pubic hair of these "sacred women" (*reifu*). See *Kasshi yawa*, quoted in Miyata 1983: 80.
14. Yanagita Kunio to Minakata Kumagusu, Meiji 44/8/11 (1911).
15. Yanagita 1990c: 43.

16. On Okinawan religion, see Kawahashi 1992, 2000a, and 2000b.

17. See Yoshie 1989.

18. According to one variant, she picked up the arrow and placed it under her bed, subsequently becoming pregnant.

19. See *Yamashiro Fudoki*, quoted in Ouwehand 1964: 153–54.

20. See Yanagita 1990c: 88.

21. Ibid., 83.

22. Ouwehand 1964: 152–53; Ishida 1984: 181–82.

23. A Buddhist variant of the *Kamo engi* is found in the biography of the priest Gyōen, in the *Genkō shakusho*. Gyōen receives wood of supernatural origin, from a zelkova tree near Kamo, to make a thousand-armed Kannon. The relation to the *Kamo engi* appears in the following episode: A maiden is impregnated by an unknown man. After she gives birth, her father gathers the villagers. The child takes a cup of wine in front of eaves, where there is a duck-feather—hence the name Kamo. He then turns into a thunderbolt and ascends to heaven, together with his mother. Mother and child eventually manifest themselves as deities at the foot of the zelkova tree. The statue, after completion, is installed at Gyōganji. See *Genkō shakusho*, trans. Ury 1971: 306–8.

24. Yanagita 1990c: 88–91.

25. See *Yuirō setsuden* for other examples in which the brother (Tamayorihiko) is punished for not believing his sister, or not obeying her. Quoted in Yanagita 1990c: 51. We even find legends of ogress-like sisters, which, according to Yanagita, seem to recount the breach of the spiritual ties between brother and sister.

26. Yanagita 1990c: 52–56.

27. See ibid., 80; and Ouwehand 1964: 155.

28. Yanagita, "Tamayorihime kō," quoted in Ouwehand 1964: 156. See also, in the *Nihon ryōiki*, the story of the girl who gave birth to two stones that continue to grow. Eventually, the Inaba deity makes it known through an oracle that these stones are his "children." See *Nihon ryōiki* 3. 31, ed. Endō and Kasuga 1967: 411; trans. Nakamura 1973: 265–66.

29. Yanagita 1990c: 52.

30. See Yoshie 1989: 51–90.

31. This functional division calls to mind the couple formed in the Edo period by the *miko* and the *yamabushi*, the former acting as medium, the latter as exorcist. A similar functional division along gender lines can be observed in various cultures: for instance, in Taiwan.

32. On this legend, see, for instance, Wakita 1997: 168–69.

33. Yoshie 1989: 77.

34. Ibid., 81.

35. See *Heike monogatari*; trans. McCullough 1988: 235–36.

36. Yoshie 1989: 82.

37. The situation may have had some similarities with the later coupling of the *miko* and the *yamabushi* in Shugendō rituals. In such tandems, however, the active role was claimed exclusively by the male *yamabushi*, who alone were entitled to enter the sacred mountains to acquire or recharge their powers; all that the *miko* retained from their alleged occult powers was their capacity as mediums. See

Blacker 1975, chapters 6 ("The ancient Sibyl," 104–26), 7 ("The Living Goddess," 127–39), and 8 ("The Blind Medium," 140–63).

38. See *Ōkagami*, trans. Yamagiwa [1966] 1977: 100–101.

39. Ibid., 102.

40. On the Kamo priestess, see Kamens 1990.

41. Tanaka 1996: 65–119.

42. According to the *Saigū no ki*, the first *saigū* was the wife of Sujin Tennō,
Toyosuki-irihime no Mikoto, who acted as an intermediary between the *kami*
Amaterasu and the people. In the next generation, Yamatohime no Mikoto, a
consort of Emperor Suinin Tennō, is said to have taken the "spirit" of Amaterasu
(that is, the sacred mirror) to Ise. See *Yamatohime no mikoto seiki* in *Shintō ronshū*, ed. Ōsumi 1977: 8–38.

43. See *Tsūkai sankeiki*, in *Nihon shomin seikatsu shiryō shūsei* 26, 1983: 460.

44. The *Nihon shoki* consulted by Chikatsune was not the original text, but a
medieval commentary. See Tanaka 1996: 105–6.

45. Orikuchi Shinobu, "Fujisan to joseishin no omokage to," quoted in Kageyama 1971: 41. Kageyama Haruki, in the case of the sun-goddess, argues that the
priestess who originally served the deity Toyouke was deified under the name
Amaterasu, becoming the main *kami*. Usually, however, scholars argue that it was
the other way around, and that Toyouke was initially the name of the goddess
(and thus, of the priestess) who served Amaterasu. On this question, see Yamamoto 1998b; and Teeuwen 1996.

46. She was the wife of Emperor Montoku, and was a *saigū* for fifteen years.
There seems to be here some similarity with the story of the seduction of Empress
Somedono (who, in some variants, was also seduced by Narihira). Even if the
circumstances are not quite the same, in both cases the woman is the weak link
in the lineage, the person through whom scandal happens.

47. See *Ise monogatari*, sect. 69, in Ōtsu and Tsukijima 1957: 150–51.

48. See *Jikkinshō*, quoted in Tanaka 1996: 83.

49. Ibid., 117.

50. Ibid., 110; see also Klein 1997; and Faure (forthcoming).

51. Tanaka 1996: 117.

52. Incidentally, the assimilation of Izumi and Narihira with the *dōsojin* (a
dual deity symbolized by yin-yang stones) makes a kind of counterpoint to the
image of Sotoba Komachi and that of the uba who turned into stone for transgressing the *nyonin kekkai*.

53. Although it is often said that *ukareme* and *asobime* were originally *miko*,
when one looks at texts such as the *Man'yōshu*, one sees no indication of this. It
seems clear that *miko* were wandering women. According to Gorai Shigeru, however, the character *yū* in *yūjo* refers to the *kuchiyose* (induced possession, as in
the case of the *oshira asobi*), not to "excursions." See Gorai 1989: 107. See also
Nakayama [1930] 1974.

54. See *Ryō no shūge*, quoted in Haguenauer [1930] 1977: 308.

55. Ame no Uzume was the ancestor of the Sarume clan, a clan originally lo-
cated in Ise and Shima before its female members came to serve the Yamato court.
The name Sarume no kimi is said to derive from her association with Sarutahiko.
According to the *Nihongi*, Uzume attended the god Sarutahiko and followed him

to the area of the Isuzu river in Ise. The archaic form of Amaterasu worship, and perhaps also the myth of the Heavenly Cave itself, was brought by the *sarume* from Ise to the Yamato court. At any rate, this myth was related to the *chinkonsai*, a ritual during which a priestess danced on the bottom of an upside-down tub called *ukefune*, stamping resoundingly on it, while occasionally striking it with the end of a sacred spear or bough as she counted from one to ten; in a variant, a Nakatomi priest tied a knot in the ruler's life-cord by counting from one to ten. Tying knots in strings was called *tamamusubi*, or "tying the soul." The striking of the tub with a spear is usually interpreted as suggesting sexual intercourse. The author of the *Kogoshūi* (808), Inbe Hironari, deplores the decline of the Sarume clan, and insists that the *ukefune* dance must be performed by a Sarume maiden, rather than by a priestess of the Nakatomi clan, as had become the case. See Gorai 1990; and Matsumae 1980.

56. On this ceremony, see in particular Haguenauer [1930] 1974.

57. See Saeki 1987: 69.

58. On this question, see Wakita 1997: 168–69.

59. See *Heike monogatari*, trans. McCullough 1988: 206.

60. See Sered 1994: 182–83.

61. *Ōkagami*, trans. Yamagiwa 1977: 147.

62. Ibid., 147–48.

63. See *Nihon kiryaku* (in *Shin kokushi taikei*), quoted in Nishiguchi 1987: 225.

64. See *Gukanshō*, trans. Brown and Ishida 1979.

65. See Waley 1932: 550.

66. See Nishiguchi 1989a: 131.

67. See *Go-Toba-in giryō takuki*, in *Zoku gunsho ruijū* 33, 1; quoted in Nishiguchi 1989c: 139.

68. *Towazugatari*, trans. Brazell 1973: 203–4.

69. Ibid.

70. See Tyler 1990: 221.

71. *Kasuga gongen genki*, quoted in ibid., 165.

72. See also *Kasuga gongen genki*, quoted in ibid., 266–67.

73. See *Kojidan*, ed. Kobayashi 1981: 239; *Ryōjin hishō* 2: 564, ed. Enoki 1979: 221; Geinōshi kenkyūkai, ed., *Nihon geinōshi*, 1981–90, vol. 2: 113. See also Marra 1993a: 54.

74. See *Yōtenki*, in *Zoku gunsho ruijū*, vol. 2, pt. 2: 619; trans. Grapard 1987: 218.

75. Tyler 1990: 269.

76. Ibid., 272–73.

77. *Genkō shakusho* 4:11, trans. Ury 1971: 250–51. See also Tyler 1990: 211; Abe 1998: 183.

78. Abe 1998: 186.

79. These schemas can still be found at work even in the analyses of otherwise more sensitive anthropologists; see, for instance, Bloch 1992: 52–61.

80. Sered 1994: 8.

81. Ibid., 9.

82. See Ishida 1956 and 1984: 173–258.

83. See Faure 1998a; and Cole 1998.

84. See Ouwehand 1964: 62–63, 129. On the relations between stone, sword, and the thunder-god, see also Reischauer 1940.

85. A derived theme, popular in ghost stories, is that of the *ubume* who appears at night, holding in her arms a child, and asks passers-by to hold it. In some legends, she is also saved by Kōbō Daishi. See Miyata 1994: 216.

86. See Kageyama 1971: 115.

87. The meaning "wet-nurse" seems more recent than that of "old woman." See Yanagita 1990c: 195.

88. See Yanagita 1990b; Orikuchi, "Mizu no onna," in Orikuchi 1975, vol. 2: 80–109.

89. See *Nihon shoki* 3.1, section "Hiko-hohodemi."

90. Orikuchi Shinobu thinks that this episode gave birth to the cult of the *uba-gami* (wet-nurse goddess), that is, of the *oba/ubagami* who raises the god. See Orikuchi 1975, loc. cit. For Yanagita, the education of the child-god born every year constitutes the primitive function of the *miko*. See Yanagita 1990c.

91. As noted earlier, in some variants of Kūkai's legend, his mother is also called Tamayorihime. These mythical elements, grafted on the legend of Kōbō Daishi (*daishi*, "Great Master," resonates with Daishi, "divine child"), transform Kūkai into a thunder-god related to the *goryō* ("vengeful spirits"). On the Kamo myth, see Yanagita 1990c: 83–88.

92. See ibid., 220.

93. McCullough 1959: 304.

94. A case in point is the story of the young Amako, ancestor of the Amako family in Izumo. When their house was destroyed by the enemy, the only survivor was this child, who was brought up by his grandmother, a nun, hence the name: *Ama-ko* (nun-child). In another version, he is the child of a celestial being, and is therefore likewise named *Ama-ko* (Heaven-child). See Yanagita 1990c: 223.

95. Ibid., 226–228.

96. Ibid., 233.

97. Ibid., 207–216.

98. See *Minakata Kumagusu zenshū*, vol. 10: 134–35.

99. This motif of the sacrifice of the woman for the man she loves can be found in various legends: for instance, in that of the Kamakura priest Mongaku, a former warrior who had become a Buddhist ascetic after killing the woman he loved by mistake, instead of her husband.

100. Yanagita 1990c: 234–35.

101. See Miyata 1983: 59–62; and 1993b: 167.

102. Miyata 1983: 64.

103. See Yanagita 1990b: 547–49.

104. The image of Datsueba calls to mind that of the Indian goddess Ieṣtha (also represented as an old woman with sagging breasts), associated with death. On this deity, see Volkmann 1995: 199.

105. See Seidel 1992–93: 128–29; and Gorai Shigeru, "Shugendō no michi," in the catalog of the exhibition "Yama to Nihonjin," Shugendō ten, Asahi shinbunsha 1973. See also Saeki Yukinaga, *Tateyama fudoki no oka*, Toyama, 1972: 66–80. Gorai thinks that this cult originated on Hakusan, a mountain southwest

of Tateyama, and more precisely at Chūgūji in Kegasa, where there was a *nuno-hashi* of the same kind as the one on Tateyama. See Gorai 1997. This would explain the similar structure of the Shirayama (Hakusan) ritual; on this ritual, see also Miyata 1994.

106. As noted earlier, this temple also claims to possess the original "stone-pillow" (*ishi-makura*).

107. Miyata 1994: 212–14. Of course, the stone is said to have been made by Kōbō Daishi.

108. See Rawlinson 1986.

109. See Faure 1987.

110. Convenient summaries are provided in Kelsey 1981b.

111. On Mélusine, see Le Goff 1980.

112. See *Fudoki*, ed. Akimoto 1958; *Kojiki*, ed. Kurano and Takeda 1958; *Nihon shoki*, ed. Sakamoto Tarō et al., 1977.

113. See Minakata 1973: 319–20.

114. The *Nihon ryōiki*, for instance, tells the outlandish story of a young girl who, having climbed a mulberry tree to pick leaves, fell to the ground when she was frightened by a large snake. The snake crept into her vagina while she laid unconscious. The girl was taken home and treated by a doctor, who had a brew poured into her vagina until the snake came out. The snake had had time to lay eggs inside her, however, and another nine gallons of brew were needed before all of the eggs came out. The girl finally awoke from a comatose state. The story does not end there, however, since the girl died three years later, after being once again violated by a snake. See *Nihon ryōiki*, 41; trans. Nakamura 1973; see also *Konjaku monogatari shū* 24, ed. Yamada Yoshio 1963, vol. 4.

115. See *Minakata Kumagusu zenshū*, vol. 4.

116. See *Konjaku monogatari shū* 24:9; ed. Yamada Yoshio, 1963, vol. 4: 290.

117. *Kokon chōmonjū* 20: 270; quoted in Tanaka 1992: 177.

118. See, for instance, the version of the *Dōjōji engi emaki* in *Konjaku monogatari shū* 14: 3, ed. Yamada Yoshio et al., 1963, vol. 3: 277.

119. See Tanaka 1992: 161.

120. Ibid., 169–70.

121. Ibid., 172–73.

122. See, for instance, *Keiran shūyōshū*, T. 76, 2410: 517c, 864a.

123. Tanaka 1992: 194–95.

124. On this dream, see Girard 1990: 329, Tanabe 1992, Faure 1996: 124.

125. After the death of Myōe, two of his male disciples, Jiben and Sonben, drowned themselves, like the two disciples of Śākyamuni, Śāriputra and Maudgalyāyana, who followed the Buddha seven days after his nirvāṇa. The fact that a statue of Maitreya was carved for the funerals of the two monks suggests that they had hoped to follow Myōe to Maitreya's Tusita Heaven. On this question, see Okuda 1997: 47.

126. Tanaka 1992: 198.

127. Abe 1998: 328–32.

128. Ibid., 333. The *Konjaku monogatari shū* contains a similar story, albeit with a happier ending, about a young monk named Tankei, who receives from Fudō Myōō a revelation that he is bound karmically to a certain girl. Tankei tries

to kill her, and believes that he has succeeded. Eventually, he breaks his monastic vows with another woman, but she turns out to be the same girl, who miraculously survived. Upon realizing this, he returns to lay life and marries his predestined lover. See *Konjaku monogatari shū* 31:3, ed. Yamada Yoshio et al., 1963: vol. 5.

129. Tanaka 1992: 191–92.

130. See *Konjaku monogatari shū*, 3:11, ed. Yamada Yoshio et al., 1963: vol. 1: 215.

131. See *Keiran shuyōshu*, T. 76, 2410: 626c.

132. The motif of the reptilian woman who comes to listen to a priest's sermon is widespread in medieval Japan. See, for example, the dialogue of the disciple of the Sōtō Zen master Tsūgen Jakurei, Ikkei Eishū, and a woman who had been reborn as a snake due to her past karma, in *Yōtakuji Tsūgen zenji gyōjō*, SZ 17, Shiden 2: 270b.

AFTERTHOUGHTS

1. See van Gennep 1960 [1909].
2. See Keyes 1986: 68.
3. Christ 1991: 91; quoted in Sered 1994: 280–81.
4. Sered 1994: 281.
5. On this question, see Fraisse 1995.
6. See, for instance, the myths of the *Shintōshū*, a text reflecting the development of the patriarchal system in medieval Japan. On this question, see Wakita 1999.
7. Sered 1994: 127.
8. Although she acknowledges that Buddhist "traditional attitudes" toward sexuality have been negative, Diana Paul, for instance, writes that "enlightenment is sexless and ageless"; see Paul 1979: 284. In so doing, she merely reiterates the "sexless view" offered by the tradition, without realizing that this view is precisely that of a certain male "descent group." At the same time, she still claims to have found in Queen Śrīmālādevī a "female buddha": female, although sexless. Rita Gross also argues for the value of androgyny as a way of going beyond what Luce Irigaray once called "this sex which is not one." Contrary to Irigaray's theory, however, for the Buddhists it is the male gender "which is not one," inasmuch as it does not carry the stigmata of sexual differentiation/duality. Indian Buddhism, inheriting the medical discourse of its times and places, has tended to consider androgyny, not so much as a transcendence of sex and gender, but as their exacerbation. As Peter Brown notes with respect to Christian ascetics, male and female: "Bodies defended with such care were not destined to melt away in some distant transformation. Far from being a superficial and transitory layer of the person, sexual differences, and the behavior appropriate to them, were validated for all eternity." See Brown 1988: 383.
9. Bloch 1987: 333.
10. See Derrida 1981.
11. Sered 1994: 8–9.

12. Contrary to Indian Vajrayāna, from which it derives, the sexual teaching of the Tachikawa-ryū is "natalist," in the sense that it emphasizes procreation and embryology, rather than mere eroticism. But it remains in other ways, precisely due to this emphasis on procreation and motherhood, dependent on patriarchy.

13. See Quignard 1997: 135.

14. Ibid., 136.

15. Moi 1985: 166.

16. See Foucault 1980a.

17. See Cixous 1976: 254.

18. On this idealization, see Faure 1998a: 241–65.

BIBLIOGRAPHY

PRIMARY SOURCES

Abbreviations

DNBZ Dai Nihon bukkyō zensho. Ed. Bussho kankōkai. 151 vols. Tokyo: Bussho kankōkai, 1912–22. Reed. Suzuki Research Foundation. 100 vols. Tokyo: Suzuki Research Foundation, 1970–73.

DZZ Dōgen zenji zenshū. Ed. Ōkubo Dōshū. Tokyo: Chikuma shobō, 1969–70.

KST Kokushi taikei. See *Shintei zōho kokushi taikei.*

NKBT Nihon koten bungaku taikei. Ed. Takagi Ichinosuke et al. 102 vols. Tokyo: Iwanami shoten, 1957–68.

NKBZ Nihon koten bungaku zenshū. Ed. Akiyama Ken et al. 51 vols. Tokyo: Shōgakkan, 1970–76.

NSTK Nihon shisō taikei. Ed. Ienaga Saburō et al. 67 vols. Tokyo: Iwanami shoten, 1970–82.

PTS Pāli Text Society. London.

SBE Sacred Books of the East. London: Pāli Text Society.

SKNS Shinchō koten Nihon shūsei. Tokyo: Shinchōsha.

SNKBT Shin Nihon koten bungaku taikei. Ed. Satake Akihiro et al. 100 vols. Tokyo: Iwanami shoten, 1989–.

ST Shintō taikei. Ed. Shintō taikei hensankai, Tokyo: Shintō taikei hensankai, 1990.

SZ Sōtōshū zensho. Reed. Sōtōshū zensho kankōkai. 18 vols. Tokyo: Sōtōshū shūmuchō, 1970–73.

T Taishō shinshū daizōkyō. Ed. Takakusu Junjirō and Watanabe Kaigyoku. 85 vols. Tokyo: Taishō issaikyō kankōkai, 1924–32.

TZ See *Zuzō.*

Zuzō Taishō shinshū daizōkyō zuzōbu. Ed. Takakusu Junjirō and Watanabe Kaigyoku. 12 vols. Tokyo: Taishō issaikyō kankōkai, 1924–35.

ZZ Dai Nihon zokuzōkyō. Ed. Nakano Tatsue. 150 vols. Kyoto: Zōkyō shoin, 1905–12. New edition, Taibei: Xinwenfeng, 1968–70.

COLLECTIONS

Chūsei shintō ron. Ed. Ōsumi Kazuo. *NSTK* 19. Tokyo, 1977.

Bukkyō daijiten. Ed. Mochizuki Shinkō. 10 vols. Sekai seiten kankō kyokai, 1933. Reedited 1973.

Bukkyō daijii. Ed. Fuzanbō henshūbu. 7 vols. Tokyo: Fuzanbō, 1973.

Dai kanwa jiten. Ed. Morohashi Tetsuji. 13 vols. Tokyo: Shōgakkan. 1960. Reedited 1986.

Dai Nihon bukkyō zensho. 100 vols. Reprint Tokyo: Suzuki Research Foundation, 1970–73.

Gunsho ruijū. Ed. Hanawa Hokiichi [*Shinkō*] Gunsho ruijū. 24 vols. Tokyo: Naigai shoseki, 1928–37.

Jōsai daishi zenshū. Ed. Kohō Chisan. 1937. Reprint Yokohama: Daihonzan Sōji-ji, 1976.

Kamakura ibun. Ed. Takeuchi Rizō. 42 vols. to date. Tokyo: Tōkyōdō shuppan, 1971–.

Kōbō Daishi zenshū. By Kūkai (774–835). Tokyo-Kyoto, 1910. Reprint 8 vols. Kōyasan daigaku, Mikkyō bunka kenkyūjo, 1965.

Muromachi jidai monogatari taisei. Ed. Yokoyama Shigeru and Matsumoto Ryūshin. 13 vols. Tokyo: Kadokawa shoten, 1973–85.

Nihon zuihitsu taisei. 23 vols. Tokyo: Yoshikawa kōbunkan, 1976.

Shintei zōho kokushi taikei. Ed. Kuroita Katsumi. 58 vols. (2 suppl. vols.) Tokyo: Yoshikawa kōbunkan, 1929–62.

Tendaishū zensho. 25 vols. Tokyo: Daiichi shobō, 1973.

Zoku gunsho ruijū. Ed. Hanawa Hokiichi. 1822. 34 vols. Tokyo: Zoku gunsho ruijū kanseikai, 1972.

Zoku zoku gunsho ruijū. Ed. Zoku gunsho ruijū kanseikai. 16 vols, 1906. Tokyo: Kokusho kankōkai, 1970.

INDIVIDUAL WORKS

Abhidharmakośa-śāstra. By Vasubandhu. T. 29, 1558. French trans. in La Vallée Poussin 1923–31. 6 vols. English trans. in Pruden 1988–89.

Ainōshō. Ed. Masamune Atsuo. Tokyo: Nihon koten senshū kankōkai, 1936.

Asabashō. DNBZ 39.

Azuma kagami. In Nagahara Keiji and Kishi Shōzō, eds., *Zenshaku Azuma Kagami*. 6 vols. Tokyo: Shinjinbutsu ōraisha, 1976–79.

Biqiuni zhuan (ca. 516). By Baochang. T. 50, 2063.

Bizei betsu. By Jien (d. 1225). In Tendai shūten hensanjo, ed. Zoku Tendaishū zensho. Mikkyō 3, Kyōten chūshakurui 2: 212–57. Tokyo: Shunjūsha, 1990.

Caṇḍamahāroṣana-tantra. Manuscript. Paris: Bibliothèque Nationale.

Chōshūki. By Minamoto no Morotoki. Vols. 16–17 in *Zōho shiryō taisei*, ed. by Zōho shiryō taisei kankōkai. Kyoto: Rinsen shoten, 1965.

Chūyū ki. By Fujiwara no Munetada (1062–1141). Vols. 9–15 in *Shiryō taisei*. Revised and expanded edition. Kyoto: Rinsen shoten.

Cullavaga. Trans. I. B. Horner, *Tripitaka*. *Vinayapiṭaka: The Book of the Discipline (Vinaya-piṭaka)*. Vol. 5. London: Luzac and Co., 1949–66.

Dahui Pujue chanshi pushuo. ZZ 1, 31, 5.

Dahui Pujue chanshi yulu. T. 47.

Dai Nihon hokkekyō genki. (ca. 1040–44). By Chingen. NSTK 7.

Dazhidulun. T. 25, 1509. French trans. in Lamotte 1944–80.

Denryaku. By Fujiwara no Tadazane. DNK ed. 5 vols.

Dīghā nikāya. Trans. T. W. and C.A.F. Rhys Davids, *Dialogues of the Buddha*. Vol. 2. Sacred Books of the Buddhists, 2–4. London: Pāli Text Society, 1899–1921.

Dīrghāgama. Chinese trans. by Buddhayaśas and Zhu Fonian. T. 1, 1.

Eiga monogatari (ca. 1092). NKBT 75. Trans. McCullough and McCullough 1980.

Engi shiki. Ed. Fujiwara no Tokihira, Fujiwara no Tadahira et al. In KST 26.

Fangyin mingyi ji. By Fayun. *T.* 54, 2131.

Fanwang jing. T. 24, 1484.

Fozu tongji. T. 49, 2035.

Fudoki. Ed. Akimoto Kichirō. *NKBT* 2. Tokyo: Iwanami shoten, 1958.

Fūga wakashū (1343–49). By Emperor Kōgon (r. 1332–33). Partial translation in Brower and Miner, *Japanese Court Poetry,* 1961.

Garbha-upaniṣad. In *Upaniṣad-Samuccaya.* Trans. in *108 Upaniṣads.* Bombay: Nirṇaya-sāgara Press, 1925.

Genji monogatari. Ed. Yamagishi Tokuhei. *NKBT* 15. Tokyo: Iwanami shoten, 1959.

Genkō shakusho (1322). By Kokan Shiren (1278–1346). *DNBZ* 62, 410 (in 1973 reprint); vol. 101 in 1921 edition.

Genpei jōsuiki. Ed. Kokumin tosho kabushiki kaisha. Nihon bungaku taikei 16. Tokyo: Kokumin tosho kabushiki kaisha, 1921.

Gikeiki. Ed. Okami Masao. *NKBT* 37. Tokyo: Iwanami shoten, 1959. See also Kajihara Masaaki, ed., *Gikeiki. NKBZ* 31. Tokyo: Shōgakkan, 1971.

Giso rokujō. By Yichu. See *Shishi liutie.*

Godanshō. In *Zoku gunsho ruijū* 27. Tokyo: Zoku gunsho ruijū kanseikai, 1931: 549–627.

Gonki. By Fujiwara no Yukinari. *ST* 4–5.

Gosen [waka] shū (ca. 951). Ed. Nakatsukasa Eijirō. [Kochū] kokka taikei, 3. Tokyo: Kokumin Toshō, 1927.

Goshūi wakashū (1086). By Fujiwara Michitoshi. Ed. Nakatsukasa Eijirō. [Kochū] kokka taikei, 3. Tokyo: Kokumin Toshō, 1927.

Goyuigō. 25-article version (ca. early to mid-10th c.) Attr. to Kūkai. *T.* 77, 2431.

Gukanshō (1219). By Jien. In Okami Masao and Akamatsu Toshihide, eds. *Gukanshō. NKBT* 86. Tokyo: Iwanami shoten, 1967. English trans. in Brown and Ishida 1979.

Gyokuyō. By Kujō Kanezane. 3 vols. Tokyo: Kokusho kankōkai, 1907. See also Takahashi Sadaichi, ed., *Kundoku Gyokuyō.* 8 vols. Tokyo: Takahashi shoten, 1988.

Hachiman gudōkun. By Kaigen (d. 1469) and Urabe Kanetomo (d. 1511). *Gunsho ruijū* 13; and *Zoku gunsho ruijū* 30.

Heike monogatari (ca. 1218). Ed. Takagi Ichinosuke et al. *NKBT* 32–33. Tokyo: Iwanami shoten, 1960. See also Ichiko Teiji, ed. *Heike monogatari.* 2 vols. *NKBZ* 29–30. Tokyo: Shōgakkan, 1973–75.

Hōbutsushū. (1179–1193). Attr. to Taira no Yasuyori. In Koizumi Hiroshi et al., eds., *Hōbutsushū, Kankyo no tomo, Hirasan kojin reitaku. SNKBT* 40. See also: Yoshida Kōichi and Koizumi Hiroshi, eds., *Hōbutsushū (kyūsatsubon).* Koten bunko 258. Koten bunko, 1969.

Hōgen monogatari. Anonymous. In Nagazumi Yasuaki and Shimada Isao, eds., *Hōgen monogatari, Heiji monogatari. NKBT* 31. Tokyo: Iwanami shoten, 1986.

Hōjōki (1212). By Kamo no Chōmei (1151–1213). In Nishio Minoru, ed. *Hōjōki, Tsurezuregusa. NKBT* 30. Tokyo: Iwanami shoten, 1957. Also: Miki Sumito, ed. *Hōjōki, Hosshinshū.* Tokyo: Shinchōsha, 1976.

Hokekyō jikidanshō. (ca. 1546). 14 vols. Kyoto: Rinsen shoten, 1989.

Hokekyō jurin shūyōshō (1512). By Sonshun. Ed. Nagai Yoshinori. 4 vols. Kyoto: Rinsen shoten, 1991.

Honchō kōsōden (1702). By Shiban. *DNBZ* 63.

Honchō shinsenden (ca. 1098). By Ōe no Masafusa (1041–1111). *NSTK* 7. *Zoku gunsho ruijū* 8. Also in Kawaguchi Hisao, ed. *Kobon setsuwashū, Honchō shinsenden*. Asahi koten zensho. Tokyo: Asahi shinbunsha, 1967.

Hōnen shōnin gyōjō ezu. By Shunshō (1255–1335). In *Jōdoshū zensho* 16.

Hōnen shōnin zenshū. Ed. Kuroda Shindō and Mochizuki Shinkō. Kyoto: Shūsuisha, 1916. Also: Kyoto: Heirakuji shoten, 1955.

Hosshinshū (ca. 1212–16). By Kamo no Chōmei (1151–1213). In Miki Sumito, ed. *Hōjōki, Hosshinshū*. *SKNS*. Tokyo: Shinchōsha, 1976.

Imakagami. Attributed to Fujiwara Tametsune. Tokyo: Kōdansha gakujutsu bunko. See also Rekishi monogatari kōza kankō iinkai, ed. 1997.

Ippen hijiri-e. In *Nihon emaki taisei*, vol. 20. Tokyo: Chūō kōronsha, 1978.

Ippen shōnin eden. Ed. Komatsu Shigemi. Tokyo: Chūō kōronsha, 1988.

Ise monogatari. Ed. Ōtsu Yūichi and Tsukishima Yū. *NKBT* 9. Tokyo: Iwanami shoten, 1957.

Jakushōdō kokkyōshū. By Unshō (1614–93). *DNBZ* 149. Tokyo: Bussho kankōkai, 1912.

Jichin ōshō musōki. In *Zoku Tendaishū zensho*, Mikkyō, vol. 3.

Jikkinshō. (1252). Attr. to Yuasa Munenari. Ed. Kuroita Katsumi. *Shintei zōho kokushi taikei*, vol. 18. Tokyo: Yoshikawa kōbunkan, 1932.

Jin shu. By Fan Xuanling (578–648). 10 vols. Beijing: Zhonghua shuju, 1974.

Jingde chuandeng lu (1004). By Daoyuan. *T.* 51, 2076.

Jingpingmei cihua. By Xiaoxiaosheng (Ming). 4 vols. Hong Kong: Xinghai wenhua, 1987.

Jōruri monogatari. In Yokoyama Shigeru and Matsumoto Ryūshin, eds., *Muromachi jidai monogatari taisei*, vol. 7: 292–333. Tokyo: Kadokawa shoten, 1973–85.

Kagerō nikki. By Fujiwara Michitsuna no haha. In Suzuki Tomotarō et al., eds., *Tosa nikki, Kagerō nikki, Izumi Shikibu nikki, Sarashina nikki*. *NKBT* 20. Tokyo: Iwanami shoten, 1965.

Kairaishi no ki. By Ōe no Masafusa (1041–1111). See *Kugutsuki*.

Kakuzenshō. By Kakuzen (12th c.). *DNBZ*, vols. 53–56 (vols. 45–51 in 1921 ed.). Also *TZ* 4–5, 3022.

Kamakura ibun. Ed. Takeuchi Rizō. 30 vols. Tokyo: Tōkyōdō shuppan, 1971–.

Kankyo no tomo. Attr. to Taira Yasuyori. In Koizumi Hiroshi, ed., *Hōbutsushū, Kankyo no tomo, Hirasan kojin reitaku*. *SNKBT* 40. Tokyo: Iwanami shoten, 1993.

Kasshi yawa (ca. 1821). By Matsuura Seizan. Tokyo: Kokusho kankōkai, 1911.

Kayoi Komachi. Attr. to Kan'ami (1333–84). In *SNKBT* 57. Trans. in Keene 1970: 52–63.

Keiran shūyōshū. By Kōjū (1276–1350). *T.* 76, 2410.

Kii zōdanshū. In *Kinsei kaii shōsetsu*. Kinsei bungei shiryō 3. Ed. Yoshida Kōichi. Koten bunko, 1955.

Kiyū shōran. By Kitamura Nobuyo. Nihon geirin sōsho, vols. 6–7. Tokyo, 1973.

Kobi ki. By Ōe no Masafusa (1041–1111). In Yamagishi Tokuhei, Takeuchi Rizō, Ienaga Saburō, and Ōsone Shōsuke, eds., *Kodai shakai shisō.* NSTK 8. Tokyo: Iwanami shoten, 1979.

Kōbō Daishi den zenshū. Attr. to Ningai (951–1046). Tokyo: Pitaka, 1977.

Kōdanshō. In Gotō Akio, Ikegami Jun'ichi, and Yamane Taisuke, eds., *Kōdanshō, Chūgaishō, Fukego.* SNKBT. Tokyo: Iwanami Shoten, 1997.

Kohon setsuwashū (ca. 1130; title given in 1943). Anonymous. SNKBT 42.

Kojidan (1212–15). By Minamoto no Akikane (1160–1215). Ed. Kuroita Katsumi. *Shintei zōho kokushi taikei,* vol. 18. See also: Kobayashi Yasuharu, ed., *Kojidan,* 2 vols. Koten bunko 60. Tokyo: Gendai shinchōsha, 1981.

Kojiki (712). Ed. Kurano Kenji and Takeda Yūkichi. NKBT 1. Tokyo: Iwanami shoten, 1958. See also: Ogihara Asao and Kōnosu Hayao, eds., NKBZ. Tokyo: Shōgakkan.

Kokon chōmonjū (1254), by Tachibana no Narisue (d. ca. 1274). Ed. Nagazumi Yasuaki and Shimada Isao. NKBT 84. See also Ed. Nishio Kōichi and Kobayashi Yasuharu. SKNS. 2 vols. Tokyo: Shinchōsha, 1983.

Komachi no sōshi. NKBT 38.

Konjaku monogatari shū. (1110–1125). Attr. to Minamoto no Takakuni (Uji Dainagon, 1004–1077) and disciples. Ed. Yamada Yoshio, Yamada Tadao, Yamada Hideo, and Yamada Toshio. NKBT 22–26. Tokyo: Iwanami shoten, 1959–63.

Konohagoromo. In Gorai Shigeru, ed. *Konoha-goromo, Suzukake-goromo, Tōun rokuji: Shugendō shiryō 1.* Tōyō bunko 273. Tokyo: Heibonsha, 1975.

Kugutsu no ki. By Ōe no Masafusa (1041–1111). In Yamagishi Tokuhei, Takeuchi Rizō, Ienaga Saburō, and Ōsone Shōsuke, eds., *Kodai shakai shisō.* NSTK 8. Tokyo: Iwanami shoten, 1979.

Lidai fabaoji. T. 51, 2075.

Linji lu (full title: *Zhenzhou Linji Huizhao chanshi yulu*). T. 47, 1985.

Majjhima Nikāya Trans. I. B. Horner, *The Middle Length Sayings* (*Majjhima-Nikāya*). 3 vols. Pāli Texts Translation Series, 19–21. London: Luzac and Co., 1954–59.

Makura no sōshi, Murasaki Shikibu nikki. Ed. Ikeda Kikan et al. NKBT 19. Tokyo: Iwanami shoten, 1965.

Masukagami (ca. 1374). Attr. to Nijō Yoshimoto.

Mizukagami (ca. 1195). Attr. to Nakayama Tadachika (1131–95). KST 21, 1. Tokyo: Kokushi taikei kankōkai, 1939.

Muchū mondō. By Musō Soseki (1275–1351). Ed. Satō Taishun. Tokyo: Iwanami shoten, 1974 (1934).

Mumyōshō (1202). By Kamo no Chōmei (1151–1216). In Hisamatsu Sen'ichi and Nishio Minoru, eds. *Karonshū, nōgaku ronshū.* NKBT 65. Tokyo: Iwanami shoten, 1961.

Muromachi monogatari shū. Nihon koten bungaku eiin sōkan 27. Tokyo: Nihon koten bungakukai, 1990.

Nihon ōjō gokuraku ki (985–86). By Yoshishige no Yasutane (d. 1002). DNBZ 107; *Zoku gunsho ruijū* 66.

Nihon ryōiki (823). By Kyōkai. Ed. Endō Yoshimoto and Kasuga Kazuo. *NKBT* 70. Tokyo: Iwanami shoten, 1967. English translation in Nakamura 1973.

Nihonshoki (or *Nihongi*, 720). Ed. Sakamoto Tarō, Ienaga Saburō, et al. *NKBT* 67–68. Tokyo: Iwanami shoten, 1977.

Ninin bikuni (1663). By Suzuki Shōsan. In Kokobun tōhō bukkyō sōsho, Bungei-bu, 104–24.

Nomori no kagami. In *Gunsho ruijū* 27. Tokyo: Gunsho ruijū kanseikai, 1936: 245–69.

Ōjō yōshū (984). By Genshin (942–1017). *T.* 84, 2682.

Ōkagami (ca. 1119). Ed. Matsumura Hiroshi. *NKBT* 21.

Otogizōshi. Ed. Ichiko Teiji. Tokyo: Iwanami shoten, 1991.

Rentian baojian (1230). By Chizhao. *ZZ* 1, 2B, 21 (Taibei ed., vol. 113).

Ryōjin hishō (1179). *NKBT* 73. Tokyo: Iwanami shoten. See also *NKBZ* 25.

Saddharmapuṇḍarīka-sūtra (Chin. *Miaofa lianhua jing*). *T.* 9, 262.

Saigū ki. By Fujiwara no Yoshifusa, Haruzumi Yoshitada, et al. *KST* 3.

Sakeiki. By Minamoto Tsuneyori (985–1039). In Zōho shiryō taisei kankōkai, ed., *Zōho shiryō taisei* 6.

Sanbō ekotoba. By Minamoto no Tamenori (984). In Yamada Yoshio, *Sanbōe ryakuchū*. Tokyo: Hōbunkan, 1951. English translation in Kamens 1988.

Sangoku denki (1431). By Gennen. *DNBZ* 148. Tokyo: Yūseidō, 1932. See also: Ikegami Jun'ichi, ed., *Sangoku denki*. 2 vols. Tokyo: Miyai shoten, 1976; and Nagoya Sangoku denki kenkyūkai, ed., *Sangoku denki*. 3 vols. Koten bunko 434, 436, 438. Tokyo: Koten bunko, 1983.

Seisuishō (1623). By Anrakuan Sakuden (1554–1642). Ed. Suzuki Tōzō. 2 vols. Tokyo: Iwanami shoten, 1986.

Sekkyōbushi. Tōyō bunko. Tokyo: Heibonsha, 1973.

Sekkyōshū. Ed. Muroki Yatarō. Shinchō Nihon koten shūsei. Tokyo: Shinchōsha, 1977.

Senjūshō (13th century). Formerly attr. to Saigyō (1118–1190). Ed. Nishio Kōichi. Tokyo: Iwanami shoten, 1970.

Shasekishū (1279–83). By Mujū Ichien (1226–1312). Ed. Watanabe Tsunaya. *NKBT* 85. Tokyo: Iwanami shoten, 1966 (reprinted 1975).

Shigisan engi. In Sakurai Tokutarō, Hagiwara Tatsuo, and Miyata Noboru, eds., *Jisha engi*, 23–28. Tokyo: Iwanami shoten.

Shinchō monjū (1749). In *Nihon zuihitsutaisei*, new ed., 2, 5.

Shinran muki. By Shinbutsu (1209–58). In *Teihon Shinran Shōnin Zenshū* 4, *Shin-gyōhen*, 201–2.

Shinsarugaku ki. By Fujiwara Akihira (989?–1066). In Yamagishi Tokuhei, Ta-keuchi Rizō, Ienaga Saburō, and Ōsone Shōsuke, eds., *Kodai shakai shisō*. *NSTK* 8. Tokyo: Iwanami shoten, 1979. See also Kawaguchi Hisao, ed. *Shin-sarugakuki*. Tokyo: Heibonsha, 1983.

Shintōshū (1361). Modern Japanese translation by Kishi Shōzō. Tōyō bunko 424. Tokyo: Heibonsha, 1967.

Shishi liutie (also known as *Yichu liutie*, Jp. *Giso rokujō*), Hangzhou: Zhejiang guji chubanshe, 1990.

Shōbōgenzō. By Dōgen (1200–53). T. 82, 2582. See also: Nishio Minoru, Kagamishima Genryū, Sakai Tokugen, and Mizuno Yaoko, eds. *Shōbogenzō, Shōbōgenzō zuimonki. NKBT.* Tokyo: Iwanami shoten, 1965; and: Terada Tōru, ed., *Dōgen. NSKT.* Tokyo: Iwanami shoten, 1974.

Shōbōgenzō zuimonki. Ed. Nishio Minoru, Kagamishima Genryū, Sakai Tokugen, and Mizuno Yaoko. *Shōbōgenzō, Shōbōgenzō zuimonki. NKBT.* Tokyo: Iwanami shoten, 1965.

Shōyūki. By Fujiwara no Sanesuke (957–1046). 3 vols. *Shiryō taisei,* bekkan 1–3.

Shūi ōjōden. By Miyoshi Tameyasu (1049–1139).

Shutsujō kōgo. By Tominaga Nakamoto (1715–46). Ed. Kyōdo Jikō. Tokyo: Ryūbunkan, 1982.

Sifen biqiuni chao. By Daoxuan (596–667). ZZ 1, 64, 1. Taibei ed., vol. 64.

Sifen lü (Dharmaguptaka vinaya). T. 22, 1428.

Sifen lü xingshi chao (full title: *Sifen lü shanfan buque xingshi chao,* 630). By Daoxuan (596–667). T. 40, 1804.

Soga monogatari (ca. 1399). *NKBT* 88. Tokyo: Iwanami shoten, 1966.

Song gaoseng zhuan. By Zanning (919–1001). T. 50, 2061.

Sotoba Komachi. Attr. to Kan'ami (1333–84). In *SNKBT* 57. English translation in Waley 1957.

Sumiyoshi monogatari. Trans. Harold Parlett, "The *Sumiyoshi Monogatari.*" *Transactions of the Asiatic Society of Japan* 29, 1 (1901): 48–90.

Taiheiki. I, II. Ed. Gotō Tanji and Kamata Kisaburō. *NKBT* 35, 36. Tokyo: Iwanami shoten, 1961.

Taiheiki. III. Ed. Yamashita Hiroaki. *SKNS.* Tokyo: Shinchōsha, 1983.

Taima mandara engi. In Sakurai Tokutarō, Hagiwara Tatsuo, and Miyata Noboru, eds., *Jisha engi,* 37–68. Tokyo: Iwanami shoten.

Tamazukuri Komachi shi sōsuisho. Ed. Tochio Takeshi. Iwanami bunko 570. Tokyo: Iwanami shoten, 1994.

Tengu zōshi. In *Shinshū emakimono zenshū,* vol. 27. Tokyo: Kadokawa shoten, 1978.

Tōkoku ki. By Keizan Jōkin (1268–1325). In Kohō Chisan, ed., *Jōsai Daishi zenshū.* 1937. Rpt. Yokohama: Daihonzan Sōjiji, 1976.

Towazugatari. By Go-Fukakusa In Nijō. Ed. Tsugita Kasumi. Nihon koten bungaku zenshū. 1966. Trans. Karen Brazell, *Confessions of Lady Nijō.* Stanford: Stanford University Press, 1973.

Tsūkai sankeiki, by Tsūkai (1234–1305). *Nihon shomin seikatsu shiryō shūsei,* vol. 26: *Jinja engi,* 453–74. Ed. Tanigawa Ken'ichi. Tokyo: San'ichi shobō, 1983. See also *Zoku gunsho ruijū* 3, 2: 759–812.

Tsuma kagami (1300). By Mujū Ichien (1226–1312). In Miyasaka Yūshō, ed., *Kana hōgo shū. NKBT* 83. Tokyo: Iwanami shoten, 1964.

Tsurezuregusa (begun 1330). By Kenkō (Yoshida Kaneyoshi, d. ca. 1352). Ed. Kidō Saizō. *SKNS* 10. Tokyo: Shinchōsha. Trans. in Keene 1967.

Uji shūi monogatari (ca. 1210–20). Ed. Watanabe Tsuneya and Nishio Kōichi. *NKBT* 27. Tokyo: Iwanami shoten, 1960.

Utsubo monogatari (ca. 982). Vol. 1. Ed. Kōno Tama. *NKBT* 10. Tokyo: Iwanami shoten, 1959.

Vimalakīrtinirdeśa. *T.* 14, 474. French translation in Lamotte 1944–80 (1962; reprinted 1987).

Visuddhimagga. Ed. C.A.F. Rhys Davids. 2 vols. London: PTS, 1920–21.

Wakan rōeishū, Ryōji hishō. Ed. Kawaguchi Hisao and Shida Nobuyoshi. *NKBT* 73. Tokyo: Iwanami shoten, 1965.

Wakan sansai zue. Compiled by Terashima Ryōan. Ed. Wakan sansai zue kōkan iinkai. 2 vols. Tokyo: Tōkyō bijutsu, 1970. Reedited 1990.

Yamatohime no mikoto seiki. In Ōsumi Kazuo, ed., *Chūsei shintō ron*, 7–38. *NSTK* 19. Tokyo: Iwanami shoten, 1977.

Yanagidaru. Ed. Hamada Giichirō et al. *Haifū Yanagidaru*. Gendai kyōyō bunko. Tokyo: Shakai shisōsha, 1985.

Yichu liutie (954). Reprinted as *Shishi liutie*. Zhejiang guji chubanshe, 1990.

Yōkyokushū. Ed. Yokomichi Mario and Omote Akira. *SNKBT*. Tokyo: Iwanami shoten, 1998.

Yōkyoku taika. Ed. Sanari Kentarō. Tokyo: Meiji shoin, 1930.

Yōtenki. In *Zoku gunsho ruijū* 48.

Yūjoki. By Ōe no Masafusa (1041–1111). In Yamagishi Tokuhei, Takeuchi Rizō, Ienaga Saburō, and Ōsone Shōsuke, eds., *Kodai shakai shisō*. *NSTK* 8. Tokyo: Iwanami shoten, 1979.

Zenkōji engi. In *Fusō ryakki*. *Kokushi taikei*, vol. 12.

Zoku honchō ōjōden (ca. 1100). By Ōe no Masafusa (1041–1111). *NSTK* 7. See also *Gunsho ruijū*, vol. 3: 734–44.

Zōtanshū (1305). By Muju Ichien (1226–1312). Ed. Yamada Shōzen and Miki Sumito. Chūsei no bungaku. Tokyo: Miyai shoten, 1973.

SECONDARY SOURCES

Abé Ryūichi. 1999. *The Weaving of Mantra: Kūkai and the Construction of Esoteric Buddhist Discourse*. New York: Columbia University Press.

Abe Shinji. 1981. *Hebigami denjōron josetsu*. Tokyo: Dentō to gendaisha.

Abe Yasurō. 1980. " 'Iruka' no seiritsu." *Geinōshi kenkyū* 69: 16–38.

———. 1984. "Jidō setsuwa no seiritsu." *Kokugo kokubun* 600–601: 1–29, 30–56.

———. 1985. "Chūsei ōken to chūsei *Nihongi*: Sokuihō to sanshū shingisetsu o megurite." *Nihon bungaku* 365: 31–48.

———. 1987. "Chūsei nanto no shūkyō to geinō: Shinnyo-ni to wakamiya haiden miko o megurite." *Kokugo to kokubungaku*.

———. 1989a. "Hōju to ōken: Chūsei ōken to mikkyō girei." In *Nihon shisō no shinsō*. Iwanami kōza tōyō shisō 16, *Nihon shisō* 2: 115–69. Tokyo: Iwanami shoten.

———. 1989b. "Nyonin kinzei to suisan." In Ōsumi Kazuo and Nishiguchi Junko, eds., *Josei to bukkyō*, vol. 4: *Miko to joshin*, 153–240. Tokyo: Heibonsha.

————. 1990. "Jien to ōken: Chūsei ōken shinwa o umidashita mono." *Bessatsu Bungei*, special issue: *Tennōsei, rekisishi, ōken, daijōsai*, 111–19. Tokyo: Kawade shobō shinsha.

————. 1995. "Irokonomi no kami: Dōsojin to aihōjin." In Yamaori Tetsuo, ed., *Nihon no kami* 1: *Kami no shigen*, 121–72. Tokyo: Heibonsha.

————. 1998. *Yūya no kōgō: Chūsei no sei to sei naru mono*. Nagoya: Nagoya daigaku shuppankai.

————. 1999 [1995]. *"The Confessions of Lady Nijō* as a "Woman's Tale and Its Layering of the Many Spheres of Medieval Literature." Trans. Maiko R. Behr. In Wakita Haruko, Anne Bouchy, and Ueno Chizuko, eds., *Gender and Japanese History* 2: 47–98. Osaka: Osaka University Press.

Ackroyd, Joyce. 1959. "Women in Feudal Japan." In *Transactions of the Asiatic Society of Japan*, 3d Series, vol. 7: 31–68.

Adamek, Wendi. 1996. "Issues in Chan Buddhist Transmission as Seen through the *Lidai fabao ji* (Record of the Dharma-Jewel through the Ages). Ph.D. Dissertation, Stanford University.

Addiss, Stephen. 1986. "The Zen Nun Ryonen Gensho (1646–1711)." In "Women in Buddhism." *Spring Wind* 6:1–3: 180–87.

Agamben, Giorgio. 1998. *Homo Sacer: Sovereign Power and Bare Life*. Trans. Daniel Heller-Roazen. Stanford: Stanford University Press.

Ahern, Emily Martin. 1974. "Affines and the Ritual of Kinship." In Arthur P. Wolf, ed., *Religion and Ritual in Chinese Society*, 279–307. Stanford: Stanford University Press.

————. 1975. "The Power and Pollution of Chinese Women." In Margery Wolf and Roxane Witke, eds., *Women in Chinese Society*, 193–214. Stanford: Stanford University Press.

————. 1988. "Gender and Ideological Differences in Representations of Life and Death." In James L. Watson and Evelyn Rawski, eds., *Death Rituals in Late Imperial and Modern China*, 164–79. Berkeley: University of California Press.

Akamatsu Toshihide. 1957. *Kamakura bukkyō no kenkyū*. Kyoto: Heirakuji shoten.

Akiyama Ken, et al., eds. 1977. *Gaki zōshi, Jigoku zōshi, Yamai no sōshi, Kusōshi emaki*. Nihon emaki taisei 7. Tokyo: Chūō kōronsha.

Albert, Jean-Pierre. 1997. *Le sang et le ciel: Les saintes mystiques dans le monde chrétien*. Paris: Aubier.

Allen, Michael. 1996 [1975]. *The Cult of Kumārī: Virgin Worship in Nepal*. Kathmandu: Maṇḍala Book Point.

Ambros, Barbara. 1997. "Liminal Journeys: Pilgrimages of Noblewomen in Mid-Heian Japan." *Japanese Journal of Religious Studies* 24, 3–4: 301–405.

Ames, Roger T. 1981. "Taoism and the Androgynous Ideal." In Richard Guisso and Stanley Johannesen, eds., *Women in China: Current Directions in Historical Scholarship*, 21–46. Youngstown, NY: Philo Press.

Amino Yoshihiko. 1978. *Muen, kugai, raku: Nihon chūsei no jiyū to heiwa*. Tokyo: Heibonsha.

Amino Yoshihiko. 1989. "Yūjo to hinin, kawaramono." In Miyata Noboru, ed., *Sei to mibun: jakusha, haisha no shōsei to hiun*, 93–128. Tokyo: Shunjūsha.

———. 1990. *Nihonron no shiza*. Tokyo: Shōgakkan.

———. 1993. *Igyō no ōken*. Tokyo: Heibonsha.

———. 1994. *Chūsei no hinin to yūjo*. Tokyo: Akashi shoten.

Amino Yoshihiko, Ishii Susumu, Kasamatsu Hiroshi, and Katsumata Shizuo. 1983. *Chūsei no tsumi to batsu*. Tokyo: Tokyo daigaku shuppankai.

Andō Fumio. 1991. "Shinran ni okeru nyonin jōbutsu no mondai." In Nihon bukkyō gakkai, ed., *Bukkyō to josei*, 43–57. Kyoto: Heirakuji shoten.

Andrews, Allan A. 1973. *The Teachings Essential for Rebirth: A Study of Genshin's Ōjōyōshū*. Tokyo: Sophia University Press.

Anzako Iwao. 1979. "Mikumano no bikuni engi." *Ronsan setsuwa to setsuwa bungaku*, 523–37. Kazama shobō.

Aotatsu Sōji. 1974. "Keizan Jōkin no nyonin sonjū shisō ni tsuite." *Shūgaku kenkyū* 16.

Arai, Paula K. R. 1993. "Sōtō Zen Nuns in Modern Japan." In Mark R. Mullins, Shimazono Susumu, and Paul L. Swanson, eds., *Religion and Society in Modern Japan*, 203–18. Nanzan Institute for Religion and Culture. Berkeley: Asian Humanities Press.

———. 1999a. *Women Living Zen: Japanese Sōtō Buddhist Nuns*. New York: Oxford University Press.

———. 1999b. "Japanese Buddhist Nuns: Innovators for the Sake of Tradition." In Karma Lekshe Tsomo, ed. 1999. *Buddhist Women Across Cultures: Realizations*, 105–22. Albany: State University of New York Press.

Arnold, Daniel. 1998. "Mapping the Middle Way: Thoughts on a Buddhist Contribution to Feminist Discussion." *Journal of Feminist Studies in Religion* 14, 1: 63–84.

Asano Miwako. 1989. "Minshū shūkyō ni okeru ryōsei guyūkan." In Ōsumi Kazuo and Nishiguchi Junko, eds., *Josei to bukkyō*, vol. 2: *Sukui to oshie*, 199–230. Tokyo: Heibonsha.

Aston, W. G., trans. 1972. *Nihongi: Chronicles of Japan from the Earliest Times to A.D. 679*. Rutland, VT: Charles E. Tuttle.

Aubert, Jean-Jacques. 1989. "Threatened Wombs: Aspects of Ancient Uterine Magic." *Greek, Roman, and Byzantine Studies* 30: 421–49.

Auerbach, Nina. 1982. *Woman and the Demon: The Life of a Victorian Myth*. Cambridge, MA: Harvard University Press.

Augé-Héritier, Françoise. 1989. "Semen and Blood: Some Ancient Theories Concerning Their Genesis and Relationship." In Michel Feher, ed., *Fragments for a History of the Human Body*, 159–75. 3 vols. New York: Urzone.

Bainbridge, Erika Ohara. 1992. "The Madness of Mothers in Japanese Noh Drama." *U.S.–Japan Women's Journal* English Supplement 3: 84–110.

Bakhtin, Mikhail. 1984. *Rabelais and His World*. Trans. Hélène Iswolsky. Bloomington: University of Indiana Press.

Bapat, P. V. 1957. "Change of Sex in Buddhist Literature." in *S. K. Belvalkar Felicitation Volume*, 209–15. Benares: Motilal Banarsidass.

Bareau, André. 1979. "Chūu." In *Hōbōgirin*, vol. 5: 558–63. Paris: Adrien Maisonneuve.

——. 1982. "Un personnage bien mystérieux: l'épouse du Buddha." In L. A. Hercus et al., eds., *Indological and Buddhist Studies, Volume in Honour of Professor J. W. de Jong on His Sixtieth Birthday*, 31–59. Delhi: Sri Satguru Publications.

Bargen, Doris G. 1988. "Spirit Possession in the Context of Dramatic Expressions of Gender Conflict: The Aoi Episode of the *Genji Monogatari.*" *Harvard Journal of Asiatic Studies* 48, 1: 95–130.

——. 1997. *A Woman's Weapon: Spirit Possession in* The Tale of Genji. Honolulu: University of Hawai'i Press.

Bartholomeusz, Tessa J. 1991. "Sri Lankan Women and the Buddhist Revival." *IRIS*, 43–48.

——. 1992. "The Female Mendicant in Buddhist Sri Lanka." In José Ignacio Cabezón, ed., *Buddhism, Sexuality, and Gender*, 37–61. Albany: State University of New York Press.

——. 1994. *Women under the Bō Tree: Buddhist Nuns in Sri Lanka*. New York: Cambridge University Press.

Bataille, Georges. 1986 (1957). *Eroticism: Death and Sexuality*. Trans. Mary Dalwood. San Francisco: City Lights Books.

——. 1991. *The Accursed Share: An Essay on General Economy*. Trans. Robert Hurley. 3 vols. New York: Zone Books.

Beillevaire, Patrick. 1986. "Le Japon, une société de la maison." In André Burguière, Christiane Klapisch-Zuber, Martine Segalen, and Françoise Zonabend, eds., *Histoire de la famille 2: Temps médiévaux: Orient/Occident*, 287–340. Paris: Armand Colin.

Bennett, Judith M. 1989. "Feminism and History." *Gender and History* 1, 3: 251–66.

——. 1993. "Medievalism and Feminism." In Nancy F. Partner, ed., *Studying Medieval Women*, 7–29. Cambridge, MA: Medieval Academy of America, Speculum.

Berthier [Baptandier], Brigitte. 1988. *La Dame-du-bord-de-l'eau: La féminité à travers un culte de la religion populaire chinoise*. Nanterre: Société d'Ethnologie.

Beyer, Stephan. 1973. *The Cult of Tara: Magic and Ritual in Tibet*. Berkeley: University of California Press.

Bharati, Agehananda. 1965. *The Tantric Tradition*. London: Rider and Company.

Bhattacharya, Narendra Nath. 1975. *Ancient Indian Rituals and Their Social Contents*. London: Curzon Press.

Biddick, Kathleen. 1993. "Genders, Bodies, Borders: Technologies of the Visible." In Nancy F. Partner, ed., *Studying Medieval Women*, 87–116. Cambridge, MA: Medieval Academy of America, Speculum.

Birnbaum, Raoul. 1979. *The Healing Buddha*. Boulder, CO: Shambhala.

Black, Alison H. 1986. "Gender and Cosmology in Chinese Correlative Thinking." In Caroline Walker Bynum, Stevan Harrell, and Paula Richman, eds., *Gender and Religion: On the Complexity of Symbols*, 166–195. Boston: Beacon Press.

Blacker, Carmen. 1975. *The Catalpa Bow: A Study of Shamanistic Practices in Japan*. London: Allen and Unwin.

Blackstone, Kathryn R. 1998. *Women in the Footsteps of the Buddha: Struggle for Liberation in the Therīgāthā*. Curzon Critical Studies in Buddhism. London: Curzon Press.

Bloch, Maurice. 1987. "Descent and Sources of Contradiction in Representations of Women and Kinship." In Jane Fishburne Collier and Sylvia Junko Yanagisako, eds., *Gender and Kinship: Essays toward a Unified Analysis*, 324–37. Stanford: Stanford University Press.

———. 1992. *Prey into Hunter: The Politics of Religious Experience*. Cambridge: Cambridge University Press.

Bloch, Maurice, and Jonathan Parry, eds. 1982. *Death and the Regeneration of Life*. Cambridge: Cambridge University Press.

Bloss, L. 1987. "The Female Renunciants of Sri Lanka: The *Dasasilmattawa*." *Journal of the International Association of Buddhist Studies* 10, 1: 7–31.

Bock, Felicia G., trans. 1970. *Engi-Shiki: Procedures of the Engi Era. Books I–IV*. Tokyo: Sophia University.

Boddy, Janice. 1989. *Wombs and Alien Spirits: Women, Men, and the Zār Cult in Northern Sudan*. Madison: University of Wisconsin Press.

Bodiford, William M. 1993. *Sōtō Zen in Medieval Japan*. Honolulu: University of Hawai'i Press.

Bokenkamp. Stephen R. 1982. "Sources of *Ling-Pao* Scriptures." In Michel Strickmann, ed., 1981–85. *Tantric and Taoist Studies in Honour of R. A. Stein*, vol. 2: 434–86. Brussels: Institut Belge des Hautes Etudes Chinoises.

———. 1998. "A Medieval Feminist Critique of the Chinese World Order: The Case of Wu Zhao (r. 690–705)." *Religion* 28: 383–92.

Bordo, Susan R. 1989. "The Body and the Reproduction of Femininity: A Feminist Appropriation of Foucault." In Alison M. Jaggar and Susan R. Bordo, eds., *Gender/ Body/ Knowledge: Feminist Reconstructions of Being and Knowing*, 13–33. New Brunswick: Rutgers University Press.

———. 1993a. *Unbearable Weight: Feminism, Western Culture, and the Body*. Berkeley: University of California Press.

———. 1993b. "Feminism, Foucault, and the Politics of the Body." In Caroline Ramazanoglu, ed., *Up against Foucault: Exploration of Some Tensions between Foucault and Feminism*, 179–202. London and New York: Routledge.

Boucher, Sandy. 1993. *Turning the Wheel: American Women Creating the New Buddhism*. Boston: Beacon Press.

Bouchy, Anne. 1996–97. "Le littoral, espace de médiations." *Cahiers d'Extrême Asie* 9: 255–98.

Bourdieu, Pierre. 1998. *La domination masculine*. Paris: Editions du Seuil.

Bourke, John Gregory. 1891. *Scatological Rites of All Nations*. Washington, D.C.: W. H. Lowdermilk.

Bowring, Richard. 1982. *Murasaki Shikibu: Her Diary and Poetic Memoirs*. Princeton: Princeton University Press.

Bray, Francesca. 1997. *Technology and Gender: Fabrics of Power in Late Imperial China*. Berkeley: University of California Press.

Brazell, Karen, trans. 1973. *The Confessions of Lady Nijō*. Stanford: Stanford University Press.

———, ed. 1988. *Twelve Plays of the Noh and Kyogen Theaters*. East Asia Papers. Ithaca: Cornell University Press.

Brock, Karen L. 1984. "Tales of Gishō and Gangyō: Editor, Artist, and Audience in Japanese Picture Scrolls." Ph.D. Dissertation, Princeton University.

———. 1990. "Chinese Maiden, Silla Monk: Zenmyō and Her Thirteenth-Century Audience." In Marsha Weidner, ed., *Flowering in the Shadows: Women in the History of Chinese and Japanese Painting*, 185–218. Honolulu: University of Hawai'i Press.

Brock, Karen L., Paula Conley, and Anne Klein. 1990. "The Questions That Won't Go: A Dialogue about Women in Buddhism and Christianity." *Journal of Feminist Studies in Religion* 6, 2: 87–120.

Brooks, Anne Page. 1981. "Mizuko kuyō and Japanese Buddhism." *Japanese Journal of Religious Studies* 8, 3–4: 119–47.

Brower, Robert H., and Earl Miner. 1962. *Japanese Court Poetry*. London: Cresset Press.

Brown, Delmer M., and Ichirō Ishida, trans. 1979. *The Future and the Past: A Translation and Study of the Gukanshō, an Interpretative History of Japan Written in 1219*. Berkeley: University of California Press.

Brown, Judith. 1986. *Immodest Acts: The Life of a Lesbian Nun in Renaissance Italy*. Oxford: Oxford University Press.

Brown, Peter. 1988. *The Body and Society: Men, Women, and Sexual Renunciation in Early Christianity*. New York: Columbia University Press.

Brown, W. N. 1940. "The Basis of the Hindu Act of Truth," *Review of Religion*, 36–45.

———. 1968. "The Metaphysics of the Truth Act (*satyakriyā*)." In *Mélanges d'Indianisme à la mémoire de Louis Renou* 171–77. Paris: Editions de Boccard.

Buffetrille, Katia. 1998. "Reflections on Pilgrimages to Sacred Mountains, Lakes and Caves." In Alex McKay, ed., *Pilgrimage in Tibet*, 18–34. London: Curzon Press.

Burguière, André, Christiane Klapisch-Zuber, Martine Segalen, and Françoise Zonabend, eds., *Histoire de la famille*, vol. 2. *Temps médiévaux: Orient/Occident*, 243–86. Paris: Armand Colin.

Burlingame, E. W. 1917. "The Act of Truth (*saccakiriya*): A Hindu Spell and Its Emplyment as a Psychic Motif in Hindu Fiction." *Journal of the Royal Asiatic Society*: 429–67.

———. 1969. [1921]. *Buddhist Legends Translated from the Original Pāli Text of the Dhammapada Commentary*. 3 vols. Harvard Oriental Series 28–30. London: Luzac.

Butler, Judith. 1993. *Bodies That Matter: On the Discursive Limits of "Sex."* New York: Routledge.

Butler, Kenneth Dean. 1966. "The Textual Evolution of the *Heike Monogatari*." *Harvard Journal of Asiatic Studies* 26: 5–51.

Bynum, Caroline Walker. 1982. *Jesus as Mother: Studies in the Spirituality of the High Middle Ages*. Berkeley: University of California Press.

———. 1991. *Fragmentation and Redemption: Essays on Gender and the Human Body in Medieval Religion*. New York: Zone Books.

Bynum, Caroline Walker, Stevan Harrell, and Paula Richman, eds. 1986. *Gender and Religion: On the Complexity of Symbols*. Boston: Beacon Press.

Cabezón, José Ignacio, ed. 1992a. *Buddhism, Sexuality, and Gender*. Albany: State University of New York Press.

———. 1992b. "Mother Wisdom, Father Love: Gender-Based Imagery in Mahāyāna Buddhist Thought." In José Ignacio Cabezón, ed., *Buddhism, Sexuality, and Gender*, 181–99. Albany: State University of New York Press.

Cahill, Suzanne E. 1986. "Performers and Female Taoist Adepts: Hsi-wang-mu as the Patron Deity of Women in Medieval China." *Journal of the American Oriental Society* 106, 1: 155–68.

———. 1990. "Practice Makes Perfect: Paths to Transcendence for Women in Medieval China." *Taoist Resources* 2, 2: 23–42.

———. 1993. *Transcendence and Divine Passion: The Queen Mother of the West in Medieval China*. Stanford: Stanford University Press.

Cao Xueqin. 1973–86. *The Story of the Stone*. Trans. David Hawkes. 5 vols. Middlesex: Penguin Books.

Carlitz, Katherine. 1986. *The Rhetoric of the Chin P'ing Mei*. Bloomington: University of Indiana Press.

———. 1991. "The Social Uses of Female Virtue in Late Ming Editions of the *Lienü Zhuan*." *Late Imperial China* 12, 2: 117–52.

———. 1994. "Desire, Danger, and the Body: Stories of Women's Virtue in Late Ming China." In Christina K. Gilmartin, Gail Hershatter, Lisa Rofel, and Tyrene White, eds., *Engendering China: Women, Culture, and the State*, 101–24. Cambridge, MA: Harvard University Press.

Cartier, Michel. 1986. "En Chine, la famille, relais du pouvoir." In André Burguière, Christiane Klapisch-Zuber, Martine Segalen, and Françoise Zonabend, eds., *Histoire de la famille*, 2: *Temps médiévaux: Orient/Occident*, 243–86. Paris: Armand Colin.

Cass, Victoria B. 1986. "Female Healers in the Ming and the Lodge of Ritual and Ceremony." *Journal of the American Oriental Society* 106, 1: 233–40.

Chan, Sin-wei. 1985. *Buddhism in Late Ch'ing Political Thought*. Boulder, CO: Westview Press.

Chayet, Anne. 1993. *La femme au temps des Dalaï-lamas*. Paris: Stock-L. Pernoud.

Chen Dongyuan. 1981. *Zhongguo funü shenghuo shi*. Shanghai: Shangwu yinshuguan.

Chen Fan Pen. 1995. "Hsing-shih Yin-yüan: Karmic versus Psychological Views of a Man's Relationships with His Women." In Morny Joy and Eva K. Neumaier-Dargyay, eds., *Gender, Genre and Religion: Feminist Reflections*, 213–24. Calgary: Wilfrid Laurier University Press.

Chen, Toyoko Yoshida. 1974. "Women in Confucian Society: A Study of Three *Tan-tz'u* Narratives." Ph.D. Dissertation, Columbia University.

Ch'en, Kenneth K. S. 1968. "Filial Piety in Chinese Buddhism." *Harvard Journal of Asiatic Studies* 28: 81–97.

———. 1973. *The Chinese Transformation of Buddhism*. Princeton: Princeton University Press.

Chikusa Masaaki. 1989. "Chūgoku ni okeru nisō kyōdan no seiritsu to hatten." In Ōsumi Kazuo and Nishiguchi Junko, eds., *Josei to bukkyō* 1: *Ama to amadera*, 43–72. Tokyo: Heibonsha.

Childs, Margaret Helen. 1991. *Rethinking Sorrow: Revelatory Tales of Late Medieval Japan*. Ann Arbor: Center for Japanese Studies, University of Michigan.

Chin, Gail. 1998. "The Gender of Buddhist Truth: The Female Corpse in a Group of Japanese Paintings." *Japanese Journal of Religious Studies* 25, 3–4: 277–317.

Cholley, Jean. 1996. *Haiku érotiques: Extraits de* La Fleur du Bout *et du* Tonneau de Saule. Arles: Editions Philippe Picquier.

Chung, Priscilla Ching. 1981. *Palace Women in the Northern Sung, 960–1126*. Leiden: E. J. Brill.

Cleary, Thomas, trans. 1989. *Immortal Sisters: Secret of Taoist Women*. Boston and London: Shambala.

Coates, Harper Havelock, and Ryugaku Ishizuka, trans. 1949. *Hōnen the Buddhist Saint: His Life and Teachings*. 5 vols. Compiled by imperial order. Kyoto: Society for the Publication of Sacred Books of the World.

Cogan, Thomas J., trans. 1987. *The Tale of the Soga Brothers*. Tokyo: University of Tokyo Press.

Cole, Alan. 1998. *Mothers and Sons in Chinese Buddhism*. Stanford: Stanford University Press.

Collcutt, Martin. 1981. *Five Mountains: The Rinzai Zen Monastic Institution in Medieval Japan*. Cambridge, MA: Harvard University Press.

Collier, Jane, and Sylvia Junko Yanagisako, eds. 1987. *Gender and Kinship: Essays toward a Unified Analysis*. Stanford: Stanford University Press.

Cooey, Paula M., William R. Eakin, Jay B. McDaniel, eds. 1991. *After Patriarchy: Feminist Reconstructions of the World Religions*. Maryknoll, N.Y.: Orbis Books.

Cornyetz, Nina. 1995 "Bound by Blood: Female Pollution, Divinity, and Community in Enchi Fumiko's *Masks*." *U.S.–Japan Women's Journal* English Supplement 9: 29–58.

Cowell, Mary-Jean. 1997. "Komachi: Medieval Legend as Modern Theater." In Amy Vladeck Heinrich, ed., *Currents in Japanese Culture: Translations and Transformations*, 309–22. New York: Columbia University Press.

Cranston, Edwin A., trans. 1969. *The Izumi Shikibu Diary: A Romance of the Heian Court*. Cambridge, MA: Harvard University Press.

———. 1975. "The Dark Path: Images of Longing in Japanese Love Poetry." *Harvard Journal of Asiatic Studies* 35: 60–100.

Czaja, Michael. 1974. *Gods of Myth and Stone: Phallicism in Japanese Folk Religion*. New York and Tokyo: Weatherhill.

Dantinne, Jean. 1987. "Féminisme et vacuité dans l'univers Abhirati." *Indo-Iranian Journal* 30: 31–34.

Darmon, Pierre. 1981. *Le mythe de la procréation à l'âge baroque*. Paris: Seuil.

Dayal, Har. 1935. *The Bodhisattva Doctrine in Buddhist Sanskrit Literature*. London: Routledge and Kegan Paul.

Delprat, Adriana. 1985. "Forms of Dissent in the *Gesaku* Literature of Hiraga Gennai (1728–1780)." Ph.D. Dissertation, Princeton University.

Demiéville, Paul. 1973. "Adieu maman." *Bulletin of the School of Oriental and African Studies* 36, 2: 271–86.

Derrida, Jacques. 1981. *Spurs: Nietzsche's Style*. Trans. Barbara Harlow. Chicago: University of Chicago Press.

Derrida, Jacques, and Christie V. McDonald. 1982. "Choreographies." *Diacritics* 12: 66–76.

———. 1992. *Points de suspension: Entretiens*. Ed. Elisabeth Weber. Paris: Galilée. English trans. by Peggy Kamuf and others, *Points. . . : Interviews 1974–1994*. Stanford: Stanford University Press, 1995.

Despeux, Catherine. 1986. "L'ordination des femmes taoïstes sous les T'ang." *Etudes chinoises* 5, 1–2: 53–100.

———. 1990. *Immortelles de la Chine ancienne: Taoïsme et alchimie féminine*. Paris: Pardès.

Dobbins, James. 1995. "Women's Birth in Pure Land as Women: Intimations from the Letters of Esshinni." *The Eastern Buddhist*, n.s. 28, 1: 108–22.

Doniger [O'Flaherty], Wendy, and Brian Smith, trans. 1991. *The Laws of Manu*. London: Penguin.

Douglas, Mary. 1966. *Purity and Danger: An Analysis of the Concepts of Pollution and Taboo*. New York: Praeger.

Dowman, Keith. 1984. *Sky Dancer: The Secret Life and Songs of the Lady Yeshe Tsogyel*. London: Routledge and Kegan Paul.

Du Fangqin. 1988. *Nüxing guannian de yanbian*. Henan: Henan renmin chubanshe.

Dudbridge, Glen. 1978. *The Legend of Miao-shan*. Oxford Oriental Monographs, no. 1. London: Ithaca Press.

———. 1992. "Women Pilgrims to T'ai Shan: Some Pages from a Seventeenth-Century Novel." In Susan Naquin and Chün-fang Yü, eds., *Pilgrims and Sacred Sites in China*, 39–64. Berkeley: University of California Press.

Dumézil, Georges. 1983. *La courtisane et les seigneurs colorés: Esquisses de mythologie*. Paris: Gallimard.

Dumont, Micheline. 1989. "The Influence of Feminist Perspectives on Historical Research Methodology." In Winnie Tomm, ed., *The Effects of Feminist Approaches on Research Methodologies*, 110–29. Calgary: Wilfred Laurier University Press.

Dundes, Alan, ed. 1982. *Cinderella: A Casebook*. Madison: University of Wisconsin Press.

Durt, Hubert. 1996. "L'apparition du Buddha à sa mère après son nirvāṇa dans le *Sūtra de Mahāmāya* et le *Sūtra de la mère du Buddha*." In Jean-Pierre Drège, ed., *De Dunhuang au Japon: Etudes chinoises et bouddhiques offertes à Michel Soymié*, 1–24. Hautes Etudes Orientales 31. Geneva: Droz.

———. 1997. "Quelques aspects de la légende du roi Ajase." *Ebisu: Etudes Japonaises* 15: 13–27.

Dykstra, Yoshiko K., trans. 1983. *Miraculous Tales of the Lotus Sūtra from Ancient Japan: The* Dainihonkoku Hokekyōkenki *of Priest Chingen*. Honolulu: University of Hawai'i Press.

———. 1986. *The Konjaku Tales, Indian Section: From a Medieval Japanese Collection*. Osaka: International Research Institute, Kansai University of Foreign Languages.

Eberhard, Wolfram. 1967. *Guilt and Sin in Traditional China*. Berkeley: University of California Press.

Ebrey, Patricia Buckley. 1993. *The Inner Quarters: Marriage and the Lives of Chinese Women in the Sung Period*. Berkeley: University of California Press.

Edou, Jerome. 1995. *Machig Labdron and the Foundations of Chod*. Ithaca: Snow Lion Publications.

Eichinger Ferro-Luzzi, Gabriella. 1980. "The Female *Liṅgam*: Interchangeable Symbols and Paradoxical Associations of Hindu Gods and Goddesses." *Current Anthropology* 21, 1: 45–68.

Eilberg-Schwartz and Wendy Doniger, eds. 1995. *Off with Her Head: The Denial of Women's Identity in Myth, Religion, and Culture*. Berkeley: University of California Press.

Eitel, E. J. 1868. "A Buddhist Purgatory for Women." *Notes and Queries on China and Japan* 5: 66–85.

Elias, Norbert. 1982 [1939]. *Power and Civility: The Civilizing Process, vol. 2.* Trans. Edmund Jephcott. New York: Basil Blackwell.

———. 1983. *The Court Society*. Trans. Edmund Jephcott. New York: Pantheon Books.

Ellwood, Robert S. 1986. "Patriarchal Revolution in Ancient Japan: Episodes from the Nihonshoki Sujin Chronicle." *Journal of Feminist Studies in Religion* 2, 2: 23–38.

Elvin, Mark. 1984. "Female Virtue and the State in China." *Past and Present* 104: 111–52.

Embree, John F., ed. 1944. *Japanese Peasant Songs*. Philadelphia: American Folklore Society. Reprint New York: Kraus Reprint Co., 1969.

Endō Hajime. 1989. "Bōmori izen no koto: otto to tsuma, shinshūshi ni okeru josei no zokusei." In Ōsumi Kazuo, and Nishiguchi Junko, eds. 1989. *Josei to bukkyō 3: Shinjin to kuyō*, 41–80. Tokyo: Heibonsha.

———. 1992. "Chūsei bukkyō ni okeru 'sei': Kōfukuji sōjō 'jōhakai ishū' o tegakari to shite." *Rekishi hyōron* 512: 19–34.

Enoki Katsurō, ed. 1979. *Ryōjin Hishō*. *SKNS* 31. Tokyo: Shinchōsha.

Fabre-Vassas, Claudine. 1997. *The Singular Beast: Jews, Christians, and the Pig*. Trans. Carol Volk. New York: Columbia University Press.

Fairchild, William P. 1962. "Shamanism in Japan." *Folklore Studies* 21: 1–122.

Falk, Nancy Auer. 1974. "An Image of Woman in Old Buddhist Literature: The Daughters of Māra." In Judith Plaskow and Joan Arnold Romero, eds., *Women and Religion*, 105–12. Missoula, MT: Scholars Press for the American Academy of Religion.

———. 1989. "The Case of the Vanishing Nun: The Fruits of Ambivalence in Ancient Indian Buddhism." In Nancy Auer Falk and Rita M. Gross, eds.,

Unspoken Worlds: Women's Religious Lives, 155–65. Belmont, CA: Wadsworth.

———. 1990. "Examplary Donors of the Pāli Tradition." In Russell F. Sizemore and Donald K. Swearer, eds., *Ethics, Wealth, and Salvation*, 124–43. Columbia: University of South Carolina Press.

Falk, Nancy Auer, and Rita M. Gross, eds. 1980. *Unspoken Worlds: Women's Religious Lives in Non-Western Cultures*. San Francisco: Harper and Row.

Farge, Arlette. 1992. "Method and Effects of Women's History." In Michelle Perrot, ed., *Writing Women's History*, 10–24. Cambridge, MA: Basil Blackwell.

Faure, Bernard. 1987. "Space and Place in Chinese Religious Traditions." *History of Religions* 26, 4: 337–56.

———. 1991. *The Rhetoric of Immediacy: A Cultural Critique of the Chan/Zen Tradition*. Princeton: Princeton University Press.

———. 1995. "Quand l'habit fait le moine: The Symbolism of the *kāṣāya* in the Sōtō Zen Tradition." *Cahiers d'Extrême Asie* 8: 335–69.

———. 1996. *Visions of Power: Imagining Medieval Japanese Buddhism*. Trans. Phyllis Brooks. Princeton: Princeton University Press.

———. 1997a. *The Will to Orthodoxy: A Critical Genealogy of Northern Chan Buddhism*. Trans. Phyllis Brooks. Stanford: Stanford University Press.

———. 1997b. "Images de la mère dans le bouddhisme médiéval japonais." In Jacqueline Pigeot and Hartmund O. Rotermund, eds., *Le vase de béryl: Etudes sur le Japon et la Chine en hommage à Bernard Frank*, 95–108. Arles: Editions Philippe Picquier.

———. 1998a. *The Red Thread: Buddhist Approaches to Sexuality*. Princeton: Princeton University Press.

———. 1998b. "Voices of Dissent: Women in Early Chan and Tiantai." *Zengaku kenkyū kiyō* 24: 25–42.

———. 1998c. "Relics, Regalia, and the Dynamics of Secrecy in Japanese Buddhism." In Elliott R. Wolfson, ed., *Rending the Veil: Concealment and Secrecy in the History of Religions*, 271–87. New York: Seven Bridges Press.

———. 2000. "Japanese Tantra, the Tachikawa-ryū, and Ryōbu Shintō." In David G. White, ed., *Tantra in Practice*, 543–56. Princeton: Princeton University Press.

———. Forthcoming. *Resilient Spirits: Buddhas, Gods, and Demons in Medieval Japan*.

Feer, Leon, trans. 1884–98. *The Samyutta-Nikāya of the Sutta-Piṭaka*. 5 vols. London.

Feher, Michel, ed. 1989. *Fragments for a History of the Human Body*. 3 vols. New York: Urzone.

Filliozat, Jean. 1991b. "The Oedipus Complex in a Buddhist Tantra." In Jean Filliozat, *Religion, Philosophy, Yoga*, 429–38. Delhi: Motilal Banarsidass.

Fischer, Felice Renee. 1972. "Ono no Komachi: A Ninth-Century Poetess of Heian Japan." Ph. D. Dissertation, Columbia University.

Fister, Patricia, ed. 1988. *Japanese Women Artists, 1600–1900*. University of Kansas, Lawrence: Spencer Museum of Art.

————. 1990. "Women Artists in Traditional Japan." In Marsha Weidner, ed., *Flowering in the Shadows: Women in the History of Chinese and Japanese Painting*, 219–40. Honolulu: University of Hawai'i Press.

Foard, James H. 1977. "Ippen Shōnin and Popular Buddhism in Kamakura Japan." Ph.D. Dissertation, Stanford University.

————. 1980. "Seiganji: The Buddhist Orientation of a Noh Play," *Monumenta Nipponica* 35, 4: 437–56.

Forte, Antonino. 1976. *Political Propaganda and Ideology in China at the End of the Seventh Century*. Naples: Istituto Universitario Orientale.

Foucault, Michel. 1975. *Surveiller et punir: Naissance de la prison*. Paris: Gallimard.

————. 1980a. *The History of Sexuality*, vol. 1: *An Introduction*. New York: Vintage-Random House.

————, ed. 1980b. *Herculine Barbin: Being the Recently Discovered Memoirs of a Nineteenth-Century French Hermaphrodite*. New York: Pantheon.

————. 1982. "Le combat de la chasteté." In P. Ariès and A. Béjin, eds., *Sexualités occidentales*, 26–40. Paris: Seuil.

————. 1984a. *Histoire de la sexualité 2: L'usage des plaisirs*. Paris: Gallimard.

————. 1984b. *Histoire de la sexualité 3: Le souci de soi*. Paris: Gallimard.

————. 1995. *Dits et écrits*. 4 vols. Paris: Gallimard.

Foucher, Alfred. 1927. *La vie du Bouddha d'après les textes et les monuments de l'Inde*. Paris: Adrien Maisonneuve.

Fowler, Sherry. 1997a. "Setting Foot on the Mountain: Mt. Murō as a Women's Alternative to Mt. Kōya." *Asian Journal of Women's Studies* 3, 4: 52–73.

————. 1997. "Nyonin Kōya to shite no Murōji no mondai." *Nihon shūkyō bunkashi kenkyū* 2, 1: 43–58.

Fracasso, Riccardo. 1988. "Holy Mothers of Ancient China: A New Approach to the Hsi-wang-mu Problem." *T'oung Pao* 74, 1–3: 1–46.

Fraisse, Geneviève. 1995. *Muse de la Raison: Démocratie et exclusion des femmes en France*. Folio Histoire. Paris: Gallimard.

————. 1996. *La différence des sexes*. Philosophies. Paris: Presses Universitaires de France.

Frank, Bernard, trans. 1968. *Histoires qui sont maintenant du passé*. Paris: Gallimard.

————. 1989. "L'expérience d'un malheur absolu: Son refus et son dépassement. L'histoire de la mère de Jōjin." *Comptes rendus de l'Académie des Inscriptions et Belles Lettres*, 472–88. Paris: Académie des Inscriptions et Belles-Lettres.

Freedberg, David. 1989. *The Power of Images: Studies in the History and Theory of Response*. Chicago: University of Chicago Press.

Freud, Sigmund. 1924 [1920]. "The Psychogenesis of a Case of Homosexuality in a Woman." In Sigmund Freud, *Collected Papers*, vol. 2: 202–31. Trans. Joan Riviere. London: Hogarth Press

Fróis, Luis, S. J. 1926. *Die Geschichte Japans (1549–78)*. Trans. George Schurhammer and E. A. Voretzsch, Leipzig: Verlag der Asia major.

Fujii Masao. 1977. "Minzoku kankō ni mirareru aka to kuro no shōchōsei." In Bukkyō minzoku gakkai, ed., *Bukkyō to girei: Katō Shōichi sensei koki kinen ronbunshū*, 203–37. Tokyo: Kokusho kankōkai.

Fukuhara Ryūzen. 1991. "Hōnen shōnin no nyonin ōjōron." In Nihon bukkyō gakkai, ed. *Bukkyō to josei*, 29–42. Kyoto: Heirakuji shoten.

Fukutō Sanae. 1991. *Heianchō no haha to ko: Kizoku to shōmin no kazoku seikatsushi*. Chūkō shinsho 1003. Tokyo: Chūō kōronsha.

———. 1995. *Heianchō no onna to otoko*. Chūkō shinsho 1240. Tokyo: Chūō kōronsha.

Furth, Charlotte. 1986. "Blood, Body, and Gender: Medical Images of the Female Condition in China, 1600–1850." *Chinese Science* 7: 43–66.

———. 1987. "Concepts of Pregnancy, Childbirth, and Infancy in Ch'ing Dynasty China." *Journal of Asian Studies* 46, 1: 7–35.

———. 1988. "Androgynous Males and Deficient Females: Biology and Gender Boundaries in Sixteenth- and Seventeenth-Century China." *Late Imperial China* 9, 2: 1–31.

———. 1994. "Rethinking Van Gulik: Sexuality and Reproduction in Traditional Chinese Medicine." In Christina K. Gilmartin, Gail Herstatter, Lisa Rofel, and Tyrene White, eds. 1994. *Engendering China: Women, Culture, and the State*, 121–46. Cambridge, MA: Harvard University Press.

———. 1995. "From Rebirth to Rebirth: The Growing Body in Chinese Medicine." In Anne Behnke Kinney, ed. *Chinese Views of Childhood*, 157–91. Honolulu: University of Hawai'i Press.

———. 1999. *A Flourishing Yin: Gender in China's Medical History, 960–1665*. Berkeley: University of California Press.

Furuta Shōkin. 1977. "Chūsei zenrin ni okeru josei no nyūshin." *Indogaku bukkyōgaku kenkyū* 26, 1: 1–13.

Gatens, Moira. 1985. "A Critique of the Sex/Gender Distinction." In J. Allen and P. Patton, eds., *Beyond Marxism?* 143–60. Leichhardt, N.S.W., Australia: Intervention Publications.

Geinōshi kenkyūkai, ed. 1981–90. *Nihon geinōshi*. 7 vols. Tokyo: Hōsei daigaku shuppankyoku.

George, Christopher S., trans. 1974. *The Caṇḍamahāroṣaṇa tantra: Chapters I–VIII*. American Oriental Series 56. New Haven: American Oriental Society.

Georgieva, Valentina. 1996. "The Representation of Buddhist Nuns in Chinese Edifying Miracle Tales during the Six Dynasties and the T'ang." *Journal of Chinese Religions* 24: 47–76.

Gernant, Karen, trans. 1995. *Imagining Women: Fujian Folk Tales*. New York: Interlink Books.

Gilmartin, Christina K., Gail Herstatter, Lisa Rofel, and Tyrene White, eds. 1994. *Engendering China: Women, Culture, and the State*. Cambridge, MA: Harvard University Press.

Girard, Frédéric. 1990. *Un moine de la secte Kegon à l'époque de Kamakura, Myōe (1173–1232) et le "Journal de ses rêves."* Paris: Ecole Française d'Extrême-Orient.

Glassman, Hank, trans. 1999. *Mokuren no sōshi*: The Tale of Mokuren." *Buddhist Literature* 1: 120–61.

———. 2001. "The Religious Construction of Motherhood in Japan." Ph.D. Dissertation, Stanford University.

———. Forthcoming. "Compassing *Mokuren no sōshi*: Textual and Thematic Approaches to a Tale from Late Medieval Japan."

Godel, Armen, and Kano Koichi, trans. 1997. *Visages cachés, sentiments mêlés: Le livre poétique de Komachi; les cinq Nô du cycle Komachi; Le Dit de Komachi*. Paris: Gallimard.

Goldfuss, Gabriele. 1994. "Gärtnerinnen der Drei Juwelen: Die *Biographien von Laienbuddhistinnen* des Peng Shaosheng (1740–1796)." *Newsletter Frauen und China* 6: 19–31.

Goldstein, Jan, ed. 1994. *Foucault and the Writing of History*. Cambridge, MA: Basil Blackwell.

Gombrich, Richard. 1972. "Feminine Elements in Sinhalese Buddhism." *Wiener Zeitschrift für die Kunde Südasiens* 16: 67–93.

Goodrich, Grace. 1937. "Nuns of North China." *Asia* 37: 90–93.

Goodwin, Janet R. 1994. *Alms and Vagabonds: Buddhist Temples and Popular Patronage in Medieval Japan*. Honolulu: University of Hawai'i Press.

———. 2000. "Shadows of Transgression: Heian and Kamakura Constructions of Prostitution." *Monumenta Nipponica* 55, 3: 327–68.

Gorai Shigeru. 1977. "Nunohashi daikanjō to Hakusan gyōji." In Takase Shigeo, ed., *Hakusan, Tateyama to Hokuriku Shugendō*, 153–76. Sangaku shūkyōshi kenkyū sōsho. Tokyo: Meicho shuppan.

———. ed. 1984. *Shugendō shiryōshū*. 2 vols. Tokyo: Meicho shuppan,

———. 1989. "Shugendō Lore." *Japanese Journal of Religious Studies* 16, 2–3: 117–42.

———. 1990. "Chūsei josei no shūkyōsei to seikatsu." In Joseishi sōgō kenkyūkai, ed., *Nihon joseishi*, vol. 2: *Chūsei*, 103–36. Tokyo: Tōkyō daigaku shuppankai.

Gotō Hiroyuki. 1984. *Nyonin jōbutsu e no kaigan: Omikuji daishi, Ryōgen no monogatari*. Tokyo: Mainichi shinbunsha.

Goux, Jean-Joseph. 1990. *Symbolic Economies: After Marx and Freud*. Ithaca: Cornell University Press.

Graham, Hilary. 1976. "The Social Image of Pregnancy: Pregnancy as Spirit Possession." *The Sociological Review* 24, 2: 291–308.

Graham, Masako Nakagawa. 1987. "The Yang Kuei-fei Legend in Japanese Literature." Ph.D. Dissertation, University of Pennsylvania.

Grant, Beata. 1989. "The Spiritual Saga of Woman Huang: From Pollution to Purification." In David Johnson, ed., *Ritual Opera, Operatic Ritual: "Mulien Rescues His Mother" in Chinese Popular Culture*, 224–311. Berkeley: Chinese Popular Culture Project, University of California.

———. 1994. "Who Is This I? Who Is That Other? The Poetry of an Eighteenth-Century Buddhist Laywoman." *Late Imperial China* 15, 1: 1–52.

Grant, Beata. 1995. "Patterns of Female Religious Experience in Qing Popular Literature." *Journal of Chinese Religions* 23: 29–58.

——. 1996. "Female Holder of the Lineage: Linji Chan Master Zhiyuan Xing-gang (1597–1654). *Late Imperial China* 17, 2: 51–76.

——. 1999. "The Red Cord Untied: Buddhist Nuns in Eighteenth-Century China." In Karma Lekshe Tsomo, ed. *Buddhist Women across Cultures: Realizations*, 91–103. Albany: State University of New York Press.

Grapard, Allan G. 1987. "Linguistic Cubism: A Singularity of Pluralism in the Sannō Cult." *Japanese Journal of Religious Studies* 14, 2–3: 211–34.

——. 1991. "Visions of Excess and Excesses of Vision: Women and Transgression in Japanese Myth." *Japanese Journal of Religious Studies* 18, 1: 3–22.

——. Forthcoming. *The Religion of Space and the Place of Religion in Japan.* Stanford: Stanford University Press.

Greenblatt, Stephen J. 1990. *Learning to Curse: Essays in Early Modern Culture.* New York: Routledge.

Groner, Paul. 1989. "The *Lotus Sūtra* and Saichō's Interpretation of the Realization of Buddhahood with This Very Body." In George J. Tanabe, Jr., and Willa Jane Tanabe, eds., *The* Lotus Sūtra *in Japanese Culture*, 53–74. Honolulu: University of Hawai'i Press.

——. 1990a. "The *Fan-wang ching* and Monastic Discipline in Japanese Tendai," in Robert Buswell, Jr., ed., *Buddhist Apocrypha*, 251–90. Honolulu: University of Hawai'i Press.

——. 1990b. "Vicissitudes in the Ordination of Japanese 'Nuns' during the Late Nara and Early Heian Periods." Unpublished ms.

Gross, Rita M. 1986. "Buddhism and Feminism: Toward Their Mutual Transformation (1)". *The Eastern Buddhist* (n. s.) 19, 1: 44–58.

——. 1987. "Yeshe Tsogyel: Enlightened Consort, Great Teacher, Female Role Model." In Janice Willis, ed., *Feminine Ground: Essays on Women and Tibet*, 11–32. Ithaca: Snow Lion Publications.

——. 1991. "'I Go for Refuge to the Saṅgha': Contemporary Reflections on Community in Buddhist Ethics." In Paula M. Cooey, William R. Eakin, and Jay B. McDaniel, eds., *After Patriarchy: Feminist Reconstructions of the World's Religions.* Orbis.

——. 1993. *Buddhism After Patriarchy: A Feminist History, Analysis, and Reconstruction of Buddhism.* Albany: State University of New York Press.

——. 1998. *Soaring and Settling: Buddhist Perspectives on Contemporary Social and Religious Issues.* New York: Continuum.

Gubar, Susan. 1998. "What Ails Feminist Criticism?" *Critical Inquiry* 24, 4: 878–902.

Guisso, Richard W. L. 1978. *Wu Tse-t'ien and the Politics of Legitimation in T'ang China.* Bellingham, WA: Western Washington University Press.

——. 1981. "Thunder over the Lake: The Five Classics and the Perception of Women in Early China." In Richard W. Guisso and Stanley Johannesen, eds., *Women in China: Current Directions in Historical Scholarship.* Youngstown, NY: Philo Press.

Guisso, Richard W. L., and Stanley Johannesen, eds. 1981. *Women in China: Current Directions in Historical Scholarship.* Youngstown, NY: Philo Press.

Gunawardana, R.A.L.H. 1988. "Subtle Silks of Ferrous Firmness: Buddhist Nuns in Ancient and Early Medieval Sri Lanka and Their Role in the Propagation of Buddhism." *Sri Lanka Journal of the Humanities* 14, 1–2: 1–59.

Gyatso, Janet. 1987. "Down with the Demoness: Reflections on Feminine Ground in Tibet." In Janice D. Willis, ed., *Feminine Ground: Essays on Women and Tibet*, 33–51. Ithaca: Snow Lion Publications.

Haddad, Yvonne Yazbeck, and Ellison Banks Findly, eds. 1985. *Women, Religion and Social Change*. Albany: State University of New York Press.

Hae-ju Sunim (Ho-Ryeon Jeon). 1999. "Can Women Achieve Enlightenment? A Critique of Sexual Transformation for Enlightenment." In Karma Lekshe Tsomo, ed. 1999. *Buddhist Women across Cultures: Realizations*, 123–41. Albany: State University of New York Press.

Hagiwara Tatsuo. 1983. *Miko to bukkyō shi: Kumano bikuni no shimei to tenkai*. Tokyo: Yoshikawa Kōbunkan.

Haguenauer, Charles. 1930. "La danse rituelle dans la cérémonie du *chinkonsai*." *Journal Asiatique* 216: 299–350. Reprinted 1974 in *Etudes choisies de Charles Haguenauer*, vol. 2: *Japon. Etudes de religion, d'histoire et de littérature*. Leiden: E. J. Brill.

Halperin, David, John J. Winkler, and Froma I. Zeitlin, eds. 1990. *Before Sexuality: The Construction of Erotic Experience in the Ancient Greek World*. Princeton: Princeton University Press.

Hamanaka Osamu, ed. 1996. *Muromachi monogatari ronkō*. Shintensha kenkyū sōsho 95. Tokyo: Shintensha kankō.

Hamburger, Jeffrey F. 1997. *Nuns as Artists*. Berkeley: University of California Press.

Hamilton, Sue. 1995. "From the Buddha to Buddhagosa: Changing Attitudes toward the Human Body in Theravāda Buddhism." In Jane Marie Law, ed., *Religious Reflections on the Human Body*, 46–63. Bloomington: University of Indiana Press.

Hammond, Charles H. 1995. "The Demonization of the Other: Women and Minorities as Weretigers." *Journal of Chinese Religions* 23: 59–80.

Harada Masatoshi. 1997. "Nyonin to zenshū." In Nishiguchi Junko, ed., *Hotoke to onna: Chūsei o kangaeru*, 140–80. Tokyo: Yoshikawa kōbunkan.

Harada Toshiaki. 1958. "Nyonin kyūzei." *Shakai to denjō* 2, 4: 24–29.

Hardacre, Helen. 1983. "The Cave and the Womb World." *Japanese Journal of Religious Studies* 10, 2–3: 149–76.

———. 1988. "Gender and the Millenium in Ōmoto Kyodan." In Michael Williams et al., eds., *Innovation in Religious Traditions*. Berlin: Mouton.

———. 1997. *Marketing the Menacing Fetus in Japan*. Berkeley: University of California Press.

———. 1999. "The Shaman and Her Transformations: The Construction of Gender in Motifs of Religious Action." In Wakita Haruko, Anne Bouchy, and Ueno Chizuko, eds., *Gender and Japanese History* 1: 87–108. Osaka: Osaka University Press.

Harris, Elizabeth J. 1997. "Reclaiming the Sacred: Buddhist Women in Sri Lanka." *Feminist Theology* 15: 83–111.

Harris, Elizabeth J. 1999. "The Female in Buddhism." In Karma Lekshe Tsomo, ed. 1999. *Buddhist Women across Cultures: Realizations*, 49–65. Albany: State University of New York Press.

Harrison, Paul. 1998. "Women in the Pure Land: Some Reflections on the Textual Sources." *Journal of Indian Philosophy* 26, 6: 553–72.

Hasegawa Kiyoko. 1980. *Onna no minzokushi*. Tokyo: Tokyo shoseki.

Hasekawa Kōzo, and Tsukikawa Kazuo, eds.. 1991. *Minakata Kumagusu nanshoku dangi: Iwata Jun'ichi ōfuku shoseki*. Tokyo: Yasaka shobō.

Havnevik, Hanna. 1990. *Tibetan Buddhist Nuns: History, Cultural Norms and Social Reality*. New York: Oxford University Press.

Hawley, John Stratton, and Donna Marie Wulff, eds. 1982. *The Divine Consort: Rādhā and the Goddesses of India*. Boston: Beacon Press.

Hayami Akira. 1983. "The Myth of Primogeniture and Impartible Inheritance in Japan." *Journal of Family History* 8: 3–29.

Hayami Tasuku. 1975. *Heian kizoku shakai to bukkyō*. Tokyo: Yoshikawa kōbunkan.

———. 1996. "On Problems Surrounding Kōya's Appearance." Trans. Robert F. Rhodes. *Japanese Religions* 21, 1: 5–27.

Hecker, Hellmuth. 1982. *Buddhist Women at the Time of the Buddha*. Kandy, Sri Lanka: Buddhist Publication Society.

Heidegger, Simone. 1995. *Die Frau in japanischen Buddhismus der Kamakura-Zeit*. SBS Monographs 4. Copenhagen: Seminar for Buddhist Studies.

Heine, Steven. 1999. *Shifting Shape, Shaping Text: Philosophy and Folklore in the Fox Kōan*. Honolulu: University of Hawai'i Press.

Henderson, Gregory, and Leon Hurvitz. 1956. "The Buddha of Seiryōji: New Finds and New Theory." *Artibus Asiae Separatum* 19, 1: 5–55.

———. 1995. *La cour du Japon à l'époque de Heian au Xe et XIe siècles*. Paris: Hachette.

Héritier-Augé, Françoise. 1989. "Semen and Blood: Some Ancient Theories concerning Their Genesis and Relationship." In Michel Feher, ed., *Fragments for a History of the Body: Part Three*, 159–75. Zone 5. New York: Urzone.

Herrmann-Pfandt, Adelheid. 1992. *Dākinīs: Zur Stellung und Symbolik des Weiblichen in Tantrischen Buddhismus*. Indica und Tibetica 20. Bonn.

———. 1992–1993. "Dākinīs in Indo-Tibetan Tantric Buddhism: Some Results of Recent Research." *Studies in Central and East Asian Religions* 5–6: 45–63.

Higuchi Seisuke. 1988. *Himitsu no Nihon-shi*. Shōdensha nonposhetto. Tokyo: Shōdensha.

Hiltebeitel, Alf, and Barbara D. Miller, eds. 1998. *Hair: Its Power and Meaning in Asian Cultures*. Albany: State University of New York Press.

Hinonishi Shinjō. 1979. "Tamayori Gozen ronkō." In *Itō Shinsei, Tanaka Junshō ryō kyōju jutoku kinen bukkyōgaku ronshū*. Tokyo: Tōhō shuppan 1979.

———. 1989. "Kōyasan fumoto Karukayadō no hassei to kinō: Tokuni Senri Gozen no mikoteki seikaku ni tsuite." In Ōsumi Kazuo and Nishiguchi Junko, eds., *Josei to bukkyō 4: Miko to joshin*, 241–90. Tokyo: Heibonsha.

Hirabayashi Bun'yu. 1978. *"Jōjin ajari no haha no shū" no kisoteki kenkyū*. Tokyo: Kasama shoin.

Hirakawa Akira. 1982. *Monastic Discipline for the Buddhist Nuns*. Tokyo and Patna: Kashi Prasad Jayaswal Research Institute.

———. 1992. "The History of Buddhist Nuns in Japan." Trans. Karma Lekshe Tsomo and Junko Miura. *Buddhist-Christian Studies* 12, 147–58.

Holmgren, Jennifer. 1981. "Myth, Fantasy or Scholarship: Images of the Status of Women in Traditional China." *The Australian Journal of Chinese Affairs* 6: 147–70.

———. 1982. "Family, Marriage, and Political Power in Sixth-Century China." *Journal of Asian History* 16, 1: 1–50.

Hongō Masatsugu. 1989. "'Kokka bukkyō' to 'kyūtei bukkyō': kyūtei josei no yakuwari." In Ōsumi Kazuo and Nishiguchi Junko, eds. *Josei to bukkyō* 3: *Shinjin to kuyō*, 207–36. Tokyo: Heibonsha.

Hori Kyotsu, ed. 1995. *St. Nichiren's Nyonin Gosho: Letters Addressed to Female Followers*. 2 vols. Tokyo: Nichiren shū, Overseas Propagation Promotion Association.

Horner, I. B. [Isabelle Blew]. [1930] 1975. *Women under Primitive Buddhism: Laywomen and Almswomen*. London: George Routledge and Sons. Reprint Delhi: Motilal Banarsidass.

———, trans. 1975–77. *The Collection of the Middle Length Sayings (Majjhima-Nikāya)*. London and Boston: Routledge and Kegan Paul.

Hosokawa Ryōichi. 1987. *Chūsei no risshū jiin to minshū*. Tokyo: Yoshikawa kōbunkan.

———. 1988a. "Chūsei ni okeru amadera no tenkai: Kyōto Tōrinji, Saga Kōdaiji, Kamakura Wasokuji, Kanazawa Kaiganji." *Kamakura* 58: 1–20.

———. 1988b. "Ōken to amadera: chūsei no sei to sharin shinkō." In Amino Yoshihiko, ed., *Rettō no bunkashi* 5. Nihon editā sukūru shuppanbu.

———. 1989a. *Onna no chūsei: Ono no Komachi, Tomoe, sono ta*. Nihon editā sukūru shuppanbu.

———. 1989b. "Sairinji Sōji to ama: Chūsei risshū to 'nyonin kyūsai.' " In Ōsumi Kazuo and Nishiguchi Junko, eds., *Josei to bukkyō* 3: *Sukui to oshie*, 121–64. Tokyo: Heibonsha.

———. 1992. "Kazoku o kōseishinai josei." In Minegishi Sumio, ed., *Kazoku to josei: Chūsei o kangaeru*, 210–40. Tokyo: Yoshikawa kōbunkan.

———. 1993. *Itsudatsu no Nihon chūsei: Kyōki, tōsaku, ma no sekai*. Tokyo: JICC.

———. 1994. *Chūsei no mibunsei to hinin*. Tokyo: Nihon editā sukūru shuppanbu.

———. 1998. *Heike monogatari no onnatachi: Dairiki, ama, shirabyōshi*. Kōdansha gendai shinsho 1424. Tokyo: Kōdansha.

———. 1999. "Kamakura Period Nuns and Convents: Exploring Hokkeji Convent." Trans. by Micah Auerback. In Wakita Haruko, Anne Bouchy, and Ueno Chizuko, eds., *Gender and Japanese History* 1: 25–51. Osaka: Osaka University Press.

Hou, Sharon Shih-jiuan. 1986. "Women's Literature." In William H. Nienhauser, Jr., ed., *The Indiana Companion to Traditional Chinese Literature*, 175–94. Bloomington: University of Indiana Press.

Hsieh, Ding-hwa E. 1999. "Images of Women in Ch'an Buddhist Literature of the Sung Period." In Peter N. Gregory and Daniel A. Getz, Jr., eds. *Buddhism in the Sung*, 149–87. Kuroda Institute, Studies in East Asian Buddhism 13. Honolulu: University of Hawai'i Press.

Hsiung Ping-chen. 1994. "Constructed Emotions: The Bond between Mothers and Sons in Late Imperial China." *Late Imperial China* 15, 1: 87–119.

Huber, Toni. 1994. "Why Can't Women Climb Pure Crystal Mountain? Remarks on Gender, Ritual, and Space at Tsa-ri." In *Tibetan Studies: Proceedings of the 6th Seminar of the International Association of Buddhist Studies (Fagernes 1992)*. 2: 350–71. Oslo: Institute for Comparative Research in Human Culture.

———. 1999. *The Cult of Pure Crystal Mountain: Popular Pilgrimage and Visionary Landscape in Southeast Tibet.* New York and Oxford: Oxford University Press.

Huizinga, Johan. 1951. *Homo Ludens: Essai sur la fonction sociale du jeu.* Paris: Gallimard.

Hurvitz, Leon, trans. 1976. *Scripture of the Lotus Sūtra Blossom of the Fine Dharma.* New York: Columbia University Press.

Ichiko Teiji, ed. 1946. *Mikan chūsei shōsetsu.* Koten bunko 12. Tokyo: Koten bunko.

Igeta Midori. 1983. "The Image of Women in Sermons: Anju in 'Sanshō Dayū.'" *Japanese Journal of Religious Studies* 10, 2–3: 247–72.

Ihara Saikaku. 1956. *Five Women Who Loved Love.* Trans. Wm. Theodore De Bary. Tokyo and Rutland, VT: Charles E. Tuttle.

Iinuma Kenji. 1990. "Chūsei zenki no josei no shōgai: jinsei no shodankai no kentō o tsūjite." In Joseishi sōgō kenkyūkai, ed. 1990. *Nihon josei seikatsu shi* 2: *Chūsei*, 31–74. Tokyo: Tōkyō daigaku shuppankai.

———. 1992. "Goke no chikara: Sono seiritsu to yakuwari o megutte." In Minogishi Sumio, ed., *Chūsei o kangaeru: Kazoku to josei*, 153–79. Tokyo: Yoshikawa kōbunko.

Imahori Taitsu. 1990. *Jingi shinkō no kaiten to bukkyō.* Tokyo: Yoshikawa kōbundō.

Inoue Takami. 1993. "Symbolic Meanings of Shinran's Dream at Rokkakudō." International Association of Shin Buddhist Studies, ed., *Papers*, 1–17. Kyoto: Ōtani University.

Irigaray, Luce. 1985. *This Sex Which Is Not One.* Trans. Catherine Porter and Carolyn Burke. Ithaca: Cornell University Press.

Ishida Eiichirō. 1956. "The Mother-Son Complex in East Asiatic Religion and Folklore." In *Wiener Schule der Völkerkunde, Festschrift zum 25-jährigen Bestand 1929–1954*, 411–19. Vienna.

———. 1964. "Mother-Son Deities." *History of Religions* 4, 1: 30–52.

———. 1984. *Momotarō no haha.* Kōdansha gakufutsu bunko 664. Tokyo: Kodansha.

Ishida Mizumaro. 1971. *Bonmōkyō.* Tokyo: Daizō shuppansha.

———. 1995. *Nyobon: Hijiri no sei.* Tokyo: Chikuma shobō.

Ishikawa Rikizan. 1984. "Chūsei Sōtōshū kirigami no bunrui shiron (4): Sōtōshū ni okeru sabetsu kirigami hassei no yūrai ni tsuite." *Komazawa daigaku bukkyōgakubu ronshū* 15: 152–69.

———. 1985. "Chūsei Sōtōshū kirigami no bunrui shiron (6): Angyabutsu kankei o chūshin to shite." *Komazawa daigaku bukkyōgakubu ronshū* 16: 102–52.

———. 1986. "Chūsei Sōtōshū kirigami no bunrui shiron (8): Tsuizen, sōsō kuyō kankei o chūshin to shite (jō)." *Komazawa daigaku bukkyōgakubu ronshū* 17: 179–213.

———. 1987. "Chūsei Sōtōshū kirigami no bunrui shiron (9): Tsuizen, sōsō kuyō kankei o chūshin to shite (chū)." *Komazawa daigaku bukkyōgakubu kenkyū kiyō* 45: 167–96.

———. 1990. "Dōgen no 'nyoshin fujōbutsu ron' ni tsuite: Jūnikanbon *Shōbōgenzō* no seikaku o meguru oboegaki." *Komazawa daigaku zen kenkyūjo nenpō* 1: 88–123.

———. 1992a. "Chūsei bukkyō ni okeru ama no isō ni tsuite (jō): Tokuni shoki Sōtōshū kyōdan no jirei o chūshin ni." *Komazawa daigaku zen kenkyūjo nenpō* 3: 141–53.

———. 1992b. "Chūsei Sōtōshū kirigami no bunrui shiron (20): Girei (jukai, tengen, segaki, sono ta) kankei o chūshin to shite." *Komazawa daigaku bukkyōgakubu ronshū* 23: 95–126.

———. 1993. "Chūsei bukkyō ni okeru ama no isō ni tsuite (ge): Toku ni shoki Sōtōshū kyōdan no jirei o chūshin to shite." *Komazawa daigaku zen kenkyūjo nenpō* 4: 63–80.

———. 1996. "Kirigami denjō to kinsei Sōtōshū: 'Beppuku' 'Botsugo sasō' kankei kirigami no kinseiteki hen'yō o megutte." In Tamamuro Fumio, ed., *Minshū shūkyō no kōzō to keifu*, 297–322. Kyoto: Yūzankaku.

Itō Kinkichi, and Donald Richie. 1967. *Danjo-zō/ The Erotic Gods: Phallicism in Japan*. Tokyo, 1967.

Itō Masayoshi. 1981. "Jidō setsuwa kō." *Kokugo kokubun* 49, 11: 1–32.

Iwai Hirosato. 1935. "The Buddhist Priest and the Ceremony of Attaining Womanhood during the Yüan Dynasty." *Memoirs of the Tōyō Bunko* 7: 105–61.

Iwamoto Yutaka. 1980. *Bukkyō to josei*. Regulus bunko. Tokyo: Daisan bunmeisha.

Iwasaki Takeo. 1994 [1973]. *Sanshō dayū kō: Chūsei no sekkyō-gatari*. Heibonsha raiburarī 1200. Tokyo: Heibonsha.

Iyanaga Nobumi. 1999. "Dākinī et l'Empereur: Mystique bouddhique de la royauté dans le Japon médiéval." *Versus: Quaderni di studi semiotici* 83–84: 41–111.

Jaffe, Richard. 1998. "Meiji Religious Policy, Sōtō Zen, and the Clerical Marriage Problem." *Japanese Journal of Religious Studies* 25, 1–2: 45–85.

Jaggar, Alison M., and Susan R. Bordo, eds. 1989. *Gender/Body/Knowledge: Feminist Reconstructions of Being and Knowing*. New Brunswick, N.J.: Rutgers University.

Jaini, Padmanabh S. 1991. *Gender and Salvation*. Berkeley: University of California Press.

Jameson, R. D. 1982. "Cinderella in China." In Alan Dundes, ed., *Cinderella: A Casebook*, 71–97. Madison: University of Wisconsin Press.

Jay, Nancy. 1992. *Throughout Your Generations Forever: Sacrifice, Religion, and Paternity.* Chicago: University of Chicago Press.

Johnson, David, ed. 1989. *Operatic Ritual, Ritual Opera:* Mu-lien Rescues His Mother *in Chinese Popular Culture.* Berkeley: University of California Press.

Jones, J. J., trans. 1949–56. *The Mahāvastu.* 3 vols. Sacred Books of the Buddhists 17–19. London: Pāli Text Society.

Joseishi sōgō kenkyūkai, ed. 1982. *Nihon josei shi.* 5 vols. Tokyo: Tōkyō daigaku shuppankai.

———, ed. 1990. *Nihon josei seikatsu shi.* 5 vols. Tokyo: Tōkyō daigaku shuppankai.

———, ed. 1983–1994. *Nihon joseishi kenkyū bunken mokuroku* [A Bibliography of Japanese Women's History]. 3 vols. [1868–1981, 1982–1986, 1987–1991]. Tokyo: Tōkyō daigaku shuppankai.

Journal of Asian Studies. 1987. "Women in the Qing Period—A Symposium." *Journal of Asian Studies* 46, 1.

Joy, Morny. 1995. "And What If Truth Were a Woman?" In Morny Joy and Eva K. Neumaier-Dargyay, eds., *Gender, Genre, and Religion: Feminist Reflections,* 277–94. Calgary: Wilfrid Laurier University Press.

Kabilsingh, Chatsumarn. 1984. *A Comparative Study of Bhikkhuni Patimokkha.* Varanasi: Chaukhambha Orientalia.

———. 1991. *Thai Women in Buddhism.* Berkeley: Parallax Press.

Kaempfer, Engelbert. 1906. *The History of Japan: Together with a Description of the Kingdom of Siam,* 1690–92. 2 vols. Glasgow: James MacLehose and Sons.

Kagawa Takao. 1975. "Bukkyō no joseikan." *Indogaku bukkyōgaku kenkyū kiyō* 23, 2: 45–53.

———. 1976. "Hōnen Shōnin no nyonin ōjōkan." *Jōdo shūgaku kenkyū* 8: 51–70.

Kageyama Haruki. 1971. *Shintaizan: Nihon no genshi shinkō o saguru.* Tokyo: Gakuseisha.

Kagiya Akiko. 1985. "Bosei no tagisei: Bunka jinruigakuteki kōsatsu." In Wakita Haruko, ed., *Bosei o tou: Rekishiteki hensen* (1), 13–42. Kyoto: Jinbun shoin.

Kaibara Ekken. 1913. *The Way of Contentment.* Trans. Ken Hoshino. London: John Murray.

Kajiyama Yuichi. 1982. "Women in Buddhism." *The Eastern Buddhist,* n. s. 15, 1: 53–70.

Kamata Hisako. 1966. "Daughters of the Gods: Shaman Priestesses in Japan and Okinawa." In *Folk Cultures of Japan and East Asia,* 56–73. Monumenta Nipponica Monographs no. 25. Tokyo: Sophia University Press.

Kamens, Edward. 1988. The Three Jewels: *A Study and Translation of Minamoto Tamenori's* Sanbōe. Ann Arbor: Center for Japanese Studies, University of Michigan.

———. 1990. *The Buddhist Poetry of the Great Kamo Priestess: Daisaiin Senshi and Hosshin Wakashū.* Michigan Monograph Series in Japanese Studies, Number 5. Ann Arbor: Center for Japanese Studies, University of Michigan.

———. 1993. "Dragon-Girl, Maidenflower, Buddha: The Transformation of a Waka Topos." *Harvard Journal of Asiatic Studies* 53, 2: 389–442.

Kaneko Sachiko, and Robert Morrell. 1983. "Sanctuary: Kamakura's Tōkeiji Convent." *Japanese Journal of Religious Studies* 10, 2–3: 195–228.

Kapani, Lakshmi, trans. 1989a. "Upaniṣad of the Embryo." In Michel Feher, ed., *Fragments for a History of the Human Body: Part Three*, 177–79. New York: Urzone.

———. 1989b. "Note on the *Garbha-Upaniṣad*." In Michel Feher, ed., *Fragments for a History of the Human Body: Part Three*, 181–96. New York: Urzone.

Kasahara Kazuo. 1975. *Nyonin ōjō shisō no keifu.* Tokyo: Yoshikawa kōbunkan.

———, ed. 1983. *Nyonin ōjō.* Rekishi shinsho 183. Tokyo: Kyoikusha.

Kasamatsu Hiroshi and Katsumata Shizuo. 1983. *Chūsei no tsumi to batsu.* Tokyo: Tōkyō daigaku shuppankai.

Katagiri Yōichi. 1975. *Ono no Komachi tsuiseki.* Tokyo: Sasama shoin.

———. 1991. *Ariwara no Narihira, Ono no Komachi: Tenkai sakka no kyōzō to jitsuzō.* Tokyo: Shintensha.

Katō Genchi. 1924. "A Study of the Development of Religious Ideas among the Japanese People as Illustrated by Japanese Phallicism." *Transactions of the Asiatic Society of Japan* 1, suppl., 2nd series, 5–22.

Katō Mieko. 1985. "'Musume' no za kara nyobōza e: Chūsei sonraku to bosei." In Wakita Haruko, ed., *Bosei o tou: Rekishiteki hensen* (1), 204–27. Kyoto: Jinbun shoin.

———. 1990. "Chūsei no josei to shinkō: miko, bikuni, kirishitan." In Joseishi sōgō kenkyūkai, ed, *Nihon josei seikatsu shi,* 2: *Chūsei,* 259–87. Tokyo: Tōkyō daigaku shuppankai.

Katsuda Itaru. 1992. "Buraku no bosei to kazoku." In Minegishi Sumio, ed., *Kazoku to josei: Chūsei o kangaeru,* 179–209. Tokyo: Yoshikawa kōbunkan.

Katsuura Noriko. 1989. "Amasogi kō: Hatsukei kara mita ama no sonzai keitai." In Ōsumi Kazuo and Nishiguchi Junko, eds., *Josei to bukkyō* 1: *Ama to amadera,* 11–42. Tokyo: Heibonsha.

———. 1992. "Josei no hosshin. shukke to kazoku: Chūsei kōki no jirei o chūshin ni." In Minogishi Sumio, ed., *Chūsei o kangaeru: Kazoku to josei,* 241–71. Tokyo: Yoshikawa kōbunkan.

———. 1995. *Onna no shinjin: tsuma ga shukkeshita jidai.* Heibonsha sensho 156. Tokyo: Heibonsha.

———. 1997. "Onna no shigo to sono kyūzai: Haha no shōsho to kinyo no dajigoku." In Nishiguchi Junko, ed., *Hotoke to onna: Chūsei o kangaeru,* 34–66. Tokyo: Yoshikawa kōbunkan.

———. 2000. *Nihon kodai no sōni to shakai.* Tokyo: Yoshikawa kōbunkan.

Kawahashi Noriko. 1992. "*Kaminchu*: Divine Women of Okinawa." Ph.D. Dissertation, Princeton University.

———. 1995. "*Jizoku* (Priests' Wives) in Sōtō Zen Buddhism: An Ambiguous Category." *Japanese Journal of Religious Studies* 22, 1–2: 161–83.

———. 2000a. "A Comparative Analysis of Female Sexuality in Religion: Buddhist Nun (Ama) and Okinawan Divine Priestess (Kaminchu)." *Nagoya kōgyō daigaku kiyō* 52: 47–54.

———. 2000b. "Religion, Gender, and Okinawan Studies." *Asian Folklore Studies* 59: 301–11.

Kawahashi Noriko. 2000c. "Seven Hindrances of Women? A Popular Discouse on Okinawan Women and Religion." *Japanese Journal of Religious Studies* 27, 1–2: 85–98.

Kawai Hayao. 1992. *The Buddhist Priest Myōe: A Life of Dreams*. Trans. Mark Unno. Venice, CA: Lapis.

Kawane Yoshiyasu. 1990. "Seikatsu no henka to josei no shakaiteki chii: Shushō-seiteki chitsujo kara kafuchōseiteki chitsujo e." In Joseishi sōgō kenkyūkai, ed. *Nihon josei seikatsu shi* 2: *Chūsei*, 1–30. Tokyo: Tōkyō daigaku shuppan-kai.

Kawashima, Terry. 2001. *Writing Margins: The Textual Construction of Gender in Heian and Kamakura Japan*. Harvard East Asian Monographs 201. Cambridge, MA: Harvard University Press.

Keene, Donald, trans. 1961. *Four Major Plays of Chikamatsu*. New York: Columbia University Press.

———. 1962. "The Hippolytus Triangle, East and West." In *Yearbook of Comparative and General Literature* 11 (Supplement): 162–71.

———, trans. 1967. *Essays in Idleness*. New York: Columbia University Press.

———, ed. 1970. *Twenty Plays of the Nō Theatre*. New York: Columbia University Press.

Keirstead, Thomas. 1995. "The Gendering and Regendering of Medieval Japan." *U.S.–Japan Women's Journal* English Supplement 9: 77–92.

Kelly, Joan. 1984. *Women, History, and Theory: The Essays of Joan Kelly*. Chicago: University of Chicago Press.

Kelsey, W. Michael. 1981a. "Salvation of the Snake, the Snake of Salvation: Buddhist-Shinto Conflict and Resolution." *Japanese Journal of Religious Studies* 8, 1–2: 83–113.

———. 1981b. "The Raging Deity in Japanese Mythology." *Asian Folklore Studies* 40, 2: 213–36.

Kendall, Laurel. 1984. *Shamans, Housewives, and Other Restless Spirits: Women in Korean Ritual Life*. Honolulu: University of Hawai'i Press.

Keswani, N. H. 1962. "The Concepts of Generation, Reproduction, Evolution, and Human Development as Found in the Writings of Indian (Hindu) Scholars during the Early Period (up to 1200 A.D.) of Indian History." *Bulletin of the National Institute of Sciences of India* 21.

Keyes, Charles F. 1984. "Mother or Mistress but Never a Monk: Buddhist Notions of Female Gender in Rural Thailand." *American Ethnologist* 11, 2: 223–41.

———. 1986. "Ambiguous Gender: Male Initiation in a Northern Thai Buddhist Society." In Caroline Walker Bynum, Stevan Harrell Paula Richman, eds., *Gender and Religion*, 66–96. Boston: Beacon Press.

Kim Insook. 1995. "A Comparison of the Buddhist Monastic Communities of Korea, Taiwan, and Japan and the Sexism of the 'Eight Rules.' " *U.S.–Japan Women's Journal* English Supplement 8, 101–28.

Kim Yung-Chung, ed. 1976. *Women of Korea: A History from Ancient Times to 1945*. Seoul: Ewha Women's University Press.

Kim Yung-Hee (Kwon), trans. 1994. *Songs to Make the Dust Dance: The* Ryōjin Hishō *of Twelfth-Century Japan*. Berkeley: University of California Press.

Kimbrough, Randle Keller. 1999. "Imagining Izumi Shikibu: Representations of a Heian Woman Poet in the Literature of Medieval Japan." Ph.D. Dissertation, Yale University.

King, Karen L., ed. 1997. *Women and Goddess Traditions in Antiquity and Today*. Minneapolis: Fortress Press.

King, Sallie B. 1987. *Passionate Journey: The Spiritual Autobiography of Satomi Myōdō*. Boston and London: Shambhala.

———. 1988. "Egalitarian Philosophies in Sexist Institutions: The Life of Satomi-san, Shinto Miko and Zen Buddhist Nun." *Journal of Feminist Studies in Religion* 4, 1: 7–26.

Kirsch, A. Thomas. 1982. "Buddhism, Sex-Roles and Thai Society." In Penny Van Esterik, ed., *Women of Southeast Asia*, 16–41. Occasional Papers no. 9. DeKalb: Center for Southeast Asian Studies, Northern Illinois University.

———. 1985. "Text and Context: Buddhist Sex Roles/ Culture of Gender Revisited." *American Ethnologist* 12, 2: 302–20.

Kitagawa Tadahiko. 1978. *Kannami no geiryū*. Tokyo: Miyai shoten.

Kitamura Mariko. 1980. "The Best Way Is to Keep Away from Them: Kamo no Chōmei's Views of Women in the *Hosshinshū*." *Journal of Asian Culture* 4: 1–20.

Kittay, Eva Feder. 1983. "Womb Envy: An Explanatory Concept." In Joyce Trebilcot, ed., *Mothering: Essays in Feminist Theory*, 94–128. Savage, MD: Rowman and Littlefield.

Kiyomoto Hideki. 1992. "Shinran ni okeru mukoku to kōsei." In Kōkakai, ed., *Shinran to ningen*, 179–208. Kyoto: Nagata bunshōdō.

Klein, Anne C. 1985. "Non-Dualism and the Great Bliss Queen: A Study in Tibetan Buddhist Ontology and Symbolism." *Journal of Feminist Studies in Religion* 1, 1: 73–98.

———. 1987. "Primordial Purity and Everyday Life: Exalted Female Symbols and the Women of Tibet." In Clarissa W. Atkinson and Margaret Miles, eds., *Immaculate and Powerful: The Female in Sacred Image and Social Reality*, 111–38. Boston: Beacon Press.

———. 1994. *Meeting the Great Bliss Queen: Buddhists, Feminists, and the Art of the Self*. Boston: Beacon Press.

Klein, Susan B. 1990. "When the Moon Strikes the Bell: Desire and Enlightenment in the Noh Play *Dōjōji*." *Journal of Japanese Studies* 17, 2: 291–322.

———. 1995. "Woman as Serpent: The Demonic Feminine in the Noh Play Dōjōji." In Jane Marie Law, ed., *Religious Reflections on the Human Body*, 100–136. Bloomington: University of Indiana Press.

———. 1997. "Allegories of Desire: Poetry and Eroticism in *Ise Monogatari Zuinō*." *Monuments Nipponica* 52, 4: 441–65.

Kloppenborg, Ria. 1995. "Female Stereotypes in Early Buddhism: The Women of the *Therīgāthā*." In Ria Kloppenborg and Wouter J. Hanegraaf, eds., *Female Stereotypes in Religious Traditions*, 151–69. Studies in the History of Religions 64. Leiden: E. J. Brill.

Ko, Dorothy. 1989. "Toward a Social History of Women in Seventeenth-Century China." Ph.D. Dissertation, Stanford University.

Ko, Dorothy. 1994. *Teachers of the Inner Chambers: Women and Culture in Seventeenth-Century China*. Stanford: Stanford University Press.

Kodate Naomi. 1991. "*Ketsubongyō* to nyōnin kyūzai: 'Chi no ike no katari' o chūshin ni." *Kokubungaku: kaishaku to kanshō* 56, 5: 124–28.

Koffman, Sarah. 1985. *The Enigma of Woman: Woman in Freud's Writings*. Trans. Catherine Porter. Ithaca: Cornell University Press.

Kohō Chisan, ed. 1976. *Jōsai daishi zenshū*, 733. Yokohama: Daihonzan Sōjiji.

Kōjin konwakai, ed. 1975. *Nihon sekibutsu jiten*. Tokyo: Yūzankaku.

Komatsu Kazuaki. 1995. "Chūsei setsuwa no Komachi." *Kokubungaku: kaishaku to kanshō* 60: 46–52.

Komatsu Shigemi and Kanzaki Mitsuharu, eds. 1981. *Hōnen Shōnin eden*. 3 vols. Zoku Nihon emaki taisei, 1–3. Tokyo: Chūō kōronsha.

Komine Kazuaki. 1995. "Amadera no shozō: Hōkyōji no baai." *Shin Nihon koten bungaku gappō* 58. Tokyo: Iwanami shoten.

Kosawa Eisaku. 1954. "Zaiaku ishiki no nishū: Ajase kompurekkusu." *Seishin bunseki kenkyū* 1, 1.

Kristeva, Julia. 1990 [1974]. *About Chinese Women*. Trans. Anita Barrows. London: Marion Boyars.

Krutzer, Robert. 1998. "Semen, Blood, and the Intermediate Existence." *Indogaku bukkyōgaku kenkyū* 46, 2: 30–36.

Ku Cheng-mei. 1984. "The Mahayanic View of Women: A Doctrinal Study." Ph.D. Dissertation, University of Wisconsin, Madison.

———. 1991. "The Mahīśāsaka View of Women." In David J. Kalupahana, ed., *Buddhist Thought and Ritual*, 103–24. New York: Paragon House.

Kubukihara Rei. 1991. "Izumi Shikibu to bukkyō." *Kokubungaku: kaishaku to kanshō* 56: 80–84.

Kuo Li-ying. 1994. *Confession et contrition dans le bouddhisme chinois du Ve au Xe siècle*. Publications de l'Ecole Française d'Extrême Orient. Paris: Ecole Française d'Extrême-Orient.

Kuratsuka Masaki. 1994. *Fujo no bunka*. Heibonsha raiburarii 1200. Tokyo: Heibonsha.

Kurausu, F. 1988. *Meicho Edai: Sei Fūzoku no Nihon shi*. Tokyo: Kawade Shobō.

Kurihara Hiromi. 1991. "Shinran no joseikan." In Nihon bukkyō gakkai, ed., *Bukkyō to josei*, 59–78. Tokyo: Heirakuji shoten.

Kuroda Hideo. 1986. *Sugata to shigusa no chūseishi: Ezu to emaki no fūkei kara*. Tokyo: Heibonsha.

Kuroda Toshio. 1975. *Nihon chūsei no kokka to shūkyō*. Tokyo: Iwanami shoten.

———. 1983. *Obō to buppō: Chūseishi no kōzu*. Kyoto: Hōzōkan.

Kuwana Tsunamasa. 1991. "Nichiren Shōnin no joseikan." In Nihon bukkyō gakkai, ed., *Bukkyō to josei*, 97–111. Tokyo: Heirakuji shoten.

Kvaerne, Per. 1975. "On the Concept of *Sahaja* in Indian Buddhist Tantric Literature." *Temenos* 11: 88–135.

Kwŏn (Kim) Yung-Hee. 1986a. "Voices from the Periphery: Love Songs in the *Ryōjin Hishō*." *Monumenta Nipponica* 41, 2: 1–20.

———. 1986b. "The Emperor's Songs: Go-Shirakawa and *Ryōjin Hishō Kudenshū* Book 10." *Monumenta Nipponica* 41, 3: 261–98.

————. 1990. "The Female Entertainment Tradition in Medieval Japan: The Case of *Asobi*." In Sue-Ellen Case, ed., *Performing Feminisms: Feminist Critical Theory and Theatre*, 316–27. Baltimore: Johns Hopkins University Press.

Kyōraku Mahoko. 1999. "Taking the Tonsure in Eleventh-Century Heian-kyō: Buddhism, Women, and the City." Translated by Gustav Heldt. In Wakita Haruko, Anne Bouchy, and Ueno Chizuko, eds., *Gender and Japanese History* 1: 3–23. Osaka: Osaka University Press.

La Vallée Poussin, Louis de, trans. 1923–31. *L'Abhidharmakośa de Vasubandhu*. 6 vols. Paris: Geuthner. English trans. by Leo Pruden. *Abhidharmakośabhāṣyam*. 3 vols. Berkeley: Asian Humanities Press, 1988–89.

Lachaud, François. 1995. "La mort aux neuf visages." *Ebisu. Etudes Japonaises* 9: 35–80.

————. 1997. "Le corps dissolu des femmes: Un autre regard sur l'impermanence." In Jacqueline Pigeot and Hartmund O. Rotermund, eds., *Le vase de béryl: Etudes sur le Japon et la Chine en hommage à Bernard Frank*, 47–62. Arles: Editions Philippe Picquier.

————. 1998. "La jeune fille et la mort. La contemplation de l'impur et celle des Neuf Notions dans le Japon classique: Une étude des représentations macabres du corps et du féminin." Ph.D. Dissertation, Institut National des Langues et Civilisations Orientales, Paris.

LaFleur, William R. 1999. *Liquid Life: Abortion and Buddhism in Japan*. Princeton: Princeton University Press.

Lafoff, Georges, and Mark Johnson. 1980. *Metaphors We Live By*. Chicago: University of Chicago Press.

Lamotte, Etienne, trans. 1944–1980. *Le Traité de la grande vertu de sagesse de Nāgārjuna*. 6 vols. Louvain: Institut Orientaliste.

————, trans. 1962. *L'enseignement de Vimalakīrti (Vimalakīrtinirdeśa)*. Louvain: Institut Orientaliste. English translation by Sara Boin., *The Teaching of Vimalakīrti*. Sacred Books of the Buddhists 32. London: PTS, 1976.

Lang, Karen C. 1986. "Lord Death's Snare: Gender-Related Imagery in the *Theragāthā* and the *Therīgāthā*." *Journal of Feminist Studies in Religion* 2, 2: 63–79.

————. 1995. "Shaven Heads and Loose Hair: Buddhist Attitudes towards Hair and Sexuality." In Howard Eilberg-Schwartz and Wendy Doniger, eds., *Off with Her Head: The Denial of Women's Identity in Myth, Religion, and Culture*, 32–52. Berkeley: University of California Press.

Laqueur, Thomas. 1990. *Making Sex: Body and Gender from the Greeks to Freud*. Cambridge, MA: Harvard University Press.

Lauwaert, Françoise. 1991. *Recevoir, conserver, transmettre: L'adoption dans l'histoire de la famille chinoise—aspects religieux, sociaux et juridiques*. Mélanges Chinois et Bouddhiques 24. Brussels: Institut Belge des Hautes Etudes Chinoises.

Law, Bimala Churn. 1939–40. "Bhikṣuṇis in Indian Inscriptions." In *Epigraphica Indica*, vol. 25: 31–34.

————. 1981 [1927]. *Women in Buddhist Literature*. Varanasi: Indological Book House.

Law, Jane Marie. 1993. "Of Plagues and Puppets: On the Significance of the Name Hyakudayū in Japanese Religion." *Transactions of the Japan Asiatic Society*, 4th Series, vol. 8: 107–31.

———. 1997. *Puppets of Nostalgia*. Princeton: Princeton University Press.

Lee, Lily Hsiao Hung. 1986–87. "The Emergence of Buddhist Nuns in China and Its Social Ramifications." *Journal of the Oriental Society of Australia* 18–19: 82–100. Reprinted in Lily Xiao Hong Lee, *The Virtues of Yin: Studies on Chinese Women*, 47–64. Sydney: Wild Peony, 1994.

Legendre, Pierre. 1985. *L'inestimable objet de la transmission*. Paris: Fayard.

Le Goff, Jacques. 1980. *Time, Work, and Culture in the Middle Ages*. Trans. Arthur Goldhammer. Chicago: University of Chicago Press.

Le Monde, ed. 1994. *Les grands entretiens du Monde*. Vol. 2. Paris: Editions Le Monde.

Leung, Angela K. C. 1984. "Autour de la naissance: La mère et l'enfant en Chine au XVIe et XVIIe siècles." *Cahiers internationaux de sociologie* 76: 51–69.

Levering, Miriam L. 1982. "The Dragon Girl and the Abbess of Mo-shan: Gender and Status in the Ch'an Buddhist Tradition." *Journal of the International Association of Buddhist Studies* 5, 1: 19–34.

———. 1992. "Lin-chi (Rinzai) Ch'an and Gender: The Rhetoric of Equality and the Rhetoric of Heroism." In José Ignacio Cabezón, ed., *Buddhism, Sexuality, and Gender*. Albany: State University of New York Press.

———. 1997. "Stories of Enlightened Women in Ch'an and the Chinese Buddhist Female Bodhisattva/Goddess Tradition." In Karen L. King, ed., *Women and Goddess Traditions in Antiquity and Today*, 137–76. Minneapolis: Fortress Press.

———. 1998. "Dōgen's *Raihaitokuzui* and Women Teaching in Sung Ch'an." *Journal of the International Association of Buddhist Studies* 21, 1: 77–110.

Lévy, André. 1978. *Inventaire analytique et critique du conte chinois en langue vulgaire*. 4 vols. Paris: Collège de France.

———. 1980. "Le moine et la courtisane, formation et évolution d'un thème littéraire d'origine Sung." In Françoise Aubin, ed., *Etudes Song in memoriam Étienne Balazs*, ser. 2, 2: 139–58. Paris: Ecole des Hautes Etudes en Sciences Sociales.

———, trans. 1985. *Fleur en Fiole d'Or (Jin Ping Mei cihua)*. Bibliothèque de la Pléiade. 2 vols. Paris: Gallimard.

Levy, Howard S. 1971. *Sex, Love, and the Japanese*. Washington, D.C.: Warm-Soft Village Press.

———, trans. 1973. *Japanese Sex Jokes in Traditional Times: The Nun Who Rubbed and Thrusted, and Other Stories*. Washington, D.C.: Warm-Soft Village Press.

Lewis, I. M. 1989 [1971]. *Ecstatic Religion: A Study of Shamanism and Spirit Possession*. London and New York: Routledge.

Li Jung-hsi, trans. 1981. *Biographies of Buddhist Nuns: Pao-Chang's Pi-ch'iu-ni chuan*. Osaka: Tōhōkai.

Li Yu. 1990a. *The Carnal Prayer Mat (Rou Putuan)*. Trans. Patrick Hanan. New York: Ballantine Books.

———. 1990b. *Silent Operas (Wusheng xi)*. Ed. Patrick Hanan. Hong Kong: The Chinese University of Hong Kong.

———. 1991. *De la chair à l'extase*. Trans. Christine Corniot. Arles: Editions Philippe Picquier.

Li Yuzhen. 1989. *Tangdai de biqiuni*. Taibei: Taiwan xuesheng shuju.

Lillehoj, Elizabeth. 1996. "Tōfukumon'in: Empress, Patron, and Artist." *Woman's Art Journal* 17, 1: 28–34.

Lincoln, Bruce. 1981. *Emerging from the Chrysalis: Studies in Rituals of Women's Initiation*. Cambridge, MA: Harvard University Press.

———. 1991. "Embryological Speculation and Gender Politics in a Pahlavi Text." In Bruce Lincoln, *Death, War, and Sacrifice: Essays in Ideology and Practice*, 218–27. Chicago: University of Chicago Press.

Liu Dalin, ed. 1993. *Zhongguo gudai xing wenhua*. 2 vols. Yinchuanshi: Ningxia renmin chubanshe.

Lloyd, Ernest R., ed. 1983 [1950]. *Hippocratic Writings*. Penguin Classics. London: Penguin Books.

Lo, Vivienne. 1993. "The Legend of the Lady Linshui." *Journal of Chinese Religions* 21: 69–96.

Mabuchi Toichi. 1964. "Spiritual Predominance of the Sister." In Allan H. Smith, ed., *Ryukyuan Culture and Society*, 79–91. Honolulu: University of Hawai'i Press.

Mackinnon, Catharine. 1982. "Feminism, Marxism, Method, and the State: An Agenda for Theory." *Signs* 7, 3: 515–44.

Macy, Joanna Rodger. 1977. "The Perfection of Wisdom: Mother of All Buddhas." In Rita Gross, ed., *Beyond Androcentrism: New Essays on Women and Religion*, 315–33. Missoula, MT: Scholars Press.

Mair, Victor A. 1986. "An Asian Story of the Oedipus Type." *Asian Folklore Studies* 45: 19–32.

Makita Tairyō. 1976. *Gikyō kenkyū*. Kyoto: Jinbun kagaku kenkyūjo.

Malamoud, Charles. 1989. "Indian Speculations about the Sex of the Sacrifice." In Michel Feher, ed., *Fragments for a History of the Body, Part One*, 74–103. New York: Urzone.

Manabe Shunshō. 1994. "Hell of the Bloody Pond and the Rebirth of Women in the Paradise." *Indogaku bukkyōgaku kenkyū kiyō* 43, 1: 34–38.

Mann, Susan. 1987. "Widows in the Kinship, Class, and Community Structures of Qing Dynasty China." *Journal of Asian Studies* 46, 1: 37–65.

———. 1997a. *Precious Records: Women's Writing in China's Long Eighteenth Century*. Stanford: Stanford University Press.

———. 1997b. "The History of Chinese Women before the Age of Orientalism." *Journal of Women's History* 8, 4: 163–76.

Marglin, Frédérique Apffel. 1982. "Types of Sexual Union and Their Implicit Meanings." In John Stratton Hawley and Donna Marie Wulff, eds., *The Divine Consort: Rādhā and the Goddesses of India*, 298–315. Boston: Beacon Press.

Marra, Michele. 1993a. "The Buddhist Mythmaking of Defilement: Sacred Courtesans of Medieval Japan." *Journal of Asian Studies* 52, 1: 49–65.

———. 1993b. *Representations of Power: The Literary Politics of Medieval Japan.* Honolulu: University of Hawai'i Press.

Mass, Jeffrey P. 1983. "Patterns of Provincial Inheritance in Late Heian Japan." *Journal of Japanese Studies* 9, 1: 67–95.

———. 1989. *Lordship and Inheritance in Early Medieval Japan: A Study of the Kamakura Sōryō System.* Stanford: Stanford University Press.

Matignon, Jean-Jacques. 1900. *Superstition, crime et misère en Chine.* Paris: Masson et Cie.

Matisoff, Susan. 1973. *The Legend of Semimaru, Blind Musician of Japan.* New York: Columbia University Press.

———. 1992. "Holy Horrors: The Sermon-Ballads of Medieval and Early Modern Japan." In James H. Sanford, William R. LaFleur, and Masatoshi Nagatomi, eds., *Flowing Traces: Buddhism in the Literary and Visual Arts of Japan,* 234–62. Princeton: Princeton University Press.

———. Forthcoming. "Barred from Paradise? Mount Kōya and the Karukaya Legend."

Matsumae Takeshi. 1980. "The Heavenly Rock-Grotto Myth and the *Chinkon* Ceremony." *Asian Folklore Studies* 39, 2: 9–22.

Matsumoto Yasushi. 1986. *Chūsei kyūtei josei no nikki:* Towazugatari *no sekai.* Chūkō shinsho 809. Tokyo: Chūō kōronsha.

Matsuo Kenji. 1988. *Kamakura shin bukkyō no seiritsu.* Tokyo: Yoshikawa kōbunkan.

———. 1989. "Tonseisō to nyonin kyūzai." In Ōsumi Kazuo and Nishiguchi Junko, eds., *Josei to bukkyō: Sukui to oshie,* 93–119. Tokyo: Heibonsha.

———. 1994. "Kamakura shin-bukkyō to nyonin kyūzai: Eizon kyōdan ni yoru ama no denpō kanjō." *Bukkyō shigaku kenkyū* 37, 2: 30–46.

———. 1995a. *Kamakura shin-bukkyō no tanjō.* Tokyo: Kōdansha.

———. 1995b. *Kanjin to hakai no chūseishi.* Tokyo: Yoshikawa kōbunkan.

———. 1996. *Kyūzai no shisō: Eizon kyōdan to Kamakura shin-bukkyō.* Kadokawa sensho 272. Tokyo: Kadokawa shoten.

———. 1997. "What Is Kamakura New Buddhism? Official Monks and Reclusive Monks." *Japanese Journal of Religious Studies* 24, 1–2: 179–89.

Matsuoka Hideaki. 1998. "Wagakuni ni okeru *Ketsubongyō* shinkō ni tsuite no ichi kōsatsu." In Sōgō joseishi kenkyūkai, ed., *Josei to shūkyō.* 257–79. Nihon joseishi ronshū 5. Tokyo: Yoshikawa kōbunkan.

Matsuoka Shinpei. 1995. "Nō ni egakareta Izumi Shikibu." *Kokubungaku: kaishaku to kanshō* 60, 8: 112–18.

Mauclaire, Simone. 1984. *Du conte au roman: un Cendrillon japonais du Xe siècle: L'Ochikubo monogatari.* Paris: Maisonneuve et Larose.

Max-Müller, Friedrich, ed. and trans. 1894. *The Larger Sukhāvatīvyūha.* Sacred Books of the East, vol. 49. Oxford: Clarendon Press.

McCullough, Helen Craig, trans. 1959. *The Taiheiki: A Chronicle of Medieval Japan.* Rutland, VT, and Tokyo: Charles E. Tuttle Company.

——— trans. 1966. *Yoshitsune: A Fifteenth-Century Japanese Chronicle.* Stanford: Stanford University Press.

———. 1988. *The Tale of the Heike.* Stanford: Stanford University Press.

McCullough, William H. 1967. "Japanese Marriage Institutions in the Heian Period." *Harvard Journal of Asiatic Studies* 27: 103–67.

McCullough, William, and Helen Craig McCullough, trans. 1980. *A Tale of Flowering Fortunes: Annals of Japanese Aristocratic Life in the Heian Period.* Stanford: Stanford University Press.

McKeon, Midori Yamamoto. 1996. "The Transformation of the Urashima Legend: The Influence of Religion on Gender." *U.S.–Japan Women's Journal* English Supplement 10: 45–102.

McMullen, I. J. 1975. "Agnatic Adoption: A Confucian Controversy in Seventeenth Century and Eighteenth Century Japan." *Harvard Journal of Asiatic Studies* 35: 134–35.

Meyer, Johann Jakob. 1995 [1930]. *Sexual Life in Ancient India.* New York: Dorset Press.

Michihata Ryōshū. 1979. *Chūgoku bukkyō shisōshi no kenkyū.* Kyoto: Heirakuji shoten.

Mikoshiba Daisuke. 1989. "Kōmyōshi no bukkyō shinkō: Sono bukkyōteki kankyō to kokubunji, kokubunniji sokken e no kan'yo ni tsuite." In Ōsumi Kazuo and Nishiguchi Junko, eds., *Josei to bukkyō: Ama to amadera,* 73–103. Tokyo: Heibonsha.

Miller, Alan L. 1984. "Ame no miso-ori me (The Heavenly Weaving Maiden): The Cosmic Weaver in Early Shintō Myth and Ritual." *History of Religions* 24: 27–48.

———. 1992. "Myth and Gender in Japanese Shamanism: The Itako of Tōhoku." *History of Religions* 32, 4: 343–67.

Mills, D. E., trans. 1970. *A Collection of Tales from Uji: A Study and Translation of Uji Shūi Monogatari.* Cambridge: Cambridge University Press.

———. 1975. "*Soga Monogatari, Shintōshū* and the Taketori Legend: The Nature and Significance of Parallels between the *manabon Soga monogatari* and *Shintōshū,* with Particular Reference to a Parallel Variant of the Taketori Legend." *Monumenta Nipponica* 30, 1: 37–68.

———. 1980. "Murasaki Shikibu: Saint or Sinner?" *Bulletin of the Japan Society of London* 90: 4–14.

Minakata Kumagusu. 1971–73. *Minakata Kumagusu zenshū.* Edited by Iwamura Shinobu. Tokyo: Heibonsha.

———. 1973. "Notes and Queries, 1899–1933." In *Minakata Kumagusu zenshū* 10: 91–398. Edited by Iwamura Shinobu. Tokyo: Heibonsha.

———. 1991. "'Mara kō' ni tsuite." In Nakazawa Shin'ichi, ed., *Jō no sekusorojī,* 195–234. Tokyo: Kawade bunko.

Minamoto Junko. 1981. *Kamakura jōdokyō to josei.* Kyoto: Nagata bunshodō.

———. 1982. "Bukkyōkai ni ikiru gendai josei." *Joseigaku nenpō* 11: 33–40.

———. 1990. "Buddhist Attitudes: A Woman's Perspective." In Jeanne Becher, ed., *Women, Religion and Sexuality,* 154–171. Geneva: WCC Publications.

———. 1991. "Nihon no hinkon sei fudō." In Yamashita Akiko, ed., *Nihonteki sekushuariti: Feminizumu kara no sei fudō hihan.* Kyoto: Hōzōkan.

———. 1993. "Buddhism and the Historical Construction of Sexuality in Japan." Trans. Hank Glassman. *U.S.–Japan Women's Journal* English Supplement 4: 87–115.

Minamoto Junko. 1996. *Bukkyō to sei: Erosu no ifu to sabetsu.* Tokyo: San'ichi shobō.

Minegishi Sumio. 1992. *Kazoku to josei: Chūsei o kangaeru.* Tokyo: Yoshikawa kōbundō.

Minobe Shigekatsu. 1982. "The World View of *Genpei Jōsuiki.*" *Japanese Journal of Religious Studies* 9, 2–3: 213–34.

Miyata Noboru. 1975. "Ryōzan shinkō to engi." In Sakurai Tokutarō and Miyata Noboru, eds. *Jisha engi,* 501–19. Tokyo: Iwanami shoten.

———. 1979. *Kami no minzokushi.* Iwanami shinsho 97. Tokyo: Iwanami shoten.

———. 1983. *Onna no seiryoku to ie no kami.* Kyoto: Jinbun shoin.

———, ed. 1989. *Sei to mibun: Jakusha, haisha no shōsei to hiun.* Tokyo: Shunjūsha.

———. 1993a. *Edo no hayarigami.* Chikuma gakugei bunko 980. Tokyo: Chikuma shobō.

———. 1993b. *Hime no minzokugaku.* Tokyo: Seidosha.

———. 1994. *Shiro no fōkuroa: Genshoteki shikō.* Heibonsha raiburarī. Tokyo: Heibonsha.

Miyatake Gaikotsu. 1996. *Waisetsu fūzoku jiten.* Kawade bunko 680. Tokyo: Kawade shobō shinsha.

Miyazaki Shōhei. 1979. *Jōjin ajari boshū.* Kodansha gakujutsu bunko. Tokyo: Kōdansha.

Mizuhara Gyōhei. 1931. *Jakyō Tachikawaryū no kenkyū.* Kyoto: Shibundō.

Moerman, David Leo. 1999. "Localizing Paradise: Kumano Pilgrimage in Medieval Japan." Ph.D. Dissertation, Stanford University.

Moi, Toril, 1985. *Sexual/Textual Politics: Feminist Literary Theory.* London and New York: Routledge.

Moore, Jean Frances. 1982. "A Study of the Thirteenth-Century Buddhist Tale Collection *Senjūshō.*" Ph.D. Dissertation, Columbia University.

Moriguchi Yasuhiko and David Jenkins, trans. 1990. *The Dance of the Dust on the Rafters: Selections from "Ryōjin-hishō."* Seattle: Broken Moon Press.

Morrell, Robert E. 1980. "Mirror for Women: Mujū Ichien's *Tsuma Kagami.*" *Monumenta Nipponica* 35, 1, 45–75.

———. 1982. "Passage to India Denied: Zeami's *Kasuga Ryūjin.*" *Monumenta Nipponica* 37, 2: 179–99.

———, trans. 1985. *Sand and Pebbles (Shasekishū): The Tales of Mujū Ichien, A Voice for Pluralism in Kamakura Japan.* Albany: State University of New York.

———. 1987. *Early Kamakura Buddhism: A Minority Report.* Berkeley: Asian Humanities Press.

Morris, Ivan, trans. 1971. *As I Crossed a Bridge of Dreams: Recollections of a Woman in Eleventh-Century Japan.* London: Penguin Books.

Mujū Ichien. 1979. *Collection de sable et de pierres (Shasekishū).* Trans. Hartmund O. Rotermund. Paris: Gallimard.

Mulhern, Chieko. 1974. " 'Otogi-zōshi': Short Stories of the Muromachi Period." *Monumenta Nipponica* 29, 2: 181–98.

————. 1985. "Analysis of Cinderella Motifs, Italian and Japanese." *Asian Folklore Studies* 44, 1: 1–37.

Muraoka Kū. 1975. *Ai no shinbutsu: Mikkyō to minkan shinkō*. Tokyo: Daizō shuppan.

Murcott, Susan. 1991. *The First Buddhist Women: Translation and Commentary on the Therīgāthā*. Berkeley: Parallax Press.

Muroki Yatarō, ed. 1977. *Sekkyōshū*. Tokyo: Shinchōsha.

Murray, Julia K. 1990. "Didactic Art for Women: The Ladies' Classic of Filial Piety." In Marsha Weidner, ed., *Flowering in the Shadows: Women in the History of Chinese and Japanese Painting*, 27–53. Honolulu: University of Hawai'i Press.

Nagahara Keiji. 1979. "Medieval Origins of the Eta-Hinin." *Journal of Japanese Studies* 5, 2: 385–403.

Nagai Yoshi 1966–67. *Nihon bukkyō bungaku kenkyū*. 2 vols. Tokyo: Toyoshima shobō.

Nagata Mizu. 1982. "*Konjaku monogatari* Tenjikubu ni okeru josei no chii." In Joseishi sōgō kenkyūkai, ed., *Nihon josei shi* 1: *Genshi, kodai*, 291–334. Tokyo: Tōkyō daigaku shuppankai.

————. 1985. "Butten ni miru boseikan: Bukkyō wa boseikū o dō toita ka." In Wakita Haruko, ed., *Bosei o tou: Rekishiteki hensen* 1: 259–86. Kyoto: Jinbun shoin.

————. 1989. "Butten ni okeru joseikan no hensen: Sanju, goshō, hakkeihō no shūen." In Ōsumi Kazuo and Nishiguchi Junko, eds., *Josei to bukkyō* 2: *Sukui to oshie*, 11–44. Tokyo: Heibonsha.

Nakamura Ikuo. 1992. "Tamayorihime to otome hinohime: Kodai ujizoku no soshin saiki to Yamato ōken." In Yamaori Tetsuo, ed., *Nihon ni okeru josei*, 5–73. Tokyo: Meicho kankōkai.

Nakamura Kyoko Motochi, trans. 1973. *Miraculous Stories from the Japanese Buddhist Tradition: The Nihon Ryōiki of the Monk Kyōkai*. Cambridge, MA: Harvard University Press.

————. 1980. "No Women's Liberation: The Heritage of a Woman Prophet in Modern Japan." In Nancy Auer Falk and Rita M. Gross, eds., *Unspoken Worlds: Women's Religious Lives in Non-Western Cultures*, 174–90. San Francisco: Harper and Row.

————. 1981. "Revelatory Experience in the Female Life Cycle: A Biographical Study of Women Religionists in Modern Japan." *Japanese Journal of Religious Studies* 8, 3–4: 187–205.

————. 1983. "Women and Religion in Japan: Introductory Remarks." *Japanese Journal of Religious Studies* 10, 2–3: 115–21.

Nakano Yuko. 1998. "Women and Buddhism: Blood Impurity and Motherhood." In Okuda Akiko and Okano Haruko, *Women and Religion in Japan*, 65–85. Trans. Alison Watts. Studies in Oriental Religions 42. Wiesbaden: Harrassowitz.

Nakayama Tarō. 1974 [1930]. *Nihon miko shi*. Tokyo: Yagi Shoten.

Nakazawa Shin'ichi, ed. 1991. *Jō no sekusorojī*. Minakata Kumagusu Collection 3. Kawade shobō shinsha. Tokyo: Kawade bunko.

Namihira Emiko. 1987. "Pollution in the Folk Belief System." *Current Anthropology* 28, 4: 65–74.

Ñanamoli, Bhikkhu, trans. 1975. *The Path of Purification (Visuddhimagga) by Bhadantācariya Buddhagosa.* 3rd ed. Kandy, Sri Lanka: Buddhist Publication Society.

Naomi Gentetsu. 1989. "Kōgo kara jotei e: Sokuten Bukō to henjō nanshi no ronri." In Ōsumi Kazuo and Nishiguchi Junko, eds. 1989. *Josei to bukkyō* 3: 167–206. Tokyo: Heibonsha.

Naylor, B. Christina. 1988. "Buddhas or Bitches: Nichiren's Attitude to Women." *Religious Traditions* 11: 63–76.

Neumaier-Dargyay, Eva K. 1995. "Buddhist Thought from a Feminist Perspective." In Morny Joy and Eva K. Neumaier-Dargyay, eds., *Gender, Genre, and Religion: Feminist Reflections*, 145–70. Calgary: Wilfrid Laurier University Press.

Ng, Vivien W. 1987. "Ideology and Sexuality: Rape Laws in Qing China." *Journal of Asian Studies* 46, 1: 57–71.

Nickerson, Peter. 1993. "The Meaning of Matrilocality: Kinship, Property, and Politics in Mid-Heian Japan." *Monumenta Nipponica* 48, 4: 429–67.

Nihon bukkyō gakkai, ed. 1991. *Bukkyō to josei.* Kyoto: Heirakuji shoten.

Niimura Taku. 1994. "Zenkindai no seishoku kan." In Wakita Haruko and S. B. Hanley, eds., *Jendā no Nihonshi I: Shukyō to minzoku; shintai to seiai*, 253–92. Tokyo: Tōkyō daigaku shuppankai.

Nishiguchi Junko. 1987. *Onna no chikara: Kodai no josei to bukkyō.* Heibonsha sensho 110. Tokyo: Heibonsha.

———. 1989a. "Ōchō bukkyō ni okeru nyonin kyūzai no ronri: shussan no shuhō to goshō no kyōsetsu." In Miyata Noboru, ed., *Sei to mibun*, 129–67. Tokyo: Shunjūsha.

———. 1989b. "'Josei to bukkyō' o meguru oboegaki: 'Ama to amadera' o megutte." In Ōsumi Kazuo and Nishiguchi Junko, eds., *Josei to bukkyō* 1: *Ama to amadera*, 279–89. Tokyo: Heibonsha.

———. 1989c. "Sei to chisuji." In Ōsumi Kazuo and Nishiguchi Junko, eds., *Josei to bukkyō.* 4: *Miko to joshin*, 127–52. Tokyo: Heibonsha.

———. 1991. "Nihon shijō no josei to bukkyō: Nyonin kyūzai to nyonin jōbutsu o megutte." *Kokubungaku: kaishaku to kanshō* 56, 5: 19–25.

———. 1993. "Jōbutsusetsu to josei: Nyobonge made." *Nihonshi kenkyū* 366: 20–38.

———, ed. 1997. *Hotoke to onna: Chūsei o kangaeru.* Tokyo: Yoshikawa kōbunkan.

Nishino Ryōhei. 1990. "Ōchō toshi to 'josei no kegare.'" In Joseishi sōgō kenkyūkai, ed., *Nihon josei seikatsu shi* 1: *Genshi, kodai*, 181–216. Tokyo: Tōkyō daigaku shuppankai.

Nishino Yukiko. "Ritsuryōseika no boshi kankei: Hachi, kyūseiki no kodaisha ni miru." In Wakita Haruko, ed., *Bosei o tou: Rekishiteki hensen* (1), 79–111. Kyoto: Jinbun shoin.

Nishio Minoru, Kagamishima Genryū, Sakai Tokugen, and Mizuno Yaoko, eds. 1965. *Shōbōgenzō zuimonki.* NKBT 81. Tokyo: Iwanami shoten.

Nishizawa Shōji and Ishiguro Kichijirō, eds. 1977. *Otogizōshi I: Oyō no ama, Tamamo no mae*. Tokyo: Shintensha.

Niwa Akiko. 1993. "The Formation of the Myth of Motherhood in Japan." Trans. Tomiko Yoda. *U.S.–Japan Women's Journal* English Supplement 4: 70–82.

Nolot, Edith. 1991. *Règles de discipline des nonnes bouddhistes: Le Bhiksunī-vinaya de l'école des Mahāsamghika-lokottaravādin*. Collège de France, Publications de l'Institut de Civilisation Indienne. Paris: Diffusion de Boccard.

Norman, K. R., trans. 1971. *The Elders' Verses II: Therīgāthā*. Pāli Text Society Translation Series 40. London: Luzac and Co.

———. 1989. *Poems of Early Buddhist Nuns*. Oxford: Pāli Text Society.

Numa Gishō. 1989. "Kannon shinkō to bosei sūhai." In Miyata Noboru, ed., *Sei to mibun*, 169–206. Tokyo: Shunjūsha.

Obara Hitoshi. 1997. "Kizoku josei no shinkō seikatsu: kizoku shakai ni okeru 'ie' no saiki." In Nishiguchi Junko, ed., *Hotoke to onna: Chūsei o kangaeru*, 5–33. Tokyo: Yoshikawa kōbunkan.

Obayashi Tarō. 1985. "*Uji* Society and *Ie* Society from Prehistory to Medieval Times." *Journal of Japanese Studies* 11, 1: 3–27.

Obeyesekere, Gananath. 1981. *Medusa's Hair*. Chicago: University of Chicago Press.

O'Brian, Mary. 1981. *The Politics of Reproduction*. London: Routledge and Kegan Paul.

O'Connor, June. 1990. "Rereading, Reconceiving and Reconstructing Traditions: Feminist Research in Religion." *Women's Studies* 17: 101–23.

O'Flaherty, Wendy (Doniger). 1973. *Śiva: The Erotic Ascetic*. New York: Oxford University Press.

———. 1980. *Women, Androgynes, and Other Mythical Beasts*. Chicago: University of Chicago Press.

Ōgoshi Aiko. 1993. "Women and Sexism in Japanese Buddhism: A Reexamination of Shinran's View of Women." *Japan Christian Review* 59: 19–25.

Ōgoshi Aiko, Minamoto Junko, and Yamashita Akiko. 1990. *Seisabetsu suru bukkyō: Feminizumu kara no kokuhatsu*. Kyoto: Hōzōkan.

Oguri Junko. 1984. "Views on Women's Salvation in Japanese Buddhism." *Young East* 10, 1: 3–11.

———. 1987. *Nyonin ōjō: Nihonshi ni miru onna no sukui*. Kyoto: Jinbun shoin.

O'Hara, Albert R. 1963. "The Confucian Ideal of Womanhood." *Journal of the China Society* 3: 76–83.

Ōishi Masaaki. 1997. "Ama no Hokkeji to sō no Hokkeji." In Nishiguchi Junko, ed., *Hotoke to onna: Chūsei o kangaeru*, 181–217. Tokyo: Yoshikawa kōbunkan.

Okano Haruko. 1976. *Die Stellung der Frau im Shintō: Eine religionsphänomenologische und -soziologische Untersuchung*. Studies in Oriental Religions. Wiesbaden: Harassowitz.

———. 1993. "Feminisuto shiten kara no Nihon shūkyō hihan." In Okuda Akiko and Okano Haruko, eds., *Shūkyō no naka no joseishi*, 19–46. Tokyo: Seikyūsha.

Okonogi Keigo. 1982. *Nihon no Ajase konpurekkusu*. Tokyo: Chūō kōronsha.

Okuda Akiko, and Okano Haruko. 1998. *Women and Religion in Japan.* Trans. Alison Watts. Studies in Oriental Religions 42. Wiesbaden: Harrassowitz.

Okuda Isao. 1978. *Myōe: Henreki yo yume.* Tokyo: Tōkyō daigaku shuppankai.

———. 1997. "Myōe to josei: *Kegon engi,* Zenmyō, Zenmyōji." *Shōshin joshi daigaku ronsō* 89: 31–51.

———. 1999. "Zenmyōji no nisō: Myōgyō, fujumon o megutte." *Shōshin joshi daigaku ronsō* 92: 157–77.

Ong, Aihwa, and Michael G. Peletz. 1995. *Bewitching Women, Pious Men: Gender and Body Politics in Southeast Asia.* Berkeley: University of California Press.

Ono Shihei. 1966. "Saiten setsuwa no seiritsu: Naikaku Bunko zō 'Sentō koin Saiten zenji goroku' ni tsuite." Reprinted in *Chūgoku kinsei ni okeru tanpen hakuwa shōsetsu no kenkyū,* 185–210. Tokyo: Hyōronsha, 1978.

Ooms, Emily Groszens. 1993. *Women and Millenarian Protest in Meiji Japan: Deguchi Nao and Omotokyo.* Ithaca: Cornell University Press.

Orikuchi Shinobu. 1975. *Orikuchi Shinobu zenshū.* 19 vols. Chūkō bunko. Tokyo: Chūō kōronsha.

Ōsumi Kazuo. 1983a. "Josei to bukkyō: kōsō to sono haha." *Shiron* 36: 1–10.

———. 1983b. "Bukkyō to josei: *Genkō shakusho* no ninyoden ni tsuite." *Rekishi hyōron* 395: 2–11.

Ōsumi Kazuo and Nishiguchi Junko, eds. 1989. *Josei to bukkyō.* 4 vols. Tokyo: Heibonsha.

Ōtsu Yūichi and Tsukijima Hiroshi, eds. 1957. *Taketori monogatari, Ise monogatari, Yamato monogatari.* NKBT 9. Tokyo: Iwanami shoten.

Ouwehand, Cornelius. 1958. "Some Notes on the God Susa-no-o." *Monumenta Nipponica* 14, 3–4: 138–61.

———. 1964. *Namazu-e: Catfish Pictures and their Themes.* Leiden: E. J. Brill.

Overmyer, Daniel L. 1985. "Values in Chinese Sectarian Literature: Ming and Ch'ing Pao-chüan." In David Johnson, Andrew J. Nathan, and Evelyn S. Rawski, eds., *Popular Culture in Late Imperial China,* 219–54. Berkeley: University of California Press.

———. 1991. "Women in Chinese Religions: Submission, Struggle, Transcendence." In Koichi Shinohara and Gregory Schopen, eds., *From Benares to Beijing: Essays on Buddhism and Chinese Religion in Honour of Prof. Jan Yün-hua,* 91–120. Oakville and New York: Mosaic Press.

Paige, Karen Ericksen, and Jeffry M. Paige. 1981. *The Politics of Reproductive Ritual.* Berkeley: University of California Press.

Pandey, Rajyashree. 1995. "Women, Sexuality, and Enlightenment: *Kankyo no Tomo.*" *Monumenta Nipponica* 50, 3: 325–56.

Paper, Jordan. 1990. "The Persistence of Female Deities in Patriarchal China." *Journal of Feminist Studies in Religion* 6, 1: 25–40.

Paul, Diana M. 1979. *Women in Buddhism: Images of the Feminine in Mahāyāna Tradition.* Berkeley: Asian Humanities Press.

———. 1980a. *The Buddhist Feminine Ideal: Queen Śrīmālā and the Tathāgatagarbha.* Missoula, MI: Scholars Press.

———. 1980b. "Empress Wu and the Historians: A Tyrant and Saint of Classical China." In Nancy Auer Falk and Rita M. Gross, eds., *Unspoken Worlds:*

Women's Religious Lives in Non-Western Cultures, 191–206. San Francisco: Harper and Row.

Pelzel, John C. 1970. "Japanese Kinship: A Comparison." In Maurice Freedman, ed., *Family and Kinship in Chinese Society*, 227–48. Stanford: Stanford University Press.

Peri, Noël. 1917. "Harītī la Mère-de-démons." *Bulletin de l'Ecole Française d'Extrême Orient* 17: 1–102.

———. 1918. "Les femmes de Çākya-muni." *Bulletin de l'Ecole Française d'Extrême Orient* 18, 2: 1–37.

Perrot, Michelle, ed. 1992. *Writing Women's History*. Trans. Felicia Pheasant. Cambridge, MA: Basil Blackwell.

Pflugfelder, Gregory M. 1992. "Strange Fates: Sex, Gender, and Sexuality in *Torikaeba Monogatari*." *Monumenta Nipponica* 47, 3: 347–68.

Philippi, Donald L., trans. 1969. *Kojiki*. Tokyo: Princeton University Press and University of Tokyo Press.

———. 1990. *Norito: A Translation of the Ancient Japanese Ritual Prayers*. Princeton: Princeton University Press.

Pigeot, Jacqueline. 1972. "Histoire de Yokobue." *Bulletin de la Maison Franco-Japonaise*, n.s. 9, 2.

———. 1998. "Des jeux d'enfants aux concerts célestes: Les représentations du divertissement dans le Japon ancien." *Extrême-Orient, Extrême-Occident* 20: 63–86.

Pitzer-Reyl, Renate. 1984. *Die Frau in frühen Buddhismus*. Berlin: Dietrich Reimer Verlag.

Plutschow, Herbert E. 1978. "Is Poetry a Sin? *Honjisuijaku* and Buddhism versus Poetry." *Oriens Extremus* 25: 206–18.

———. 1990. *Chaos and Cosmos: Ritual in Early and Medieval Japanese Literature*. Leiden: E. J. Brill.

Plutschow, Herbert E., and Fukuda Hideichi, trans. 1981. *Four Travel Diaries of the Middle Ages*. Ithaca: Cornell University Press.

Powers, John, and Deane Curtin. 1994. "Mothering in Buddhist and Feminist Ethics." *Philosophy East and West* 44, 1: 1–18.

Quignard, Pascal. 1994. *Le sexe et l'effroi*. Paris: Gallimard.

———. 1997. *Vie secrète*. Paris: Gallimard.

Ramanujan, A. K. 1982. "On Women Saints." In J. Hawley and D. M. Wulff, eds., *The Divine Consort: Rādhā and the Goddesses of India*. Berkeley: Berkeley Religious Studies Series.

Rambelli, Fabio. Forthcoming. "Power Spots: Poetics and Politics of the Maṇḍala."

Raphals, Lisa. 1998. *Sharing the Light: Representations of Women and Virtue in Early China*. Albany: State University of New York Press.

Rawlinson, Andrew. 1986. "Nāgas and the Magical Cosmology of Buddhism." *History of Religions* 16, 2: 135–53.

Ray, Reginald A. 1980. "Accomplished Women in Tantric Buddhism of Medieval India and Tibet." In Nancy Auer Falk and Rita M. Gross, eds., *Unspoken Worlds: Women's Religious Lives in Non-Western Cultures*, 227–42. San Francisco: Harper and Row.

Raymond, Janice G. 1998. *Women as Wombs: Reproductive Technology and the Battle over Women's Freedom.* Spinifex Press.

Reischauer, Edwin. 1940. "The Thunder-Weapon in Ancient Japan." *Harvard Journal of Asiatic Studies* 5: 137–41.

Renondeau, Georges. 1960. *Le bouddhisme dans les Nô.* Publications de la Maison Franco-Japonaise. Tokyo: Hosokawa Printing Co.

Revel, Jacques. "Masculine and Feminine: The Historiographical Use of Sexual Roles." In Michelle Perrot, ed., *Writing Women's History,* 90–105. Trans. Felicia Pheasant. Cambridge, MA: Basil Blackwell.

Rhodes, Robert F. 1996. "A New Approach to Medieval Pure Land Buddhism." *Japanese Religions* 21, 1: 163–81.

Rhys Davids, C.A.F., and K. R. Norman, trans. 1989. *Poems of Early Buddhist Nuns: Therīgāthā.* London: Pali Text Society.

Richman, Paula. 1986. "The Portrayal of a Female Renouncer in a Tamil Buddhist Text." In Caroline Walker Bynum, Stevan Harrell, and Paula Richman, eds., *Gender and Religion: On the Complexity of Symbols,* 143–65. Boston: Beacon Press.

———. 1992. "Gender and Persuasion: The Portrayal of Beauty, Anguish, and Nurturance in an Account of a Tamil Nun." In José Ignacio Cabezón, ed., *Buddhism, Sexuality, and Gender,* 111–36. Albany: State University of New York Press.

Roberts, Dorothy. 1997. *Killing the Black Body: Race, Reproduction, and the Meaning of Liberty.* New York: Pantheon Books.

Robertson, Jennifer. "The Shingaku Woman: Straight from the Heart." In Gail Lee Bernstein, ed., *Recreating Japanese Women, 1600–1945,* 88–107. Berkeley: University of California Press.

Robertson, Maureen. 1992. "Voicing the Feminine: Constructions of the Gendered Subject in Lyric Poetry by Women of Medieval and Late Imperial China." *Late Imperial China* 13, 1: 63–110.

Ropp, Paul. 1976. "The Seeds of Change: Reflections on the Condition of Women in the Early and Mid Ch'ing." *Signs* 2: 5–23.

Rosaldo, Michelle Zimbalist, and Louise Lamphere, eds. 1974. *Woman, Culture, and Society.* Stanford: Stanford University Press.

Rotermund, Hartmund O. 1991. *Hōsōgami ou la petite vérole aisément.* Paris: Maisonneuve et Larose.

Roth, Gustav, ed. 1970. *Bhikṣuṇī Vinaya [of the Mahāsaṅghikas]: Manual of Discipline for Buddhist Nuns.* Patna: K. P. Jayaswal Research Institute.

Rousselle, Aline. 1988. *Porneia: On Desire and the Body in Antiquity.* Cambridge, MA: Basil Blackwell.

Ruch, Barbara. 1965. "*Otogi bunko* and Short Stories of the Muromachi Period." Ph.D. Dissertation, Columbia University.

———. 1977. "Medieval Jongleurs and the Making of a National Literature." In John W. Hall and Toyoda Takeshi, eds., *Japan in the Muromachi Age,* 279–309. Berkeley: University of California Press.

———. 1990. "The Other Side of Culture in Medieval Japan." In Kozo Yamamura, ed., *The Cambridge History of Japan,* vol. 3: *Medieval Japan,* 500–543. Cambridge: Cambridge University Press.

———. 1991. *Mō hitotsu no chūseizō: Bikuni, otogi Zōshi, raise*. Tokyo: Shibunkaku shuppan.

———. 1997. "Transformation of a Heroine: Yokobue in Literature and History." In Amy Vladeck Heinrich, ed., *Currents in Japanese Culture: Translations and Transformations*, 99–116. New York: Columbia University Press.

———, ed. Forthcoming. *Engendering Faith: Women and Buddhism in Premodern Japan*. Ann Arbor: Center for Japanese Studies, University of Michigan.

Ruppert, Brian D. 1999. *Jewel in the Ashes: Buddha Relics and Power in Early Medieval Japan*. Cambridge, MA: Council on East Asian Studies Publications, Harvard University.

Ryūkoku daigaku, ed. 1997. *Bukkyō daijii*. Tokyo: Fusanbō.

Sadakata Akira. 1989. "Bukkyō ni okeru kaikyūkan to joseikan." In Miyata Noboru, ed., *Sei to mibun*, 39–68. Tokyo: Shunjūsha.

Saeki Junko. 1987. *Yūjo no bunkashi*. Chūō shinsho 853. Tokyo: Chūō kōronsha.

Saigō Nobutsuna. 1993. *Kodaijin to yume*. Tokyo: Heibonsha.

Saitō Eiko. 1989. *Die Frau in alten Japan*. Düsseldorf: Brücken Verlag.

Saitō Kōjun. 1973. "*Shakuon shirin*." In *Kōsōden no kenkyū: Kushida Hakushi shoju kinen*, 839–40. Tokyo: Sankibō busshorin.

Sakurai Yoshirō. 1986. *Jisha engi no sekai*. Tokyo: Shunjūsha.

Sanday, Peggy Reeves. 1981. *Female Power and Male Dominance: On the Origins of Sexual Inequality*. Cambridge: Cambridge University Press.

Sanday Peggy Reeves, and Ruth Gallagher Goodenough, eds. 1990. *Beyond the Second Sex: New Directions in the Anthropology of Gender*. Philadelphia: University of Pennsylvania Press.

Sanford, James H. 1981. *Zen-Man Ikkyū*. Chico, CA: Scholars Press.

———. 1988. "The Nine Faces of Death: "Su Tung-po's *Kuzō-shi*." *The Eastern Buddhist* n.s. 21, 2: 54–77.

———. 1991. "The Abominable Tachikawa Skull Ritual." *Monumenta Nipponica* 46, 1: 1–20.

———. 1997. "Winds, Waters, Stupas, Mandalas: Fetal Buddhahood in Shingon." *Japanese Journal of Religious Studies* 24, 1–2: 1–38.

Sangren, Steven P. 1983. "Female Gender in Chinese Religious Symbols: Kuan Yin, Ma Tsu, and the 'Eternal Mother.' " *Signs* 9, 1: 4–25.

———. 1996. "Myths, Gods and Family Relations." In Meir Shahar and Robert P. Weller, eds., *Unruly Gods: Divinity and Society in China*, 150–83. Honolulu: University of Hawai'i Press.

Sasaki Kokan. 1984. "Spirit Possession as an Indigenous Religion in Japan and Okinawa." In George A. De Vos and Takao Sofue, eds., *Religion and the Family in East Asia*, 75–84. Berkeley: University of California Press.

Sasaki, Ruth Fuller, et al. trans. 1971. *A Man of Zen: The Recorded Sayings of Layman P'ang*. New York: Weatherhill.

Sasama Yoshihiko. 1989. *Kangiten (Shōten) shinkō to zokushin*. Tokyo: Yūzankaku.

———. 1991. *Benzaiten shinkō to zokushin*. Tokyo: Yūzankaku.

Satō Kazuhiko. 1995. "'Des gens étranges à l'allure insolite': Contestation et valeurs nouvelles dans le Japon médiéval." *Annales: Histoire, Sciences Sociales* 50, 2: 307–40.

Satō Noriaki. 1981. "The Initiation of the Religious Specialists 'Kamisan': A Few Observations." *Japanese Journal of Religious Studies* 8, 3–4: 149–86.

Sawada Mizuho. 1968. *Jigoku hen: Chūgoku no meikaisetsu.* Ajia no shūkyō bunka 3. Kyoto: Hōzōkan.

———. 1975a. *Bukkyō to Chūgoku bungaku.* Tokyo: Kokusho kankōkai.

———. 1975b. *Hōkan no kenkyū.* Tokyo: Kokusho kankōkai.

Sawicki, Jana. 1991. *Disciplining Foucault: Feminism, Power, and the Body.* New York and London: Routledge.

Sax, W. S. 1991. *Mountain Goddess: Gender and Politics in an Himalayan Pilgrimage.* New York: Oxford University Press.

Schafer, Edward H. 1980. *The Divine Woman: Dragon Ladies and Rain Maidens.* San Francisco: North Point Press.

Schalow, Paul G., and Janet A. Walker, eds. 1996. *The Woman's Hand: Gender and Theory in Japanese Women's Writing.* Stanford: Stanford University Press.

Schmidt, Uta. 1993. "Problems of Theory and Method in Feminist History." In Joanna deGroot and Mary Manard, eds., *Women's Studies in the 1990's: Doing Things Differently?* New York: St. Martin's Press.

Schopen, Gregory. 1988–1989. "On Monks, Nuns and 'Vulgar' Practices: The Introduction of the Image Cult into Indian Buddhism." *Artibus Asiae* 49, 1–2: 153–68.

———. 1995. "Deaths, Funerals, and the Division of Property in a Monastic Code." In Donld Lopez, Jr., ed. *Buddhism in Practice,* 473–502. Princeton: Princeton University Press.

———. 1996. "The Suppression of Nuns and the Ritual Murder of Their Special Dead in Two Buddhist Monastic Texts." *Journal of Indian Philosophy* 24: 563–92.

Schuster (Barnes), Nancy. 1981. "Changing the Feminine Body: Wise Women and the Bodhisattva Career in Some *Mahāratnakūṭasūtras.*" *Journal of the International Association of Buddhist Studies* 4, 1: 24–69.

———. 1984. "Yoga-Master Dharmamitra and Clerical Misogyny in Fifth Century China." *The Tibet Journal* 9, 4: 33–46.

———. 1985. "Striking a Balance: Women and Images of Women in Early Chinese Buddhism." In Yvonne Yazbeck Haddad and Ellison Banks Findly, eds., *Women, Religion and Social Change,* 87–111. Albany: State University of New York Press.

———. 1987. "Women in Buddhism." In Arvind Sharma, ed., *Women in World Religions.* Albany: State University of New York Press.

———. 1996. "Buddhist Women and the Nuns' Order in Asia." In Christopher S. Queen and Sallie B. King, eds., *Engaged Buddhism: Buddhist Liberation Movements in Asia.* Albany: State University of New York Press.

Scott, Joan Wallach. 1988. "Gender: A Useful Category of Historical Analysis." In Joan Wallach Scott, *Gender and the Politics of History,* 29–50 and 206–11. New York: Columbia University Press.

Seaman, Gary. 1981. "The Sexual Politics of Karmic Retribution." In Emily Martin Ahern and Hill Gates, eds., *The Anthropology of Taiwanese Society,* 381–96. Stanford: Stanford University Press.

———. 1992. "Winds, Waters, Seeds and Souls: Folk Concepts of Physiology and Etiology in Chinese Geomancy." In Charles Leslie and Allan Young, eds., *Paths to Asian Medical Knowledge*, 74–97. Berkeley: University of California Press.

Segawa Kiyoko. 1963. "Menstrual Taboos Imposed upon Women." In Richard M. Dorson, ed., *Studies in Japanese Folklore*, 239–50. Bloomington: University of Indiana Press.

Seidel, Anna K. 1992–93. "Mountains and Hells: Religious Geography in Japanese *mandara* Paintings." *Studies in Central and East Asian Religions* 5–6: 122–33.

Seidensticker, Edward G., trans. 1988 [1964]. *The Gossamer Years* (Kagerō Nikki): *The Diary of a Noblewoman of Heian Japan*. Tokyo: Tuttle.

Seigle, Cecilia Segawa. 1993. *Yoshiwara: The Glittering World of the Japanese Courtesan*. Honolulu: University of Hawai'i Press.

Seki Keigo. 1963. "The Spool of Thread: A Subtype of the Japanese Serpent-Bridegroom Tale." In Richard M. Dorson, ed., *Studies in Japanese Folklore*, 267–88.

Sekiguchi Hiroko. 1982. "Kodai ni okeru Nihon to Chūgoku no shoyū, kazoku keitai no sōi ni tsuite: joshi shoyūken o chūshin to shite." In Joseishi sōgō kenkyūkai, ed., *Nihon josei shi* 1: *Genshi. kodai*, 249–90. Tokyo: Tōkyō daigaku shuppankai.

Selby, Martha Ann. 1994. "Sanskrit Gynecologies: The Semiotics of Femininity in the *Caraka-* and *Suśrutā-saṃhitās*." Unpublished ms.

Sered, Susan. 1992. *Women as Religious Experts: The Religious Lives of Elderly Jewish Women in Jerusalem*. New York: Oxford University Press.

———. 1994. *Priestess, Mother, Sacred Sister: Religions Dominated by Women*. New York: Oxford University Press.

———. 1999. *Women of the Sacred Groves: Divine Priestesses of Okinawa*. New York: Oxford University Press.

Sharma, Arvind. 1977. "How and Why Did the Women in Ancient India Become Buddhist Nuns?" *Sociological Analysis* 38, 3: 239–51.

———, ed. 1987. *Women in World Religions*. New York: State University of New York Press.

———, ed. 1993. *Religion and Women*. New York: State University of New York Press.

Shaw, Miranda. 1994. *Passionate Enlightenment: Women in Tantric Buddhism*. Princeton: Princeton University Press.

———. 1997. "Worship of Women in Tantric Buddhism: Male Is to Female as Devotee Is to Goddess." In *Women and Goddess Traditions*, 111–36. Minneapolis: Fortress Press.

Shimizu Akitoshi. 1987. "*Ie* and *Dōzoku*." *Current Anthropology* 28, 4: 85–90.

Shimizu Hōgon. 1978 [1915]. *Josei to Zen*. Sōsho "*Zen*" 20. Tokyo: Kokusho kankōkai.

Shimizu Yoshiko. 1982. "Ōchō joryū bungaku no keisei to haikei: *Sarashina nikki no baai*." In Joseishi sōgō kenkyūkai, ed., *Nihon josei shi* 1: *Genshi, kodai*, 177–206. Tokyo: Tōkyō daigaku shuppankai.

Shimomi Takao. 1989. *Ryū Kō "Retsujo den" no kenkyū*. Tokyo: Tōkyō daigaku shuppankai.

Shinno Toshikazu. 1988. "Kōbō Daishi no haha." In Hinonishi Shinjō, ed., *Kōbō Daishi shinkō*. Tokyo: Yūzankaku.

Shirai Yūko. 1989. "Heian jidai shotō no bukkyō to josei." In Ōsumi Kazuo and Nishiguchi Junko, eds., *Josei to bukkyō* 1: *Ama to amadera*, 105–39. Tokyo: Heibonsha.

Shirane Haruo. 1987. *The Bridge of Dreams: A Poetics of* The Tale of Genji. Stanford: Stanford University Press.

Skord, Virginia, trans. 1991. *Tales of Tears and Laughter: Short Fiction of Medieval Japan*. Honolulu: University of Hawai'i Press.

Smith, Robert J. "Gender Inequality in Contemporary Japan." *Journal of Japanese Studies* 13, 1: 1–25.

Smith, Robert J., and Ella Wisewell. 1982. *The Women of Suye Mura*. Chicago: University of Chicago Press.

Smyers, Karen A. 1983. "Women and Shinto: The Relation between Purity and Pollution." *Japanese Religions* 12, 4: 7–19.

———. 1999. *The Fox and the Jewel: Shared and Private Meanings in Contemporary Japanese Inari Worship*. Honolulu: University of Hawai'i Press.

Sōtōshū nisōshi hensankai, ed. 1955. *Sōtōshū nisōshi*. Tokyo: San'yōsha.

Souyri, Pierre F. 1998. *Le Monde à l'envers: La dynamique de la société médiévale*. Histoire du Japon. Paris: Maisonneuve et Larose.

Soymié, Michel. 1965. "*Ketsubongyō* no shiryō-teki kenkyū." In Yoshioka Yoshitoyo, *Dōkyō kenkyū*, 1: 109–65. Tokyo: Shōrinsha.

Spiro, Melford E. 1982. *Buddhism and Society: A Great Tradition and Its Burmese Vicissitudes*. 2d. ed. Berkeley: University of California Press.

———. 1984. "Some Reflections of Family and Religion in East Asia." In George A. De Vos and Takao Sofue, eds., *Religion and the Family in East Asia*, 35–54. Berkeley: University of California Press.

Sponberg, Alan. 1992. "Attitudes toward Women and the Feminine in Early Buddhism." In José Ignacio Cabezón, ed., *Buddhism, Sexuality, and Gender*, 3–36. New York: State University of New York Press.

Stein, Rolf A. 1972. *Vie et chants de 'Brug-pa Kun-legs le Yogin*. Paris: Maisonneuve et Larose.

———. 1986. "Avalokiteśvara/Kouan-yin, un exemple de transformation d'un dieu en déesse." *Cahiers d'Extrême-Asie* 2: 17–80.

———. 1988. *Grottes-matrices et lieux saints de la déesse en Asie Orientale*. Paris: Ecole Française d'Extrême-Orient.

Stone, Jacqueline I. 1999. *Original Enlightenment and the Transformation of Medieval Japanese Buddhism*. Kuroda Institute, Studies in East Asian Buddhism 12. Honolulu: University of Hawai'i Press.

Strickmann, Michel, ed. 1981–85. *Tantric and Taoist Studies in Honour of R. A. Stein*. 3 vols. Brussels: Institut Belge des Hautes Etudes Chinoises.

———. 1996. *Mantras et mandarins: Le bouddhisme tantrique en Chine*. Paris: Gallimard.

———. 2002. *Chinese Magical Medicine*. Ed. Bernard Faure. Stanford: Stanford University Press.

Strong, John S. 1992. *The Legend and Cult of Upagupta: Sanskrit Buddhism in North India and Southeast Asia*. Princeton: Princeton University Press.

———. 1997. "A Family Quest: The Buddha, Yaśodharā, and Rāhula in the *Mū-lasarvāstivāda Vinaya.*" In Juliane Schober, ed., *Sacred Biography in the Buddhist Traditions of South and Southeast Asia,* 113–28. Honolulu: University of Hawai'i Press.

———. Forthcoming. "Aśoka's Wives and the Ambiguities of Buddhist Kingship."

Strong, Sarah M. 1994. "The Making of a Femme Fatale: Ono no Komachi in the Early Medieval Commentaries." *Monumenta Nipponica* 49, 4: 391–412.

Sugano Mieko. 1985. "Ōchō kizoku no boseikan: Bungaku no kataru shosō." In Wakita Haruko, ed., *Bosei o tou: Rekishiteki hensen,* 1: 112–42. Kyoto: Jinbun shoin.

Sugimoto Shunryū. 1938. *Zōtei Tōjō shitsunai kirigami narabini sanwa no kenkyū.* Reedited 1982. Tokyo: Sōtōshū shūmucho.

Sugiyama Jirō. 1965. "Denkōji hada Jizō bosatsu-zō ni tsuite." *Museum* 167: 23–34.

Tabata Yasuko. 1985. "Kamakura ki ni okeru boshi kankei to boseikan: Kafuchō-sei kazoku no seiritsu o megutte." In Wakita Haruko, ed., *Bosei o tou: Rekishiteki hensen* (1), 143–71. Kyoto: Jinbun shoin.

———. 1994. *Nihon chūsei josei shiron.* Tokyo: Hanawa shobō.

———. 1999 [1994]. "Female Attendants and Wives of the Medieval Warrior Class." Trans. Christina Laffin. In Wakita Haruko, Anne Bouchy, and Ueno Chizuko, eds., *Gender and Japanese History* 2: 313–47. Osaka: Osaka University Press.

Tagami Taishū. 1990. "Henjō nanshi shisō no kenkyū." *Komazawa daigaku zen kenkyūjo nenpō* 1: 41–61.

Taira Masayuki. 1989. "Kyū bukkyō to josei." In Tsuda Hideo sensei koki kinenkai, ed., *Hōken shakai to kindai,* 3–29. Kyoto: Dōmeisha.

———. 1990. "Chūsei bukkyō to josei." In Joseishi sōgō kenkyūkai, ed, *Nihon josei seikatsu shi,* 2: *Chūsei,* 75–108. Tokyo: Tōkyō daigaku shuppankai.

———. 1992. *Nihon chūsei no shakai to bukkyō.* Tokyo: Hanawa shobō.

Takagi Tadashi. 1992. *Mikudarihan to Enkiridera: Edo no rikon o yominaosu.* Kōdansha gendai shinsho 1092. Tokyo: Kōdansha.

Takagi Yutaka. 1988. *Bukkyōshi no naka no nyonin.* Heibonsha sensho 126. Tokyo: Heibonsha.

Takakusu Junjirō. 1928–29. "Le voyage de Kanshin en Orient." Bulletin de l'Ecole Française d'Extrême-Orient 28: 1–41 and 441–72; 29: 47–62.

———. 1966 [1986]. *A Record of the Buddhist Religion as Practiced in India and the Malay Archipelago (A.D. 671–695) by I-tsing.* Delhi: Munshiram Manoharlal.

Takamure Itsue. 1963. *Nihon kon'in-shi* Tokyo: Shibundō.

———. 1966. *Nihon josei shakai-shi.* In *Takamure Itsue zenshū.* Tokyo: Rironsha.

———. 1975 [1966]. *Shoseikon no kenkyū.* 2 vols. Tokyo: Miraisha.

Takatori Ayumi. 1993. *Shintō no seiritsu.* Tokyo: Heibonsha.

Takemi Tomoko. 1983. "'Menstruation Sūtra' Belief in Japan." Trans. W. Michael Kelsey. *Japanese Journal of Religious Studies* 10, 2–3: 229–46.

Takigawa Masajirō. 1965. *Yūjo no rekishi*. Nihon rekishi shinsho. Tokyo: Shibundō.

Talim, Meena. 1972. *Women in Early Buddhist Literature*. Bombay: University of Bombay.

Talim, T. V. 1965. "Buddhist Nuns and Disciplinary Rules." *Journal of the University of Bombay* 34, 2: 98–137.

Tamamuro Taijō. 1963. *Sōshiki bukkyō*. Tokyo: Daihōrinkaku.

Tamanoi, Mariko Asano. 1991. "Songs as Weapons: The Culture and History of Komori (Nursemaids) in Modern Japan." *Journal of Asian Studies* 50, 4: 793–814.

Tanabe, George J., Jr., 1992. *Myōe the Dreamkeeper: Fantasy and Knowledge in Early Kamakura Buddhism*. Harvard East Asian Monographs. Cambridge, MA: Harvard University Press.

Tanabe, Willa Jane. 1984. "The Lotus Lectures: The *Hokke hakkō* in Heian Japan." *Monumenta Nipponica* 39, 4: 393–407.

Tanaka Takako. 1989. "'Gyokunyo' no seiritsu to genkai: 'Jishin oshō musōki' kara 'Shinran yume no ki' made." In Ōsumi Kazuo and Nishiguchi Junko, eds. *Josei to bukkyō* 4: *Miko to joshin*, 91–126. Tokyo: Heibonsha.

———. 1992. *"Akunyo" ron*. Tokyo: Kinokuniya shoten.

———. 1993. *Gehō to aihō no chūsei*. Tokyo: Sunakoya shobō.

———. 1996: *Sei-naru onna: Saigū, joshin, Chūjōhime*. Kyoto: Jinbun shoin.

———. 1999 [1995]. "Medieval Literature and Women: Focusing on *Mumyō-zōshi*." Trans. Christina Laffin. In Wakita Haruko, Anne Bouchy, and Ueno Chizuko, eds. 1999. *Gender and Japanese History* 2: 99–129. Osaka: Osaka University Press.

Tatelman, Joel. 1998. "The Trials of Yaśodharā and the Birth of Rāhula: A Synopsis of *Bhadrakalpāvadāna* II–IX." *Buddhist Studies Review* 15, 1: 3–42.

Tatz, Mark. 1986. *Asaṅga's Chapter on Ethics with the Commentary of Tsong-kha-pa, The Basic Path to Awakening: The Complete Bodhisattva*. New York: Edwin Mellen Press.

Tay, C. N. 1976. "Kuan-yin, the Cult of Half Asia." *History of Religions* 16, 2: 147–77.

Teele, Roy E., Nicholas J. Teele, and H. Rebecca Teele, trans. 1993. *Ono no Komachi: Poems, Stories, Nō Plays*. New York and London: Garland Publishing.

Teeuwen, Mark. 1996. *Watarai Shintō: An Intellectual History of the Outer Shrine in Ise*. CNWS Publications 52. Leiden: Research School CNWS.

Ten Grotenhuis, Elisabeth. 1983. "Rebirth of an Icon: The Taima Mandala in Medieval Japan." *Archives of Asian Art* 36: 59–87.

———. 1985. *The Revival of the Taima Mandala in Medieval Japan*. New York: Garland Publishing.

———. 1992. "Chūjōhime: The Weaving of Her Legend." In James H. Sanford, William R. LaFleur, and Masatoshi Nagatomi, eds., *Flowing Traces: Buddhism in the Literary and Visual Arts of Japan*, 180–200. Princeton: Princeton University Press.

Teng, Jinhua Emma. 1996. "The Construction of the 'Traditional Chinese Woman' in the Western Academy: A Critical Review." *Signs* 22, 1: 115–51.

Terada Tōru and Mizuno Yaeko, eds. 1974. *Dōgen*. 2 vols. Tokyo: Iwanami shoten.

Terasaki Etsuko. 1984. "Images and Symbols in *Sotoba no Komachi*: A Critical Analysis of a Nō Play." *Harvard Journal of Asiatic Studies* 44, 1: 155–84.

———. 1992. "Is the Courtesan of 'Eguchi' a Buddhist Metaphorical Woman? A Feminist Reading of a Nō Play in the Japanese Medieval Theater." *Women's Studies* 21, 4: 4–31.

Teruoka Yasutaka. 1989a. *Nihonjin no ai to sei*. Iwanami shinsho 92. Tokyo: Iwanami shoten.

———. 1989b. "The Pleasure Quarters and Tokugawa Culture." In C. Andrew Gerstle, ed., *Eighteenth Century Japan*. Sydney: Allen and Unwin.

Thurman, Robert A. F., trans. 1976. *The Holy Teaching of Vimalakīrti: A Mahāyāna Scripture*. University Park and London: Pennsylvania State University Press.

T'ien Ju-k'ang. 1988. *Male Anxiety and Female Chastity: A Comparative Study of Chinese Ethical Values in Ming-Ch'ing Times*. Leiden: E. J. Brill.

Tochio Takeshi. 1991. *Tamatsukuri Komachi shi sōsui-sho no kenkyū*. 2 vols. Tokyo: Rinsen shoten.

Tokuda Kazuo. 1994. "Chūsei nyonin shukke-banashi 'Chiyono monogatari' ni tsuite." *Kokugo kokubun ronshū* 23.

———1997. "Kumano ni mōderu Izumi Shikibu." *Nihon no bigaku* 25: 74–85.

———. Forthcoming. "Chiyono monogatari to Mugai Nyodai no denki densetsu."

Tominaga Nakamoto. 1990. *Emerging from Meditation*. Trans. Michael Pye. Honolulu: University of Hawai'i Press.

Tonomura Hitomi. 1990. "Women and Inheritance in Japan's Early Warrior Society." *Comparative Studies in Society and History* 32, 2: 592–623.

———. 1994a. "Black Hair and Red Trousers: Gendering the Flesh in Medieval Japan." *The American Historical Review* 99, 1: 129–54.

———. 1994b. "Nikutai to yokubō no keiro." In Wakita Haruko and Susan B. Henley, eds., *Jendā no Nihonshi* 1. Tokyo: Tōkyō daigaku shuppankai, 1994.

———. 1997. "Re-envisioning Women in the Post-Kamakura Age." In Jeffrey P. Mass, ed., *The Origins of Japan's Medieval World: Courtiers, Clerics, Warriors, and Peasants in the Fourteenth Century*, 138–69. Stanford: Stanford University Press.

Topley, Marjorie. 1974. "Cosmic Antagonisms: A Mother-Child Syndrome." In Arthur P. Wolf, ed., *Religion and Ritual in Chinese Society*, 233–49. Stanford: Stanford University Press.

———. 1975. "Marriage Resistance in Rural Kwangtung." In Margery Wolf and Roxane Witke, eds., *Women in Chinese Society*, 67–88. Stanford: Stanford University Press.

Tsai, Kathryn Ann. 1981. "The Chinese Buddhist Monastic Order for Women: The First Two Centuries." In Richard W. Guisso and Stanley Johannesen, eds., *Women in China: Current Reflections in Historical Scholarship*, 1–20. Youngstown, NY: Philo Press.

Tsai, Kathryn Ann, trans. 1994. *Lives of the Nuns: Biographies of Chinese Buddhist Nuns from the Fourth to Sixth Centuries: A Translation of the Pi-ch'iu-ni chuan, compiled by Shih Pao-ch'ang*. Honolulu: University of Hawai'i Press.

Tsomo, Karma Lekshe. 1987. "Tibetan Nuns and Nunneries." In Janice D. Willis, ed., *Feminine Ground: Essays on Women and Tibet*, 118–34. Ithaca: Snow Lion Publications.

———. 1996. *Sisters in Solitude: Two Traditions of Buddhist Monastic Ethics for Women. A Comparative Analysis of the Chinese Dharmagupta and the Tibetan Mūlasarvāstivāda Bhikṣuṇī Prātimokṣa Sūtras*. Albany: State University of New York Press.

———, ed. 1999. *Buddhist Women across Cultures: Realizations*. Albany: State University of New York Press.

Tsuchiya Megumi. "Ganshū to ama: Daigoji no josei." In Ōsumi Kazuo and Nishiguchi Junko, eds., *Josei to bukkyō* 1: *Ama to amadera*, 175–219. Tokyo: Heibonsha.

Tsunoda Bun'ei. 1985. *Taikenmon'in Tamako no shōgai: Shōtei hishō*. Asahi sensho 281. Tokyo: Asahi shinbunsha.

Tsurumi, Patricia E. 1983. "The Male Present versus the Female Past: Historians and Japan's Ancient Female Emperors." *Bulletin of Concerned Asian Scholars* 14: 71–75.

Tyler, Royall, trans. 1977. *Selected Writings of Suzuki Shōsan*. Ithaca: Cornell University Press.

———, trans. *The Miracles of the Kasuga Deity*. New York: Columbia University Press.

Uchino Kumiko. 1983. "The Status Elevation Process of Sōtō Sect Nuns in Modern Japan." *Japanese Journal of Religious Studies* 10, 2–3: 177–94. Reprinted in Diana Eck and Devaki Jain, eds., *Speaking of Faith*, 75–83. Philadelphia: New Society Publishing.

Ueno Chizuko. 1987. "The Position of Japanese Women Reconsidered." *Current Anthropology* 28, 4: 75–84.

Ury, Marian Bloom. 1971. "*Genkō shakusho*: Japan's First Comprehensive History of Buddhism." Ph. D. Dissertation, University of California, Berkeley.

———. 1972. "Recluses and Eccentric Monks." *Monumenta Nipponica* 27, 2: 149–73.

———. trans. 1979. *Tales of Times Now Past: Sixty-Two Stories from a Medieval Japanese Collection*. Berkeley: University of California Press.

———. 1981. "Stepmother Tales in Japan." *Children's Literature* 9: 61–72.

Ushiyama Yoshiyuki. 1982. "Ritsuryō sei tenkaiki ni okeru ama to amadera." *Minshūshi kenkyū* 23: 1–26.

———. 1984. "Kodai ni okeru ama to amadera no mondai." *Minshūshi kenkyū* 27: 1–23.

———. 1989. "Chūsei no amadera to ama." In Ōsumi Kazuo and Nishiguchi Junko, eds., *Josei to bukkyō* 1: *Ama to amadera*, 221–69. Tokyo: Heibonsha.

———. 1990. *Kodai chūsei jiin soshiki no kenkyū*. Tokyo: Yoshikawa kōbunkan.

———. 1994. "Nyonin kinzei." In Nihon bukkyō kenkyūkai, ed., *Nihon no bukkyō* 6: 74–79. Kyoto: Hōzōkan.

Vanden Broucke, Pol. 1992. *Hōkyōshō: 'The Compendium of the Precious Mirror' of the Monk Yūkai*. Ghent: Ghent National University.

Van Gennep, Arnold. 1960 [1909]. *The Rites of Passage*. Trans. M. B. Wizedom anf G. L. Caffee. Chicago: University of Chicago Press.

Van Gulik, Robert H. 1971. *La vie sexuelle dans la Chine ancienne*. Paris: Gallimard. English trans. *Sexual Life in Ancient China: A Preliminary Survey of Chinese Sex and Society from ca. 1500 B.C. till 1644 A.D.* Leiden: E. J. Brill, 1961.

Varley, H. Paul, trans. 1980. *A Chronicle of Gods and Sovereigns: Jinnō Shōtoki of Kitabatake Chikafusa*. New York: Columbia University Press.

Verdier, Yvonne. 1979. *Façons de dire, façons de faire: La laveuse, la couturière, la cuisinière*. Paris: Gallimard.

———. 1995. *Coutumes et destins: Thomas Hardy et autres essais*. Bibliothèque des Sciences Humaines. Paris: Gallimard.

Vincent, Claire. 1997. "La psychanalyse selon Ajase." *Ebisu: Etudes japonaises* 15: 29–60.

Volkmann, Rosemarie. 1995. "Female Stereotypes in Tibetan Religion and Art: The Genitrix/Progenitress as the Exponent of the Underworld." In Ria Kloppenborg and Wouter J. Hanegraaf, eds., *Female Stereotypes in Religious Traditions*, 171–211. Studies in the History of Religions 64. Leiden: E. J. Brill.

Wakabayashi Haruko. 1995. "Tengu: Images of the Buddhist Concepts of Evil in Medieval Japan." Ph.D. Dissertation, Princeton University.

Wakita Haruko. 1984. "Marriage and Property in Premodern Japan from the Perspective of Women's History." Trans. Susanne Gay. *Journal of Japanese Studies* 10, 1: 77–99.

———, ed. 1985a. *Bosei o tou: Rekishiteki hensen*. Vol. 1. Tokyo: Jinbun shoin.

———. 1985b. "Bosei sonjū shisō to zaigyōkan: Chūsei no bungei o chūshin ni." In Wakita Haruko, ed., *Bosei o tou: Rekishiteki hensen* 1: 172–203. Kyoto: Jinbun shoin.

———. 1990. "Chūsei kōki, machi ni okeru 'onna no isshō.'" In Joseishi sōgō kenkyūkai, ed., *Nihon josei seikatsu shi* 2: *Chūsei*, 147–86. Tokyo: Tōkyō daigaku shuppankai.

———. 1992. *Nihon chūsei joseishi no kenkyū: Seibetsu yakuwari buntan to bosei, kasei, seiai*. Tokyo: Tōkyō daigaku shuppankai.

———. 1993. "Women and the Creation of the *Ie* in Japan: An Overview from the Medieval Period to the Present." Trans. David P. Phillips. *U.S.–Japan Women's Journal* English Supplement 4, 83–105.

———. 1994. "Ie no seiritsu to chūsei shinwa." In Wakita Haruko and Susan B. Hanley, eds. 1994. *Jendā no Nihonshi*. Vol. 1: *Shūkyō to minzoku, shintai to seiai*. Vol. 2: *Chūtai to hyōgen, shigoto to seikatsu*, 87–118. Tokyo: Tōkyō daigaku shuppankai.

———. 1995. *Chūsei ni ikiru onnatachi*. Iwanami shinsho 377. Tokyo: Iwanami shoten.

———. 1997. "La montée du prestige impérial dans le Japon du XVIe siècle." *Bulletin de l'Ecole Française d'Extrême-Orient* 84: 159–79.

———. 1999. "The Formation of the *Ie* and Medieval Myth: The *Shintōshū*, Nō Theater, and Picture Scrolls of Temple Origins." Trans. Micah Auerback. In

Wakita Haruko, Anne Bouchy, and Ueno Chizuko, eds., *Gender and Japanese History* 1: 53–85. Osaka: Osaka University Press.

Wakita Haruko, and Susan B. Hanley, eds. 1994. *Jendā no Nihonshi.* Vol. 1: *Shūkyō to minzoku, shintai to seiai.* Vol. 2: *Chūtai to hyōgen, shigoto to seikatsu.* Tokyo: Tōkyō daigaku shuppankai.

Wakita Haruko, Anne Bouchy, and Ueno Chizuko, eds. 1999. *Gender and Japanese History.* 2 vols. Osaka: Osaka University Press.

Waley, Arthur. 1932. "An Eleventh Century Correspondence." In *Etudes d'Orientalisme offerts par le Musée Guimet à la mémoire de Raymonde Linossier,* vol. 2: 531–62. Paris: Librairie Ernest Leroux.

———. 1947. "The Chinese Cinderella Story." *Folk-lore* 58: 226–38.

Walters, Jonathan S. 1994. "A Voice from the Silence: The Buddha's Mother's Story." *History of Religions* 33, 4: 358–79.

———. 1996. "Gotamī's Story." In Donald S. Lopez, Jr., ed., *Buddhism in Practice,* 113–38. Princeton: Princeton University Press.

Walthall, Anne. 1991. "The Life Cycle of Farm Women in Tokugawa Japan." In Gail Lee Bernstein, ed., *Recreating Japanese Women, 1600–1645,* 42–70. Berkeley: University of California Press.

Waltner, Ann. 1990. *Getting an Heir: Adoption and the Construction of Kinship in Late Imperial China.* Honolulu: University of Hawai'i Press.

Wang Jing. 1992. *The Story of the Stone: Intertextuality, Ancient Chinese Stone Lore, and the Stone Symbolism of* Dream of the Red Chamber, Water Margin, *and* The Journey to the West. Durham and London: Duke University Press.

Watanabe Hōyō. 1991. "Nichiren Shōnin to josei shintō." In Nihon bukkyō gakkai, ed., *Bukkyō to josei,* 113–25. Kyoto: Heirakuji shoten.

Watson, Burton, trans. 1993. *The Lotus Sūtra.* New York: Columbia University Press.

Watson, James L. 1982. "Of Flesh and Bones: The Management of Death Pollution in Cantonese Society." In Maurice Bloch and Jonathan Parry, eds., *Death and the Regeneration of Life.* Cambridge: Cambridge University Press.

———. 1985. "Standardizing the Gods: The Promotion of T'ien Hou ("Empress of Heaven") along the South China Coast." In David Johnson, Andrew J. Nathan, and Evelyn Rawski, eds., *Popular Culture in Late Imperial China,* 292–324. Berkeley: University of California Press.

Watson, Rubie S., and Patricia B. Ebrey, eds. 1991. *Marriage and Inequality in Chinese Society.* Berkeley: University of California Press.

Wawrytko, Sandra A. 1994. "Sexism in the Early Saṅgha: Its Social Basis and Philosophical Dissolution." In Charles Wei-hsun Fu and Sandra Wawrytko, eds., *Buddhist Behavioral Codes and the Modern World,* 277–97. Westport, CT: Greenwood Press.

Wayman, Alex. 1983. "Male, Female, and Androgyne: Per Buddhist Tantra, Jacob Boehme, and the Greek and Taoist Mysteries." In Michel Strickmann, ed., *Tantric and Taoist Studies in Honour of R. A. Stein* 2: 592–631. Mélanges chinois et bouddhiques, vol. xxi. Brussels: Institut Belge des Hautes Etudes Chinoises.

———. 1984. "The Intermediate-State Dispute in Buddhism." In *Buddhist Insight: Essays by Alex Wayman*, 251–66. Ed. George R. Elder. Delhi: Motilal Banarsidass.

———. 1991. "The Position of Women in Buddhism." *Studia Missionalia* 40: 259–85.

Wayman, Alex, and Hideko Wayman, trans. 1974. *The Lion's Roar of Queen Śrīmālā: A Buddhist Scripture on the Tathāgatagarbha Theory*. New York: Columbia University Press.

Weber, Max. 1963. *The Sociology of Religion*. Boston: Beacon Press.

Weber, Samuel. 1987. *Institution and Interpretation*. Minneapolis: University of Minnesota Press.

Weidner, Marsha, ed. 1990. *Flowering in the Shadows: Women in the History of Chinese and Japanese Painting*. Honolulu: University of Hawai'i Press.

Weidner, Marsha, et al., eds. 1988. *Views from Jade Terrace: Chinese Women Artists 1300–1912*. Indianapolis: Indianapolis Museum of Art.

Weiner, Annette B. 1976. *Women of Value, Men of Renown: New Perspectives in Trobriand Exchange*. Austin: University of Texas Press.

Weinstein, Stanley. 1973. "The Concept of Reformation in Japanese Buddhism." In Saburo Ota, ed., *Studies in Japanese Culture*, 2. Tokyo: P.E.N. Club.

Werblowsky, R. J. Zwi. 1991. "*Mizuko kuyō*: Notulae on the Most Important "New Religion" of Japan." *Japanese Journal of Religious Studies* 18: 295–354.

White, David Gordon. 1996. *The Alchemical Body: Siddha Traditions in Medieval India*. Chicago: University of Chicago Press.

———. 1999. "Tantric Sects and Tantric Sex: The Flow of Secret Tantric Gnosis." In Elliott R. Wolfson, ed., *Rending the Veil: Concealment and Secrecy in the History of Religions*, 249–70. New York: Seven Bridges Press.

Whitehouse, Wilfrid, and Yanagisawa Eizo, trans. 1974. *Lady Nijō's Own Story: Towazu-gatari, the Candid Diary of a Thirteenth-Century Japanese Imperial Concubine*. Rutland, VT: Tuttle.

Widmer, Ellen, and Kang-i Sun Chang, eds. 1997. *Writing Women in Late Imperial China*. Stanford: Stanford University Press.

Wieger, Léon. 1910. *Bouddhisme chinois: Vinaya, Monachisme et Discipline; Hīnayāna, Véhicule inférieur*. Vol. 1. Hien-Hien: Imprimerie de la mission catholique. Reprint, Paris: Cathasia, 1951.

Wijayaratna, Mohan. 1991. *Les moniales bouddhistes: Naissance et développement du monachisme féminin*. Paris: Editions du Cerf.

Wile, Douglas. 1992. *Art of the Bedchamber: The Chinese Sexual Yoga Classics, Including Women's Solo Meditation Texts*. Albany: State University of New York Press.

Willis, Janice Dean. 1985. "Nuns and Benefactresses: The Role of Women in the Development of Buddhism." In Yvonne Yazbeck Haddad and Ellison Banks Findly, eds., *Women, Religion, and Social Change*, 59–85. Albany: State University of New York Press.

———. ed. 1987a. *Feminine Ground: Essays on Women and Tibet*. Ithaca: Snow Lion Publications.

Willis, Janice Dean. 1987b. "Dākiṇī: Some Comments on Its Nature and Meaning." *Feminine Ground: Essays on Women and Tibet*, 57–75. Ithaca: Snow Lion Publications.

———. 1987c. "Tibetan Ani-s: The Nun's Life in Tibet." In Janice D. Willis, ed., *Feminine Ground: Essays on Women and Tibet*, 96–117. Ithaca: Snow Lion Publications.

Wilson, Elisabeth. 1995a. "The Female Body as a Source of Horror and Insight in Post-Ashokan Indian Buddhism." In Jane Marie Law, ed., *Religious Reflections on the Human Body*, 76–99. Bloomington: University of Indiana Press.

———. 1995b. "Seeing through the Gendered 'I': The Self-Scrutiny and Self-Disclosure of Nuns in Post-Ashokan Buddhist Hagiographic Literature." *Journal of Feminist Studies in Religion*. 11: 41–80.

———. 1996. *Charming Cadavers: Horrific Figurations of the Feminine in Indian Buddhist Hagiographic Literature*. Chicago: University of Chicago Press.

Wilson, William R., trans. 1971. *Hōgen monogatari: The Tale of the Disorder in Hōgen*. Tokyo: Sophia University Press.

Winkler, John J. 1990. *The Constraints of Desire: The Anthropology of Sex and Gender in Ancient Greece*. New York and London: Routledge.

Wisewell, Ella. 1988. "Suye Mura Fifty Years After." *American Ethnologist* 15, 2: 369–84.

Wolf, Margery. 1972. *Women and Family in Rural Taiwan*. Stanford: Stanford University Press.

———. 1975. "Women and Suicide in China." In Margery Wolf and Roxane Witke, eds., *Women in Chinese Society*, 111–41. Stanford: Stanford University Press.

Wolf, Margery, and Roxane Witke, eds. 1975. *Women in Chinese Society*. Stanford: Stanford University Press.

Woodward, F. L. 1942. *Tripiṭaka Suttapiṭaka: Some Sayings of the Buddha according to the Pāli Canon*. London and New York: Oxford University Press.

Woodward, F. L., and E. R. Hare, trans. 1932–36. *The Book of the Gradual Sayings (Anguttara-Nikāya)*. 5 vols. Pāli Texts Society Translation Series, 22, 24–27. London: Pāli Texts Society.

Wright, Arthur F. 1952. "Biography of the Nun An-ling-shou." *Harvard Journal of Asiatic Studies* 15: 192–96.

Wu Pei-yi. 1978. "Self-Examination and Confession of Sins in Traditional China. *Harvard Journal of Asiatic Studies* 39, 1: 5–38.

Wu Yenna. 1988. "The Inversion of Marital Hierarchy: Shrewish Wives and Henpecked Husbands in Seventeenth-Century Chinese Literature." *Harvard Journal of Asiatic Studies* 48: 363–82.

———. 1995. The *Chinese Virago: A Literary Theme*. Cambridge, MA: Council on East Asian Studies, Harvard University.

Yamada Meiji, ed. 1984. *The Sūtra of Contemplation on the Buddha of Immeasurable Life as Expounded by Śākyamuni Buddha*. Kyoto: Ryūkoku University.

Yamagami Izumo. 1981. *Miko no rekishi*. Kyoto: Yūzankaku.

Yamagishi Tokuhei, Takeuchi Rizō, Ienaga Saburō, and Ōsone Shōsuke, eds. 1977. *Kodai seiji shakai shisō*. NSTK 8. Tokyo: Iwanami shoten.

Yamagiwa, Joseph K., trans. 1977 [1966].*The Ōkagami: A Japanese Historical Tale*. Rutland, VT, and Tokyo: Charles E. Tuttle.

Yamakami Izumo. 1994. *Miko no rekishi: Nihon shūkyō no botai*. Tokyo: Yūzankaku.

Yamamoto Hiroko. 1987. "Yōshu to gyokunyo: chūsei ōken no kurayami kara." *Gekkan hyakka* 313: 7–16.

———. 1993. *Henjō fu: Chūsei shinbutsu shūgō no sekai*. Tokyo: Shunjūsha.

———. 1998a. *Ijin: chūsei Nihon no hikyōteki sekai*. Tokyo: Heibonsha.

———. 1998b. *Chūsei shinwa*. Iwanami shinsho 593. Tokyo: Iwanami shoten.

Yamamoto Takashi. 1980. "Dōmyō to Izumi Shikibu no setsuwa." *Kokugo to kokubungaku* 57, 3: 41–57.

Yamanaka Kyōko. 1995. *Kyōko zuihitsu*. Tōyō bunko 588. Tokyo: Heibonsha.

Yamaori Tetsuo. 1991. *Kami to okina no minzokugaku*. Kōdansha gakujutsu bunkō. Tokyo: Kōdansha.

———, ed. 1992. *Nihon ni okeru josei*. Tokyo: Meicho kankōkai.

Yamashita Akiko. 1990. "Tenrin-ō and Henjō-nansi: Two Women—Founders of New Religions." *Japanese Religions* 16, 2: 1–23.

Yampolsky, Philip B. trans. 1967. *The Platform Sūtra of the Sixth Patriarch*. New York: Columbia University Press.

———, ed. 1990. *Selected Writings of Nichiren*. New York: Columbia University Press.

Yanagida Seizan. 1981. *Chūsei hyōhaku*. Kyoto: Hōzōkan.

Yanagita Kunio. 1990a. *Momotarō no tanjō*. In *Yanagita Kunio zenshū*, vol. 10: 7–421. Chikuma bunko. Tokyo: Chikuma shobō.

———. 1990b. *Josei to minkan denjō*. In *Yanagita Kunio zenshū*, vol. 10: 423–589. Chikuma bunko. Tokyo: Chikuma shobō.

———. 1990c. *Imōto no chikara*. In *Yanagita Kunio zenshū*, vol. 11: 7–304. Chikuma bunko. Tokyo: Chikuma shobō.

———. 1990d. *Miko kō*. In *Yanagita Kunio zenshū*, vol. 11: 305–415. Chikuma bunko. Tokyo: Chikuma shobō.

———. 1990e. *Oshiragami kō*. In *Yanagita Kunio zenshū*, vol. 15: 201–419. Chikuma bunko. Tokyo: Chikuma shobō

Yang Lien-sheng. 1960–61. "Female Rulers in Imperial China." *Harvard Journal of Asiatic Studies* 23: 47–61.

Yokoi Yūhō. 1976. *Zen Master Dōgen: An Introduction with Selected Writings*. New York: Weatherhill.

Yokomichi Mario, and Omote Akira, eds. 1960. *Yōkyoku shū*. 2 vols. NKBT 40. Tokyo: Iwanami shoten.

Yoshida Dōkō. 1991. "Dōgen zenji no bikuni, nyoninkan." In Nihon bukkyō gakkai, ed., *Bukkyō to josei*, 79–96. Kyoto: Heirakuji shoten.

Yoshida Kazuhiko. 1989. "Ryūnyo no jōbutsu." In Ōsumi Kazuo and Nishiguchi Junko, eds., *Josei to bukkyō* 2: *Sukui to oshie*, 45–91. Tokyo: Heibonsha.

Yoshida Teigo. 1990. "The Feminine in Japanese Folk Religion: Polluted or Divine?" In Eyal Ben-Ari, Brian Moeran, and James Valentine, eds., *Unwrapping Japan*, 58–77. Manchester: Manchester University Press.

Yoshie Akiko. 1989. "'Tamayorihime' saikō: 'Imōto no chikara' hihan." In Ōsumi Kazuo and Nishiguchi Junko, eds., *Josei to bukkyō* 4: *Miko to joshin*, 51–90. Tokyo: Heibonsha.

Yoshie Akio. 1995. "Eviter la souillure: Le processus de civilisation dans le Japon ancien." *Annales: Histoire, Sciences Sociales* 50, 2: 283–306.

Yoshikai Naoto. 1987. "Jōjin no haha: Rōbo no kanashimi." *Kokubungaku: kaishaku to kanshō* 52, 3: 125–30.

Yoshikawa Shinji. 1999 [1994]. "Ladies-in-Waiting in the Heian Period." Trans. Paul S. Atkins. In Wakita Haruko, Anne Bouchy, and Ueno Chizuko, eds. *Gender and Japanese History* 2: 283–311. Osaka: Osaka University Press.

Yoshino Hiroko. 1995. *Daruma no minzokugaku.* Iwanami shinsho 378. Tokyo: Iwanami shoten.

Yü Chün-fang. 1990. "Feminine Images of Kuan-yin in Post-T'ang China." *Journal of Chinese Religions* 18: 61–89.

Yusa Michiko. 1994. "Women in Shinto: Images Remembered." In Arvind Sharma, ed., *Religion and Women*, 93–119. Albany: State University of New York Press.

Zinsser, Judith P. 1992. *History and Feminism: A Glass Half Full.* New York: Twayne.

Zürcher, Erik. 1959. *The Buddhist Conquest of China: The Spread and Adaptation of Buddhism in Early Medieval China.* 2 vols. Leiden: E. J. Brill.

———. 1991. *Bouddhisme, Christianisme et société chinoise.* Conférences, essais et leçons du Collège de France. Paris: Julliard.

INDEX

BUDDHISMS: A PRINCETON UNIVERSITY PRESS SERIES

Buddhist Learning and Textual Practice in Eighteenth-Century Lankan Monastic Culture, by Anne M. Blackburn

The Red Thread: Buddhist Approaches to Sexuality, by Bernard Faure

Neither Monk nor Layman: Clerical Marriage in Modern Japanese Buddhism, by Richard M. Jaffe

The Power of Denial: Buddhism, Purity, and Gender, by Bernard Faure